Along Interstate 75

13th Edition
(for year 2005)

by Dave Hunter

2005 is the centenary of Einstein's Special Theory of Relativity, which presented the famous equation $E=MC^2$ to the World

"Local Knowledge" and ***"Insider Information"***
for interstate travelers between
Detroit and the Florida Border

Along Interstate-75 is updated annually and available from:

- bookstores in the USA, Canada and on the Internet
- **American Automobile Association** (AAA) offices in Ohio
- **Canadian Automobile Association** (CAA) in Ontario
- or by phoning 1-800-431-1579
  (Visa, MasterCard & Discover accepted
  - all order shipped within 24 hours)

Visit our internet site at:
www.i75online.com
for late breaking Interstate-75 travel information such as **detours, gas prices, construction, road and traffic information**, and much more.

i75online.com now includes a complete **state-wide information section for Florida**, with links to Florida **tourist information, accommodation, attractions, museums, golf, parks, historical sites**, etc.

for further information, please contact:
Mile Oak Publishing Inc.
Suite 81, 20 Mineola Road East,
Mississauga, ON Canada L5G 4N9

e.mail: mile_oak@compuserve.com
phone: 905-274-4356
fax: 905-274-8656

This book is dedicate to the **Memory of Bill Hone**, who on December 21, 1977 at the official Opening Ceremony, drove the first vehicle on the newly completed Interstate-75. The vehicle, a new Ford CL-9000 truck with Bill at the wheel cut the ribbon stretched across I-75, in the northbound lanes at exit 271, Cobb County, Georgia.

Many thanks to Bill's sons who lent me memorabilia, photos and press clipping of the I-75 Opening Ceremony. Fred and Clif, you have helped keep your Dad's Spirit alive.

13th Annual Edition of *"Along Interstate-75"* by Dave Hunter, Mile Oak Publishing Inc.

Editor and research assistance: Kathy Hunter

Cover: design by Margrie Wallace and Dave Hunter

Cover Background - Wild flowers and stratified rock beside a small waterfall on the road from Clay's Ferry, Kentucky (exit 99).

Cataloging in Publication Data

Hunter, Dave, 1941 -

"Along Interstate-75, 12th edition. Local knowledge, Insider Information and Entertainment for those traveling between Detroit & the Florida Border."

ISBN 1-896819-26-5

1. Interstate-75 - Guidebooks. 2. United States - Guidebooks
3. Automobile Travel - United States - Guidebooks I. Title II. Series

Graphic Credits:

Artwork courtesy of Softkey Clipmaster Pro and Corel Corporation's Gallery, Gallery 2, Mega Gallery and IMSI USA including: Image Club Graphics Inc., One Mile Up Inc., Techpool Studios Inc. and Totem Graphics Inc.

All Photos and Photo Illustrations taken or drawn by Dave Hunter, except as follows:

Booth Western Art Museum (125), FHA, DC (70), Florida DOT (142), Hofbräuhaus (86), KY Artisan Center (21 & 177), Macon (38), Marietta Diner (129), Monroe CVB, MI (8,190), NASA (75), Neil Armstrong Museum, Ohio (12, 186), Richmond, Kentucky (page 53), Road to Tara (132), Toyota, Ohio (179), US Marine Corps (12, 75, 186).

A Word of Praise for our Printer . . .

Once again, *Along Interstate-75* has been printed by our favorite printing company, ***Gerrie-Young Lithography*** of Mississauga, Ontario, who uses a Computer-to-Plate (CTP) process to produce the shiny finished book now in your hands.

Each year since 1996, Gerrie-Young has consistently produced an excellent product which has helped *Along Interstate-75* win major awards such as the national *Alcuin Award for "Excellence in Book Design"* and last year's *ForeWord Magazine Bronze "Travel Book of the Year"* award

Thank you everyone at Gerrie-Young. You all take such a personal interest in producing *Along Interstate-75*; you're a great team to work with. Dave.

Printed in Canada

Contents at a Glance

*Note: based on the past trip observations; prices could increase due to reasons beyond our control.

Hello and Welcome to the 13th Annual Edition of Along I-75

Hello once again to all my I-75 friends,

Throughout the year I get many wonderful and helpful e.mail messages from you, my reader-friends ... thank you, I treasure ever one of them. This past summer I received a very special message from two brothers, Fred and Clif Hone. Sadly, their mother had passed away and while clearing her house in California, they came across a scrapbook put together by their late father, Bill. Knowing of my interest in the Interstate, Fred contacted me right away.

You see, on December 21, 1977, an official Ceremony was held to open the newly completed Interstate-75, and Bill, who worked for the Ford Motor Company was selected to be the driver who cut the ribbon stretched across the interstate in the northbound lanes at Georgia's exit 271. He did it at the wheel of a brand new Ford CL-9000 truck and thereby became the first person to drive the newly completed interstate ... all the way northwards to Sault Ste Marie, Michigan. During the trip, Bill delivered official "Greetings" to various mayors and dignitaries along the way.

Fred and Clif kindly lent me their Dad's scrapbook which contains the Interstate-75 Opening Ceremony program, a 45rpm record with a lilting *Ballad of I-75* song specially composed for the event and many photos of the ceremony, as well as various newspaper clippings. They also very generously gave me their Dad's I-75 medallion, a memento of the ceremony. The scrapbook is a real treasure trove to a '75 enthusiast such as myself. I thought you might also enjoy some of these memories so I've reproduced several of the items on page 62 for you.

In other news, there have been many changes along the interstate since the last (12th, 2004 edition) so I've started an "annual trend" section to summarize these. This starting on page 63. A new addition to our maps this year is our "low priced gas" symbol - the result of our "gas price" observations over many years of I-75 travel, hopefully these will save you some gas money ... but no guarantees.

Finally, I want you to know that the profits from *"Along I-75"* are being put to good use. Kathy and I do not want to become wealthy ... we enjoy life just as it is ... so last year, we decided that *we* (Kathy, myself and you, our readers) should start to drill water wells for villages in Africa which currently have no fresh water. They get their water–often polluted–from nearby rivers. Through the Oprah Winfrey show, we contacted Ryan Hreljac, the young schoolboy who appeared on her show after collecting money for water wells as a class project (see www.ryanswell.ca), and are pleased to report that *we* have drilled our first water well in Uganda.

We had some money left over so through the Heifer International (www.Heifer.org), we purchased five goats for poor families in India who can use the goat's milk for subsistence, as well as a means of raising income by selling extra milk to others. Some of those goats have already had kids...so our program is expanding!

We hope you approve of these "extra I-75" programs; I know the villages and families affected, do.

"INTY"

Safe travels,

Dave

Where Are We? . . . a visual index to I-75

"A picture's worth a thousand words" – so I've replaced the *"Contents"* page with a visual index of the book's information. The next two pages relate the 25-mile maps (by page #) to an aerial view of I-75. Features and attractions are similarly referenced.

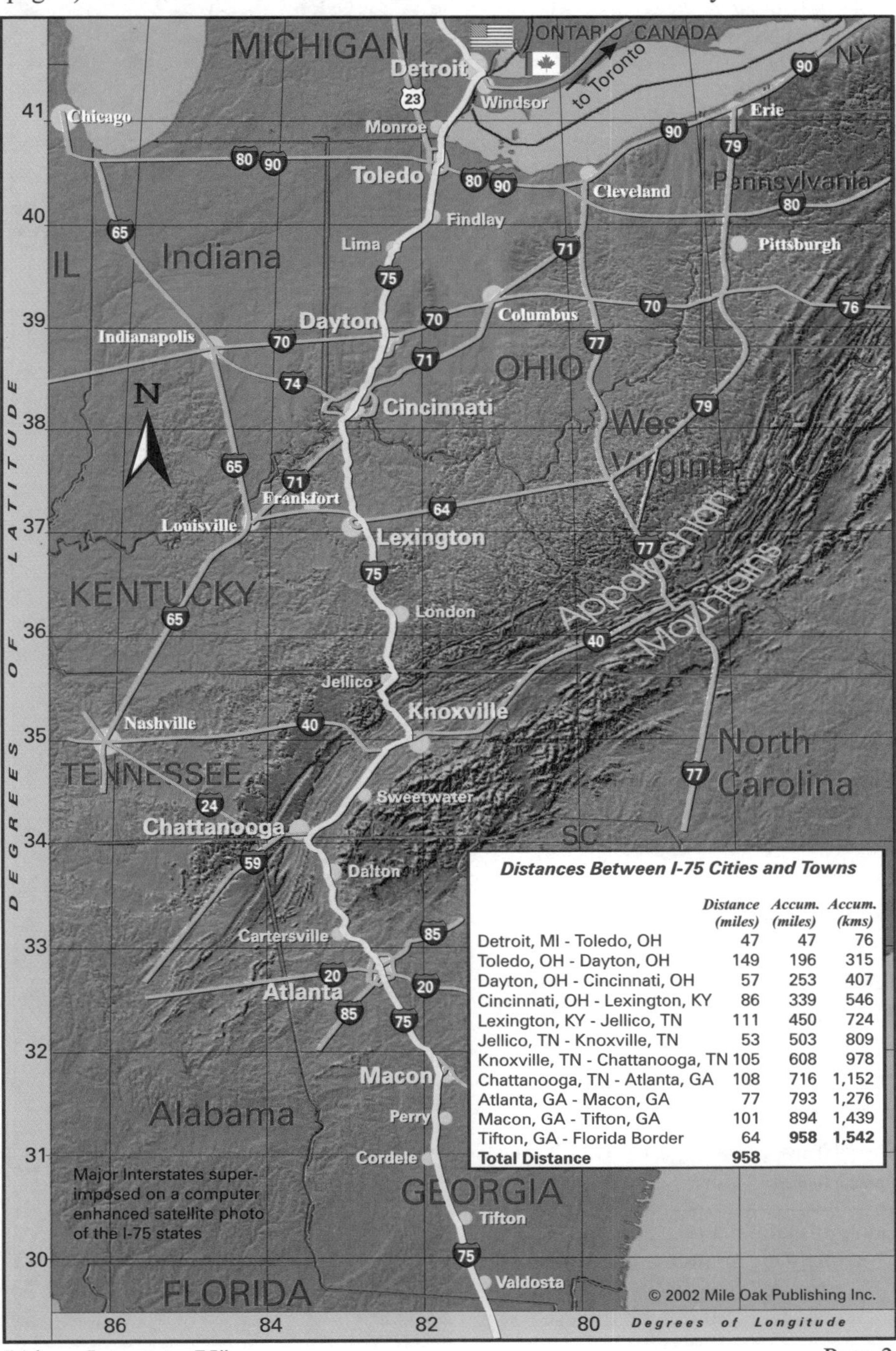

Distances Between I-75 Cities and Towns

	Distance (miles)	*Accum. (miles)*	*Accum. (kms)*
Detroit, MI - Toledo, OH	47	47	76
Toledo, OH - Dayton, OH	149	196	315
Dayton, OH - Cincinnati, OH	57	253	407
Cincinnati, OH - Lexington, KY	86	339	546
Lexington, KY - Jellico, TN	111	450	724
Jellico, TN - Knoxville, TN	53	503	809
Knoxville, TN - Chattanooga, TN	105	608	978
Chattanooga, TN - Atlanta, GA	108	716	1,152
Atlanta, GA - Macon, GA	77	793	1,276
Macon, GA - Tifton, GA	101	894	1,439
Tifton, GA - Florida Border	64	**958**	**1,542**
Total Distance	**958**		

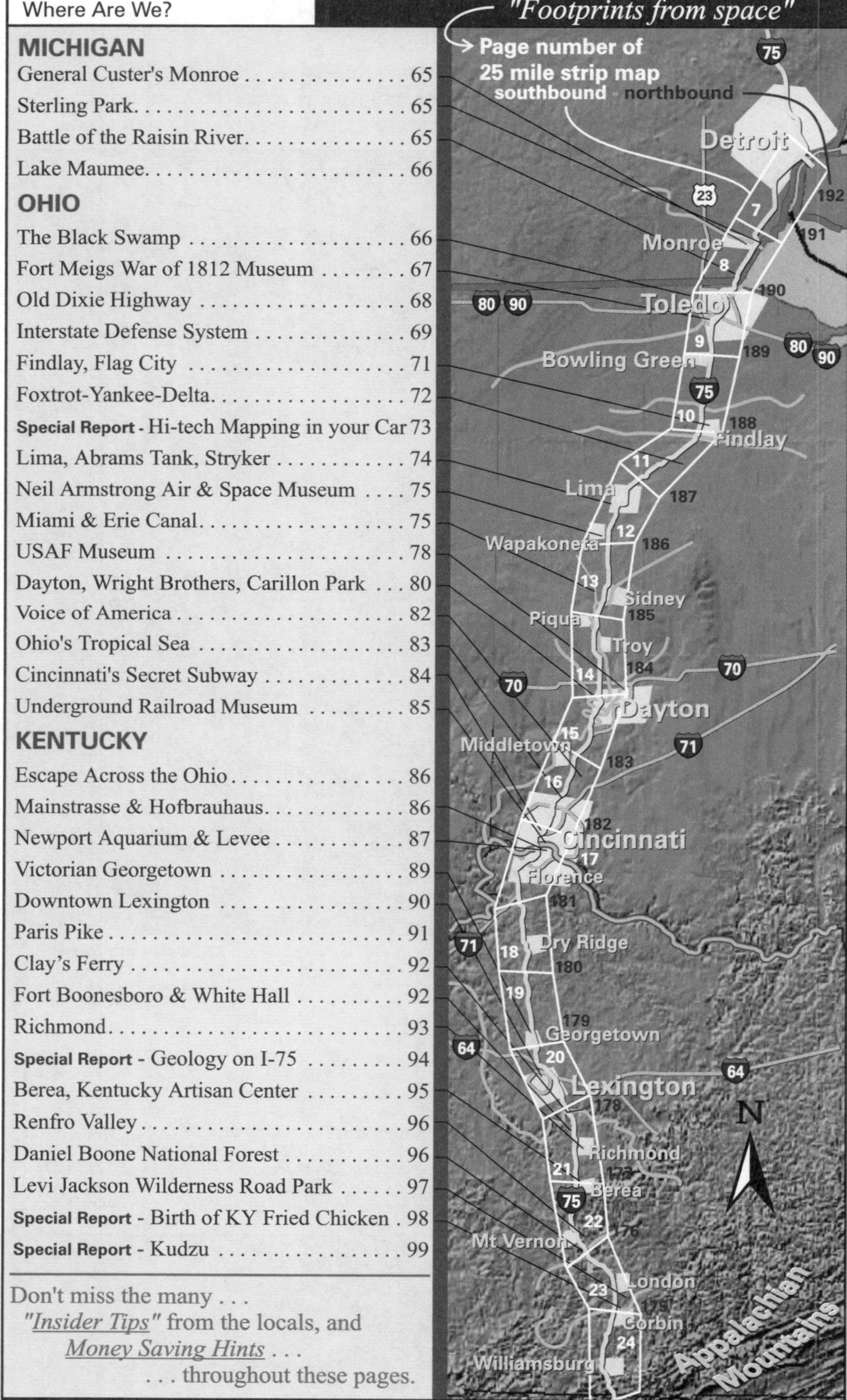

Where Are We?

Don't miss the many . . .
"Insider Tips" from the locals, and
Money Saving Hints . . .
. . . throughout these pages.

"Footprints from space"

Where Are We?

TENNESSEE

GEORGIA

Southbound Route

First time readers: please read the *"Quick Start Hints"* on the inside of the front cover - this will quickly explain how the book is laid out in sections to help you on your journey. The Key to the road speed colors and map symbols is located on the front cover flap.

To get the maximum benefit from the 25 mile-per-page maps, remember . . .

- It takes approximately ½ hour to drive each page. The actual drive time for each page - at posted speeds - is shown at the foot of each map.
- **Count Pages rather than miles.** In other words, if you are heading for a specific stop or destination, count the number of pages between your current position and the destination, and divide by 2. This gives you your approximate driving time in hours.
- **Plan your day by the page.** I suggested a *"drive by the page"* strategy. Here it is (see top of next column) based on a 400 mile (16 page or 8 hour) day:

Leave motel at 8:30am, and then drive . . .

four pages before 10:30am coffee break
**15 minute coffee break*
four pages before lunch at 12:45pm
** 1 hour lunch*
four pages before 3:45pm coffee break
** 15 minute coffee break*
four pages before the night stop at 6:00pm

Of course, the page strategy can be changed to meet your specific needs. "Morning" people may want to get an earlier start and drive for a few pages before stopping for breakfast; families with young children may need to "time shift" to provide more frequent breaks.

- **Find the lowest priced gas:** After driving I-75 for many years, I've learned where to find the lowest priced, branded gas. To help you save some money, I've marked the cheaper fill-up spots on the colored maps. No guarantees though. The oil market, gas station management and pricing strategies can change overnight!

Insider Tip for Southbound Travelers
Avoiding "Drive South" Sunburn

Did you know that you can get a sunburn and dangerous overload of cancer causing ultraviolet (UV) light while driving south, especially if you are not used to being outdoors for long periods of time? Three days of driving into the sun - the average run from Michigan to Florida on I-75 - can create a very high exposure to UV light on the face and arms, even on cloudy days.

The thick glass and plastic laminate of car windshields help filter UV light so that only about 15% of UVA* and virtually no UVB* reach the car's interior, but the extra long hours of constant exposure and UV light coming through the thinner, non-laminated side windows can mean that you are receiving too much higher UV radiation than under normal circumstances.

To protect yourself from these harmful rays, wear long sleeves and use a sunscreen with protection factor of at least SPF15 on your face - and of course, keep your side windows rolled up.

***Note: UVA ages the skin and can cause skin cancer; UVB causes burning.**

All information updated as of September, 2004

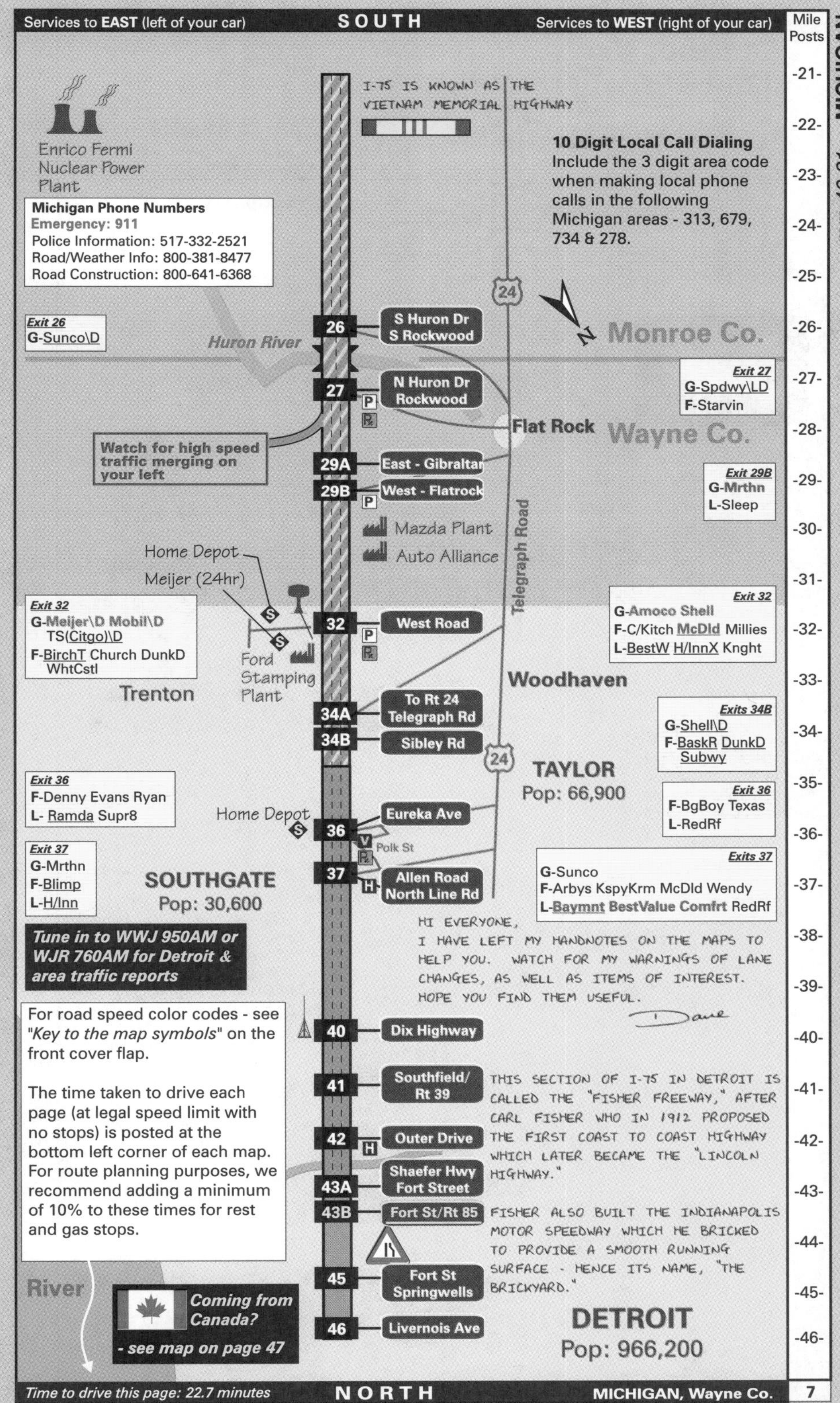
Mile Posts
-21- -22- -23- -24- -25- -26- -27- -28- -29- -30- -31- -32- -33- -34- -35- -36- -37- -38- -39- -40- -41- -42- -43- -44- -45- -46-
I-75 IS KNOWN AS THE VIETNAM MEMORIAL HIGHWAY
Enrico Fermi Nuclear Power Plant
Michigan Phone Numbers
Emergency: 911
Police Information: 517-332-2521
Road/Weather Info: 800-381-8477
Road Construction: 800-641-6368
10 Digit Local Call Dialing
Include the 3 digit area code when making local phone calls in the following Michigan areas - 313, 679, 734 & 278.
24
Exit 26
G-Sunco\D
Huron River
26 S Huron Dr S Rockwood
Monroe Co.
27 N Huron Dr Rockwood
Exit 27
G-Spdwy\LD
F-Starvin
Flat Rock
Wayne Co.
Watch for high speed traffic merging on your left
29A East - Gibraltar
29B West - Flatrock
Exit 29B
G-Mrthn
L-Sleep
Mazda Plant
Auto Alliance
Telegraph Road
Home Depot
Meijer (24hr)
Exit 32
G-Meijer\D Mobil\D TS(Citgo)\D
F-BirchT Church DunkD WhtCstl
32 West Road
Exit 32
G-Amoco Shell
F-C/Kitch McDld Millies
L-BestW H/InnX Knght
Ford Stamping Plant
Trenton
Woodhaven
34A To Rt 24 Telegraph Rd
34B Sibley Rd
Exits 34B
G-Shell\D
F-BaskR DunkD Subwy
24
TAYLOR
Pop: 66,900
Exit 36
F-Denny Evans Ryan
L- Ramda Supr8
Home Depot
36 Eureka Ave
Polk St
Exit 36
F-BgBoy Texas
L-RedRf
Exit 37
G-Mrthn
F-Blimp
L-H/Inn
SOUTHGATE
Pop: 30,600
37 Allen Road North Line Rd
Exits 37
G-Sunco
F-Arbys KspyKrm McDld Wendy
L-Baymnt BestValue Comfrt RedRf
HI EVERYONE,
I HAVE LEFT MY HANDNOTES ON THE MAPS TO HELP YOU. WATCH FOR MY WARNINGS OF LANE CHANGES, AS WELL AS ITEMS OF INTEREST. HOPE YOU FIND THEM USEFUL.
Dave
Tune in to WWJ 950AM or WJR 760AM for Detroit & area traffic reports
For road speed color codes - see "Key to the map symbols" on the front cover flap.
The time taken to drive each page (at legal speed limit with no stops) is posted at the bottom left corner of each map. For route planning purposes, we recommend adding a minimum of 10% to these times for rest and gas stops.
40 Dix Highway
41 Southfield/ Rt 39
THIS SECTION OF I-75 IN DETROIT IS CALLED THE "FISHER FREEWAY," AFTER CARL FISHER WHO IN 1912 PROPOSED THE FIRST COAST TO COAST HIGHWAY WHICH LATER BECAME THE "LINCOLN HIGHWAY."
42 Outer Drive
43A Shaefer Hwy Fort Street
43B Fort St/Rt 85
FISHER ALSO BUILT THE INDIANAPOLIS MOTOR SPEEDWAY WHICH HE BRICKED TO PROVIDE A SMOOTH RUNNING SURFACE - HENCE ITS NAME, "THE BRICKYARD."
45 Fort St Springwells
River
Coming from Canada?
- see map on page 47
46 Livernois Ave
DETROIT
Pop: 966,200

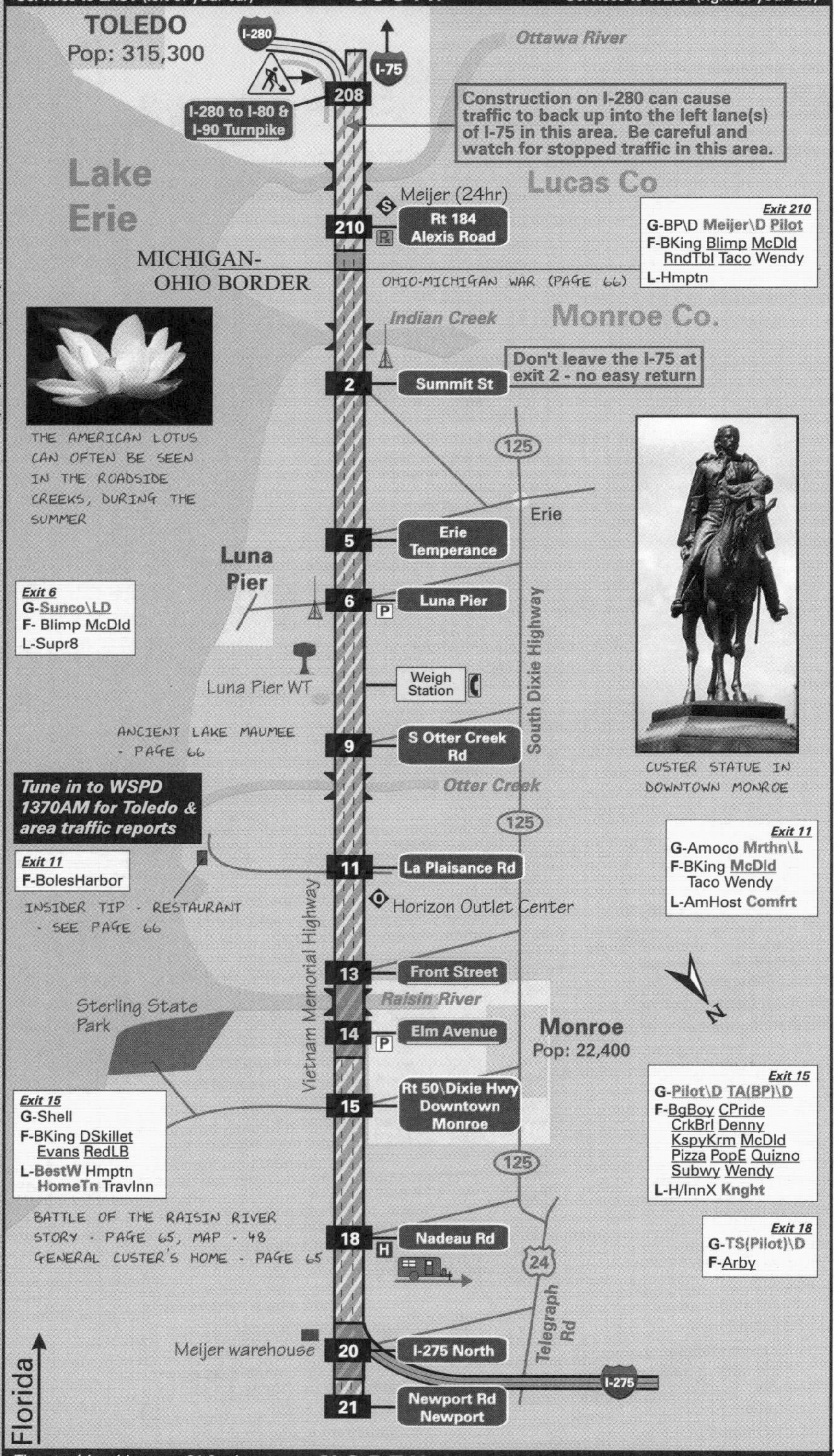

Mile Posts

TOLEDO
Pop: 315,300

I-280 to I-80 & I-90 Turnpike

Construction on I-280 can cause traffic to back up into the left lane(s) of I-75 in this area. Be careful and watch for stopped traffic in this area.

Lake Erie

Lucas Co

Meijer (24hr)

208

210 Rt 184 Alexis Road

Exit 210
G-BP\D Meijer\D Pilot
F-BKing Blimp McDld RndTbl Taco Wendy
L-Hmptn

MICHIGAN-OHIO BORDER

OHIO-MICHIGAN WAR (PAGE 66)

Indian Creek

Monroe Co.

2 Summit St

Don't leave the I-75 at exit 2 - no easy return

THE AMERICAN LOTUS CAN OFTEN BE SEEN IN THE ROADSIDE CREEKS, DURING THE SUMMER

125

Erie

5 Erie Temperance

Luna Pier

Exit 6
G-Sunco\LD
F- Blimp McDld
L-Supr8

6 Luna Pier

South Dixie Highway

Luna Pier WT

Weigh Station

CUSTER STATUE IN DOWNTOWN MONROE

ANCIENT LAKE MAUMEE - PAGE 66

9 S Otter Creek Rd

Otter Creek

Tune in to WSPD 1370AM for Toledo & area traffic reports

Exit 11
F-BolesHarbor

11 La Plaisance Rd

Exit 11
G-Amoco Mrthn\L
F-BKing McDld Taco Wendy
L-AmHost Comfrt

INSIDER TIP - RESTAURANT - SEE PAGE 66

Horizon Outlet Center

Vietnam Memorial Highway

13 Front Street

Raisin River

Sterling State Park

14 Elm Avenue

Monroe
Pop: 22,400

Exit 15
G-Shell
F-BKing DSkillet Evans RedLB
L-BestW Hmptn HomeTn TravInn

15 Rt 50\Dixie Hwy Downtown Monroe

Exit 15
G-Pilot\D TA(BP)\D
F-BgBoy CPride CrkBrl Denny KspyKrm McDld Pizza PopE Quizno Subwy Wendy
L-H/InnX Knght

BATTLE OF THE RAISIN RIVER STORY - PAGE 65, MAP - 48
GENERAL CUSTER'S HOME - PAGE 65

18 Nadeau Rd

Exit 18
G-TS(Pilot)\D
F-Arby

24

Telegraph Rd

Meijer warehouse

20 I-275 North

I-275

21 Newport Rd Newport

Florida

-207- -208- -209- -210- -0- -1- -2- -3- -4- -5- -6- -7- -8- -9- -10- -11- -12- -13- -14- -15- -16- -17- -18- -19- -20- -21-

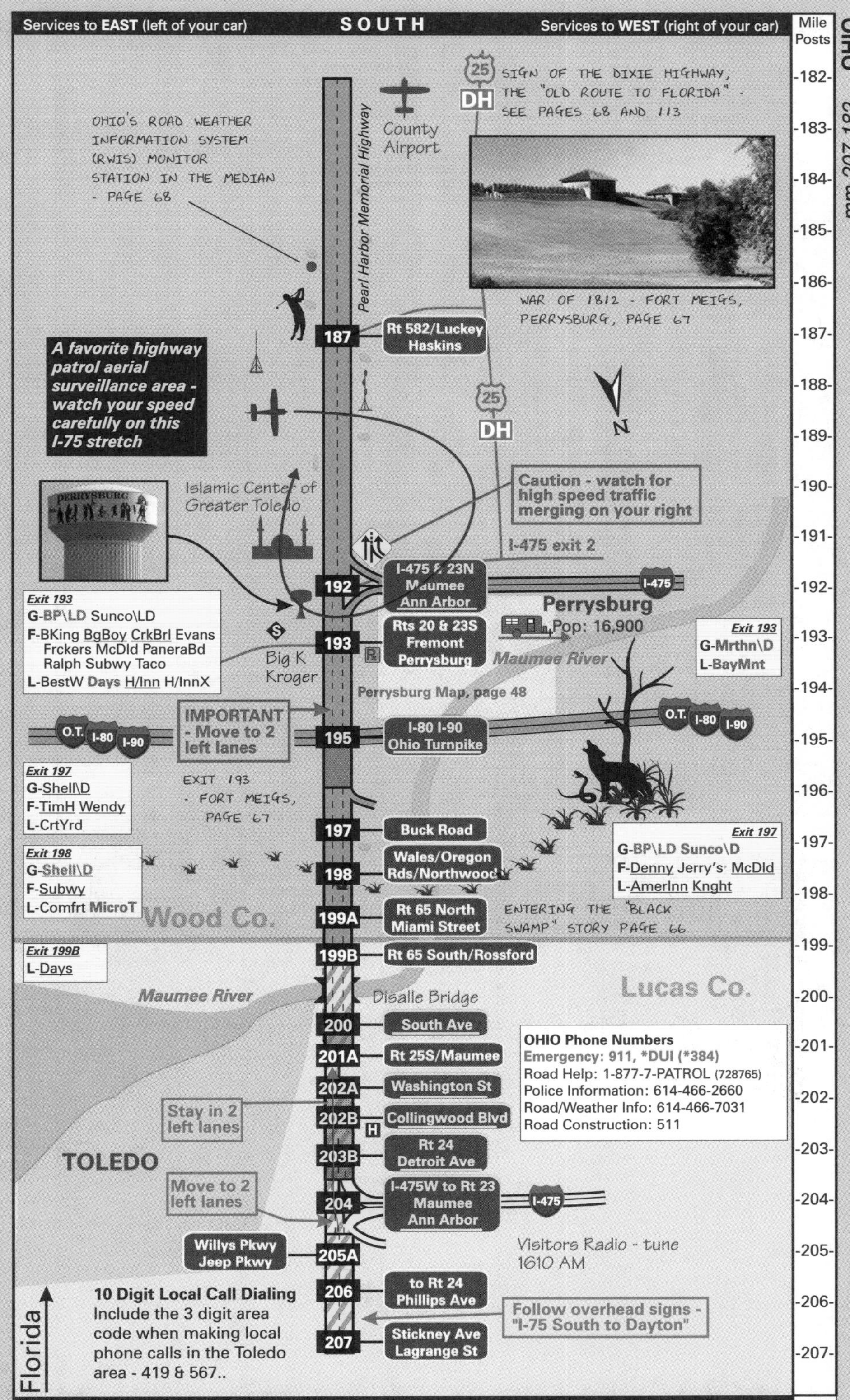
25 DH
SIGN OF THE DIXIE HIGHWAY, THE "OLD ROUTE TO FLORIDA" - SEE PAGES 68 AND 113
County Airport
OHIO'S ROAD WEATHER INFORMATION SYSTEM (RWIS) MONITOR STATION IN THE MEDIAN - PAGE 68
Pearl Harbor Memorial Highway
WAR OF 1812 - FORT MEIGS, PERRYSBURG, PAGE 67
187
Rt 582/Luckey Haskins
A favorite highway patrol aerial surveillance area - watch your speed carefully on this I-75 stretch
N
Islamic Center of Greater Toledo
PERRYSBURG
Caution - watch for high speed traffic merging on your right
I-475 exit 2
192
I-475 & 23N Maumee Ann Arbor
I-475
Perrysburg
Pop: 16,900
Exit 193
G-BP\LD Sunco\LD
F-BKing BgBoy CrkBrl Evans Frckers McDld PaneraBd Ralph Subwy Taco
L-BestW Days H/Inn H/InnX
193
Rts 20 & 23S Fremont Perrysburg
Maumee River
Exit 193
G-Mrthn\D
L-BayMnt
Big K Kroger
Perrysburg Map, page 48
O.T. I-80 I-90
IMPORTANT - Move to 2 left lanes
195
I-80 I-90 Ohio Turnpike
Exit 197
G-Shell\D
F-TimH Wendy
L-CrtYrd
EXIT 193 - FORT MEIGS, PAGE 67
197
Buck Road
Exit 197
G-BP\LD Sunco\D
F-Denny Jerry's McDld
L-AmerInn Knght
Exit 198
G-Shell\D
F-Subwy
L-Comfrt MicroT
198
Wales/Oregon Rds/Northwood
Wood Co.
199A
Rt 65 North Miami Street
ENTERING THE "BLACK SWAMP" STORY PAGE 66
Exit 199B
L-Days
199B
Rt 65 South/Rossford
Maumee River
DiSalle Bridge
Lucas Co.
200
South Ave
201A
Rt 25S/Maumee
202A
Washington St
Stay in 2 left lanes
202B
Collingwood Blvd
203B
Rt 24 Detroit Ave
OHIO Phone Numbers
Emergency: 911, *DUI (*384)
Road Help: 1-877-7-PATROL (728765)
Police Information: 614-466-2660
Road/Weather Info: 614-466-7031
Road Construction: 511
TOLEDO
Move to 2 left lanes
204
I-475W to Rt 23 Maumee Ann Arbor
I-475
Willys Pkwy Jeep Pkwy
205A
Visitors Radio - tune 1610 AM
206
to Rt 24 Phillips Ave
10 Digit Local Call Dialing
Include the 3 digit area code when making local phone calls in the Toledo area - 419 & 567..
Follow overhead signs - "I-75 South to Dayton"
207
Stickney Ave Lagrange St
Florida
-182- -183- -184- -185- -186- -187- -188- -189- -190- -191- -192- -193- -194- -195- -196- -197- -198- -199- -200- -201- -202- -203- -204- -205- -206- -207-

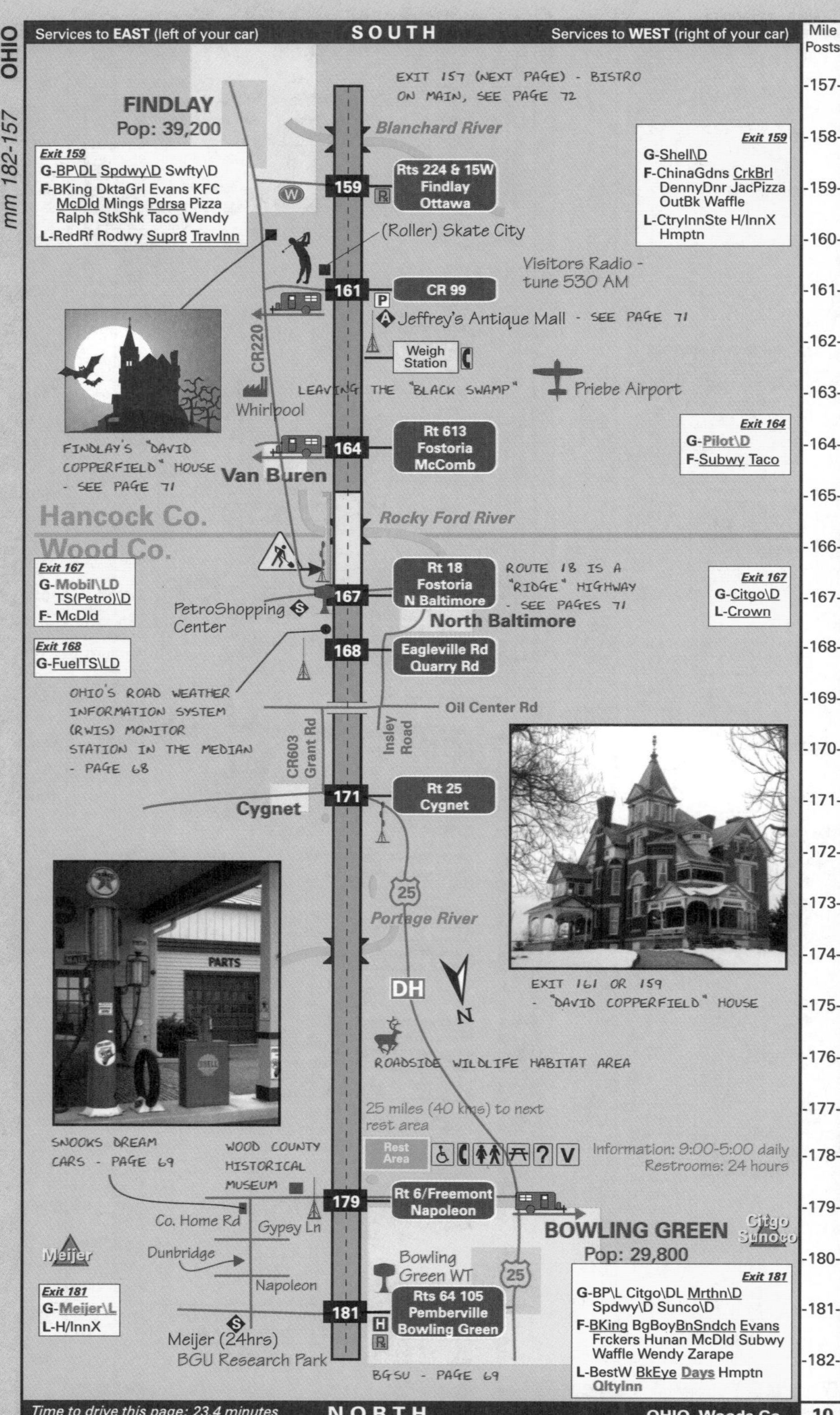
Services to EAST (left of your car)
SOUTH
Services to WEST (right of your car)
Mile Posts
EXIT 157 (NEXT PAGE) - BISTRO ON MAIN, SEE PAGE 72
FINDLAY
Pop: 39,200
Blanchard River
Exit 159
G-BP\DL Spdwy\D Swfty\D
F-BKing DktaGrl Evans KFC McDld Mings Pdrsa Pizza Ralph StkShk Taco Wendy
L-RedRf Rodwy Supr8 TravInn
159
Rts 224 & 15W Findlay Ottawa
Exit 159
G-Shell\D
F-ChinaGdns CrkBrl DennyDnr JacPizza OutBk Waffle
L-CtryInnSte H/InnX Hmptn
(Roller) Skate City
Visitors Radio - tune 530 AM
161
CR 99
Jeffrey's Antique Mall - SEE PAGE 71
CR220
Weigh Station
Whirlpool
LEAVING THE "BLACK SWAMP"
Priebe Airport
164
Rt 613 Fostoria McComb
Exit 164
G-Pilot\D
F-Subwy Taco
FINDLAY'S "DAVID COPPERFIELD" HOUSE - SEE PAGE 71
Van Buren
Hancock Co.
Wood Co.
Rocky Ford River
Exit 167
G-Mobil\LD TS(Petro)\LD
F- McDld
167
Rt 18 Fostoria N Baltimore
ROUTE 18 IS A "RIDGE" HIGHWAY - SEE PAGES 71
Exit 167
G-Citgo\D
L-Crown
PetroShopping Center
North Baltimore
Exit 168
G-FuelTS\LD
168
Eagleville Rd Quarry Rd
OHIO'S ROAD WEATHER INFORMATION SYSTEM (RWIS) MONITOR STATION IN THE MEDIAN - PAGE 68
Oil Center Rd
CR603 Grant Rd
Insley Road
171
Rt 25 Cygnet
Cygnet
25
Portage River
DH
N
EXIT 161 OR 159 - "DAVID COPPERFIELD" HOUSE
ROADSIDE WILDLIFE HABITAT AREA
25 miles (40 kms) to next rest area
Rest Area
Information: 9:00-5:00 daily
Restrooms: 24 hours
SNOOKS DREAM CARS - PAGE 69
WOOD COUNTY HISTORICAL MUSEUM
179
Rt 6/Freemont Napoleon
Co. Home Rd
Gypsy Ln
BOWLING GREEN
Pop: 29,800
Citgo Sunoco
Meijer
Dunbridge
Napoleon
Bowling Green WT
Exit 181
G-Meijer\L
L-H/InnX
181
Rts 64 105 Pemberville Bowling Green
Meijer (24hrs)
BGU Research Park
BGSU - PAGE 69
Exit 181
G-BP\L Citgo\DL Mrthn\D Spdwy\D Sunco\D
F-BKing BgBoyBnSndch Evans Frckers Hunan McDld Subwy Waffle Wendy Zarape
L-BestW BkEye Days Hmptn QltyInn
PARTS
-157- -158- -159- -160- -161- -162- -163- -164- -165- -166- -167- -168- -169- -170- -171- -172- -173- -174- -175- -176- -177- -178- -179- -180- -181- -182-

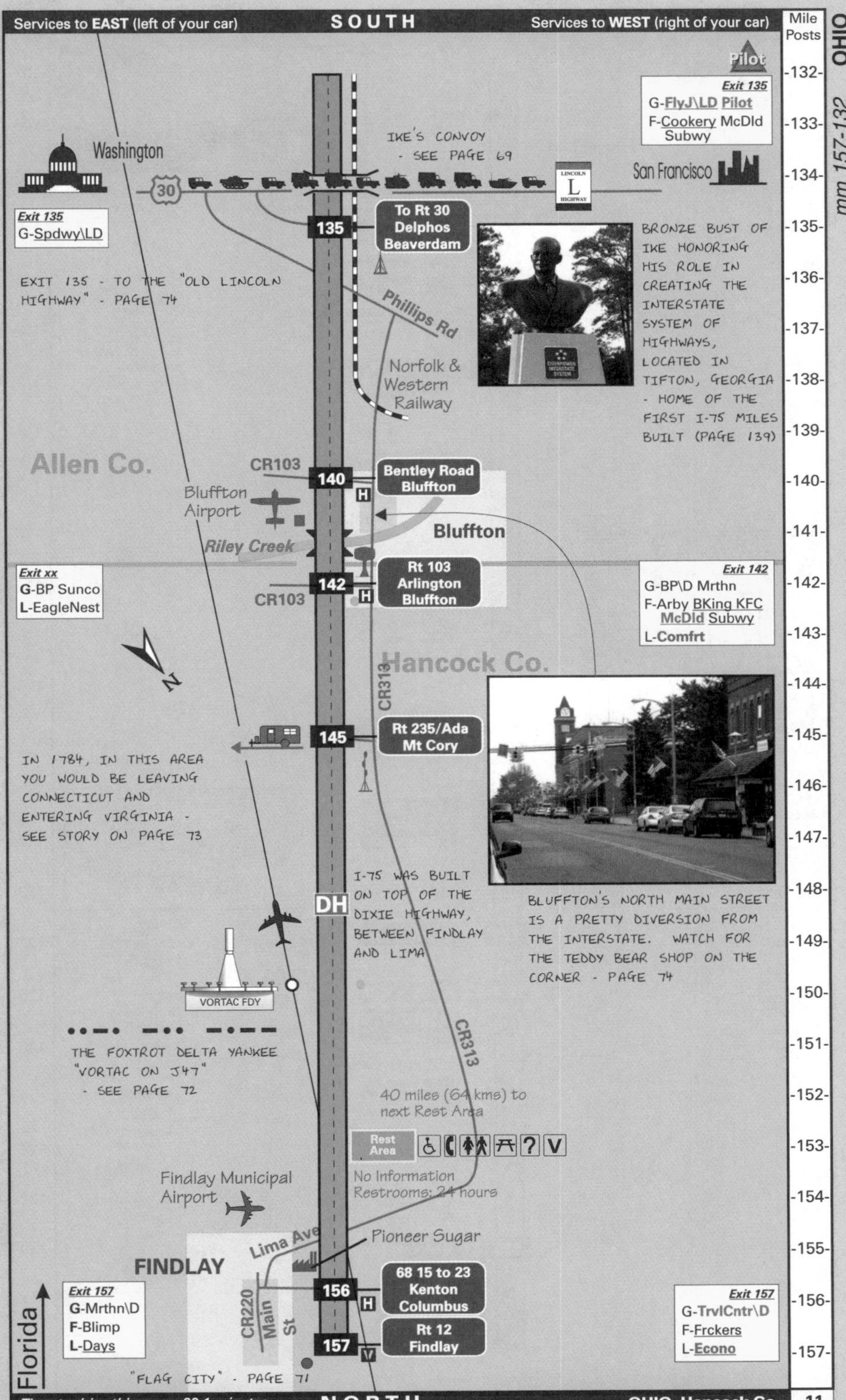

Services to EAST (left of your car)
SOUTH
Services to WEST (right of your car)
Mile Posts
OHIO
mm 157-132
Pilot
Exit 135
G-FlyJ\LD Pilot
F-Cookery McDld Subwy
IKE'S CONVOY - SEE PAGE 69
Washington
30
LINCOLN L HIGHWAY
San Francisco
Exit 135
G-Spdwy\LD
135
To Rt 30 Delphos Beaverdam
BRONZE BUST OF IKE HONORING HIS ROLE IN CREATING THE INTERSTATE SYSTEM OF HIGHWAYS, LOCATED IN TIFTON, GEORGIA - HOME OF THE FIRST I-75 MILES BUILT (PAGE 139)
EXIT 135 - TO THE "OLD LINCOLN HIGHWAY" - PAGE 74
Phillips Rd
Norfolk & Western Railway
Allen Co.
CR103
140
Bentley Road Bluffton
Bluffton Airport
Bluffton
Riley Creek
Exit xx
G-BP Sunco
L-EagleNest
142
Rt 103 Arlington Bluffton
CR103
Exit 142
G-BP\D Mrthn
F-Arby BKing KFC McDld Subwy
L-Comfrt
Hancock Co.
N
CR313
145
Rt 235/Ada Mt Cory
IN 1784, IN THIS AREA YOU WOULD BE LEAVING CONNECTICUT AND ENTERING VIRGINIA - SEE STORY ON PAGE 73
I-75 WAS BUILT ON TOP OF THE DIXIE HIGHWAY, BETWEEN FINDLAY AND LIMA
DH
BLUFFTON'S NORTH MAIN STREET IS A PRETTY DIVERSION FROM THE INTERSTATE. WATCH FOR THE TEDDY BEAR SHOP ON THE CORNER - PAGE 74
VORTAC FDY
THE FOXTROT DELTA YANKEE "VORTAC ON J47" - SEE PAGE 72
CR313
40 miles (64 kms) to next Rest Area
Rest Area
? V
No Information
Restrooms: 24 hours
Findlay Municipal Airport
Lima Ave
Pioneer Sugar
FINDLAY
CR220
Main St
156
68 15 to 23 Kenton Columbus
157
Rt 12 Findlay
Exit 157
G-Mrthn\D
F-Blimp
L-Days
Exit 157
G-TrvlCntr\D
F-Frckers
L-Econo
Florida
"FLAG CITY" - PAGE 71
-132-
-133-
-134-
-135-
-136-
-137-
-138-
-139-
-140-
-141-
-142-
-143-
-144-
-145-
-146-
-147-
-148-
-149-
-150-
-151-
-152-
-153-
-154-
-155-
-156-
-157-
Time to drive this page: 23.1 minutes
NORTH
OHIO, Hancock Co.
11

Services to **EAST** (left of your car) **SOUTH** Services to **WEST** (right of your car) Mile Posts

THE BEAUTIFUL NEIL ARMSTRONG AIR & SPACE MUSEUM - SEE PAGE 75

RADAR

25A

DH

110 St Marys Belfontaine

RV HEAVEN - PAGE 75

111 Belfontaine Street

Exit 111
G-LGTS\LD
L-Days

Exit 111
G-BP\L Shell
F-Arby BKing CaptD DQ Evans LampLghtr LkyStr McDld Pizza Taco Waffle Wendy YangGdns
L-BestW H/InnX Supr8 TravL

Wapakoneta
Pop: 9,500

113 Rt 67 Unipolis Wapakoneta

Rest Area

33 miles (53 kms) to next Rest Area

No Information
Restrooms: 24 hours

OHIO ICE AGE - PAGE 75

For local weather information, tune to 1610 AM

Auglaize Co.

Caution - The Ohio State Police run very active aerial speed patrols from a small airport a few miles west of milepost 106. This stretch of the I-75 is heavily patroled from the air. On clear days, watch for low flying, high wing single engine aircraft flying parallel to the interstate.

Dixie Hwy

DH

118 Cridersville

Cridersville

Exit 118
G-FuelTS/D Spdwy\LD
F-Subwy

Allen Co.

120 Breese Rd Fort Shawnee

Exit 122
G-Shell\LD

McClain Rd

Exit 122
G-Spdwy\LD

122 Rt 65 Lima Uniopolis

Exit 125A
G-BP\D Spdwy\LD
F-Arbys BKing CaptD CrkBrl Evans Grindr Hunan McDld Olive Pdrsa Pizza Rally Ralph RedLb Ryan SkyInStk Taco TexStk Wendy
L-H/Inn Hmptn Motel6

124 Fourth Street

HOME OF THE SECRET "KRYPTONITE" ROOM - PAGE 74

Wal-Mart

125A Rt 309 & 117E

125B Rt 309 & 117W Lima

LIMA
Pop: 40,300

Exit 125B
G-Shell
F-DmnRibs IgnaGrl Kwpee PJPizza
L-Econmy Supr8

Ottawa River

STRIP MINING OPERATIONS

127 Rt 81 Ada Lima

Exit 127
G-BP Mrthn\D
F-Waffle
L-Comfrt Days Econo

US Plastics Retail Outlet
(on Neubrecht Rd - ½ mile) SEE STORY ON PAGE 74

Dixie Hwy

DH

Norfolk & Western Railway

Exit 130
G-Mrthn
L-BestValue

130 Blue Lick Rd

Power Grid Substation

Florida

-107- -108- -109- -110- -111- -112- -113- -114- -115- -116- -117- -118- -119- -120- -121- -122- -123- -124- -125- -126- -127- -128- -129- -130- -131- -132-

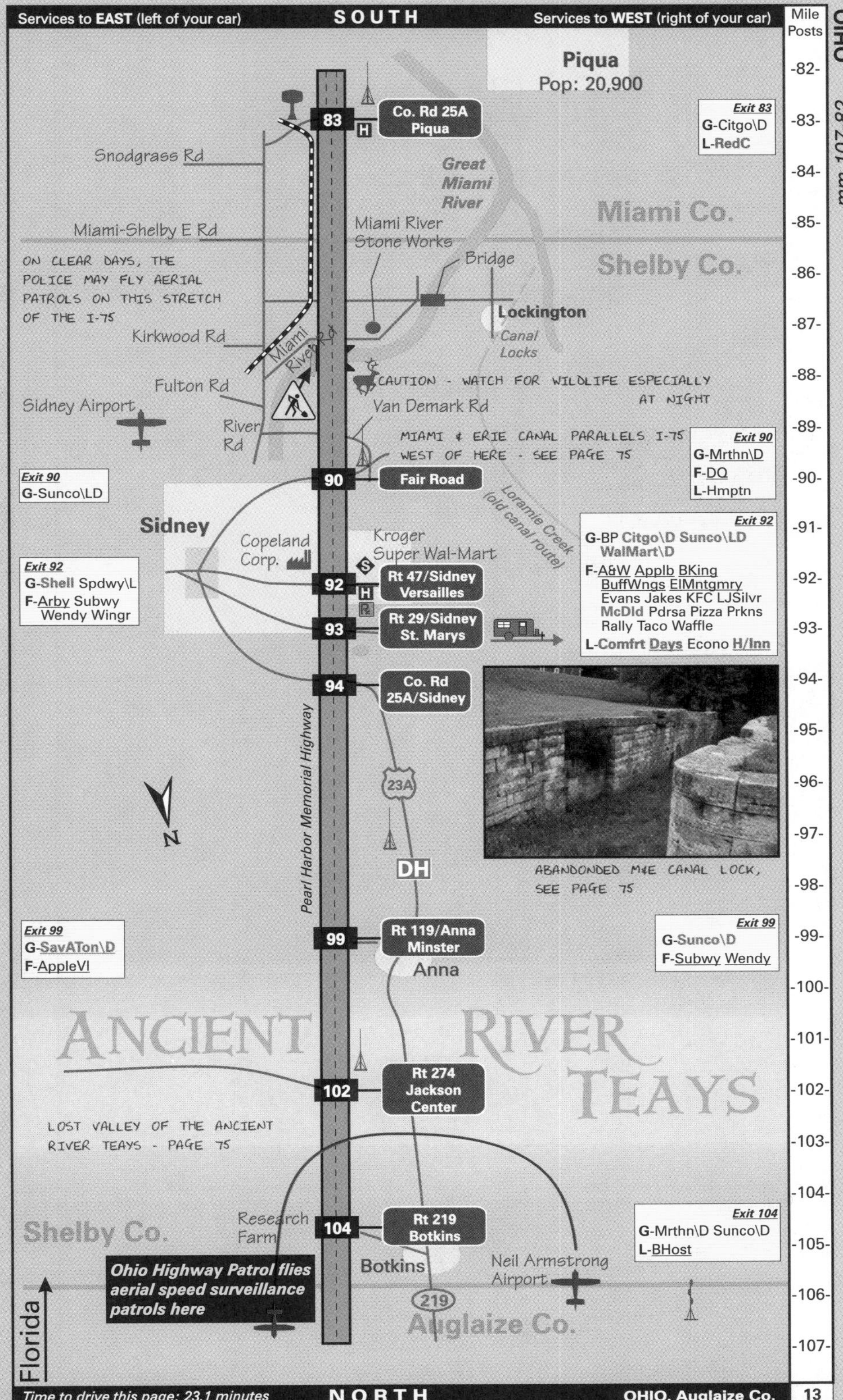
Services to EAST (left of your car)
SOUTH
Services to WEST (right of your car)
Mile Posts
OHIO
mm 107-82
Piqua
Pop: 20,900
Exit 83
G-Citgo\D
L-RedC
83
Co. Rd 25A Piqua
Snodgrass Rd
Great Miami River
Miami Co.
Miami-Shelby E Rd
Miami River Stone Works
Shelby Co.
Bridge
ON CLEAR DAYS, THE POLICE MAY FLY AERIAL PATROLS ON THIS STRETCH OF THE I-75
Lockington
Canal Locks
Kirkwood Rd
Miami River Rd
Fulton Rd
CAUTION - WATCH FOR WILDLIFE ESPECIALLY AT NIGHT
Sidney Airport
Van Demark Rd
River Rd
MIAMI & ERIE CANAL PARALLELS I-75 WEST OF HERE - SEE PAGE 75
Exit 90
G-Mrthn\D
F-DQ
L-Hmptn
Exit 90
G-Sunco\LD
90
Fair Road
Loramie Creek (old canal route)
Sidney
Copeland Corp.
Kroger Super Wal-Mart
Exit 92
G-BP Citgo\D Sunco\LD WalMart\D
F-A&W Applb BKing BuffWngs ElMntgmry Evans Jakes KFC LJSilvr McDld Pdrsa Pizza Prkns Rally Taco Waffle
L-Comfrt Days Econo H/Inn
Exit 92
G-Shell Spdwy\L
F-Arby Subwy Wendy Wingr
92
Rt 47/Sidney Versailles
93
Rt 29/Sidney St. Marys
94
Co. Rd 25A/Sidney
Pearl Harbor Memorial Highway
23A
N
DH
ABANDONDED M&E CANAL LOCK, SEE PAGE 75
Exit 99
G-SavATon\D
F-AppleVl
99
Rt 119/Anna Minster
Anna
Exit 99
G-Sunco\D
F-Subwy Wendy
ANCIENT RIVER TEAYS
102
Rt 274 Jackson Center
LOST VALLEY OF THE ANCIENT RIVER TEAYS - PAGE 75
Shelby Co.
Research Farm
104
Rt 219 Botkins
Exit 104
G-Mrthn\D Sunco\D
L-BHost
Botkins
Neil Armstrong Airport
Ohio Highway Patrol flies aerial speed surveillance patrols here
219
Auglaize Co.
Florida
-82- -83- -84- -85- -86- -87- -88- -89- -90- -91- -92- -93- -94- -95- -96- -97- -98- -99- -100- -101- -102- -103- -104- -105- -106- -107-
Time to drive this page: 23.1 minutes
NORTH
OHIO, Auglaize Co.
13

Services to **EAST** (left of your car) — **SOUTH** — Services to **WEST** (right of your car) — Mile Posts

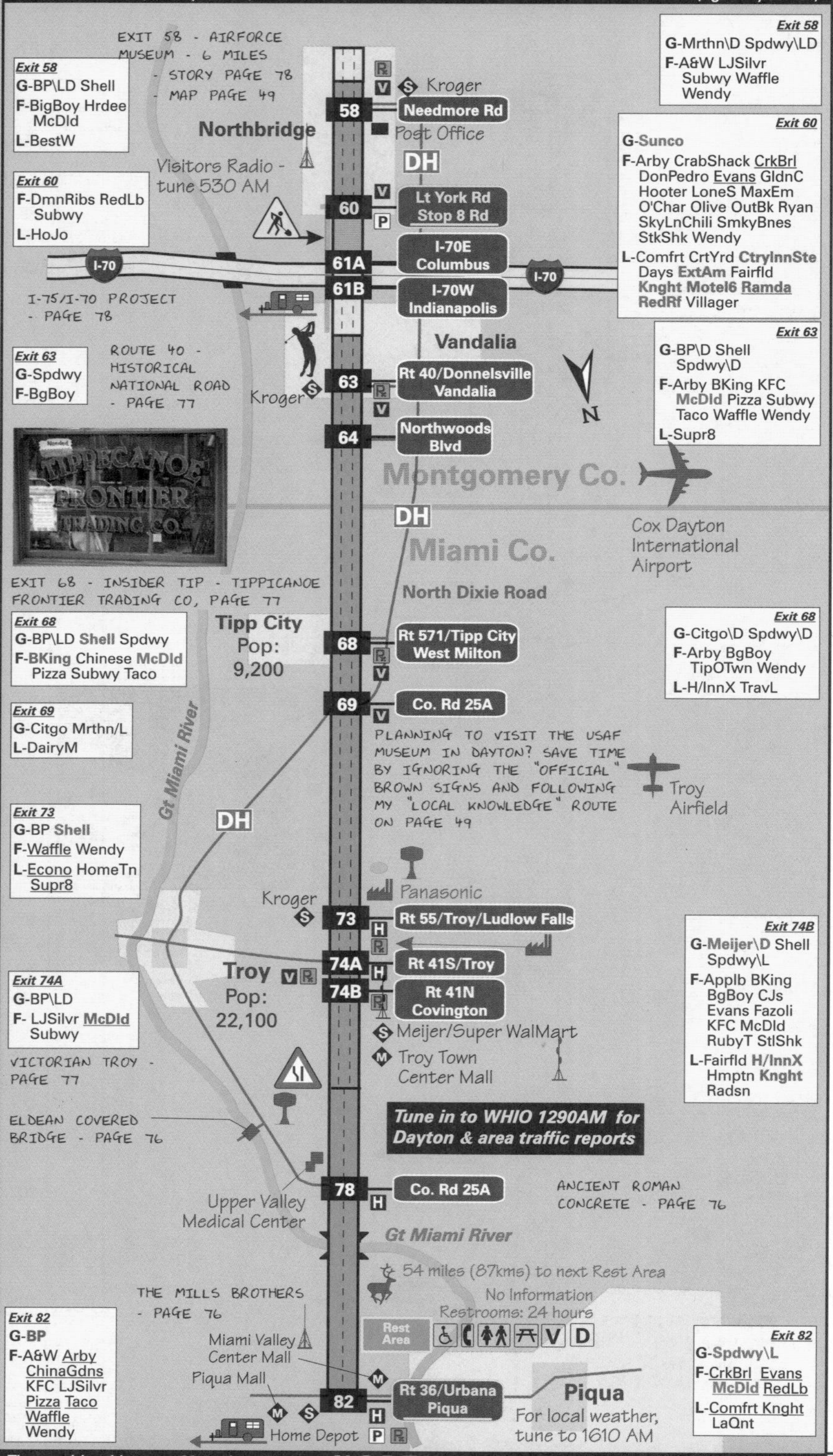

EXIT 58 - AIRFORCE MUSEUM - 6 MILES
- STORY PAGE 78
- MAP PAGE 49

Exit 58
G-BP\LD Shell
F-BigBoy Hrdee McDld
L-BestW

Exit 60
F-DmnRibs RedLb Subwy
L-HoJo

Northbridge

Visitors Radio - tune 530 AM

58 Needmore Rd — Kroger — Post Office
60 Lt York Rd / Stop 8 Rd
61A I-70E Columbus
61B I-70W Indianapolis

I-70

I-75/I-70 PROJECT - PAGE 78

Exit 58
G-Mrthn\D Spdwy\LD
F-A&W LJSilvr Subwy Waffle Wendy

Exit 60
G-Sunco
F-Arby CrabShack CrkBrl DonPedro Evans GldnC Hooter LoneS MaxEm O'Char Olive OutBk Ryan SkyLnChili SmkyBnes StkShk Wendy
L-Comfrt CrtYrd CtryInnSte Days ExtAm Fairfld Knght Motel6 Ramda RedRf Villager

ROUTE 40 - HISTORICAL NATIONAL ROAD - PAGE 77

Exit 63
G-Spdwy
F-BgBoy

Vandalia

63 Rt 40/Donnelsville Vandalia — Kroger
64 Northwoods Blvd

Exit 63
G-BP\D Shell Spdwy\D
F-Arby BKing KFC McDld Pizza Subwy Taco Waffle Wendy
L-Supr8

N

TIPPECANOE FRONTIER TRADING CO.

Montgomery Co.

Miami Co.

Cox Dayton International Airport

EXIT 68 - INSIDER TIP - TIPPICANOE FRONTIER TRADING CO, PAGE 77

North Dixie Road

Exit 68
G-BP\LD Shell Spdwy
F-BKing Chinese McDld Pizza Subwy Taco

Tipp City Pop: 9,200

68 Rt 571/Tipp City West Milton

Exit 68
G-Citgo\D Spdwy\D
F-Arby BgBoy TipOTwn Wendy
L-H/InnX TravL

Exit 69
G-Citgo Mrthn/L
L-DairyM

69 Co. Rd 25A

PLANNING TO VISIT THE USAF MUSEUM IN DAYTON? SAVE TIME BY IGNORING THE "OFFICIAL" BROWN SIGNS AND FOLLOWING MY "LOCAL KNOWLEDGE" ROUTE ON PAGE 49

Troy Airfield

Gt Miami River

DH

Exit 73
G-BP Shell
F-Waffle Wendy
L-Econo HomeTn Supr8

Panasonic

Kroger

73 Rt 55/Troy/Ludlow Falls
74A Rt 41S/Troy
74B Rt 41N Covington

Troy Pop: 22,100

Exit 74A
G-BP\LD
F- LJSilvr McDld Subwy

Meijer/Super WalMart
Troy Town Center Mall

Exit 74B
G-Meijer\D Shell Spdwy\L
F-Applb BKing BgBoy CJs Evans Fazoli KFC McDld RubyT StlShk
L-Fairfld H/InnX Hmptn Knght Radsn

VICTORIAN TROY - PAGE 77

ELDEAN COVERED BRIDGE - PAGE 76

Tune in to WHIO 1290AM for Dayton & area traffic reports

78 Co. Rd 25A

Upper Valley Medical Center

ANCIENT ROMAN CONCRETE - PAGE 76

Gt Miami River

54 miles (87kms) to next Rest Area
No Information
Restrooms: 24 hours
Rest Area

THE MILLS BROTHERS - PAGE 76

Exit 82
G-BP
F-A&W Arby ChinaGdns KFC LJSilvr Pizza Taco Waffle Wendy

Miami Valley Center Mall
Piqua Mall
Home Depot

82 Rt 36/Urbana Piqua

Piqua
For local weather, tune to 1610 AM

Exit 82
G-Spdwy\L
F-CrkBrl Evans McDld RedLb
L-Comfrt Knght LaQnt

Mile Posts: -57- -58- -59- -60- -61- -62- -63- -64- -65- -66- -67- -68- -69- -70- -71- -72- -73- -74- -75- -76- -77- -78- -79- -80- -81- -82-

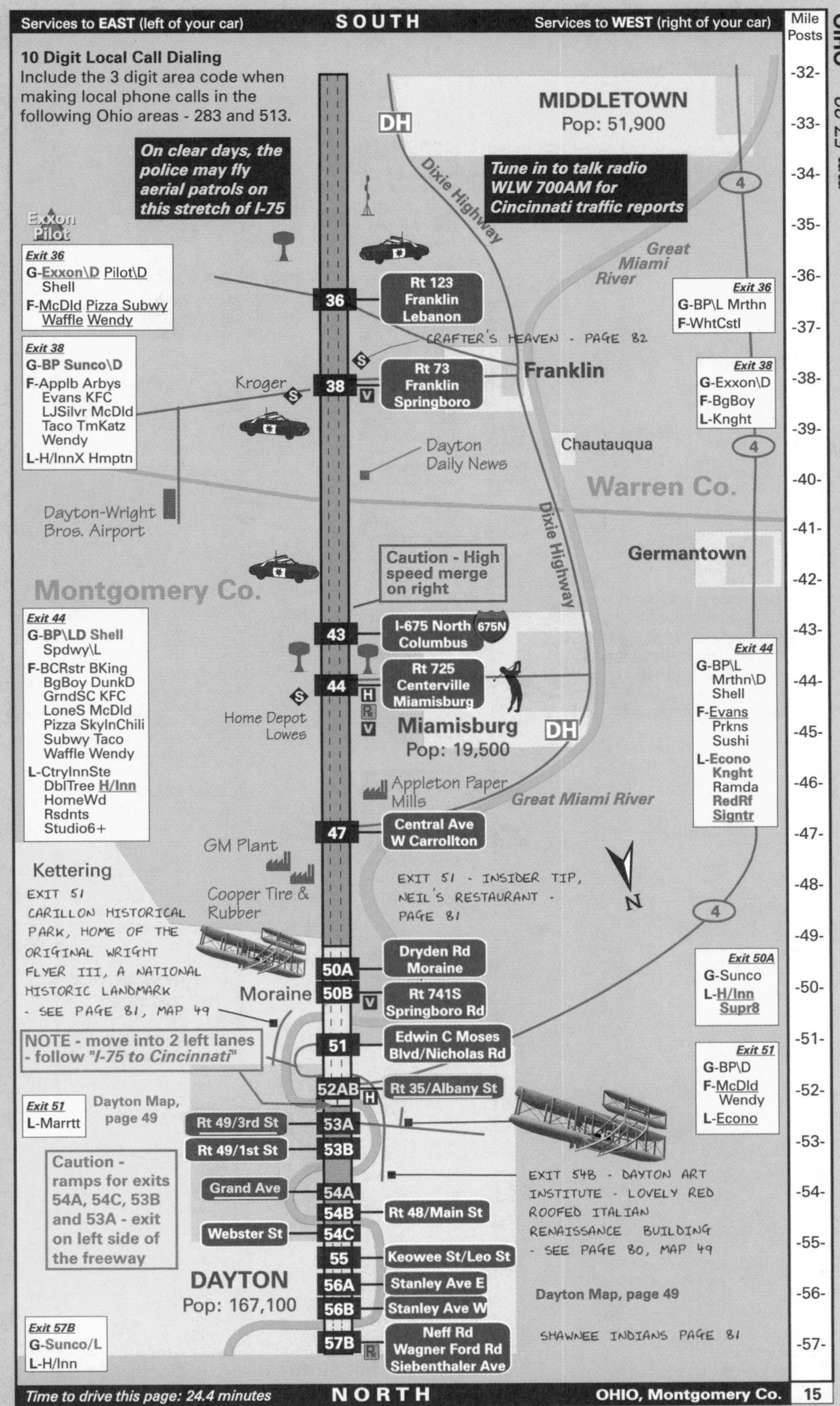
Services to EAST (left of your car)
SOUTH
Services to WEST (right of your car)
Mile Posts
OHIO
mm 57-32
10 Digit Local Call Dialing
Include the 3 digit area code when making local phone calls in the following Ohio areas - 283 and 513.
On clear days, the police may fly aerial patrols on this stretch of I-75
MIDDLETOWN
Pop: 51,900
DH
Dixie Highway
Tune in to talk radio WLW 700AM for Cincinnati traffic reports
4
Great Miami River
Exxon Pilot
Exit 36
G-Exxon\D Pilot\D Shell
F-McDld Pizza Subwy Waffle Wendy
36
Rt 123 Franklin Lebanon
Exit 36
G-BP\L Mrthn
F-WhtCstl
CRAFTER'S HEAVEN - PAGE 82
Exit 38
G-BP Sunco\D
F-Applb Arbys Evans KFC LJSilvr McDld Taco TmKatz Wendy
L-H/InnX Hmptn
Kroger
38
Rt 73 Franklin Springboro
Franklin
Exit 38
G-Exxon\D
F-BgBoy
L-Knght
Dayton Daily News
Chautauqua
Warren Co.
Dayton-Wright Bros. Airport
Dixie Highway
Germantown
Caution - High speed merge on right
Montgomery Co.
Exit 44
G-BP\LD Shell Spdwy\L
F-BCRstr BKing BgBoy DunkD GrndSC KFC LoneS McDld Pizza SkylnChili Subwy Taco Waffle Wendy
L-CtryInnSte DblTree H/Inn HomeWd Rsdnts Studio6+
43
I-675 North Columbus
675N
44
Rt 725 Centerville Miamisburg
Exit 44
G-BP\L Mrthn\D Shell
F-Evans Prkns Sushi
L-Econo Knght Ramda RedRf Signtr
Home Depot Lowes
Miamisburg
Pop: 19,500
DH
Appleton Paper Mills
Great Miami River
GM Plant
47
Central Ave W Carrollton
Kettering
EXIT 51 CARILLON HISTORICAL PARK, HOME OF THE ORIGINAL WRIGHT FLYER III, A NATIONAL HISTORIC LANDMARK - SEE PAGE 81, MAP 49
Cooper Tire & Rubber
EXIT 51 - INSIDER TIP, NEIL'S RESTAURANT - PAGE 81
N
4
50A
Dryden Rd Moraine
Exit 50A
G-Sunco
L-H/Inn Supr8
Moraine
50B
Rt 741S Springboro Rd
NOTE - move into 2 left lanes - follow "I-75 to Cincinnati"
51
Edwin C Moses Blvd/Nicholas Rd
Exit 51
G-BP\D
F-McDld Wendy
L-Econo
52AB
Rt 35/Albany St
Exit 51
L-Marrtt
Dayton Map, page 49
Rt 49/3rd St
53A
Rt 49/1st St
53B
Caution - ramps for exits 54A, 54C, 53B and 53A - exit on left side of the freeway
Grand Ave
54A
54B
Rt 48/Main St
EXIT 54B - DAYTON ART INSTITUTE - LOVELY RED ROOFED ITALIAN RENAISSANCE BUILDING - SEE PAGE 80, MAP 49
Webster St
54C
55
Keowee St/Leo St
DAYTON
Pop: 167,100
56A
Stanley Ave E
Dayton Map, page 49
56B
Stanley Ave W
Exit 57B
G-Sunco/L
L-H/Inn
57B
Neff Rd Wagner Ford Rd Siebenthaler Ave
SHAWNEE INDIANS PAGE 81
-32- -33- -34- -35- -36- -37- -38- -39- -40- -41- -42- -43- -44- -45- -46- -47- -48- -49- -50- -51- -52- -53- -54- -55- -56- -57-
Time to drive this page: 24.4 minutes
NORTH
OHIO, Montgomery Co.
15

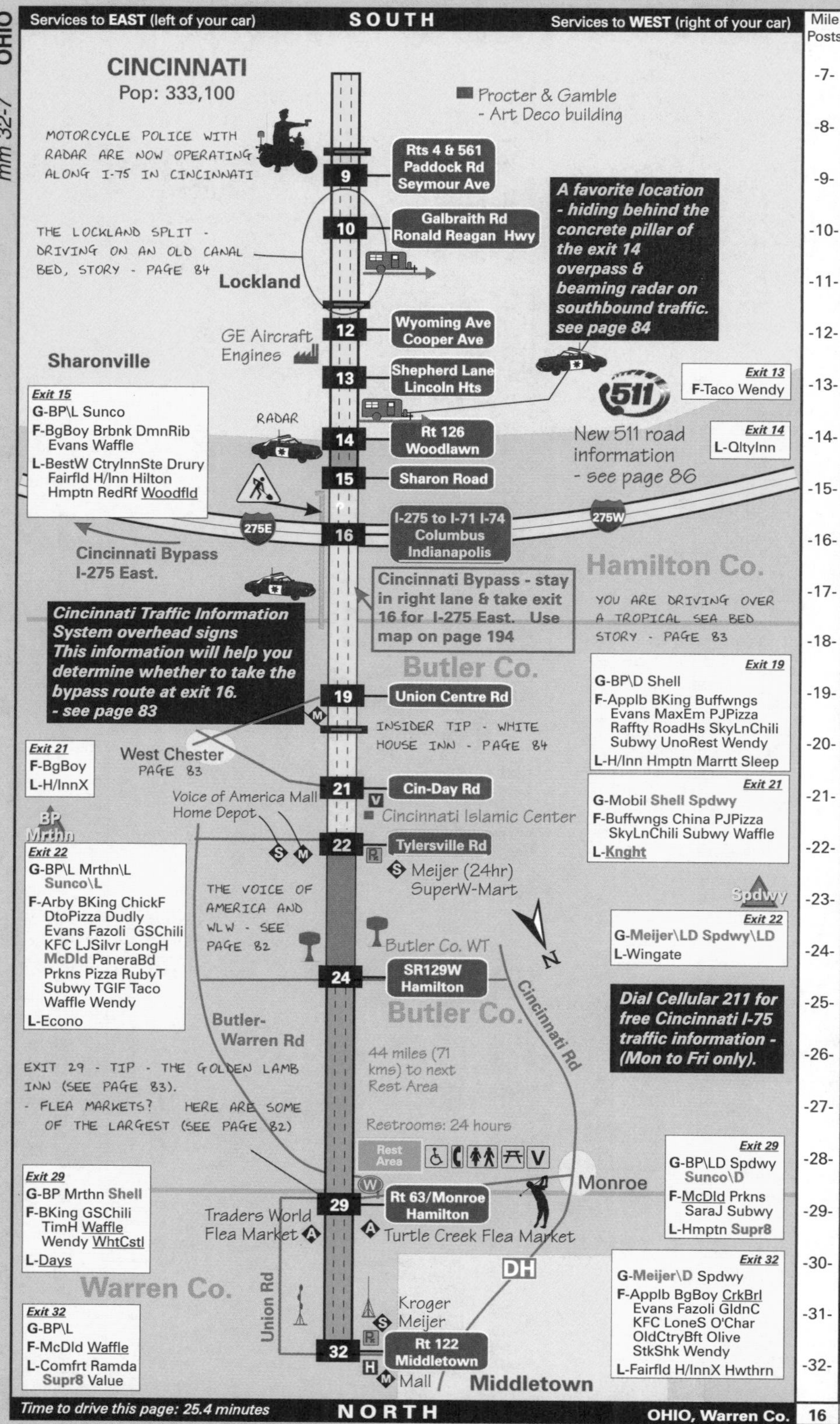
Services to EAST (left of your car)
SOUTH
Services to WEST (right of your car)
Mile Posts
CINCINNATI
Pop: 333,100
Procter & Gamble - Art Deco building
MOTORCYCLE POLICE WITH RADAR ARE NOW OPERATING ALONG I-75 IN CINCINNATI
9
Rts 4 & 561 Paddock Rd Seymour Ave
A favorite location - hiding behind the concrete pillar of the exit 14 overpass & beaming radar on southbound traffic. see page 84
10
Galbraith Rd Ronald Reagan Hwy
THE LOCKLAND SPLIT - DRIVING ON AN OLD CANAL BED, STORY - PAGE 84
Lockland
12
Wyoming Ave Cooper Ave
GE Aircraft Engines
Sharonville
13
Shepherd Lane Lincoln Hts
Exit 13
F-Taco Wendy
Exit 15
G-BP\L Sunco
F-BgBoy Brbnk DmnRib Evans Waffle
L-BestW CtryInnSte Drury Fairfld H/Inn Hilton Hmptn RedRf Woodfld
RADAR
14
Rt 126 Woodlawn
New 511 road information - see page 86
Exit 14
L-QltyInn
15
Sharon Road
16
I-275 to I-71 I-74 Columbus Indianapolis
275E
275W
Cincinnati Bypass I-275 East.
Hamilton Co.
Cincinnati Bypass - stay in right lane & take exit 16 for I-275 East. Use map on page 194
YOU ARE DRIVING OVER A TROPICAL SEA BED STORY - PAGE 83
Cincinnati Traffic Information System overhead signs This information will help you determine whether to take the bypass route at exit 16. - see page 83
Butler Co.
19
Union Centre Rd
Exit 19
G-BP\D Shell
F-Applb BKing Buffwngs Evans MaxEm PJPizza Raffty RoadHs SkyLnChili Subwy UnoRest Wendy
L-H/Inn Hmptn Marrtt Sleep
INSIDER TIP - WHITE HOUSE INN - PAGE 84
Exit 21
F-BgBoy
L-H/InnX
West Chester PAGE 83
21
Cin-Day Rd
Exit 21
G-Mobil Shell Spdwy
F-Buffwngs China PJPizza SkyLnChili Subwy Waffle
L-Knght
Voice of America Mall
Home Depot
Cincinnati Islamic Center
BP Mrthn
22
Tylersville Rd
Meijer (24hr) SuperW-Mart
Exit 22
G-BP\L Mrthn\L Sunco\L
F-Arby BKing ChickF DtoPizza Dudly Evans Fazoli GSChili KFC LJSilvr LongH McDld PaneraBd Prkns Pizza RubyT Subwy TGIF Taco Waffle Wendy
L-Econo
THE VOICE OF AMERICA AND WLW - SEE PAGE 82
Spdwy
Exit 22
G-Meijer\LD Spdwy\LD
L-Wingate
Butler Co. WT
N
24
SR129W Hamilton
Butler Co.
Cincinnati Rd
Butler-Warren Rd
Dial Cellular 211 for free Cincinnati I-75 traffic information - (Mon to Fri only).
44 miles (71 kms) to next Rest Area
EXIT 29 - TIP - THE GOLDEN LAMB INN (SEE PAGE 83).
- FLEA MARKETS? HERE ARE SOME OF THE LARGEST (SEE PAGE 82)
Restrooms: 24 hours
Rest Area
Exit 29
G-BP\LD Spdwy Sunco\D
F-McDld Prkns SaraJ Subwy
L-Hmptn Supr8
Exit 29
G-BP Mrthn Shell
F-BKing GSChili TimH Waffle Wendy WhtCstl
L-Days
29
Rt 63/Monroe Hamilton
Monroe
Traders World Flea Market
Turtle Creek Flea Market
DH
Exit 32
G-Meijer\D Spdwy
F-Applb BgBoy CrkBrl Evans Fazoli GldnC KFC LoneS O'Char OldCtryBft Olive StkShk Wendy
L-Fairfld H/InnX Hwthrn
Warren Co.
Union Rd
Kroger
Meijer
Exit 32
G-BP\L
F-McDld Waffle
L-Comfrt Ramda Supr8 Value
32
Rt 122 Middletown
Mall
Middletown
-7- -8- -9- -10- -11- -12- -13- -14- -15- -16- -17- -18- -19- -20- -21- -22- -23- -24- -25- -26- -27- -28- -29- -30- -31- -32-
Time to drive this page: 25.4 minutes
NORTH

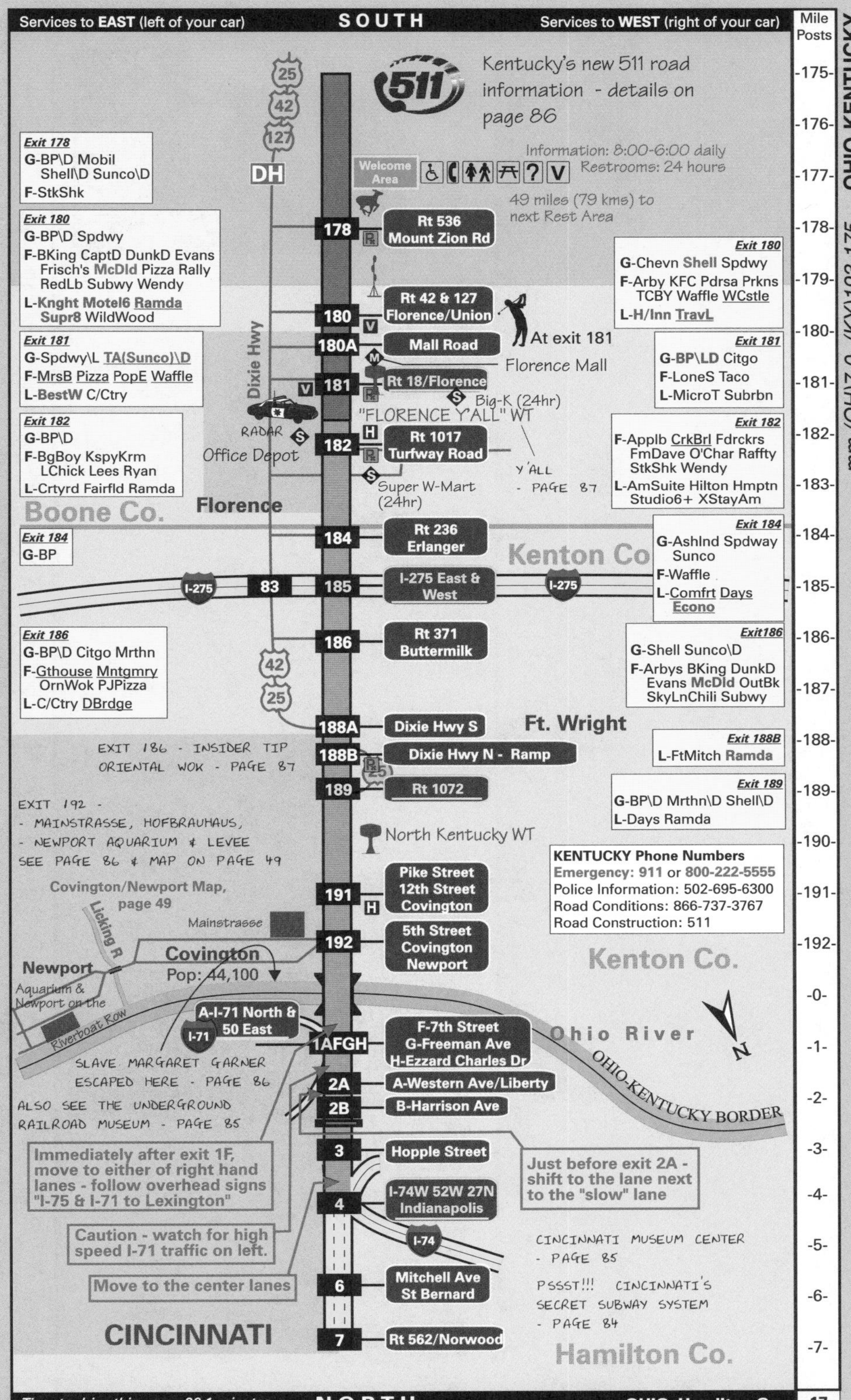

Services to EAST (left of your car)
SOUTH
Services to WEST (right of your car)
Mile Posts
OHIO-KENTUCKY
mm (OH)7-0 (KY)193-175
Kentucky's new 511 road information - details on page 86
Information: 8:00-6:00 daily
Restrooms: 24 hours
49 miles (79 kms) to next Rest Area
Welcome Area
DH
Exit 178
G-BP\D Mobil Shell\D Sunco\D
F-StkShk
178 Rt 536 Mount Zion Rd
Exit 180
G-BP\D Spdwy
F-BKing CaptD DunkD Evans Frisch's McDld Pizza Rally RedLb Subwy Wendy
L-Knght Motel6 Ramda Supr8 WildWood
Exit 180
G-Chevn Shell Spdwy
F-Arby KFC Pdrsa Prkns TCBY Waffle WCstle
L-H/Inn TravL
180 Rt 42 & 127 Florence/Union
At exit 181
180A Mall Road
Florence Mall
Exit 181
G-Spdwy\L TA(Sunco)\D
F-MrsB Pizza PopE Waffle
L-BestW C/Ctry
Exit 181
G-BP\LD Citgo
F-LoneS Taco
L-MicroT Subrbn
181 Rt 18/Florence
Big-K (24hr)
"FLORENCE Y'ALL" WT
Dixie Hwy
Exit 182
G-BP\D
F-BgBoy KspyKrm LChick Lees Ryan
L-Crtyrd Fairfld Ramda
RADAR
Office Depot
182 Rt 1017 Turfway Road
Y'ALL - PAGE 87
Super W-Mart (24hr)
Exit 182
F-Applb CrkBrl Fdrckrs FmDave O'Char Raffty StkShk Wendy
L-AmSuite Hilton Hmptn Studio6+ XStayAm
Boone Co.
Florence
Exit 184
G-BP
184 Rt 236 Erlanger
Kenton Co
Exit 184
G-Ashlnd Spdway Sunco
F-Waffle
L-Comfrt Days Econo
I-275
83
185 I-275 East & West
Exit 186
G-BP\D Citgo Mrthn
F-Gthouse Mntgmry OrnWok PJPizza
L-C/Ctry DBrdge
186 Rt 371 Buttermilk
Exit186
G-Shell Sunco\D
F-Arbys BKing DunkD Evans McDld OutBk SkyLnChili Subwy
188A Dixie Hwy S
Ft. Wright
188B Dixie Hwy N - Ramp
Exit 188B
L-FtMitch Ramda
EXIT 186 - INSIDER TIP ORIENTAL WOK - PAGE 87
189 Rt 1072
Exit 189
G-BP\D Mrthn\D Shell\D
L-Days Ramda
EXIT 192 -
- MAINSTRASSE, HOFBRAUHAUS,
- NEWPORT AQUARIUM & LEVEE
SEE PAGE 86 & MAP ON PAGE 49
North Kentucky WT
KENTUCKY Phone Numbers
Emergency: 911 or 800-222-5555
Police Information: 502-695-6300
Road Conditions: 866-737-3767
Road Construction: 511
Covington/Newport Map, page 49
Licking R
Mainstrasse
191 Pike Street 12th Street Covington
192 5th Street Covington Newport
Newport
Covington Pop: 44,100
Kenton Co.
Aquarium & Newport on the Riverboat Row
A-I-71 North & 50 East
I-71
1AFGH F-7th Street G-Freeman Ave H-Ezzard Charles Dr
Ohio River
OHIO-KENTUCKY BORDER
N
SLAVE MARGARET GARNER ESCAPED HERE - PAGE 86
2A A-Western Ave/Liberty
2B B-Harrison Ave
ALSO SEE THE UNDERGROUND RAILROAD MUSEUM - PAGE 85
Immediately after exit 1F, move to either of right hand lanes - follow overhead signs "I-75 & I-71 to Lexington"
3 Hopple Street
Just before exit 2A - shift to the lane next to the "slow" lane
4 I-74W 52W 27N Indianapolis
I-74
Caution - watch for high speed I-71 traffic on left.
CINCINNATI MUSEUM CENTER - PAGE 85
Move to the center lanes
6 Mitchell Ave St Bernard
PSSST!!! CINCINNATI'S SECRET SUBWAY SYSTEM - PAGE 84
CINCINNATI
7 Rt 562/Norwood
Hamilton Co.
-175- -176- -177- -178- -179- -180- -181- -182- -183- -184- -185- -186- -187- -188- -189- -190- -191- -192- -0- -1- -2- -3- -4- -5- -6- -7-

Services to **EAST** (left of your car) **SOUTH** Services to **WEST** (right of your car)

Mile Posts

-150- -151- -152- -153- -154- -155- -156- -157- -158- -159- -160- -161- -162- -163- -164- -165- -166- -167- -168- -169- -170- -171- -172- -173- -174- -175-

City of Williamstown WT

Exit 154
G-Citgo\LD
Shell\D
F-EZStop

154 Rt 36 Williamstown

Exit 154
G-BP\D Mrthn\D
F-ClassK
L-BestValue Days

Williamstown

Rock Cut

A CIVIL WAR EXECUTION TOOK PLACE HERE - SEE PAGE 88

PHOTO OPPORTUNITY JUST AHEAD AS YOU COME OVER THE BROW OF THE HILL AFTER MILEPOST 156

156 Barnes Road

DH

Exit 159
G-BP Mrthn
Shell\D
F-Arby BKing-I
DQ HpyDragn
KFC LJSilvr
McDld Pizza
Subwy Taco
Waffle Wendy
L-MicroT Supr8

Dry Ridge WT

159 Rt 22 Dry Ridge

Exit 159
G-Spdwy\D
Sunco\D
F-CrkBrl CntryGrill
Shony
L-H/InnX Hmptn

Dry Ridge

Dry Ridge Outlet Mall

Super W-Mart (24hr)

Arnold's River

EXIT 159 - THE COUNTRY GRILL - AN EXCELLENT RESTAURANT - SEE INSIDER TIP ON PAGE 88

N

Grant Co.

Exit 166
G-Chevn
Shell\D
F-BKing
CntyPumkin
Subwy

Exit 166
G-BP Citgo\D
EZstop
Mrthn\D
F-A&W McDld
Taco

166 Rt 491 Crittenden

Crittenden

Weigh Station

ADVANTAGE-75? SEE PAGE 88

ADVANTAGE 75
FOLLOW
IN-CAB SIGNALS

Kenton Co.

Boone Co.

Exit 171
G-BP Citgo
F-DQ

Walton

171 Rts 14 16 Walton Verona

Exit 171
G-Conco FlyJ\DL
F-Cookery

Walton WT

I-71

173 I-71 South to Louisville

Exit 175
G-BP PilotTS\D
Shell\LD
F-GSChili HngKng
McDld PapaDino
PennStn Raymnd
SkyLnChili Subwy
Waffle Wendy
L-Days Econo

Exit 175
G-TA(BP)\D
TS(Pilot)
F-Arby BKing
CPride
KspyKrm Taco
WhtCstl
L-H/InnX

175 Rt 338 Richwood

Richwood

EXIT 175 - INSIDER TIP - TOM'S PAPA DINO'S - PAGE 88

Time to drive this page: 23.9 minutes **NORTH**

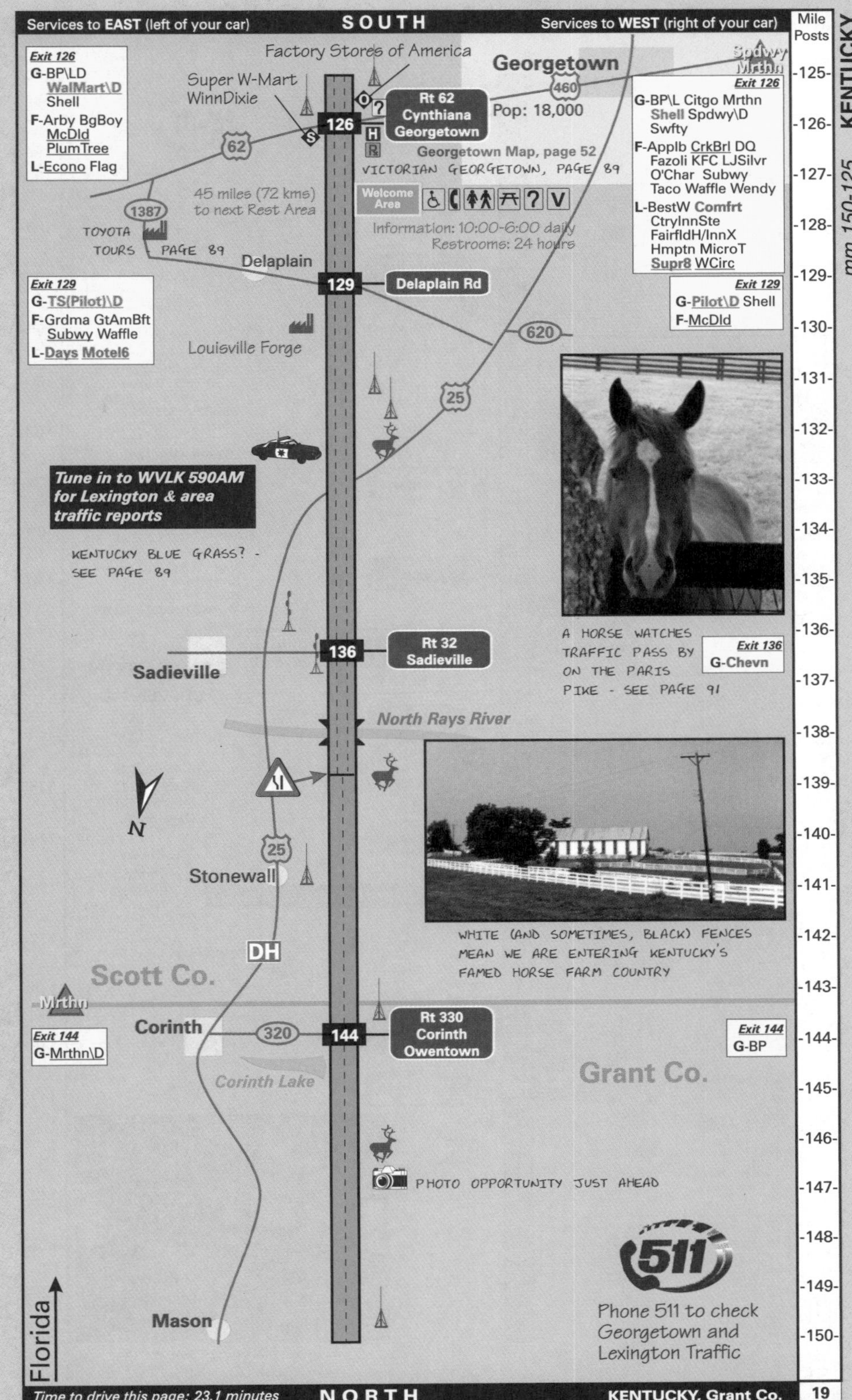
Mile Posts
Exit 126
G-BP\LD
WalMart\D
Shell
F-Arby BgBoy
McDld
PlumTree
L-Econo Flag
Factory Stores of America
Super W-Mart
WinnDixie
Georgetown
460
126
Rt 62
Cynthiana
Georgetown
Pop: 18,000
62
Georgetown Map, page 52
VICTORIAN GEORGETOWN, PAGE 89
Spdwy
Mrthn
Exit 126
G-BP\L Citgo Mrthn
Shell Spdwy\D
Swfty
F-Applb CrkBrl DQ
Fazoli KFC LJSilvr
O'Char Subwy
Taco Waffle Wendy
L-BestW Comfrt
CtryInnSte
FairfldH/InnX
Hmptn MicroT
Supr8 WCirc
1387
45 miles (72 kms)
to next Rest Area
Welcome Area
Information: 10:00-6:00 daily
Restrooms: 24 hours
TOYOTA TOURS - PAGE 89
Delaplain
129
Delaplain Rd
Exit 129
G-TS(Pilot)\D
F-Grdma GtAmBft
Subwy Waffle
L-Days Motel6
Louisville Forge
620
Exit 129
G-Pilot\D Shell
F-McDld
25
Tune in to WVLK 590AM
for Lexington & area
traffic reports
KENTUCKY BLUE GRASS? - SEE PAGE 89
136
Rt 32
Sadieville
Sadieville
A HORSE WATCHES TRAFFIC PASS BY ON THE PARIS PIKE - SEE PAGE 91
Exit 136
G-Chevn
North Rays River
N
25
Stonewall
WHITE (AND SOMETIMES, BLACK) FENCES MEAN WE ARE ENTERING KENTUCKY'S FAMED HORSE FARM COUNTRY
DH
Scott Co.
Mrthn
Corinth
320
144
Rt 330
Corinth
Owentown
Exit 144
G-Mrthn\D
Exit 144
G-BP
Corinth Lake
Grant Co.
PHOTO OPPORTUNITY JUST AHEAD
511
Phone 511 to check
Georgetown and
Lexington Traffic
Mason
Florida
-125- -126- -127- -128- -129- -130- -131- -132- -133- -134- -135- -136- -137- -138- -139- -140- -141- -142- -143- -144- -145- -146- -147- -148- -149- -150-

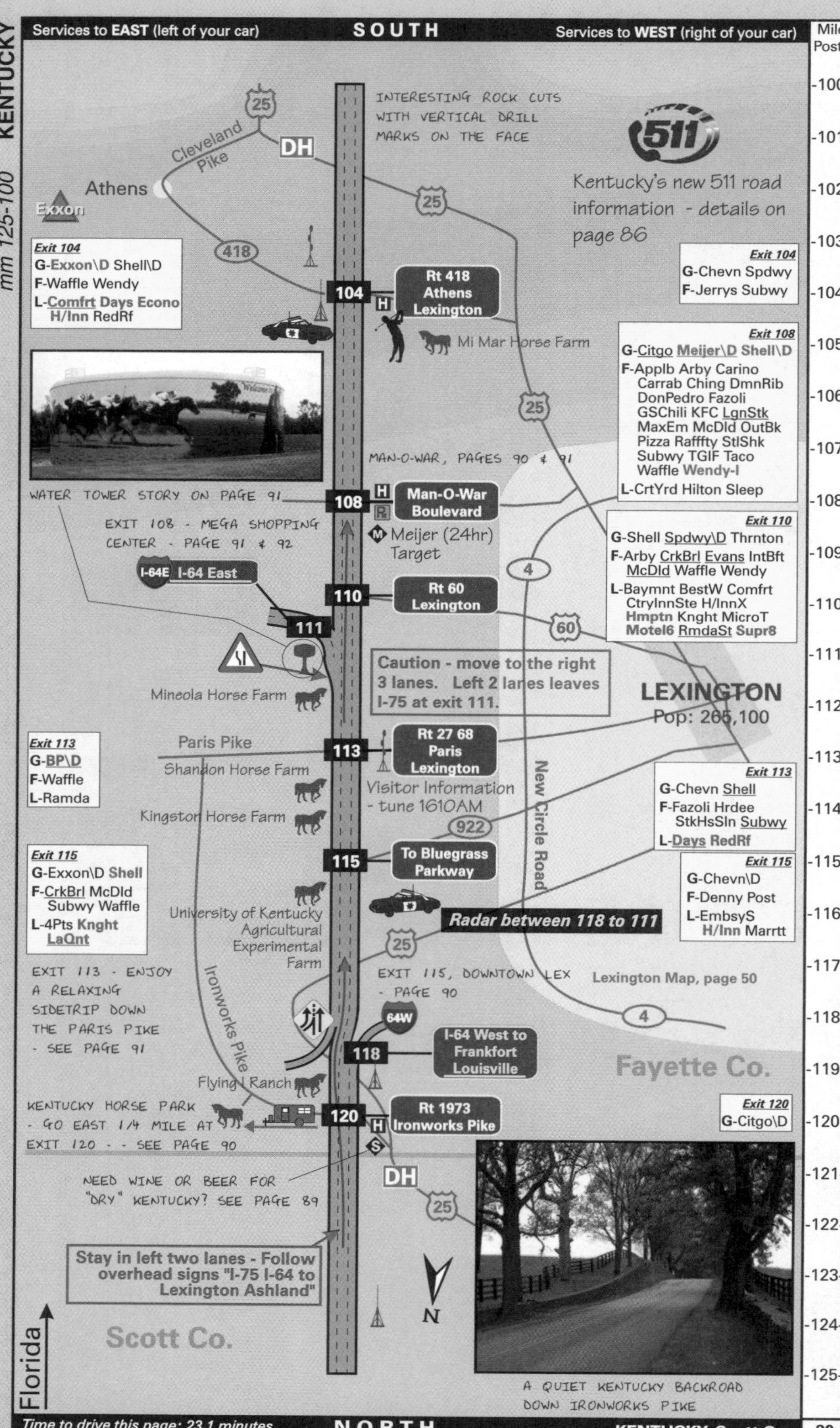
Services to EAST (left of your car)
SOUTH
Services to WEST (right of your car)
Mile Posts
INTERESTING ROCK CUTS WITH VERTICAL DRILL MARKS ON THE FACE
Cleveland Pike
Athens
Exxon
DH
Kentucky's new 511 road information - details on page 86
Exit 104
G-Exxon\D Shell\D
F-Waffle Wendy
L-Comfrt Days Econo H/Inn RedRf
104
Rt 418 Athens Lexington
Exit 104
G-Chevn Spdwy
F-Jerrys Subwy
Mi Mar Horse Farm
Exit 108
G-Citgo Meijer\D Shell\D
F-Applb Arby Carino Carrab Ching DmnRib DonPedro Fazoli GSChili KFC LgnStk MaxEm McDld OutBk Pizza Rafffty StlShk Subwy TGIF Taco Waffle Wendy-I
L-CrtYrd Hilton Sleep
MAN-O-WAR, PAGES 90 & 91
WATER TOWER STORY ON PAGE 91
108
Man-O-War Boulevard
Meijer (24hr) Target
EXIT 108 - MEGA SHOPPING CENTER - PAGE 91 & 92
Exit 110
G-Shell Spdwy\D Thrnton
F-Arby CrkBrl Evans IntBft McDld Waffle Wendy
L-Baymnt BestW Comfrt CtrylnnSte H/InnX Hmptn Knght MicroT Motel6 RmdaSt Supr8
I-64E I-64 East
110
Rt 60 Lexington
111
Caution - move to the right 3 lanes. Left 2 lanes leaves I-75 at exit 111.
LEXINGTON
Pop: 265,100
Mineola Horse Farm
Exit 113
G-BP\D
F-Waffle
L-Ramda
Paris Pike
113
Rt 27 68 Paris Lexington
Shandon Horse Farm
Visitor Information - tune 1610AM
Kingston Horse Farm
New Circle Road
Exit 113
G-Chevn Shell
F-Fazoli Hrdee StkHsSln Subwy
L-Days RedRf
Exit 115
G-Exxon\D Shell
F-CrkBrl McDld Subwy Waffle
L-4Pts Knght LaQnt
115
To Bluegrass Parkway
Exit 115
G-Chevn\D
F-Denny Post
L-EmbsyS H/Inn Marrtt
University of Kentucky Agricultural Experimental Farm
Radar between 118 to 111
EXIT 113 - ENJOY A RELAXING SIDETRIP DOWN THE PARIS PIKE - SEE PAGE 91
Ironworks Pike
EXIT 115, DOWNTOWN LEX - PAGE 90
Lexington Map, page 50
64W
118
I-64 West to Frankfort Louisville
Fayette Co.
Flying J Ranch
KENTUCKY HORSE PARK - GO EAST 1/4 MILE AT EXIT 120 - - SEE PAGE 90
120
Rt 1973 Ironworks Pike
Exit 120
G-Citgo\D
NEED WINE OR BEER FOR "DRY" KENTUCKY? SEE PAGE 89
Stay in left two lanes - Follow overhead signs "I-75 I-64 to Lexington Ashland"
N
Scott Co.
Florida
A QUIET KENTUCKY BACKROAD DOWN IRONWORKS PIKE
Time to drive this page: 23.1 minutes
NORTH
KENTUCKY, Scott Co.

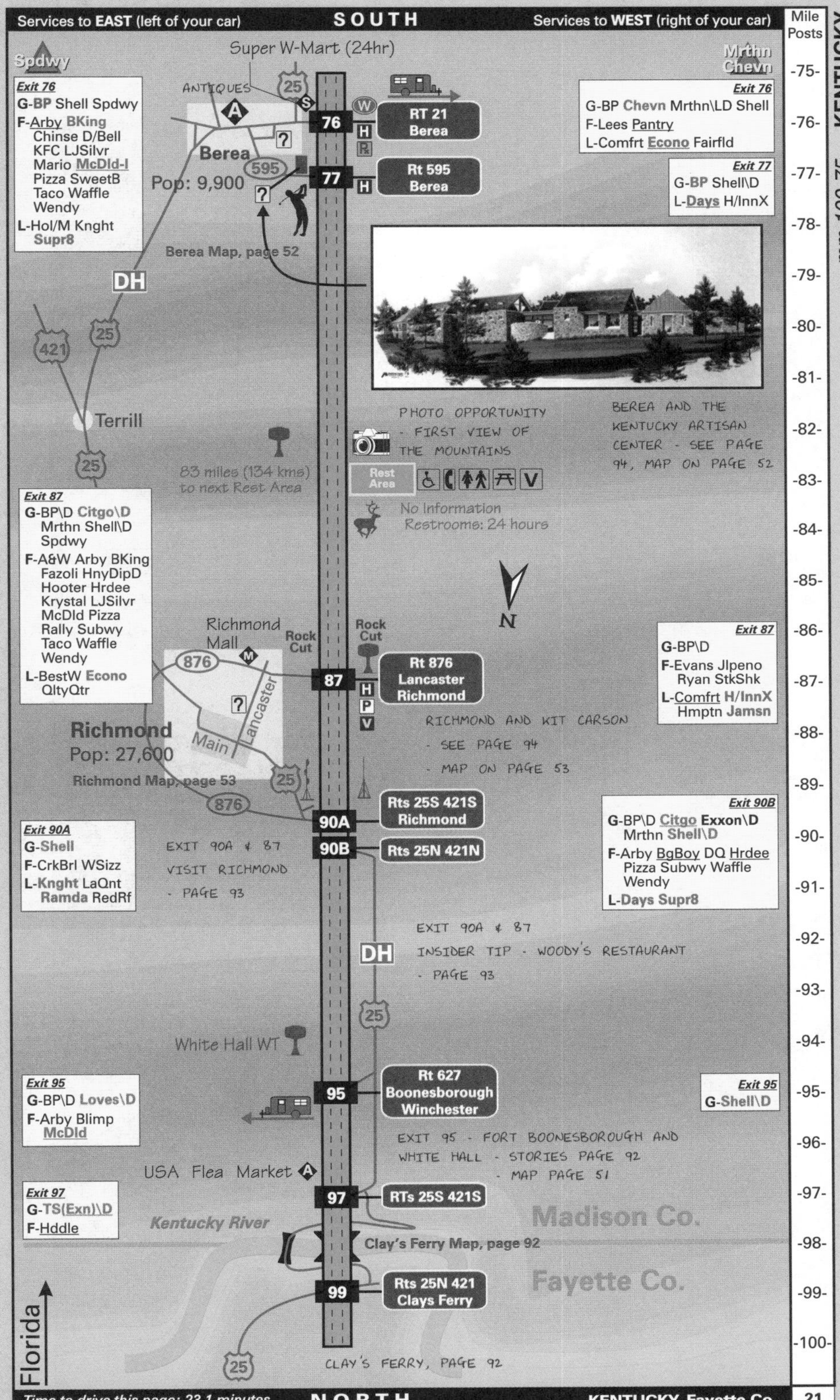
Services to EAST (left of your car)
SOUTH
Services to WEST (right of your car)
Mile Posts
KENTUCKY
mm 100-75
Spdwy
Super W-Mart (24hr)
Mrthn Chevn
Exit 76
G-BP Shell Spdwy
F-Arby BKing Chinse D/Bell KFC LJSilvr Mario McDld-I Pizza SweetB Taco Waffle Wendy
L-Hol/M Knght Supr8
ANTIQUES
Berea
Pop: 9,900
76
RT 21 Berea
77
Rt 595 Berea
Exit 76
G-BP Chevn Mrthn\LD Shell
F-Lees Pantry
L-Comfrt Econo Fairfld
Exit 77
G-BP Shell\D
L-Days H/InnX
Berea Map, page 52
DH
Terrill
PHOTO OPPORTUNITY - FIRST VIEW OF THE MOUNTAINS
BEREA AND THE KENTUCKY ARTISAN CENTER - SEE PAGE 94, MAP ON PAGE 52
83 miles (134 kms) to next Rest Area
Rest Area
No Information
Restrooms: 24 hours
N
Exit 87
G-BP\D Citgo\D Mrthn Shell\D Spdwy
F-A&W Arby BKing Fazoli HnyDipD Hooter Hrdee Krystal LJSilvr McDld Pizza Rally Subwy Taco Waffle Wendy
L-BestW Econo QltyQtr
Richmond Mall
Rock Cut
Rock Cut
87
Rt 876 Lancaster Richmond
Exit 87
G-BP\D
F-Evans Jlpeno Ryan StkShk
L-Comfrt H/InnX Hmptn Jamsn
Lancaster
Main
Richmond
Pop: 27,600
Richmond Map, page 53
RICHMOND AND KIT CARSON - SEE PAGE 94 - MAP ON PAGE 53
90A
Rts 25S 421S Richmond
90B
Rts 25N 421N
Exit 90A
G-Shell
F-CrkBrl WSizz
L-Knght LaQnt Ramda RedRf
EXIT 90A & 87 VISIT RICHMOND - PAGE 93
Exit 90B
G-BP\D Citgo Exxon\D Mrthn Shell\D
F-Arby BgBoy DQ Hrdee Pizza Subwy Waffle Wendy
L-Days Supr8
EXIT 90A & 87 INSIDER TIP - WOODY'S RESTAURANT - PAGE 93
White Hall WT
Exit 95
G-BP\D Loves\D
F-Arby Blimp McDld
95
Rt 627 Boonesborough Winchester
Exit 95
G-Shell\D
EXIT 95 - FORT BOONESBOROUGH AND WHITE HALL - STORIES PAGE 92 - MAP PAGE 51
USA Flea Market
Exit 97
G-TS(Exn)\D
F-Hddle
97
RTs 25S 421S
Kentucky River
Madison Co.
Clay's Ferry Map, page 92
Fayette Co.
99
Rts 25N 421 Clays Ferry
Florida
CLAY'S FERRY, PAGE 92
Time to drive this page: 23.1 minutes
NORTH
KENTUCKY, Fayette Co.
21

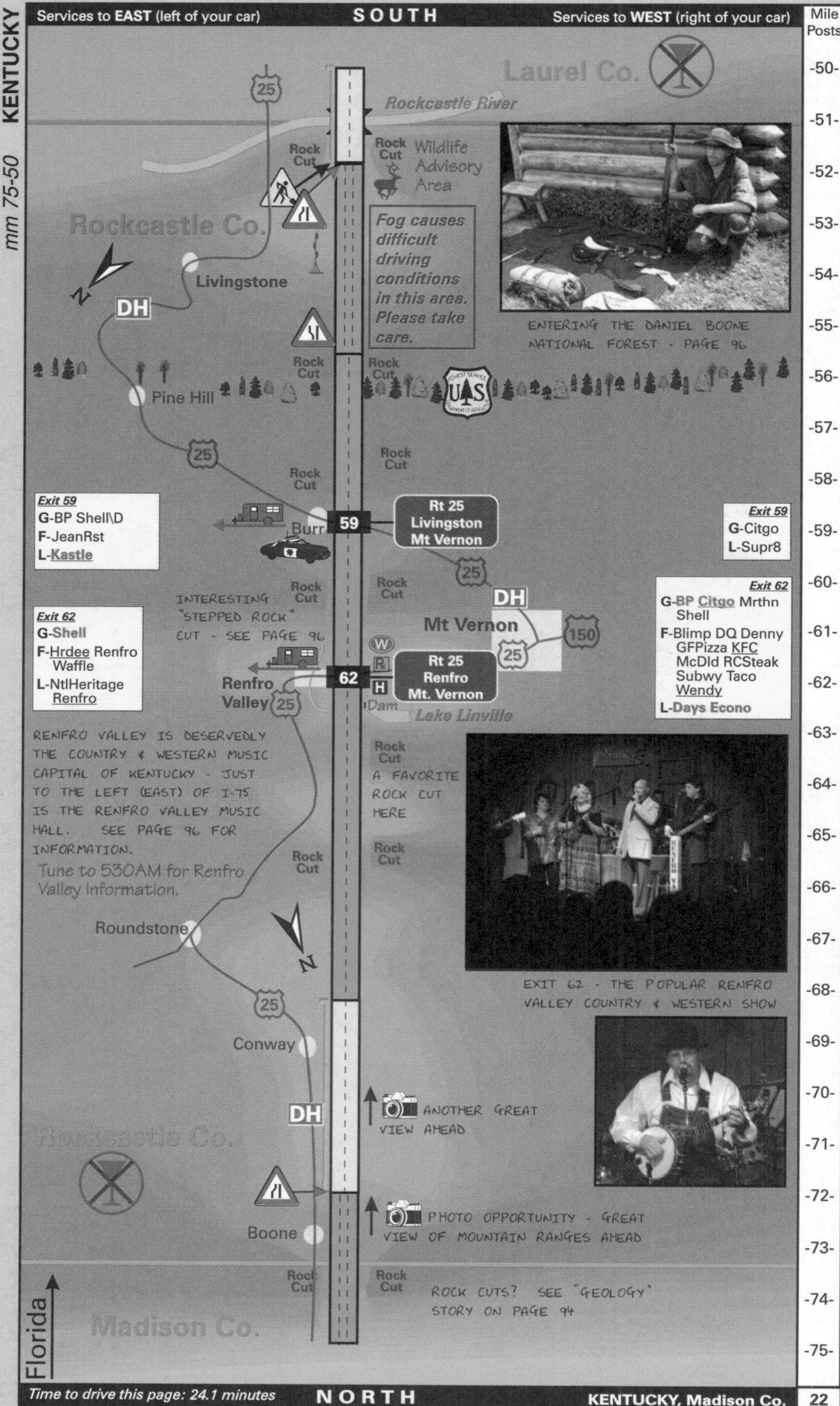
Services to EAST (left of your car)
SOUTH
Services to WEST (right of your car)
Mile Posts
-50- -51- -52- -53- -54- -55- -56- -57- -58- -59- -60- -61- -62- -63- -64- -65- -66- -67- -68- -69- -70- -71- -72- -73- -74- -75-
Laurel Co.
Rockcastle River
Rock Cut
Wildlife Advisory Area
Rockcastle Co.
Livingstone
DH
Fog causes difficult driving conditions in this area. Please take care.
ENTERING THE DANIEL BOONE NATIONAL FOREST - PAGE 96
Pine Hill
25
Exit 59
G-BP Shell\D
F-JeanRst
L-Kastle
Burr
59
Rt 25 Livingston Mt Vernon
Exit 59
G-Citgo
L-Supr8
INTERESTING "STEPPED ROCK" CUT - SEE PAGE 96
Mt Vernon
150
Exit 62
G-Shell
F-Hrdee Renfro Waffle
L-NtlHeritage Renfro
Exit 62
G-BP Citgo Mrthn Shell
F-Blimp DQ Denny GFPizza KFC McDld RCSteak Subwy Taco Wendy
L-Days Econo
Renfro Valley
62
Rt 25 Renfro Mt. Vernon
Dam
Lake Linville
RENFRO VALLEY IS DESERVEDLY THE COUNTRY & WESTERN MUSIC CAPITAL OF KENTUCKY - JUST TO THE LEFT (EAST) OF I-75 IS THE RENFRO VALLEY MUSIC HALL. SEE PAGE 96 FOR INFORMATION.
A FAVORITE ROCK CUT HERE
Tune to 530AM for Renfro Valley information.
Roundstone
EXIT 62 - THE POPULAR RENFRO VALLEY COUNTRY & WESTERN SHOW
Conway
ANOTHER GREAT VIEW AHEAD
Rockcastle Co.
PHOTO OPPORTUNITY - GREAT VIEW OF MOUNTAIN RANGES AHEAD
Boone
ROCK CUTS? SEE "GEOLOGY" STORY ON PAGE 94
Florida
Madison Co.
NORTH

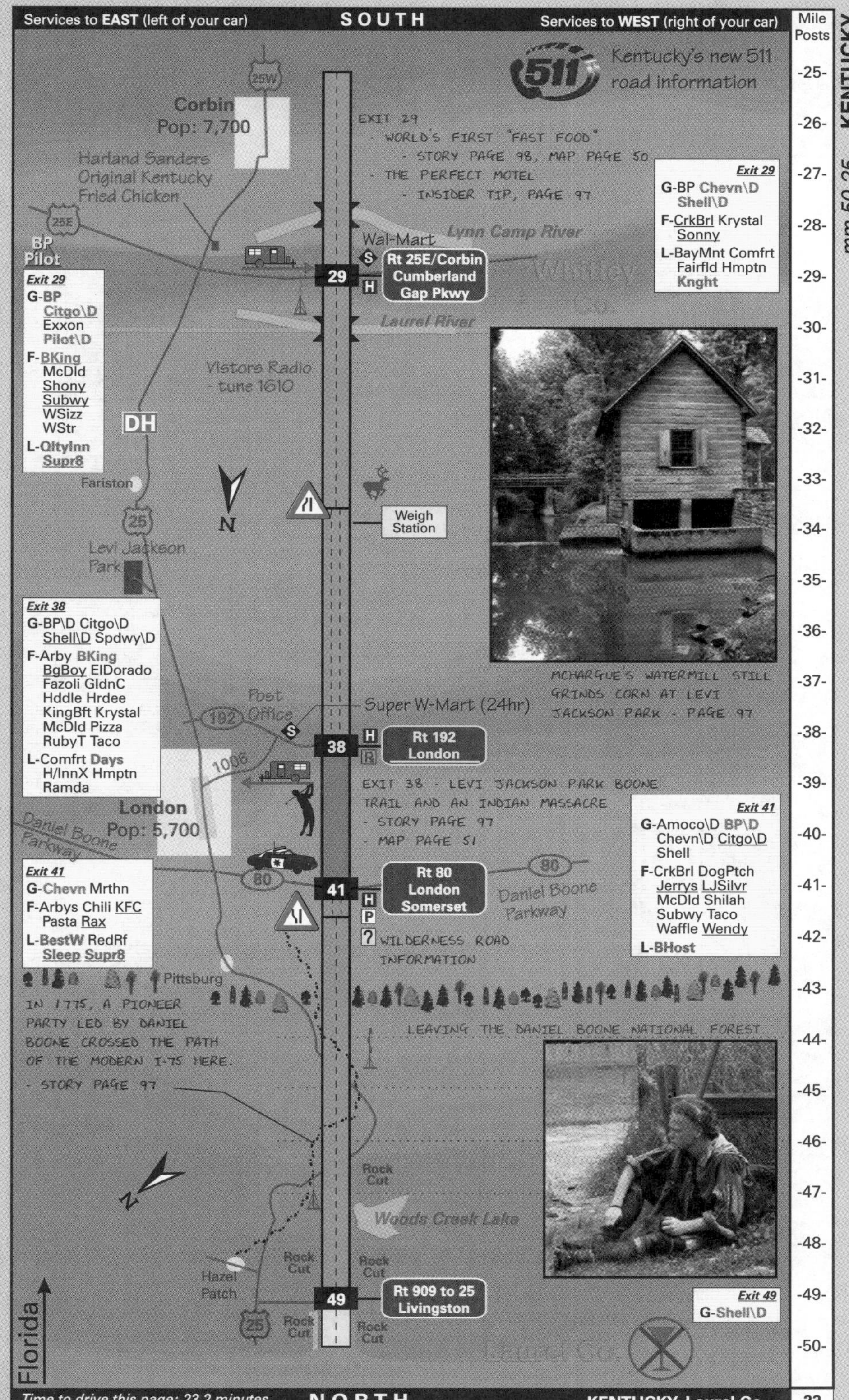
Mile Posts
KENTUCKY
mm 50-25
Kentucky's new 511 road information
Corbin
Pop: 7,700
Harland Sanders Original Kentucky Fried Chicken
EXIT 29
- WORLD'S FIRST "FAST FOOD"
- STORY PAGE 98, MAP PAGE 50
- THE PERFECT MOTEL
- INSIDER TIP, PAGE 97
Exit 29
G-BP Chevn\D Shell\D
F-CrkBrl Krystal Sonny
L-BayMnt Comfrt Fairfld Hmptn Knght
BP Pilot
Wal-Mart
Lynn Camp River
Rt 25E/Corbin Cumberland Gap Pkwy
29
Whitley Co.
Exit 29
G-BP Citgo\D Exxon Pilot\D
F-BKing McDld Shony Subwy WSizz WStr
L-QltyInn Supr8
Laurel River
Vistors Radio - tune 1610
DH
Fariston
N
Weigh Station
Levi Jackson Park
Exit 38
G-BP\D Citgo\D Shell\D Spdwy\D
F-Arby BKing BgBoy ElDorado Fazoli GldnC Hddle Hrdee KingBft Krystal McDld Pizza RubyT Taco
L-Comfrt Days H/InnX Hmptn Ramda
MCHARGUE'S WATERMILL STILL GRINDS CORN AT LEVI JACKSON PARK - PAGE 97
Post Office
Super W-Mart (24hr)
38
Rt 192 London
1006
London
Pop: 5,700
EXIT 38 - LEVI JACKSON PARK BOONE TRAIL AND AN INDIAN MASSACRE
- STORY PAGE 97
- MAP PAGE 51
Daniel Boone Parkway
Exit 41
G-Amoco\D BP\D Chevn\D Citgo\D Shell
F-CrkBrl DogPtch Jerrys LJSilvr McDld Shilah Subwy Taco Waffle Wendy
L-BHost
Exit 41
G-Chevn Mrthn
F-Arbys Chili KFC Pasta Rax
L-BestW RedRf Sleep Supr8
80
41
Rt 80 London Somerset
Daniel Boone Parkway
WILDERNESS ROAD INFORMATION
Pittsburg
IN 1775, A PIONEER PARTY LED BY DANIEL BOONE CROSSED THE PATH OF THE MODERN I-75 HERE.
- STORY PAGE 97
LEAVING THE DANIEL BOONE NATIONAL FOREST
Rock Cut
Woods Creek Lake
Hazel Patch
49
Rt 909 to 25 Livingston
Exit 49
G-Shell\D
Laurel Co.
Florida
-25- -26- -27- -28- -29- -30- -31- -32- -33- -34- -35- -36- -37- -38- -39- -40- -41- -42- -43- -44- -45- -46- -47- -48- -49- -50-

Services to **EAST** (left of your car) **SOUTH** Services to **WEST** (right of your car)

Mile Posts

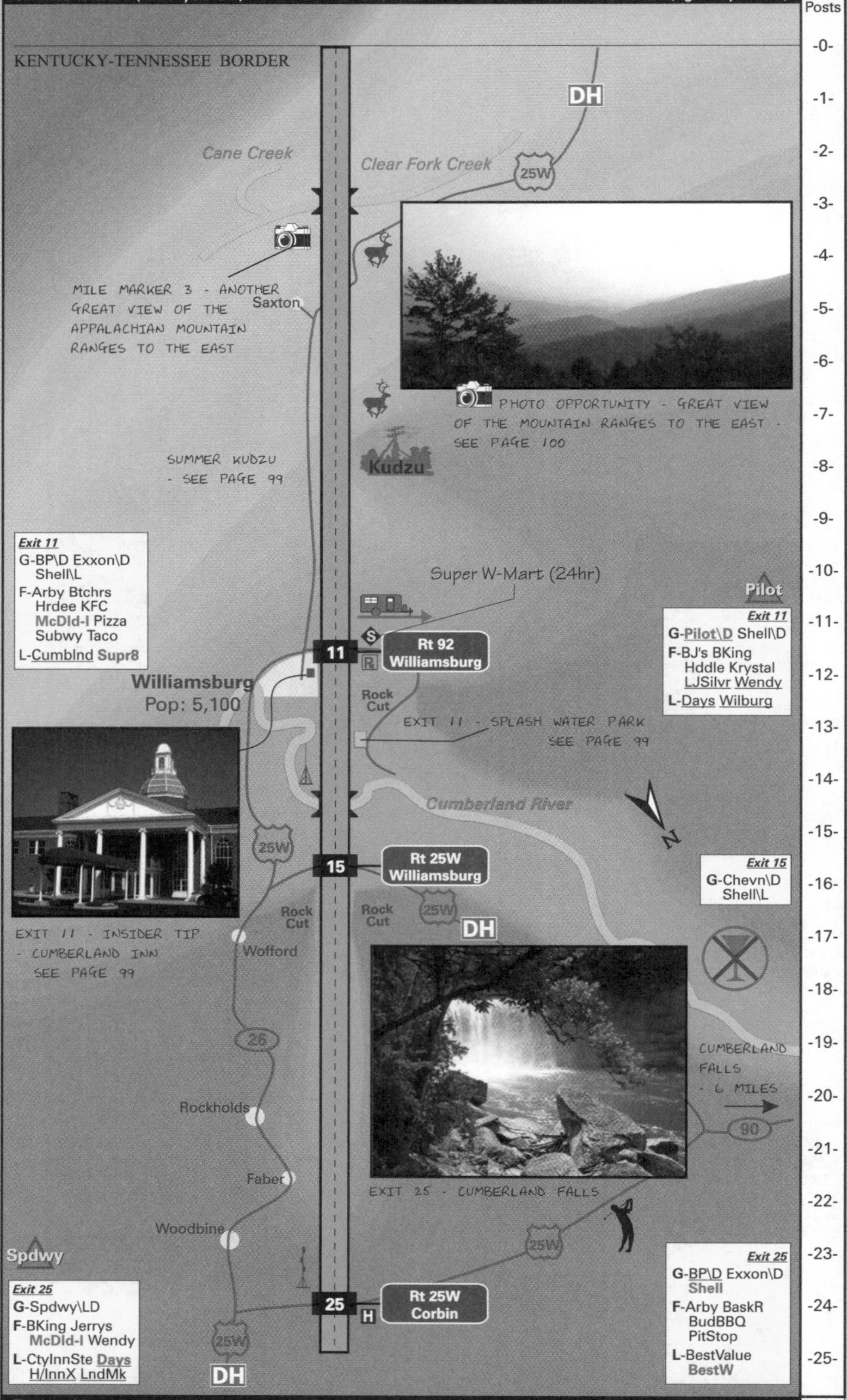

KENTUCKY-TENNESSEE BORDER

DH

Cane Creek

Clear Fork Creek

25W

MILE MARKER 3 - ANOTHER GREAT VIEW OF THE APPALACHIAN MOUNTAIN RANGES TO THE EAST

Saxton

PHOTO OPPORTUNITY - GREAT VIEW OF THE MOUNTAIN RANGES TO THE EAST - SEE PAGE 100

SUMMER KUDZU - SEE PAGE 99

Kudzu

Exit 11
G-BP\D Exxon\D Shell\L
F-Arby Btchrs Hrdee KFC **McDld-I** Pizza Subwy Taco
L-Cumblnd **Supr8**

Super W-Mart (24hr)

Pilot

Exit 11
G-Pilot\D Shell\D
F-BJ's BKing Hddle Krystal LJSilvr Wendy
L-Days Wilburg

11 Rt 92 Williamsburg

Williamsburg
Pop: 5,100

Rock Cut

EXIT 11 - SPLASH WATER PARK SEE PAGE 99

Cumberland River

N

25W

15 Rt 25W Williamsburg

Exit 15
G-Chevn\D Shell\L

Rock Cut

Rock Cut

25W

DH

EXIT 11 - INSIDER TIP - CUMBERLAND INN SEE PAGE 99

Wofford

26

Rockholds

Faber

Woodbine

CUMBERLAND FALLS - 6 MILES

90

EXIT 25 - CUMBERLAND FALLS

25W

Spdwy

Exit 25
G-Spdwy\LD
F-BKing Jerrys **McDld-I** Wendy
L-CtyInnSte Days H/InnX LndMk

25 Rt 25W Corbin

H

Exit 25
G-BP\D Exxon\D **Shell**
F-Arby BaskR BudBBQ PitStop
L-BestValue **BestW**

25W

DH

-0- -1- -2- -3- -4- -5- -6- -7- -8- -9- -10- -11- -12- -13- -14- -15- -16- -17- -18- -19- -20- -21- -22- -23- -24- -25-

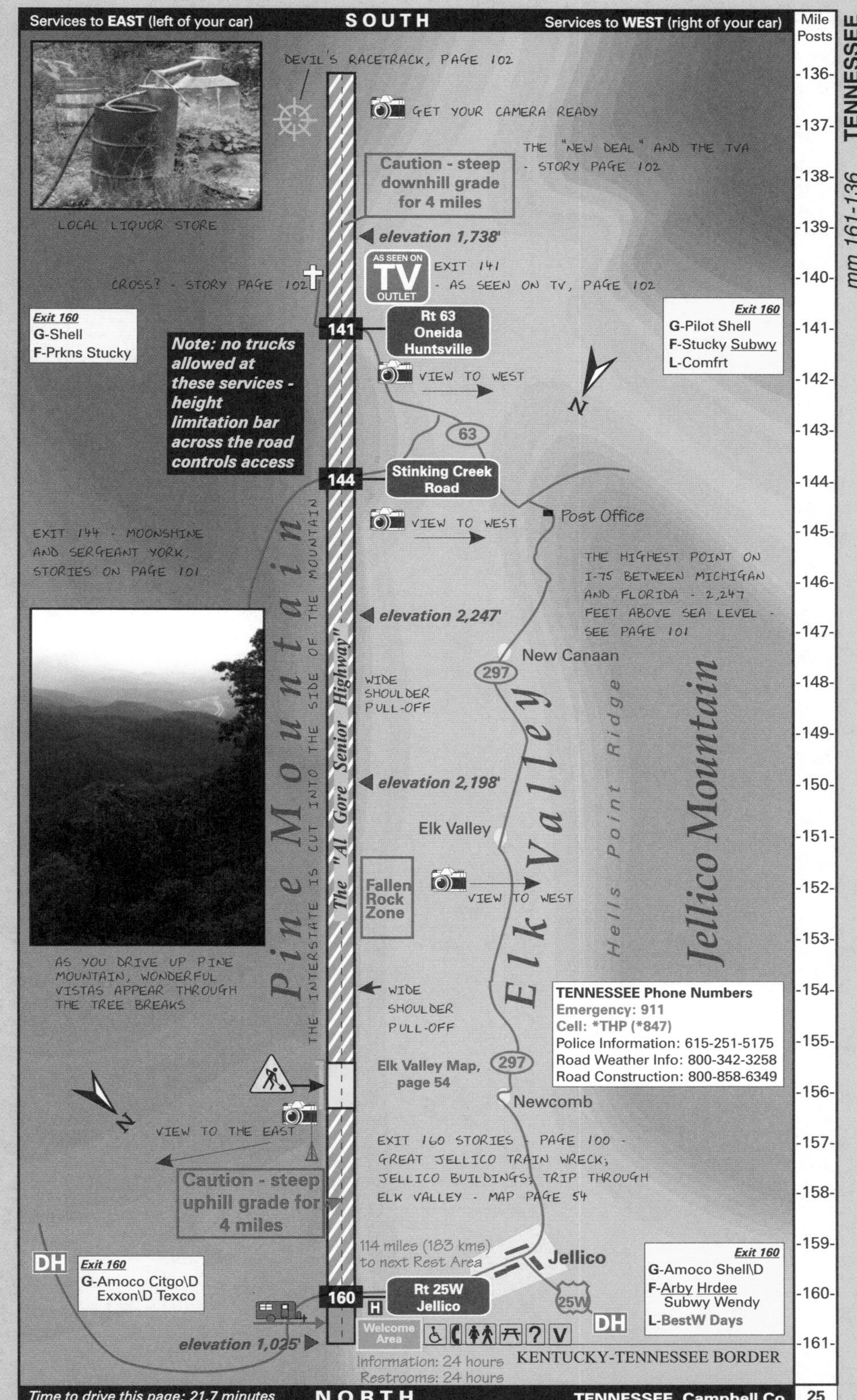
Services to EAST (left of your car)
SOUTH
Services to WEST (right of your car)
Mile Posts
-136-
-137-
-138-
-139-
-140-
-141-
-142-
-143-
-144-
-145-
-146-
-147-
-148-
-149-
-150-
-151-
-152-
-153-
-154-
-155-
-156-
-157-
-158-
-159-
-160-
-161-
LOCAL LIQUOR STORE
DEVIL'S RACETRACK, PAGE 102
GET YOUR CAMERA READY
THE "NEW DEAL" AND THE TVA - STORY PAGE 102
Caution - steep downhill grade for 4 miles
elevation 1,738'
AS SEEN ON TV OUTLET
EXIT 141 - AS SEEN ON TV, PAGE 102
CROSS? - STORY PAGE 102
Exit 160
G-Shell
F-Prkns Stucky
Note: no trucks allowed at these services - height limitation bar across the road controls access
141
Rt 63 Oneida Huntsville
VIEW TO WEST
Exit 160
G-Pilot Shell
F-Stucky Subwy
L-Comfrt
N
63
144
Stinking Creek Road
VIEW TO WEST
Post Office
EXIT 144 - MOONSHINE AND SERGEANT YORK, STORIES ON PAGE 101
THE HIGHEST POINT ON I-75 BETWEEN MICHIGAN AND FLORIDA - 2,247 FEET ABOVE SEA LEVEL - SEE PAGE 101
elevation 2,247'
New Canaan
297
WIDE SHOULDER PULL-OFF
Pine Mountain
THE INTERSTATE IS CUT INTO THE SIDE OF THE MOUNTAIN
The "Al Gore Senior Highway"
elevation 2,198'
Elk Valley
Elk Valley
Hells Point Ridge
Jellico Mountain
Fallen Rock Zone
VIEW TO WEST
AS YOU DRIVE UP PINE MOUNTAIN, WONDERFUL VISTAS APPEAR THROUGH THE TREE BREAKS
WIDE SHOULDER PULL-OFF
TENNESSEE Phone Numbers
Emergency: 911
Cell: *THP (*847)
Police Information: 615-251-5175
Road Weather Info: 800-342-3258
Road Construction: 800-858-6349
Elk Valley Map, page 54
297
Newcomb
N
VIEW TO THE EAST
EXIT 160 STORIES - PAGE 100 - GREAT JELLICO TRAIN WRECK; JELLICO BUILDINGS; TRIP THROUGH ELK VALLEY - MAP PAGE 54
Caution - steep uphill grade for 4 miles
114 miles (183 kms) to next Rest Area
Jellico
DH
Exit 160
G-Amoco Citgo\D Exxon\D Texco
160
H
Rt 25W Jellico
25W
DH
Exit 160
G-Amoco Shell\D
F-Arby Hrdee Subwy Wendy
L-BestW Days
Welcome Area
elevation 1,025'
Information: 24 hours
Restrooms: 24 hours
KENTUCKY-TENNESSEE BORDER
Time to drive this page: 21.7 minutes
NORTH
TENNESSEE, Campbell Co.

Exit 112
G-BP\D Chevn Pilot\D
F-Aubreys BudBBQ DQ Krystal McDld-I StkShk Taco Wendy
L-CtylnnSte H/InnX

Exit 112
G-Exxon Shell\D
F-Hrdee Shony Waffle
L-Comfrt

112 Rt 131 Emory Rd Powell

Emory Rd

Heiskell Rd

EXIT 112 - INSIDER TIP AUBREY'S RESTAURANT

EXIT 112 - WATCH FOR LOW FLYING PLANES COMING IN OVER I-75. THE RUNWAY STARTS JUST BY THE SOUTHWEST SIDE OF THIS EXIT

Rock Cut

Exit 117
G-BP Pilot\D

Knox Co.

117 Rt 170 Raccoon Valley

170

Anderson Co.

to I-75 via Oak Ridge

Clinton

CLINTON - STORY ON PAGE 104

441

Clinton and Oak Ridge Maps, page 56

Sevier Blvd

61

Exit 122
G-Exxon\D GitnGo\D Mrthn Phil66\D Texco\D
F-Arby BKing BaskR GitnGo GldnGirls Harrisn Hrdee Krystal McDld Subwy Waffle Wendy
L-BestW Comfrt H/InnX Supr8

Museum of the Appalachia

Exit 122
G-Shell
F-Shony

122 Rt 61/Norris Clinton

Twin Gables Antique Mall

Bypass Knoxville? See page 104; map on page 56

25S

Norris

Wildlife Sanctuary

Norris Dam Map, page 55

EXIT 122
MUSEUM OF THE APPALACHIA
- STORY PAGE 103, MAP ON PAGE 55
GOLDEN GIRLS RESTAURANT
- INSIDER TIP ON PAGE 103

DH

Clinch River

Lenoir Museum

Grist Mill & Threshing Barn

Exit 128
G-BP Sunco

Lake City

Norris Dam

Norris Park

Norris Park

128 Rt 44 Lake City

Exit 129
G-Citgo Exxon\LD Shell
F-BKing Blimp CrkBrl KFC McDld-I Subwy
L-Days Lambs LkCty

129 Rt S25W Lake City

116

Anderson Co.

Campbell Co.

Kudzu

Truck Inspect

NO FACILITIES

Kudzu

Tune in to WNOX 990AM for Knoxville & area traffic reports

N

EXIT 128 - TAKE A SHORT BUT FASCINATING SIDE TRIP OVER NORRIS DAM
- STORY PAGE 102
- MAP PAGE 55

134 Rts N25W/E63 Caryville Jacksboro La Follette

Exit 134
G-Amoco BP
F-Scottys Shony
L-BHost

Exit 134
G-Exxon\D Shell
F-D/Bell Family Louies Waffle
L-Family Hmptn Lkview Supr8

COVE LAKE STATE PARK

Caryville

VIEW - OFF TO THE WEST

elevation 1,093'

-111- -112- -113- -114- -115- -116- -117- -118- -119- -120- -121- -122- -123- -124- -125- -126- -127- -128- -129- -130- -131- -132- -133- -134- -135- -136-

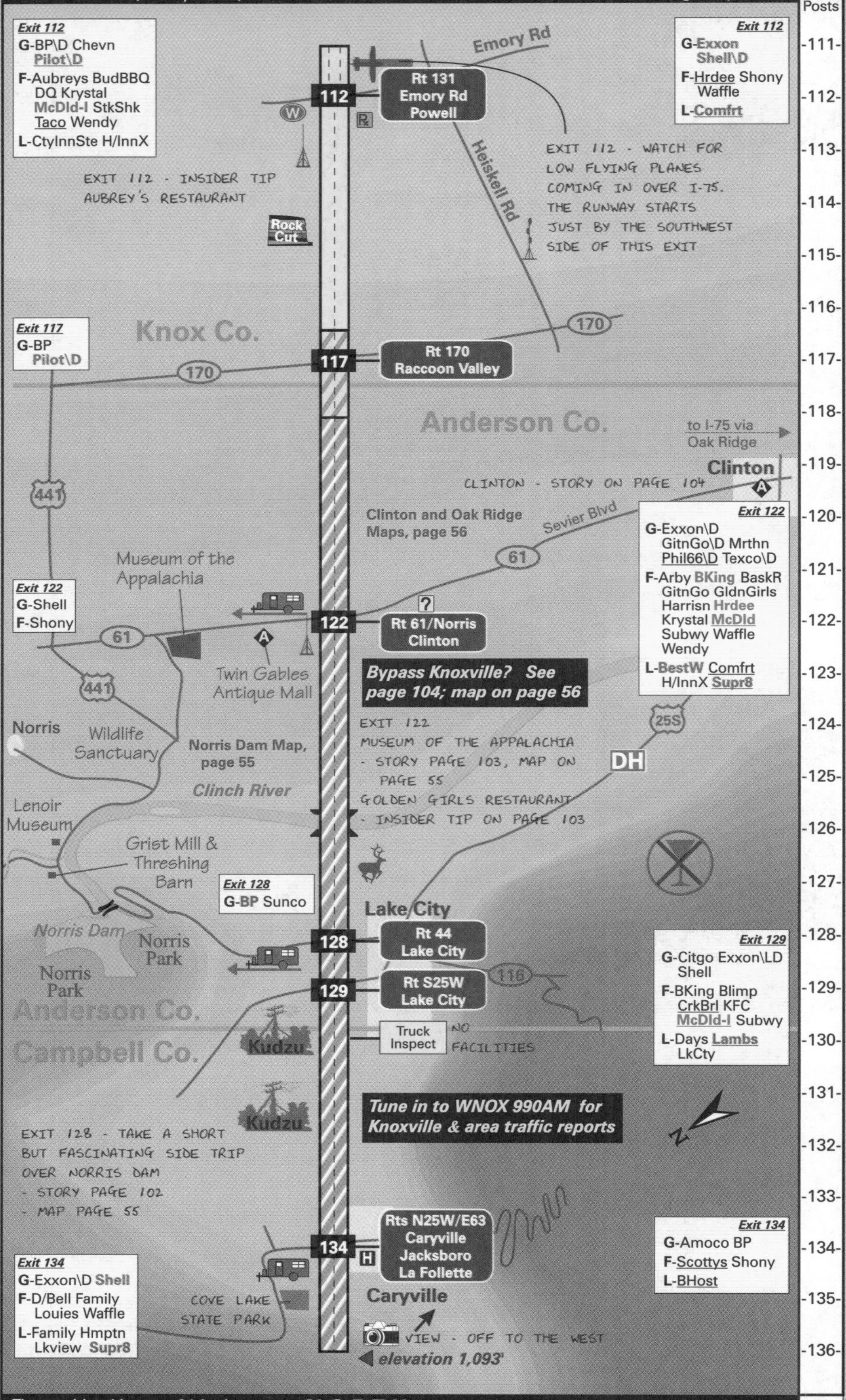

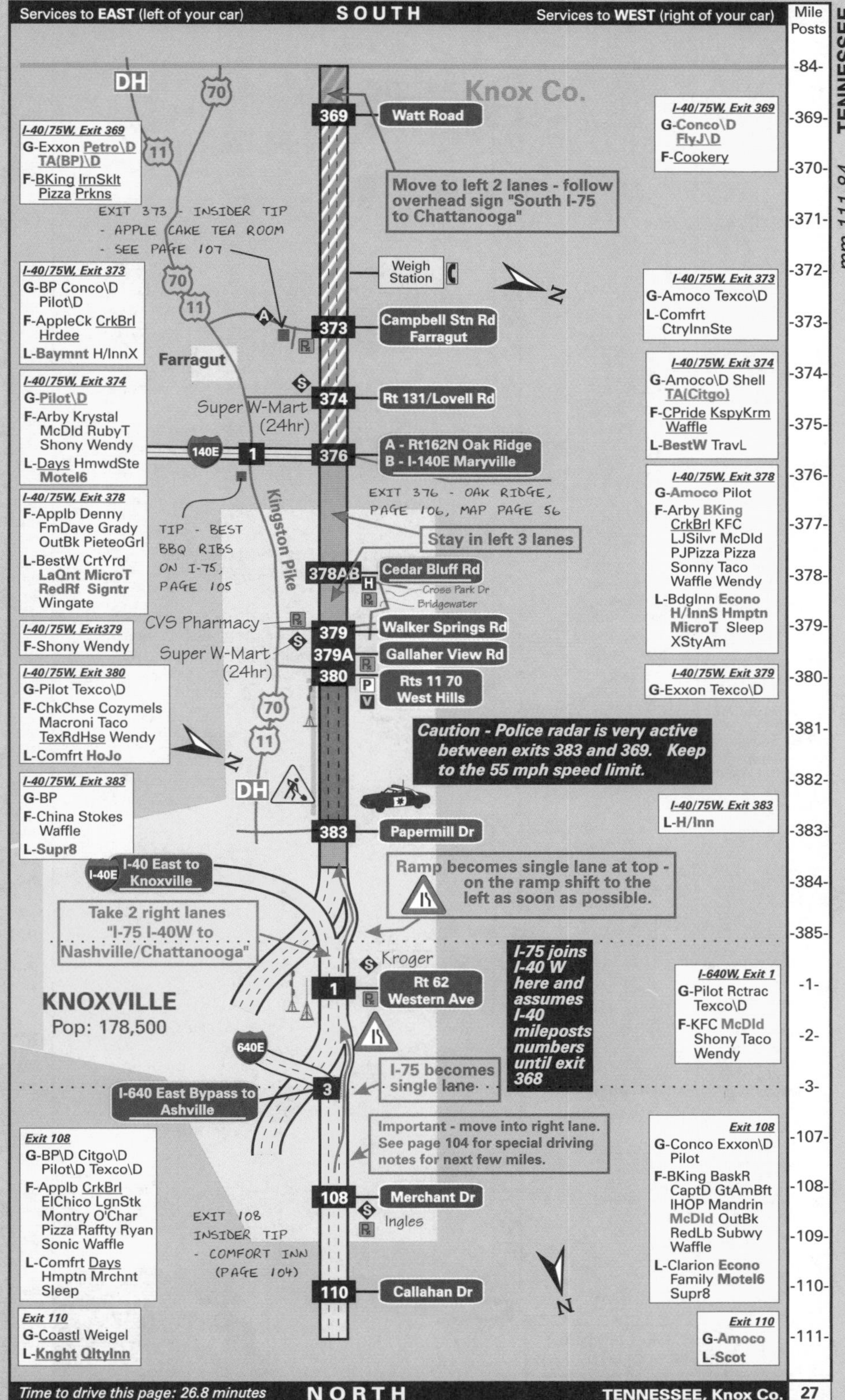
Services to EAST (left of your car)
SOUTH
Services to WEST (right of your car)
Mile Posts
TENNESSEE
mm 111-84
Knox Co.
-84-
369
Watt Road
I-40/75W, Exit 369
G-Exxon Petro\D TA(BP)\D
F-BKing IrnSklt Pizza Prkns
I-40/75W, Exit 369
G-Conco\D FlyJ\D
F-Cookery
-369-
-370-
Move to left 2 lanes - follow overhead sign "South I-75 to Chattanooga"
-371-
EXIT 373 - INSIDER TIP - APPLE CAKE TEA ROOM - SEE PAGE 107
Weigh Station
-372-
I-40/75W, Exit 373
G-BP Conco\D Pilot\D
F-AppleCk CrkBrl Hrdee
L-Baymnt H/InnX
373
Campbell Stn Rd Farragut
I-40/75W, Exit 373
G-Amoco Texco\D
L-Comfrt CtryInnSte
-373-
Farragut
I-40/75W, Exit 374
G-Pilot\D
F-Arby Krystal McDld RubyT Shony Wendy
L-Days HmwdSte Motel6
374
Rt 131/Lovell Rd
Super W-Mart (24hr)
I-40/75W, Exit 374
G-Amoco\D Shell TA(Citgo)
F-CPride KspyKrm Waffle
L-BestW TravL
-374-
-375-
140E
1
376
A - Rt162N Oak Ridge
B - I-140E Maryville
-376-
EXIT 376 - OAK RIDGE, PAGE 106, MAP PAGE 56
I-40/75W, Exit 378
F-Applb Denny FmDave Grady OutBk PieteoGrl
L-BestW CrtYrd LaQnt MicroT RedRf Signtr Wingate
TIP - BEST BBQ RIBS ON I-75, PAGE 105
Kingston Pike
Stay in left 3 lanes
I-40/75W, Exit 378
G-Amoco Pilot
F-Arby BKing CrkBrl KFC LJSilvr McDld PJPizza Pizza Sonny Taco Waffle Wendy
L-BdgInn Econo H/InnS Hmptn MicroT Sleep XStyAm
-377-
378AB
Cedar Bluff Rd
Cross Park Dr
Bridgewater
-378-
CVS Pharmacy
I-40/75W, Exit379
F-Shony Wendy
379
Walker Springs Rd
-379-
Super W-Mart (24hr)
379A
Gallaher View Rd
I-40/75W, Exit 380
G-Pilot Texco\D
F-ChkChse Cozymels Macroni Taco TexRdHse Wendy
L-Comfrt HoJo
380
Rts 11 70 West Hills
I-40/75W, Exit 379
G-Exxon Texco\D
-380-
Caution - Police radar is very active between exits 383 and 369. Keep to the 55 mph speed limit.
-381-
-382-
I-40/75W, Exit 383
G-BP
F-China Stokes Waffle
L-Supr8
DH
383
Papermill Dr
I-40/75W, Exit 383
L-H/Inn
-383-
I-40E
I-40 East to Knoxville
Ramp becomes single lane at top - on the ramp shift to the left as soon as possible.
-384-
Take 2 right lanes "I-75 I-40W to Nashville/Chattanooga"
-385-
Kroger
I-75 joins I-40 W here and assumes I-40 mileposts numbers until exit 368
1
Rt 62 Western Ave
I-640W, Exit 1
G-Pilot Rctrac Texco\D
F-KFC McDld Shony Taco Wendy
-1-
KNOXVILLE
Pop: 178,500
640E
-2-
I-75 becomes single lane
I-640 East Bypass to Ashville
3
-3-
Important - move into right lane. See page 104 for special driving notes for next few miles.
Exit 108
G-BP\D Citgo\D Pilot\D Texco\D
F-Applb CrkBrl ElChico LgnStk Montry O'Char Pizza Raffty Ryan Sonic Waffle
L-Comfrt Days Hmptn Mrchnt Sleep
Exit 108
G-Conco Exxon\D Pilot
F-BKing BaskR CaptD GtAmBft IHOP Mandrin McDld OutBk RedLb Subwy Waffle
L-Clarion Econo Family Motel6 Supr8
-107-
108
Merchant Dr
Ingles
-108-
EXIT 108 INSIDER TIP - COMFORT INN (PAGE 104)
-109-
110
Callahan Dr
-110-
Exit 110
G-Coastl Weigel
L-Knght QltyInn
Exit 110
G-Amoco
L-Scot
-111-
Time to drive this page: 26.8 minutes
NORTH
TENNESSEE, Knox Co.
27

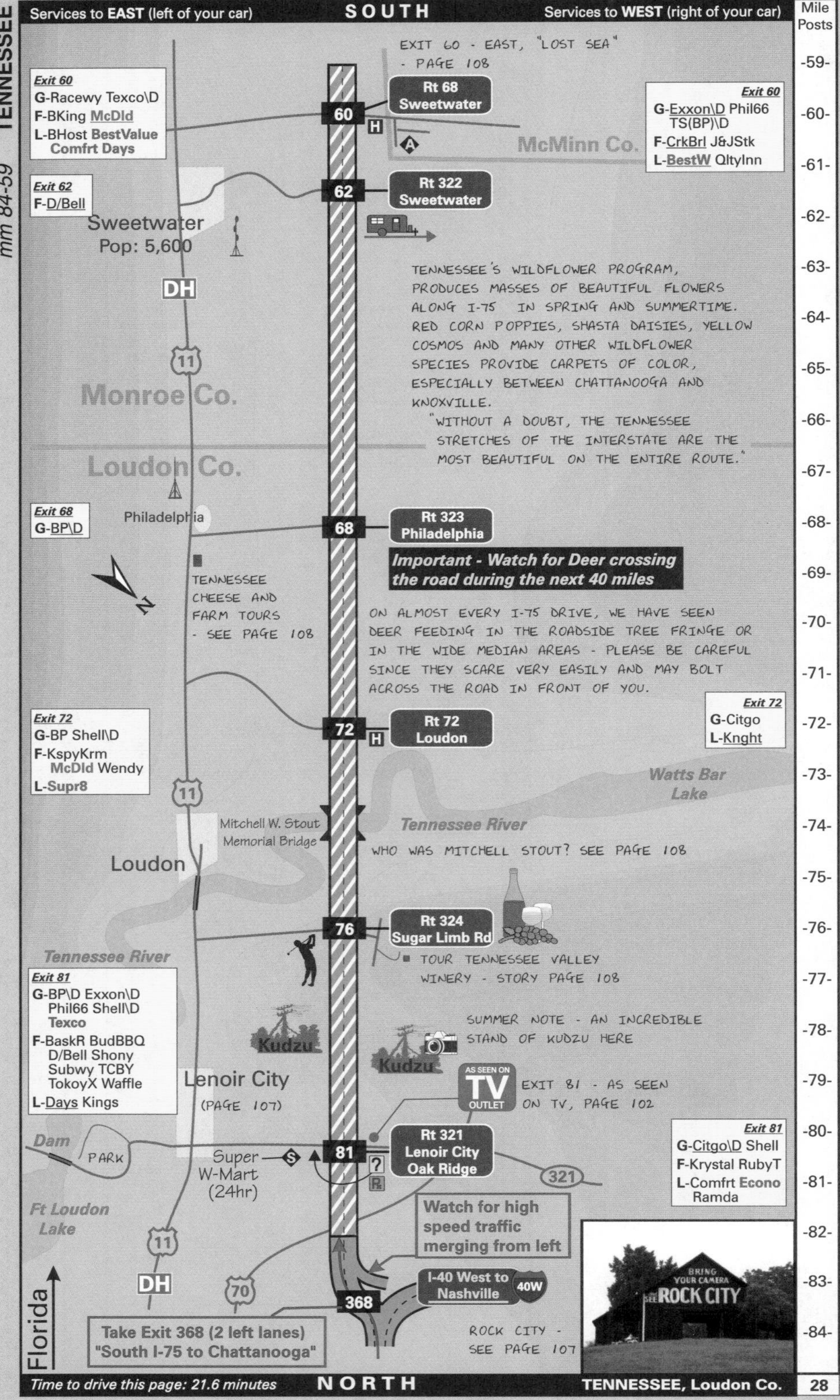

Services to EAST (left of your car)
SOUTH
Services to WEST (right of your car)
Mile Posts
EXIT 60 - EAST, "LOST SEA" - PAGE 108
Exit 60
G-Racewy Texco\D
F-BKing McDld
L-BHost BestValue Comfrt Days
60
Rt 68 Sweetwater
Exit 60
G-Exxon\D Phil66 TS(BP)\D
F-CrkBrl J&JStk
L-BestW QltyInn
McMinn Co.
Exit 62
F-D/Bell
62
Rt 322 Sweetwater
Sweetwater Pop: 5,600
DH
TENNESSEE'S WILDFLOWER PROGRAM, PRODUCES MASSES OF BEAUTIFUL FLOWERS ALONG I-75 IN SPRING AND SUMMERTIME. RED CORN POPPIES, SHASTA DAISIES, YELLOW COSMOS AND MANY OTHER WILDFLOWER SPECIES PROVIDE CARPETS OF COLOR, ESPECIALLY BETWEEN CHATTANOOGA AND KNOXVILLE.
"WITHOUT A DOUBT, THE TENNESSEE STRETCHES OF THE INTERSTATE ARE THE MOST BEAUTIFUL ON THE ENTIRE ROUTE."
11
Monroe Co.
Loudon Co.
Exit 68
G-BP\D
Philadelphia
68
Rt 323 Philadelphia
Important - Watch for Deer crossing the road during the next 40 miles
TENNESSEE CHEESE AND FARM TOURS - SEE PAGE 108
N
ON ALMOST EVERY I-75 DRIVE, WE HAVE SEEN DEER FEEDING IN THE ROADSIDE TREE FRINGE OR IN THE WIDE MEDIAN AREAS - PLEASE BE CAREFUL SINCE THEY SCARE VERY EASILY AND MAY BOLT ACROSS THE ROAD IN FRONT OF YOU.
Exit 72
G-BP Shell\D
F-KspyKrm McDld Wendy
L-Supr8
72
Rt 72 Loudon
Exit 72
G-Citgo
L-Knght
Watts Bar Lake
11
Mitchell W. Stout Memorial Bridge
Tennessee River
WHO WAS MITCHELL STOUT? SEE PAGE 108
Loudon
76
Rt 324 Sugar Limb Rd
TOUR TENNESSEE VALLEY WINERY - STORY PAGE 108
Tennessee River
Exit 81
G-BP\D Exxon\D Phil66 Shell\D Texco
F-BaskR BudBBQ D/Bell Shony Subwy TCBY TokoyX Waffle
L-Days Kings
Kudzu
Kudzu
SUMMER NOTE - AN INCREDIBLE STAND OF KUDZU HERE
Lenoir City (PAGE 107)
AS SEEN ON TV OUTLET
EXIT 81 - AS SEEN ON TV, PAGE 102
Dam
PARK
Super W-Mart (24hr)
81
Rt 321 Lenoir City Oak Ridge
321
Exit 81
G-Citgo\D Shell
F-Krystal RubyT
L-Comfrt Econo Ramda
Ft Loudon Lake
Watch for high speed traffic merging from left
11
DH
70
I-40 West to Nashville
40W
368
BRING YOUR CAMERA SEE ROCK CITY
Take Exit 368 (2 left lanes) "South I-75 to Chattanooga"
ROCK CITY - SEE PAGE 107
Florida
-59- -60- -61- -62- -63- -64- -65- -66- -67- -68- -69- -70- -71- -72- -73- -74- -75- -76- -77- -78- -79- -80- -81- -82- -83- -84-

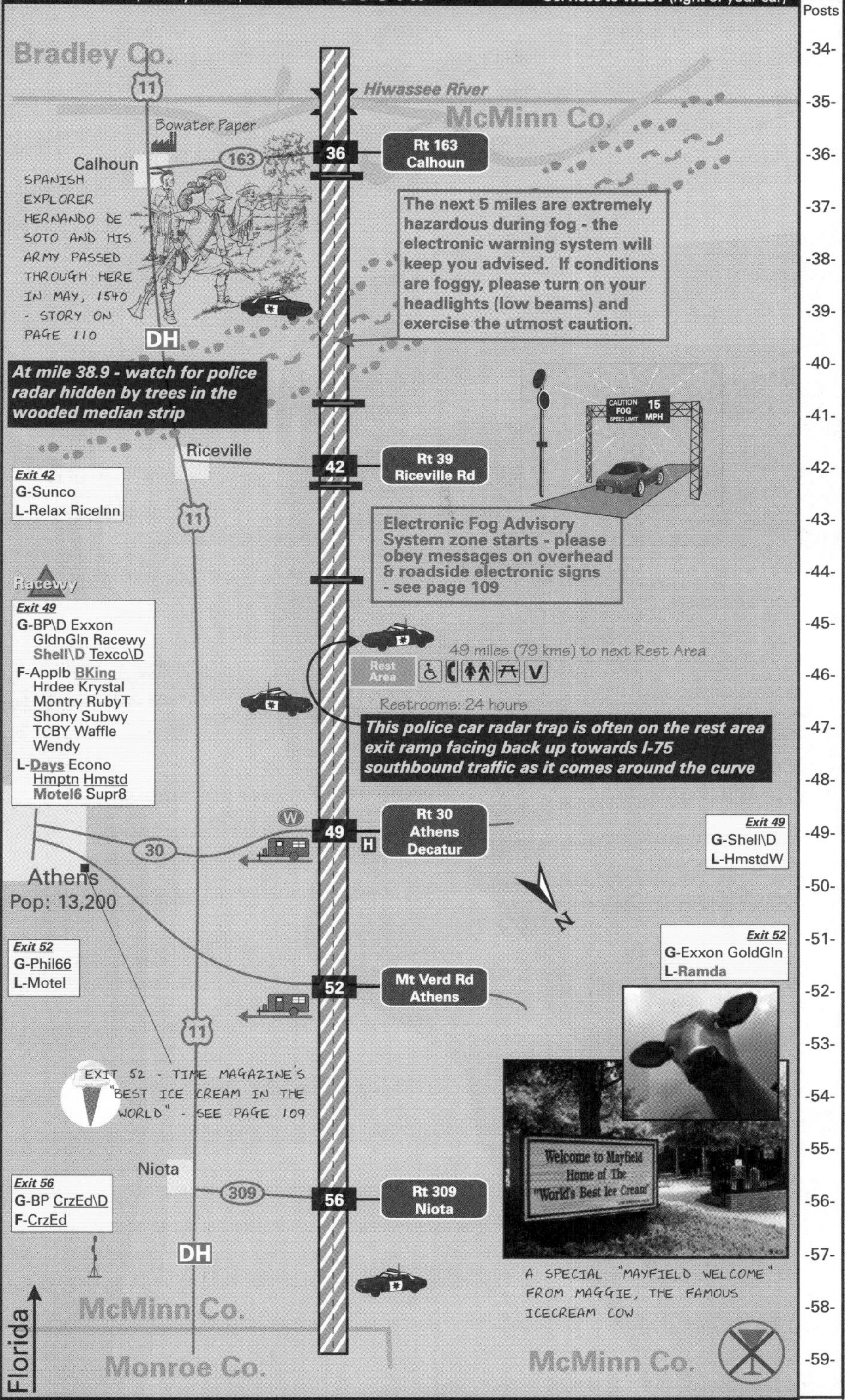

Bradley Co.
11
Hiwassee River
McMinn Co.
Bowater Paper
Calhoun
163
36 Rt 163 Calhoun

SPANISH EXPLORER HERNANDO DE SOTO AND HIS ARMY PASSED THROUGH HERE IN MAY, 1540 - STORY ON PAGE 110

DH

The next 5 miles are extremely hazardous during fog - the electronic warning system will keep you advised. If conditions are foggy, please turn on your headlights (low beams) and exercise the utmost caution.

At mile 38.9 - watch for police radar hidden by trees in the wooded median strip

CAUTION FOG SPEED LIMIT 15 MPH

Riceville
42 Rt 39 Riceville Rd

Exit 42
G-Sunco
L-Relax RiceInn

11

Electronic Fog Advisory System zone starts - please obey messages on overhead & roadside electronic signs - see page 109

Racewy

Exit 49
G-BP\D Exxon GldnGln Racewy **Shell\D** Texco\D
F-Applb **BKing** Hrdee Krystal Montry RubyT Shony Subwy TCBY Waffle Wendy
L-**Days** Econo Hmptn Hmstd **Motel6** Supr8

Rest Area
49 miles (79 kms) to next Rest Area
V
Restrooms: 24 hours

This police car radar trap is often on the rest area exit ramp facing back up towards I-75 southbound traffic as it comes around the curve

W
30
49 Rt 30 Athens Decatur
H

Exit 49
G-Shell\D
L-HmstdW

Athens
Pop: 13,200

N

Exit 52
G-Phil66
L-Motel

Exit 52
G-Exxon GoldGln
L-**Ramda**

52 Mt Verd Rd Athens

11

EXIT 52 - TIME MAGAZINE'S "BEST ICE CREAM IN THE WORLD" - SEE PAGE 109

Welcome to Mayfield Home of The "World's Best Ice Cream"

Niota
309
56 Rt 309 Niota

Exit 56
G-BP CrzEd\D
F-CrzEd

DH

A SPECIAL "MAYFIELD WELCOME" FROM MAGGIE, THE FAMOUS ICECREAM COW

McMinn Co.
Florida
Monroe Co.
McMinn Co.

-34- -35- -36- -37- -38- -39- -40- -41- -42- -43- -44- -45- -46- -47- -48- -49- -50- -51- -52- -53- -54- -55- -56- -57- -58- -59-

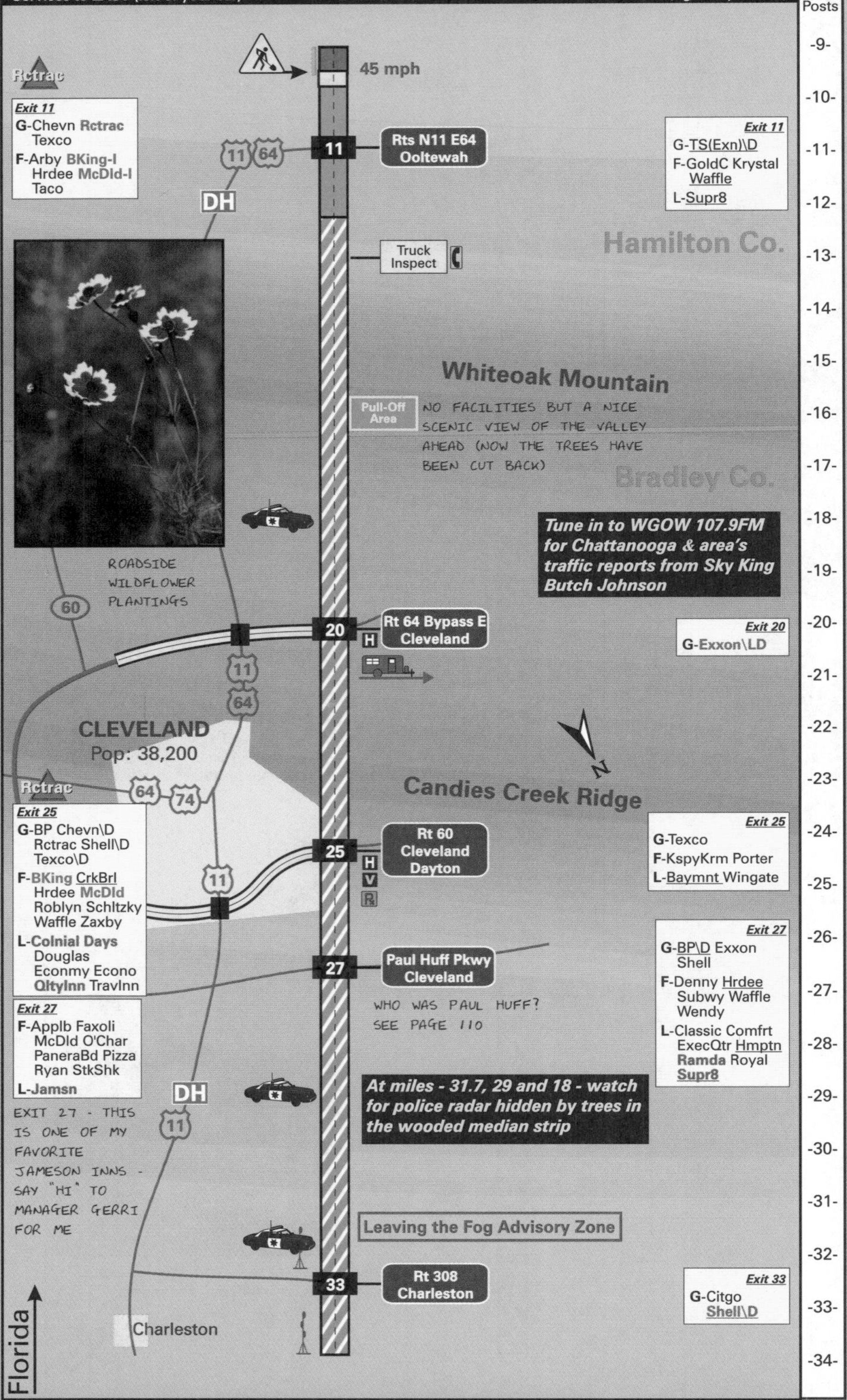

Services to **EAST** (left of your car) **SOUTH** Services to **WEST** (right of your car) Mile Posts

Rctrac

45 mph

Exit 11
G-Chevn Rctrac Texco
F-Arby BKing-I Hrdee McDld-I Taco

11 64

11 Rts N11 E64 Ooltewah

Exit 11
G-TS(Exn)\D
F-GoldC Krystal Waffle
L-Supr8

DH

Truck Inspect

Hamilton Co.

Whiteoak Mountain

Pull-Off Area

NO FACILITIES BUT A NICE SCENIC VIEW OF THE VALLEY AHEAD (NOW THE TREES HAVE BEEN CUT BACK)

Bradley Co.

Tune in to WGOW 107.9FM for Chattanooga & area's traffic reports from Sky King Butch Johnson

ROADSIDE WILDFLOWER PLANTINGS

60

20 Rt 64 Bypass E Cleveland

H

Exit 20
G-Exxon\LD

11 64

CLEVELAND
Pop: 38,200

N

Candies Creek Ridge

Rctrac

64 74

Exit 25
G-BP Chevn\D Rctrac Shell\D Texco\D
F-BKing CrkBrl Hrdee McDld Roblyn Schltzky Waffle Zaxby
L-Colnial Days Douglas Econmy Econo QltyInn TravInn

25 Rt 60 Cleveland Dayton

H V Rx

Exit 25
G-Texco
F-KspyKrm Porter
L-Baymnt Wingate

11

27 Paul Huff Pkwy Cleveland

Exit 27
G-BP\D Exxon Shell
F-Denny Hrdee Subwy Waffle Wendy
L-Classic Comfrt ExecQtr Hmptn Ramda Royal Supr8

Exit 27
F-Applb Faxoli McDld O'Char PaneraBd Pizza Ryan StkShk
L-Jamsn

WHO WAS PAUL HUFF? SEE PAGE 110

DH

11

EXIT 27 - THIS IS ONE OF MY FAVORITE JAMESON INNS - SAY "HI" TO MANAGER GERRI FOR ME

At miles - 31.7, 29 and 18 - watch for police radar hidden by trees in the wooded median strip

Leaving the Fog Advisory Zone

33 Rt 308 Charleston

Exit 33
G-Citgo Shell\D

Charleston

Florida

-9- -10- -11- -12- -13- -14- -15- -16- -17- -18- -19- -20- -21- -22- -23- -24- -25- -26- -27- -28- -29- -30- -31- -32- -33- -34-

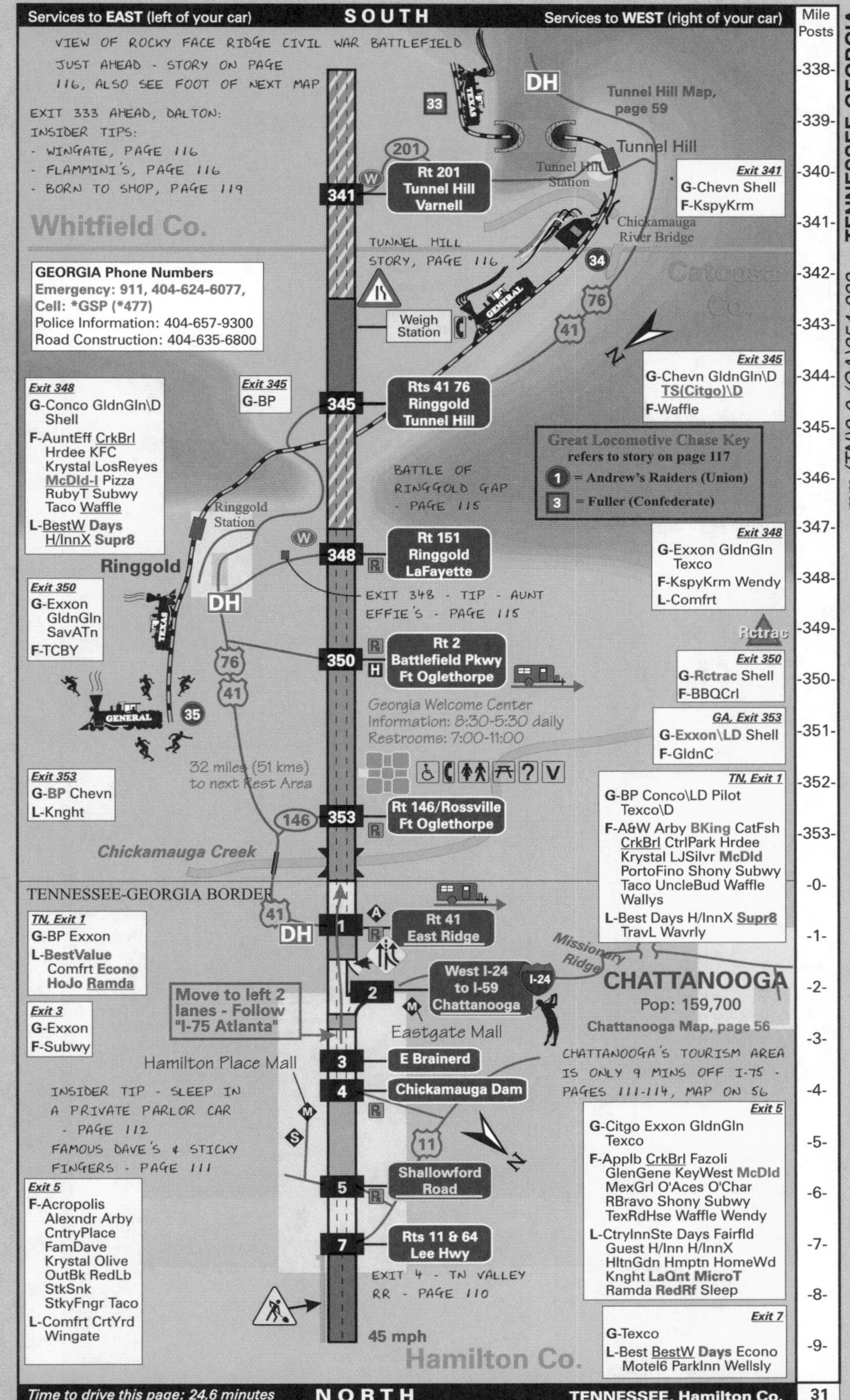

Services to EAST (left of your car)
SOUTH
Services to WEST (right of your car)
Mile Posts
TENNESSEE-GEORGIA
mm (TN)9-0 (GA)354-338
VIEW OF ROCKY FACE RIDGE CIVIL WAR BATTLEFIELD JUST AHEAD - STORY ON PAGE 116, ALSO SEE FOOT OF NEXT MAP
EXIT 333 AHEAD, DALTON:
INSIDER TIPS:
- WINGATE, PAGE 116
- FLAMMINI'S, PAGE 116
- BORN TO SHOP, PAGE 119
Whitfield Co.
DH
Tunnel Hill Map, page 59
Tunnel Hill
Tunnel Hill Station
Chickamauga River Bridge
Catoosa Co.
33
34
201
341
Rt 201 Tunnel Hill Varnell
Exit 341
G-Chevn Shell
F-KspyKrm
TUNNEL HILL STORY, PAGE 116
GEORGIA Phone Numbers
Emergency: 911, 404-624-6077,
Cell: *GSP (*477)
Police Information: 404-657-9300
Road Construction: 404-635-6800
Weigh Station
76
41
Exit 345
G-Chevn GldnGln\D
TS(Citgo)\D
F-Waffle
Exit 348
G-Conco GldnGln\D Shell
F-AuntEff CrkBrl Hrdee KFC Krystal LosReyes McDld-I Pizza RubyT Subwy Taco Waffle
L-BestW Days H/InnX Supr8
Exit 345
G-BP
345
Rts 41 76 Ringgold Tunnel Hill
Great Locomotive Chase Key refers to story on page 117
1 = Andrew's Raiders (Union)
3 = Fuller (Confederate)
BATTLE OF RINGGOLD GAP - PAGE 115
Ringgold Station
Ringgold
348
Rt 151 Ringgold LaFayette
Exit 348
G-Exxon GldnGln Texco
F-KspyKrm Wendy
L-Comfrt
EXIT 348 - TIP - AUNT EFFIE'S - PAGE 115
Exit 350
G-Exxon GldnGln SavATn
F-TCBY
Rctrac
350
Rt 2 Battlefield Pkwy Ft Oglethorpe
Exit 350
G-Rctrac Shell
F-BBQCrl
35
Georgia Welcome Center
Information: 8:30-5:30 daily
Restrooms: 7:00-11:00
GA, Exit 353
G-Exxon\LD Shell
F-GldnC
32 miles (51 kms) to next Rest Area
Exit 353
G-BP Chevn
L-Knght
146
353
Rt 146/Rossville Ft Oglethorpe
TN, Exit 1
G-BP Conco\LD Pilot Texco\D
F-A&W Arby BKing CatFsh CrkBrl CtrlPark Hrdee Krystal LJSilvr McDld PortoFino Shony Subwy Taco UncleBud Waffle Wallys
L-Best Days H/InnX Supr8 TravL Wavrly
Chickamauga Creek
TENNESSEE-GEORGIA BORDER
TN, Exit 1
G-BP Exxon
L-BestValue Comfrt Econo HoJo Ramda
1
Rt 41 East Ridge
Missionary Ridge
CHATTANOOGA
Pop: 159,700
Chattanooga Map, page 56
2
West I-24 to I-59 Chattanooga
I-24
Move to left 2 lanes - Follow "I-75 Atlanta"
Exit 3
G-Exxon
F-Subwy
Eastgate Mall
Hamilton Place Mall
3
E Brainerd
CHATTANOOGA'S TOURISM AREA IS ONLY 9 MINS OFF I-75 - PAGES 111-114, MAP ON 56
4
Chickamauga Dam
INSIDER TIP - SLEEP IN A PRIVATE PARLOR CAR - PAGE 112
FAMOUS DAVE'S & STICKY FINGERS - PAGE 111
11
Exit 5
G-Citgo Exxon GldnGln Texco
F-Applb CrkBrl Fazoli GlenGene KeyWest McDld MexGrl O'Aces O'Char RBravo Shony Subwy TexRdHse Waffle Wendy
L-CtryInnSte Days Fairfld Guest H/Inn H/InnX HltnGdn Hmptn HomeWd Knght LaQnt MicroT Ramda RedRf Sleep
Exit 5
F-Acropolis Alexndr Arby CntryPlace FamDave Krystal Olive OutBk RedLb StkSnk StkyFngr Taco
L-Comfrt CrtYrd Wingate
5
Shallowford Road
7
Rts 11 & 64 Lee Hwy
EXIT 4 - TN VALLEY RR - PAGE 110
Exit 7
G-Texco
L-Best BestW Days Econo Motel6 ParkInn Wellsly
45 mph
Hamilton Co.
-338- -339- -340- -341- -342- -343- -344- -345- -346- -347- -348- -349- -350- -351- -352- -353- -0- -1- -2- -3- -4- -5- -6- -7- -8- -9-
Time to drive this page: 24.6 minutes
NORTH
TENNESSEE, Hamilton Co.

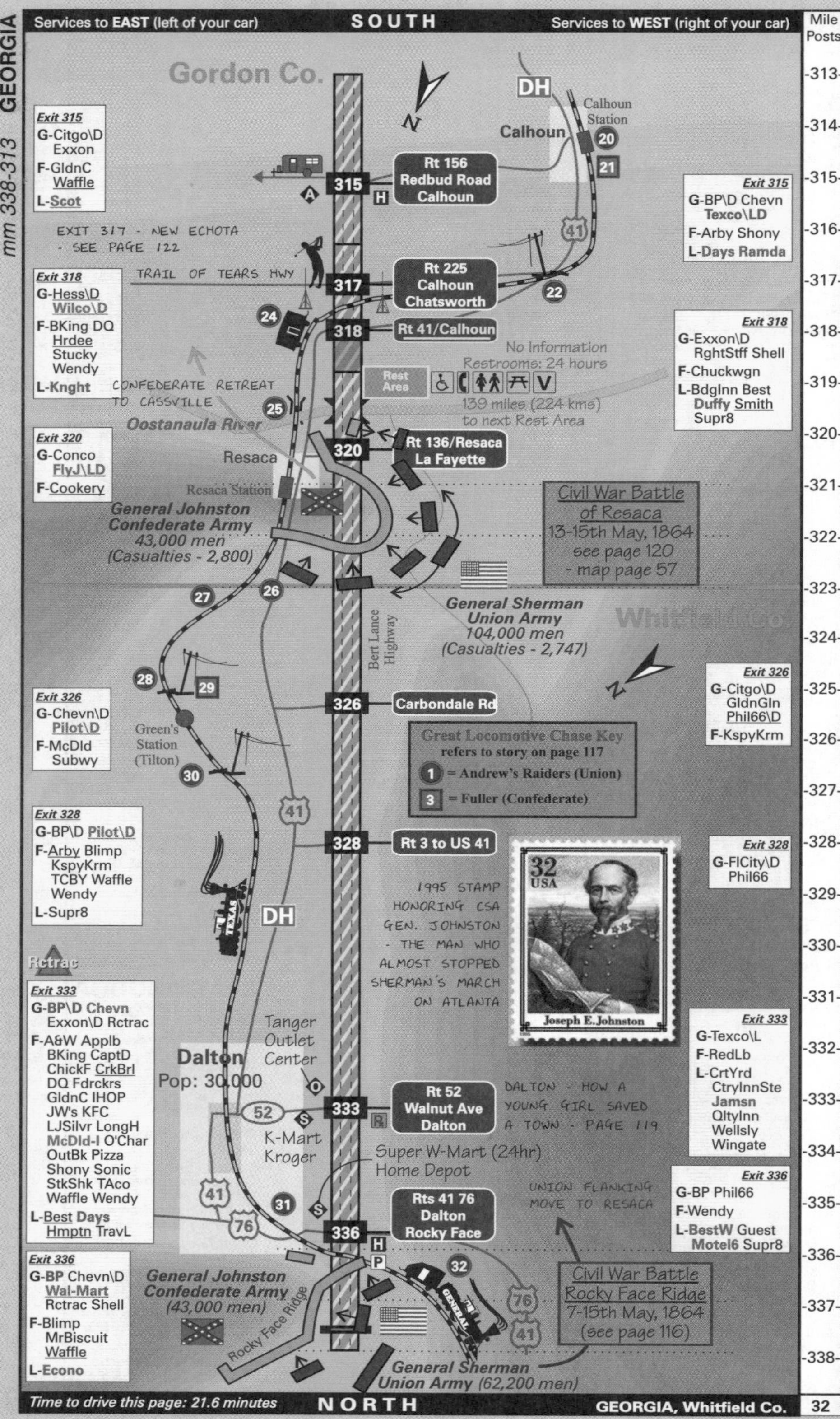
Services to EAST (left of your car)
SOUTH
Services to WEST (right of your car)
Mile Posts
Gordon Co.
N
DH
Calhoun Station
Calhoun
20
21
Exit 315
G-Citgo\D Exxon
F-GldnC Waffle
L-Scot
315
Rt 156 Redbud Road Calhoun
A
H
Exit 315
G-BP\D Chevn Texco\LD
F-Arby Shony
L-Days Ramda
41
EXIT 317 - NEW ECHOTA - SEE PAGE 122
Exit 318
G-Hess\D Wilco\D
F-BKing DQ Hrdee Stucky Wendy
L-Knght
TRAIL OF TEARS HWY
317
Rt 225 Calhoun Chatsworth
22
24
318
Rt 41/Calhoun
Exit 318
G-Exxon\D RghtStff Shell
F-Chuckwgn
L-BdgInn Best Duffy Smith Supr8
No Information
Restrooms: 24 hours
Rest Area
139 miles (224 kms) to next Rest Area
CONFEDERATE RETREAT TO CASSVILLE
25
Oostanaula River
Exit 320
G-Conco FlyJ\LD
F-Cookery
Resaca
320
Rt 136/Resaca La Fayette
Resaca Station
General Johnston Confederate Army 43,000 men (Casualties - 2,800)
Civil War Battle of Resaca
13-15th May, 1864
see page 120
- map page 57
27
26
General Sherman Union Army 104,000 men (Casualties - 2,747)
Whitfield Co.
Bert Lance Highway
28
29
Exit 326
G-Chevn\D Pilot\D
F-McDld Subwy
Green's Station (Tilton)
326
Carbondale Rd
Exit 326
G-Citgo\D GldnGln Phil66\D
F-KspyKrm
Great Locomotive Chase Key
refers to story on page 117
1 = Andrew's Raiders (Union)
3 = Fuller (Confederate)
30
41
Exit 328
G-BP\D Pilot\D
F-Arby Blimp KspyKrm TCBY Waffle Wendy
L-Supr8
328
Rt 3 to US 41
Exit 328
G-FlCity\D Phil66
32 USA
Joseph E. Johnston
1995 STAMP HONORING CSA GEN. JOHNSTON - THE MAN WHO ALMOST STOPPED SHERMAN'S MARCH ON ATLANTA
TEXAS
DH
Rctrac
Exit 333
G-BP\D Chevn Exxon\D Rctrac
F-A&W Applb BKing CaptD ChickF CrkBrl DQ Fdrckrs GldnC IHOP JW's KFC LJSilvr LongH McDld-I O'Char OutBk Pizza Shony Sonic StkShk TAco Waffle Wendy
L-Best Days Hmptn TravL
Dalton
Pop: 30,000
Tanger Outlet Center
52
333
Rt 52 Walnut Ave Dalton
K-Mart Kroger
DALTON - HOW A YOUNG GIRL SAVED A TOWN - PAGE 119
Exit 333
G-Texco\L
F-RedLb
L-CrtYrd CtrylnnSte Jamsn QltyInn Wellsly Wingate
Super W-Mart (24hr)
Home Depot
41
31
76
336
Rts 41 76 Dalton Rocky Face
UNION FLANKING MOVE TO RESACA
Exit 336
G-BP Phil66
F-Wendy
L-BestW Guest Motel6 Supr8
Exit 336
G-BP Chevn\D Wal-Mart Rctrac Shell
F-Blimp MrBiscuit Waffle
L-Econo
H
P
32
General Johnston Confederate Army (43,000 men)
Rocky Face Ridge
GENERAL
76
41
Civil War Battle Rocky Face Ridge
7-15th May, 1864
(see page 116)
General Sherman Union Army (62,200 men)
-313- -314- -315- -316- -317- -318- -319- -320- -321- -322- -323- -324- -325- -326- -327- -328- -329- -330- -331- -332- -333- -334- -335- -336- -337- -338-
Time to drive this page: 21.6 minutes
NORTH
GEORGIA, Whitfield Co.
32

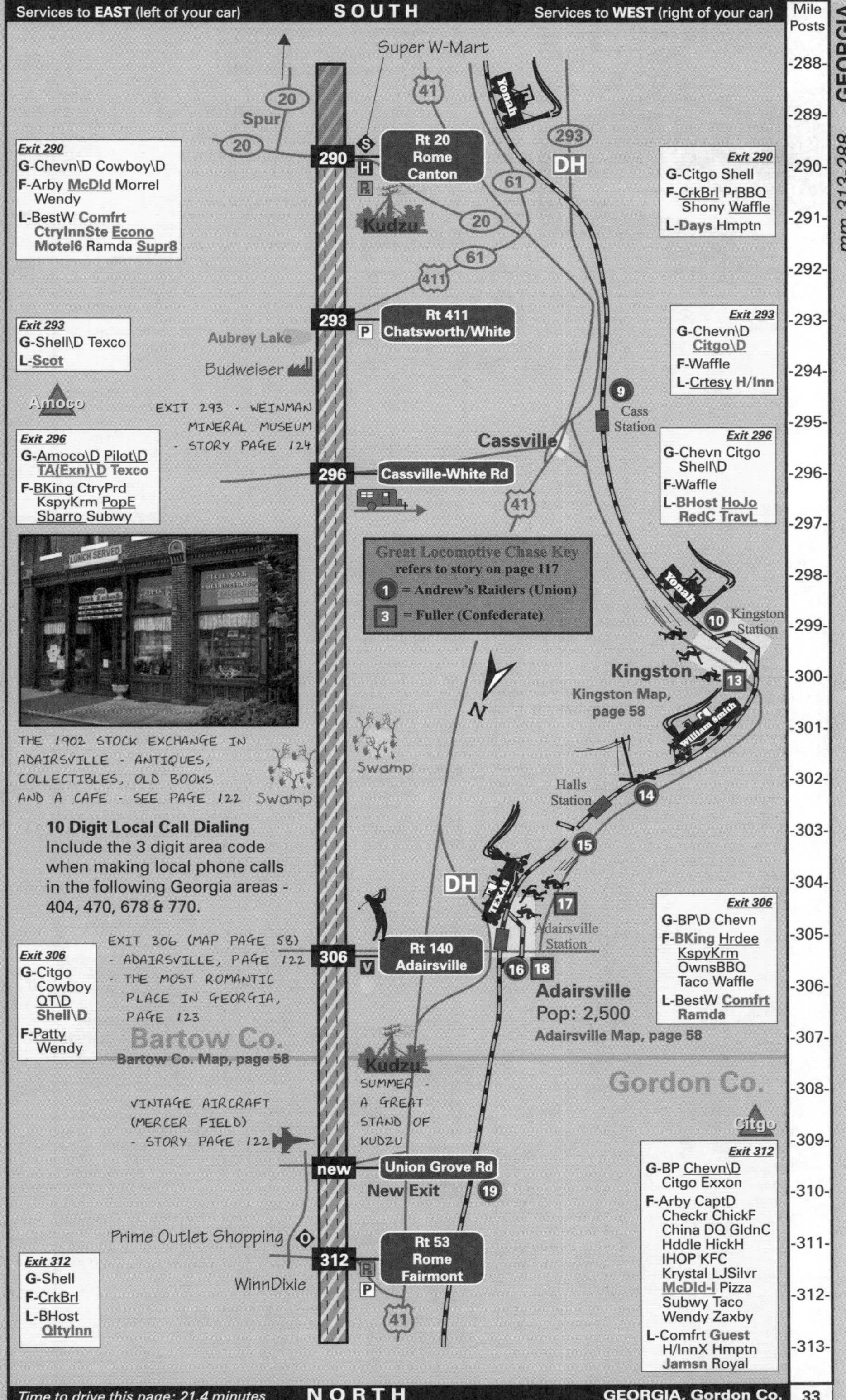
Services to EAST (left of your car)
SOUTH
Services to WEST (right of your car)
Mile Posts
GEORGIA
mm 313-288
Super W-Mart
Spur
20
41
293
DH
290
Rt 20 Rome Canton
Exit 290
G-Chevn\D Cowboy\D
F-Arby McDld Morrel Wendy
L-BestW Comfrt CtryInnSte Econo Motel6 Ramda Supr8
Exit 290
G-Citgo Shell
F-CrkBrl PrBBQ Shony Waffle
L-Days Hmptn
Kudzu
61
411
293
Rt 411 Chatsworth/White
Exit 293
G-Shell\D Texco
L-Scot
Aubrey Lake
Budweiser
Exit 293
G-Chevn\D Citgo\D
F-Waffle
L-Crtesy H/Inn
Amoco
EXIT 293 - WEINMAN MINERAL MUSEUM - STORY PAGE 124
9
Cass Station
Cassville
296
Cassville-White Rd
Exit 296
G-Amoco\D Pilot\D TA(Exn)\D Texco
F-BKing CtryPrd KspyKrm PopE Sbarro Subwy
Exit 296
G-Chevn Citgo Shell\D
F-Waffle
L-BHost HoJo RedC TravL
LUNCH SERVED
CIVIL WAR COLLECTIBLES
Great Locomotive Chase Key
refers to story on page 117
1 = Andrew's Raiders (Union)
3 = Fuller (Confederate)
Yonah
10
Kingston Station
Kingston
13
Kingston Map, page 58
N
William Smith
THE 1902 STOCK EXCHANGE IN ADAIRSVILLE - ANTIQUES, COLLECTIBLES, OLD BOOKS AND A CAFE - SEE PAGE 122
Swamp
Swamp
Halls Station
14
15
10 Digit Local Call Dialing
Include the 3 digit area code when making local phone calls in the following Georgia areas - 404, 470, 678 & 770.
DH
Texas
17
Adairsville Station
EXIT 306 (MAP PAGE 58) - ADAIRSVILLE, PAGE 122 - THE MOST ROMANTIC PLACE IN GEORGIA, PAGE 123
306
Rt 140 Adairsville
16
18
Adairsville
Pop: 2,500
Adairsville Map, page 58
Exit 306
G-Citgo Cowboy QT\D Shell\D
F-Patty Wendy
Exit 306
G-BP\D Chevn
F-BKing Hrdee KspyKrm OwnsBBQ Taco Waffle
L-BestW Comfrt Ramda
Bartow Co.
Bartow Co. Map, page 58
Kudzu
SUMMER - A GREAT STAND OF KUDZU
Gordon Co.
Citgo
VINTAGE AIRCRAFT (MERCER FIELD) - STORY PAGE 122
new
Union Grove Rd
New Exit
19
Prime Outlet Shopping
312
Rt 53 Rome Fairmont
WinnDixie
41
Exit 312
G-Shell
F-CrkBrl
L-BHost QltyInn
Exit 312
G-BP Chevn\D Citgo Exxon
F-Arby CaptD Checkr ChickF China DQ GldnC Hddle HickH IHOP KFC Krystal LJSilvr McDld-I Pizza Subwy Taco Wendy Zaxby
L-Comfrt Guest H/InnX Hmptn Jamsn Royal
-288- -289- -290- -291- -292- -293- -294- -295- -296- -297- -298- -299- -300- -301- -302- -303- -304- -305- -306- -307- -308- -309- -310- -311- -312- -313-
Time to drive this page: 21.4 minutes
NORTH
GEORGIA, Gordon Co.
33

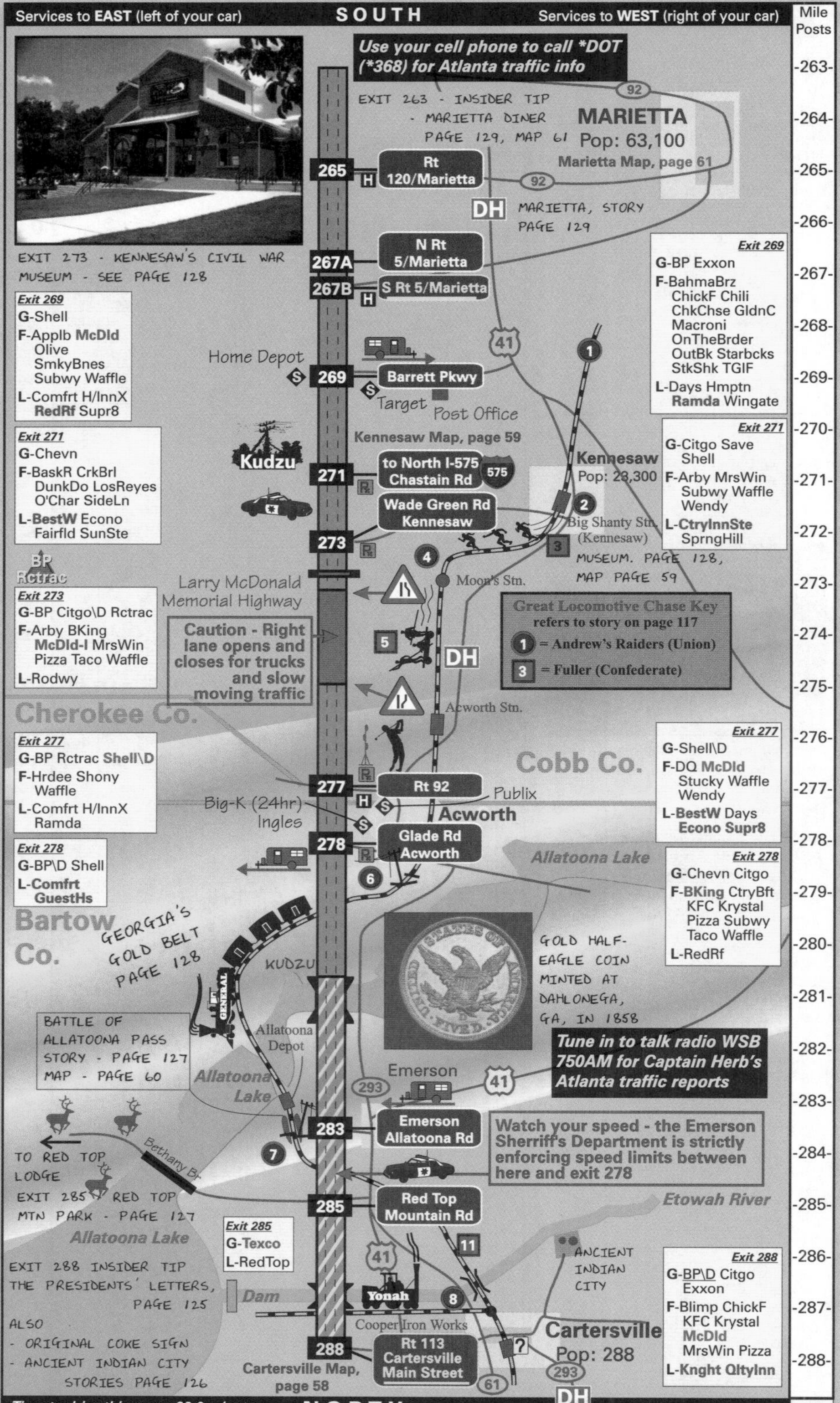
Services to EAST (left of your car)
SOUTH
Services to WEST (right of your car)
Mile Posts
Use your cell phone to call *DOT (*368) for Atlanta traffic info
EXIT 263 - INSIDER TIP - MARIETTA DINER PAGE 129, MAP 61
MARIETTA Pop: 63,100
Marietta Map, page 61
92
265 H Rt 120/Marietta
DH MARIETTA, STORY PAGE 129
EXIT 273 - KENNESAW'S CIVIL WAR MUSEUM - SEE PAGE 128
267A N Rt 5/Marietta
267B H S Rt 5/Marietta
Exit 269
G-Shell
F-Applb McDld Olive SmkyBnes Subwy Waffle
L-Comfrt H/InnX RedRf Supr8
Home Depot
269 Barrett Pkwy
Target
Post Office
41
Exit 269
G-BP Exxon
F-BahmaBrz ChickF Chili ChkChse GldnC Macroni OnTheBrder OutBk Starbcks StkShk TGIF
L-Days Hmptn Ramda Wingate
Kennesaw Map, page 59
Kudzu
271 to North I-575 Chastain Rd
575
Kennesaw Pop: 23,300
Exit 271
G-Chevn
F-BaskR CrkBrl DunkDo LosReyes O'Char SideLn
L-BestW Econo Fairfld SunSte
Wade Green Rd Kennesaw
273
Big Shanty Stn. (Kennesaw)
MUSEUM. PAGE 128, MAP PAGE 59
Exit 271
G-Citgo Save Shell
F-Arby MrsWin Subwy Waffle Wendy
L-CtryInnSte SprngHill
BP Rctrac
Exit 273
G-BP Citgo\D Rctrac
F-Arby BKing McDld-I MrsWin Pizza Taco Waffle
L-Rodwy
Larry McDonald Memorial Highway
Moon's Stn.
Great Locomotive Chase Key refers to story on page 117
1 = Andrew's Raiders (Union)
3 = Fuller (Confederate)
Caution - Right lane opens and closes for trucks and slow moving traffic
DH
Acworth Stn.
Cherokee Co.
Cobb Co.
Exit 277
G-BP Rctrac Shell\D
F-Hrdee Shony Waffle
L-Comfrt H/InnX Ramda
277 Rt 92
Publix
Big-K (24hr)
Ingles
Acworth
Exit 277
G-Shell\D
F-DQ McDld Stucky Waffle Wendy
L-BestW Days Econo Supr8
278 Glade Rd Acworth
Allatoona Lake
Exit 278
G-BP\D Shell
L-Comfrt GuestHs
Exit 278
G-Chevn Citgo
F-BKing CtryBft KFC Krystal Pizza Subwy Taco Waffle
L-RedRf
Bartow Co.
GEORGIA'S GOLD BELT PAGE 128
KUDZU
GOLD HALF-EAGLE COIN MINTED AT DAHLONEGA, GA, IN 1858
GENERAL
BATTLE OF ALLATOONA PASS STORY - PAGE 127 MAP - PAGE 60
Allatoona Depot
Allatoona Lake
Tune in to talk radio WSB 750AM for Captain Herb's Atlanta traffic reports
Emerson
293
41
283 Emerson Allatoona Rd
Watch your speed - the Emerson Sherriff's Department is strictly enforcing speed limits between here and exit 278
TO RED TOP LODGE
Bethany Br.
EXIT 285 RED TOP MTN PARK - PAGE 127
285 Red Top Mountain Rd
Etowah River
Allatoona Lake
Exit 285
G-Texco
L-RedTop
11
ANCIENT INDIAN CITY
EXIT 288 INSIDER TIP THE PRESIDENTS' LETTERS, PAGE 125
ALSO
- ORIGINAL COKE SIGN
- ANCIENT INDIAN CITY STORIES PAGE 126
Dam
Yonah
Cooper Iron Works
Exit 288
G-BP\D Citgo Exxon
F-Blimp ChickF KFC Krystal McDld MrsWin Pizza
L-Knght QltyInn
288 Rt 113 Cartersville Main Street
Cartersville Pop: 288
Cartersville Map, page 58
61
293
DH
NORTH
-263- -264- -265- -266- -267- -268- -269- -270- -271- -272- -273- -274- -275- -276- -277- -278- -279- -280- -281- -282- -283- -284- -285- -286- -287- -288-

Time to drive this page: 23.0 minutes

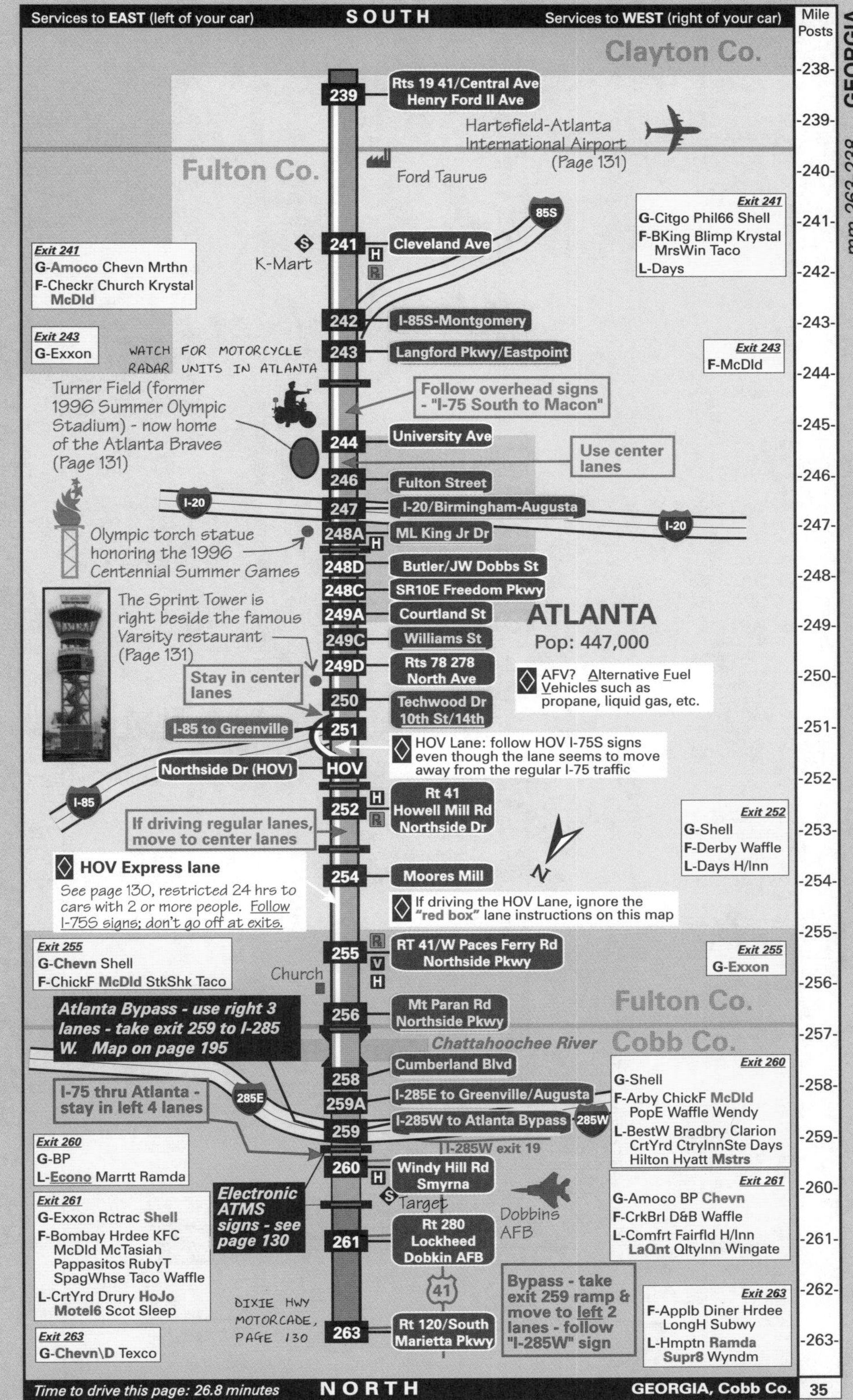
Clayton Co.
239 Rts 19 41/Central Ave Henry Ford II Ave
Hartsfield-Atlanta International Airport (Page 131)
Fulton Co.
Ford Taurus
Exit 241
G-Citgo Phil66 Shell
F-BKing Blimp Krystal MrsWin Taco
L-Days
85S
Exit 241
G-Amoco Chevn Mrthn
F-Checkr Church Krystal McDld
K-Mart
241 Cleveland Ave
242 I-85S-Montgomery
Exit 243
G-Exxon
WATCH FOR MOTORCYCLE RADAR UNITS IN ATLANTA
243 Langford Pkwy/Eastpoint
Exit 243
F-McDld
Turner Field (former 1996 Summer Olympic Stadium) - now home of the Atlanta Braves (Page 131)
Follow overhead signs - "I-75 South to Macon"
244 University Ave
Use center lanes
246 Fulton Street
I-20
247 I-20/Birmingham-Augusta
Olympic torch statue honoring the 1996 Centennial Summer Games
248A ML King Jr Dr
248D Butler/JW Dobbs St
248C SR10E Freedom Pkwy
The Sprint Tower is right beside the famous Varsity restaurant (Page 131)
249A Courtland St
ATLANTA
Pop: 447,000
249C Williams St
249D Rts 78 278 North Ave
AFV? Alternative Fuel Vehicles such as propane, liquid gas, etc.
Stay in center lanes
250 Techwood Dr 10th St/14th
I-85 to Greenville
251
HOV Lane: follow HOV I-75S signs even though the lane seems to move away from the regular I-75 traffic
Northside Dr (HOV)
HOV
I-85
252 Rt 41 Howell Mill Rd Northside Dr
Exit 252
G-Shell
F-Derby Waffle
L-Days H/Inn
If driving regular lanes, move to center lanes
HOV Express lane
See page 130, restricted 24 hrs to cars with 2 or more people. Follow I-75S signs; don't go off at exits.
254 Moores Mill
N
If driving the HOV Lane, ignore the "red box" lane instructions on this map
Exit 255
G-Chevn Shell
F-ChickF McDld StkShk Taco
Church
255 RT 41/W Paces Ferry Rd Northside Pkwy
Exit 255
G-Exxon
Atlanta Bypass - use right 3 lanes - take exit 259 to I-285 W. Map on page 195
256 Mt Paran Rd Northside Pkwy
Fulton Co.
Chattahoochee River
Cobb Co.
258 Cumberland Blvd
Exit 260
G-Shell
F-Arby ChickF McDld PopE Waffle Wendy
L-BestW Bradbry Clarion CrtYrd CtryInnSte Days Hilton Hyatt Mstrs
I-75 thru Atlanta - stay in left 4 lanes
285E
259A I-285E to Greenville/Augusta
259 I-285W to Atlanta Bypass
285W
I-285W exit 19
Exit 260
G-BP
L-Econo Marrtt Ramda
260 Windy Hill Rd Smyrna
Target
Exit 261
G-Amoco BP Chevn
F-CrkBrl D&B Waffle
L-Comfrt Fairfld H/Inn LaQnt QltyInn Wingate
Exit 261
G-Exxon Rctrac Shell
F-Bombay Hrdee KFC McDld McTasiah Pappasitos RubyT SpagWhse Taco Waffle
L-CrtYrd Drury HoJo Motel6 Scot Sleep
Electronic ATMS signs - see page 130
261 Rt 280 Lockheed Dobkin AFB
Dobbins AFB
41
Bypass - take exit 259 ramp & move to left 2 lanes - follow "I-285W" sign
Exit 263
F-Applb Diner Hrdee LongH Subwy
L-Hmptn Ramda Supr8 Wyndm
DIXIE HWY MOTORCADE, PAGE 130
263 Rt 120/South Marietta Pkwy
Exit 263
G-Chevn\D Texco
-238- -239- -240- -241- -242- -243- -244- -245- -246- -247- -248- -249- -250- -251- -252- -253- -254- -255- -256- -257- -258- -259- -260- -261- -262- -263-

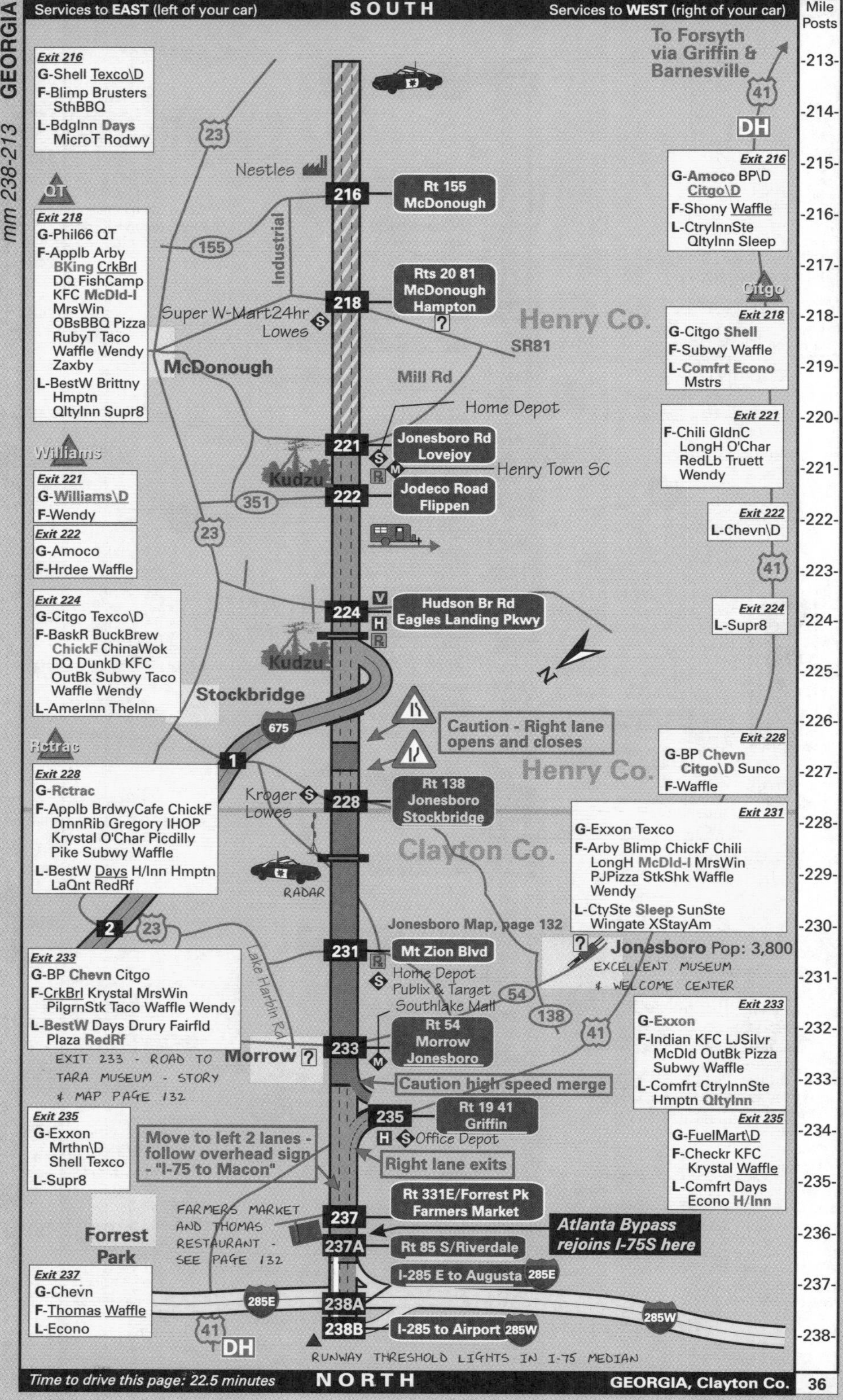

Services to EAST (left of your car)
SOUTH
Services to WEST (right of your car)
Mile Posts
To Forsyth via Griffin & Barnesville
Exit 216
G-Shell Texco\D
F-Blimp Brusters SthBBQ
L-BdgInn Days MicroT Rodwy
Nestles
216
Rt 155 McDonough
Exit 216
G-Amoco BP\D Citgo\D
F-Shony Waffle
L-CtryInnSte QltyInn Sleep
QT
Exit 218
G-Phil66 QT
F-Applb Arby BKing CrkBrl DQ FishCamp KFC McDld-I MrsWin OBsBBQ Pizza RubyT Taco Waffle Wendy Zaxby
L-BestW Brittny Hmptn QltyInn Supr8
155
Industrial
Super W-Mart24hr
Lowes
218
Rts 20 81 McDonough Hampton
Citgo
Exit 218
G-Citgo Shell
F-Subwy Waffle
L-Comfrt Econo Mstrs
Henry Co.
SR81
McDonough
Mill Rd
Home Depot
Exit 221
F-Chili GldnC LongH O'Char RedLb Truett Wendy
Williams
221
Jonesboro Rd Lovejoy
Henry Town SC
Kudzu
Exit 221
G-Williams\D
F-Wendy
351
222
Jodeco Road Flippen
Exit 222
L-Chevn\D
Exit 222
G-Amoco
F-Hrdee Waffle
Exit 224
G-Citgo Texco\D
F-BaskR BuckBrew ChickF ChinaWok DQ DunkD KFC OutBk Subwy Taco Waffle Wendy
L-AmerInn TheInn
224
Hudson Br Rd Eagles Landing Pkwy
Exit 224
L-Supr8
Kudzu
Stockbridge
675
Caution - Right lane opens and closes
Rctrac
1
Exit 228
G-BP Chevn Citgo\D Sunco
F-Waffle
Henry Co.
Exit 228
G-Rctrac
F-Applb BrdwyCafe ChickF DmnRib Gregory IHOP Krystal O'Char Picdilly Pike Subwy Waffle
L-BestW Days H/Inn Hmptn LaQnt RedRf
Kroger
Lowes
228
Rt 138 Jonesboro Stockbridge
Exit 231
G-Exxon Texco
F-Arby Blimp ChickF Chili LongH McDld-I MrsWin PJPizza StkShk Waffle Wendy
L-CtySte Sleep SunSte Wingate XStayAm
Clayton Co.
RADAR
Jonesboro Map, page 132
2
23
Lake Harbin Rd
231
Mt Zion Blvd
Jonesboro Pop: 3,800
EXCELLENT MUSEUM & WELCOME CENTER
Exit 233
G-BP Chevn Citgo
F-CrkBrl Krystal MrsWin PilgrnStk Taco Waffle Wendy
L-BestW Days Drury Fairfld Plaza RedRf
Home Depot
Publix & Target
Southlake Mall
54
138
Exit 233
G-Exxon
F-Indian KFC LJSilvr McDld OutBk Pizza Subwy Waffle
L-Comfrt CtryInnSte Hmptn QltyInn
41
233
Rt 54 Morrow Jonesboro
Morrow
EXIT 233 - ROAD TO TARA MUSEUM - STORY & MAP PAGE 132
Caution high speed merge
Exit 235
G-Exxon Mrthn\D Shell Texco
L-Supr8
235
Rt 19 41 Griffin
Office Depot
Exit 235
G-FuelMart\D
F-Checkr KFC Krystal Waffle
L-Comfrt Days Econo H/Inn
Move to left 2 lanes - follow overhead sign - "I-75 to Macon"
Right lane exits
FARMERS MARKET AND THOMAS RESTAURANT - SEE PAGE 132
237
Rt 331E/Forrest Pk Farmers Market
Atlanta Bypass rejoins I-75S here
Forrest Park
237A
Rt 85 S/Riverdale
Exit 237
G-Chevn
F-Thomas Waffle
L-Econo
I-285 E to Augusta
285E
238A
285W
238B
I-285 to Airport
41
DH
RUNWAY THRESHOLD LIGHTS IN I-75 MEDIAN
-213- -214- -215- -216- -217- -218- -219- -220- -221- -222- -223- -224- -225- -226- -227- -228- -229- -230- -231- -232- -233- -234- -235- -236- -237- -238-
Time to drive this page: 22.5 minutes
NORTH

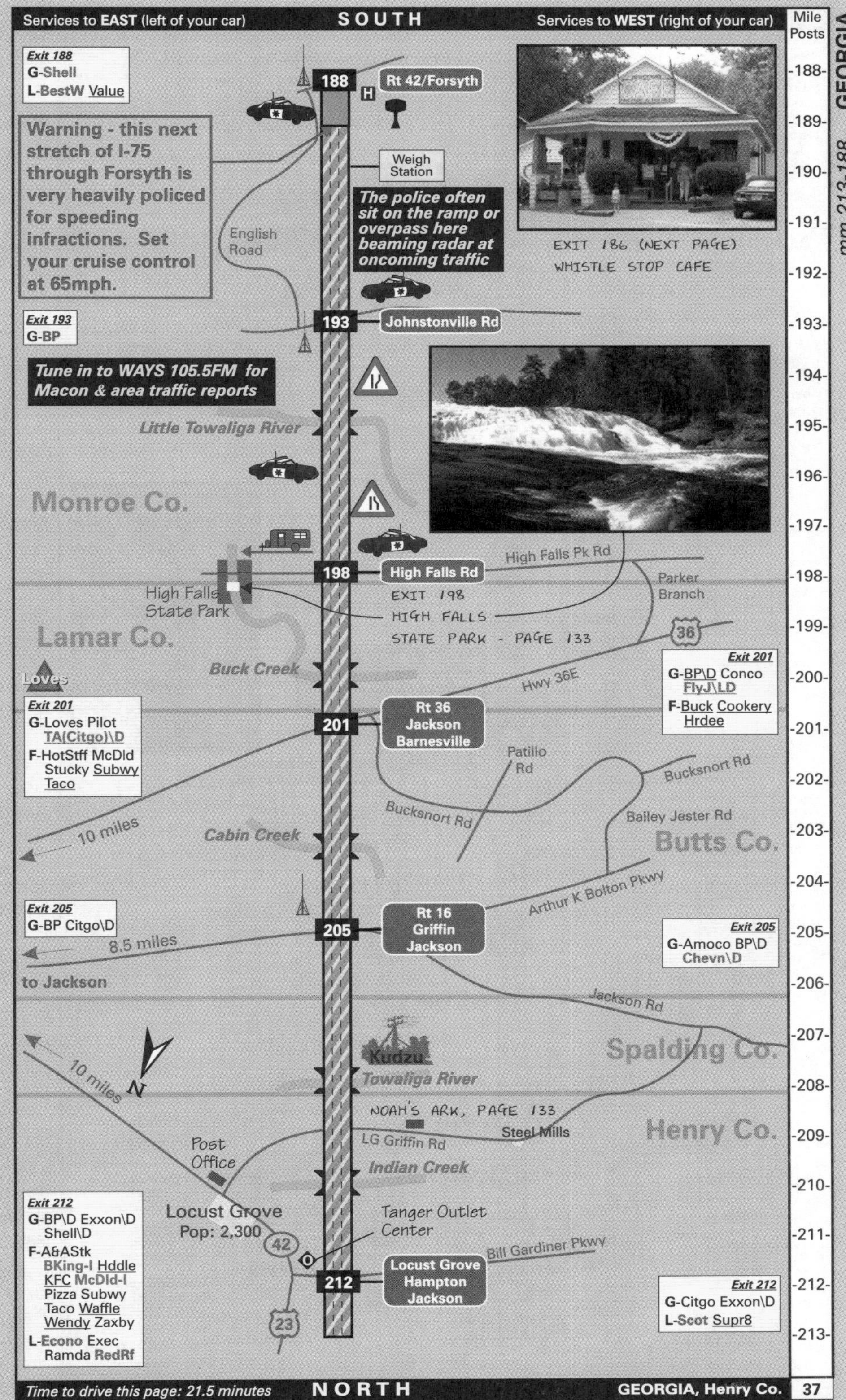
Services to EAST (left of your car)
SOUTH
Services to WEST (right of your car)
Mile Posts
GEORGIA
mm 213-188
Exit 188
G-Shell
L-BestW Value
188
Rt 42/Forsyth
Warning - this next stretch of I-75 through Forsyth is very heavily policed for speeding infractions. Set your cruise control at 65mph.
Weigh Station
The police often sit on the ramp or overpass here beaming radar at oncoming traffic
English Road
EXIT 186 (NEXT PAGE)
WHISTLE STOP CAFE
Exit 193
G-BP
193
Johnstonville Rd
Tune in to WAYS 105.5FM for Macon & area traffic reports
Little Towaliga River
Monroe Co.
198
High Falls Rd
High Falls Pk Rd
High Falls State Park
EXIT 198
HIGH FALLS
STATE PARK - PAGE 133
Parker Branch
Lamar Co.
36
Buck Creek
Loves
Hwy 36E
Exit 201
G-BP\D Conco
FlyJ\LD
F-Buck Cookery
Hrdee
Exit 201
G-Loves Pilot
TA(Citgo)\D
F-HotStff McDld
Stucky Subwy
Taco
201
Rt 36
Jackson
Barnesville
Patillo Rd
Bucksnort Rd
Bucksnort Rd
Bailey Jester Rd
10 miles
Cabin Creek
Butts Co.
Arthur K Bolton Pkwy
Exit 205
G-BP Citgo\D
205
Rt 16
Griffin
Jackson
Exit 205
G-Amoco BP\D
Chevn\D
8.5 miles
to Jackson
Jackson Rd
N
10 miles
Kudzu
Spalding Co.
Towaliga River
NOAH'S ARK, PAGE 133
Steel Mills
Henry Co.
LG Griffin Rd
Post Office
Indian Creek
Locust Grove
Pop: 2,300
Tanger Outlet Center
42
Bill Gardiner Pkwy
Exit 212
G-BP\D Exxon\D
Shell\D
F-A&AStk
BKing-I Hddle
KFC McDld-I
Pizza Subwy
Taco Waffle
Wendy Zaxby
L-Econo Exec
Ramda RedRf
212
Locust Grove
Hampton
Jackson
23
Exit 212
G-Citgo Exxon\D
L-Scot Supr8
-188- -189- -190- -191- -192- -193- -194- -195- -196- -197- -198- -199- -200- -201- -202- -203- -204- -205- -206- -207- -208- -209- -210- -211- -212- -213-
Time to drive this page: 21.5 minutes
NORTH

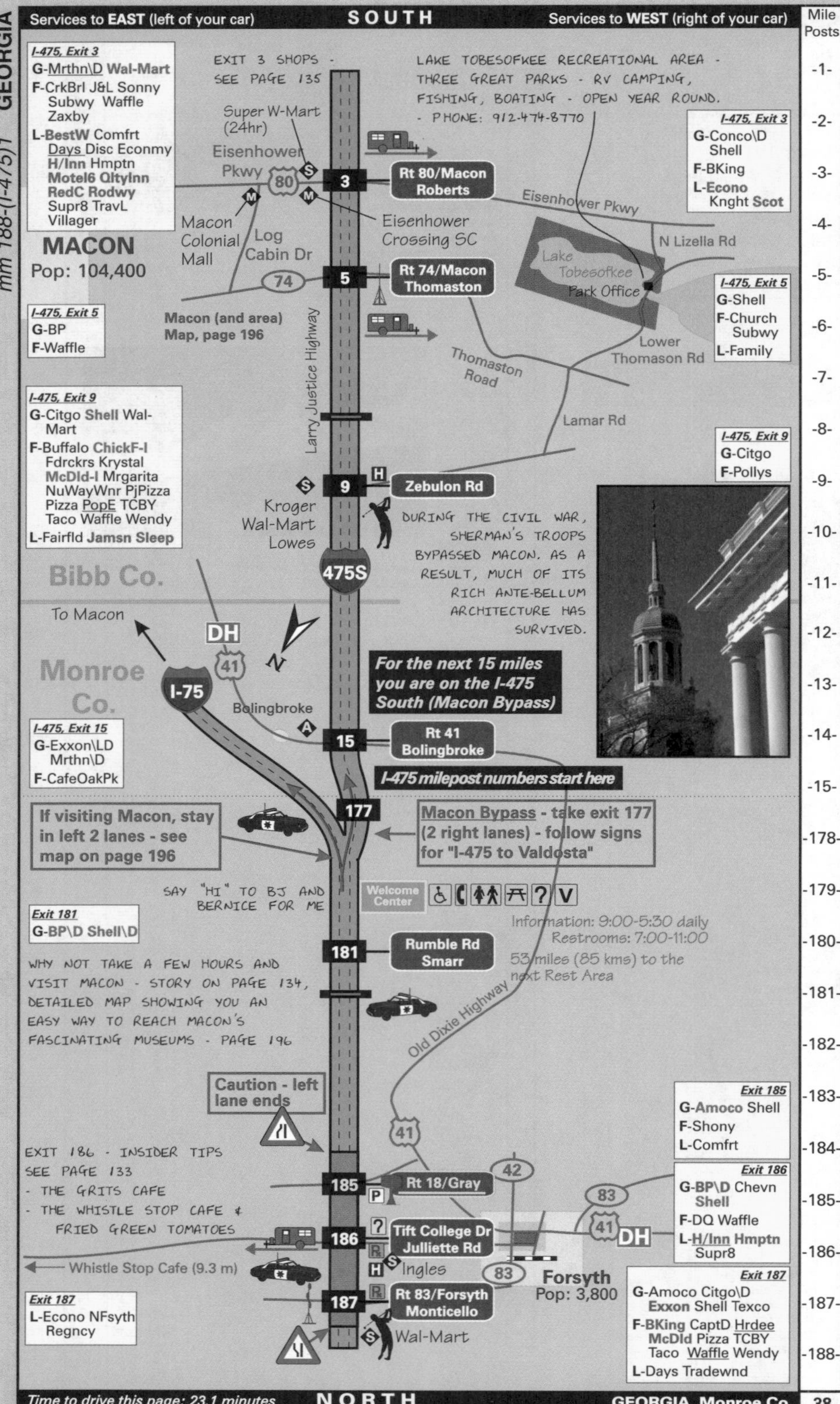
Services to EAST (left of your car)
SOUTH
Services to WEST (right of your car)
Mile Posts
I-475, Exit 3
G-Mrthn\D Wal-Mart
F-CrkBrl J&L Sonny Subwy Waffle Zaxby
L-BestW Comfrt Days Disc Econmy H/Inn Hmptn Motel6 QltyInn RedC Rodwy Supr8 TravL Villager
EXIT 3 SHOPS - SEE PAGE 135
LAKE TOBESOFKEE RECREATIONAL AREA - THREE GREAT PARKS - RV CAMPING, FISHING, BOATING - OPEN YEAR ROUND. - PHONE: 912-474-8770
Super W-Mart (24hr)
Eisenhower Pkwy
80
3
Rt 80/Macon Roberts
I-475, Exit 3
G-Conco\D Shell
F-BKing
L-Econo Knght Scot
Macon Colonial Mall
Log Cabin Dr
Eisenhower Crossing SC
Eisenhower Pkwy
N Lizella Rd
Lake Tobesofkee
Park Office
MACON
Pop: 104,400
74
5
Rt 74/Macon Thomaston
I-475, Exit 5
G-Shell
F-Church Subwy
L-Family
I-475, Exit 5
G-BP
F-Waffle
Macon (and area) Map, page 196
Larry Justice Highway
Thomaston Road
Lower Thomason Rd
Lamar Rd
I-475, Exit 9
G-Citgo Shell Wal-Mart
F-Buffalo ChickF-I Fdrckrs Krystal McDld-I Mrgarita NuWayWnr PjPizza Pizza PopE TCBY Taco Waffle Wendy
L-Fairfld Jamsn Sleep
I-475, Exit 9
G-Citgo
F-Pollys
9
Zebulon Rd
Kroger Wal-Mart Lowes
DURING THE CIVIL WAR, SHERMAN'S TROOPS BYPASSED MACON. AS A RESULT, MUCH OF ITS RICH ANTE-BELLUM ARCHITECTURE HAS SURVIVED.
475S
Bibb Co.
To Macon
DH
41
N
Monroe Co.
I-75
For the next 15 miles you are on the I-475 South (Macon Bypass)
Bolingbroke
I-475, Exit 15
G-Exxon\LD Mrthn\D
F-CafeOakPk
15
Rt 41 Bolingbroke
I-475 milepost numbers start here
If visiting Macon, stay in left 2 lanes - see map on page 196
177
Macon Bypass - take exit 177 (2 right lanes) - follow signs for "I-475 to Valdosta"
SAY "HI" TO BJ AND BERNICE FOR ME
Welcome Center
Exit 181
G-BP\D Shell\D
Information: 9:00-5:30 daily
Restrooms: 7:00-11:00
181
Rumble Rd Smarr
53 miles (85 kms) to the next Rest Area
WHY NOT TAKE A FEW HOURS AND VISIT MACON - STORY ON PAGE 134, DETAILED MAP SHOWING YOU AN EASY WAY TO REACH MACON'S FASCINATING MUSEUMS - PAGE 196
Old Dixie Highway
Caution - left lane ends
Exit 185
G-Amoco Shell
F-Shony
L-Comfrt
41
EXIT 186 - INSIDER TIPS SEE PAGE 133
- THE GRITS CAFE
- THE WHISTLE STOP CAFE & FRIED GREEN TOMATOES
185
Rt 18/Gray
42
83
Exit 186
G-BP\D Chevn Shell
F-DQ Waffle
L-H/Inn Hmptn Supr8
186
Tift College Dr Juliette Rd
41
DH
Whistle Stop Cafe (9.3 m)
Ingles
83
Forsyth
Pop: 3,800
Exit 187
L-Econo NFsyth Regncy
187
Rt 83/Forsyth Monticello
Wal-Mart
Exit 187
G-Amoco Citgo\D Exxon Shell Texco
F-BKing CaptD Hrdee McDld Pizza TCBY Taco Waffle Wendy
L-Days Tradewnd
-1- -2- -3- -4- -5- -6- -7- -8- -9- -10- -11- -12- -13- -14- -15- -178- -179- -180- -181- -182- -183- -184- -185- -186- -187- -188-
Time to drive this page: 23.1 minutes
NORTH
GEORGIA, Monroe Co.

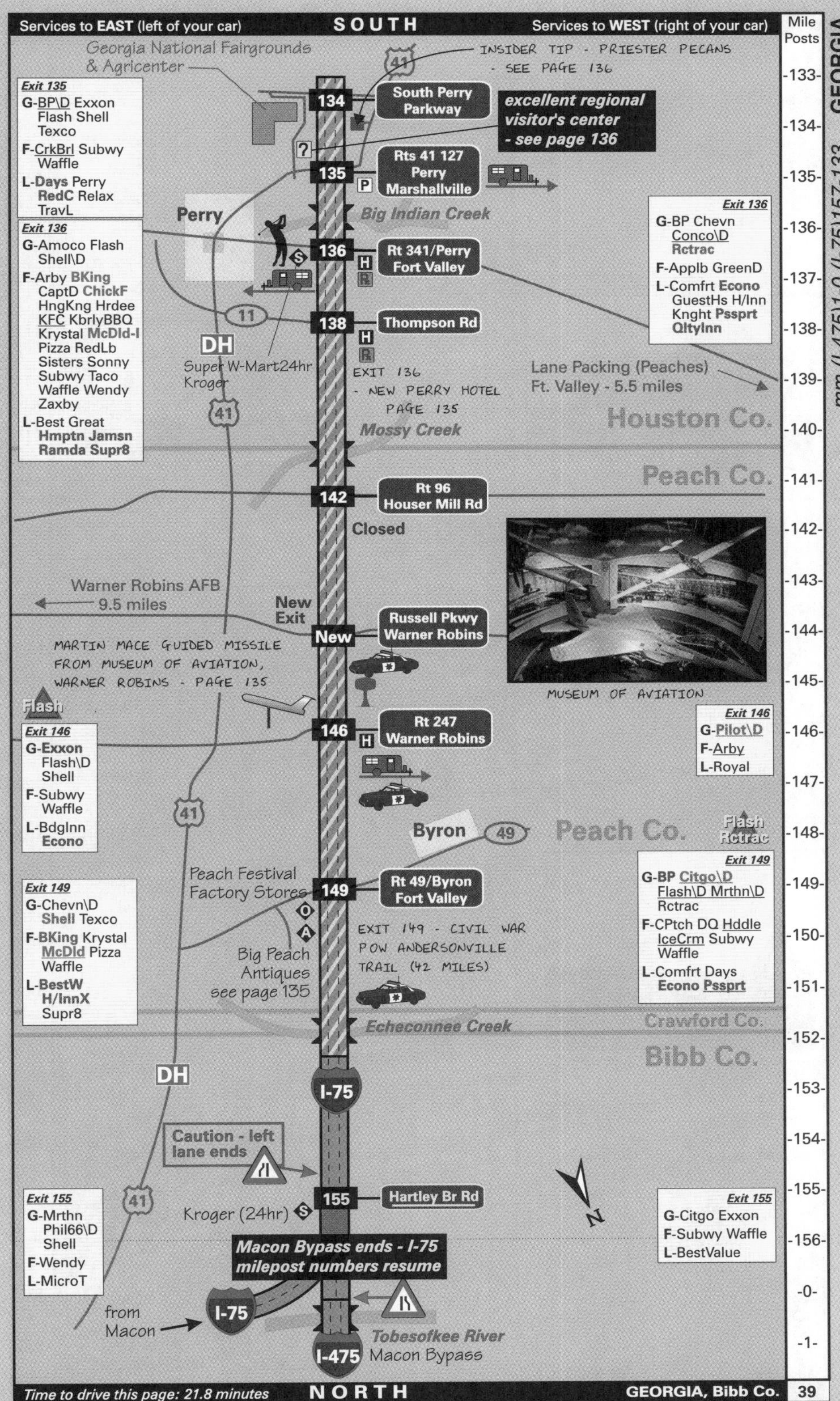
Services to EAST (left of your car)
SOUTH
Services to WEST (right of your car)
Mile Posts
GEORGIA
mm (I-475)1-0 (I-75)157-133
Georgia National Fairgrounds & Agricenter
INSIDER TIP - PRIESTER PECANS - SEE PAGE 136
41
134
South Perry Parkway
excellent regional visitor's center - see page 136
Exit 135
G-BP\D Exxon Flash Shell Texco
F-CrkBrl Subwy Waffle
L-Days Perry RedC Relax TravL
135
Rts 41 127 Perry Marshallville
Perry
Big Indian Creek
Exit 136
G-Amoco Flash Shell\D
F-Arby BKing CaptD ChickF HngKng Hrdee KFC KbrlyBBQ Krystal McDld-I Pizza RedLb Sisters Sonny Subwy Taco Waffle Wendy Zaxby
L-Best Great Hmptn Jamsn Ramda Supr8
136
Rt 341/Perry Fort Valley
Exit 136
G-BP Chevn Conco\D Rctrac
F-Applb GreenD
L-Comfrt Econo GuestHs H/Inn Knght Pssprt QltyInn
11
138
Thompson Rd
DH
Super W-Mart24hr Kroger
EXIT 136 - NEW PERRY HOTEL PAGE 135
Lane Packing (Peaches) Ft. Valley - 5.5 miles
41
Mossy Creek
Houston Co.
Peach Co.
142
Rt 96 Houser Mill Rd
Closed
Warner Robins AFB 9.5 miles
New Exit
New
Russell Pkwy Warner Robins
MARTIN MACE GUIDED MISSILE FROM MUSEUM OF AVIATION, WARNER ROBINS - PAGE 135
MUSEUM OF AVIATION
Flash
Exit 146
G-Exxon Flash\D Shell
F-Subwy Waffle
L-BdgInn Econo
146
Rt 247 Warner Robins
Exit 146
G-Pilot\D
F-Arby
L-Royal
41
Byron
49
Peach Co.
Flash Rctrac
Peach Festival Factory Stores
149
Rt 49/Byron Fort Valley
Exit 149
G-Chevn\D Shell Texco
F-BKing Krystal McDld Pizza Waffle
L-BestW H/InnX Supr8
Exit 149
G-BP Citgo\D Flash\D Mrthn\D Rctrac
F-CPtch DQ Hddle IceCrm Subwy Waffle
L-Comfrt Days Econo Pssprt
Big Peach Antiques see page 135
EXIT 149 - CIVIL WAR POW ANDERSONVILLE TRAIL (42 MILES)
Echeconnee Creek
Crawford Co.
Bibb Co.
DH
I-75
Caution - left lane ends
41
Exit 155
G-Mrthn Phil66\D Shell
F-Wendy
L-MicroT
Kroger (24hr)
155
Hartley Br Rd
Exit 155
G-Citgo Exxon
F-Subwy Waffle
L-BestValue
N
Macon Bypass ends - I-75 milepost numbers resume
from Macon
I-75
Tobesofkee River
I-475 Macon Bypass
-133- -134- -135- -136- -137- -138- -139- -140- -141- -142- -143- -144- -145- -146- -147- -148- -149- -150- -151- -152- -153- -154- -155- -156- -0- -1-
Time to drive this page: 21.8 minutes
NORTH
GEORGIA, Bibb Co.
39

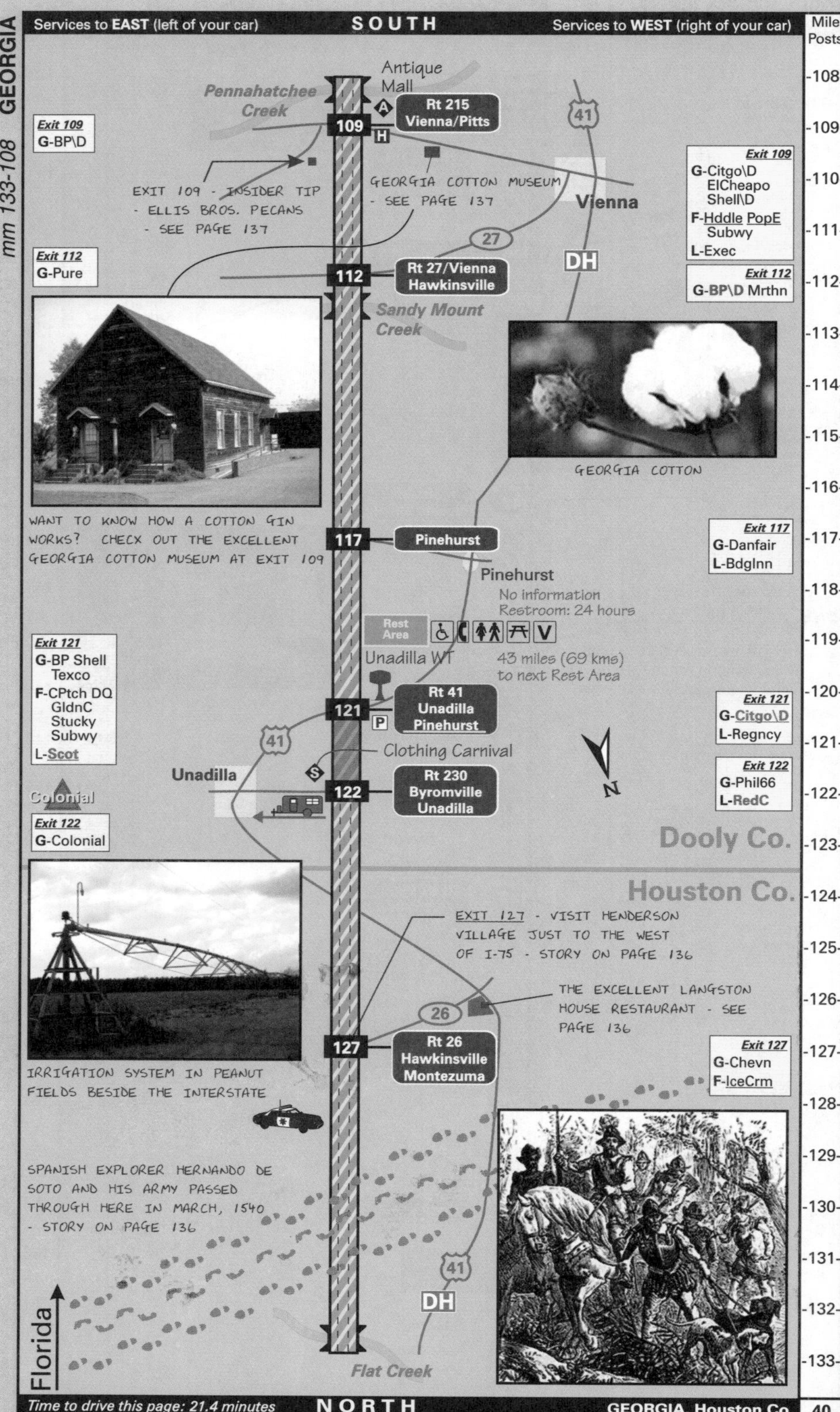

GEORGIA
mm 133-108
Services to EAST (left of your car)
SOUTH
Services to WEST (right of your car)
Mile Posts
-108-
-109-
-110-
-111-
-112-
-113-
-114-
-115-
-116-
-117-
-118-
-119-
-120-
-121-
-122-
-123-
-124-
-125-
-126-
-127-
-128-
-129-
-130-
-131-
-132-
-133-
Antique Mall
Pennahatchee Creek
109
Rt 215 Vienna/Pitts
41
Exit 109
G-BP\D
EXIT 109 - INSIDER TIP - ELLIS BROS. PECANS - SEE PAGE 137
GEORGIA COTTON MUSEUM - SEE PAGE 137
Vienna
Exit 109
G-Citgo\D
ElCheapo
Shell\D
F-Hddle PopE
Subwy
L-Exec
27
DH
Exit 112
G-Pure
112
Rt 27/Vienna Hawkinsville
Exit 112
G-BP\D Mrthn
Sandy Mount Creek
GEORGIA COTTON
WANT TO KNOW HOW A COTTON GIN WORKS? CHECK OUT THE EXCELLENT GEORGIA COTTON MUSEUM AT EXIT 109
117
Pinehurst
Exit 117
G-Danfair
L-BdgInn
Pinehurst
No information
Restroom: 24 hours
Rest Area
Unadilla WT
43 miles (69 kms) to next Rest Area
Exit 121
G-BP Shell
Texco
F-CPtch DQ
GldnC
Stucky
Subwy
L-Scot
121
Rt 41 Unadilla Pinehurst
Exit 121
G-Citgo\D
L-Regncy
41
Clothing Carnival
Unadilla
122
Rt 230 Byromville Unadilla
Exit 122
G-Phil66
L-RedC
Colonial
Exit 122
G-Colonial
N
Dooly Co.
Houston Co.
EXIT 127 - VISIT HENDERSON VILLAGE JUST TO THE WEST OF I-75 - STORY ON PAGE 136
THE EXCELLENT LANGSTON HOUSE RESTAURANT - SEE PAGE 136
26
127
Rt 26 Hawkinsville Montezuma
Exit 127
G-Chevn
F-IceCrm
IRRIGATION SYSTEM IN PEANUT FIELDS BESIDE THE INTERSTATE
SPANISH EXPLORER HERNANDO DE SOTO AND HIS ARMY PASSED THROUGH HERE IN MARCH, 1540 - STORY ON PAGE 136
41
DH
Florida
Flat Creek
Time to drive this page: 21.4 minutes
NORTH
GEORGIA, Houston Co.
40

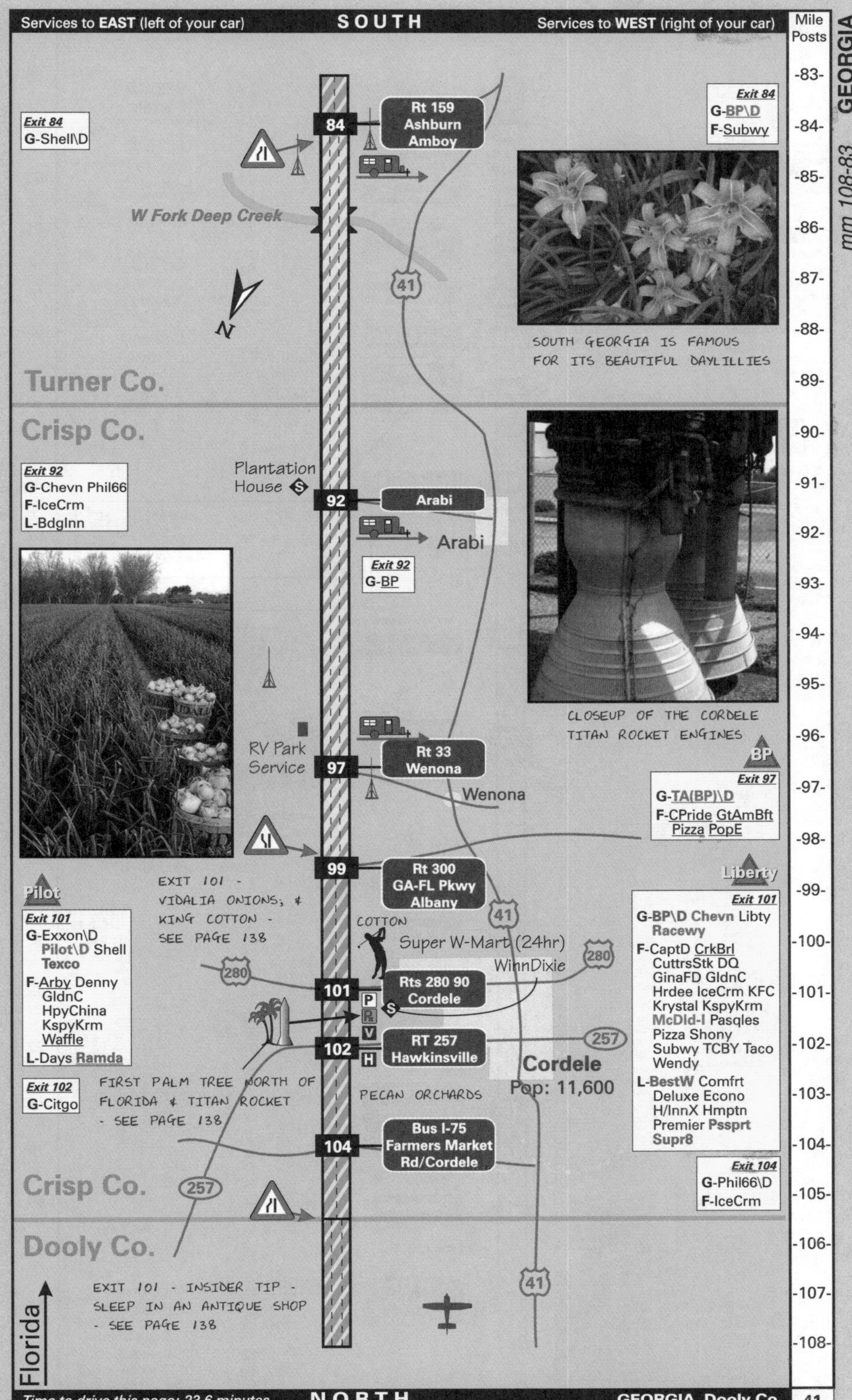
Services to EAST (left of your car)
SOUTH
Services to WEST (right of your car)
Mile Posts
GEORGIA
mm 108-83
-83-
-84-
-85-
-86-
-87-
-88-
-89-
-90-
-91-
-92-
-93-
-94-
-95-
-96-
-97-
-98-
-99-
-100-
-101-
-102-
-103-
-104-
-105-
-106-
-107-
-108-
Exit 84
G-Shell\D
84
Rt 159
Ashburn
Amboy
Exit 84
G-BP\D
F-Subwy
W Fork Deep Creek
41
N
SOUTH GEORGIA IS FAMOUS
FOR ITS BEAUTIFUL DAYLILLIES
Turner Co.
Crisp Co.
Exit 92
G-Chevn Phil66
F-IceCrm
L-BdgInn
Plantation
House
92
Arabi
Arabi
Exit 92
G-BP
CLOSEUP OF THE CORDELE
TITAN ROCKET ENGINES
RV Park
Service
97
Rt 33
Wenona
Wenona
BP
Exit 97
G-TA(BP)\D
F-CPride GtAmBft
Pizza PopE
99
Rt 300
GA-FL Pkwy
Albany
Liberty
Pilot
EXIT 101 -
VIDALIA ONIONS; &
KING COTTON -
SEE PAGE 138
COTTON
Super W-Mart (24hr)
WinnDixie
Exit 101
G-Exxon\D
Pilot\D Shell
Texco
F-Arby Denny
GldnC
HpyChina
KspyKrm
Waffle
L-Days Ramda
280
101
Rts 280 90
Cordele
Exit 101
G-BP\D Chevn Libty
Racewy
F-CaptD CrkBrl
CuttrsStk DQ
GinaFD GldnC
Hrdee IceCrm KFC
Krystal KspyKrm
McDld-I Pasqles
Pizza Shony
Subwy TCBY Taco
Wendy
L-BestW Comfrt
Deluxe Econo
H/InnX Hmptn
Premier Pssprt
Supr8
102
RT 257
Hawkinsville
257
Cordele
Pop: 11,600
Exit 102
G-Citgo
FIRST PALM TREE NORTH OF
FLORIDA & TITAN ROCKET
- SEE PAGE 138
PECAN ORCHARDS
104
Bus I-75
Farmers Market
Rd/Cordele
Exit 104
G-Phil66\D
F-IceCrm
Crisp Co.
257
Dooly Co.
EXIT 101 - INSIDER TIP -
SLEEP IN AN ANTIQUE SHOP
- SEE PAGE 138
Florida
Time to drive this page: 23.6 minutes
NORTH
GEORGIA, Dooly Co.
41

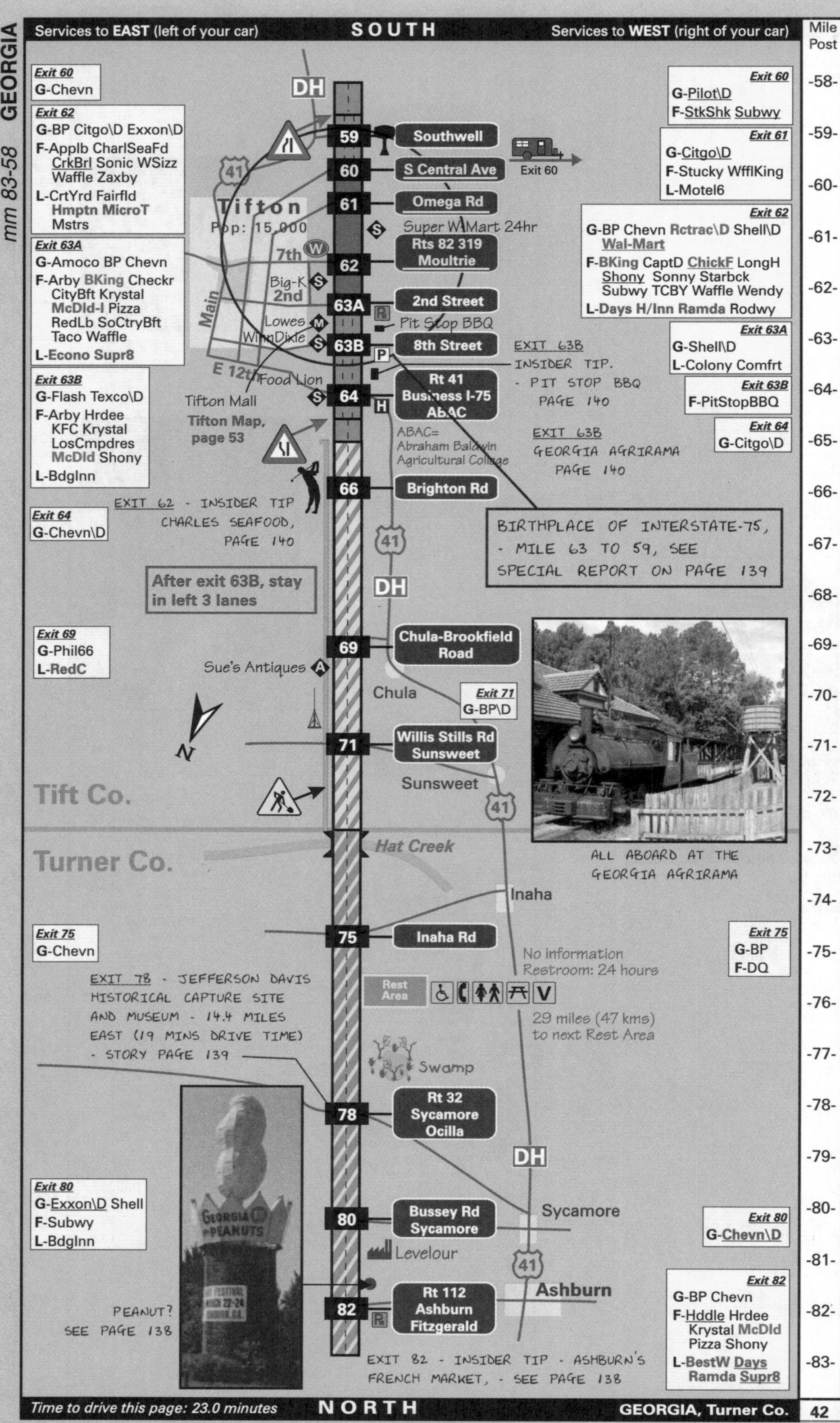
Services to EAST (left of your car)
SOUTH
Services to WEST (right of your car)
Mile Post
Exit 60
G-Chevn
Exit 62
G-BP Citgo\D Exxon\D
F-Applb CharlSeaFd CrkBrl Sonic WSizz Waffle Zaxby
L-CrtYrd Fairfld Hmptn MicroT Mstrs
Exit 63A
G-Amoco BP Chevn
F-Arby BKing Checkr CityBft Krystal McDld-I Pizza RedLb SoCtryBft Taco Waffle
L-Econo Supr8
Exit 63B
G-Flash Texco\D
F-Arby Hrdee KFC Krystal LosCmpdres McDld Shony
L-BdgInn
Exit 64
G-Chevn\D
Exit 69
G-Phil66
L-RedC
Exit 75
G-Chevn
Exit 80
G-Exxon\D Shell
F-Subwy
L-BdgInn
Exit 60
G-Pilot\D
F-StkShk Subwy
Exit 61
G-Citgo\D
F-Stucky WfflKing
L-Motel6
Exit 62
G-BP Chevn Rctrac\D Shell\D Wal-Mart
F-BKing CaptD ChickF LongH Shony Sonny Starbck Subwy TCBY Waffle Wendy
L-Days H/Inn Ramda Rodwy
Exit 63A
G-Shell\D
L-Colony Comfrt
Exit 63B
F-PitStopBBQ
Exit 64
G-Citgo\D
Exit 71
G-BP\D
Exit 75
G-BP
F-DQ
Exit 80
G-Chevn\D
Exit 82
G-BP Chevn
F-Hddle Hrdee Krystal McDld Pizza Shony
L-BestW Days Ramda Supr8
DH
59 Southwell
60 S Central Ave
61 Omega Rd
62 Rts 82 319 Moultrie
63A 2nd Street
63B 8th Street
64 Rt 41 Business I-75 ABAC
66 Brighton Rd
69 Chula-Brookfield Road
71 Willis Stills Rd Sunsweet
75 Inaha Rd
78 Rt 32 Sycamore Ocilla
80 Bussey Rd Sycamore
82 Rt 112 Ashburn Fitzgerald
Exit 60
Tifton
Pop: 15,000
41
7th
2nd
Big-K
Main
Lowes
WinnDixie
E 12th
Food Lion
Super WalMart 24hr
Pit Stop BBQ
Tifton Mall
Tifton Map, page 53
ABAC= Abraham Baldwin Agricultural College
EXIT 63B INSIDER TIP. - PIT STOP BBQ PAGE 140
EXIT 63B GEORGIA AGRIRAMA PAGE 140
EXIT 62 - INSIDER TIP CHARLES SEAFOOD, PAGE 140
BIRTHPLACE OF INTERSTATE-75, - MILE 63 TO 59, SEE SPECIAL REPORT ON PAGE 139
After exit 63B, stay in left 3 lanes
Sue's Antiques
Chula
Sunsweet
Tift Co.
Turner Co.
Hat Creek
Inaha
No information Restroom: 24 hours
Rest Area
29 miles (47 kms) to next Rest Area
EXIT 78 - JEFFERSON DAVIS HISTORICAL CAPTURE SITE AND MUSEUM - 14.4 MILES EAST (19 MINS DRIVE TIME) - STORY PAGE 139
Swamp
Sycamore
Leveloür
Ashburn
PEANUT? SEE PAGE 138
EXIT 82 - INSIDER TIP - ASHBURN'S FRENCH MARKET, - SEE PAGE 138
ALL ABOARD AT THE GEORGIA AGRIRAMA
-58- -59- -60- -61- -62- -63- -64- -65- -66- -67- -68- -69- -70- -71- -72- -73- -74- -75- -76- -77- -78- -79- -80- -81- -82- -83-
Time to drive this page: 23.0 minutes
NORTH

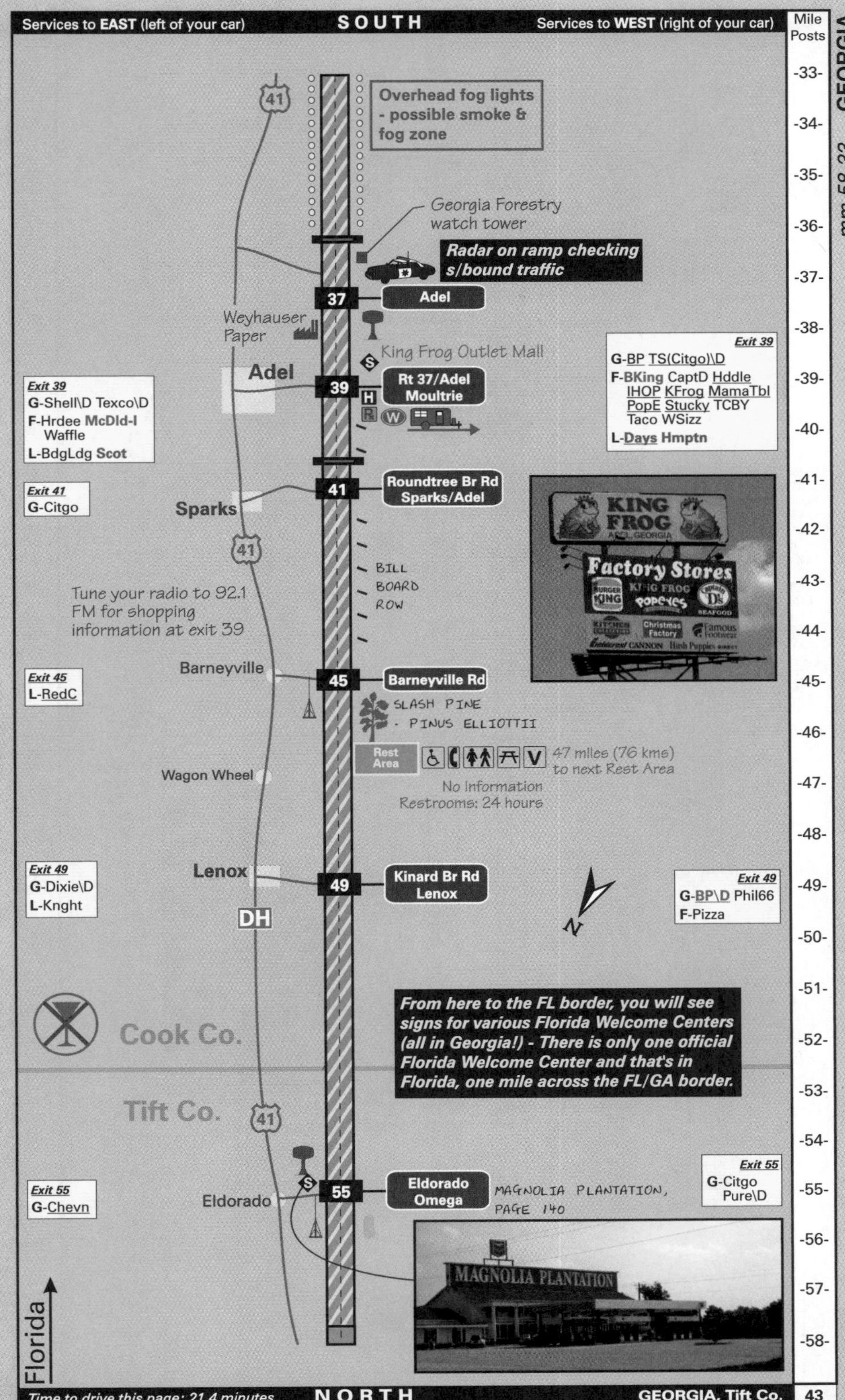
Services to EAST (left of your car)
SOUTH
Services to WEST (right of your car)
Mile Posts
GEORGIA
mm 58-33
-33-
-34-
-35-
-36-
-37-
-38-
-39-
-40-
-41-
-42-
-43-
-44-
-45-
-46-
-47-
-48-
-49-
-50-
-51-
-52-
-53-
-54-
-55-
-56-
-57-
-58-
41
Overhead fog lights - possible smoke & fog zone
Georgia Forestry watch tower
Radar on ramp checking s/bound traffic
37
Adel
Weyhauser Paper
King Frog Outlet Mall
Adel
39
Rt 37/Adel Moultrie
H
R
W
Exit 39
G-Shell\D Texco\D
F-Hrdee McDld-I Waffle
L-BdgLdg Scot
Exit 39
G-BP TS(Citgo)\D
F-BKing CaptD Hddle IHOP KFrog MamaTbl PopE Stucky TCBY Taco WSizz
L-Days Hmptn
Exit 41
G-Citgo
41
Roundtree Br Rd Sparks/Adel
Sparks
KING FROG
Factory Stores
BURGER KING
KING FROG
POPEYES
Captain D's SEAFOOD
KITCHEN COLLECTION
Christmas Factory
Famous Footwear
CANNON
Hush Puppies
41
BILL BOARD ROW
Tune your radio to 92.1 FM for shopping information at exit 39
Barneyville
Exit 45
L-RedC
45
Barneyville Rd
SLASH PINE - PINUS ELLIOTTII
Rest Area
V
47 miles (76 kms) to next Rest Area
Wagon Wheel
No Information
Restrooms: 24 hours
Exit 49
G-Dixie\D
L-Knght
Lenox
49
Kinard Br Rd Lenox
DH
Exit 49
G-BP\D Phil66
F-Pizza
N
From here to the FL border, you will see signs for various Florida Welcome Centers (all in Georgia!) - There is only one official Florida Welcome Center and that's in Florida, one mile across the FL/GA border.
Cook Co.
Tift Co.
41
Exit 55
G-Chevn
Eldorado
55
Eldorado Omega
MAGNOLIA PLANTATION, PAGE 140
Exit 55
G-Citgo Pure\D
MAGNOLIA PLANTATION
Florida
Time to drive this page: 21.4 minutes
NORTH
GEORGIA, Tift Co.
43

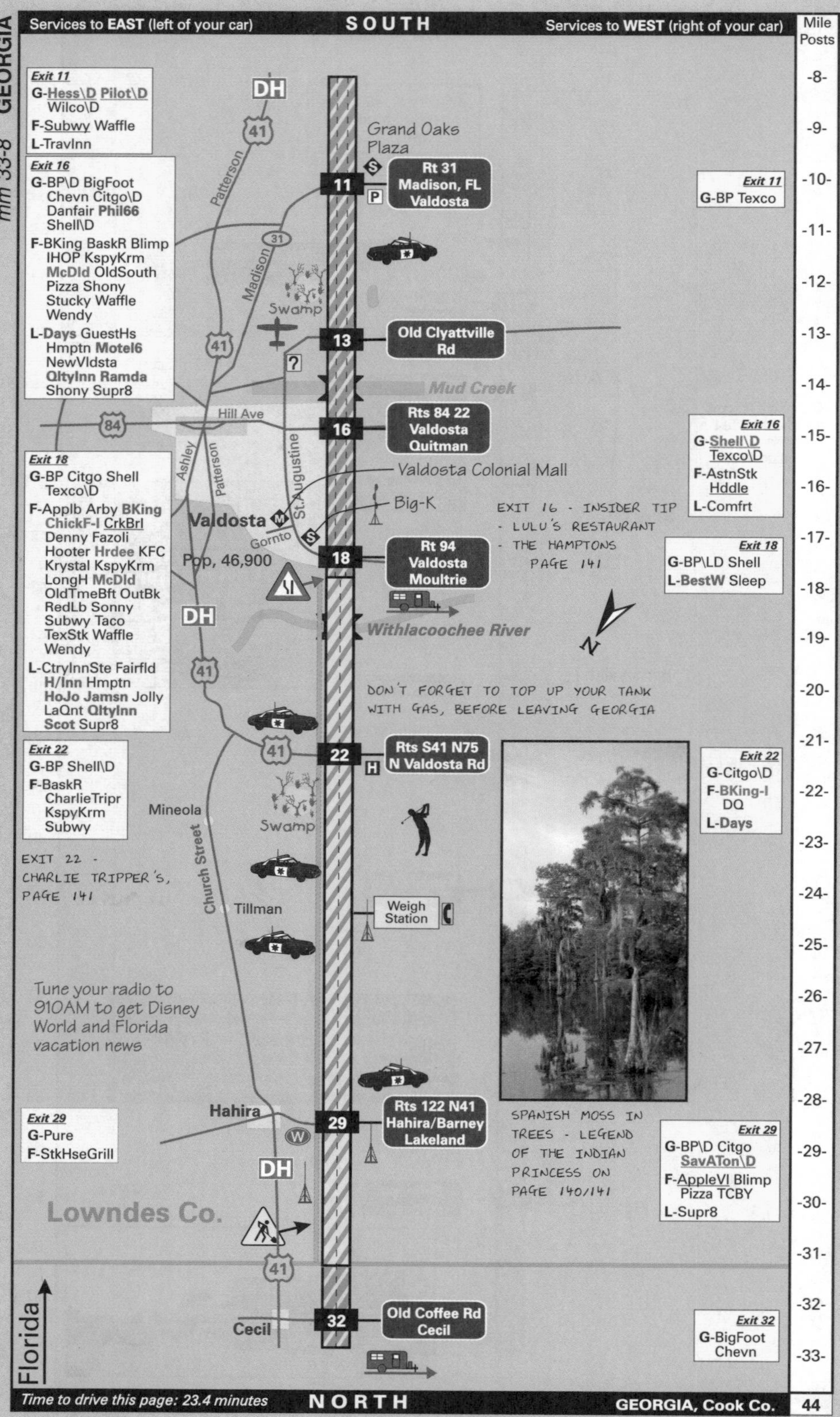
Services to EAST (left of your car)
SOUTH
Services to WEST (right of your car)
Mile Posts
Exit 11
G-Hess\D Pilot\D Wilco\D
F-Subwy Waffle
L-TravInn
Exit 16
G-BP\D BigFoot Chevn Citgo\D Danfair Phil66 Shell\D
F-BKing BaskR Blimp IHOP KspyKrm McDld OldSouth Pizza Shony Stucky Waffle Wendy
L-Days GuestHs Hmptn Motel6 NewVldsta QltyInn Ramda Shony Supr8
Exit 18
G-BP Citgo Shell Texco\D
F-Applb Arby BKing ChickF-I CrkBrl Denny Fazoli Hooter Hrdee KFC Krystal KspyKrm LongH McDld OldTmeBft OutBk RedLb Sonny Subwy Taco TexStk Waffle Wendy
L-CtryInnSte Fairfld H/Inn Hmptn HoJo Jamsn Jolly LaQnt QltyInn Scot Supr8
Exit 22
G-BP Shell\D
F-BaskR CharlieTripr KspyKrm Subwy
EXIT 22 - CHARLIE TRIPPER'S, PAGE 141
Tune your radio to 910AM to get Disney World and Florida vacation news
Exit 29
G-Pure
F-StkHseGrill
Lowndes Co.
Florida
DH
41
Patterson
Madison
31
Swamp
84
Hill Ave
Ashley
St. Augustine
Valdosta
Pop. 46,900
Gornto
Mineola
Church Street
Tillman
Hahira
Cecil
Grand Oaks Plaza
11
Rt 31 Madison, FL Valdosta
13
Old Clyattville Rd
Mud Creek
16
Rts 84 22 Valdosta Quitman
Valdosta Colonial Mall
Big-K
18
Rt 94 Valdosta Moultrie
Withlacoochee River
22
Rts S41 N75 N Valdosta Rd
Weigh Station
29
Rts 122 N41 Hahira/Barney Lakeland
32
Old Coffee Rd Cecil
EXIT 16 - INSIDER TIP
- LULU'S RESTAURANT
- THE HAMPTONS PAGE 141
N
DON'T FORGET TO TOP UP YOUR TANK WITH GAS, BEFORE LEAVING GEORGIA
SPANISH MOSS IN TREES - LEGEND OF THE INDIAN PRINCESS ON PAGE 140/141
Exit 11
G-BP Texco
Exit 16
G-Shell\D Texco\D
F-AstnStk Hddle
L-Comfrt
Exit 18
G-BP\LD Shell
L-BestW Sleep
Exit 22
G-Citgo\D
F-BKing-I DQ
L-Days
Exit 29
G-BP\D Citgo SavATon\D
F-AppleVl Blimp Pizza TCBY
L-Supr8
Exit 32
G-BigFoot Chevn
-8- -9- -10- -11- -12- -13- -14- -15- -16- -17- -18- -19- -20- -21- -22- -23- -24- -25- -26- -27- -28- -29- -30- -31- -32- -33-
Time to drive this page: 23.4 minutes
NORTH

HAVE A SAFE TRIP TO YOUR FLORIDA DESTINATION. DON'T FORGET TO STOP AT THE WELCOME CENTER AND GET YOUR FREE ORANGE OR GRAPEFRUIT JUICE DRINK! ALSO, PICK UP YOUR DISCOUNT COUPON BOOKS FROM THE BOXES NEAR THE VENDING MACHINES. I'LL SEE YOU ON THE WAY BACK.

Dave

FLORIDA DESTINATIONS - Routes & Mileage

DESTINATION	ROUTE	MILES/*Km*
ORLANDO	FL Border (I-75)>Wildwood (FL Tpk)>Orlando	210/*338*
TITUSVILLE	FL Border (I-75)>Wildwood (FL Tpk)>Orlando (Rts528/427) Orlando (Rts528/427)>Titusville	250/*402*
JACKSONVILLE	Fl Border (I-75)>Lake City (I-10)>Jacksonville	113/*182*
DAYTONA BCH	FL Border (I-75)>I-10>I-295>I-95>Daytona	188/*303*
FT LAUDERDALE	FL Border (I-75)>Wildwood (FL Tpk)>Fort Lauderdale	407/*655*
MIAMI	FL Border (I-75)>Wildwood (FL Tpk)>Miami	422/*679*
TAMPA	FL Border (I-75)>Junction I-275> Tampa	226/*364*
St. PETERSBURG	FL Border (I-75)>St. Petersburg	247/*397*
FORT MYERS	FL Border (I-75)>Fort Myers	346/*557*
NAPLES	FL Border (I-75)>Naples	388/*624*
KEY WEST	FL Border (I-75)>Wildwood (FL Tpk)>Miami> >Miami (FL Tpk/US 1)>Key West	578/*930*

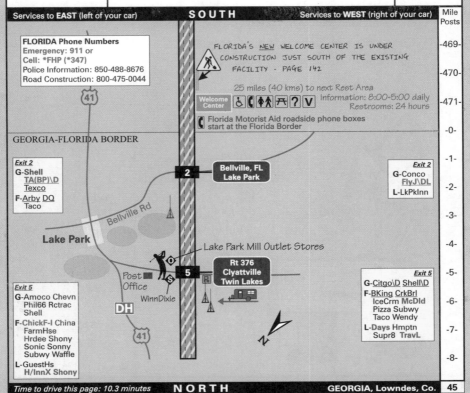

Services to **EAST** (left of your car) — **SOUTH** — Services to **WEST** (right of your car)

Mile Posts: -469- -470- -471- -0- -1- -2- -3- -4- -5- -6- -7- -8-

FLORIDA Phone Numbers
Emergency: 911 or
Cell: *FHP (*347)
Police Information: 850-488-8676
Road Construction: 800-475-0044

FLORIDA'S NEW WELCOME CENTER IS UNDER CONSTRUCTION JUST SOUTH OF THE EXISTING FACILITY - PAGE 142

25 miles (40 kms) to next Rest Area
Welcome Center — Information: 8:00-5:00 daily; Restrooms: 24 hours

Florida Motorist Aid roadside phone boxes start at the Florida Border

GEORGIA-FLORIDA BORDER

41

Exit 2 (East)
G-Shell TA(BP)\D Texco
F-Arby DQ Taco

2 Bellville, FL Lake Park

Exit 2 (West)
G-Conco FlyJ\DL
L-LkPkInn

Bellville Rd

Lake Park

Lake Park Mill Outlet Stores

Post Office

WinnDixie

DH

5 Rt 376 Clyattville Twin Lakes

Exit 5 (East)
G-Amoco Chevn Phil66 Rctrac Shell
F-ChickF-I China FarmHse Hrdee Shony Sonic Sonny Subwy Waffle
L-GuestHs H/InnX Shony

Exit 5 (West)
G-Citgo\D Shell\D
F-BKing CrkBrl IceCrm McDld Pizza Subwy Taco Wendy
L-Days Hmptn Supr8 TravL

N

Off The Beaten Path

One of the most enjoyable aspects of a journey along Interstate-75 is the abundance of interesting places you can visit within just a few minutes of an exit ramp. Yet many travelers don't take advantage of this because of the fear of becoming lost in unfamiliar territory.

On the following pages we provide you with short side trips you can take - perhaps as a brief evening tour after checking into your motel or as a short excursion during your day's drive. Why not take an extra day on your journey, and enjoy the countryside around you?

Enjoy your drive . . . after all, getting there is half the fun!

All information updated as of September, 2004

Detroit's Ambassador Bridge to Canada - and Back

Finding the Ambassador Bridge to Canada from I-75 is easy - just take exit 47B, drive across the lights at Lafayette and you are at the bridge toll booths. Watch for trucks on your left as you enter the Toll Plaza - they have to cross to get to the right hand lane.

Getting back onto I-75 South is not so easy. This is nothing to do with Customs or Immigration, it is more to do with finding I-75 again (incidentally, this section of I-75 is called the *"Fisher Freeway"*). The signs are quite confusing and depending upon the season, covered by foliage in some cases. We have included this map to help you.

Finding the I-75 South

1. After clearing Customs, drive across the lights at Porter. Do not go down the I-75 ramp to your left - it goes north!
2. After passing Bristol (a small side street on your right, move into left turn lane.
3. Turn left at the Vernor intersection lights.
4. On Vernor, move **immediately** into the left turn lane as you cross the bridge over the I-75.
5. At the next lights, turn left onto Fisher Freeway W. Ignore sign at the corner that says *"Bridge to Canada."*
6. Stay on *"Fisher Freeway West"* - past Bagley, Lambie, Howard, 25th St, to the lights at Grand Boulevard.
7. Pass Vinewood, Hubbard and Scotten. Immediately after the lights at Clark, move to the left lane and go down the ramp onto the I-75 South.
8. If this ramp is closed for construction, continue on along the service road - there are at least 3 more I-75 Southbound ramps ahead.

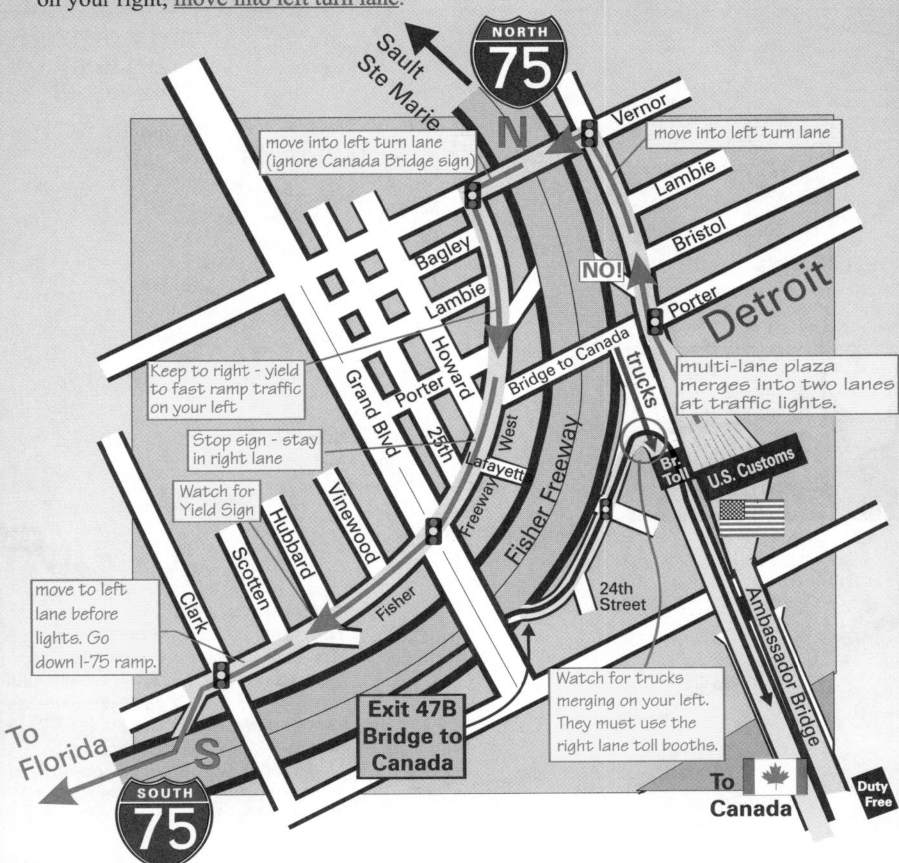

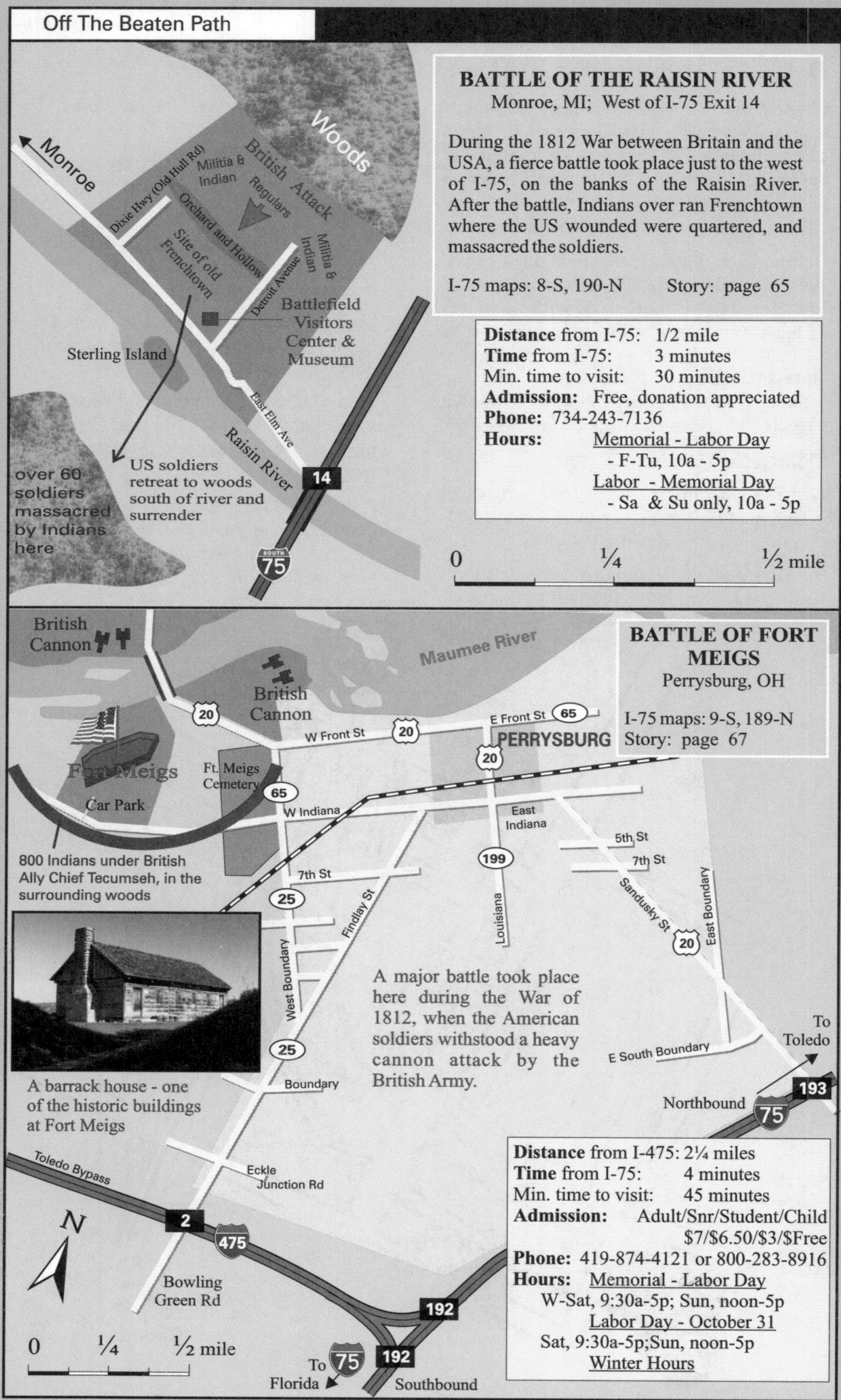
BATTLE OF THE RAISIN RIVER
Monroe, MI; West of I-75 Exit 14
During the 1812 War between Britain and the USA, a fierce battle took place just to the west of I-75, on the banks of the Raisin River. After the battle, Indians over ran Frenchtown where the US wounded were quartered, and massacred the soldiers.
I-75 maps: 8-S, 190-N
Story: page 65
Distance from I-75: 1/2 mile
Time from I-75: 3 minutes
Min. time to visit: 30 minutes
Admission: Free, donation appreciated
Phone: 734-243-7136
Hours: Memorial - Labor Day
- F-Tu, 10a - 5p
Labor - Memorial Day
- Sa & Su only, 10a - 5p
Woods
Monroe
British Attack
Militia & Indian
Regulars
Dixie Hwy (Old Hull Rd)
Orchard and Hollow
Site of old Frenchtown
Militia & Indian
Detroit Avenue
Battlefield Visitors Center & Museum
Sterling Island
East Elm Ave
Raisin River
14
US soldiers retreat to woods south of river and surrender
over 60 soldiers massacred by Indians here
75
0
¼
½ mile
BATTLE OF FORT MEIGS
Perrysburg, OH
I-75 maps: 9-S, 189-N
Story: page 67
British Cannon
Maumee River
British Cannon
20
W Front St
20
E Front St
65
PERRYSBURG
20
Fort Meigs
Ft. Meigs Cemetery
65
Car Park
W Indiana
East Indiana
5th St
7th St
199
800 Indians under British Ally Chief Tecumseh, in the surrounding woods
7th St
25
Findlay St
Louisiana
Sandusky St
East Boundary
20
West Boundary
A major battle took place here during the War of 1812, when the American soldiers withstood a heavy cannon attack by the British Army.
25
Boundary
E South Boundary
To Toledo
193
Northbound
75
Toledo Bypass
Eckle Junction Rd
N
2
475
Bowling Green Rd
192
0
¼
½ mile
To Florida
75
192
Southbound
Distance from I-475: 2¼ miles
Time from I-75: 4 minutes
Min. time to visit: 45 minutes
Admission: Adult/Snr/Student/Child
$7/$6.50/$3/$Free
Phone: 419-874-4121 or 800-283-8916
Hours: Memorial - Labor Day
W-Sat, 9:30a-5p; Sun, noon-5p
Labor Day - October 31
Sat, 9:30a-5p;Sun, noon-5p
Winter Hours

A barrack house - one of the historic buildings at Fort Meigs

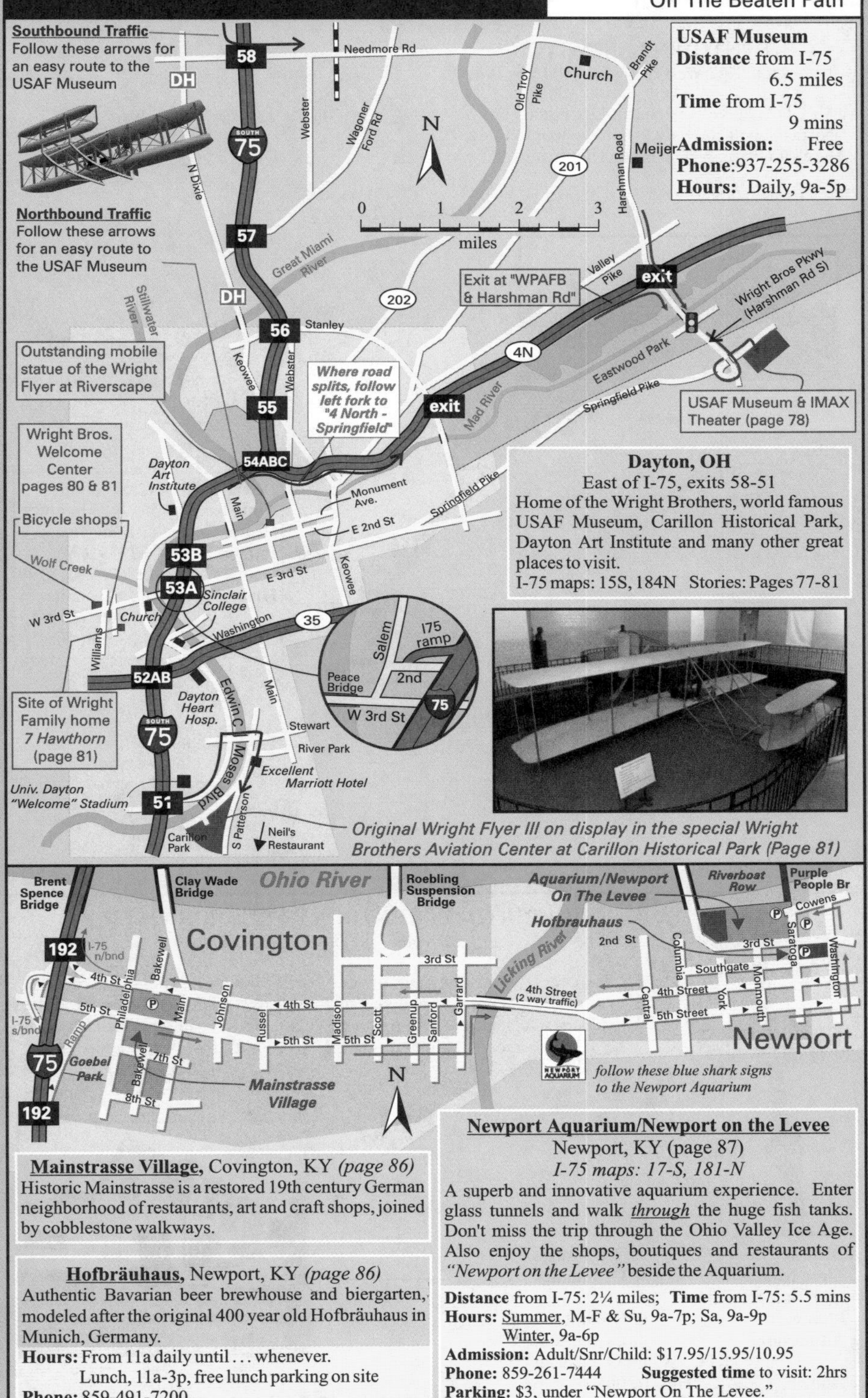

USAF Museum
Distance from I-75 6.5 miles
Time from I-75 9 mins
Admission: Free
Phone:937-255-3286
Hours: Daily, 9a-5p

Dayton, OH
East of I-75, exits 58-51
Home of the Wright Brothers, world famous USAF Museum, Carillon Historical Park, Dayton Art Institute and many other great places to visit.
I-75 maps: 15S, 184N Stories: Pages 77-81

Mainstrasse Village, Covington, KY *(page 86)*
Historic Mainstrasse is a restored 19th century German neighborhood of restaurants, art and craft shops, joined by cobblestone walkways.

Hofbräuhaus, Newport, KY *(page 86)*
Authentic Bavarian beer brewhouse and biergarten, modeled after the original 400 year old Hofbräuhaus in Munich, Germany.
Hours: From 11a daily until . . . whenever.
Lunch, 11a-3p, free lunch parking on site
Phone: 859-491-7200

Newport Aquarium/Newport on the Levee
Newport, KY (page 87)
I-75 maps: 17-S, 181-N
A superb and innovative aquarium experience. Enter glass tunnels and walk *through* the huge fish tanks. Don't miss the trip through the Ohio Valley Ice Age. Also enjoy the shops, boutiques and restaurants of *"Newport on the Levee"* beside the Aquarium.
Distance from I-75: 2¼ miles; **Time** from I-75: 5.5 mins
Hours: Summer, M-F & Su, 9a-7p; Sa, 9a-9p
Winter, 9a-6p
Admission: Adult/Snr/Child: $17.95/15.95/10.95
Phone: 859-261-7444 **Suggested time** to visit: 2hrs
Parking: $3, under "Newport On The Levee."

DOWNTOWN LEXINGTON

Lexington, KY; West of I-75 Exit 115 or 104

Most I-75 travelers bypass Lexington, but a short visit will add only ½ hour to your journey. Here's how to navigate through this historic city.

I-75 maps: 20-S, 178-N Story: page 90

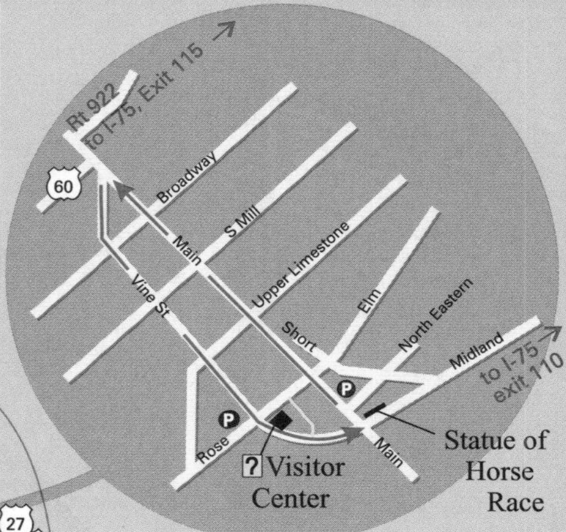

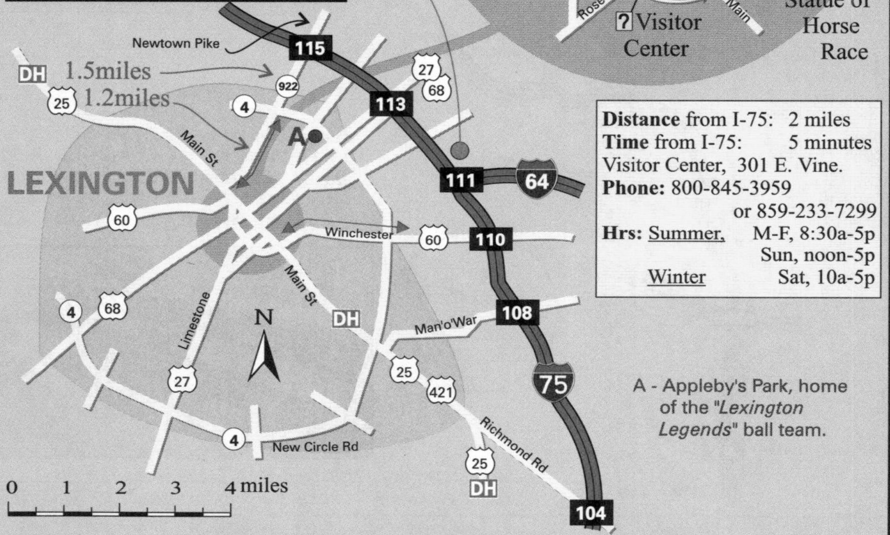

Distance from I-75:	2 miles
Time from I-75:	5 minutes
Visitor Center, 301 E. Vine.	
Phone: 800-845-3959	
	or 859-233-7299
Hrs: Summer,	M-F, 8:30a-5p
	Sun, noon-5p
Winter	Sat, 10a-5p

A - Appleby's Park, home of the "*Lexington Legends*" ball team.

Statue of Horse Race

Visitor Center

BIRTH OF KENTUCKY FRIED CHICKEN

Corbin, KY; East of I-75 Exit 29

Here on Hwy 25 (the main route to Florida before I-75) Harland Sanders owned a motel. When construction plans for I-75 were announced he developed food for travelers - his famous Kentucky Fried Chicken recipe - which resulted in the world's first fast food operation.

I-75 maps: 23-S, 175-N

Story: page 98

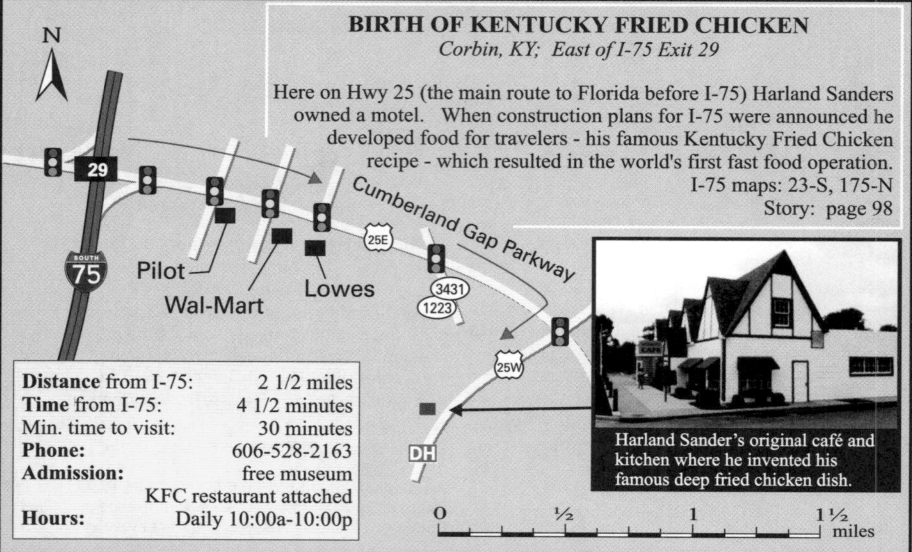

Harland Sander's original café and kitchen where he invented his famous deep fried chicken dish.

Distance from I-75:	2 1/2 miles
Time from I-75:	4 1/2 minutes
Min. time to visit:	30 minutes
Phone:	606-528-2163
Admission:	free museum
	KFC restaurant attached
Hours:	Daily 10:00a-10:00p

WHITE HALL

Richmond, KY; West of I-75 Exit 95

Home of Abraham Lincoln's friend, and Kentucky's most colorful historical figure - Cassius Marcellus Clay. This magnificent Georgian style home dates from 1798 and is open to the public.

I-75 maps: 21-S, 178-N Story: page 93

0 1 2 3 miles

River
Fort Boonesborough State Park
Coones Ferry Road
627E
Old Boonesborough Rd
McKinney Lane
N
75
627E
Rt 3377 Lost Fork Rd
White Hall
95
627W

FORT BOONESBOROUGH

Richmond, KY; East of I-75 Exit 95

Here in 1775 Daniel Boone established his frontier homesite on the bank of the Kentucky River. The reconstructed log fort is now a state park.

I-75 maps: 21-S, 178-N
Story: page 92

Distance from I-75: 1.9 miles
Time from I-75: 3 1/2 mins
Min.time to visit: 1 hour
Phone: 859-623-9178
Admission: Adult/Child: $6/$3
Hrs: Apr 1-Labor Day, daily, 9-5:30
LabrDay-Oct 31, W-Su, 9-5:30

Catching up with daily chores at Fort Boonesboro

Distance from I-75: 5.2 miles
Time from I-75: 6 minutes
Min.time to visit: 1 hour
Admission: Adult/Child $6/$4
Phone: 859-527-3131
Hours:
Apr 1-Oct 31 - Daily 9a-5p
Winter (weather permitting) -Wed-Sun 10a-4p

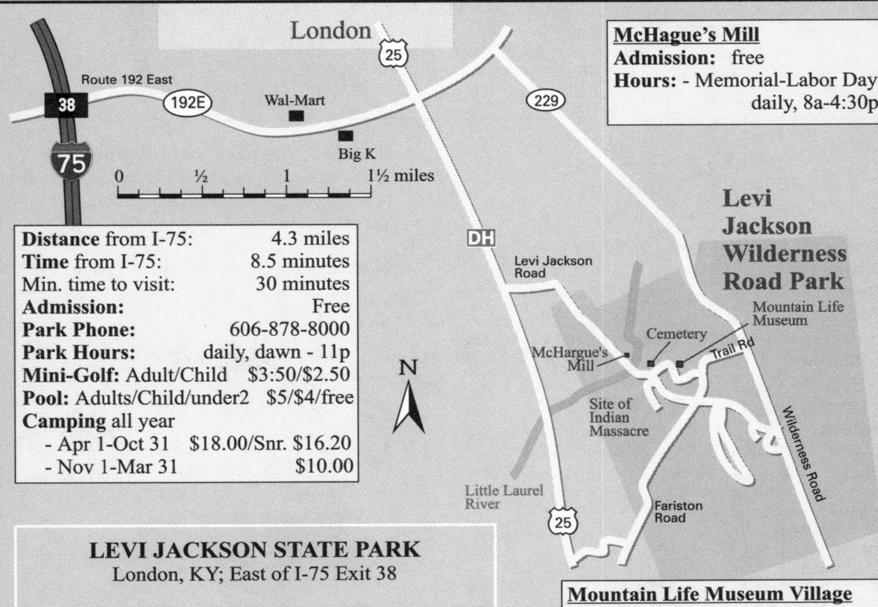

McHague's Mill
Admission: free
Hours: - Memorial-Labor Day daily, 8a-4:30p

Distance from I-75: 4.3 miles
Time from I-75: 8.5 minutes
Min. time to visit: 30 minutes
Admission: Free
Park Phone: 606-878-8000
Park Hours: daily, dawn - 11p
Mini-Golf: Adult/Child $3:50/$2.50
Pool: Adults/Child/under2 $5/$4/free
Camping all year
- Apr 1-Oct 31 $18.00/Snr. $16.20
- Nov 1-Mar 31 $10.00

LEVI JACKSON STATE PARK

London, KY; East of I-75 Exit 38

Levi Jackson Wilderness Road State Park is situated on a portion of Daniel Boone's pioneer trail which started at the Cumberland Gap.

I-75 maps: 23-S, 175-N Story: page 97

Mountain Life Museum Village
Min. time to visit: 30 minutes
Admission:
Adult/Child, $2.50/$1.25
Phone: 606-878-8000
Hours: April-October, daily 9a-5p

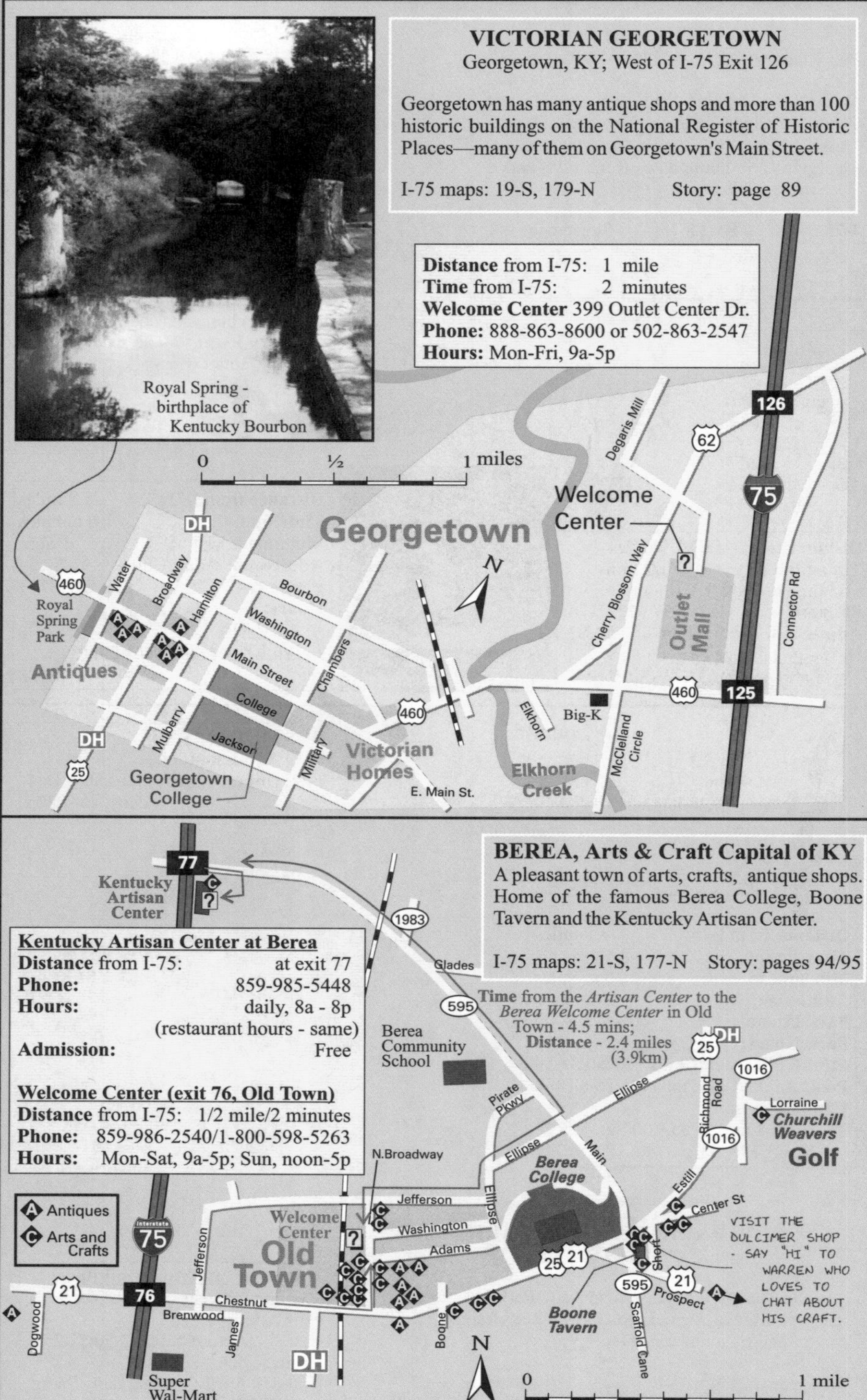
VICTORIAN GEORGETOWN
Georgetown, KY; West of I-75 Exit 126
Georgetown has many antique shops and more than 100 historic buildings on the National Register of Historic Places—many of them on Georgetown's Main Street.
I-75 maps: 19-S, 179-N
Story: page 89
Distance from I-75: 1 mile
Time from I-75: 2 minutes
Welcome Center 399 Outlet Center Dr.
Phone: 888-863-8600 or 502-863-2547
Hours: Mon-Fri, 9a-5p
Royal Spring - birthplace of Kentucky Bourbon
0
½
1 miles
Georgetown
Welcome Center
Degaris Mill
126
62
75
DH
460
Royal Spring Park
Water
Broadway
Hamilton
Bourbon
Washington
Main Street
Chambers
College
Jackson
Mulberry
Military
Antiques
Cherry Blossom Way
Outlet Mall
Connector Rd
460
125
Elkhorn
Big-K
McClelland Circle
Victorian Homes
Elkhorn Creek
E. Main St.
Georgetown College
25
BEREA, Arts & Craft Capital of KY
A pleasant town of arts, crafts, antique shops. Home of the famous Berea College, Boone Tavern and the Kentucky Artisan Center.
I-75 maps: 21-S, 177-N
Story: pages 94/95
77
Kentucky Artisan Center
1983
Glades
Kentucky Artisan Center at Berea
Distance from I-75: at exit 77
Phone: 859-985-5448
Hours: daily, 8a - 8p (restaurant hours - same)
Admission: Free
Welcome Center (exit 76, Old Town)
Distance from I-75: 1/2 mile/2 minutes
Phone: 859-986-2540/1-800-598-5263
Hours: Mon-Sat, 9a-5p; Sun, noon-5p
595
Time from the Artisan Center to the Berea Welcome Center in Old Town - 4.5 mins;
Distance - 2.4 miles (3.9km)
Berea Community School
25
DH
1016
Pirate Pkwy
Ellipse
Richmond Road
Lorraine
Churchill Weavers
Golf
Main
Berea College
N.Broadway
Estill
Center St
Antiques
Arts and Crafts
Jefferson
Washington
Adams
Welcome Center
Old Town
VISIT THE DULCIMER SHOP - SAY "HI" TO WARREN WHO LOVES TO CHAT ABOUT HIS CRAFT.
Short
21
76
Chestnut
Brenwood
Dogwood
James
Boone
Boone Tavern
Scaffold Cane
Prospect
Super Wal-Mart
N
0
1 mile

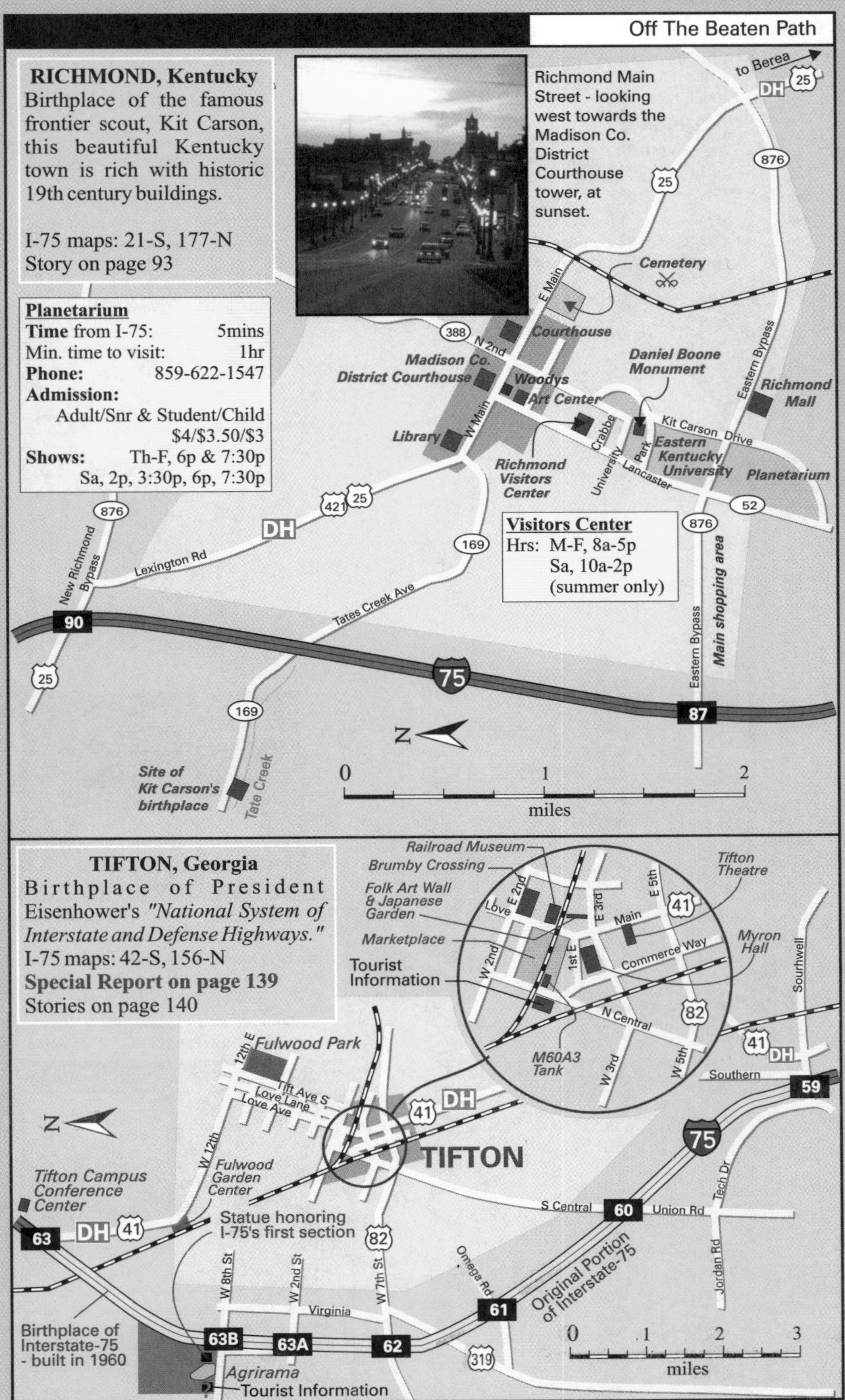
RICHMOND, Kentucky
Birthplace of the famous frontier scout, Kit Carson, this beautiful Kentucky town is rich with historic 19th century buildings.
I-75 maps: 21-S, 177-N
Story on page 93
Richmond Main Street - looking west towards the Madison Co. District Courthouse tower, at sunset.
Planetarium
Time from I-75: 5mins
Min. time to visit: 1hr
Phone: 859-622-1547
Admission:
Adult/Snr & Student/Child
$4/$3.50/$3
Shows: Th-F, 6p & 7:30p
Sa, 2p, 3:30p, 6p, 7:30p
Visitors Center
Hrs: M-F, 8a-5p
Sa, 10a-2p
(summer only)
to Berea
Cemetery
Courthouse
Madison Co. District Courthouse
Woodys
Art Center
Daniel Boone Monument
Richmond Mall
Library
Richmond Visitors Center
Eastern Kentucky University
Planetarium
Kit Carson Drive
Lancaster
University
Crabbe
Park
E Main
W Main
N 2nd
Eastern Bypass
Main shopping area
New Richmond Bypass
Lexington Rd
Tates Creek Ave
Tate Creek
Site of Kit Carson's birthplace
miles
TIFTON, Georgia
Birthplace of President Eisenhower's *"National System of Interstate and Defense Highways."*
I-75 maps: 42-S, 156-N
Special Report on page 139
Stories on page 140
Railroad Museum
Brumby Crossing
Folk Art Wall & Japanese Garden
Marketplace
Tourist Information
Tifton Theatre
Myron Hall
M60A3 Tank
Love
E 2nd
E 3rd
E 5th
Main
Commerce Way
1st E
W 2nd
N Central
W 3rd
W 5th
Sourwell
Southern
Fulwood Park
12th E
Tift Ave S
Love Lane
Love Ave
W 12th
TIFTON
Fulwood Garden Center
Tifton Campus Conference Center
Statue honoring I-75's first section
S Central
Union Rd
Tech Dr
Jordan Rd
Omega Rd
Original Portion of Interstate-75
W 8th St
W 2nd St
W 7th St
Virginia
Birthplace of Interstate-75 - built in 1960
Agrirama
Tourist Information
miles

ELK VALLEY

Tennessee - S/Bound: exit 160, N/Bound: exit 141

An alternative route to I-75. An excellent paved, but winding road leading through tunnels of trees in the valley immediately to the west of I-75. Caution - a great drive on a good day but do not use in bad weather or if you do not enjoy narrow twisting roads. Not suitable for large Rvs. If northbound on I-75, take exit 141 and drive US63 west for 4.3 miles (6.9km); watch for the sharp right turn onto SR297 just past the Post Office.

I-75 maps: 25-S, 173-N Stories: page 100/101

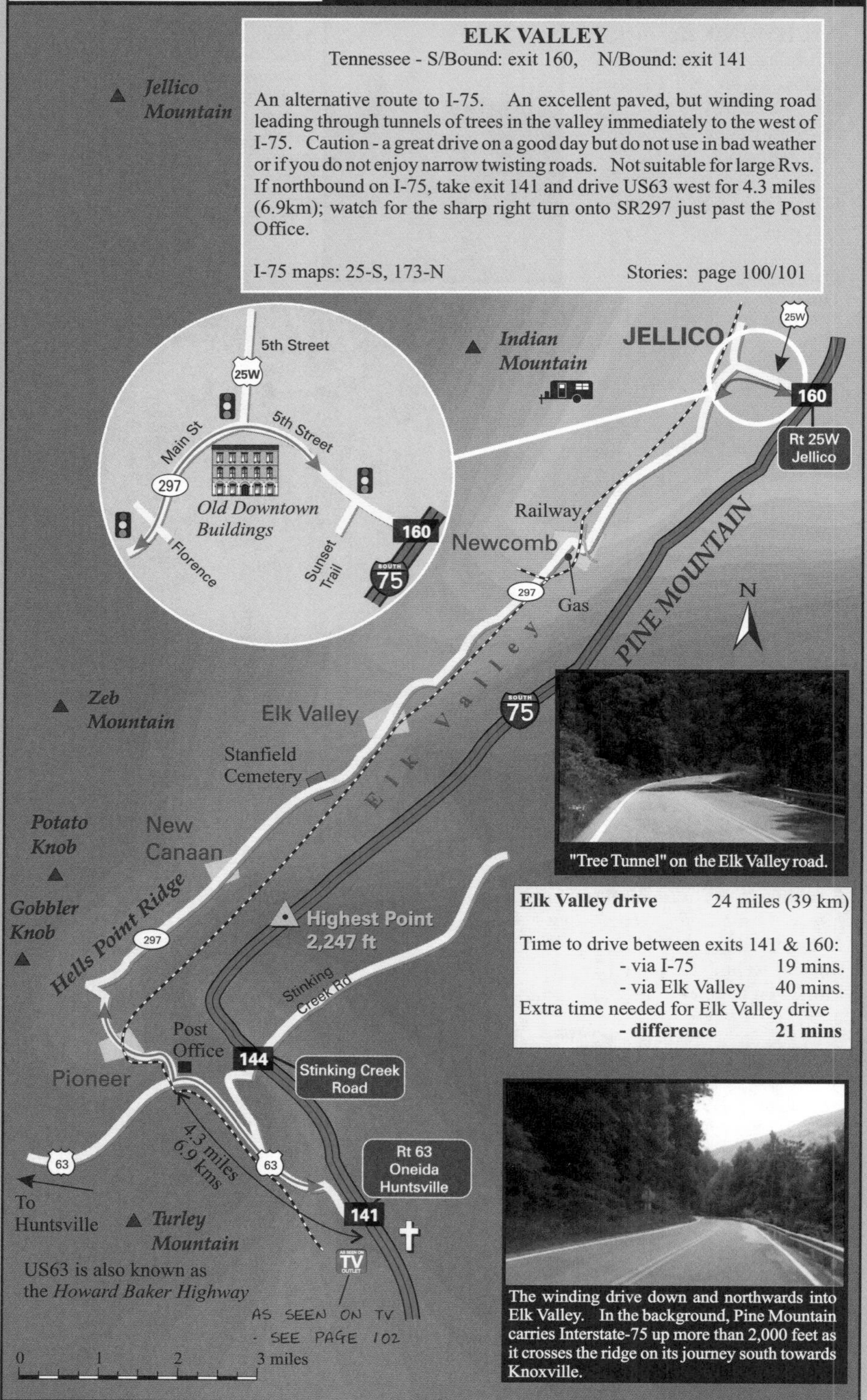

Jellico Mountain
Indian Mountain
JELLICO
25W
160
Rt 25W Jellico
5th Street
25W
Main St
5th Street
297
Old Downtown Buildings
Florence
Sunset Trail
160
South 75
Railway
Newcomb
297
Gas
Elk Valley
PINE MOUNTAIN
N
Zeb Mountain
Elk Valley
South 75
Stanfield Cemetery
Potato Knob
New Canaan
Gobbler Knob
Hells Point Ridge
297
Highest Point 2,247 ft
Stinking Creek Rd
Post Office
144
Stinking Creek Road
Pioneer
4.3 miles 6.9 kms
63
63
Rt 63 Oneida Huntsville
To Huntsville
141
Turley Mountain
TV Outlet
US63 is also known as the *Howard Baker Highway*
AS SEEN ON TV - SEE PAGE 102
0 1 2 3 miles

"Tree Tunnel" on the Elk Valley road.

Elk Valley drive	24 miles (39 km)
Time to drive between exits 141 & 160:	
- via I-75	19 mins.
- via Elk Valley	40 mins.
Extra time needed for Elk Valley drive	
- difference	**21 mins**

The winding drive down and northwards into Elk Valley. In the background, Pine Mountain carries Interstate-75 up more than 2,000 feet as it crosses the ridge on its journey south towards Knoxville.

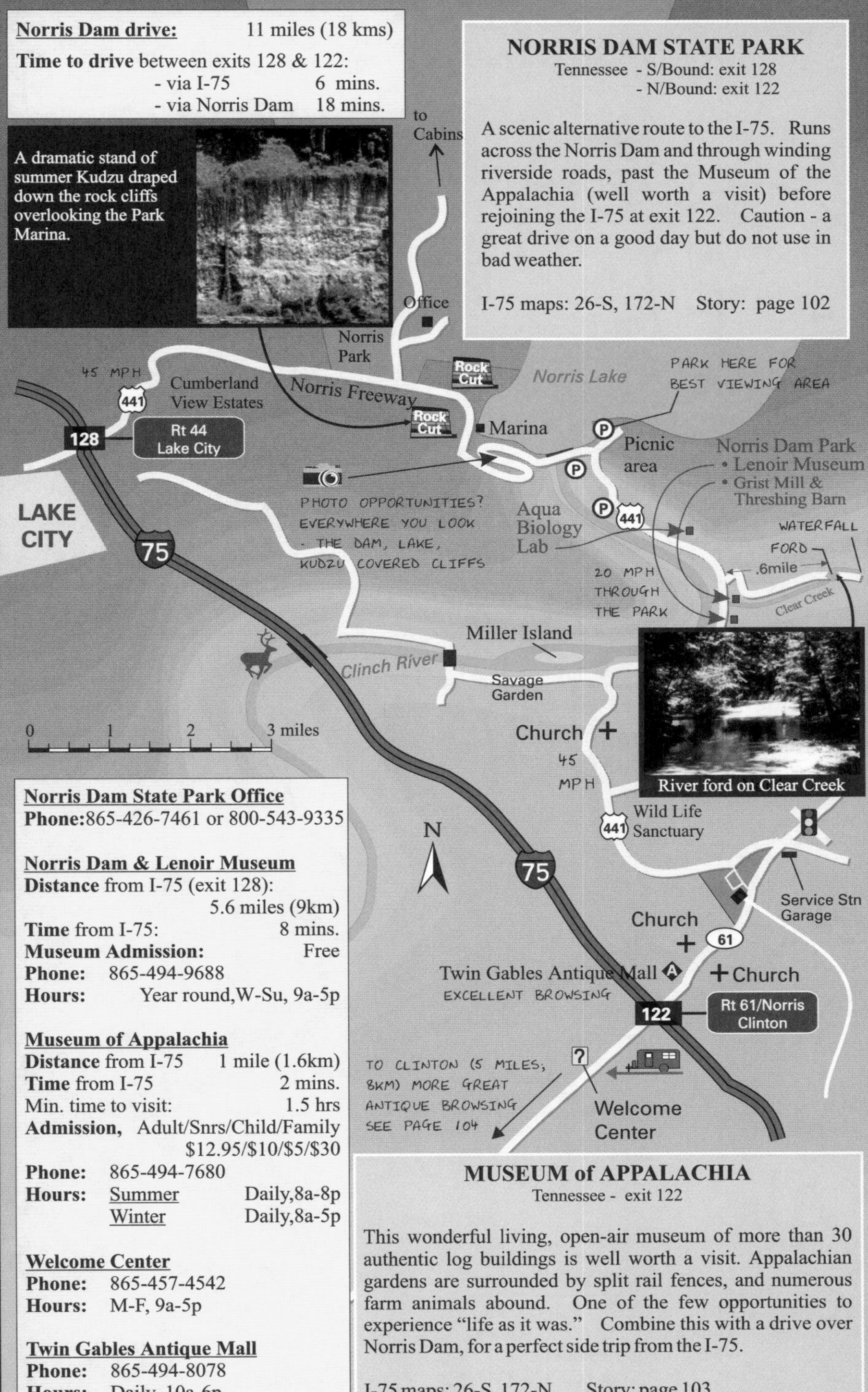

A dramatic stand of summer Kudzu draped down the rock cliffs overlooking the Park Marina.

River ford on Clear Creek

Norris Dam drive: 11 miles (18 kms)

Time to drive between exits 128 & 122:
- via I-75 6 mins.
- via Norris Dam 18 mins.

NORRIS DAM STATE PARK

Tennessee - S/Bound: exit 128
- N/Bound: exit 122

A scenic alternative route to the I-75. Runs across the Norris Dam and through winding riverside roads, past the Museum of the Appalachia (well worth a visit) before rejoining the I-75 at exit 122. Caution - a great drive on a good day but do not use in bad weather.

I-75 maps: 26-S, 172-N Story: page 102

Norris Dam State Park Office
Phone: 865-426-7461 or 800-543-9335

Norris Dam & Lenoir Museum
Distance from I-75 (exit 128): 5.6 miles (9km)
Time from I-75: 8 mins.
Museum Admission: Free
Phone: 865-494-9688
Hours: Year round, W-Su, 9a-5p

Museum of Appalachia
Distance from I-75 1 mile (1.6km)
Time from I-75 2 mins.
Min. time to visit: 1.5 hrs
Admission, Adult/Snrs/Child/Family $12.95/$10/$5/$30
Phone: 865-494-7680
Hours: Summer Daily, 8a-8p
Winter Daily, 8a-5p

Welcome Center
Phone: 865-457-4542
Hours: M-F, 9a-5p

Twin Gables Antique Mall
Phone: 865-494-8078
Hours: Daily, 10a-6p,

MUSEUM of APPALACHIA

Tennessee - exit 122

This wonderful living, open-air museum of more than 30 authentic log buildings is well worth a visit. Appalachian gardens are surrounded by split rail fences, and numerous farm animals abound. One of the few opportunities to experience "life as it was." Combine this with a drive over Norris Dam, for a perfect side trip from the I-75.

I-75 maps: 26-S, 172-N Story: page 103

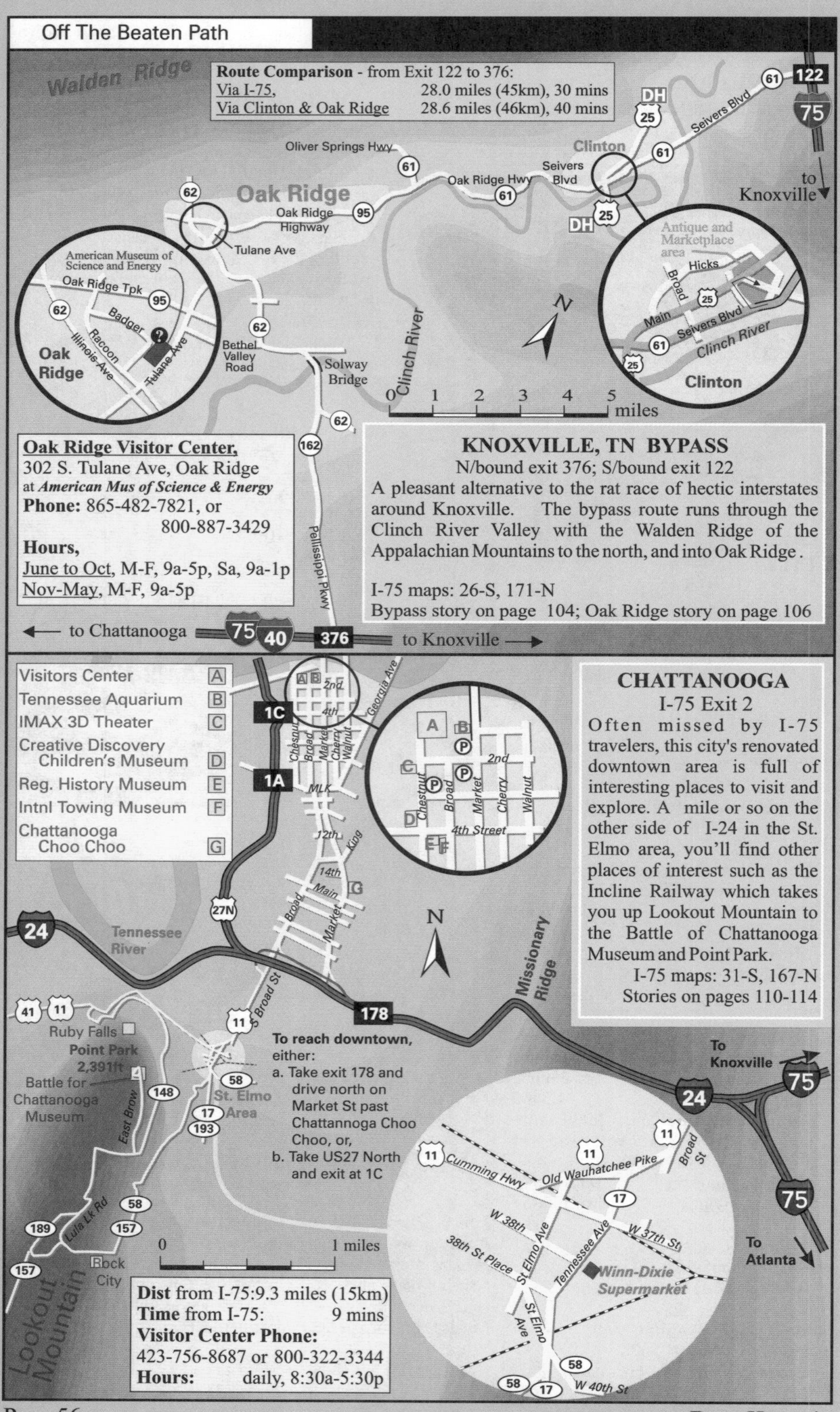
Route Comparison - from Exit 122 to 376:
Via I-75, 28.0 miles (45km), 30 mins
Via Clinton & Oak Ridge 28.6 miles (46km), 40 mins
Walden Ridge
Oliver Springs Hwy
Oak Ridge
Oak Ridge Highway
Oak Ridge Hwy
Tulane Ave
Seivers Blvd
Clinton
Seivers Blvd
to Knoxville
Antique and Marketplace area
Hicks
Broad
Main
Seivers Blvd
Clinch River
Clinton
American Museum of Science and Energy
Oak Ridge Tpk
Badger
Racoon
Illinois Ave
Tulane Ave
Oak Ridge
Bethel Valley Road
Solway Bridge
Clinch River
0 1 2 3 4 5 miles
Oak Ridge Visitor Center,
302 S. Tulane Ave, Oak Ridge
at American Mus of Science & Energy
Phone: 865-482-7821, or
800-887-3429
Hours,
June to Oct, M-F, 9a-5p, Sa, 9a-1p
Nov-May, M-F, 9a-5p
Pellissippi Pkwy
KNOXVILLE, TN BYPASS
N/bound exit 376; S/bound exit 122
A pleasant alternative to the rat race of hectic interstates around Knoxville. The bypass route runs through the Clinch River Valley with the Walden Ridge of the Appalachian Mountains to the north, and into Oak Ridge.
I-75 maps: 26-S, 171-N
Bypass story on page 104; Oak Ridge story on page 106
to Chattanooga
to Knoxville
Visitors Center A
Tennessee Aquarium B
IMAX 3D Theater C
Creative Discovery Children's Museum D
Reg. History Museum E
Intnl Towing Museum F
Chattanooga Choo Choo G
Georgia Ave
2nd
4th
Chestnut
Broad
Market
Cherry
Walnut
MLK
12th
King
14th
Main
4th Street
CHATTANOOGA
I-75 Exit 2
Often missed by I-75 travelers, this city's renovated downtown area is full of interesting places to visit and explore. A mile or so on the other side of I-24 in the St. Elmo area, you'll find other places of interest such as the Incline Railway which takes you up Lookout Mountain to the Battle of Chattanooga Museum and Point Park.
I-75 maps: 31-S, 167-N
Stories on pages 110-114
Tennessee River
Missionary Ridge
S Broad St
Ruby Falls
Point Park 2,391ft
Battle for Chattanooga Museum
East Brow
St. Elmo Area
To reach downtown, either:
a. Take exit 178 and drive north on Market St past Chattannoga Choo Choo, or,
b. Take US27 North and exit at 1C
To Knoxville
To Atlanta
Cumming Hwy
Old Wauhatchee Pike
Broad St
W 38th
St Elmo Ave
Tennessee Ave
W 37th St
38th St Place
Winn-Dixie Supermarket
W 40th St
Lula Lk Rd
Rock City
Lookout Mountain
0 1 miles
Dist from I-75: 9.3 miles (15km)
Time from I-75: 9 mins
Visitor Center Phone:
423-756-8687 or 800-322-3344
Hours: daily, 8:30a-5:30p

BATTLE OF RESACA & CONFEDERATE CEMETERY

Resaca, GA; Cemetery east of I-75 Exit 320

A bloody Civil War battle (5,547 men killed or injured) was fought here, between the 13th and 15th of May, 1864, as the Confederate Army was beaten back towards Atlanta. To help you understand the scope of this large battlefield, the mile markers are shown on the I-75. Directions and distances refer to the Confederate Cemetery which is well worth visiting.

Recent research has led to much greater knowledge of this battle; this revised map reflects that new knowledge.

I-75 maps: 32-S, 166-N Story and Civil War Sidebar, page 120

Confederate Cemetery

Distance from I-75: 2.5 miles (4km)

Time from I-75: 4 minutes

Min. time to visit: 20 minutes.

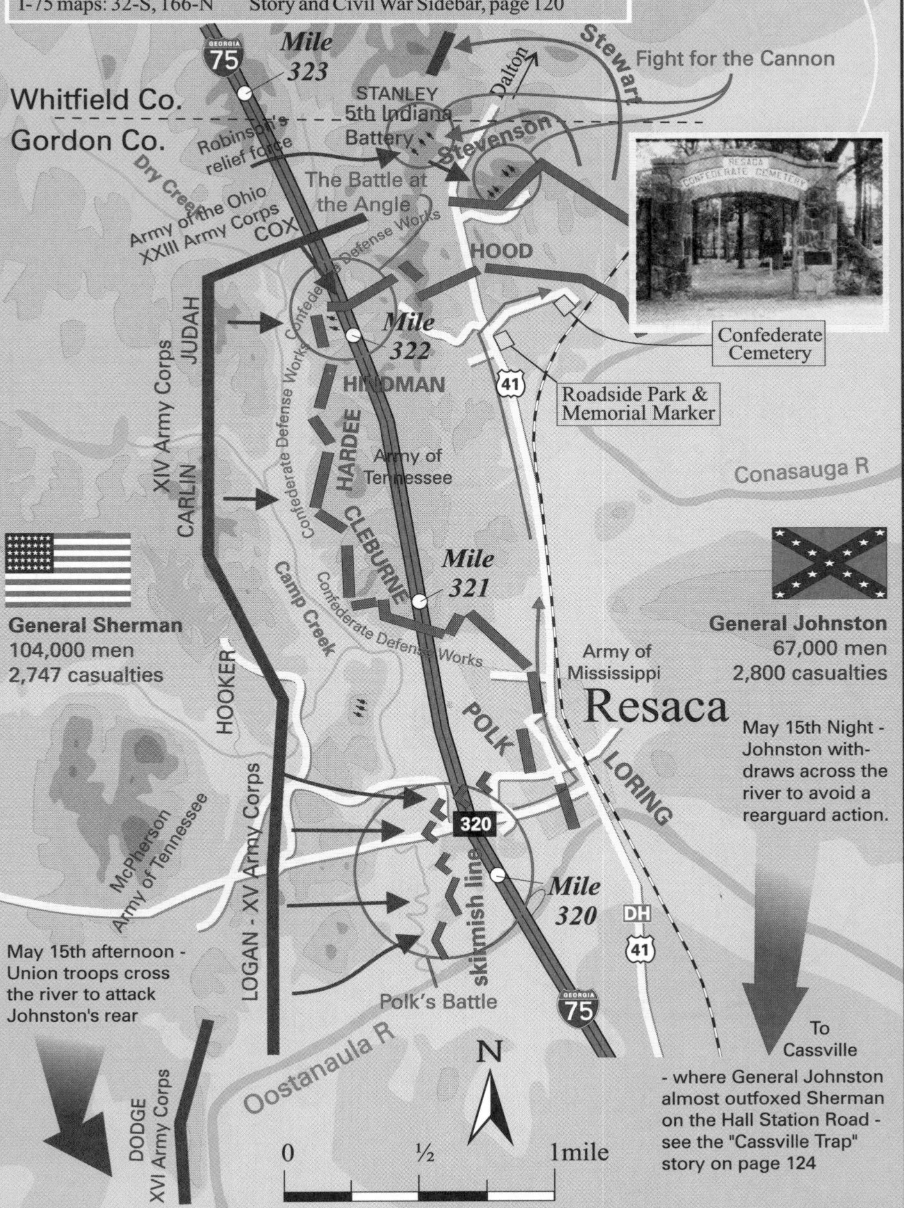

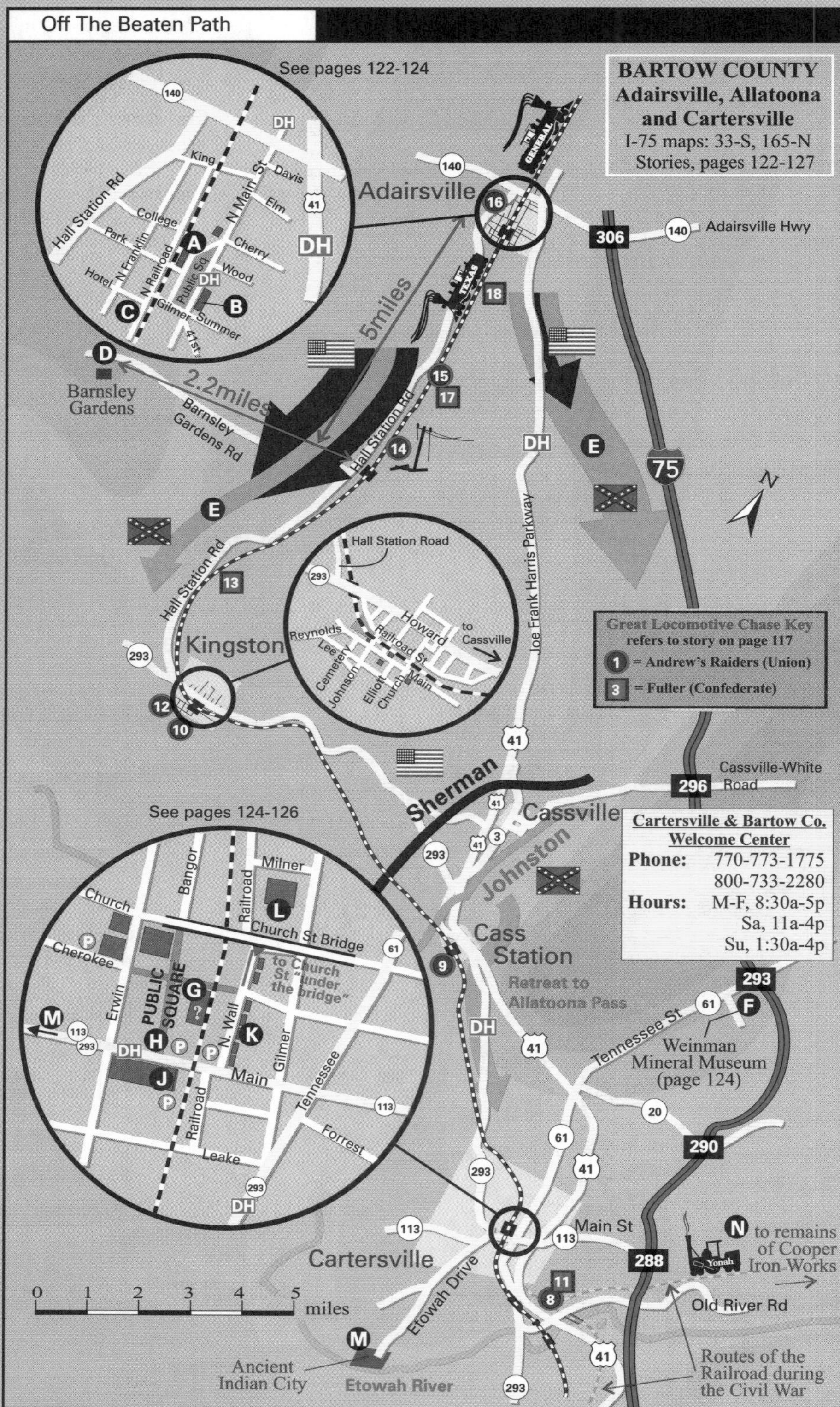
BARTOW COUNTY
Adairsville, Allatoona and Cartersville
I-75 maps: 33-S, 165-N
Stories, pages 122-127
See pages 122-124
Adairsville
Adairsville Hwy
5miles
2.2miles
Barnsley Gardens
Barnsley Gardens Rd
Hall Station Rd
Kingston
Hall Station Road
Joe Frank Harris Parkway
Great Locomotive Chase Key refers to story on page 117
1 = Andrew's Raiders (Union)
3 = Fuller (Confederate)
Sherman
Cassville
Cassville-White Road
Johnston
Cartersville & Bartow Co. Welcome Center
Phone: 770-773-1775
800-733-2280
Hours: M-F, 8:30a-5p
Sa, 11a-4p
Su, 1:30a-4p
See pages 124-126
Church St Bridge
to Church St "under the bridge"
PUBLIC SQUARE
Cass Station
Retreat to Allatoona Pass
Weinman Mineral Museum (page 124)
Tennessee St
Main St
to remains of Cooper Iron Works
Old River Rd
Cartersville
Etowah Drive
Ancient Indian City
Etowah River
Routes of the Railroad during the Civil War
miles

SOUTHERN MUSEUM of CIVIL WAR & LOCOMOTIVE HISTORY

Kennesaw, GA; I-75 Exit 273

Kennesaw was the starting point of the Great Locomotive Chase. Walk the grounds where the "General" was stolen and then cross the road and visit the newly renovated Museum, home of the famous locomotive.

Opened last summer, this world class museum is now associated with the Smithsonian Museum in Washington, DC, and now has one of the finest collections of Civil War artefacts in North America.

I-75 maps: 34-S, 164-N; Story page 128

Admission:	Adult/Snr/Child $7.50/$6.50/$5.50
Phone:	770-427-2117
Hours:	Mon-Sat, 9:30a-5p Sun, noon-5p

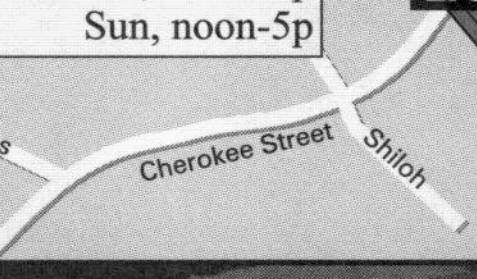

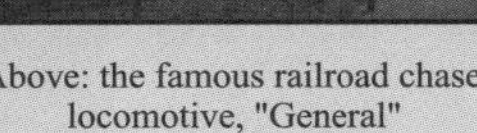

Above: the famous railroad chase locomotive, "General"

Left: don't miss the fabulous reconstruction of a 19th century locomotive factory. Tour the Engineering office, Tool & Pattern shop, and Assembly ("Works") area.

TUNNEL HILL

Tunnel Hill, GA; I-75 Exit 341

This 1849 tunnel became the scene of dramatic action during the Civil War's Great Locomotive Chase. The Tunnel Hill Heritage Center houses a Museum with much information about the tunnel, and its role in the epic railroad chase. The Visitors Center is across the road in the old General Store building.

I-75 maps: 31-S, 167-N

Stories: pages 115 and 119(32)

Heritage Center/Museum

Dist from I-75:	2.1mile (3.4km)
Time from I-75:	32.mins
Phone:	800-331-3258
Hours:	
Summer:	M-Sa, 10a-6p
Winter:	M-Sa, 9a-5p
Admission:	
Adult/Child	$2.50/$1.50

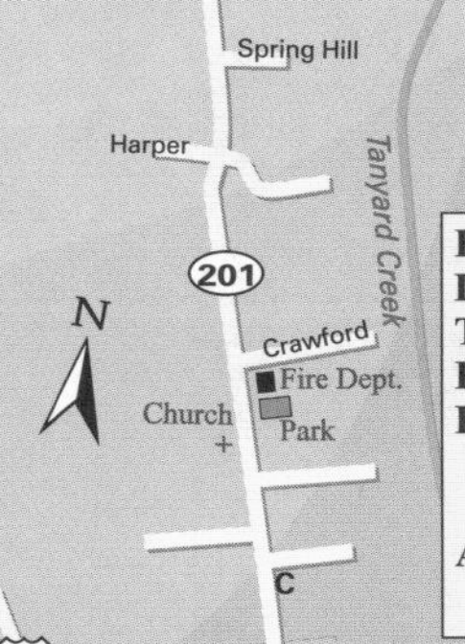

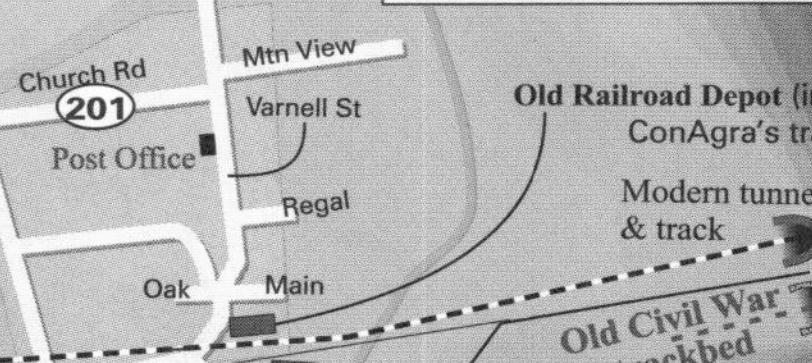

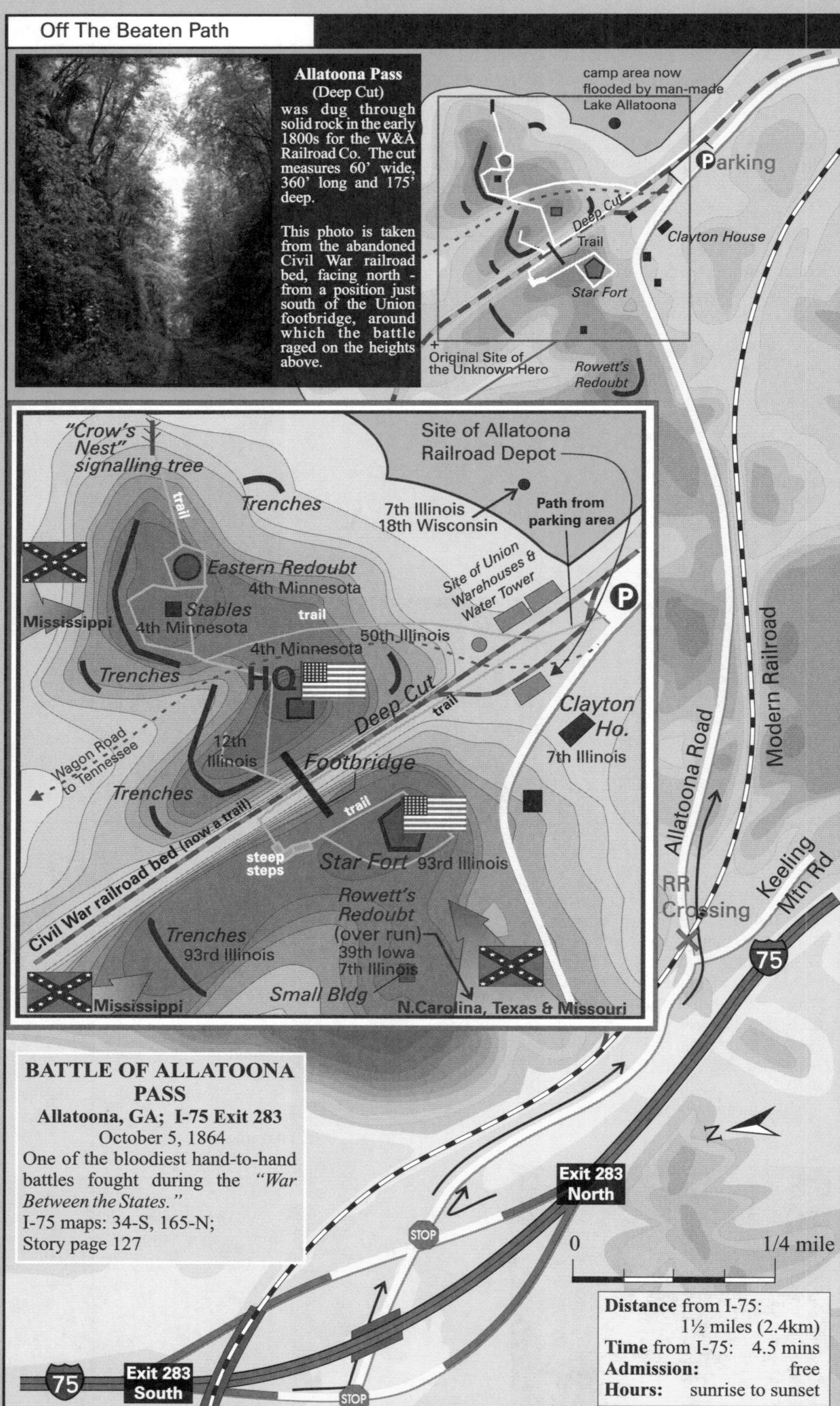

Allatoona Pass
(Deep Cut)
was dug through solid rock in the early 1800s for the W&A Railroad Co. The cut measures 60' wide, 360' long and 175' deep.

This photo is taken from the abandoned Civil War railroad bed, facing north - from a position just south of the Union footbridge, around which the battle raged on the heights above.

BATTLE OF ALLATOONA PASS
Allatoona, GA; I-75 Exit 283
October 5, 1864
One of the bloodiest hand-to-hand battles fought during the *"War Between the States."*
I-75 maps: 34-S, 165-N;
Story page 127

Distance from I-75: 1½ miles (2.4km)
Time from I-75: 4.5 mins
Admission: free
Hours: sunrise to sunset

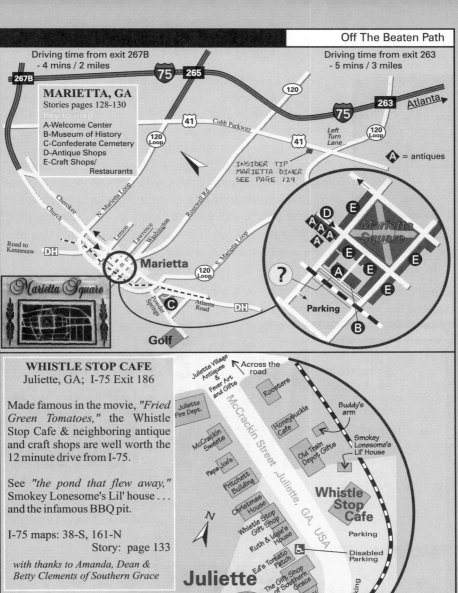

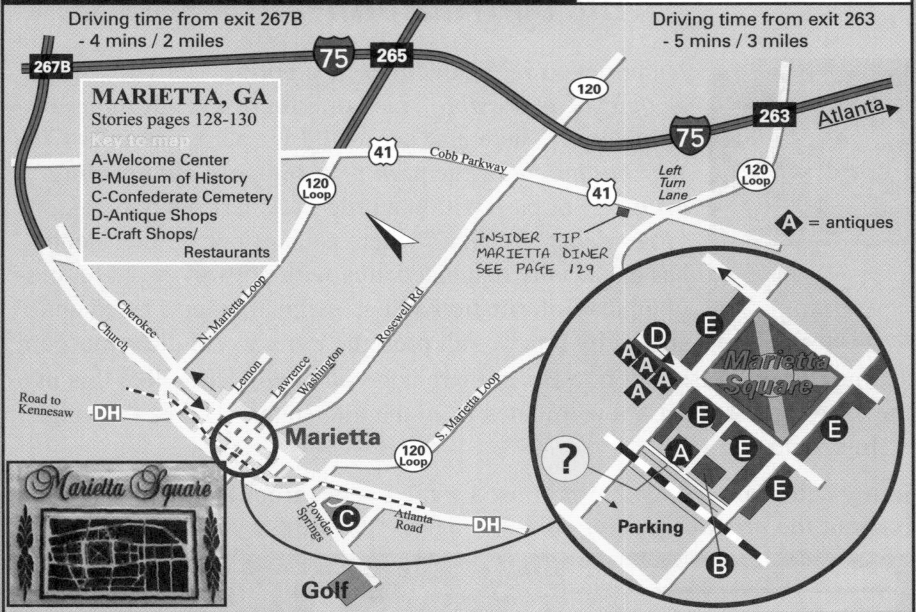

Driving time from exit 267B
- 4 mins / 2 miles
Driving time from exit 263
- 5 mins / 3 miles
MARIETTA, GA
Stories pages 128-130
Key to map
A-Welcome Center
B-Museum of History
C-Confederate Cemetery
D-Antique Shops
E-Craft Shops/
Restaurants
267B
75
265
120
263
Atlanta
41
Cobb Parkway
120 Loop
41
Left Turn Lane
A = antiques
INSIDER TIP
MARIETTA DINER
SEE PAGE 129
Cherokee
Church
N. Marietta Loop
Rosewell Rd
Lemon
Lawrence
Washington
Road to Kennesaw
DH
Marietta
S. Marietta Loop
120 Loop
Marietta Square
Powder Springs
C
Atlanta Road
DH
Golf
Parking
?
B
A
D
E

WHISTLE STOP CAFE

Juliette, GA; I-75 Exit 186

Made famous in the movie, *"Fried Green Tomatoes,"* the Whistle Stop Cafe & neighboring antique and craft shops are well worth the 12 minute drive from I-75.

See *"the pond that flew away,"* Smokey Lonesome's Lil' house . . . and the infamous BBQ pit.

I-75 maps: 38-S, 161-N

Story: page 133

with thanks to Amanda, Dean & Betty Clements of Southern Grace

Distance from I-75: 9.3 miles
Time from I-75: 11.2 mins
Cafe phone: 478-992-8886
Hours: Tu-Sun, 11a-6p
closed Mondays
Juliette **stores hours** vary but normally all will be open between 11a-4p.

Juliette Village Antiques & Fever Art and Gifts
Across the road
Roosters
Juliette Fire Dept.
McCrackin Street, Juliette, GA, USA
Honeysuckle Cafe
Buddy's arm
McCrackin Sweets
Smokey Lonesome's Lil' House
Old Train Depot Gifts
Papa Joe's
Pritchett Building
Whistle Stop Cafe
Christmas House
Whistle Stop Gift Shop
Ruth & Idgie's House
Parking
N
Disabled Parking
Ed's Tomato Patch
Juliette
The Gift Shop of Southern Grace
Parking
The pond that flew away
Habersham Winery tasting room
alternate route back to US23
Newton Rd
Parking
Byars
23
Ponder Tramwell
Juliette Road
75
Rum Creek Wildlife Mgmt
Forsyth Landing
Johnson Lane
Juliette Road
Hester
Holly Grove
186
Conifer
Joe Chambers
Dillard
Maynard Church
45mph
Forsyth
0
1
2
3 miles
CAFE

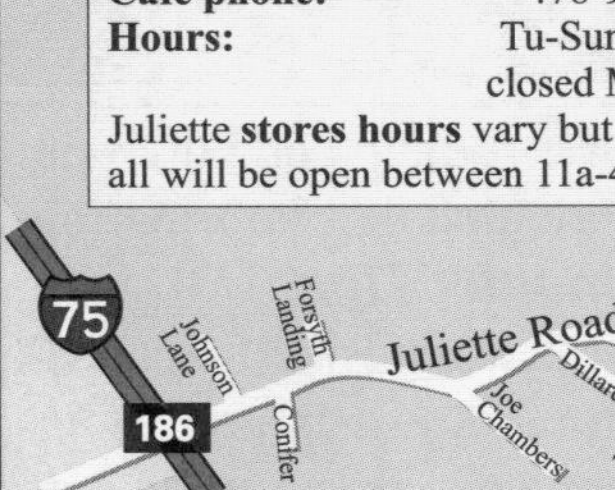

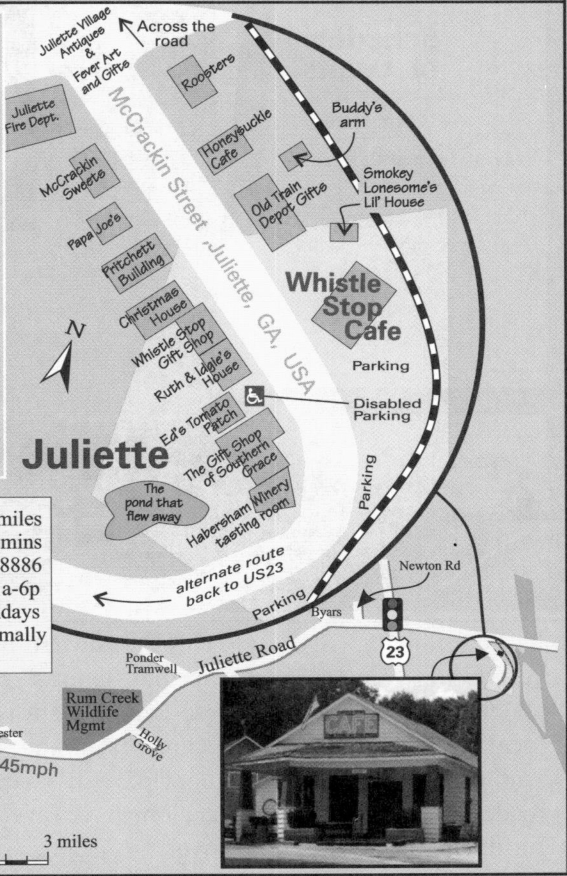

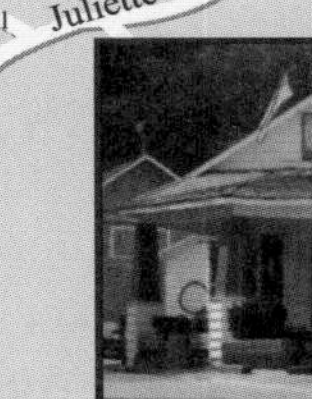

Mile by Mile on I-75

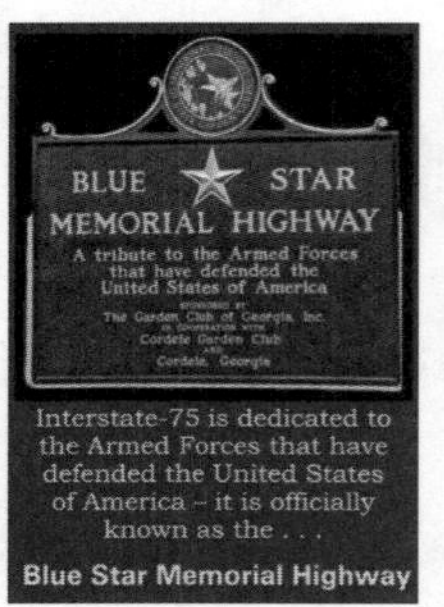

Interstate-75 is dedicated to the Armed Forces that have defended the United States of America – it is officially known as the . . .

Blue Star Memorial Highway

A journeyon I-75 can either be a boring *"let's get there as quickly as possible"* race or a fun-filled adventure of discovery. Where else can you drive across a major ***Civil War battlefield*** or the ***path of a 466 year old invading army*** . . . or pass within a mile of America's <u>only</u> ***"Presidents' Gallery,"*** where each of our 42 Presidents has a specially dedicated area with portrait or photo, biographical information and an original letter written and signed by him . . . all presented in a world-class museum setting. From Washington to Bush, there is no other collection like this in the USA, and it's just a few minutes from the interstate. This is the magic of Interstate-75.

In my editorial on page 2, I promised some images from Bill Hone's scrapbook of the ***official opening of I-75***. Here they are for you to enjoy:

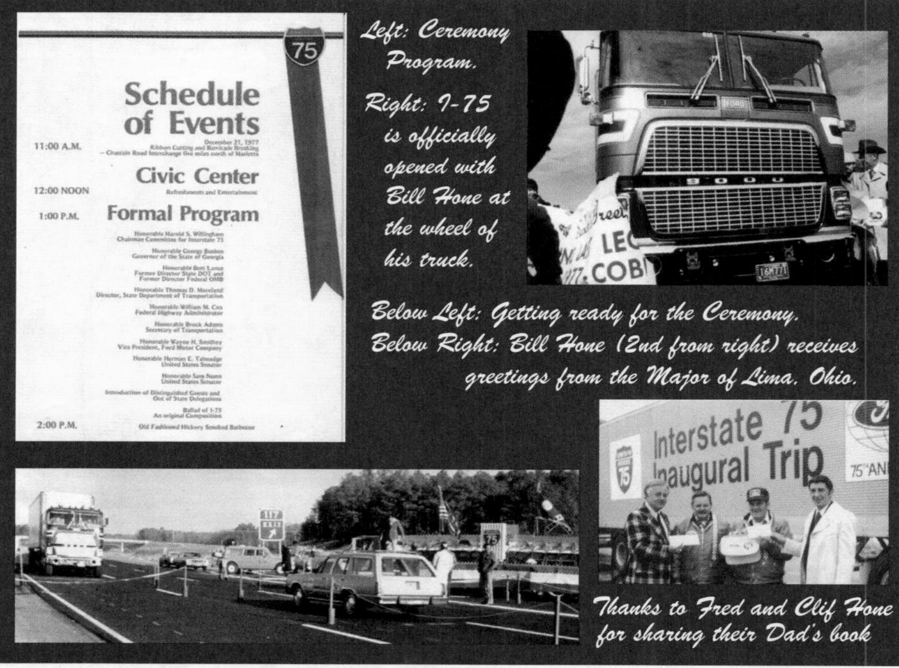
75

Schedule of Events

December 21, 1977

11:00 A.M. Ribbon Cutting and Barricade Breaking – Chastain Road Interchange five miles north of Marietta

Civic Center

12:00 NOON Refreshments and Entertainment

1:00 P.M. **Formal Program**

Honorable Harold S. Willingham
Chairman Committee for Interstate 75

Honorable George Busbee
Governor of the State of Georgia

Honorable Bert Lance
Former Director State DOT and
Former Director Federal OMB

Honorable Thomas D. Moreland
Director, State Department of Transportation

Honorable William M. Cox
Federal Highway Administrator

Honorable Brock Adams
Secretary of Transportation

Honorable Wayne H. Smithey
Vice President, Ford Motor Company

Honorable Herman E. Talmadge
United States Senator

Honorable Sam Nunn
United States Senator

Introduction of Distinguished Guests and
Out of State Delegations

Ballad of I-75
An original Composition

2:00 P.M. Old Fashioned Hickory Smoked Barbecue

Left: Ceremony Program.

Right: I-75 is officially opened with Bill Hone at the wheel of his truck.

Below Left: Getting ready for the Ceremony.
Below Right: Bill Hone (2nd from right) receives greetings from the Major of Lima, Ohio.

Thanks to Fred and Clif Hone for sharing their Dad's book

In the following pages, you will find several features to help and entertain you during your I-75 trip. "Special Reports" provide detailed information about sights of particular interest along the way, "***Insider Tips***" will share local knowledge about interesting restaurants and other roadside "secrets." And our tried and true $aving Tip$ will save you money ... many of our readers have told us that these alone have saved them enough money to pay for this book, several times over! All information updated as of September, 2004

I-75 Changes and Trends for 2004/2005

Since writing the 2004 edition of this book, I've driven Interstate-75 six times and on each trip, have been amazed at the significant differences I found in its services and facilities. For instance, our 12th edition (2004) book recorded 3,226 gas stations, food outlets and lodging services between Detroit and the Florida border. In this book (2005), we have added 331 new services and removed 208, for a total of 539 changes - representing a "turnover" rate of almost 17%.

Within these services and on I-75, there have also been some interesting new trends developing; here is a summary of these findings:

♦ There has been a significant increase in the number of ***motels now accepting pets***. All are highlighted in blue on my colored "25-mile-per-page" maps.

♦ More gas stations are now ***open 24 hours***. These are shown in green on the maps.

♦ There is ***less road construction***. In fact, until you reach southern Georgia, construction is hardly noticeable.

♦ In Georgia's Valdosta's notorious speed trap zone–***police radar activity*** has been greatly curtailed, in part due to the new 13 mile concrete median wall which limits the number of places police cars can cross the median strip and pursue offenders.

♦ ***Motorcycle radar or laser*** equipped police *(see colored maps)* are now being used in several I-75 cities. Often monitoring traffic from the median area, these are much more likely to pull over a marginal speeder (5-10mph over the limit) than a police car, since they can "chase" very effectively in close or dense traffic.

Lane Talk - L1 to L4 . . . and more

I want to share the official lane numbering codes with you since I will sometimes use them in the driving (lane changing) directions, in these pages.

In police or DOT reports, the **lanes number from the center (median) strip, to the right with the "Fast"** lane (truckers *"hammer"* lane) as **L1**.

For instance in a three lane stretch, the "fast" lane is L1, the **middle** (also the truck overtaking lane) is **L2** and the **"slow"** or **"inside"** lane is **L3**.

Therefore, if I suggest you move from L3 to L1/2, you know that I mean you should move from the slow lane in a 3 lane stretch, to the center or fast lanes.

Some other changes worthy of note . . .

▲ several new ***Cracker Barrel*** restaurants have opened, or are under construction.

▲ at time of writing, all ***Tennessee rest areas*** servicing northbound traffic are planned for renovation (i.e., closed), leaving a 209 mile (336km) stretch with no state operated facilities.

▲ three brand ***new exits*** are in the final stages of completion.

▲ long time a favorite with I-75 travelers, the ***Holiday Motel in Berea***, KY, is in final negotiations with *Cracker Barrel* to sell part of its property to the chain, which plans the construction of a new *Cracker Barrel* at exit 76.

▲ another favorite, the ***Holiday Inn*** at ***Dalton***, GA has gone out of business.

▲ ***10 digit telephone number dialing*** (area code + local number) has become necessary in a number of I-75 communities. Useful information to know when making local calls from your motel.

New Child Restraint Laws: And finally, two I-75 states (Tennessee & Georgia) have enacted significant new legislation to amend their "child restraint device" laws. In each case, "booster" seats are now required for children too old (or too big) for the smaller child restraint devices. I have summarized these changes for you on page 146.

Where are the best I-75 gas prices? (a new money saving feature): As an I-75 driver for more than 36 years, I've always been aware that certain gas stations price their product lower than their neighbors, and have taken advantage of this knowledge to save money.

But times are changing. Since the previous book edition, state gas taxes have increased and as a result, price patterns from previous years are no longer relevant. For instance, for the first time this year, we found it cheaper to buy our gas in Tennessee than in North Georgia - a major change from earlier years since Georgia has always had the cheapest gas.

So this summer, Kathy and I drove I-75 and recorded regular gas prices along the interstate (335 observations). We gathered these data in a three day period when the prices were stable and upon return to our office, entered and analyzed them on our computer. Since there are 743 gas stations on the maps of this book, this represents a 45% sampling - excellent for statistical purposes. What we found was very interesting.

For instance, we found as much as a 10 cent/gallon difference between east and west gas stations at one exit. A phone call to friends in that area indicated that regardless of the actual pump price on a given day, these differentials were always there and well known by the "locals."

Also, comparing pricing in different stretches of I-75 (eg. Lexington vs. mid-Kentucky) within the same state and on the same day showed some very specific differences.

I have shared some of these findings with you on the colored map pages by indicating "lower price/gallon" stations with a green triangle.

Exxon

I can't guarantee these savings though since much depends upon the local operators (you wouldn't believe the inter-station "politics" involved in setting the gas prices at a given exit). Also ownership may change . . . but the trends do indicate some significant savings.

So at the very least, the information provided may save you some money on your I-75 trips. I would be very interested in your feedback *(use the form on page 203),* or e.mail me at:

mile_oak@compuserve.com

Changes to make the 25 mile maps easier to read: As a result of reader suggestions, I've made several changes to the color coding and layout of the 25 mile colored strip maps.

1. To make the maps appear less cluttered, I've eliminated the lines "tying" the exit services to the exit number box. Instead, the exit number has been included in the "services" box. Where space permits, the "services" box has been elongated to make it easier to scan the services at a given exit while providing more space for comment in the center of the map page.
2. When driving an RV in the "slow" lane it's very important to know when you are close to an exit where this lane becomes the off ramp. This year, to make these exits even more visible than on past maps, I've colored the exit number and exit signage, yellow.

Construction Delays: In a construction zone, it's the presence of lane merges which create delays . . . not the fact that it's a construction area with a reduced speed limit (normally a reduction of 10mph.

The Ohio DOT recently published the following stats, which upholds this opinion:

Every minute a traffic lane is blocked results in 8 minutes of delay.

Every 5 minutes a traffic lane is blocked creates a 1 mile backup.

So there you have it.

Well, it's now time to travel so let's fasten our seatbelts and start our trip down I-75 to Florida. You drive and I'll sit in the back and regale you with a rich tapestry of stories to entertain you as we roll southward.

INSIDER TIPS

Throughout the following sections, you will find our famous **"Insider Tips"**– hints of special significance to help you save money and have a more enjoyable journey. In many instances, we recommend specific I-75 facilities (often first brought to our attention by our readers–see page 203) which, from our personal inspections have proven to offer exceptional value and service to interstate travelers.

No business has paid to be recommended in *"Along I-75."* There is no commercial content in this guide. In fact, none of our "recommendations" knew they were being inspected at the time of our visit.

You can trust our **"Insider Tips"** -here's where you get the **real local knowledge**.

WHAT'S IN A NAME?

Indian terms, historical characters, national heroes, town site descriptions–place names weave a colorful tapestry as we journey along Interstate-75. In some cases, early pioneers and settlers from east coast regions transferred the names of their original home towns to their new settlements (e.g.. Milford, Ohio), thereby perpetuating British and European names in the U.S. interior.

Throughout the following pages, we explain the meanings behind some of the more interesting place names encountered as we travel southbound to Florida:

Insider Tip - Lodging Freebies

The lodging industry continues to rebuild itself following the recent years of restrained travel. Here are some new incentives being offered to attract customers:

Free local phone calls: I hate having to pay $1 to $1.50 (plus taxes) to make a local phone call or dial a 1-800 number so I can use my phone card. For some reason, it really rankles me way beyond the actual cost. Several smaller Inn companies - ***Baymont***, ***Jameson*** and ***Signature*** Inns - recognize this and offer the service free to guests at all their properties.

Free Coffee or bottled water: You don't have to be a guest at ***Baymont*** to take advantage of their new safety driven ***"DriveRevived"*** program. You just have to be a tired driver. If you find yourself feeling weary behind the wheel, stop at a Baymont and receive a free reviving coffee or water bottle.

Express Start is the new breakfast cafe bar concept for ***Holiday Inn Express*** guests. With warm cinnamon rolls and Smart Roast (100% Arabica) coffee, who would ever want to leave!

MICHIGAN - Exit 15-Monroe & General Custer: This exit leads to one of the oldest communities in Michigan, the historic town of Monroe settled by the French in 1780. General George Custer (of Civil War and Little Bighorn fame) lived here for many years before joining the army and making a name for himself in the cavalry.

Custer and his brother, Nevin, owned the Nevin Custer farm (now privately owned), just west of Monroe on the north bank of the Raisin River. The brothers purchased the farm in 1871, five years before George's death at Little Bighorn. George's favorite horse, Dandy is buried in the orchard near the barn. Visitors to the farm have included Buffalo Bill Cody and Annie Oakley.

Today, Monroe remembers Custer with a bronze statue of him astride his restless horse, Dandy, in downtown Monroe at the corners of Elm and Monroe Streets.

Milepost 15 to the Ohio Border-American Lotus: For the next 15 miles (24.1km), I-75 parallels Lake Erie and every so often, the Lake's inlets and river estuaries can be seen east of the freeway.

If you are traveling in July or August, watch for beds of the creamy yellow blossoms of the American Lotus (nelumbo lutea), which until recently was on the endangered species list.

The Lotus, with an extensive underwater root system will only grow in clean water and it's a tribute to the City of Monroe that an active Lotus protection program is in place.

Exit 15-Sterling State Park: If you drive a mile east towards the Lake you'll find Sterling Park, the State's 4th most visited recreational facility. The park has a display about the American Lotus.

Exit 14-Battle of the Raisin River: *(see map on page 48)*. Just west of this exit on the north bank of the Raisin River, lies the site of an early settlement called Frenchtown. It was here that one of largest battles between the British and American Armies took place during the War of 1812.

On the evening of January 18, 1813, Frenchtown was occupied by an American force, mainly from Kentucky. The 700 men had faced a small British force earlier that day and after hours of tree to tree fighting, had driven them back north towards Detroit.

Several days later their leader, Gen. Winchester, arrived with the remainder of the troops, bringing the army to a strength of 934 men.

In the quiet pre-dawn of January 21st, a huge British force of 597 British soldiers support-

MICHIGAN - *an old Indian word of unknown origins. It could come from Mishi-mikin-nac or "swimming turtle," a descriptive term used to describe the shape of some of Michigan's land, or from Mitchisawgyegan (michi gama), an Indian term meaning "Great Lake."*

DETROIT - *from the French word "d'etroit" (of the strait). Founded on July 24th, 1701, by French explorer Antoine Cadillac, the early settlement lay on the stretch of land between Lake Erie and Lake St.Clair.*

ed by 800 Indians, crept towards Frenchtown to take their revenge. The attack lasted less than twenty minutes before the American right (closest to the I-75) was outflanked and the men retreated to the river. Of the 400 men who fled, over 200 were killed and 147 were captured–including General Winchester.

The remaining 500 Kentuckians, fighting from behind Frenchtown's picket fences, were unaware of the collapse on their right, and drove off three fierce British attacks with their rifles. When they saw a British officer come towards them with a white flag, they thought that the British were going to surrender. They were surprised when the officer gave them orders from their own General, now a prisoner of the British, to surrender.

After the surrender, the British withdrew and the Americans gathered their dying and injured to the settlers' homes in Frenchtown. The following morning, the Indian forces attacked, burning and plundering the homes and scalping the American wounded. Over 60 were killed–the action became known as the *"Massacre of the Raisin River."*

The massacre shocked and enraged settlers throughout the Old Northwest Territory (today's Michigan). Ten months later, American troops chased the British army from Detroit to Ontario where a major battle took place on the banks of another river–the Thames. During this battle, the famous Indian chief and friend of the British, Tecumseh, was killed. The American battle cry at this engagement? *"Remember the Raisin!"* [Battlefield hours and other details on page 48].

Milepost 10 (N/bound)-Monroe Welcome Center: When traveling into Michigan, you'll find this Center well stocked with brochures for all areas of the State.

Insider Tip
Bolles Harbor Restaurant

Psst–this is why you bought this book ... for local knowledge! Hidden just half a mile to the east of exit 11 and overlooking the marina is the Bolles Harbor Café, voted by the AAA as the #2 Best New Restaurant in Michigan. Fresh perch and other lake fish are their specialties.

Stop by and say *"hi"* from me to owners and chef, Silverio and Georgianna. I know you'll enjoy their hospitality.

Hours, Tu-Th,Sun, 6am-2pm; F-Sat, 6am-8pm; closed M; ☎ 734-457-2233

Exit 9-Lake Maumee: We cross through the plains south of Monroe giving little thought to the scene a million years ago when melting glaciers hundreds of feet thick formed an ancient lake which ran right across this section of Michigan and down as far as Exit 159 (Findlay) in Ohio. Geologists named it Lake Maumee and its water surface was about 230 feet above the present position of our car.

How can scientists tell? They found the beach ridges of the lake permanently etched into rock at an elevation of 800 feet above sea level (we are driving at 570 feet above sea level)–see page 71. The lake finally flooded the Grand River Valley in Michigan and as its water level fell, the current shoreline of Lake Erie appeared.

OHIO - Exit 210-Toledo and the Ohio-Michigan war: It is 1835 and this is where we find a forgotten war. The land between this exit and Ohio Exit 199 is disputed territory and both Ohio and Michigan have laid claim to it. That large crowd of men over there marching down the road with flintlock muskets slung over their shoulders is Michigan's Army led southward by Governor Mason (the stout, black hatted fellow on the roan horse). They are on their way to attack the small settlement of Toledo and settle this question once and for all. They don't know yet but before the week is out, they will capture one of Toledo's founding fathers and hold him as a prisoner of war. Congress will finally have to intervene. The war that has broken out will be resolved by awarding the territory to Ohio, and granting Michigan full statehood in 1837 along with all the copper and iron rights in the peninsula to their north.

The issue of "who owns Toledo" will not go away. In 1992, an editorial appeared in the *Toledo Blade*, questioning the ownership of Toledo by Ohio. It seems that some would still like to cede the city to Michigan!

Miles 198 to 163-The Black Swamp: You wouldn't have wanted to be here 125 years ago, for this entire region (about the size of Connecticut) was the dreaded Black Swamp. A dense, dank, gloomy forest populated mainly by deer, panthers, rattlesnakes, wolves and bear. The ground was an evil boggy quagmire of black muck which sucked pioneers to their knees and if the animals and insects did not get them, then malaria probably would. In 1850, farmers decided to try to drain the area, and by 1890 more than 22,000 miles of ditches had drained the land and revealed the rich fertile farmland beneath. In 40 years, the stinking swamp had been transformed into the productive farms of today's Ohio.

Exit 192-Fort Meigs: *(see map on page 48)*. To set you in the mood, you enter the fort through the impressive new Gift Shop and Museum. Take your time to go through the Museum first; it will greatly enhance your understanding of the War of 1812, and the actions which took place at this historical site.

After the massacre of the Kentucky troops at the Raisin River in January, 1813 *(see Michigan, Exit 14)*, fighting between the British and the Americans came to a temporary halt. U.S. Maj Gen. Harrison decided to build a new fort on the south banks of the Maumee River, named after Gov. Meigs of Ohio.

The fort quickly became central to the protection of Ohio for if it fell, Michigan & Ohio would become conquered British territory. At its peak it housed more than 2,000 American regulars from Ohio, Kentucky, Pennsylvania and Virginia. Let's go back in time and visit the fort.

It's late April, 1813; the fort is badly undermanned with twelve hundred troop of which only 850 are fit for duty. Will they be able to withstand the coming British attack? To protect his forces, Harrison orders long embankments of earth built across the fort parade grounds so his troops can burrow down into the muddy earth, behind them.

At 11 a.m. on May 1st, a British force of two thousand lays siege to Fort Meigs with 20-30 artillery pieces, pounding its earthworks and wooden blockhouses continuously for four days. Twenty-four pound cannon balls, red hot 12 pounders, mortar shells and fragmentation bombs rain down on the fort sending deadly iron and wood splinter fragments in all directions.

Six days later, American reinforcements arrive and although the buildings and earthworks have been badly mauled, the American flag still flies. The garrison has held tight; the British lift the siege and withdraw northward into Ontario.

In a curious footnote to history, one and a half years later on September 14, 1814, a similar circumstance occurred at Fort McHenry in Baltimore Harbor, Maryland. After a heavy 24 hour pounding by British canon and mortar, the Fort survived and the American flag remained flying *"by the dawn's early light"*

Insider Tip - Coffee Fill-up

Did you know that Cracker Barrel will fill your coffee thermos for $2.49? We've also heard that if you eat there, some will waive the charge.

Insider Tip - Cruise Control

An insidious danger has recently been identified for those driving cars equipped with cruise control. Highway patrol officers have been surprised by the number of cars they find which have skidded or overturned for no apparent reason.

The culprit? Using cruise control on a wet or slippery road surface.

If you have your cruise control turned on and one or more of your wheels starts to spin due to a slippery surface, the control unit detects a decrease in forward motion and applies more power to the car's wheels. This is a vicious circle. You are now skidding but your car is accelerating. Worst still, this cycle starts and you lose control before you know it! By the time, you become consciously aware of your "unbalanced" drive train . . . it's too late with an inevitable result.

OHIO - *early French explorers discovered the Ohio River, and used Iroquois words such as Oheo (beautiful) to describe it. The explored territory later acquired the name.*

TOLEDO - *because of its industrial heritage, named after the Spanish town of Toledo famous throughout history for "Toledo Steel."*

as immortalized by Francis Scott Key in *"The Star Spangled Banner."* But first honors for "survival under heavy British attack" should probably go to Fort Meigs!

Today, you can wander around this historic eight acre stockade overlooking the Maumee River, peer into the gloomy interiors of the log blockhouses and cast your mind back to the heroes who held this fort against a far superior force. Guides in period costume explain the actions which took place, and demonstrate some of the crafts of the time. [Hours and other details on page 48.]

Escape Routes-The Old Road to Florida: By now, you will have noticed that our maps show not only I-75, but parallel side roads (in brown–*please note that these are not necessarily to scale on the east/west across-the-map axis*) so that should the traffic become heavy ahead, you know how and where to get off I-75 to bypass potential problems.

Most of these "escape" routes follow the traditional north-south route used by Florida snowbirds long before I-75 was constructed, the– ***"Old Dixie Highway."*** In some stretches, the interstate was built right on top of the old route but you can still follow the *"Old Dixie"* when US25 (in the North), and US411, US41 and US19(in the South) parallel the interstate.

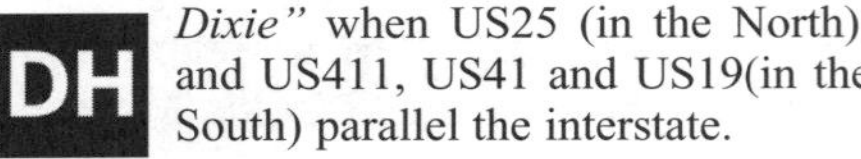

During the I-75's construction, many lands and buildings were expropriated to make way for the "super slab." Some survived physically but died as business disappeared.

Radar

When compared to national highway safety statistics, I-75 is a very safe freeway. State police mean to keep it that way by actively monitoring speed and issuing tickets for infractions as little as 5 mph over the limit.

Now, I *know* you have absolutely no intention of speeding but it is good to know where the regular I-75 radar traps are positioned. That way, you can be prepared for those speeders who sweep past you and throw on their brakes when they spot the patrol car in the bushes.

The "radar" symbols on our colored maps are very accurate–as many of our readers will attest.

Mile 186-RWIS: I bet you thought that the road surface beneath your wheels was just that–a road surface. Wrong! In this section of Ohio, and in sections north of Cincinnati and on Atlanta's I-75 in Georgia, the road surface acts as part of a giant input device which feeds information to traffic computers. Wire loops in the road record traffic information; cameras and other roadside devices send other types of data to a central computer.

This is all part of Ohio's multi-million dollar Traffic Information System (OTIS).

Money Saving Tip

After entering a new state, stop at the Welcome or Traveler Information Center and get copies of the free motel coupon books–the green Traveler Discount Guide and the red Market America Motel Discount Guide. They can usually be found lying in a pile on the counter or a rack inside the door. Ask the staff, if you don't see them.

These publications will save you many $$$$ on your overnight accommodation. They are chock full of discount coupons for motels (independents as well as major chains) along the way. Typically, you will find discounts in the 20-45% range. Bargains we have seen recently were $65 rooms discounted to $36, and $42 rooms to $28. We use the books all the time on each trip (including our vacation stays in Florida) and save literally hundreds of dollars.

Here's how they work. Every day, each motel listed in the coupon books sets aside a certain number of discount rate rooms based on their occupancy experience from the previous night. The discounts are provided on a first-come first-served basis to travelers with the discount book coupons. What are your chances of getting a discount room? We normally pull off the road around 6 p.m. and in all our years of traveling have only been turned down three times at a motel of our choice. We quickly found another one nearby which accepted their coupon from the book.

Insider Tip - Signature & Jameson Inns, Clean and Friendly

Consistency in the quality of accommodation & service is very important to me as a traveler. I much prefer staying at a regional inn chain, than the large franchise-operated "Nationals." "Regionals" are often managed by the company's own staff–and this ensures consistency. "Nationals" tend to be franchise operations and the franchisee can be an absent owner/investor. When traveling in Ohio, Kentucky or Tennessee, ***Signature Inns*** is my choice (owned by the Jameson Inn folk in Atlanta), and in Kentucky, Tennessee, Georgia and Florida, I find the parent company's ***Jameson Inns*** to be superb. All are trained, staffed and managed by Signature/Jameson employees.

Both "flags" (brands) focus on safe, quality accommodations at a reasonable price. The Signature Inns are corridor hotels where night access is past the front desk or outer locked doors. Both brands feature electronic door locks and 24/7 front desk. Additionally, Signature Inns are noted for their large rooms which all include coffeemaker, iron & ironing board, 2 phones and computer data ports, microwave & fridge . . . and free HBO TV.

Front desk service is always excellent, friendly and helpful. A breakfast of fresh fruit, Belgian waffles, baked pastries, cereal, juices, coffee, etc., is included with your overnight stay, as is a free *"USA Today."* Local phone calls (including 1-800 access) is also free. When comparing motel rates, don't overlook all these extras. For instance, if you buy a morning paper, making a couple of phone calls and have breakfast "on the road," you are probably spending another $14 per couple–a stay at Signature or Jameson Inns saves you these additional costs.

In fact, you are just about to pass one of the input devices at mile marker 186. The pole with the weather vane and wind cups (known as an anemometer) in the median strip and the coils of wire you've just passed over are gathering information and sending it electronically to the Road and Weather Information System (RWIS), all part of OTIS.

By the way, if you missed the sensor at this mile marker, you have a chance to see another one in the median strip just after exit 168.

Exit 181-BGSU: As we run southward, we pass the stadium and campus of Bowling Green State University. Founded in 1914, BGSU has developed into a major college campus of more than 100 buildings spread over 1,300 acres, and providing a diversity of programs to approximately 18,000 students.

Exit 179-Snook's Dream Cars: Believe it or not you will find a 1940s era Texaco gas station less than a mile to the east of this exit. What started as a hobby for Bill Snook and his son, Jeff, has turned into a wonderful living museum of vintage automobiles and memorabilia, and a restored 1930s general store. See the colored maps for simple directions. If you love the 1940s and old cars, you'll love Snook's! [Daily, 11a-4p; Adults/Snrs/Child, $5/$4/$3 ☎ 419-353-8338].

Milepost 178-Ohio Traveler Information Centers: I always make a point of pulling into the TIC at mile 178 and say "hello" to the knowledgeable counter staff of Blanca, Mindy and Quinn. Northbounders, say *"hi"* to Rose, Mary and Kate.

Incidentally, while here look for the marker designating Ohio's stretch of I-75 as the ***"Pearl Harbor Memorial Highway,"*** in memory of the many Americans who fought and died during the surprise attack.

Milepost 178-Interstate Defense System: As you pulled into the rest area, you may have noticed a historical marker which refers to the interstate as the *"National System of Interstate and Defense Highways."*

Here's the story behind this long title:

Just after World War I, the War Department in Washington wanted to "wave the flag" and thank the people of America who had generously supported the war effort in many ways. The Department decided that a "train" of America's military might–tanks, trucks, field guns–driven 3,251 miles across the continent from Washington to San Francisco would be a suitable event. Named the Trans-Continental Motor Truck Trip, the convoy consisting of 79 vehicles & 282 men, would visit various towns on the way and give the public a closer view of the equipment which had help win the European war.

They turned to a young lieutenant colonel in the Tank Corps to lead this mission which he did with much enthusiasm. The convoy set off on July 7, 1919 and arrived on the Coast 62 days later.

From the first day, the expedition was a disaster. Heavy vehicles collapsed many wooden rural bridges and trucks were frequently mired to the axles in mud. Two months after the journey started, the convoy limped into Oakland, California–an average speed of 6 mph. Nine vehicles were so badly damaged they couldn't complete the trip.

The officer recorded in his memoirs,

"efforts should be made to get our people interested in producing better roads."

A typical "road" from the cover of 1919 *Better Roads Magazine*

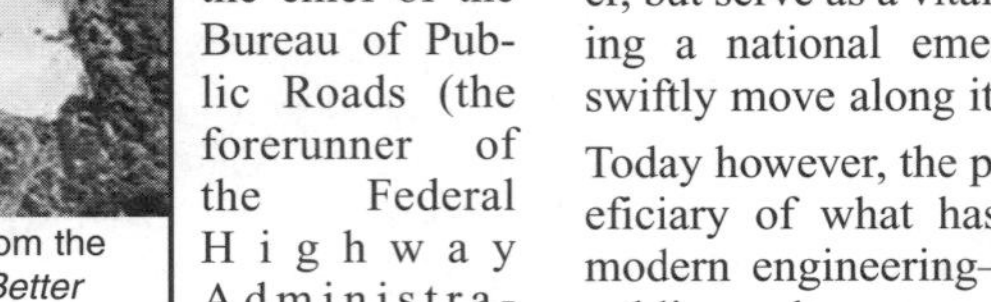

Others were also concerned about the state of the nation's roads and in the late 1930's during Roosevelt's administration, legend has it that during a meeting with the chief of the Bureau of Public Roads (the forerunner of the Federal Highway Administration), the President took a map of North America, drew equidistant three lines across the nation and three north-south lines ... and then handed the map over so roads could be built as indicated! Finally, plans were being laid for a national grid of high speed freeways.

Urban section of a 1950s interstate

And then came World War II. The young Lt. Colonel who led the 1919 convoy had risen in rank and had become the Supreme Allied Commander with responsibility for coordinating the invasion of "Fortress Europe." He and his generals watched Hitler's ability to rapidly deploy his troops via the German super-freeway Autobahn system.

The commander of course, was Dwight Eisenhower who in 1953 became President of the United States. On June 29, 1956–the "official birth date" of the Interstate system–he signed legislation creating a ***"National System of Interstate and Defense Highways"*** – an extensive multi-lane limited-access freeway system designed not only to move people quickly from one place to another, but serve as a vital element of defense during a national emergency, so armies can swiftly move along its arteries.

Today however, the public at large is the beneficiary of what has become a miracle of modern engineering–the largest coordinated public works program in the entire history of mankind.

Defense isn't entirely forgotten though; sec-

Insider Tip - Cracker Barrel's Talking Books

Tired of the radio and need something different to pass the time as you drive? Then stop at the nearest Cracker Barrel Store *(see our maps for the closest "Cracker Barrel" exit to you)* and rent a tape or CD–yes ... Cracker Barrel now has some of the books on CDs–from their "Book on Audio" program. Pay for it–take it with you and after you've finished listening to it, drop it off at the next Cracker Barrel stop on your journey. Your total cost if you return it within a week? Three dollars & fifty cents!

Here's how the Cracker Barrel tape\CD-book program works. Go to the revolving stand in any Cracker Barrel store (usually just beside the counter) and choose the audio book you want. You pay Cracker Barrel the full price (marked on the tape\CD), and they give you a special receipt for this amount. After enjoying the book on your journey you stop at another Cracker Barrel, turn the audio-book in and receive your money back less $3.50 (per week) to cover the rental. A great way to catch-up with the "bestsellers."

tions of interstates have been designed to serve as tactical airstrips during times of crisis. During the 1960's, there was a concern that Soviet forces might attempt an invasion of the US mainland via Cuba. Sections of I-75 in lower Georgia would have been converted to airstrips to help meet this threat.

Incidentally, let me lay one myth about interstate highways to rest. There is absolutely no truth to the persistent rumor that one out of every five miles of freeway must be straight to accommodate the possibility of aircraft landings. It just isn't so. The rumor was born out of a study made in the 1950s to see if this was feasible. It wasn't and so the requirement was never designed into the freeway system.

The familiar blue and white interstate logo, honoring President Eisenhower

Prior to the Interstate System, traveling long distances could be painful; a trip from Detroit to Florida would take 5 to 6 days. Primary roads did not always go in straight lines–they often meandered around the countryside. Frequently they were single lane and at every community along the way, traffic lights, stop signs and local cross traffic slowed the journey. Today, however, I-75 makes the drive to Florida a comfortable & pleasant experience.

Exits 167, 164 & 157-Ancient Ridge Highway: As the ancient Lake Maumee slowly receded to existing lake levels, it left beach ridges and sand dunes which can still be seen. Since these were on high ground, the Indians used the ridges for their trails through areas such as the Black Swamp. Pioneers cut their paths on top of Indian tracks, and these eventually evolved into the early roads and then the highways of today. I-75 crosses three highways which have been built on the backs of ancient Lake Maumee beach ridges–Route 18 at Exit 167, Route 613 at Exit 164, and Route 12 at Exit 157.

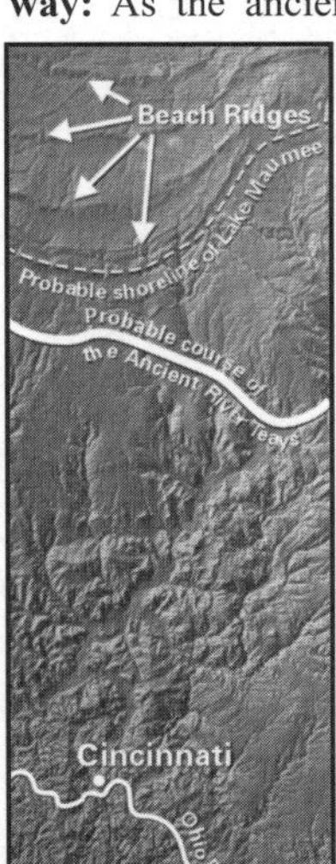

Exit 161-I75's Antique Roadshow: Those who watch this popular TV program will know that valuable treasures can still be found hiding among the bric-a-brac of antique malls and flea markets–and I-75 is particularly rich with such places.

To the right at this exit is Jeffrey's, Ohio's largest antique mall. Over 700 feet long (2 football fields end to end) and occupying 40,000 square feet. It is home to 300 dealers who are there from 10-6pm daily, year round. ☎ 419-423-7500

Exit 159-Findlay: This is not exactly on I-75 but since so many people break their journey here, I thought I would mention something that has fascinated me for many years.

At that time, because of an accident I was routed off I-75 and had to drive down County Road 220 which eventually runs into Findlay's Main Street. That's when I saw it! It's has to be the most grotesque and yet beautiful Victorian house in the world–best viewed in the evening as the sun is slowly sinking behind it in the west. A perfect Halloween property–go and judge for yourself.

The house was built in 1883 on part of a 300 acre farm owned by the Bigelow family and has only had a few owners since. It has seven fireplaces and many of the original gas jets, including one on the staircase newel post shaped like a dragon, which breathes actual fire through its nostrils! The beautiful main staircase of carved butternut wood, curves up to the second story in front of a magnificent stained glass window.

The *"House on the Hill"* is so impressive that master magician David Copperfield used it as a setting for his spectacular "burning house" illusion, in his 1995 TV special.

To find "my" house, take exit 159 east (Trenton Avenue) for 1 mile until you reach Main Street. Turn left at the lights and go north 1 mile until you reach the point just above the Bigelow Avenue traffic lights where Main Street changes from

FINDLAY - *after James Findlay and a fort he built in this area during the 1812 War. Findlay later became the Mayor of Cincinnati for two terms and a Brigadier-General with the state militia.*

Insider Tip - Bistro on Main, Findlay

Don't miss this lovely restaurant with its distinctive green awning housed in an old Victorian building on Main Street in Findlay. From the moment you pass under the green awning and enter the warm interior with its mellow wooden booths, etched glass, old brickwork walls and tin ceiling, you know you are in for a treat. But it doesn't stop with the decor. The staff is friendly and welcoming–and the Northern Italian and American food is out of this world.

Owner Sam Fittante has a passion for people. His hospitality is exceptional and as his guests you will no doubt receive a friendly table visit from this affable restaurateur. The menu is extensive and all entrees reasonably priced, and supported with an excellent wine list. As many know, I love desserts and Sam's Tiramasu, double Truffle cake or chocolate dipped strawberries are very much worth the short trip in from the interstate. Say "hi" to Sam for me.

Bistro on Main is easily reached from I-75 exit 157: travel east along W Main Cross St (Rt37) for 1.2 miles (1.9km) ; turn right onto S. Main St and drive south 1 block. Bistro on your left at number 407. Open for lunch M-F, 11-2:30; dinner M-Th, 5-10; F-Sa, 5-11; closed Sunday ☎ 419-425-4900.

two lanes to one–the house is immediately to your left. Catch it silhouetted in front of a sinking sun and you'll never forget it.

Some other notes of interest about Findlay. It was originally founded when natural gas was discovered in the area during the 1800's. This period was known as the great Ohio Natural Gas Boom.

Mile 157-The Flag Tank: Findlay also bills itself as ***"Flag City, USA"***–a "tip o' the hat" to the patriotism of Findlay's citizens. A drive down Main Street in the summertime will attest to Findlay's claim since virtually every building is dressed with a flag or red, white and blue bunting.

And congratulations to Marathon Oil, whose magnificently painted tank beside I-75 leaves no doubt that Findlay really is "Flag City."

Mile 150-Foxtrot Delta Yankee: Just to the east of I-75 at mile 150 is a round squat building with radio antennas on top. This is a signpost of sorts–an electronic signpost for aircraft called a VOR, or VHF Omnidirectional Range. It sits there transmitting its identification code, FDY in morse to anyone tuned into its navigation frequency.

Why does it do this? Just as interstates guide our car from city to city, aircraft are guided from place to place along invisible highways in the sky called, "airways." And just as interstates are given "I" numbers, airways are given "V" numbers, and their intersections are marked with VORs and other radio aids to navigation, to keep the aircraft on course.

For instance, if we were traveling the air-route from Toledo to Cincinnati, which overflies just to the east of I-75 for most of the journey, our flight plan would be as follows:

VWV
V47 30
FDY
V47 42
ROD
V47 82
CVG

Take off at Toledo and join the airway V47 at the Victor-Whiskey-Victor VOR - fly 30 miles to the Foxtrot-Delta-Yankee VOR (the one beside you at mile marker 150) - continue airway V47 for 42 miles to Romeo-Oscar-Delta VOR–and continue V47 for 82 miles to the Charlie-Victor-Golf VOR and Cincinnati's air traffic control zone.

As the journey proceeds, the pilot tunes in the frequency of the next VOR on the plane's navigational equipment, and displays indicate the distance away, the bearing towards, and whether the plane is on (or off) course for the next VOR–"highways in the sky."

And if you wish this sort of assistance was available for cars on the ground, well it is.

For many years now, I've been navigating the interstates with a Global Positioning System, or GPS *(see sidebar - "Hi Tech Mapping")*, which picks up radio signals from satellites in

Hi Tech Mapping in your Car

Did you know that you can have in-car colored digital mapping for under $150? With it, you'll never be lost again. All it requires is a GPS unit readily available at most electronic stores, a laptop computer (or Palm style PDA) with a 12volt converter, and appropriate software.

My favorite is DeLorme Mapping's new *Earthmate* GPS unit which costs $129.95, including powerful *Street Atlas USA 2004* software, which covers the entire Nation.

It's very impressive. Not only is this GPS unit so tiny (about 2"x2"x1") you can place it on your dashboard or as I did, tuck it between your sunroof and ceiling lid and forget it's there–but its state-of-the-art technology uses 12 channels and the very accurate WAAS signals. Bottom line? My mapped position was often recorded quickly and within six feet of my actual location!

The Street Atlas USA software, a favorite I have used since it was first introduced many years ago, works extremely well with this mini GPS. I love the software's mapped one-way streets when I'm driving in an I-75 city such as Cincinnati or Atlanta.

Lately, I've even been using the unit while on walking tours. I clip the tiny GPS unit to my backpack strap (using the additional powerpack - $49.95) and connect it to my Palm (Tungsten C) PDA unit with a short cable. This allows me to walk around various I-75 towns and city with a colored street map on the Palm screen. As the GPS receives its satellite signals from space, it updates the map to show me exactly where I am. Now, I only get lost if I want to and never have to ask for directions!

Finally, I added an expensive toy-Garmin's on-the-dash *GPSMap 176C* car unit. This is a superb piece of equipment but certainly not within the $150 budget. It also requires additional *MapSource* software for map applications. Strangely though, I tend to use this unit for waypoint routing-telling me how long it will take to reach my destination-or recording highway speeds and altitudes, while driving. I much prefer the DeLorme products for map work.

If you would like to start using this fascinating technology and you have a laptop or PDA, I highly recommend the DeLorme combination of the Earthmate GPS and *Street Atlas USA 2004* software. To reach DeLorme, phone 1-800-561-5105. You can order the system kit over the phone with a credit card, or at www.delorme.com.

space and tells me exactly where I am, how fast I am going, which direction and how far away is my next destination point ,and what time will I arrive given my current speed.

And now let's step back several hundred years in terms of navigation . . .

Mile 142-Yesterday's Virginia: What a difference a few hundred years make. If it had been possible to travel the I-75 route southward in 1784, you would now be leaving Connecticut and entering Virginia–and after leaving Virginia 300 miles south of here, you would enter the Carolinas before arriving in the Spanish territory of Florida.

According to a map drawn in 1784 by Abel Buell, the four Atlantic states of Connecticut, Virginia, North and South Carolina stretched westward from the sea to the Mississippi River. Territorial disputes led to much of this land being designated as *"Northwest Territory"* (present day Michigan, Indiana, Ohio, Kentucky and Tennessee) in 1787. Virginian Congressman Thomas Jefferson, proposed that the land be sliced into fourteen new states, with names such as Cherronesus, Assenesipia, Illinoia, Michigania and Polypotamia. Congress rejected this proposal however and granted statehood to Kentucky and Tennessee in 1792 and 1796, respectively. In 1803, the eastern part of the remaining Territory gained statehood – with the Iroquois Indian name for beauty– *"Ohio."*

Mile 141-Wildflowers: If you are driving through here in summertime, you cannot help noticing the masses of wildflowers along the banks and median of I-75. Blues, mauves, pinks and whites. Like many other states, Ohio's Department of Transportation has an active wildflower planting program which provides motorists with a rainbow of colors at more than 200 sites throughout the State.

Begun in 1984, the Ohio program now annually plants more than 2,000 pounds of wildflower seed along the roadsides. In addition to providing carpets of red, blue and yellow flowers, the program helps preserve native vegetation and reduces costs along the way.

Between mile markers 137 and 138, you'll notice an ODOT sign announcing the Tree Source program, which is a similar initiative–planting trees for Ohio.

Mile 140-Bluffton: I know you are heading south, but as a small break from freeway driving, I'm going to suggest that you head off at exit 140 and drive the short distance west to County Road 313 (S Main St), turn right and drive north through the very pleasant town of Bluffton. There are only a couple of traffic lights so it's a very pleasant drive of about 2.3 miles (3.7km). At the intersection of Jefferson, turn right onto Route 103 to rejoin I-75.

If you have children in the car, don't miss Grove's Bears, the teddy bear store on the corner of Main and Jefferson. Just around the corner is also an interesting wall painting.

Mile 133-Old Lincoln Highway: On an overpass above us is US Highway 30–the Granddaddy of all of our super-roads–the old *"Lincoln Highway."*

It's the route which taught young 29 year old Dwight Eisenhower that America's roads were inadequate for heavy transportation *(see "The Interstate Defense System"–page 69)*. The first of the trans-continental roads, it was originally a Dutch settler's trail called the *"Old Plank Road"* starting near Philadelphia and linking with Indian paths through Ohio and the midwest. It connected with the Oregon Trail in the Platte Valley and then ran through the mountains and past Salt Lake for the Overland Stage Route into California.

In 1912, Carl Fisher, a visionary from Indianapolis, tried to raise funds to develop this route into the first proper road across the nation–but little progress was made. Eventually, Fisher's dream came true as the Federal Government began its freeway building program, and the Old Lincoln Highway became the US 30 and I-80, a continuous modern route from Philadelphia to San Francisco.

Exit 127-US Plastics Corp: As you approach exit 127, you cannot miss the huge US Plastics Corporation plant on the right-hand side of the interstate. We decided to go in and have a closer look, and found ourselves in an incredible world of plastic. The US Plastics retail outlet covers 18,000 square feet and according to one of their sales staff, has the largest assortment of plastic goods in the world. If you have a plastic product need–no matter how unusual–you will probably find it here.

To reach US Plastics, go west at exit 127 and turn right on to Neubrecht Road. Run north parallel to I-75 for ½ mile and US Plastics is on your right. It's well sign-posted. [Hrs, M-F, 8-5; ☎ 800-537-9724 or 419-228-2242].

Mile 124 -Lima's Kryptonite Room: A mile or so to the west of I-75 is a manufacturing factory of General Dynamics Land Systems Division, the Lima Army Tank Plant (LATP). Here they build, unarguably the best army tank in the world–the famed M1 Abrams Main Battle Tank.

The 70 ton tanks were used extensively during Operation Iraqi Freedom, and it must have been an awesome sight to see them rapidly deploy into the Saddam Hussein Airport and the streets of Baghdad while Iraqi Information Minister Muhammad Saeed al-Sahaf held press conferences stating, *"I triple guarantee you, there are no American soldiers in Baghdad. There are no infidel tanks at the International Airport. None!"*

During this conflict, the sophisticated M1 once again proved itself to be unstoppable and virtually indestructible. The secret of this super strength armor is just beyond the I-75, which brings us to Lima's "kryptonite" room.

In his excellent book, *"Armored Cav,"* Tom Clancy takes us for a tour of the plant and gives insight into the manufacturing processes. Based on a British innovation called

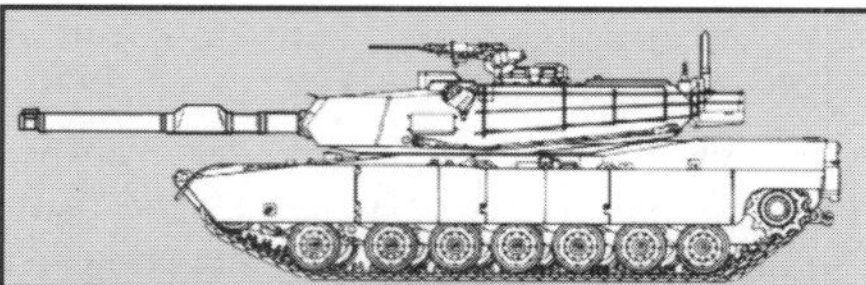

LIMA - *pronounced "lime-uh"...although named after Lima, Peru (pronounced "lee-mer")*

WAPAKONETA - *possibly named for the distinguished daughter of a Shawnee Chief.*

PIQUA - *the French explorer derivation of the name of a local Shawnee Indian tribe, from which the famous Indian Chief Tecumseh rose to fame.*

Chobham armor, the M1's outer shell uses interleaved layers of high quality steel alloys and ceramic. But that's not all, using a secret "black art" process in the Kryptonite room, a layer of depleted uranium is somehow bound to the armor shell, more than doubling its effectiveness. Superman would be proud!

LATP also builds the hull portion of what is another awesome machine –the eight-wheeled Stryker Combat Vehicle. With the upper deck built in London, Ontario, and the final assembly in Anniston, Alabama, this 19 ton assault vehicle will greatly enhance the speed at which the US military will be able to deploy on the battlefield.

Miles 116 to 91-Ohio's Ice Age: During a winter drive, a glance out of the window at the snow laden landscape gives a sense of what it must have been like during the Pleistocene Ice Age. At that time, huge glaciers rumbled southward from Canada dragging boulders, rocks and other debris which slowly ground the Ohio countryside down under their massive weight. As the earth warmed and the glaciers melted and receded, the rubble was left in large ridges known as "end moraines"–gigantic piles of debris which were slowly assimilated into the surrounding landscape. The interstate between Lima and Piqua is rich with such moraines–a good view of a typical glacial moraine can be seen by looking behind your car and to the right (northward) at Mile 114.

Exit 111-Neil Armstrong Air & Space Museum: If you are older than 29, I am sure you remember the hazy TV pictures on July 20, 1969, of Neil Armstrong climbing down the ladder of the Lunar Exploration Module, "Eagle," and saying–*"That's one small step for a man; one giant leap for mankind."* Neil Armstrong was the first human to set foot on the moon.

Neil was born and raised in Wapakoneta, just to the west of I-75. Here as a boy, he built model aircraft and worked part-time delivering for the local pharmacy.

Today, there is a magnificent museum just to the west of I-75, to honor his achievements and showcase exhibits from America's space program. Built by the state of Ohio, the museum is housed in the low gray concrete building that looks like it has a white golf ball on top. Inside, there are seven galleries devoted to the history of space exploration. Exhibits include moon rock and meteorite samples, rocket engines, space suits, actual space rockets and spacecraft.

A special display records the early days of space exploration, including many personal items and Russian space artifacts.

Aspiring astronauts can try their hand at the new space shuttle landing simulator. This unit uses computer programs designed to help train the shuttle crew. After a short training session, you take over the controls and have command of the shuttle on its final approach.

The Neil Armstrong Air and Space Museum is very easy to find. Simply take exit 111 west; turn right at the first road and you are in the museum parking area. [Hrs: Tu-Sa, 9:30a-5p; Sun, noon-5p; Closed Mon & holidays; Adults/Snrs/ Child-$7/$6.50/$3. ☎ 800-860-0142 or 419-738-8811]

Exit 110-RV Heaven: It's been a few years since I headed off on an RV trip but I remember enough to recognize an above average campsite when I see one. John and Debbie Schuettler, the owners of the Wapakoneta KOA, run an excellent campsite; I heartily recommend it. Non-RVers, they have 6 cabins available–a great change to a night at a motel.

Miles 104 to 99-Lost River Teays: Ohio is rich in its ancient geological history. Between these mile markers, you are crossing the location of the lost River Teays. It was a major North American river of pre-glacial times and its valley was as much as 400 feet deep below the present position of the I-75. But the glaciers spelled its death. The rubble they dragged along blocked the course of the Teays, burying the valley–erasing it from the landscape forever.

Mile 88-The M&E: A few pages ago, I mentioned the invisible "highways in the sky" – the "airways" used to guide commercial aircraft. For several miles now, I-75 has been paralleling a much older transportation system and just before crossing the Great Miami River Bridge, we traversed the abandoned and dried course of the Miami & Erie feeder canal from Sidney. This branch used to join the Miami and Erie canal just above Piqua.

This old stone lock was moved from the Miami Canal just north of Dayton, and relocated at the city's historical Carillon Park

Opened in 1841, the M&E canal system provided valuable barge transportation between Lake Erie at Toledo and the Ohio River at Cincinnati but the growth of much faster railroad transportation spurred on by the needs of the Civil War, quickly made canals obsolete.

Capacity and speed of delivery have always been the main keys driving the constant improvement in transport systems, whether carrying goods or people. Consider the much greater capacity of a canal barge over a horse drawn cart, it's little wonder that canal routes were built as rapidly as possible when the only alternative was the horse and buggy.

And then along came the steam locomotive with its network of railroads, and of course far greater capacity and delivery speed than the canal barge. The canal era was over.

Mile 87-Lockington: To the west lies the small village of Lockington. Here you will find impressive remains of the five Lockington Locks which in the mid-19th century lowered canal barges 67 feet within 1/2 mile. Today, the stone walls remain in almost original condition.

Unfortunately, although so close to the interstate (about a mile away), there is no easy access from I-75 other than through various county roads running west from exits 90 or 82. I've added these roads to the colored maps (brown lines) so if you feel adventurous, leave the interstate at either of these exits and head over to Lockington.

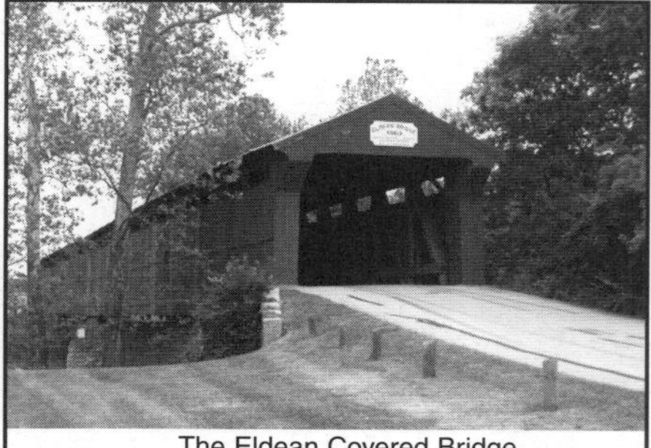
The Eldean Covered Bridge

Exit 82-The Mills Brothers: John Jr., Herbert, Harry F.and Donald F. Mills were born in Piqua. Their famous "sound" started when, during a talent contest at the Piqua Mays Opera House, Harry discovered that he had lost his kazoo and, cupping his hands around his mouth, imitated a trumpet. *"Paper Doll"* and *"Glow Worm"* are among their international hits.

Exit 78-The Eldean Covered Bridge: If you would like a little diversion from the interstate, let's go and visit another of Ohio's covered bridges. It's only a mile or so out of our way and perhaps we'll meet a photographer or maybe Francecsa, from the movie *"Bridges of Madison County."*

Eldean Covered Bridge was built in 1860 to cross the Great Miami River; its 224 foot span makes it the second longest covered bridge still in use in Ohio (the longest is in Brown Co.) To reach the bridge, go east of I-75 on CR25A South (past the Medical Center and towards Troy). In 1.6 miles (2.6km, just past concrete silos on the right), turn left on to CR33 (Eldean Road)–the bridge is ahead.

After, you can either backtrack the 1.8 miles to I-75 or continue down CR25A to return to I-75 via Victorian Troy (4.9 miles/7.9km).

If this is your choice then continue south on CR25A. When you reach Main Street (Route 41), turn left and drive south-east towards Troy Public Square where routes 41 & 55 meet.

Mile 75-Concrete: We are now running on a concrete road top, one of the most enduring (and expensive) methods of surfacing a freeway. How enduring-well, did you know that concrete was used extensively by the ancient Romans and many of their buildings are still around?

In 20CE, the Roman architect, Vitruvius. described the process in detail. Equal parts of powdered burnt limestone, pozzolan volcanic ash and small stones were mixed with a little water, and the resulting stiff grey mixture was tamped heavily into the cracks and spaces between rocks laid in wooden forms, layer by layer. A chemical reaction took place in this ancient mortar which resulted in a long lasting concrete, as strong as any modern roller compacted material.

Many ancient Roman aqueducts, cisterns and buildings-such as the famous Pantheon in Rome-were built in this manner and are still standing today. I wonder if this road surface so carefully built by Ohio DOT a few years ago will still be here 2,000 years from now?

Exit 74-Troy: Here you will find many historical buildings listed on the National Register of Historical Places, such as the lovely red brick Dye building, fronted with the fountain and flower beds. Where Market Street meets the Square are some excellent restaurants and antique & collectible shops.

The Miami County Visitors Bureau is located at 405 SW Public Square, Suite 272 ☎ 800-348-8993; pick up their map of the downtown area–and stroll around for a while.

Once back in your car, leave the Square via Market Street (Route 55), and drive in a south-west direction towards I-75 exit 73.

Exit 68-Tipp City: A mile is all it takes to drive along the pleasant Main Street of Tipp City (Old Tippecanoe), with its many antique & craft shops, cafes and 89 historical buildings. If you have a chance, pick up a copy of the "Visitors Walking Tour" map from the Information Kiosk at 12 East Main.

Tipp City is another 1840s M&E Canal town and when you reach the river just past First St, you'll see a canal "narrow" boat on the left, in a small grassy park where you can turn around.

This short drive is a very pleasant diversion from I-75, and will take less than 5 minutes if you don't stop and shop.

Mile 67-Dayton Traffic: Turn on your car radio to 1290AM and see if you can get a Dayton traffic report. Check to see if traffic is slow around the I-70/I-75 Interchange *(see below)*.

If traffic is busy, get off the interstate at exit64 or 63, and drive south through the small town of Vandalia on the old Dixie Highway *(see map page 14)*. It's an easy drive. After 4.5 miles (7.2km), watch for Needmore Rd. Cross Needmore and Wagoner roads, watch for easy to see I-75 signs. Follow I-75 South and rejoin the interstate at exit 56 (Stanley).

Exit 63-Ohio's Historical National Road: We are just passing US Route 40 which has been designated a Historical National Road.

Insider Tip - Tippicanoe Frontier Trading Company

When you walk through the door of the Tippecanoe Frontier Trading Company at Tipp City, you will quickly realize you have traveled back in time. Old lanterns hang from the ceiling, wall racks hold swords and flintlock guns and a sign in the window announces that black powder cartridges are available. In a corner is a tub of lye soap beside a rack of men and women's 1700 style clothing. From old Indian arrows to hunting knives, gun flints and musket balls, this store has everything for the frontier country.

No, it's not a museum; it's a real frontier trading company and everything is for sale. Owner Mara, says that she specializes in the 1700-1840 and 1870 to 1898 eras, mainly for re-enactors, but anybody can shop there. I was surprised how reasonably priced many of the reproduction items were. For instance, men's American Revolutionary shirts and breeches are about $45; women's long dresses of the same era are about $60.

For anybody with a love of American frontier history, a stop at this store is a must.

At I-75 exit 68 (Tipp City), go east for about 8/10ths mile (1.3km); the store is on your right at 114 E Main. Hrs: Tu-Fri, 10-6; Sat, 10-5; sun-Mon, closed. ☎ 937-667-1816

George Washington and Thomas Jefferson believed that a trans-Appalachian road was essential for expanding the young nation and in 1806, their dreams were realized when a road was constructed (the first road to be federally funded) running from Maryland to the Ohio River. US 40 is the later extension of this route and now runs to the border of Illinois. Today, the route has been designated as one of significant historic value.

USAF Museum visitors: ignore the brown roadside signs instructing you to take exit 61. There is a much better "local" route to the museum; it's shorter and avoids heavy traffic. Just follow my map and details on page 49.

Exit 61 I-70/I-75 Interchange: Built in the late 1960s, $145 million is being spent on a three phase construction project to transform this exit into one of the safest and most modern interchanges in the Nation. Work is well along on Phase II which includes I-70/I-75 ramp work, and Ohio DOT have assured us that there will be minimal disruption to I-75 traffic with all three lanes being kept open for most of the project time.

Dayton and the Wright Brothers: In 2003, we celebrated the 100th Anniversary of the Brothers famous first powered flight-120 feet in length and 12 seconds in duration-at Kitty Hawk, in North Carolina.

But it is really a Dayton, Ohio story since this is where the brothers went to school, grew up and as young men discovered the principles behind "heavier than air" flight. This is where they ran their printing and bicycle businesses, and where they built their famous Wright Flyer which was then taken to pieces and transported to Kitty Hawk for its 1903 flight.

Why was Kitty Hawk chosen? According to a report written by Orville Wright in 1920, the Brothers decided upon Kitty Hawk for their experiments after consultation with the US Weather Bureau, looking for the *"windiest place in the country."*

It was here at Dayton where the Wright Brothers developed by experimentation the principles of flight, built practical airplanes capable of sustained and steerable flight, the first airport, the first permanent flying school and the first airplane factory.

Exit 58 (N/bound-54C)-USAF Museum: *(see map and details on page 49)*. You must visit this awesome museum if you have any interest in flight. Nearly 350 military aircraft and missiles fill its four huge halls, and range from very early wooden biplanes to the most modern non-secret and experimental aircraft-and admission is absolutely free!

The Museum has recently expanded with the addition of a new hangar creating 17 acres of indoor exhibition space. Exhibits have been rearranged in a more logical and spacious manner thereby eliminating the past crowding. The extra space gives you a much better appreciation of each aircraft and has allowed the staff to add dioramas and other small dis-

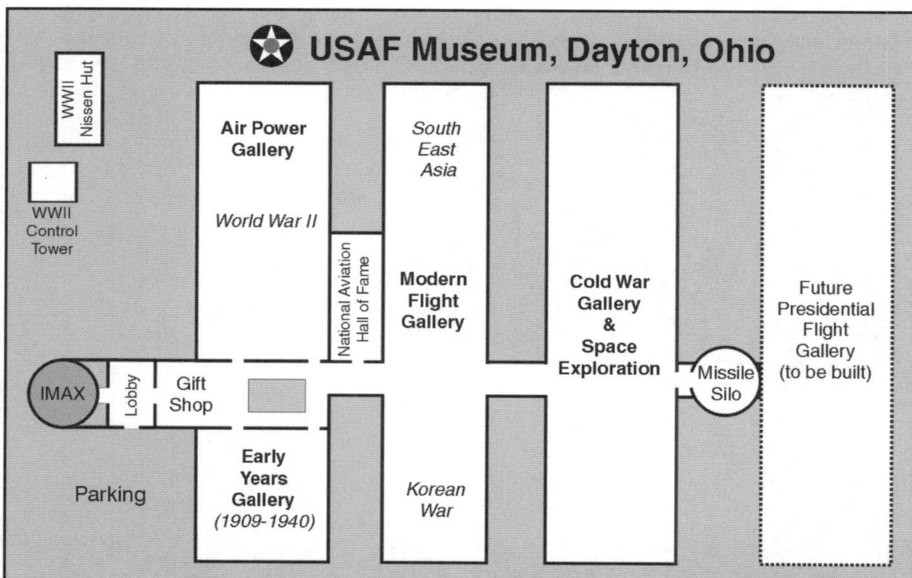

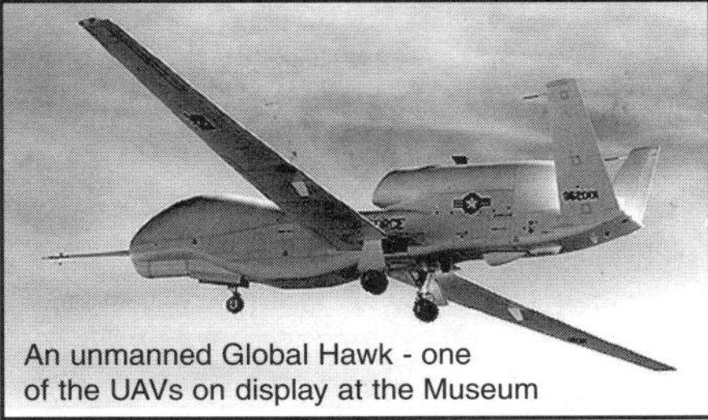
An unmanned Global Hawk - one of the UAVs on display at the Museum

plays of particular interest to specific aircraft.

Let's have a quick look at the Museum's galleries:

The *Early Years Gallery* features many aircraft from the "pioneer of flight" days, through WWI and on through the 1930s into WWII-from the Wright 1909 Military Flyer, Bleriot monoplane to a superb British WWII Hawker Hurricane. A huge barrage balloon brought memories of a wartime childhood on the southeast coast of England, flooding back to me. A recent addition to this gallery is a WWI Spad XIII fighter, in mint condition.

The *Air Power Gallery* tells the World War II story, from the European and Pacific theaters, to China-Burma-India and of course, the home front.

Next is the *Modern Flight Gallery* with aircraft from the Korean Conflict and War in Vietnam eras, to the present. Here you will find classics such as the F86 Sabrejet and the latest modern aircraft such as the YF-22, prototype of the F/A-22 Raptor.

As you enter the last hangar, the *Cold War Gallery*, you cannot help but be impressed by its 200,000 sq.ft. The space is dominated by the massive B-36J, the largest bomber ever built-but it is the spaceship appearance of the B2 stealth bomber just inside the door which will probably capture your attention. Also on display are the F-117 stealth fighter, B-1B *"Lancer"* bomber, the awesome SR-71 *"Blackbird"* and a U-2 spy plane.

Walk through this gallery past the thermonuclear bomb sitting insidiously on its cradle, to the other side of the hangar and enter the small space missile ante-room. Just beyond the far door is an authentic missile launch silo with a Minuteman ready to rocket up into space to defend against enemy ICBMs (intercontinental ballistic missiles).

Throughout the museum complex, you will find other special exhibits such as the tribute to *Bob Hope*. Here you can sit and watch him entertaining the troops overseas.

Everyone should visit the *Holocaust Exhibit*. Chillingly, you enter it under the stark wrought iron sign–*"Arbeit Macht Frei"* meaning *"Work Brings Freedom."* Nazi Rudolph Hess required that these words be installed over the entrance gates of Auschwitz, and other concentration camps. Beyond is a very rare concentration camp uniform, which was worn by prisoner 114600 Moritz Bomstein.

In another section, a *VE Day* diorama shows bomb ruins in Berlin. Amidst the rubble lies a golden eagle with its outspread wings–the icon of the Nazi party. This eagle was one of two which stood either side of the entrance to Hitler's office in the Reich Chancellery. Several feet away, is a battered bust of Hitler, with bullet holes through the head.

Veterans from the European theater of WWII, shouldn't miss the *Nissen Hut* and *Control Tower* exhibits just outside the main museum building. As you enter the hut, you walk into a briefing for a bomb run over Germany-a very authentic visual and sound presentation.

Finally, it's time to rest your feet and enjoy the awesome experience of the *IMAX Theater*. With its high six-story, wide screen, you feel as if you are actually strapped into the cockpit and it is here that you can come the closest to experiencing flight as you fly a helicopter on a mercy mission in Europe or fly as a passenger with the Blue Angels. [Museum-see page 49 for details].

Huffman Prairie Flying Field: Two miles (3.2km) to the east of the Museum is the National Park Service Huffman Prairie Flying Field Interpretive Center and the Wright Brothers Memorial.

Huffman Prairie was the field where the Wright Brothers conducted most of their post-Kitty Hawk flights. They made hundreds of flights from here and also ran a flying

World War I Spad XIII, the "Early Years" Gallery

Model of the 1903 Wright Flyer 1, built and owned by the author

school training the first military flyers for the US Army Signal Corps.

While there, make sure you chat with Ranger Bob; he's very knowledgeable about the early days of flight and loves to share his Wright Brother stories with visitors to the shop.

From the USAF Museum, turn right on to Springfield Pike. Go to second traffic light and turn right on to Kauffman Road, and then immediately right into the first driveway;the park entrance is on your right. [Open all year, daily, 8:30am-5pm ☎ 937-425-0008].

Mile 55-Dayton Inventors: Dayton must be the #1 city in the World for inventors;if society needed it–it was probably invented here. The downtown RiverScape Park, located where Dayton's five rivers meet (Twin Creek, Wolf Creek, Gt. Miami, Mad and Stillwater), honors many of these inventors with gold stars set into the park's paths.

So what did these Dayton inventors invent? Of course, you already know about the Wright Brothers inventing powered flight, but how about Dayton's other inventors and these everyday items: parking meters (ugh!), office building mail chutes, parachute, cash register, pull tab & pop top soda cans, microfiche, stepladder, cellophane tape, movie projector, ice cube tray, gas mask, auto starter motor, price tag machine... and the list goes on.

Exit 54B-Dayton Art Institute & Jonathan Winters: *(see map on page 49)* While driving through here I must mention the Dayton Art Institute–the beautiful red tile-roofed, warm stone Romanesque building you see to your right just north of this exit. It's well worth a visit–free parking, free admission and world-class special exhibitions. I particularly enjoy the incredible beauty of the modern glass sculptures in the *Eileen Dicke Gallery of Glass*-each piece is dramatically displayed with hidden lights. My favorite? *"Bold Endeavor"* by Jon Kuhn.

Incidentally, *comedian Jonathan Winters* (remember Ma Fricker) lived in an apartment just behind the Institute. He studied art and met his wife, Eileen, here. Later, Winters entered a local talent contest and as a result, started working as an early morning disc-jockey at local radio station, WING.

[Hrs, Daily 10-4, Th, open until 8pm; Admission-free; ☎ 937-223-5277].

Exit 53-Wright Welcome Center: *(see map on page 49)*. A visit to the Wright Welcome Center is a must for those following the footsteps of the famous brothers. Located at 22 Williams Street, the center is housed in one of the original buildings used by the Wrights for their printing business, and includes a 1900s grocery shop on the street level and the Wright's print shop on the second. The information desk on the ground floor is an excellent place to start your visit to the Wright's Dayton. Say "hi" to Ranger Judi for me...and don't forget the gift shop.

Next door is the building used by the Wrights as one of their bicycle shops. It's hard to imagine that this small red-brick 19th century building with its original wood plank flooring, located on a quiet Dayton side street was the birthplace of aviation. And yet this is where, from 1895 to 1897, Orville and Wilbur ran their printing and bicycle repair business in the day–and by evening's oil-lamp light developed the concepts of powered flight.

The second of four locations for the brothers' bicycle business, it was here they read about experiments in Germany, analyzed and rejected the concepts involved, designed and built a wooden wind tunnel with which they developed a set of radically new pressure tables and started drafting what would eventually be the first flying machine, the Wright Flyer 1.

The Wright Welcome Center is administered by the National Park Service as part of the Dayton Aviation Heritage National Historical Park. [Hrs: daily 8:30am-5pm, ☎ 937-225-7705].

22 Williams Street

<u>1127 West Third St</u>-the Wright Brothers moved here from 22 Williams, in 1897 and occupied the premises until 1916. While continuing their bicycle business, they continued research into flight and on these

premises built their kites, gliders and the first flying machine–the Wright Flyer 1–which was successfully flown at Kitty Hawk, NC, on December 17, 1903.

In 1936, the building was acquired by Henry Ford, who moved it to the Henry Ford Museum & Greenfield Village, in Dearborn, MI, where it is open to public display.

7 Hawthorn Street-the Wright family home from 1869-1878 and 1885-1914. Bishop Milton Wright and his wife, Susan, purchased this new home in 1869, and raised their family of 4 boys and a girl. It was here that Bishop Wright brought home a small flying top toy which motivated Wilbur and Orville's interest in flight.

This building was also acquired by Henry Ford, and can now be visited at the Greenfield Village, in Dearborn, MI.

Incidentally, all these Wright Brother sites are all within a couple of blocks of each other, and only a few minutes from I-75.

Designed by Orville Wright, The John W Berry Sr. Wright Bros Aviation Center is located in Carillon Park *(see below)*. After walking through a faithful replica of the 1127 W Third St Bicycle Shop, and enjoying a multi-media movie about flight, you enter a hall housing the actual 1905 Wright Flyer III–the world's first practical airplane which was flown at Huffman Prairie.

The Brothers felt that this was their most definitive craft since it could not only sustain heavier-than-air flight for a long time but it was completely maneuverable. This is the only airplane which has been recognized as a National Historic Landmark.

As with the other local Wright Brother sites, the Aviation Center is administered by the Dayton Aviation Heritage National Historical Park. Between Nov 1st and March 31st, when Carillon Park is closed for the winter, phone the National Park folk at 937-225-7705 to arrange your visit. Winter admission is $3.00.

Exit 51-Carillon Historical Park: *(see map on page 49)* Carillon Historical Park is a "feast" of historic Ohio buildings and transportation exhibits, arranged in a bygone street scene. Twenty-three buildings include the 1796 Newcom Tavern, gristmill, covered bridge, 1924 gas station, canal office & locks, 1894 railroad station and vintage vehicles dating back to 1835. Culp's Cafe, a 1930s era restaurant serves excellent soup & sandwiches.

All the buildings are open to the public and suitably equipped and furnished. Each is staffed by knowledgeable guides who enjoy demonstrating some of the machines and relating to life at that time.

The exhibits are diverse–from early transportation such as locomotives and luxury passenger cars, canals, bicycles, automobiles, to many of the major inventions created by area entrepreneurs, such as the famous Barn Gang who, with Charles Kettering, invented the electric starter for automobiles.

[The park is only open from April 1 to October 31st; Hrs, Tu-Sa, 9:30a-5p; Sun & Holidays, noon-5p. Adult/Seniors/Children-$8/$7/$5 ☎ 937-293-2841].

Exit 50-Shawnee War Parties: Two hundred years ago you would be in the heart of Indian country, for the main Shawnee camp of Old Chillicothe lay on the banks of the Little Miami River, just thirteen miles (21km) to the east. The Shawnee were the most fierce of the Ohio tribes. Their war parties ranged the

Insider Tip - Neil's Restaurant

In 1946, a GI returning from WWII fulfilled his dreams over opening a quiet restaurant. The result was Neil's which has been a popular Dayton dining spot since.

Decorated with country style furnishings and wall hangings, it is quiet and clean. Linen covered tables and excellent service makes Neil's an enjoyable dining experience.

Owner Walter Schaller always gives his guest a warm greeting; I think it is the sort of dining experience you will enjoy. The cuisine is American and Continental with entrees in the $12-$20 range.

To find Neil's, follow the directions from I-75, exit 51, to Carillon Park *(see map on page 49)*, but instead of turning right at the traffic lights on to Carillon Blvd, continue forward on South Patterson and up the hill for 1/2 mile (.8km). At Schantz Ave, turn left and then immediately turn left again on to Heritage Point Dr (S. Dixie). Neil's is in the Heritage House building on the corner so park in the parking area on your left. [Hrs: Tu-Su, 11a-8p; Sunday Brunch, 11-1:30p; closed Mon. ☎ 937-298-8611]

countryside down to the mountains in South Kentucky (Cherokee lands), often attacking the white settlers who were invading their lands from the east.

In 1778, the famous frontiersman Daniel Boone was captured by the Shawnee Chief Black Fish, and for four months lived as a member of the Shawnee tribe at Little Chillicothe. Learning of an Indian plan to attack his home at Boonesborough (just east of exit 95 in Kentucky) he escaped and made his way through the country alongside today's I-75 route, to warn the Boonesborough settlers.

Exit 38-Crafter's Heaven: (parking not suitable for large RVs) It would probably be easier to list all handcraft supplies that are not carried–leathercraft and woodworking, for instance–but supplies for virtually everything else can be found in this huge warehouse retail outlet just west of the interstate.

Pick up a free catalog just inside the door–and if you are reading it in your motel room that evening and find something else you need–they have a mail order service.

Right next door is *"Crafty Deals"* where surplus supplies from Crafter's Heaven go on sale for a maximum price of $1.49!

Factory Direct Craft Supply is at 315 Conover Drive. From the exit, turn west on to State Route 73 then left on to Conover Drive. The craft supply outlet is halfway down on the right. [Hrs, M-Sa 9a-6p; Su 11a-5p. ☎ 937-743-5855].

Exit 29-Flea Market Paradise: If you enjoy flea markets, then the north-east and north-west sides of exit 29 must be pure paradise. Trader's World (to the east) and Turtle Creek (to the west) markets are open on weekends from 9-5pm, all year round.

Exit 29-Tim Horton: Canadian travelers will be delighted to find one of the few I-75 outlets of their favorite Tim Horton coffee and doughnut chain, just east at exit 29. Named after the Toronto Maple Leaf hockey star, the Tim Horton chain was purchased by Wendy's International in 1995–so of course, the Tim Horton is right alongside the Wendy's!

Mile 28-Travelers Information Center: The southbound no longer has a travel information desk - just restrooms and vending machines - but for those northbound on I-75, Jerome, Sheila and Todd await you on the other side of the freeway, ready to help with free Ohio travel information. To find them, go past the restrooms to the center of the building where you will find them "hidden" in a corner. This Center also has a Family restroom - one of only two on I-75.

Mile 24-Voice of America (VOA) & WLW: On your left once stood the tall towers and curtain antenna arrays of the former VOA Bethany Relay station. For more than 50 years, this facility transmitted its signals to the World.

Early photo of VOA Bethany's powerful transmission towers

During WWII, the station played a major part beaming messages of freedom into the heart of Nazi Europe. As you drive by now, it's strange to think that this tiny parcel of land east of I-75 once incensed Hitler so much that he screamed during a Reichstag speech, *"the lying propagandists in Cincinnati."*

Exit 22-Voice of America Center: For a number of years now, the VOA land has been cleared of its antenna towers but has stood vacant. But all that is changing now for a huge shopping area-the Voice of America Center- is already under construction with many of its "big box" stores already open.

Exit 22-WLW: While on the subject of radio transmitters, I must mention what was once the most powerful radio station in North America–Cincinnati's WLW. Between 1934-39, WLW's transmission tower at Mason, OH (on the ridge about 3 miles (3.2km) east of exit 22) radiated 500,000 watts! This is much more powerful than the 50,000 watt "clear" AM radio stations currently allowed by the FCC, which can easily reach 10-16 states at nighttime. In the 1930s, local residents complained that they could receive WLW on their "water taps" and "fence posts"!

The huge glass valve transmitters generated so much heat that they had to be water cooled and ponds for the cooling outflow were built on the transmitter's premises.

The original 1933 antenna is still in use. Weighing about 135 tons of steel, this massive antenna reaches 747 feet into the sky and is 35 square feet wide at its midpoint.

Insider Tip - The Golden Lamb Inn

If you enjoy dining in the elegance of a past era with a little "main street browsing" before or after your meal or perhaps partake in a pint at the Black Horse Tavern, then the *Golden Lamb Inn* and the town of Lebanon's twenty-four antique shops are for you.

Better still, if you would enjoy staying in Ohio's oldest inn which has hosted Ulysses Grant, Henry Clay, Charles Dickens, Mark Twain and more recently, Charles Kurault, before its open fireplace–then one of the inn's comfortable period-decorated eighteen guest rooms awaits you.

Established by Jonas Seaman in a log cabin as *"a house of publik entertainment"* in 1803, the Golden Lamb has long been a traveler's favorite. In its time, it has seen guests arrive by foot, horse and carriage–and more recently by automobile.

Today, your genial host general manager Paul Reseter will greet you with a warm smile and if you wish, some local history. If you would like to enjoy this very unusual hostelry, give the inn a phone call at 513-932-5065. Dining room hours are, M-Sa, 11a-3p, 5-9p; Su, noon-3p; 4-8p; Breakfast served Sa/Su, 8a-10a.

The drive to the inn take about 9 minutes (distance is 6.7 miles (10.8km) from I-75 eastwards through rolling Ohio countryside–it's a joy to drive. At exit 29, take Route 63 east; cross State Route 741 in 3 miles (4.8km). In Lebanon, route 741 becomes Main Street–go through the West St. & Sycamore St. traffic lights. Watch for the next lights–the junction of US Routes 42/48 (Broadway) and Main. Turn left at the Main/Broadway traffic lights and the Golden Lamb Inn is immediately on your left.

Exit 21-West Chester Village: Just east of the Interstate less than half a mile down the Cin-Day Road lies a small community where time seems to have stood still since founded in 1805–the village of West Chester. Several antique stores and craft shops make their home here, in original West Chester buildings–there's even a piano restoration studio.

A pleasant place to take a short break from the huge antique malls along the freeway–go off at exit 21, drive through the village then follow the signs to bring you back onto I-75 at exit 19.

Mile 25-Cincinnati's Traffic System: The Greater Cincinnati area has implemented the 511 traffic information system now in use in Kentucky *(see page 86)*. So you can now obtain Cincy traffic information at any time by dialing 511 from any phone (including your cell phone). The service is available on a 24/7 basis, the information is completely up-to-date...and it's free!

Miles 20 to 14-Ohio's Tropical Sea: You are now traveling across the ancient bed of a warm, shallow tropical sea *(see Geology chart on page 94; Paleozoic Era–Ordovician Period–400 million years ago*). The shale and limestone outcrops along I-75 are rich in fossils, particularly around Miles 20.5 to 19.5 and 14.8 to 14.3. As the teeming sea-life of small animals (examples, trilobites, primitive fish) and other life forms died, they settled to the bottom and slowly over millions of years, became the familiar layered (geologists call it sedimentary) rock that you see in exposed roadside rock cuts on your journey down the I-75. Often, the ancient animals' hard shells and skeletons remained intact in the rock, creating the fossils of today.

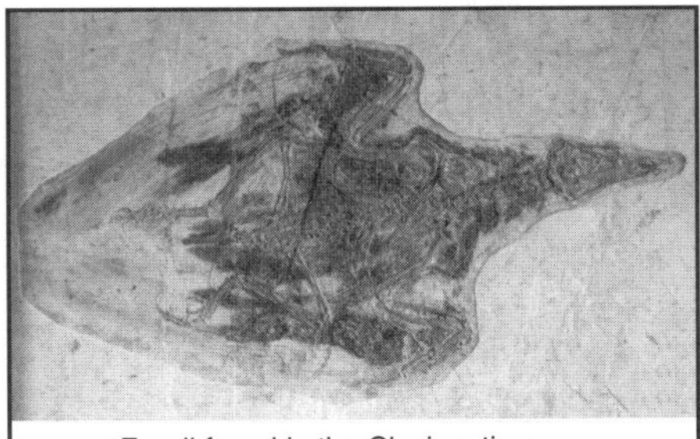

Fossil found in the Cincinnati area while building the interstate

Insider Tip - The White House Inn

Just a few miles west of exit 19 is a wonderful inn, serving excellent lunches and dinners in an "old world" setting. Owner/Chef Michael welcomes you to enjoy his *"heartland cooking and fireside spirits"* (entrees $7.50-$18.95) and the ambience of this lovely house surrounded by sweeping lawns, flower beds, herb gardens, patios and gazebos–six acres of heaven in Ohio.

The White House Inn is 2 miles from I-75. Go west at exit 19 (Union Center Rd), turn left at the traffic lights by the Marriott, through the lights at Allen Road and International Boulevard. Pass the Totes-Isotoner plant (no retail outlet) on the left and the pale blue "Butler Co." tank on your right. Up the hill passing the homes of Meadowridge on your right; in half-a-mile, turn right into the White House Inn driveway. The Inn is open Mon-Thu, 11am-9pm; Fri-Sat, 11am-10pm; Sun, noon-9pm. ☎ 513-860-1110

One of the best places to find extensive fossil beds is at the Hueston Woods State Park (near Oxford, OH), but this is 22 miles (35km) west of here. Phone the park office at 513-523-6347 for further information.

Exit 19-Streets of West Chester: Hmm, what's going on in the northeast corner of this exit? It looks like a new mall of boutiques, gift stores and restaurants. We'll certainly keep an eye on this and report more in next year's book.

Exit 14-Hidden Radar: As you approach the concrete pillars of the overpass by exit 14, watch your speed *very* carefully. The pillar near the slow lane soft shoulder is a favorite hiding place for a radar equipped patrol car, beaming its radar gun at oncoming southbound traffic as it leaves the 65 mph zone and enters the 55 mph speed reduction.

Incidentally, Cincinnati has started monitoring its city interstate routes using motorcycle police equipped with radar guns. Motorcycles are much more effective than police cars in urban areas since the officer can sit in the concrete median area beaming back over their shoulder... and then chase through heavy traffic easily to catch an offender.

Mile 14-Driving the Old M-E Canal: Few will remember that from mile 14 southward, Interstate-75 actually runs on the bed of the old Miami-Erie Canal (drained in 1910). South of mile 13 where the southbound lanes veer away from the northbound and become separated by high concrete walls (known locally as the *"Lockland Split"*) you are driving in a very old part of the freeway system which has not changed that much over the years. In this area stood the series of canal locks (hence, *"Lockland"*) which once took the barges down to the level of the Ohio River!

The first freeway built here was not I-75, but the *"Wright-Lockland Highway,"* a 1941 WWII project to help Cincinnati workers reach the Wright Aeronautical Plant (now GE Engine Plant) where they built engines for RAF fighters and the American B29 bomber.

As I drive through here, I'm often reminded of what it was like to drive I-75 when it was first constructed –as you came around the blind curve of the *"Split"* surrounded by the high walls, you had to be very careful you didn't hit slow traffic pulling into your path from the several gas stations which were still open on the right-hand side of the road. A drive through the "Lockland Split" is still very much a "time warp" experience.

Exit 3-Cincinnati Subway System: If you ask most Cincinnatians where you can find the closest subway station, they will probably look at you as if you are crazy. Cincinnati doesn't have a subway ... or does it?

Well actually, it does, but it has been silent and abandoned since it ran out of money in 1927, before it could be put into operation. In fact, it was so badly in

Subway tunnel entrances just before I-75, exit 3

CINCINNATI - *settled in 1788 and called Losantiville, the Governor of the then Northwest Territories renamed the village after a Revolutionary War officers' association called the Society of Cincinnatus, which in turn was named after Lucius Quinctius Cincinnatus (519 B.C.), a Roman dictator and soldier who was also a keen farmer.*

debt that it took until 1966 for the City to make its final payment on the original 1916 $6 million bond issue.

In 1916, the scheme sounded like a good idea. The old M&E canal running down to the Ohio River had been drained and there was a perceived need to build a transportation system to move people out from the downtown area of the Queen City. What would be more logical than to build a railroad on the old canal bed, and burying it!

Eleven miles of the 16 mile subway project-including two miles of downtown tunnels and three stations with platforms-were completed and ready for the track laying crews, before the money ran out.

Some of the finished sections between the River and mile marker 3 were used during Interstate-75's construction, but most of the other sections were abandoned.

Northbound drivers can see the sealed tunnel entrances where the proposed subway right-of-way was to curve off the path of today's freeway and disappear underground, just to their right as they approach Interstate-75's Hopple St, exit 3.

So today, under the streets of Cincinnati lie subway tunnels and stations, and nobody knows what to do with them.

Mile 2-*"Pardon me boy, is this the Cincinnati Choo Choo"*: "Cincinnati *Choo Choo*, Dave...surely that should be *Chattanooga Choo Choo*?"

Well, actually...no...but you'll have to wait until we arrive at Chattanooga for me to explain.

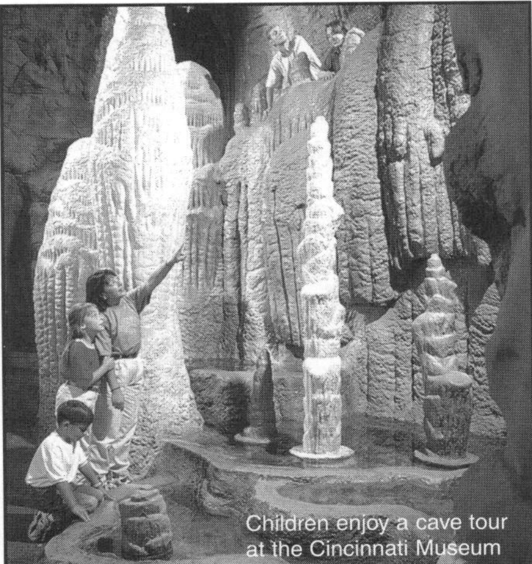
Children enjoy a cave tour at the Cincinnati Museum

Exit 2A (s/bound), or 1G (northbound)-Cincinnati Museum Center: I rarely recommend leaving the interstate in large cities because it is so easy to become lost, but the Cincinnati Museum Center, housed in the beautiful 1933 Art Deco Railroad Terminal is not to be missed.

It's really three museums in one-Cincinnati History, hands-on Children's Museum and the Museum of Natural History & Science. The Center includes an OMNIMAX Theater showing the latest in giant-screen movies.

I find the *Cincinnati History* galleries the most fascinating of the three. As you step through its doors, you enter *Cincinnati in Motion*-a huge moving model of the city. Streetcars glide down urban streets, locomotives haul freight and passengers along the many railroad tracks through the city and traffic is moving everywhere. There's even an airplane flying overhead. You actually walk through the model so you are surrounded by this city throbbing with miniature life.

Continuing down a tunnel we come out into the dark, starlit ancient hills of prehistoric Ohio and then slowly work our way through time until we step out into a Cincy street of the 1850s. Ahead is a paddle-wheeler being loaded ready for its run down river.

This wonderful museum is well worth the short trip from I-75. To reach the museum: S/bound traffic take exit 2A (Western Ave). N/bound traffic take exit 1G (US50W - River/Linn Sts), take Gest St exit on left, go north to Freeman, then north to Ezzard Charles Dr, turn left museum is at end of road. [Museum Hrs, M-Sa, 10-5, Su, 11-6; Adult/Snr/Student/Child, $6.75/$5.75/$3.75 /free ☎ 513-287-7000; OMNIMAX-phone 513-287-7001 for show times and prices].

Exit 1A, National Underground Railroad Freedom Center: A new $110 million Museum has just opened on the north banks of the Ohio River, on the very location where many fugitives first set foot on free soil in the 1800s *(see following story–Garner Slave Escape)*. The Center commemorates the secret *Underground Railroad*, the human network which helped slaves escape from the South, to the free North and Canada. This Museum is so important in helping us understand our society's roots that last month, Oprah Winfrey donated $1 million to the project and is narrating the Center's orientation film.

Whatever your color, whatever your ethnic

background and whatever your age, this is a "must see" museum for us all.

From I-75 take exit 1A (Downtown-2nd St) & follow signs to *Freedom Center*. ☎ 513-333-7500

Mile 0-Escape Across the Ohio: As you cross the busy Brent Spence Bridge, it's hard to imagine how desolate and lonely the river to your left would have been on a wintery night in late January, 1856. It was...and an historical marker on the south bank of the Ohio records a very tragic event which took place below you, that evening:

> *"On a snowy night in January, 1856, seventy slaves fled at the foot of Main Street (in Covington, Kentucky) across the frozen Ohio River. A Margaret Garner was in the group. When arrested in Ohio, she killed her little daughter rather than see her returned to slavery. This much publicized slave capture became the focus of national attention because it involved the issues of Federal and State authority"*

Here is the story behind the escape.

On that snowy January night, 22 year old freed-slavewoman Margaret Garner, gathered her children and met with twelve other slaves at a nearby church. Here they boarded a horse drawn sled and galloped through the darkness north to Covington, where they crossed the frozen Ohio on foot.

The Garners sought the "safe" house cabin of a friend, but this was their undoing since their "owners" were in hot pursuit and quickly discovered the Garners' whereabouts.

Surrounding the cabin, a battle commenced during which one of the deputies was shot. The door was broken down and seeing no escape, Margaret took a knife and killed her youngest daughter, Mary, so she would no longer have to suffer the horrors of slavery.

The trial that followed raised many legal and moral questions about slave ownership since one of the key arguments was that Margaret and her children were not slaves, but free due to earlier circumstances. Sadly however, the Court's decision was to return her to slavery in Kentucky. She died in 1858, still a slave.

KENTUCKY - State Wide 511: We all recognize 911 and 411 as standard telephone numbers in use throughout North America for emergency and directory information services, respectively. Now a new one is entering our lives, and the State of Kentucky (with the Cincinnati) is among the first to implement it–511 road conditions & travel information.

The service is free and can be dialed from any phone within the area for information about travel in your vicinity. It uses voice-recognition technology but has a live operator override in case you experience difficulty.

It really works. We were able to get traffic conditions on I-75 ahead of us (using a cell phone in the car) while southbound above Lexington and lower in the State near Corbin.

Exits 192-MainStrasse, Hofbräuhaus Newport and the Newport Aquarium: Exit 192 (5th Street; Covington/Newport) opens the door to some very interesting attractions just east of the Interstate.

Mainstrasse Village: this picturesque 5 block area of restored 19th century German buildings will make you think you have landed in Europe. Antique, art and craft shops abound, and of course, restaurants serve the finest Bavarian food such as sauerbraten, schnitzel and wurst, washed down with German lager.

Mainstrasse people are proud of their heritage and offer old world service. Summer or winter, it's fun to wander the cobbled walkways and visit establishments such as the Linden Noll Gift Haus or MainStrasse Arts. Or sit under the trees near the Goose Girl fountain watching others go by while listening to the glockenspiel tower playing its 43 bell carillon in the nearby park.

Hofbräuhaus Newport: After visiting Mainstrasse, we drove a few minutes further east along 5th Street and across the Licking River, to the only authentic Bavarian beer hall outside Munich, Germany.

Modeled after (and licensed by) the famous 400 year old HofbräuHaus in Munich, this

traditional bräuhaus brews its own München beers-from creamy and dark Hofbräu Dunkel & Weizen to lighter Kunzel Lager, and seasonal favorites such as Maibock, Doppel Bock and Weizenbock. Traditional bräuhaus lunches and dinners are also served. I also noted that they were serving that wonderful *Gemütlichkeit* (fun & good times) which you often find in Baverian beer halls - *Ein Prosit*.

The parent, Munich Hofbräuhaus has done everything to ensure the authenticity of this Newport location. Most of the fittings come from Munich; even the chairs (dating from the 1930s) were shipped from the original Bavarian beer hall.

Every day is Oktoberfest in the Hofbräuhaus Newport - Wunderbar!

Newport Aquarium & Newport on the Levee: Just a block away is one of the finest aquariums in North America. If driving, park your car in the indoor parking area beneath *"Newport on the Levee"* and take the elevator up to the Levee and Aquarium level.

"Inside" a tank tunnel

If you are traveling with "children" this is a "must see" attraction. Not only do you walk around the seventeen dramatic themed galleries–*Dangerous and Deadly, Bizarre & Beautiful, Jellyfish, Shore, River Bank and Penguins*–to name a few, but you also can wander through the huge tanks by means of 200 feet of acrylic tunnels. One 85 foot tunnel takes you to the middle of a shark feeding ground, and if the fish don't provide enough excitement, the scuba divers you will see in most tank, probably will!

Look up! A hungry shark swims overhead

While your car is parked for the aquarium why not also enjoy *Newport on the Levee* and nearby *Riverboat Row*. The *Levee* has some interesting shops, a cafe and a great seafood restaurant, *Mitchell's Fish Market*.

Insider Tip - Oriental Wok

When readers write to say that they not only enjoyed a wonderful meal at a restaurant...but that the owner is "quite a character," I just have to check it out for myself. And that's how I met Mike Wong, his wife, Helen.

I love Chinese food and Mike's Oriental Wok is certainly one of the finest Chinese restaurants I've visited for a long time. Everything is sumptuous and beautifully clean. Service is excellent and the food superb and reasonably priced. I was very impressed when I learned that Mike had actually designed the building himself, especially for his restaurant.

But if you can get Mike to sit down at your table with you, you are in for a special surprise! He really enjoys his customers who he proudly calls his friends...and yes, he is *"quite a character."*

To find the Oriental Wok, go east at I-75 exit 186 until the road bends. Just past the lights, turn into the restaurant's parking lot. Hrs: Su-Th, 11a-10p; F, 11a-11p; Sa, 4p-11p ☎ 859-331-3000

To find all of the Covington/Newport attractions described in the last few paragraphs, use the map on page 49. You will also find hours and phone numbers on the map.

Mile 182-*"Florence Y'all"*: Do you see the warm welcome on the side of the water tower to our right? Now–y'all know you are in the "South;" on the sunny side of the famous Mason-Dixon line (if extended this far west).

But there is an interesting story behind the

Children feed tropical birds in the new Rain Forest Gallery

KENTUCKY - *a Wyandot Indian name "Kentahteh" meaning "land of tomorrow," or as early settlers used to call it - Caintuck.*

Money Saving Tip

Pickup your free copies of the green Traveler Discount Guide (old EIG) and the red Market America motel coupon books at the Kentucky Welcome Center (mile 177). Coupons in these books can save you as much as 45% off of regular motel rates.

greeting, *"Florence Y'all."* It was never intended as a sign of welcome to Northerners. Originally, a local company used the publicly owned water tower to advertise their nearby business, the Florence Mall. Other area retailers were upset that public property was being used for this purpose and convinced the authorities that the tower should be repainted removing the offensive advertising. But although it agreed, the City lacked the budget to pay for the work.

Then an enterprising city employee suggested removing the "M" from "Mall" & replacing it with "Y'"–that's how it remains to this day.

Exit 180-Wildwood Inn: Kathy and I spent an interesting evening in an African Safari hut here last summer. We could have slept in a cave or by a waterfall but opted for a kraal in our own African village. If you are traveling with children, you will certainly find a night in one of the Wildwood Inn theme rooms something they will remember for a long time to come. ☎ 859-371-6300 or 800-758-2335.

Mile 177-Welcome Center: Need Kentucky information or discount coupons? Then this is the place to get them. Say "hi" to Manager Jeff, and Judy, Bonnie or Brad. They all know Kentucky well and would love to help you.

Insider Tip - Tom's PaPa Dino's

In the mood for a pizza lunch? If so, I'm sure you will enjoy this small restaurant which has been run by the Schwartz family for 40 years. Pizza's from the stone ovens, spaghetti smothered with secret sauce brought from Italy by Grandma Magdaline, Italian Hoagies–washed down with a beer. Owners Mary, Rich and John will look after you. As the menu says, It is a place of *"good food and old-fashioned hospitality."*

To find Tom's PaPa Dino's Pizza, drive west from exit 175, and turn right just past McDonalds. The Restaurant is in the small "Shoppes in Richmond" plaza. Hrs: M-Th, 11a-9p; F-Sa, 11a-11p; Su, 4p-9p
☎ 859-493-5567

Insider Tip-The Country Grill

Every year we stop and eat at the Country Grill family restaurant, and can report that it's just as good as the first time we recommended it, in 1996.

It's easy to spot the Country Grill as you come off the interstate; it sits on the side of a small hill on the south (your left) side of the road. Parking is provided both in front of the restaurant and in a lower level (inc. RV parking) just below the building.

All meals are prepared from fresh ingredients by Chef Edward Smain; "front of house" operations are run by owners Edward and Greg Melcher–Greg will probably seat you at your table.
Hrs: Su-Th, 8a-9p; F-Sa, 8a-10p;
☎ 859-824-6000

Mile 169-Advantage-75: Are you curious about the *"Advantage-75"* signs you see at truck weigh stations? This is an electronic scanning system which uses computers to automatically identify the equipment rolling through the weigh scales. Introduced in 1994 at a cost of $150,000 per weigh station, it is now speeding trucks through the documentation process at many of I-75's weigh stations.

This is the beginning of the elimination of interstate weigh stations. Eventually, all trucks will carry mini-transmitters (transponders) similar to those used by aircraft for traffic control purposes. A truck will roll down I-75 without slowing down, pass a road side scanner which reads the truck's load and destination data, drive over an electronic plate in the right lane road surface to record the load's weight, and get a green signal in their cab which indicates that they may continue–or a red signal to pull over for an inspection. Electronic sensors will monitor the other lanes to ensure that no trucks bypass this invisible data collection system.

Exit 154-A Civil War Execution: Just a quarter of a mile east of this exit is an historical marker commemorating a sad Civil War event which took place in 1864. Three Confederate soldiers were brought here from the Union prison in Lexington. At this spot, the three were hanged as a reprisal for the guerrilla murder of two Union sympathizers.

Insider Tip - Picnic

Tired of the fast food "factories" and their consistently predictable food? Recently we've been trying another way of handling lunch while on the road. Most rest areas have picnic areas away from their main buildings so–we look on our 25 mile strip maps for such a facility ahead of us (look for the picnic table symbol) which we will reach about lunch time, and then a Subway (or similar fresh food outlet) at an exit before it. Stopping at the Subway, we get our sandwiches and drinks–and then head of for our picnic. No crowds, no fuss–just us, food and pleasant surroundings. A great stress reliever.

Mile 132-Blue Grass: Sixty miles back we passed over the mighty Ohio River and into Kentucky. The scenery is very pleasant as we drive through the gently rolling Kentucky countryside, but try as we might, we cannot see any famous bluegrass–and yet it is supposed to be all around us–but the grass is distinctly green!

So what is Kentucky Bluegrass? It is a type of grass which grows lushly in the State's rich limestone soil. It is not really blue–it's green, but in the spring, Bluegrass develops bluish-purple buds which, when coated with early morning dew and viewed from a distance, appear as a rich, blue blanket cast across a meadow. Early pioneers found it growing in abundance when they crossed the Appalachian Mountains in their wagons. They shipped it back east and soon traders began asking for the "blue grass seeds from Kentucky"–and the name stuck.

Exit 129 or 126-Toyota: Toyota Motor Manufacturing in Georgetown is huge. Its 1,300 acres property includes a test track, 8 million square foot plant and administration offices. Two vehicle production lines produce the popular Camry, Avalon and Solara vehicles, as well as engine and axle components.

The Visitor Center Lobby, is open M-Fr, 9a-4p (to 7p on Thurs). Here you can book a free tour of the plant where you'll have a chance to see some of the 400,000 cars and 350,000 engines which are built here, annually. After an introductory video, you are taken on a guided tram ride through the stamping, body welding and assembly shops. Here is your chance to watch robots at work!

Drive east from exit 129 towards the plant chimneys–you can't miss them.

Plant's tours depart the Center M-Fr, at 10am, noon and 2pm. On Thursday there is also a 6pm tour. The plant is closed holidays & the third week in July. There is a maximum of 64 people/tour so reservations are required. Children must be at least 8 years old. No shorts. ☎ 502-868-3027 or 800-866-4485

Mile 128-Georgetown/Lexington Welcome Center: If stopping for Georgetown or Lexington information, say hello to Manager Jean, and Gaynell and Pat at counter.

Exit 126-Georgetown: *(see map on page 52)*. Just west of I-75 at this exit is the pleasant community of Georgetown–the *"Antiques Capital of Kentucky."* If you have a few minutes to spare, a drive down and back up Main Street is well worthwhile (I-75 is easy to rejoin). Main between Hamilton and Water Streets is an antique shopper's heaven. Brick sidewalks, old-fashioned lamp posts and more than 100 buildings listed on the National Register of Historic Places make this short sidetrip a visit to a bygone era.

Incidentally, an historical marker at the west end of Main Street tells us that the first Bourbon whiskey was distilled here using fine limestone water from nearby Royal Spring.

Named after the county name *"Bourbon"* when this land was part of Virginia, in 1789 Georgetown founder Rev. Elijah Craig, set up a still at the spring and brewed the first batch of this potent potion.

Tree trunk statue

You can still visit the spring which is in a small park just behind the Historical Marker. The park also contains the 1874 log cabin of former slave, Milton Leach, and an interesting "statue" of Elijah Craig, carved out of a tree trunk.

Exit 120-Time to Top Up: With wine and beer, that is. Soon you will be in Kentucky "dry county" country, and just to the west of this exit is the perfect place to pickup "supplies." Not only does *Post Time Liquors* have an excellent selection of wines but next door's convenience store has a whole refrigeration section of ice cold beer. *Post Time Liquors* even has a drive through window! ☎ 859-255-7277

Store hours are M-Th, 10-10; F-Sa, 10-12, Su closed. This exit is an "easy off-easy on" (i.e., little traffic; just a stop sign on the exit ramp).

Exit 120-Kentucky Horse Park: Kentucky is famous for its horses and horse breeding, and Lexington is at the heart of horse country. If you enjoy anything to do with horses (and even if you don't) then you owe it to yourself to stop at the Kentucky Horse Park (exit 120, Iron Works Pike–go east for ¼ mile).

Here you will be welcomed by a statue of that most famous horse of all–Man O'War *(see story at Kentucky, exit 108)*, who is buried at the park. The Visitor Center has a spectacular film presentation, *"Thou Shalt Fly Without Wings."* Journey through time and trace the history of horses from prehistoric to modern times, along the spiral ramp of the International Museum of the Horse.

Afterwards, take the park shuttle, horse-drawn carriage or horseback (in snowy winter, horse-drawn sleigh) and enjoy the beautiful Kentucky park with its many horse related activities. The park houses an educational department where students are trained in skills to enter careers in the horse industry, so there is always something going on.

[Hrs, Winter: W-Su, 9-5; Summer: Daily, 9-5; Admission, includes the American Saddlebred Museum: Adult/Snr/Child (summer)-$14/$13/$7 (winter)-$9/$8/$6. Parking $2. ☎ 859-233-4303].

Exit 120-Ironworks Pike: This road got its name from the early 1800's transport route which ran from the Slate Creek Ironworks about 40 miles (64km) east of Lexington, to Frankfort on the Kentucky River. War materials from the Ironworks were carried along this road for shipment by river down the Mississippi to Andrew Jackson in New Orleans during the War of 1812.

Mile 117-Ice Storm of the Century: As we approach Lexington, I'm reminded of a drive I made through here in February, 2003. The Lexington area had been hit with a tremendous ice storm. Trees were broken or uprooted, house roofs had caved in, power had been out for days–everything was covered with sheets of ice. I took photos of the devastation.

While visiting the area again in June, I took photos from some of the same locations, and find it remarkable how Nature is able to repair herself so well. Unless you knew what to look for, you would not know that this area had been so heavily ice damaged.

Exit 115-Lexington Downtown area: *(map on page 50)*. One and a quarter miles (2km - south on Newtown Pike - route 922) will bring you to the Lexington downtown area. Lexington was a settlers' campsite in 1775 and yet had become a bustling commercial center within twenty-five years. Turn onto West Main Street, bear right onto Vine (one way), cross Broadway, S Mill, Upper, Limestone and stop at the Visitor Center at Vine and Rose [301 E. Vine St; ☎ 800-845-3959 or 859-233-7299. Hours–see map on page 50].

While there, pick up a map and a guide book for there is lots to see and do in Lexington. Also, ask for a free copy of *"Lexington Walk & Bluegrass Country Driving Tour."* One side of this folded map details a walking tour of the downtown area with descriptions of the history and architecture; the other side provides driving plans for short but spectacular car trips around Lexington's nearby horse country. The accompanying maps are beautifully drawn in colored pastel–the brochure is in itself, a work of art.

While at the Visitors Center, a few minutes to walk over to Thoroughbred Park and see what I consider to be one of the most fascinating statues in the world! If you are in your car, you can park in the area just behind the statue *(see map on page 50)*.

This bronze statue by Gwen Reardon is of a "frozen" horse race, and you can easily spend

Lexington's superb horse race statue

LEXINGTON - *named in 1775 after Lexington, Massachusetts, by a group of colonial hunters who camped close by after the first skirmish with British troops during the War of Independence.*

a half-hour wandering around between the horses just looking at the expressions on the riders' faces. Colored in subtle earth tones, you can see the supreme effort on the faces of the leading jockeys as they attempt to eke out just one more inch of horse flesh on the finish line. And don't miss the look of desperation on the face of the tail end jockey who already knows that he has lost. Take your camera–the close-ups you take will be memorable.

Exit 113-Paris Pike: (not suitable for large RVs) If you have time on your hands and would like to see some of the lush Kentucky horse farm land close up, you might enjoy a country drive east of this exit, along Paris Pike–routes 27 & 68. But first a caution. This route is used heavily in the "rush hours" by commuters traveling between Paris and Lexington so best not to do this drive in peak travel periods.

This section of the Pike was recently widened and this caused a very unusual problem since the new right-of-way cut through some heritage lands which have dry-laid stone walls, some dated back to the late 1800s. These walls were moved by hand and rebuilt stone-by-stone as the road construction proceeded eastward. Well, back to the drive.

Designated a "Scenic Route" you will travel past the old stone walls and white fenced meadows of horse farms such as Walmac International, Bittersweet, Clovelly, C.V. Whitney, Elmendorf, Normandy, Spendthrift and Domino Stud. Many of these farms have bred thoroughbred champions running in major events around the world, most notably in the USA and France. Man o' War's sire, Fair Play and dam, Mahubah, are buried on Normandy Farm. CV Whitney's Farm is often host to film stars, international business and political figures.

The drive takes you 3 miles (4.8km) to the junction of Rt1973 (Ironworks Pike), in a further 2 miles (3.2km) turn left on to Hughes Lane. Turn left again in 1 1/3 miles (2.8km) onto Kenny Lane and drive to the junction of Ironworks Rd in 2 miles (3.2km).

Here you can either turn left to rejoin the Paris Pike in 1 mile (1.5km) where you turn right to drive the 3 miles (4.8km) back to I-75, or, turn right to head north on historic Ironworks Pike. After 1.2 miles (1.9km) you will reach the junction of Russell Cave Rd (route 353). Cross the intersection and continue on Ironworks Pike for 2.4 miles (3.9km) until you reach the Newtown Pike (route 922). Turn left and drive 2.3 miles (3.7km) until you rejoin I-75 at exit 115.

Total mileage? Thirteen miles (21km) if you took the shorter route or 15 miles (24.1km) for the longer route–both of wonderful Kentucky countryside–20 mins of pure pleasure.

If short of time, just drive the 3 miles (4.8km) to the junction of Rt 1973, carefully turn around and drive back to the interstate.

Exit 111-Blue Water Tower: Speaking of monuments, if you have any doubts that Lexington is the center of the horse world, check

the blue water tower on the east side of I-75 just north of exit 111. This project was a joint effort on the part of nine organizations.

Exit 108-Man O'War: Man O'War Boulevard is of course, named after the famous Kentucky thoroughbred-foaled in 1917-who put many new records into the book. Man O'War (WWI was in progress at the time) was said to have had a 25 foot stride and was once clocked at 43 MPH during a workout. He was only beaten once in his racing career, ironically by a horse named, *"Upset."*

In retirement, Man O'War and his groom, Will Harbot, became inseparable friends for 17 years. Will died in 1947; Man O'War died one month later–many said of a broken heart.

Lexington is thoroughbred horse country. The

2.3 miles
115
922
2.4 miles
Ironworks Pike
353
Russel Cave Rd
1.2 miles
1973
Dixiana Road
8
7
Kenny Lane
6
75
Swigert Ave
1 mile
Hughes Lane
2
4
5
113
68
Paris Pike
1
3
1973
Johnson Road
Nonamed St
3 miles
2 miles

Key to Farms
1-KY Horse Center
2-Walmac Intnl.
3-CV Witney
4-Elmendorf
5-Normandy
6-Clovelly
7-Domino Stud
8-Spendthrift

lush grass meadows growing on limestone soil make ideal horse grazing conditions. As you travel the I-75, the neat horse farms to the east with their trim plank fences–Kingston, Shandon, Winter Hill and Meadowcrest–are a delight to the eye. Check our I-75 maps–we have named them for you.

Check out an I-75 mega shopping experience. Hidden from the freeway but just west of this exit, Hamburg Pavilion contains many "big box" stores, anchored by a huge Meijer 24 hour superstore and Target.

A Barnes & Noble super bookstore is here (need another copy of this book? B&N has it in stock!)–and so are many other well known stores such as Office Max, Radio Shack, Old Navy, Garden Ridge, etc.

A multi screen movie theatre (Regal Cinema) has opened and with all sorts of new lodging facilities across from the mall, this exit is fast becoming one of the favorite stop-over spots for the Florida bound "snowbird."

Exit 99-Clay's Ferry: (not suitable for large RVs). If you're getting a bit tired of the freeway, I've got a small diversion for you. It will only take a few extra minutes-the entire distance is 2.9 miles (4.7km). Let's go down and visit the Kentucky River and see the site of historical Clay's Ferry.

I-75 crosses the Kentucky River

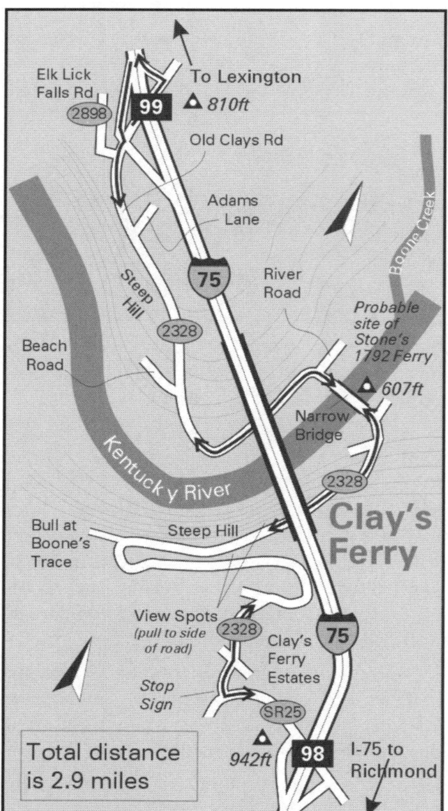

Actually, there's very little to see now but the scenery is pretty and the drive interesting (don't try this if icy!). After leaving I-75 at exit 99, follow the winding road down 200 ft into the river valley. Here you'll find a narrow single-lane road bridge-drive across this carefully after yielding to any oncoming traffic.

As you drive across the bridge, glance to your left (east) for it was here that Valentine Stone operated his ferry in 1792. Stone sold the ferry to Gen. Clay in 1798 and it stayed in the Clay family ferrying people and carts back and forth until 1865.

As you drive up the hill away from the river there are several impressive views of the valley below. If you park by the side of the road, pull well off even though there's not a lot of traffic here. Do you hear that rumbling overhead? It's I-75 traffic on the bridge high above you.

Finally, drive around the hairpin bend at Boone's Trace and follow the winding road to the stop sign at SR25. A left turn will bring you back to I-75.

Mile 98-The Kentucky Knobs: Now we have crossed the Kentucky River, the road becomes hillier for we are in the region known as the Kentucky Knobs. Geologists refer to this area as the Jessamine Dome, an area of sedimentary rock which was uplifted millions of years ago.

Exit 95-Fort Boonesborough: *(see map on page 51 for details)*. Just five miles (8km) east (about an eight minute drive) along route 627 lies Fort Boonesborough–a reconstruction of the wooden fortified settlement built by Daniel Boone in 1775. As you wander around inside the wooden stockade you may visit the settlers in their period costumes and

watch them make soap, spin wool, & practice many other frontier arts and crafts. This is a "hands-on" experience so if there is something you would like to try, just ask.

In 1778, Boone escaped from an Indian village in Ohio (Little Chillicothe–Ohio exit 52) and returned here to warn the settlers of an impending Indian attack. With the help of the British Army, the Indians lay siege to this fort for ten days. Heavy rains and the strong defense by Boone and his men broke the siege. On the tenth day the Indians gave up, disappearing into the trees around the fort.

As you peer through the half opened gateway into the dappled sunlight of the still green forest beyond, it's easy to imagine that the cawing sound you just heard was not a bird but one of a Shawnee war party signaling the band to move closer to the stockade walls.

Exit 69-Driving Tip: Don't forget to use the brown "escape routes" shown on the colored maps. They can save you lots of time and stress. While driving in this area last summer, we heard on the radio that the interstate traffic had backed up several miles at mile 94, due to an accident. So, I checked the map and found that we could cut off of I-75 at exit 97 and come back on at exit 90B. It was a great drive. We came back to an almost empty road and avoided all the stress of bumper-to-bumper traffic.

Exit 95-White Hall: *(see map on page 51 for details)*. In the opposite direction just 1.9 miles (3km - 3½ minutes) to the west lies the famous White Hall. This magnificent Georgian and Italianate building was the home of Cassius Marcellus Clay, Clay is one of Kentucky's most colorful and historical figures–a noted abolitionist, publisher, ambassador to Russia and friend of Abraham Lincoln.

White Hall is really two houses in one. The original Georgian building–Clermont–was built in 1798, by Clay's father. In the 1860s while Clay was on service in Russia, his wife, Mary Jane supervised the construction of the second house over the original. The transformed building designed by prominent architects Lewinski and McMurtry became known as *"White Hall."*

Exit 90A-Richmond: *(see map on page 53)* Home of East Kentucky University, Richmond is an attractive town which has done an excellent job of protecting its 19th century heritage with more than 100 buildings on the National Register of Historic Places. Many of these fine homes and public buildings can be seen in the "downtown" area on East and West Main, Lancaster, Water & Irvine streets.

South of East Main Street just past Baker Court lies the old Cemetery. This was the scene of Civil War action, during the Battle of Richmond in August, 1862.

Having been beaten in two skirmishes between Berea and Richmond on the previous days, the Union forces retreated to the Richmond Cemetery. Their commander, Maj. General Nelson, a huge man of 300 pounds, rode up and down in front of them, brandishing his sword and berating them as cowards for retreating.

"Boys," he said, *"if they can't hit something as big as I am, they can't hit anything."*

Insider Tip - Woody's

The ground floor of the historical Glydon Hotel (1892) at the corner of Richmond's Main & Third Streets *(see map on page 53)*, is occupied by a delightful restaurant, *Woody's*. Opened in 1991, it quickly became a favorite of local folk by offering local dishes such as the Kentucky pioneer delicacy, *"Spoon Bread."*

The menu is varied and well balanced with entrees in the $8-$21 range. Owner Andrew has even added a special *Light Choice* section, showing the calories, fat, carbohydrate and protein content–a thoughtful idea for those on a diet.

The restaurant is small and intimate so it's best to call to ensure they have a table available. Andrew promises you a warm welcome, and if you arrive with this edition of *"Along I-75"* in hand, you'll get a free glass of wine. ☎ 859-623-5130
Hrs: M-Sa, 11a-10:30p, closed Su.

RICHMOND - *named by early settlers after the capital of Virginia, which in turn was named after Richmond, Surrey, England.*

Geology and Dinosaurs along I-75.

The I-75 winds its way across an ancient land with many rock cuts revealing the geology of very early times.To help you understand the age of the land around you and the life forms which were present at that time, here is a simplified chart of the Geological Time Scale.

Period	From	To	Life forms
Quaternary	1	Today	Modern man, modern animals & birds
Tertiary	65	1	Horses, apes, monkeys, early man
KT Boundary	65	65	KT Boundary - Why did all dinosaurs die?
Cretaceous	145	65	Dinosaurs (T-Rex; Triceratops)
Jurassic	208	145	Dinosaurs, early birds
Triassic	245	208	Reptiles, early dinosaurs
Paleozoic	570	245	Fish, trilobites (life in warm seas)
Precambrian	3,800?	570	Single & multi cell organisms

Road Surface (cut down through rocks)

Think of the Time Scale as an eight layer cake; each layer representing a period of time (numbers are in millions of years). The oldest layer is at the bottom and the newest (today) is at the top:

Incidentally did you notice that according to the chart, Tyrannosaurus Rex, the huge flesh eating monster in the "Jurassic Park" movies, was not around in the Jurassic period? It did not appear until the Cretaceous Period, 63 million years later–the movie should have been called, "Cretaceous Park."

continued top or next page

Insider Tip -KY Artisan Center

To the east of I-75 at exit 77 is Kentucky's Artisan Center (see map on page 52). Built in a French Chateau style from limestone quarried near Harrodsburg, KY, this 20,000 sq feet showcases the finest of Kentucky arts and crafts, as static displays and hands-on demonstrations by crafts folk from all over the State. Whether it's music, pottery, weaving or one of the other many Kentucky art forms, you will find it here.

The magnificent building with its high pine-beam ceiling also has a tourist counter with well-stocked information racks and a cafe serving Kentucky food for breakfast, lunch and dinner. Oh yes, and the restrooms are super clean!

The Center is open from 8a to 8p daily; admission is free. There is loads of parking space (including RVs and buses) outside, so why not stop and say hello to manager Victoria, and the friendly info counter folk–Brian, Elizabeth, Glenna, Jennifer, Lisa, Lucian, Marj, Sandra, Toby and Todd–they would love to share stories about their beautiful state with you.

Suddenly, a gun was heard and Nelson fell, shot in the thigh. He was carried off the field.

The Confederates overran the Cemetery resulting in a significant Confederate victory which opened the way for the CSA's advance to the North. The Union suffered 80% losses.

Route 169 (Tates Creek Road) runs west out of Richmond where in about 12 miles (19.3km) it reaches the Kentucky River and the famous Valley View Car Ferry, Kentucky's oldest continuous business.

It's along this road that the famous pioneer and explorer, *Christopher "Kit" Carson* was born in a small log cabin beside Tates Creek, on Christmas Eve, 1809. Kit Carson, went on to become a living legend as a frontiersman.

His skill as a hunter and rifleman was thought by many to be second to none. The publication of his adventures during his 1842-1844 exploration of the West was widely read in the eastern cities and spurred many on to life on the new frontier.

Mile 86-Sedimentary Rock: We pass through an interesting cut of stratified limestone–successive layers of sedimentation from an ancient tropical sea which have been heaved up by the Earth's colossal, mountain folding forces. In summer, this cut is particu-

Special Report–continued from top of previous page

Dinosaurs disappeared 65 million years ago, possibly as the result of a major natural catastrophe. Geologists have identified a dark narrow band of material called the KT Boundary, which appears in rock strata of that time. This layer contains iridium, an element rare on earth but common in asteroids. It also contains tectites, small beads of glass fused under tremendous pressure and heat (most powerful nuclear bomb times 500,000). One theory is that a 6 mile wide asteroid collided with the earth (the Chicxulub Crater) in the ocean off the Yucatan Peninsula, Mexico, causing a massive, earth circling cloud of sulphur fog and debris. This blocked the sun plunging the world into a dark cold ice age, killing all land animals in the process. The KT Boundary may consist of debris from this cloud which settled back onto the earth's surface and was gradually covered by later geological layers.

As we drive along I-75 we travel over an ancient section of landscape, for time has seen many of the more recent geological layers eroded away. Today, the surface geology is often the rocks of the seventh Paleozoic period–a time when warm tropical salt seas covered the land. During that period, sediment suspended in the sea water continually dropped to the bottom accompanied by dead fish, shell invertebrates and vegetation debris. Over time, the ocean bed hardened layer by layer into sedimentary rock such as limestone and shale; the trapped fish and shell remains became the fossils which can be found today in the sedimentary (many-layered) rocks of the cuts along the I-75. All the way from Ohio, through Kentucky and Tennessee and down into Georgia, the surface geology is of this Paleozoic period.

But what about the Dinosaurs? Did they ever stalk the lands through which the I-75 now runs? Not according to the surface geology for this is too old. But marine dinosaur bones of the late Cretaceous period have been found in southwest Georgia.

larly pretty–topped with stands of young lush trees and carpets of wildflowers.

Exit 77-Kentucky Artisan Center: *(see* **Insider Tip** *and map on page 52).*

Exit 76-Berea: *(see map on page 52)*. Literally seconds to the east of I-75, the town of Berea is a hidden jewel that many drive by in their haste to reach Florida. If you enjoy crafts and antiques, make sure you plan an overnight stop here for Berea is exciting and vibrant. In 1988, it was designated the *"Folk Arts and Craft Capital of Kentucky"* by the State Legislature. More recently, Southern Living magazine recognized it as a *"favorite small town"* in America.

The largest concentration of working studios and craft galleries can be found in "Old Town Berea," located near the Berea Welcome Center on North Broadway.

Head to the Welcome Center housed in the town's original 1917 L&N Railroad Depot building and get a copy of the excellent Berea guide and fold-out map–it's a great help in navigating around the town. When leaving, don't forget to say *"goodbye"* to Tux the black and white Depot Cat. Tux and her kittens owe their lives to Berea's cat rescue unit. Ask Center Director Belle, or her staff to tell you the story.

Don't miss the historic Boone Tavern located in the heart of College Square along with numerous galleries and shops.

Berea, where the bluegrass meadows meet the rugged mountains, is truly a living celebration of the Appalachian culture. Stop for a night and enjoy it.

Exit 76-Holiday Motel & Cracker Barrel: Here's some I-75 scuttlebutt for you. We hear that the Holiday Motel-a long time Berea favorite with I-75 travelers-is in negotiations with Cracker Barrel, who wish to purchase the northern part of the motel's property to build one of their popular restaurants. Decision time is late this year.

Mile 73-Rock Springlets: We are approaching the Cumberland Mountain region of Kentucky, an area rich with timbered ridge scenery, dense stands of forest, and interesting rock cuts. A favorite of mine is on the west side of the interstate at Mile 63. The face of the cliff is covered with vines and the rock often weeps from hidden springlets of ground water. In the warm sunlight of a spring day, it is magical.

BEREA - *for the Biblical city in ancient Syria.*

Hawks: Two or three hawks glide above us, riding the air currents of the ridges, their sharp eyes focused on the ground looking for the tiny, almost imperceptible movement of a delectable field mouse or baby rabbit. Suddenly, one of them swoops down–sharp talons extended earthward– dropping like a stone. You look away knowing that once again a small animal has given its life to ensure that in death, life goes on. Such is Nature's food chain.

Exit 62-Renfro Valley: Renfro Valley Entertainment Center is one of Kentucky's best loved places and is less than a minute east of I-75 at this exit. Known as *"Kentucky's Country Music Capital,"* the Renfro Valley complex has everything you need for an enjoyable stay– restaurant, gift shops and its most recent addition, the world class *"Kentucky Music Hall of Fame & Museum."*

But it's the stage shows in the entertainment Barn Theater which brings most people to Renfro Valley. Fiddling, banjo picking, singing, clogging, bluegrass, and vaudeville comedy make up the best country music and entertainment show this side of Nashville. Over the years, many stars have graced the Renfro Valley stages . . from Red Foley to the Osborne Brothers, or Loretta Lynn to Patty Loveless. Enjoy the Renfro Valley Barn Dance, Jamboree, Mountain Gospel Jubilee and traditional Festivals.

The newly opened Music Hall of Fame & Museum is outstanding. Among the 12 first inductees are Merle Travis, The Osborne Bros., Loretta Lynn, Rosemary Clooney and Clyde Julian "Red" Foley. Here you will find special exhibits honoring these folk–their costumes and dresses, instruments, etc.

The Valley's musical venues run from March to December. From May to October, the entertainment of various forms, runs from Wednesday to Sunday. The programs and stars vary, so it's best to call ahead at 1-800-765-7464 for your reservations. At the very least, there is a Barn Dance and Jamboree every Saturday night and a Sunday Gatherin' every Sunday morning at 8:30 am.

Funny man, Bun Wilson harasses show host, Jim Gaskin during the Renfro Valley Music show

Mile 61-Interstate Engineering: As we drive through more rock cuts, we cannot help wondering about the massive engineering and construction task presented to I-75 road builders. The roadbed was built through anything which stood in its path. At times, I-75 cuts deep into the side of a hill and at others, it traverses a short valley on top of an embankment.

At this mile marker, you notice how the rock face on both sides of the road has been blasted and cut back in steps. If you look carefully, you will often see evidence of drill holes running vertically down the rock face. These holes were drilled down through the rock a few feet apart; dynamite charges dropped down each hole were set off at the same time slicing the earth away from the face where it could be gathered and trucked away at the road bed.

The building of America's Interstate system is often quoted as the largest public works project of all human times–larger than the building of the Egyptian Pyramids; broader in scope than the digging of the Suez Canal.

As we whiz by on our way to Florida, we take our hat off to you, the builders of I-75. Thank you for your Herculean work.

Mile 56-Daniel Boone National Forest: We are about to cross into the Daniel Boone National Forest. From I-75, it doesn't look very big; most of it lies to the east and west of us covering 21 counties and over 670,000 acres of rugged terrain–steep slopes, narrow valleys, picturesque lakes, rocks and cliffs. The Forest is a primary recreation area with many miles of hiking trails and opportunities for outdoor activities such as picnicking, camping, fishing and water sports.

As we cruise down the freeway on automatic control at 65 MPH, I often think about the hard life of the early pioneers as they pushed their way inland from the settlements of the Atlantic shore. The Appalachian (pronounced locally as, "App-er-latch-urns") Mountains blocked their path and until the Cumberland and Pine Mountain gaps were discovered in 1750 by Dr. Thomas Walker, the journey by ox-drawn wagon laden with all their household possessions was next to impossible. Measuring their forward progress in days–not minutes–they overcame obstacle after obstacle to finally emerge into that wonderful land just beyond the next misty horizon-*Caintuck*.

The difficult terrain of the settlers' journey was not the only hazard. As the War of Independence raged up and down the Atlantic Coast the British Army incited the warlike Indians tribes of Ohio and Kentucky to attack the pioneers and turn them eastward again. Soon small warbands of Cherokee, Shawnee, Miami and Wynadot braves were treading the paths in the forests beside which we travel, to ambush and tomahawk the settlers.

In 1775, a man called Henderson formed the Transylvania Company and purchased the lands we now know as Kentucky from the Cherokee Indians–his wish was to sell land grants to white settlers from the east, and he hired Daniel Boone to help with this mission.

The country we are now passing through is named in honor of Boone, for it was he who blazed the original trail across the mountain passes and into Kentucky, in 1775. Later, with 30 axe-men, he broadened the trail cutting trees down below wagon axle height, so that settlers could follow his path, known as the *Wilderness Trace*. He and his men opened the entire trail in less than three weeks!

In the next few miles, I-75 crosses the original path of Boone's pioneer trail *(see map pages 23-S and 175/176-N)*. The modern terrain matches the 200 year old frontier trail well. It is still easy to imagine those deerskin clad woodsmen with their wide brimmed beaverskin hats and flintlock muskets crooked over their arms, near the rocks beside the freeway. We can still hear the rumbling of the wagon wheels and snorting of the pack horses as the first settlers move northward on their journey to Boonesborough, Kentucky.

Exit 41-Wilderness Rd: This is the "official" intersection of I-75 and the Wilderness Road although research has shown that the actual path was a few miles to the north of here.

Exit 38-Levi Jackson Wilderness Road State Park: *(see map for details on page 51)*. Nine minutes to the east of this exit lies the Levi Jackson Wilderness Road State Park, honoring both the first judge in Laurel County and the famous pioneer trail which runs through the property.

The park is home to McHargue's Mill where you can enjoy the nearby mill pond and watch corn being ground on the millstone.

Nearby is the Mountain Life Museum, a living collection of old log buildings representing the different aspects of pioneer life in

Insider Tip - We find the Perfect Motel

I've been recommending this Inn–the Baymont west at exit 29, since Kathy and I first visited it many years ago while escaping from a terrible I-75 snow storm. Since then, owner Bob Adkins has won many awards; the Inn is always clean and the staff, friendly.

The well decorated, high ceiling rooms have a full reclining armchair, large 25" screen TV, and coffee maker with full supplies. Heavy noise-killing drapes ensure a quiet stay even though next to the interstate. The separate vanity-bathroom (very important for traveling couples and fast morning getaways) has a modular shower with an excellent shower head and a GREAT steam extractor fan–the perfect room in a perfect motel.

But there is more. On the ground floor is an indoor/outdoor swimming pool which is maintained at a tepid 97°F (36°C); an even warmer bubble spa is right alongside.

We often eat at the Cracker Barrel within walking distance next door. The following morning, we enjoyed a free breakfast and paper in the Baymont "breakfast room," enabling us to make an early start. I continue to highly recommend this motel. ☎ 606-523-9040.

Birth of the World's Fast Food Business

Special Report

Hidden in the valley just to the east of the Interstate in south Kentucky is a gem of a discovery–the birth place of America's (and the world's) fast food industry. For this is where Harland Sanders ran his Sanders Court Motel and Restaurant for many years (long famous with travelers for its clean rooms, country hams and pecan pie), right alongside the main route to Florida–Highway 25 *(see map on page 50).*

The Colonel's original kitchen - note the tub of secret herbs and spices in the corner.

Imagine Mr. Sanders' consternation in 1956 when he learned about the Government's plan to build a super highway (the I-75) to Florida just two miles to the west of his property. Sixty-six year old Sanders decided that his reputation for good wholesome food could continue to attract customers so he set about developing a new type of food for the traveler which they could take along on the road with them–deep fried chicken.

The rest, of course, is history. His 11 secret herbs and spices combined with pressure frying techniques, developed into his famous Kentucky Fried Chicken, the first fast food business in the world. Later, the Commonwealth of Kentucky honored him by granting him the title of Colonel, and the name "Colonel Sanders Kentucky Fried Chicken" was born.

How much money did Harland Sanders' Motel and Restaurant make? Here are his financial results for 1945:

RESTAURANT	- Food Sales	$1,847	
	- Cost of Sales	1,081	
	- Net Food Sales	$766	
	- Expenses	777	
	- **LOSS**	$10	**$11**
MOTEL	- Revenue	$906	
	- Expenses	542	
	- PROFIT	**$364**	**364**
TOTAL PROFIT FOR 1945			**$353**

Today, you may visit the free museum which includes a typical Sanders Court motel room, the Colonel's office and the kitchen where he developed his special recipe. You sit in the original restaurant which was restored and re-opened in September 1990, and eat where it all began! Order the Colonel's original recipe from the adjoining modern KFC store.

Caintuck. The 19th century folk (actors) bake bread, make candles and carry on with their life as usual while enjoy a chat with their "visitors from the future." Be careful if you go there and you're a man though. On the day I visited, the mother tried to marry her daughter off to me. I thought I was in serious trouble until Kathy rescued me!

On a sadder note, within the park lies the site of Kentucky's worst Indian massacre, Defeated Camp. During the night of October 3, 1786, under a hunter's moon, the McNitt party became the victims of a bloody Indian massacre in which at least 24 of the travelers were killed.

"Unmarried" daughter with Levi Jackson Mother

The group of approximately 60 pioneers, representing 24 families, had been traveling for over a month and had stopped for the night on the Boone Trace near the Little Laurel River.

Unknown to them, Indians–Shawnee and Chickamauga–were in the area to observe religious ceremonies. A war band may have become disturbed when it observed the settlers singing and playing cards at their overnight camp–also a sacred Indian place beside the river.

The scalped bodies were found later by local settlers, who buried the remains by the camp. During the raid, up to ten pioneers were taken prisoner, including 8 year old Polly Ford who spent nearly 15 years living with the Indians before being rescued.

Exit 29 & 25-Corbin: In May, 2003, Corbin held a "liquor" referendum and to the surprise of virtually all residents, the town voted "wet" after more than 60 years of temperance. However, the new law will only allow sale of alcohol by the glass and only in restaurants which have more than 100 seats.

Insider Tip - Cumberland Inn

Cumberland Inn is such a great find that I am almost reluctant to share it.

Less than two minutes east of the I-75 at exit 11, Cumberland Inn was built–with absolutely no expenses spared–by Cumberland College to serve as a full service hotel that would introduce visitors to the College and its students. Winter room rates start at $74.00 but General Manager Jim has offered a special discount rate of $69 to *"Along Interstate-75"* snowbird readers, so be sure to take this book with you when you check in. The inn's phone number is 800-315-0286 (606-539-4100).

And the rooms are exactly what you would expect at an up-scale full-service facility. Quiet, wonderfully clean and very well equipped. Hair drier, iron and ironing board, coffee equipment, an electronic calendar on the TV–no detail is missed, even the shower curtain rings have bearings! But would you expect less?

The Athenaeum dining room is superb–friendly service by the college's students, real table linen, napkin rings, shining silverware–and great food. Surrounded with library shelves bearing more than 400 books and entertained by an automatic grand piano, I can't think of a better way to spend an evening after a day on the interstate. The price? Our evening meal for two people came to just more than $25, less tip.

The Inn setting is so peaceful–it really is a wonderful way to break your interstate journey–this is truly our "Tranquillity Base" in Kentucky.

As of press time for this edition, no restaurant has risen to this challenge although I have heard a rumor that one of the locally owned restaurants at exit 25 is considering selling to a large chain which serves liquor.

Exit 29-KFC: *(see* **Insider Tip** . *Also see the map on page 50).*

Exit 25-Inn on top of the Hill: Another piece of I-75 scuttlebutt. The off-track betting which forced so many travelers away from this property, is no longer there. They just forgot to take their sign with them.

Exit 11-Splash Water Park: Kentucky's largest family attraction is just 1/2 mile west of exit 11. Twenty-five acres of fun–Wave Pool, 900ft long Castaway (driftin') River, Tad Pole Island, three water slides of varying intensity, 300 gallon dump bucket–ensure all will enjoy themselves.

And if this is not enough, try the go-kart track, batting cages or 18 hole championship miniature golf.

I should also tell you from my own personal experience that if you are a chocolate lover, you must try Mrs. Whitey's locally made chocolate chip brownies! You can get them from the concession stand beside the ticket counter. [Entertainment Center open all year, Hrs, M-Th, 11a-7p; F/Sa, 11a-10p; Su, 12:30-6p. Water Park open Memorial Day to Sep-

Kudzu

If it is summer and you look at the hillside ahead at Kentucky mile 8, you will see an incredible stand of Kudzu (pronounced *cut-zoo*, with the stress on the first syllable). This prolific vine (Pueraria) grows rapidly, covering everything in its path. You often see it in South Tennessee or Georgia covering telephone poles, fences and surrounding trees. Brought to America from Japan in 1876, it was first grown in the Japanese Pavilion at the Philadelphia Centennial Exposition and then became popular as a house plant.

Until 1955, it was used to stop soil erosion in the South, but it escaped and rapidly became a menace to the point where it has been described as a "national disaster." Growing as much as a foot a day in hot weather, the vine develops roots wherever its leaves touch the ground. In one season, it can easily grow 100 feet away from its original stem, enveloping everything in its path. The good news, however, is that cattle like to eat it. It has been used for its herbal and medicinal properties; recently, it has been found to be very useful in alcohol addiction therapy.

tember 7. Hrs, M-Sa, 11-7, Su, 12:30-6:30. Phone 606-549-6065 for admission options].

Mile 8 & 3-Mountains: Soon we will be crossing the Kentucky–Tennessee border and climbing from Jellico up into the sky. At Kentucky Miles 8 and 3, the freeway ahead gives us a glimpse of what is to come–a panoramic view of the mountain ridges to the south. Taylor, Patterson, Vanderpool, Chestnut Oak, Walnut and Brushy Mountains march across the horizon and recede into the bluish hazy distance.

Mile 1 (N/bound)-Welcome Center: Say hello to Claude, Debbie, Dallas or Jeff if they are at the counter.

TENNESSEE - Mile 161 (N/bound)-Graveyard: Notice the tiny graveyard beside I-75 just before this mile marker? Here is stark evidence of the way the interstate planners slashed the new freeway across landscape, dividing businesses, farms, homesteads, and in this case–separating the local folk from their departed loved ones. The graveyard is lovingly maintained by the Gibson, Hyslope, Corbin and Parrott families; the cemetery is always well groomed and the flowers fresh.

Tennessee-the State that almost wasn't: Did you know that Tennessee would have been called *Franklin* if a Rhode Island delegate to an 18th century Congress had not been too late to vote? Here's what happened:

In 1769, settlers from Virginia illegally crossed the mountains and moved into the protected lands of the Cherokee, homesteading along the banks of the Watauga river.

Neighboring North Carolina refused the settlers appeals for help against the Cherokees who attacked the settlers so, four years before the American Revolution, they formed the Watauga Association, wrote the first American constitution (the Watauga Compact) and later in 1784, created the State of Franklin (after Ben of the same name).

In 1788, the state approached the Philadelphian Congress requesting entry into the Union as the 14th state, but the motion was lost by a single vote (remember that tardy delegate from RI?) and the State of Franklin disappeared forever–except in the hearts of Tennesseans. For being a descendant of a Watauga Association settler is as revered in Tennessee as a proven genealogy back to the *Mayflower* is in Massachusetts.

Over the next few years, Congress annexed Franklin to North Carolina, then designated it as part of the "SW Territory." The settlers finally achieved statehood in 1796, when Tennessee was admitted as the 16th state. The first Governor was John Sevier, one of the leaders of the original efforts for statehood.

Mile 161-Welcome Center: It's always a joy to stop at this well maintained Welcome Center. Say hello to Rick, Debbie, Linda or Joyce, who are usually at the counter helping travelers with their journeys through Tennessee.

Exit 160-Jellico: The small town of Jellico guards the northern gateway to the southernmost range of the massive Appalachian Mountains chain which sweeps across the northeast U.S.A., from New Brunswick, Canada to the Carolinas and Tennessee. Jellico, possibly named after the mountain Angelica plant which was used by settlers to brew an intoxicating drink called "Jelca," was settled in 1795 and incorporated in 1883. Some say the town was incorporated to provide a legal means of selling Tennessee whiskey.

It is remembered for a terrible train crash which occurred here during WWII. A speeding train hauling 15 cars loaded with over 600 soldiers on their way to army camp, derailed and crashed into the deep gorge of the Clear Fork River, about 1½ miles (2.4km) to the east. More than 35 men were killed.

Elk Valley: *(see map on page 54 - although paved all the way, the route is not suitable for*

TENNESSEE - *after the major Cherokee Indian town of Tanasi, located on the river which is now known as the Little Tennessee, in the eastern part of the State.*

large RVs). If you have time-this will only take you an extra 21 minutes-and the weather is reasonable, I suggest you turn off I-75 at exit 160, drive through Jellico and take the Elk Valley road which parallels the interstate. It rejoins I-75 at exit 141. For those who ply the freeway year after year, this might be a refreshing break. As you drive through the Jellico main street, note the old storefronts on either side. This is an unusual opportunity to see some really old buildings in their original state. Although they are designated as historical landmarks, they have not been renovated.

Route 297 continues on past the buildings and becomes a very pleasant country byway through leafy tunnels formed by overhanging trees, winding corners and occasional vistas to the east of I-75 as it climbs over Pine Mountain.

Mile 159-Pine Mountain: The road seems to climb forever as it starts its four mile (6.4km) ascent toward the highest point on our southward journey. We are climbing the Pine Mountain Ridge of the Appalachian chain with Elk Fork Valley and Jellico Mountain to our right; the Cumberland Mountain range to our left. The interstate tops at Mile 147 *(see next paragraph)*, and then, as it descends to Caryville, we come across one of the most famous exit signs on our journey–the one that everybody remembers– Stinking Creek.

Mile 147-the highest point on your journey: You are now at the highest point on your journey to Florida-2,247 feet above sea level-from now on it's all downhill!

Exit 144-"Stinking Creek Road": With all the names available to county planners, how did *"Stinking Creek"* ever get its name? As usual, the answer is rooted in history.

Years ago, there was a very harsh winter in the Tennessee mountains and wildlife were unable to forage and find food. They gathered at the local creek where water and sustenance had always been plentiful but the creek was frozen; eventually the animals died of starvation and thirst. In the Spring, all the carcasses thawed out and soon a horrible stench pervaded the area. So with great imagination, the creek was named, *"Stinking Creek."*

Moonshiners: (note - don't try this without a local map or GPS system in your car - see page 73). On past trips I've wandered around the backwood tracks leading off of Stinking Creek Road – among the hills, valleys and hollows with their sweetwater creeks and room for a small corn patch. It's not difficult to imagine the smell and sounds of a different time–wood smoke, sour mash and the hiss of a copper still. The clink as another wide-mouthed Mason jar is set aside after receiving its potent fill of "white lightning," which trickles from the still's copper pipe.

Here is a photo of an abandoned still we found traveling on back mountain roads (somewhere in Tennessee!) several years ago.

One evening, I was having dinner with some of the local folk when the conversation turned to moonshine. My neighbor asked if I'd ever tasted it. I told him I hadn't and thought little more about it as we continued our meal. Just as dessert was being served, I felt something heavy drop in my lap–it was a Mason Jar of clear liquid. I don't know where it came from–I think I had my eyes closed at the time. Well, of course, later that evening I had to try it to make sure it wasn't just water...and let me tell you ... we will never have another fuel crisis...that stuff is *very, very* potent.

Many say that stock car racing owes its roots to these early moonshine activities since the moonshiners were often outracing the Revenue men, in their constant battle of outwitting each other. Soon, bragging rights for the fastest car were established by racing each other–is this how NASCAR was born?

Sergeant York: A famous World War I hero lived and hunted in the mountains just beyond Elk Valley to our west–Sergeant Alvin York. He grew up with guns and as a boy, was a crack shot and had the reputation of making every single bullet he fired, count.

Drafted into the Army in 1917, he struggled with the moral issue of shooting humans, but all this changed in Europe's Argonne Forest, on a cool day in October, 1918.

While attempting to move forward, York's platoon was trapped and surrounded by a large German force of machine gunners. In the next few minutes, York single-handedly took out 35 machine gun nests and captured 132 enemy soldiers–all in one action and with only 18 rifle shots and 6 shots from his .45 Colt pistol.

At one point, he was charged by a German

The "New Deal" and Tennessee Valley Authority (TVA)

As you travel through Tennessee, you will encounter the massive works (Norris Dam & Chickamauga Dam, for example) of the Tennessee Valley Authority, the TVA...what's it all about?

In the 1930's, the country was hurting from the effects of the Great Depression, and no where was this more evident than in the state of Tennessee. Newly elected President Franklin Roosevelt decided that the answer was to put the country back to work, and in 1933 proposed a "New Deal" which created many public works agencies and projects thus producing employment, and jump starting the economy.

Tennessee needed electrical power so work projects were implemented to build dams and generating plants on the Tennessee River. Senator George Norris of Nebraska led a fight to create an agency to keep such projects out of private hands, and the Tennessee Valley Authority (TVA) was born.

During the Second World War, the TVA's ability to produce massive amounts of electrical energy was crucial to the development of the atomic bomb (see Oak Ridge story on page 106). Today, the TVA is a powerful agency controlling all water issues such as power generation, flood control and navigation on the state's river system.

Major and six men with fixed bayonets. York coolly picked them off one by one with his pistol, starting at the rear so the men in front weren't aware of their fallen comrades. He then captured the lone survivor, the Major!

Sergeant York was awarded the Medal of Honor for his heroic stand. Every single shot from his rifle and pistol had counted–a legacy from his hunting days in these mountains beside I-75.

Exit 141-As Seen on TV (also at **TN exit 81**): How can you not stop when you see the enticing red and white *"As Seen on TV"* sign? Sheer curiosity took me off I-75 recently. Do they really have TV specials? Is the selection current or are they just leftovers? Well, the answer to all the above is a resounding, "yes."

The store is jammed with just about every "special" I've seen advertised on TV over the last 10 years; the diversity of the store's stock is huge. And yes, they have the most recent merchandise as well as items from *"As seen on TV"* history.

You pay the same price as was advertised in the TV offer, but with no waiting or shipping and handling. Be aware that there is a local tax of 9.5% though.

I left proudly carrying a wire thing which I am assured, slices and dices faster and more efficiently than anything else on the Planet! [Hrs: Daily, 8a-10p. ☎ 423-562-7777]

Mile 142-The Cross: What's that huge cross on the east side of the road? There are no churches nearby, just a building which very visibly advertises that it sells "adult" products. And that's exactly what it's all about.

According to local people, a wealthy Tennessean travels the state trying to stamp out such shops. Whenever one opens, he buys a small plot of land close by and erects one of his crosses.

I spoke to the owner of the RV park at the top of the lane which starts near the foot of the cross. He isn't very happy with the "Adult" shop either. Although he has no ties with the "Cross" man, he says it does provide a convenient landmark to guide RVs in to his site.

Mile 137-Devil's Racetrack: About 1/4 mile to the east of the interstate is a cone-shaped hill with vertical runs of sandstone rock up its sides. This is the "Devil's Racetrack," a formation of Pennsylvanian rock (late Paleozoic Age–see the geological strata diagram on page 94), about 340 million years old. People come from miles to explore this unique geological feature, rich with fossils.

Exit 128-Norris Dam: *(see map on page 55)*. Here is another opportunity to take a short scenic trip off the I-75, for very little extra investment in time. This side trip across the picturesque Norris Dam will only add an

NORRIS - *named after George William Norris, Senator and a great champion of public electric power. Norris was instrumental in promoting the Tennessee Valley Authority (TVA) as the agency to harnessing the power of water. Norris was built to house the builders of the Dam.*

Insider Tip - A Mountain Man's Gift to the Future

When you arrive at the ***Museum of Appalachia*** and enter the main building, you know this is a special place. The smell of warm, freshly baked bread wafts by as you purchase your tickets. You follow the signs to this huge outdoor museum, passing the brick fireplace where flaming logs pop and snap on ancient andirons. These are all good omens.

As you move out into the bright mountain sunlight, you have stepped back into time. Nestled close to rounded hay stacks are a few sheep while a small herd of Scottish Longhorn cattle drink from a pond. The faint sounds of fiddle and banjo waft across the meadow on the still morning air as a group on the verandah of an old mountain house, enjoy a few moments away from field chores.

This is a living mountain village–the *Museum of Appalachia*. A wonderful experience of 38 original mountain buildings, displayed in such a way that you would believe the inhabitants have just stepped out back for a few moments.

Barns contain museum displays of Appalachian mountain living. Of particular interest are the many different types of musical instruments, including a long horn which was used by Grandma for warning everybody within miles, that "revenue men" were in the valley.

To John Rice Irwin, founder of this wonderful museum, it has been a lifetime labor of love and this dedication shows in the detail around you. John Rice has created a true gift for future generations–we heartily recommend it. See the map on page 55 for details.

extra 12 minutes to your journey, and bring you back to I-75 at exit 122.

For a really interesting time, you might wish to visit the Lenoir Museum at the Norris Dam State Park or the Museum of Appalachia *(see* **Insider Tip**, *page 103)*, both are excellent.

Several years ago, Kathy and I stopped at the Grist Mill, just below the Museum on the east side of the dam, and chatted with a Park Ranger. She told us that the road below the Grist Mill led to a ford and waterfall–so off we went. We discovered a narrow leafy road which ran alongside Clear Creek. After driving slowly through the shallow ford, we found the waterfall. Below it, the creek meandered across a bed of small rocks and pebbles, in a small valley speckled with yellow winged butterflies–a beautiful sight on a warm, sunny day. The whole adventure only took fifteen minutes; if you would like to repeat our adventure, just follow our "waterfall" road on the Norris Dam map on page 55.

Just to the west of Norris Dam lies the Norris Dam State Park where you can rent a cabin. Ten of them are labeled deluxe or "AAA," 19 are rustic or "AA." If interested, give the Park office a call at 865-426-7461.

Mile 126.5 and 125 (Northbound): As we start to leave the relative flat lands of the Clinch River Valley, ahead you will see the Pine and Walden Mountain Ridges with the Vowell Mountain peak at 2,603 ft, and far to the left is the Flag Pole at 3,500 ft.

We will leave these peaks on our left as we continue to climb northbound towards the

Insider Tip Golden Girls Restaurant

No, not TV's "Golden Girls" but the Golden family sisters who really know how to operate a great restaurant.

Owners Ann & Jeanné, and sisters Becky and Kathy run a restaurant that is very popular locally. Excellent food, attentive service and reasonable prices add up to superb value. You know it's good when you see the many police cars parked outside at meal time. By the way, if you get Kathy as your server - watch out. She's the cheeky one!

Go west at exit 122. The Golden Girls restaurant is a log building (set back a bit) on your right hand side. Hours: 6am-10pm; ☎ 865-457-3302

Cumberland Mountain Ridge at mile 136.

Exit 122-Museum of Appalachia: *(see* **Insider Tip,** *map on page 55).*

Exit 122-Welcome Center: Right next door to the Golden Girls, is the Anderson County log cabin Welcome Center. Stop by and say hello to Stephanie and her helpers. If you decide to take the Knoxville bypass via Clinton and Oak Ridge, they will be able to help you. [Hrs, M-F, 9a-5p; ☎ 865-457-4542].

Exit 122-Bypass Knoxville via Oak Ridge: *(see route map on page 56)* Sometimes it would be great to get off I-75 for a little while–and exit 122 provides such an opportunity while still moving you ahead in your journey. Rather than continue running south and through the sometimes heavy traffic of Knoxville's I-40, you could "cut the corner" and taking the *"Oak Ridge"* route.

The bypass leaves west from exit 122 on SR61-Seivers Blvd, crosses the Clinch River and cuts through the "antique shop" town of Clinton *(see next topic).*

After crossing US25, SR61 (now called the *Oakridge Hwy*) the road follows the northern bank of the Clinch with the Walden Ridge of the Appalachian Mountain chain to the north- and becomes the *"Oak Ridge Parkway."*

Just east of Oak Ridge, the *Parkway* becomes SR95 and you enters the secret WWII town of Oak Ridge *(see Tennessee exit 376A for the story of Oak Ridge and the Atomic Bomb).*

Here you take Tulane Ave to pass the *Museum of Science & Energy* buildings, and join SR62-Illinois/Kerr Hollow Rd which leads to SR162-the *Pellissippi Parkway.* The *Parkway* joins I-75 west of Knoxville at I-40/I-75, Exit 376.

The total distance from exit 122 to exit 376 is 28.6 miles (46km) and takes about 40 minutes to drive. Alternatively, staying on I-75 will take about 30 minutes (depending upon construction activity and traffic), but the Oak Ridge route is much more interesting and will only cost you an extra 10 minutes.

Exit 122-Clinton: this old Tennessee town, five miles (8km) west of I-75 is an antique hunters heaven. Clustered around Main and Market streets are eleven antique shops and a large mall. Enjoy!

Here you will also find the marketplace where in 1895-1936, freshwater pearl producers traded their wares harvested from the Clinch River. Clinton pearls were so well known that dealers came from New York to buy; pearls from this area have even been featured at the International Exposition, in Paris.

Mile 107-Southbound Driving Notes: If continuing on I-75 past exit 122, you will need the following notes.

As Interstate-75 swings south and around Knoxville to the west, it briefly joins and assumes the mile post numbers of two other freeways (I-640 and I-40). It can be a little tricky driving through here without local knowledge, so let me "talk" you through it. You'll find all the lane change instructions clearly marked on the colored map page 27 (pp171-172 for northbounders).

Insider Tip - Aubrey's

If it's time to stop for a meal then I know you will enjoy Aubrey's Restaurant at exit 112. As soon as you enter the door, you know this is going to be a wonderful dining experience-the greeting could not be friendlier. Aubrey's meets all our criteria for a *"Dave Hunter* **Insider Tip.**" Service is excellent, a wide choice of entrees are reasonable priced ($9-$22) and the food, tasty. Try the Potato Soup topped with cheese, with crispy sweet rolls to start - yummy!

Take time to check out the unusual artwork hanging from the ceiling. Artist Bobbie Crews has decorated 4'x8' blackboards with pictures from bygone times, in colored chalk. They are quite a feature.

To find Aubrey's, go east at exit 112 and turn left up the hill towards the Holiday Inn Express; the restaurant is across the road. Hrs: 11a-10p daily ☎ 865-938-2724

Insider Tip - Comfort Inn

East of exit 108 (Merchant Drive) is a reasonably priced Comfort Inn with clean, large rooms furnished with a soft chair/foot rest, sofa, and desk with free internet. A firm bed, fluffy towels, excellent shower and other amenities ensure a comfortable stay. If you decide to stop here, try and get a ground floor room, and don't forget that you'll find their best rates in the Tennessee motel discount coupon book. ☎ 865-688-1010

First, we want the westbound branch of I-640 (Knoxville's northern "ring road")–here's how we join it. Several miles after exit 108, you will see an *"Exit 3 I-640 East"* sign.

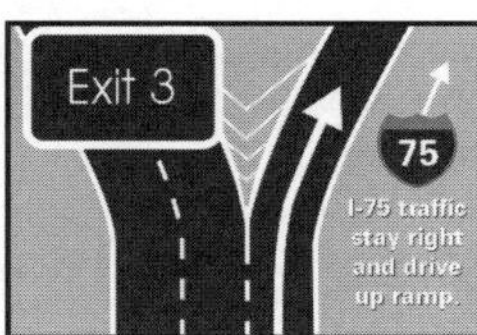

As you approach it, make sure you stay well over to the right. At exit 3, the left 2 lanes bear off to the east and continues on to downtown Knoxville–don't follow it! Instead, stay over in the right lane (the *I-75 South* lane) which becomes a single lane ramp until you join merge with the traffic of I-640 West. The mile posts now change to Interstate-640's numbering system.

After three miles (4.8km), the left lanes continue ahead to *I-40 East-Knoxville*. Move into the right two lanes and follow the *I-40West/I-75 South - Nashville/Chattanooga* sign.

On the ramp, the two lanes quickly become one, so move left as soon as possible–and move left again once you are on I-40 since the ramp lane disappears.

The mile posts numbers change once again–this time to I-40's "380" series.

Watch for police along this stretch since it is actively patrolled for out of state speeders (the "locals" seem to whiz by at excessive speeds with complete immunity).

Well, how did we do? You should now be driving westward along I-75/I-40. If you see exit 383-Papermill Dr ahead of you, you know you are going the right way.

Mile 383-The Body Farm: Now, if you are squeamish (or just about to stop for a meal), please skip the following paragraphs. If you continue to read, I make no apology for the subject matter . . .

About 2 miles (3.2km) south-east of where you are right now is the 3 acre Bass Anthropological Research Facility. Also known by its initials BARF (I kid you not!), or the *"Body Farm."* Made famous in crime writer Patricia Cornwell's novel of the same name, the Body Farm is a highly secured area where corpses are placed in various situations (in the open, buried under leaves, in water, etc.) and in different environments (burnt out cars, old trunks,)–and in the interests of forensic science, left to deteriorate.

Operated by the University of Tennessee, the facility is famous in the world of crime detection. Organizations such as Interpol, the FBI and regional police authorities use the Farm's findings to determine how long a corpse might have been dead (given climate and environment of the discovery site).

How is this done? Well, out of a sense of propriety I'm not going to tell you unless you ask me in person–or better still, read Patricia Cornwell's best selling book. You'll find the answers in lurid detail.

Oh! by the way, you cannot visit the Body Farm–it's not an "attraction" and is surrounded by razor wire fences. However, since this book claims to be a complete guide to I-75–I just wanted you to know it was there.

Exit 376-Exit Letters: Some travelers have found this exit confusing. I-75, exit 376 services a short multi lane "service road" which

Insider Tip - Best BBQ Ribs on I-75

Calhouns: locals flock to Calhouns which claims to be the *"Home of America's Best Ribs."* As soon as you step through the front door, you know that manager Lisa Clark is ready for our challenge. Food is fresh, service is warm and friendly; it's a popular spot for the locals and was rated MMMM by the Knoxville media. Thoughtfully, the menu provides a number of *"Health Smart"* selections.

Calhoun's is just 2 minutes off the interstate and easy to find-take exit 376B (I-140E-Pellissippi Parkway) and leave it after 6/10th mile at exit 1A (Kingston Pike N, US11E, US70). Go through traffic lights at Mabry Hood, and Calhoun's–a wooden barn-style building with dark red roof–is immediately on your right. Calhouns - 10020 Kingston Pike, Knoxville, TN 37923. Hrs: M-Th, 11-10; F-Sa, 11-11; Su, 11-9:30 ☎ 865-673-3444

KNOXVILLE - *originally called White's Fort, in 1791 it was renamed after General Henry Knox (1750-1806), a soldier during the American Revolution. General Knox was the army Commander in Chief (1783-84) and the Nation's first Secretary of War under President Washington (1785-95). The main depository of the Nation's gold bullion, Fort Knox, is also named after him.*

Was Albert Einstein really the genius behind Relativity?

I love historical mysteries and here's a great one for the Centenary of Albert Einstein's famous $E=MC^2$ equation, which led to development of the atomic bomb.

Did you know that...Albert Einstein was married to a brilliant mathematician-physicist, Mileva Einstein-Marity and that they had first met in 1896 at university while attending the same mathematics & physics lectures together? That in 1898, Mileva wrote to Albert about her fascination and studies involving molecular motion, time and distance? Later, Albert wrote to Mileva, *"how happy and proud I will be when we two have led our work on relative motion to an end?"*

In 1903, the Einsteins moved into an apt in Berne while work proceeded on the *Special Theory of Relativity*. Did they work on it together? It's almost certain since Albert's closest friends remarked that the relationship was "an intellectual partnership." Was Mileva the *real* genius behind Relativity? Maybe...she did all the mathematics according to Albert. It's also a fact that she had previously authored other scientific papers which Albert later claimed as his.

The famous *"Relativity"* paper was published in 1905 and the Editor later reported that the submitted manuscript bears both Albert's and Marity's names as co-authors, but only Mileva signed it- *"Marity."* For reasons unknown, Mileva's name was suppressed and the World assumed it was the sole work of Albert Einstein. The couple were divorced in 1919. In 1922, Albert won the Nobel Prize for "his" work on *"Relativity;"* he gave all his prize money to Mileva. Why?

2005 is the 100th Anniversary of the "Special Theory of Relativity," a scientific paper which literally changed the world we live in. In light of these recent finding among the Einstein-Marity private papers, the mystery of who really authored *Relativity* might be soon resolved.

then splits into exits 376A-to Oak Ridge, and 376B-Maryville. So if you are looking for the "lettered" exits, you must take exit 376 first.

Exit 376A-Oak Ridge: *(see map on page 56 for details)*. 12.3 miles (19.8km) to the north of the I-40/I-75 lies a city built in 1942, for the workers of Clinton Engineering Works. A city so "secret" that it was on no map and anybody asking casual questions about it would be arrested as a possible spy.

One hundred years ago, Albert Einstein published his Special Theory of Relativity (see *Special Report for an intriguing mystery related to this paper)* and revealed his famous equation $E=MC^2$. In essence, this formula states that there is an incredible amount of energy locked up in matter.

But how to unlock it? In 1939, the US Government realized that the Nazis in Germany understood the possibilities of unlocking this energy and creating an atomic bomb. Their scientists had recently succeeded in splitting atoms of uranium at Berlin's Kaiser Wilhelm Institute. An atomic bomb in the hands of the Nazis would have guaranteed their world domination so it was vital that the USA protect itself by beating the Germans by developing the bomb first.

President Roosevelt authorized a full-scale atomic bomb program, code named the *Manhattan Project*; work started in 1942.

Three top secret sites were chosen to perform different phases of the project. Plutonium production was located at site W (Hanford, WA); Uranium (U235) extraction at site X in Tennessee, and site Y, a lonely mesa in New Mexico called *Los Alamos* where the various components from "W" and "X" would be assembled under the direction of Robert Oppenheimer, and the finished bomb tested.

Site X was to become the secret city of *Oak Ridge*. Named after *Black Oak Ridge*, one of a series of three valleys northwest of Knoxville, it was chosen because of the availability of huge amounts of hydro-electricity generated by the TVA dams; the valleys offered shelter to adjacent operations should one of the atomic plants explode, and finally, it was very sparsely populated by farmers who could be easily relocated. Its remoteness also ensured security from Nazi spies.

So the secret city of Oak Ridge was born and scientists & workers moved in. Very few residents were allowed to leave and until 1949 it could only be visited by special permit.

Three plants with code names K25–uranium extraction and enrichment, X10–atomic pile and Y12–uranium atom separation were built in parallel valleys under a secret organization, the Clinton Engineering Works. The entire area, including the town of Oak Ridge with housing and amenities for all the workers, was enclosed by barbed-wire with access controlled by seven gates. Life in the area was very basic and made difficult by the ever present mud.

Today things are much different, an excellent visitors' center and several attractions –the *American Museum of Science and Energy*, *New Bethel Church* (where the Project scientists used to meet), the *Graphite Reactor* and the K-25 visitor overlook–are well worth a visit for those interested in the birth of the Nuclear Age. Since 9/11, security has been tightened at some of the sites so if planning to visit them, I suggest you phone or visit the *Visitors Center* first *(See map and other details on page 56)*.

Exit 373-Apple Cake Tea Room: *(see* **Insider Tip***).*

Exit 368-Driving Notes: Here I-75 leaves the I-40, and continues south towards Chattanooga. I-75 mile marker numbers resume.

Exit 81-Wild Flowers: I happened to drive through this stretch of I-75 last May which is an unusual time of year for me, and was awed by the profusion of flowers. Carpets of red corn poppies, white and yellow shasta daisies and yellow cosmos blanketed the ramp slopes and median strips along the interstate.

In fact, the Tennessee Department of Transport plants more than 700 acres of wildflowers along interstate routes, under the State's Bicentennial Beautification Act. As somebody recently remarked,

> *"Without a doubt, Tennessee stretches of the interstate were the most beautiful of the entire journey."*

Exit 81: Lenoir City: 1/5th mile east of I-75, just below the Phillips 66 station is the pleasant Lenoir City (pronounced, "Len-ore") Visitor Center, with its waterfall and koi pond. Say "hi" to Becky, Betty, Helen and Virginia who have all sorts of area information to share.

While here, you might consider taking a side tour to the City Park near the Loudon Dam (there is another Calhouns Restaurant there), or perhaps continue your journey southward by using Route 11 through Loudon, Philadelphia and Sweetwater. Whatever you decide, they can provide you with maps and directions.

Mile 81-Rock City: Those who drove to Florida in the pre-I-75 days will remember the classics of roadside advertising–*Burma Shave* and *Rock City*. Most of these were discontinued when federal legislation required the removal of all private roadside signs along the interstates, but several have survived.

"Rock City" signs were very prolific and adorned the roofs of barns, outhouses, and farm buildings throughout the South (Rock City is an attraction in Chattanooga), announcing the number of miles you had to travel to *"See Rock City."* If you

Insider Tip - Apple Cake Tea Room

I cannot rave enough about the Apple Cake Tea Room, just south of the interstate at exit 373. Housed in a cozy log cabin, the minute you enter the door you know this is going to be a special occasion. Tasty home cooking aromas greet your senses and prepare you for the meal to follow. Take a look around the interior. The Henry family has lived here for many generations and owner Mary Henry furnished the interior with many of her treasured family heirlooms.

Now to the lunch menu. First, a very presentable chicken soup and then on to the main course. There are a number of sandwich choices; I enjoyed the grilled chicken sandwich on a fresh croissant. Side orders of honey butter, cheese toast and banana nut bread help round out the course. Don't miss trying the Cornucopia for dessert–a wonderful blending of vanilla ice cream, sauteed bananas and homemade chocolate or butterscotch sauce nested in a crunchy basket. Scrumptious!

To find this wonderful restaurant, take exit 373 south towards Farragut. The Apple Cake is in Appalachian Log Square plaza on the left side of Campbell Station Road, almost immediately opposite the Pilot gas station. Hrs: M-Sa, 11-2:30 ☎ 865-966-7848

look very carefully to the left at mile marker 81, you will see a barn with an original *"Rock City"* sign painted on its roof.

Exit 76-TN Valley Winery: A quarter of a mile to the west of exit 76 (Sugar Limb Road) lies the entrance to the Tennessee Valley Winery. Here, for 21 years the Reed family – Jerry & Tom Reed, and Christine – have practiced the Tennessee wine making tradition, producing more than 22,000 gallons of table wines each year from their 22 acres of plantings at the Wildwood Vineyards, located 15 miles (24.1km) south in Roane County. Wine-maker, Tom, is proud of the fact that the family's estate has won medals and awards from all over the United States. Last year they entered 22 wines into competition and walked away with 22 medals!

Tom and Christine sample one of their gold medal wines

Tastings and picnic facilities are all available here; Tom invites you to stay a while and enjoy a picnic lunch on the sun-deck where you can relax and take in the magnificent view across the Loudon Valley. Wine tastings, from 10:00-6:00pm, Mon-Sat, and from 1:00-5:00pm on Sun. ☎ 865-986-5147

Mile 74-Mitchell W. Stout Bridge: You are just about to pass over the wide Tennessee River, on a bridge named after a Korean War hero, Sergeant Stout. Here's what happened:

While his unit's bunker came under heavy attack while guarding the Khe Gio Bridge, a grenade was thrown into their midst. Stout, knowing that it might explode at any moment and kill them all, grabbed it and hugging it close to his body like a football to shield them all, ran for the door. It exploded killing him–but his action saved his fellow soldiers.

Mitchell Stout was awarded the Medal of Honor, posthumously. He died at age 20.

Exit 68-Tennessee Cheddar: As a youth, I spent several months living on an English dairy farm which owned a huge herd of black & white cows, or *"Freisans"* as we called them. Kathy, my Canadian wife, calls the same breed, *"Holsteins."* Who is right?

This question arose again recently when we drove in to Sweetwater Valley Farm to meet owners John and Celia Harrison and to sample the famous Tennessee cheese we had been hearing so much about.

Let me say, the question of b&w cows (I still call them *Freisans*!) quickly disappeared as I sank my teeth into nibblets of Sweetwater's award winning *1999 Tennessee Aged, Mountain White, Hickory Smoked* and *Burch's Champion Reserve*. These cheeses are so good the Harrisons actually mail them to customers in Wisconsin! By the way, while you are tasting the cheese, you can watch it being made through the large glass windows of the cheese "Make" room.

Manager Rita Ritchey then took us on a tour where we saw the farm's baby calves in their "nursery" pens. Next, we visited the farm's milking facility where machines milk the herd of 700 *"Freisans"* three times daily. Dairy farming has become so sophisticated that computers track how far each cow has walked during the day and her milk yield.

If you are traveling with children–who have never seen a cow and believe that all milk comes in bottles–this farm visit and tour is an absolute must!

The farm is only a 4 minute drive from I-75. Take exit 68 and drive east for 2 miles (3.2km) on Pond Creek Rd (SR323), turn left on to US 11 and drive 1/5th mile to the farm entrance which is on your left. [Store Hrs, 8:30a-5p, all year. Farm walking tours: M-Sa, weather permitting, subject to change. ☎ toll free 877-862-4332, 865-458-9192].

Exit 60-Lost Sea: Seven miles (11.3km) to the east of I-75 (91/2 minutes along Route 68) lies North America's largest underground lake–the *"Lost Sea"*–4.5 acres of water deep within the Craighead Caverns.

As you glide across the mirror lake in the dimly lit cavern, unusual rock formations, limestone deposits and strange cave flowers heighten the mystery; through the glass bottomed boat, speckled trout can be seen in the crystal clear water below.

During the Civil War, the caves were a source of saltpeter for gunpowder. Close your eyes and imagine smoky lanterns casting their flickering shadows on the cavern walls as Confederate soldiers swing their pickaxes. Listen to the ring of metal against stone. These are spooky surroundings.

If you decide to tour the caves, dress warmly

because below ground, the air is a constant 58 degrees summer or winter. Also wear solid shoes–the tour includes a walk of about 3/4 mile. [Daily Hrs. Summer, 9a-8p, Winter, 9a-5p; Adult/Child- $12.00/$5.50;
☎ 423-337-6616.

Exit 52-"The World's Best Ice Cream: It's that time again...the time when for you, dear reader, I must sit down in front of a table covered with cups of different flavored ice-creams, to sample them and ensure that Mayfield Dairy is still churning out (pun intended) what Time Magazine reported as the *"World's Best Ice Cream."*

So once again, I leave I-75 at Tennessee's exit 52 (Mt. Verd Road) and follow route 305 eastwards for 4.3 miles (6.9 km) through pleasant countryside towards Athens, TN.

Mayfield Dairy is well marked on the left side of the road, you can't miss the big round brown and yellow billboard at Mayfield Lane stating:

"Mayfield Dairy Farms–Home of the World's Best Ice Cream."

As usual, I head right for the Ice Cream Parlor to interview Chad and the Mayfield counter staff...and sample the wares.

There's a new Mayfield product this year-*"Snowcream"*-old fashioned vanilla. Reminiscent of drinks we used to make as children by flavoring freshly fallen snow, Snowcream is light, with very few carbohydrates. Made with frozen milk, sugar and flavoring, it's very refreshing.

While on a low-carb kick, I also tried the new *Vanilla-Chocolate*, *Butter Pecan* and *Neapolitan* ice-creams. Love them all!

It's now time to cleanse my palate with a sip of water, and check out some new flavors - *Jamocha* (coffee flavor with a rich swirl of dark chocolate fudge). Surprisingly it tastes more like chocolate to begin with and then you get a burst of coffee on your tongue - delightful.

Somebody has to do it!

Luckily, I left room to try the new *Caramel Popcorn* ice-cream-popcorn base flavor with a dulce caramel swirl and dark chocolate chunks-delicious...and for the new *Cream Bar (Orange Sherbet)* treat.

I was going to try some of my favorites from last year–Brown Cow (vanilla dipped in chocolate), Cherry Brown Cow, Mint Brown Cow and Peanut Butter Brown Cow but Kathy decided that I'd had enough (calories) for one day. Besides, we are going to be reviewing a BBQ rib restaurant in another couple of hours, and I want to be at my best!

You too can have a Mayfield Dairy tasting experience. The ice cream parlor is open year round: M-F, 9-5, Sa, 9-2p, closed Su & major holidays. Ice cream prices are very reasonable, starting at $1 for a single scoop & $2 for a double.

Plant tours are held Monday to Saturdays, every half-hour. The last tour is 1 hour before closing time. Admission is free; comfortable slip-resistant shoes are recommended for the plant tour. Further information?
☎ 423-745-2151 or 1-800-629-3435.

Mile 44-Electronic Fog Detection & Warning System: You are about to enter a "high-tech" portion of the freeway. Born out of tragedy–the Hiwassee River Valley electronic Fog Detection and Warning system.

Man-made fog is a frequent problem on this five mile section, caused primarily by industry east of here–and it can be deadly.

Since the opening of this stretch of highway in 1973, there have been 18 fatalities and 130 injuries in more than 200 fog related crashes. In December, 1990, a terrible traffic accident of massive proportions was caused by fog rapidly enveloping I-75. On the southbound downgrade towards the River, 83 cars and trucks piled into one another. The end result? Thirteen killed and 50 injured.

This tragedy provided the impetus needed to deal with this deadly section, and the fog advisory system was born. The Fog Detection and Warning system uses eight fog sensors and 44 speed detectors to constantly monitor visibility and traffic flow. In the same manner as an optical smoke detector, the fog sensors measure the clarity of the air between its detection cells–if you look closely you will

HIWASSEE RIVER - *Cherokee Indian word meaning "meadow."*

CHATTANOOGA - *a Cree Indian word meaning "rock rising to a point" (Lookout Mountain).*

see the two arms of the sensors on some of the roadside poles.

Data from the monitors are relayed to a central computer at the Highway Patrol office where it is analyzed and translated into messages displayed on the overhead electronic signs. If it senses heavy fog, the system can even activate barriers at six I-75 entry ramps, closing off the fog shrouded freeway to traffic.

Since installation in late 1993, there have been no fog related accidents or fatalities in this area.

Mile 42-Spanish Explorers: And now for a change of pace. In May, 1539, the Governor of Cuba, Don Hernando de Soto landed in Tampa and started an extensive exploration of North America with an army of 600 men.

For more than four years, he traveled over 4,000 miles while searching for gold and silver–and a north passage to China. Ranging up the US mainland through Georgia, he led his army into the Carolinas, Tennessee–and as far away as modern Chicago, until he turned southward through Missouri and into Arkansas where he died in 1542.

Extensive journals were kept documenting his exploration. Since most of the Indian sites mentioned are known today and many modern roads are built over early Indian trails, the track taken by his expedition is well known. The path of I-75 crosses the path of de Soto's army in two places–Athens, TN & Perry, GA.

From his journals for May, 1540, we know that while in Tennessee he spent a night at Madisonville. The next day an Indian chief visited him and led him to Athens. Here he was joined by a scouting party he had sent up the Tennessee Valley towards Knoxville, where they discovered Indian mines.

He and his army then traveled to, and camped on, Hiwassee Island, at the confluence of the Hiwassee & Tennessee Rivers. Examination of the terrain indicates that he would have crossed the modern path of I-75 in the vicinity of this mile marker.

Mile 18-Radar Alert: Be careful here in case the traffic ahead of you suddenly brakes! The interstate runs downhill and gently curves to the left–trees line the median.

At the bottom of the hill an emergency vehicle path cuts through the trees between the south and northbound I-75 lanes, and the police love to hide here with radar beamed up the hill. Cars cannot see them until they are right on top of the trap and speeders violently brake to avoid getting caught. Watch the traffic ahead of you as you descend this hill. We don't want you to rear-end a speeder.

Exit 27-Paul Huff Pkwy: Tennessee sure has its fair share of Medal of Honor winners.

Infantryman and Cleveland resident Cpl. Paul Huff was awarded the Medal for intrepid leadership and daring combat skills during the US attack on Carano, Italy, in 1944.

Exit 4-Tennessee Valley Railroad: As a kid, I loved the smell and noise of steam locomotives as they chugged their way through the countryside. Now you can experience it (again...if you are over 40 years old!) with a ride on the Tennessee Valley Railroad.

You board your coach *(see* **Insider Tip***)* at the Grand Junction Station where your locomotive–Southern Railway #4501, old Central Georgia #349 or perhaps Engines #610 or #630–waits to follow the Civil War track of the Tennessee & Georgia Railroad; once a vital supply link, first for the Confederacy and then for the Union as the tides of war shifted.

You can sense the Civil War atmosphere as the train winds through the Chattanooga country and plunges into the darkness of the 1858 Missionary Ridge tunnel, on its way to the East Chattanooga Terminus where the locomotive is turned around on the turn table ready for the trip back again.

Afterwards,

View from the cab as we head into the tunnel

Insider Tip - Ride in the Cab

Psst! If you are planning to ride the TN Valley Railroad, few know you can ride up front in the cab with the engineer. It costs $10 extra but is well worth it. Phone ahead to makes sure cab space is available–there are only two spaces per trip.

Insider Tip - Famous Dave's

With a name like this, I just had to try it. We arrived around 7pm, so had to wait with a paging unit (they wouldn't let me go to the front of the list when I told them my name was Dave, too) but sitting outside chatting with local folk until the pager's lights started flashing, was just fine.

The wait was definitely worth it. The pit BBQ food (ribs, steaks, etc) was well prepared and very tender; our server's name was also Dave, so table service was excellent too!

We later found that Famous Dave's has several branches along I-75 (KY, exit 182 and TN, exit 378). We visited the Chattanooga location at exit 5. Go east from the exit for 1/2 mile (.8km); turn right at the Gunbarrel Rd traffic lights and drive for 1/2 mile. FamousDave's is on your right at 2122 Gunbarrel.

Hrs, Su-Th, 11a-10p; Fr & Sa, 11a-11p; closed Sun. ☎ 423-954-3227

enjoy the audio-visual show and railroad exhibits, visit the repair shop or browse the gift store.

Grand Junction Station is 3.8 miles (6.1km) from I-75, take exit 4 (Chickamauga Dam) and follow Rt153N to the fourth (Jersey Pike) exit. Turn left and follow the "TVRM" signs to Cromwell Rd. [Hrs, M-Sa, 10am-5pm; Su, 11:30am-5pm; Adult/Child, $12.50/$6.50; ☎ 423-894-8028].

Old Number 349

Exit 2-Chattanooga: *(see map on page 56).* Many people bypass Chattanooga because it seems such a long trek to the west of I-75, but a <u>9 minute trip</u> along I-24 will get you to the area attractions. It's a scenic and interesting drive as the excellent freeway winds down the face of historic Missionary Ridge.

The Interstate physically separates Chattanooga's two tourist areas. As you approach Chattanooga, the ***Lookout Mountain/St. Elmo area*** is on your left, and ***Downtown Tourist area*** is to your right. Let me quickly summarize the driving directions and attractions for you and then we will go back and visit several in more detail.

I-24 exit 178-Lookout Mtn/St. Elmo: follow the sign for <u>Lookout Mountain</u>–turn left on to Broad St–pass back under I-24–follow the enlarged section on my map on page 56.

<u>Attractions:</u> On the mountain–Rock City, Ruby Falls, Battle for Chattanooga Museum and Point Park. You need to drive to the first two; I suggest you take a ride up the Incline Railway from its St. Elmo station and at the top, walk the 2 blocks along to the museum and park–the view over Chattanooga with the river winding around, is spectacular.

I-24 exit 178-Downtown: Downtown Chattanooga is based on a square grid pattern so it's very easy to navigate–just watch for one-way signs. Use the distinctive Aquarium building (brown angular building with glass triangles on top) as your area landmark.

To reach it, take I-24, exit 178 and take the first ramp on your right following signs for Downtown/Market Street. Drive along Market Street, past the Chattanooga Choo Choo Holiday Inn *(see* **Insider Tip**) until you see the *Tennessee Aquarium* with the *Visitors Center* in the building to its right. There is lots of parking ahead or to your left. Stop at the Visitors Center for one of their excellent maps.

<u>Attractions:</u> TN Aquarium, Imax 3D Theater (incredible!!!), Regional History Museum, Creative Discovery Museum, Tow & Recovery Hall of Fame, "Southern Belle" Riverboat, African-American Museum, Houston Museum, Hunter Museum of American Art, Medal of Honor Museum and...Candyland.

To me, the whole of the downtown area is now an attraction–with easy parking, great

Insider Tip - Sticky Fingers

One of my favorite restaurant, *Sticky Fingers* in downtown Chattanooga, has opened a branch here just south of Hamilton Place. If you enjoy ribs, you'll understand its name although they serve many other entrees as well. Enjoy!

Take exit 5 and go east to the first traffic light. Turn right and drive past Best Buy and to the right around Hamilton Place. Hrs, Su-Th, 11a-10p; Fr & Sa, 11a-11p ☎ 423-899-7427

restaurants and shops, and excellent sidewalks for walking–downtown Chattanooga has experienced a renaissance and grown into a wonderfully interesting place for visitors. Now let me share a few specifics with you:

Tennessee Aquarium: Gone are the days of dark, dank rooms with small thick glass apertures separating fish and viewer. The Tennessee Aquarium is a "4th generation facility," an aquarium which tells a story as you wander through its thematic galleries.

You ride to the top of the building and start your self-guided tour by following the flow of the Tennessee River, from its beginnings in the Appalachians down into the great Mississippi and onward towards the salt waters of the Gulf of Mexico. Fabulous vistas of birds, animal and marine life accompany your journey as you descend through the aquarium building.

First, the Appalachian Cove Forest with its dripping rocks, ferns, moss covered trees, mountain streams and otter pool. Then to the Tennessee River Gallery where you examine (above and below water) the huge *"Nickajack"* and *"Reelfoot"* lakes. *"Discovery Falls"* takes you through an interactive educational gallery where children (and adults) may examine various specimens at close range. And finally, on to the *Mississippi Delta*–a recreated cypress swamp where

Insider Tip - a Private Parlor Car for the Night

How would you like to spend a night in your own private railroad Parlor car? All this is possible at the 1909 Chattanooga Railroad Terminus, now operated by Holiday Inn. Several Victorian platforms have been retained an waiting at each, personal Parlor Sleeping cars await lucky guests. Each is well appointed with a large bedroom (including TV & phone), and a separate toilet/shower compartment. And before you ask, yes, it's OK to flush while the train is standing in the station–the cars are permanently attached to the hotel's plumbing system. After spending a night in Car 764, I can appreciate what a magnificent life style the railroad barons of the 19th century lived! Call ahead to ensure a car is available for you–they are very popular.

Our personal luxury Parlor Car

As darkness settled, I sat under a flickering gas lamp on the old platform reflecting upon a wonderful evening dining in the station's restaurant. I'm sure I sensed the rustle of petticoats as ghostly passengers swished by–and then I heard what I'd been waiting for, *"Pardon me boy, is this the Cincinnati Choo Choo?"* Was it the wine? I knew it was time to climb the iron steps up into my mahogany furnished sleeping car–and go to bed.

. . . and so to bed

The Holiday Inn Chattanooga Choo Choo is just north of I-24 (exit 178), at 1400 Market St *(see map page 56)*. A free shuttle operates between the hotel and downtown; you can be at the Aquarium and other Chattanooga attractions in less than 5 minutes. If you are traveling with children the "Choo Choo" is an experience they will never forget. ☎ 423-266-5000 or 1-800-872-2529

People often stop and ask us what's inside the Parlor Car. Here's a plan for you. . .

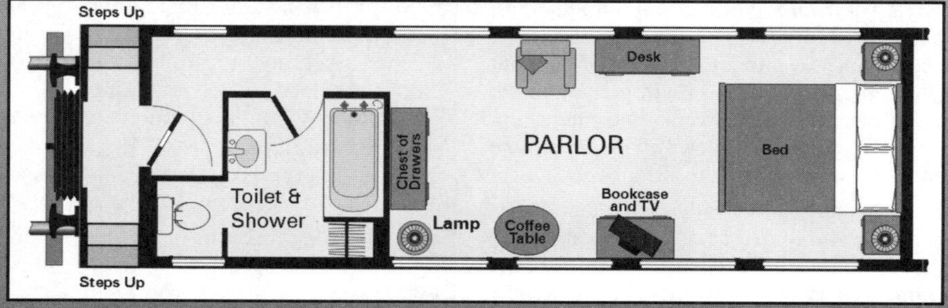

A misty Tennessee valley and full-size waterfall recreated in one of the Aquarium galleries

snakes, alligators and other fearsome reptiles live–and the *Gulf of Mexico*, the aquarium's only salt water tank.

[Hrs, May 1-Labor Day: M-Th, 9-6; F-Su, 9-8, Rest of year; 10-6 daily; Adult/Child-$14/$7.50–children under 3yrs are free].

The Aquarium also operates an IMAX 3D theater showing nature oriented films with images that leap off the screen.

[Tickets $7.75/$5.25. Combination aquarium & theater are also available at $18/$10.50. ☎ 800-262-0695 or 423-265-0695].

Chattanooga and the Old Dixie Highway: While visiting the excellent Regional History Museum (4th & Chestnut Sts), I was fascinated to discover that the famous Dixie Highway–the route all snowbirds used before I-75 was built, was actually started as an initiative of the Chattanooga Auto Club (now part of the AAA). In 1915, the Club organized a meeting of the governors of seven states to discuss the possibility of creating a north-south route, and the Dixie Highway was born.

Each section was financed by local communities along the way and this led to some problems–but by 1927, most of the route from Detroit to Miami had been opened. Red & white "DH" signs nailed to telephone and telegraph poles along the way, marked the route since in those early days, there were no route numbers. The Chattanooga Regional History Museum is open, M-F, 10-4:30; Sa-Sun, 11-4:30. ☎ 423-265-3247].

DH

Chattanooga and Coca-Cola: As we head towards the Georgia border, I have to remind Kathy that we will soon be entering "Coca-Cola Country." She is such a Pepsi fan, she's liable to ask for diet Pepsi in the *"World of Coca-Cola"* museum in Atlanta! But Coca-Cola is so strongly identified with Georgia that in days gone, the State's welcome centers handed out free Coca-Colas to greet tourists.

However, if it hadn't been for two Chattanooga business men, you might never have heard of this drink! For it was here that changes were made to the marketing of the beverage which helped Coca-Cola change from being a local soda fountain drink, to the huge international success it is today.

In 1899, Benjamin Thomas and Joseph Whitehead sat in the Atlanta office of Coca-Cola owner, Asa Chandler, explaining how they would like to take the drink and sell the brown liquid in little green straight-sided bottles. Chandler laughed and said it would never work. He was convinced that Coca-Cola's future lay in drug store soda fountain sales, so–he sold the two men the rights to bottle and distribute Coca-Cola within the USA, for $1!

Thomas and Whitehead set up the first bottling plant in Chattanooga on the ground floor of a pool hall, and the rest is history.

"Cincy Choo Choo"

Remember when we were driving in Ohio and I was singing, *"Pardon me boy, is this the Cincinnati Choo Choo?* Well, here's the story I promised.

The famous train actually ran between the termini in Chattanooga and the Queen City–so there's no point in being at the Pennsylvania Station at a quarter to four. It won't be there! According to an historical marker at the Chattanooga Railroad Terminal,

"On March 5, 1880, the first passenger train leaving for Cincinnati was called the "Chattanooga Choo Choo. This historical occasion opened the first major link in public transportation from the North to the South. "Choo Choo" was operated by the Cincinnati Southern Railroad."

Don't you just love historical markers?

Bottling a soda to increase sales may sound like basic common sense today, but in the late 1800's it was a novel approach for a soda fountain drink. Soon, the Chattanooga group sold bottling franchises to other businessmen across the Nation, became rich beyond their wildest dream–and Coca-Cola was on its way to become a national and then international, success. The original bottling plant (just opposite the Aquarium at the corners of 2nd and Broad) is currently under renovation to become a museum, with boutiques and restaurants.

RC Cola and Moonpie: a final Chattanooga thought I cannot resist before we leave.

Moonpies, a combination of rich, sugary chocolate covered marshmallow on a round graham cookie were created by the Chattanooga Bakery in 1917 and have been a strong Chattanooga favorite ever since.

Royal Crown Cola, cool & sweet, more affectionately known as RC Cola or just RC, has also been around the South for many years.

Both came together as a combo strongly identified with the southern middle-class lifestyle through song and word in the 1950s. As one old-timer said, *"RC and moonpie are as southern as grits and chicken-fried steak."*

St. Elmo and Lookout Mountain: *(see map on page 56)*. On the other side of I-24 rises Lookout Mountain, peaking at 2,391 feet. On the mountain you'll find other Chattanooga attractions–Battle of Chattanooga Museum, Incline Railway, Ruby Falls and Rock City. The drive up the mountain *(see map)* to the Point Park at the top is well worth the effort.

Exit 1-East Town Antiques: Just to the west of this exit (behind the Cracker Barrel) is an interesting mall of eight antique shops, including a rare and used book store.

Mile 1- (N/bound)-Welcome Center: Sad news for northbound travelers. At press time, the TDOT has decided to closed the Welcome Center for much needed renovations. It's scheduled to re-open in late summer, 2005. I've also heard that the McMinn Rest Area at mile marker 45 will be closed for the same time period. in 2005, it's going to be a long 160 miles to the next stop (in Kentucky at mile 1). Better find a McDonalds!

Money Saving Tip

Fill up with gas as soon as you can–even if you only need a 1/4 of a tank. Georgia still has the cheapest gasoline in the USA.

GEORGIA- Mile 352-Welcome Center: One of my very favorite stops is to pull in here and chat with my friends–and find out what's new in Georgia. Teresa and Janice have been sharing their knowledge with me since I started to write *"Along I-75"* in 1992–we actually met in Tampa but that's another story. Betty, Donna, Jane, Jean and Linda have also become special I-75 friends over the years. Betty always bakes cookies for me if she knows we are coming. Please say *"hi"* to them for me.

Exit 350-Georgia Wine Tasting: A new winery center is being built just west of this exit., providing tours and tastings. Planned opening is winter, 2005. ☎ 706-931-2851

Exit 350-KOA: Those who have used this convenient RV park before will be interested to know that it's under new ownership. A new shower, laundry and utility building is under construction and should be completed soon.

Exit 350-Firing Pits: In 1898, America went to war with Spain and one of the conflict's theaters was Cuba, with its protecting Spanish army of almost 200,000 men. At the time, US army strength was 26,000 but a Mobilization Act called for a further 125,000 volunteers who of course, needed training.

Many volunteers came from the Southeast, and to the west of I-75, down the hill just behind the Racetrac gas station are the target

Money Saving Tip

Pickup your <u>free copies</u> of the green Traveler Discount Guide and the red Market America motel coupon books at the Georgia Welcome Center (mile 352). Coupons in these books can <u>save you as much as 45%</u> off of regular motel rates.

GEORGIA - *in honor of King George II of England, by early explorer James Oglethorpe who received a Royal Charter in 1733, to settle the area.*

RINGGOLD - *in memory of Samuel Ringgold, professional soldier and Indian fighter who died of wounds received in action during the Mexican War, 1846.*

War Between the States - the Ringgold Gap

Special Report

There is much history just to the east of I-75 in Ringgold, so let's leave the freeway for a while and drive the 5.2 miles (8.4km) through the town and the Gap where the Battle of Ringgold took place, until we rejoin the freeway at exit 345. Because of a narrow bridge with an 11' 7" height restriction, this sidetrip is not suitable for large RVs.

Exit 348 - at the bottom of the s/bound ramp, turn left to cross the interstate bridge heading east. On the bridge, look south at the Ringgold Gap. It was on the sides of these hills in November, 1863, that Gen. Cleyburne's 4,100 men stopped the 12,000 Union soldiers of "Fighting Joe" Hooker long enough to allow the Confederate forces under General Bragg to reorganize at Dalton. Although this battle only lasted six hours, hostilities did not recommence until 6 May, 1864, when south of Ringgold Gen. Sherman gave his famous orders to *"Advance on Atlanta."*

For the next .6 mile (10km) we are driving east along the old Alabama Road used by Andrew Jackson as a supply route in his war against the Creek Indians. Pass "Aunt Effie's" *(see* **Insider Tip***)* on your right and turn right at the next set of traffic lights, on to Nashville St, or US41S.

Drive south on US41 towards Ringgold for .7 miles (1.1km), you will cross Maple Street and enter the main street area of Ringgold. Imagine the street scene on the night of Nov 27, 1863 the town was occupied with the thousands of Union troops who had not been able to get through the Gap during the day's battle.

Two tenths of a mile (.3 km) further on is the Train Depot where Generals Grant, Sherman and Hooker rested their maps on barrels on the porch and planned their next moves. After the battle they attempted to blow it up but were only successful in destroying the roof.

Just beyond the Depot is the narrow railway bridge. Drive through it following US41. Half a mile (.8km) is a small park on your right, commemorating the battle.

Continue driving for 1.8 miles (2.9km) until you reach the Stone Church at the junction of US41 and GA Route 2. Built in 1850, the Confederates used it as a hospital during the battle. You can still see blood stains on the floor and teeth marks on the benches, which date from its founding.

After leaving the Church, continue along US41 for a mile (1.6km). where you will rejoin I-75 at exit 345.

pits used for live ammunition training exercises. Apparently, a great place for those with metal detectors.

Exit 348-Ringgold & the Great Locomotive Chase: *(see Special Report on page 117, side trip maps on page 59, Bartow Co. map on page 58, and detailed 25 mile maps between exit 348 and exit 273)*. One of the best known adventures of the Civil War–made even more famous by a Walt Disney movie, *"The Great Locomotive Chase,"* starring Fess Parker, and Buster Keaton's classic of the Silent era, The General–was exactly that–an epic chase where a steam locomotive stolen by Union soldiers, was chased through the Georgia countryside by its Southern crew, who used their feet, a push car, and three other locomotives before they successfully recaptured their errant ward.

But best of all, the route of this chase from Kennesaw in the south, to Ringgold in the north, criss-crossed the path of the modern I-75 as it winds its way from the Tennessee-Georgia border towards Atlanta. We have

Insider Tip - Aunt Effie's

Just a few blocks east of exit 348 is Aunt Effie's Restaurant, a very popular favorite with the locals. Serving Southern and American meals, it can be noisy and crowded at times but definitely a good place to meet the folk from Ringgold.
Hrs, M-F, 11a-8p, Su, 11a-3p closed Sat.
☎ 706-935-6525

Insider Tip - Wingate

As you approach exit 333 from the north, you will see several inns to your right on a side road. There are some excellent lodging bargains here.

Our favorite is the Wingate, with the largest, most tastefully decorated rooms in town. Their coupon book rate of $59 includes an excellent breakfast and morning newspaper. ☎ 706-272-9099

mapped this chase alongside the modern interstate for you on southbound map pages 31 to 34 & northbound map pages 164 to 167.

Exit 341-Tunnel Hill: *(map with details on page 59)*. The famous 1850 railroad tunnel at Tunnel Hill played a very significant role in the Civil War's Great Locomotive Chase *(see page 117)* and in General Sherman's 1864 Atlanta Campaign.

Across the field, the Clisby-Austin House is also a special Civil War site. It was used as a hospital during the war and later, as General Sherman's HQ during his campaign against Atlanta. After General John Hood lost his leg at the battle of Chickamauga, he and the limb were transferred to the House; the leg was buried in a nearby cemetery.

During last Summer, the Dalton Visitors Center moved into the old General Store across the road from the new Tunnel Hill Heritage Center Museum, which is now operated by the Visitor Center staff.

Mile 339-Battle of Rocky Face Ridge: Ahead of you looms the craggy heights of Rocky Face Ridge, shielding the strategic town of Dalton behind. Here, for eight days starting on May 7th, 1864, Confederate General Joseph Johnston held off General Sherman's Army of the Ohio, under the command of Major General Schofield. The Rebs were well entrenched along the ridge (known locally as "Buzzards Roost") and as you can see, the terrain was very difficult for the attacking forces. In places, the men could only advance along its precipitous paths in single file; General Sherman described this gap as "the door of death."

While General Schofield pursued his attack, Sherman decided to outflank the Confederates and sever the railroad further south. On May 9th, he sent his Army of the Tennessee to the west through Snake Creek Gap and down towards the sleepy town of Resaca (mile marker 320). On May 11th, realizing the assault on the Ridge was impossible, Sherman left a token attacking force and fol-

continued on page 119

Insider Tip
Flammini's - An Italian Family Dining Experience

Have you ever been to an Italian family feast–one where everybody knows everybody, people wander around and talk to people at other tables, everybody is happy, smiling and laughing. Well, *Flammini's* Cafe Italia in Dalton is just like that. Even if you are far from home, the minute you poke your head through the door and past all the family photos, you are made warmly welcome by owner Pete, or perhaps his mother, Pat. You know you are going to have a wonderfully, enjoyable evening among new friends. Tiny lights twinkle throughout the dining area, and everybody–from the staff to the patrons is obviously having a good time.

The Flammini's are from the Marche region of Italy near the Adriatic Sea, and serve traditional foods from the small towns in the region. After our tasty main course of Veal Marsala (veal sauteed in marsala wine with mushrooms) and capellini (angel hair) pasta, Pat Flammini insisted that I sample a taste of traditional Tirami Su dessert (ladyfingers, soaked in rum, layered with mascarpone cheese and coffee whipped cream)–it's to die for! Incidentally, the Flammini's haven't forgotten those with dietary concerns, and offer a number of light and children's' meals. Buon Appetito.

Flammini's Cafe Italia is at 1205 W. Walnut Ave, Dalton. To find it, take exit 333 and drive east along Walnut Avenue, through the lights at Tibbs Road–look for the yellow sign with black writing on your right–7/10ths of a mile from I-75. ☎ 706-226-0667
Hours: Mon-Sat, 5pm-10pm. Closed Sunday.

DALTON - *in honor of Tristram Dalton (politician & Senator from Maine), whose grandson was the engineer who laid out the town and donated land.*

War Between the States - The Great Locomotive Chase

During the Civil War, the Western & Atlantic railway line between Chattanooga and Atlanta was of great importance to the Confederacy, moving freight and soldiers between these two important railway centers. This vital link was a single track railway with passing tracks at various stations along the route. Kentuckian James Andrews, a Federal spy, devised a plan to steal a train near Atlanta and destroy the track and bridges along this line as he traveled northward. Andrew's tiny band of Union soldiers became known as Andrew's Raiders, and the subsequent actions of Saturday, April 12, 1862–the "Great Locomotive Chase."

Note: This Special Report tells the story of the chase from the theft of the "General" at Big Shanty (Kennesaw–exit 273) to its conclusion at Ringgold (exit 348). The chase therefore ran from south to north. If southbound on I-75, I suggest you read this report first so you understand the significance of the various locations as you run south towards Kennesaw. The entire adventure is shown on the I-75 map pages covering the exits mentioned above, supported by special sidetrip maps on pages 58 and 59. Numbers in the report refer to the locations marked on the maps–numbers in circles represent Andrew's Raiders (Union) actions; numbers in squares represent Fuller's (Confederate) actions.

1. 5:30 a.m.–on a wet, rainy day, James Andrews and 23 Union soldiers from Ohio ride from Marietta to Big Shanty (Kennesaw) as passengers on a northbound train pulled by the locomotive, *General*. William Fuller is the train's conductor
2. 6:00 a.m.–while the train stops for breakfast at Big Shanty, Andrews' Raiders capture the *General* and with three box-cars, head north towards Chattanooga. Andrews and two men ride the locomotive while the rest of the armed band are hidden inside the box-cars.
3. 6:10 a.m.–Fuller, disturbed at breakfast and believing that Confederate conscripts had stolen his train to get clear of Big Shanty's army camp and would shortly abandon it, decides to give chase on foot. The General's engineer, Jeff Cain and a railroad engineering foreman, Anthony Murphy run with him.
4. The *General* runs out of steam a few miles up the track from Big Shanty. Andrews did not realize that the boiler dampers had been closed while the crew were at breakfast. The dampers were quickly opened and fires re-stoked with oil-soaked wood while the Raiders cut trackside telegraph wires to prevent "intercept" messages going north.

   After a quick run north, the *General* arrives at Moon's Station, and the Raiders "borrow" an iron bar from a track repair crew. The Raiders intend to remove rail sections behind them to halt pursuit, but later find the bar is inadequate for the task.
5. A breathless Fuller and companions arrive at Moon's Station, and take a *pole-car*. The three continue their pursuit by poling the car northward at 7-8 mph.
6. After passing through Acworth Station, the Raiders stop and cut more telegraph wires and damage a rail section.
7. The *General* halts just below Allatoona to cut telegraph wires.
8. Andrews sees the *Yonah*, a work locomotive belonging to the Cooper Iron Works on the north banks of the Etowah River, with steam up. He is concerned since he knows that if a pursuit message gets this far north, there is now an operational locomotive and armed crew, to give chase. He does not stop since destroying the Etowah Bridge would not fill a purpose now.
9. The *General* pulls up at Cass Station (near Cartersville). Andrews convinces a suspicious railway worker that he is carrying much needed gunpowder north to the Confederate Army. The patriotic worker gives Andrews his only railway schedule so that Andrews can plan his northbound run to meet and pass southbound trains at appropriate stations.
10. The Raiders pull into Kingston Station, a major passing point on the railroad. Here they wait for a southbound train but when it finally arrives, they find that there are two unscheduled southbounds on the same track section. The Raiders are forced to wait until the next section of track is clear.

In the meantime, the station personnel are getting very suspicious of the northbound "gunpowder" train.

11. Fuller cannot stop the pole-car in time and it runs off the track at the broken rail section, dumping the crew and car down an embankment. Uninjured, they carry the car back up and resume the chase. After an epic pole-car journey of 20 miles, Fuller and crew arrive at the Etowah River and commandeer the *Yonah*.

12. After a wait of more than an hour, the *General* pulls out of Kingston to continue its northbound journey, just eight minutes before the arrival of Fuller aboard the *Yonah*. Andrews is now aware that pursuit is close since he has heard the frantic whistle of the *Yonah* as it approaches Kingston.

13. Fuller cannot get past the southbound trains so once again, he and his companions take to foot, running across the Kingston railroad yards to commandeer another locomotive, the *William R. Smith*. They give chase northwards alongside Hall Station Road towards Adairsville Station. To warn of obstructions, Fuller hangs onto the locomotive's cowcatcher while scanning the track ahead.

14. Aware that a chase is now on hand, the Raiders stop to cut wires and pile railroad ties across the track as a delaying tactic.

15. Several miles further, the Raiders stop to remove a rail section but find that their crowbar is too small to easily pull the spikes. By brute strength, the men manage to bend and snap a rail and throw it in the bushes.

16. Feeling safe once more, the Raiders pull into Adairsville Station where they find a long southbound train pulled by the locomotive, *Texas*. The suspicious engineer refuses to pull his train forward to clear the north switch of the passing track. After another delay, Andrews manages to convince the driver, and tries to send him southbound to either collide with their pursuers or derail on the broken section.

17. The *William R. Smith* is stopped in time to avoid being derailed by the missing section of rail. Fuller and company take off on foot for the third time, running up the track where they manage to flag down the southbound train pulled by the *Texas*.

18. They hear the engineer's story and commandeer the *Texas* for their chase–running in reverse. As they pass through Adairsville, Fuller, without stopping the train, uncouples the cars, runs ahead, turns the switch to a side track diverting the cars into it, returns the switch for the mainline movement, jumps back on board the *Texas* and the pursuit continues unencumbered by the weight of the cars.

19. The Raiders hear the whistle of the *Texas* to the south. They create as high a head of steam as possible by burning wood soaked in oil. The *General* careens up the railroad, leaning out and almost toppling on the curves.

20. The *General* and the last train southbound from Chattanooga pass at Calhoun Station without incident.

21. As the *Texas* steams through Calhoun a few minutes behind the General, Fuller spots a 13 year old telegraph boy, and grabs him onto the moving train. He writes a telegram to the Confederate commander in Chattanooga.

22. Desperately, the Raiders stop and attempt to remove a rail section but are only able to bend it slightly out of shape. They also cut the telegraph wire. They quickly scramble back on board when they see their pursuer for the first time–the reversed *Texas* with a full head of steam charging in their direction.

23. The *Texas* miraculously rides right over the damaged rail section.

24. Around a curve and out of sight, the Raiders uncouple a box car and let it run down a grade onto Fuller, who reverses his direction of travel to "catch" the box-car. He couples it to the *Texas'* tender and resumes the chase with the box car leading.

25. The Raiders do not have time to burn and destroy the covered Oostanaula River Bridge (a major target) so drop the second box-car in its center span hoping to slow down the pursuers. As before, the Fuller "catches" the box-car, couples it and later drops them both at a siding near Resaca Station.

26. A mile north of Resaca Station, Andrews cuts the Calhoun-Dalton telegraph wire and piles ties across the track.

27. The tactic of dropping railroad ties onto the track works to delay the *Texas*. Each time, the engineer must throw the locomotive into full reverse, skid to a halt while Fuller and his men jump down, clear the track and start on their way again. Seeing this, Andrews decided to punch a hole through the rear wall of the remaining box-car, and drop a succession of ties on the track behind him.

28. Aware their pursuers are close again, the Raiders stop to cut wires and pile railroad ties across the track as a delaying tactic. Just south of Green's Station (Tilton), the Raiders stop again and attempt to remove a rail. They can only pry it out of shape, however. Andrews puts another rail underneath the bent rail, to try and derail the fast approaching *Texas*.

29. Thinking the damaged rail will have stopped the pursuit, a mile north of Tilton, Andrews' Raiders stop to take on much needed wood and water, but have to cut this short when they hear the whistle from the fast approaching *Texas* again. For the second time that day, the *Texas* has managed to run over damaged railway track without derailing.

30. After two more miles, the *General* stops again. Telegraph wires are cut and the track obstructed.

31. The Raiders decide to speed through Dalton, a major Confederate camp. A mile north of Dalton, they stop to cut the telegraph wire to stop messages getting through but they are unaware that minutes behind them, Fuller has dropped off the boy telegraph operator, who manages to get a portion of the message through to Chattanooga.

32. A few miles ahead is the Tunnel Hill railroad tunnel, and the Raiders discuss whether to ambush the *Texas* or perhaps travel through the tunnel and then reverse the *General* locomotive back towards the pursuing *Texas* for a collision. They decide to speed on northwards.

33. The *Texas* approaches the smoke filled tunnel. They cannot see ahead and are aware of what the Raiders might plan. Fuller decides to plunge into the tunnel's darkness at full speed, regardless of safety.

34. To their horror, Andrews looks back and sees the *Texas* emerge from the tunnel hard on their heels. They are approaching a covered wooden bridge across the Chickamauga River so he orders the last box car set on fire and then uncoupled in the middle of the bridge. Wet wood and the driving rain of the hour prevents this last attempt to escape, from working.

35. After a frantic dash through Ringgold, the Raiders are out of wood and oil and the *General* is slowing down. Andrews orders his men to jump from the train and find their own ways back to Union lines.

The mission failed because of the dogged pursuit by the General's conductor, William Fuller. Of the Raiders, sixteen were captured and eight were able to escape back to the safety of the Union. Of the captured men, eight were taken to Atlanta (including James Andrew) where they were hanged. Six were exchanged and two "enlisted" in the Confederate Army. After the war, most of the surviving Raiders were awarded the first Medals of Honor.

continued from page 116

lowed his main army down towards Resaca. Johnston found out about this flanking movement from prisoners a day later, and rapidly pulled his troops from the *"Door of Death"* and retreated to defend the railroad at Resaca.

Exit 333-Carpet Capital of North America: Dalton is the *"Carpet Capital of North America,"* and it all started in the early 1900s with a young farm girl, Catherine Whitener, who supported her family by making tufted bedspreads & scatter rugs at home. Other women joined her and soon Dalton had a booming cottage industry, saving the area from the pangs of the Depression.

In these early days, one of the most popular designs incorporated two colorful peacocks

Insider Tip
Born to Shop, Dalton Style

In case you didn't already know, there's excellent factory outlet shopping–the West Point Pepperill Mall–on the east side of Exit 333. And with great forethought Hampton built an excellent inn within easy walking distance right alongside the mall. So, you can park your car at the inn–shop–go back to your room–shop–go back to your room–shop, etc. Note: a ground floor room might be your best bet. The inn also provides an excellent free breakfast. An outlet shopper's dream come true! ☎ 706-226-4333

The War Between the States - Resaca

Special Report

As you drive through north Georgia, you will pass a number of nearby Civil War battlefields–Chickamauga and Chattanooga's Lookout Mountain. Interstate-75 follows the route of Sherman's march toward Atlanta with its resulting destruction by flame–and you will actually drive through two of the battlefields *(see Resaca map on page 57).*

Imagine the scene–it is May 13,1864. Strung out across the path of the southbound I-75 a few yards south of mile marker 323 is a thin line of young men crouched in hurriedly constructed trenches cut deep into the red Georgian earth. Banks of rubble have been thrown forward to give added protection from the whining Minie balls which zip overhead like angry hornets waiting to administer the sting of death. A fountain of red soil suddenly shoots skyward in front of them, followed by the vibration of the ground shock wave and deep crumping sound of a distant explosion. A Confederate field gun is ranging in on their position.

Sweltering under the hot Georgian sun in their heavy flannel uniforms of dark blue, they wait their officer's command to rise up and charge over the rough ground toward the wooded rise where they can see the gray hunched shapes of the Confederates behind log spiked palisades. Behind the wooden barriers, the distinctive saltire cross of the red and blue Battle Flag floats lazily overhead.

On closer look, the mud and sweat streaked faces are of very young men–frightened, quietly exchanging comments of bravado in nervous, throat-tightened voices. Many, only in their sixteenth or seventeenth year, will not see nightfall.

Continued top of next page

facing each other. Since the women used to hang the newly made carpets and rugs on lines strung near the old US 41route to Florida, the Dalton section of the *"Dixie Highway"* became known as *"Peacock Alley."*

By the 1950s advances in machinery and dyeing opened the door to the modern carpet industry. The entrepreneurial spirit of the local residents turned the cottage bedspread industry into multi-billion dollar carpet manufacturing. Today, more than 65% of the world's carpets are made in Dalton!

GA-Bert Lance Highway: This section of I-75 is named in honor of Thomas Bertram Lance, a Georgian "native son" who favorite phrase was, *"If it ain't broke, don't fix it."*

Bert was Director of the Georgia State Highway Department during the those years when I-75 was under construction through here. Later, he served under President Carter in Washington as Director of the Office of Management and Budget.

Miles 323 to 319.8-Battle of Resaca: *(see battle map on page 57).* We are just entering the Resaca battlefield, which involved over 171,000 men and boys for three days, in May, 1864. During the construction of this stretch of I-75, in the Fall, 1960, many artifacts were uncovered but unfortunately much of the field's earthworks and trenches which lay in the path of the interstate, were destroyed. Archaeologists were given eleven weeks prior to construction, to excavate the three mile long site–an impossible task.

Last year, we heard that the State has purchased the battlefield lands to the west of I-75 and is funding a park to be developed here, with signs interpreting the events of the day. I'll keep you posted. In the meantime, here's a mile-by-mile account of the battle action:

Mile 322.8-*"Fight for the Cannon"* - just to the left on the hill, the six cannon batteries of the Union's 35th Indiana held the northern boundary of the field. This position was

RESACA- *originally called Dublin by Irish railroad workers, renamed after the Mexican town of Resaca de la Palma, by returning Mexican War veterans.*

OOSTANAULA RIVER - *Cherokee name, "place of the rocks across the stream," for a shallow place to ford.*

They are showing the strain of the Atlanta campaign–many escaped death only a few days earlier facing the same enemy in the battle of Rocky Face Ridge, 14 miles north of here. They were lucky, for they survived and flanked General Johnston's Gray forces who have now retreated southward to make yet another stand here–at Resaca–as the Rebels fall back toward Atlanta's main defense line in a losing war.

These are the men and boys of the General Sherman's 35th Indiana, under the command of Brigadier General Stanley. Little do they know that the Confederates have already spotted a weakness to the left of their line and at 4 o'clock that afternoon, six divisions of General Hood's best Rebs will charge down the slope and drive them from their position. The situation will be saved by the 5th Indiana gunners firing double-shotted canister into the Grays, and the timely arrival of General William's Union Army of the Cumberland, currently positioned a mile to their right.

Before the end of this battle three days later, 5,547 men and boys will have been killed or injured, and the Confederates will have pulled back across the Oostanaula River to make yet another retreating stand at Cassville (just west of I-75 at exit 296, opening the door to Sherman's Union victories at New Hope Church, Kennesaw Mountain–and ultimately, Atlanta.

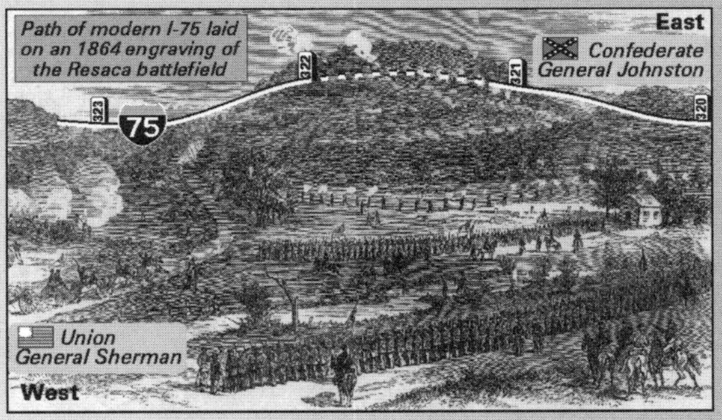

All this action took place across the modern I-75 as you approach Exit 320 *(see page 57).*

attacked by Confederate forces using bayonets; the attack was turned by a relief Union force - Col. Robinson's 20th Corp. which rode across the I-75 path at this point.

Mile 322.2-*"Battle at the Angle"* - a bloody attack by the Union forces of Generals Cox and Judah took place right here on the path of I-75 as they attempted to breach the Confederate defenses of Generals Hood and Hardee.

Mile 322-*Confederate Territory* - although the interstate is running through cuts in the hills, we are now driving across what would have been the Confederate Army of the Tennessee encampments.

Mile 321-*Southern edge of the Confederate Defense line* - here we leave the Confederate high ground and run down towards the "no-man's land" in the valley of Camp Creek. Polk's Confederate Army is to our left and Logan's Union XV Army Corp is to our right.

Exit 320-*Resaca Confederate Cemetery* - nowhere can the atmosphere of that day in 1864 be better felt than at the Confederate Cemetery just a few minutes east of the I-75. The map on page 57 will help you find it.

The first time I visited this site it was dusk and I was by myself. It was lonely yet somehow peaceful–just row upon row of old but tidy graves–in the soft fading light filtered through the leafy boughs of the trees above.

The United Daughters of the Confederacy had recently put tiny flags by many of the tombstones; even 130 years later, the men are still cared for. Imagine the anguish of wives and daughters, of families left behind who didn't know where their men had gone. But we know where they went–their journey ended here.

Exit 320-*The Skeleton at the Exit Ramp* - Several years ago, new research about the battlefield came to light and was published in a book I highly recommend, *"The Battle of Resaca,"* by Philip Secrist (Kennesaw State University). One of the intriguing stories Prof. Secrist recounts is the discovery of a grave by a local Resaca resident, working ahead of the bulldozers grading the land for the exit 320 (south-west quadrant) ramps.

The grave contained a brass-lined tobacco pipe, a few unfired minie-ball cartridges–and a skeleton with an amputated foot. Just above the knee around the femur lay an iron tourniquet buckle. The skeleton was reburied in the Confederate Cemetery.

Mile 320-*Polk/Logan Skirmish Line* - the open muddy land north of the Oostanaula River with small hill fortifications left a very vulnerable section in the Confederate defenses. The Union capitalized on this. After a pounding bombardment by General Logan's artillery (fired from the west and in the direction of the modern I-75), nine Union regiments charged the small hills held by Polk's mainly untried recruit troops.

The Union troops won the positions; Polk counter-attacked several times with little success and the hills were still in Federal hands by nightfall. These hills now posed a major threat to the Confederate's southern flank but Sherman did not grasp this tactical situation and the following day was spent in repairing and improving the hill defenses. Wisely, General Johnston decided to move his forces back across the river that night before the Union forces realized the situation. Thus began the Confederate retreat to Cassville.

Exit 317-New Echota and the Cherokee Nation: Route 225 crosses I-75 here and for very good reasons is known as the *"Trail of Tears"* highway. During the early 1800's, north Georgia was the heart of the sovereign Cherokee Indian Nation. By this time, the Cherokee was one of the most progressive Indian tribe in North America.

In 1821, they became the first American Indians with a written language, invented by *Sequoyah*. New Echota (pronounced "air-chot-er"), the Cherokee national capital, was located just 1/2 mile from here (take exit 317–and follow Rt 225 east for 1 minute). There, a constitutional government with executive, legislative and judicial branches ruled the nation. Once the largest town in this area, New Echota consisted of houses, stores, taverns, a Council house, Supreme Courthouse, and a printing office which published a bilingual newspaper, the *Cherokee Phoenix*.

In 1838, the Cherokee were rounded up at gun point and imprisoned by state and federal armies. Later that year, these peaceful people were forced to what is now Oklahoma. Four thousand Cherokee died on the terrible march west known as the *"Trail of Tears."*

Today, you can visit New Echota where the State of Georgia maintains an excellent museum and seven of the original houses. [Hrs. Tu-Sa, 9-5; Su 2-5:30; Adults/Senior/Child–$3:50/$3/$2:50; ☎ 706-624-1321].

Mile 310-Mercer Air Field: Across the freeway beside the northbound lanes is a field containing vintage aircraft. Representing aircraft from WWII, the Korean War and Vietnam eras, this private collection has sadly deteriorated over the years.

Miles 307-277-Bartow County: This next stretch of I-75 has so many things to see that I've drawn a special map for you on page 58, with the various attractions identified by letters of the alphabet. I've used these reference letters in the next few pages.

Exit 306-Adairsville: *(see map on page 58)*. Just 1.3 miles (2.1km) west of I-75 lies the historical town of Adairsville. Leave I-75 at exit 306 and drive west, through the traffic lights at US 41. Just past Citgo (1/10th mile), turn left to Adairsville Main St.

Adairsville lies on the strategic Atlanta-Chattanooga railroad line which during the Civil War, became a bustling supply depot. This ended abruptly when Sherman marched through on his way to Cassville. Today though, it's enjoying a renaissance and has become a great place to stop and relax for a while. The entire town with its many heritage buildings, is listed on the National Register of Historic Places.

I suggest you park in the public square just outside the historic **Train Depot *(A)***. This original Western & Atlantic Depot pre-dates the Civil War and played a part in the Great Locomotive Chase *(see page 118, item 16)*, for it was here that the Conductor Fuller commandeered the southbound Texas and started chasing the stolen General backwards, towards the north.

Across the square the **1902 Stock Exchange *(B)*** (124 Public Sq.) is a fine example of an historical restoration. Inside, you'll find antiques, gifts, crafts, used hardcover quality books, a cafe-style gourmet tea room and an Antebellum dinner theater. Owner Rita Pritchard loves chatting with visitors and showing them her architectural treasure. She invites you in to use her clean restroom and also enjoy free coffee. [Hrs, Tu-Sa, 10-5; Su, 1-5; closed Mondays ☎ 770-773-1902].

Insider Tip - BJ's

BJ's, a pleasant family style restaurant lies just west of exit 312 here at US41, in Calhoun. I know Barbara, Jimi or Aletia will welcome you with good food at a reasonable price. Hrs., Mon-Sat, 11am-9pm, Sun, 11am-2:30pm ☎ 706-629-3461

Turn around, look across the railroad track and you will see a white frame house with a silver roof. This is the **childhood home of Charles Arthur Floyd *(C)***, who became better known as *"Pretty Boy" Floyd* when his career of crime started in the mid-1920s.

Wanted for robbing banks and killings armed with a machine gun in the mid '30s, he quickly became the FBI's "Public Enemy No. 1." To the impoverished farmers & share-croppers of the Depression though, he became a folk-hero since he often took time to destroy all the mortgage records in banks he robbed. Finally shot to death while avoiding capture in Ohio, in Oct., 1934.

Incidentally, you've crossed paths with "Pretty Boy" before. In 1931, he drove north (on the Dixie Highway?) to Mt. Zion, a small town just outside Lexington, Kentucky, where he robbed a bank and fled to Bowling Green, Ohio, with the proceeds–$2,262.22!

Before leaving Adairsville to return to I-75, read the **Insider Tip** about the most romantic place in Georgia. It's not too far from here

Insider Tip - the Most Romantic Place in Georgia

Let's visit one the most romantic place in Georgia–the haunting ruins and beautiful Antebellum roses of **Barnsley Gardens (*D*).** Add a Civil War action, *"Gone With The Wind"* connections, a ghost, acres of flowers and a water garden–and I think you will have to agree that this is a place you will never want to leave.

And if that is your wish and you're in a mood to "splurge," Barnsley is also a five star resort with a village of "cottages" styled in 19th century architecture and a first class restaurant beside a championship golf course. But let me tell you Barnsley's story:

In 1824, penniless Godfrey Barnsley, arrived in North America, where he rose to become a prominent and rich cotton planter. Needing an estate, he purchased this property and named it *Woodlands*. During his business travels abroad, Barnsley collected rare and exotic plants, brought them back and planted the famous Woodlands gardens–perhaps best known for their countless varieties of roses.

The untimely death of his wife, Julia and the Civil War bought an end to his fortunes, and sadly, Godfrey died as penniless as the day he arrived on these shores. Disaster struck again in 1906 when a tornado ruined the main house and nearby gardens. In later years, Margaret Mitchell was a visitor and some believe that Godfrey Barnsley's Woodlands provided inspiration and background to Tara in *"Gone With The Wind."*

Today, thanks to Prince Hubertus of Bavaria, we can enjoy Barnsley's roses, ferns, fruit trees, rockeries and woodland gardens–over 30 acres of cultivated delight surrounding the ruins of Godfrey's Italianate villa.

Don't miss the excellent museum to the right of the ruins. Here you will find Barnsley's knowledgeable historian, my friend Clent Coker. I'll leave it to Clent to explain the stain from a large pool of blood on the floor of the old building–and the hauntings!

Admission to the gardens, ruins & museum-Adults/Snrs/Student: $10/$8/$5; Hrs, M-Sat 9am-6pm; Sun, noon-5pm. The ruins are sometimes closed for special functions–phone ahead to ensure they are open ☎ 770-773-7480 or 1-877-773-2447.

To find Barnsley Gardens, take Hall Station Rd from Adairsville, in 5 miles turn right on to Barnsley Garden Rd and drive 2½ miles to the Barnsley Gardens gate; at the gatehouse, they will direct you to the gardens, the ruined manor house and museum.

The War Between the States - the Cassville Trap

On the west side of Adairsville is Hall Station Road. It parallels the railroad track down to Kingston and a number of events during the Great Locomotive Chase *(see page 117)* took place along this stretch as Andrews' Raiders attempted to stop their pursuers.

The road was also witness to a Civil War trap set by CSA General Johnston's which, if successful, might have turned the tide against Sherman possibly saving Atlanta *(see item **(E)** on the map on page 58).*

Withdrawing from the Battle of Resaca, Johnston decided to fool Sherman into thinking that the entire Confederate army was retreating down Hall Station Rd towards Kingston. He did this by sending a third of his men–24,000 noisy soldiers, heavy artillery and wagons, down the road while his main force moved quietly down another route to the east.

Sherman fell for the ruse, sending most of his troops "chasing the Rebs" down this road. A much smaller force traveled the eastern route not realizing that the main Confederate army was just ahead.

On arrival just north of Cassville, both Confederate armies regrouped and with superior numbers, made a stand across the east route. The plan was to quickly annihilate the small Union army and then swing around to the west to deal with the remainder of Sherman's troops.

But just before the trap was sprung, a small detachment of Federal cavalry was sighted to the right of the CSA; they assumed they were being outflanked by the main Union force. Abandoning their trap, they fell back to the long ridge just southeast of Cassville.

That evening, several generals convinced Johnston that the two mile long ridge was untenable. He agreed to withdraw which he did during the night, heading southward towards Allatoona Pass.

This non-battle could have been a key turning point in the Battle for Atlanta; it later became known as the Cassville Affair. What if the detachment of Federal Cavalry had not appeared–what if they had been assessed as what they were–a small lost detachment of Union cavalry–would Johnston have sprung his trap and defeated Sherman? Possibly–and if so, Atlanta might not have fallen, Savannah might not have been delivered to President Lincoln as a Christmas present . . .and the South might have come back to a strength which would have enabled them to win the war and successfully cede from the Nation.

(see map on page 58) and I wouldn't want you to miss it.

Exit 293-Weinman Mineral Museum *(F)*: This museum has just undergone an extensive renovation, and is now bigger and better than ever. If you enjoy rocks and gem stones, there's a treat in store for you here.

More than 2,000 exhibits are displayed in three halls. The Georgia room contains many specimens native to the State, as well as a simulated cave and waterfall. Indian artifacts dated back to 8,000 BC and fossils as early as the Paleozoic Era *(see chart on page 94)* are displayed in a second room, while a third contains the international Mayo collections.

Children can touch the skull (replica) of a 30 foot Triceratops Horridus dinosaur or try their hands at gold panning and mineral classification while parents peruse the Gift Shop. To find the museum, take exit 293 and go west for a few yards on route 411–turn left onto Mineral Museum Drive which is just past the motel. [☎ 770-387-3747; Hrs: Tu-Sa, 9a-5p; Su, 2-5:30p, closed Mon.; Adult/Senior/Child-$3/$2.50/$2].

Exit 288-Cartersville: *(see map on page 58)* A few minutes to the west lies Cartersville, with many interesting things to see and do. Let's go for a quick tour of the highlights.

Park your car between the railroad tracks and North Wall St, and walk over to the **Cartersville Visitors Center (*G*)** housed in the old **Cartersville Train Depot**. Here you'll find all sorts of information about this historic town, in particular, pick up the self-guided walking tour map.

Many visitors incorrectly think that Cartersville was named after President Carter. It was named after Col. Farish Carter (1780-1861), an early landowner.

Before leaving, say *"hi"* to Donna or Susie on the reception desk. Director Ellen, her

Insider Tip - the Presidents' Letters

One does not expect to find a world-class museum in the busy Interstate-75 town of Cartersville, but the multi-million dollar, purpose-built building of the **Booth Western Art Museum *(L)*,** with 80,000 sq.ft of quiet galleries innovatively and dramatically lit to draw the finest detail out of its 200 Western American works of art, would be right at home in New York's Manhattan or London, England. Focussed primarily on the art of western life, it also holds a unique and very unusual treasure which makes the two mile trip off I-75, well worth the effort. But more on that later.

Let's go for a tour of the Museum. We start on the ground floor in the *Grand Hall* where a beautifully restored original *1889 stage coach* draws your attention just outside the *Presentation and Orientation theatres*. We'll check the *Museum Gift* shop and perhaps have lunch in the *Café* after spending time in the core of the Museum's permanent collection, the *American West Gallery*. Here finely detailed bronzes and superb paintings by well known artists re-tell the story of the American West.

A quick look in the lower level reveals the *Research Library* and the *Sagebrush Ranch*-a hands-on, interactive gallery for the young at heart, organized like a working ranch.

A glass elevator ride takes us up to the Second Floor where two smaller galleries beside the *Cowboy* exhibits introduce us to the wild west of Hollywood through Western movie stars and posters. To our left is the *Special Exhibit Gallery* and just ahead is a large room devoted to contemporary Civil War painting and other artwork-the *War Is Hell Gallery*.

But it's the ***President's Gallery*** at the end of the hall which I believe is the Museum's real treasure...for here you will find a letter written and signed by each of the forty-two men who have served as the Nation's Chief Executive.

Lifesize Bronze of Thomas Jefferson sits pensively in the President's Gallery.

From George Washington to George W Bush, they are all here with painting or photo, a short bio and an original letter and brief details describing the circumstances behind the letter. In many cases, a transcription of the letter is included-Andrew Jackson's handwriting for instance, presents quite a challenge!

Lincoln's 1862 letter to the US Judge Advocate General is quite poignant; it questions the reasons for the pending execution of 300 Indians. Jefferson's letter deals with a personal matter-the conveyance by cart of a spinning machine he recently purchased in Washington, to his home in Monticello. JFK's letter is to an "admirer" who had presented him with a book titled, "How to be President." Kennedy's droll reply gives wonderful insight to his dry sense of humor.

Arguably, this priceless collection of President's Letters is the only one of its kind in the World. In my opinion, it's a National treasure . . . and a "must see" for anybody driving past Cartersville on Interstate-75.

The Museum is open Tu,W,Fr,Sa, 10am-5pm; Th, 10am-8pm, Sun, 1-5pm; closed Mon. Admit, Adult/Snr/Student/Child under 12, $6/$5/$4/free ☎ 770-387-1300.

(Both photos courtesy of the Museum; the "shadow" sculpture is *An Honest Day's Work*, by Fred Fellows; The lifesized sculpture of *Thomas Jefferson* is by George Lundeen).

deputy, Regina, are personal friends of ours so if you see them, please give them our best wishes. All the staff here love to meet and help visitors to this interesting and very historical area. [Hours, Mon-Fri, 8:30a-5p; Sa, 11a-2p; Su, 1:30-4p. ☎ 770-387-1357].

As you leave the Depot and walk towards Main St across the Public Square, take note of the white marble **Friendship Monument** *(H)*–until recently, this was at the top of a nearby hill where nobody could see it. The monument was originally erected as a *"thank you"* by local iron maker, Mark Cooper, who in 1857 stood in danger of losing the nearby Etowah Iron Works. Thirty-eight friends raised the funds to clear his debt. Later, after Cooper had repaid them all, he raised this monument–an unusual case of a debtor honoring his creditors.

Across Main St you'll see the Young Brothers Pharmacy. On its eastern outside wall is the **first outdoor Coca-Cola advertisement** *(J)* in the World, painted by a Coca-Cola syrup salesman in 1894.

Cross the road again towards your car and let's stroll along **North Wall St.** *(K)*. Here you will find the **1929 Grand Theater**, home of the famed Cartersville Opera Co. [☎ 770-386-7343], **Etowah Art Gallery** [11 N. Wall; ☎ 770-382-8277] & the **Bartow History Center** [13 N. Wall; Hrs, Tu-Sat, 10a-5p; Adult/Senior/Child-$3/$2.50/$2 ☎ 770-382-3818]. The latter is well worth a visit to get a glimpse of life in the 1900s. I was particularly taken with the display of the dentist's office with the treadle drill. Ouch!

Continue walking along N Wall St., under the Church St bridge and ahead you will see the beautiful building of the **Booth Western Art Museum** *(L)*. Here you will find a national treasure, arguably the only collection in the world of letters and signatures of the 42 men who became our Nation's Presidents *(see* **Insider Tip***)*.

Return through the Museum's gates and turn left into Church St. *"Under the Bridge."* You'll find some very special treats waiting for you in this unusual subterranean street which I call, **"Underground Cartersville"**

First ... food. Wonderful lunch treats await at the **Appalachian Grill**. [Hrs, M-Th, 11-9p; F-Sa, 11a-10p; closed Su. ☎ 770-607-5357].

Next door is a one-of-a-kind shop, **The Shaving Gallery**, owned and operated by a most unusual (in the nicest of senses) person, Lauren Cross. Lauren (an expatriate from New Zealand, via London) is an expert at hot lather shaving men. She's done it for years and it is a wonderfully relaxing experience. She and her staff have many other services as well–most of them for the ladies.

Drop in and say *"hello"* to Lauren–tell her, Dave sent you–and by the way, don't call her an *"Aussie"* when she has a razor in her hand! [Hours, M-Sat, 10:30a-5:30p; ☎ 770-387-1200].

For a wonderful antique, gift & craft browsing experience, I'm sure you'll enjoy Patty Richardson's **Periwinkle**. I was particularly taken by the artistic way Patty displays her merchandise. I know you will enjoy her store. [Hrs, M-Th, 10a-6p; F-Sa, 10a-8p ☎ 770-607-7171].

Finally, just 3 miles (4.8km) (11 minutes) south-west of Cartersville is the "not to be missed" **Ancient Indian City** *(M)*–the 1,000 year old Etowah Mounds.

From where you parked your car, follow Main St. west (away from I-75). Continue forward on SR 113 at the traffic lights where Bartow St. (SR293) leaves to the right. Watch for the branching of route 113 West and Etowah Drive. At these lights, take the left branch (Etowah Dr.) and follow the road for 2.4 miles (3.9km) until you reach the Etowah Indian Mound State Park. The route is well marked.

Dated from 1000–1500 AD, this entire area was once a huge Indian village. Today, you may explore the remains of three flat topped ceremonial mounds and a moat which encircled the town remain.

Archeological digs have yielded many finds which are on display at the park's Visitor Center. Ranger Steve is very knowledgeable and can answer your questions about this mysterious site. [Hours, Tu-Sat, 9am-5pm, Sun 2pm-5:30pm; Adult/Child; $3/$2; ☎ 770-387-3747.

The War Between the States–Allatoona Pass

Special Report

A small but significant battle took place about a 1¾ miles east of exit 283 *(see map page 60)*. Known only to the locals, the battlesite is undisturbed with trenches, redoubts and a fort in situ. It has now been opened to the public by the Etowah Valley Historical Society and the Corps of Engineers, and you are invited to wander its wooded trails, but first let me take you back to 1864 and set the scene for you:

By early September, General Sherman had successfully captured Atlanta and the single track Western & Atlantic railroad running through North Georgia had become a vital link for bringing supplies to the occupied city. But Southern President Jeff Davis had announced that he intended to disrupt the route using Confederate raiders. One of the most vulnerable stretches of track was the section at Allatoona where it cuts through a 175ft deep, 360ft long man-made pass; it would be easy work for a small contingent of "Rebs" to block it at this point. For protection, Sherman posted a small detachment of men to fortify Allatoona. Trenches were dug and earthwork defenses built on the high ground either side of the cut–both camps joined by a wooden foot-bridge 170 feet in the air.

On October 4th, Confederate commander General Hood issued several conflicting orders to General Samuel French, one of which told him to "fill up the deep cut at Allatoona . . ." (an impossible feat of engineering given the 30 hours allowed for the task).

Sherman received early warnings of this as Confederate troop movements were reported in the area. He dispatched reinforcements to Allatoona under the command of General Corse but due to railroad damage inflicted by the "Rebs," only a portion of them arrived. With the scene set for the battle, Corse had a total force of only 2,025 men to defend the Pass against French's force of 3,276.

What developed as the Battle of Allatoona Pass was one of the most vicious and deadliest of the entire war. Its intense hand-to-hand fighting produced many heroes. The Star Fort on the western side of the Pass was the scene of the most intensive action. The defenders under the personal command of Corse, fired their Henry 15 shot repeater rifles so fast that they became too hot to hold. As the fort ran out of ammunition, Pvt. Edwin Fullington crossed the footbridge three times as he was fired upon by enemy snipers, to resupply the defenders. Another defender, Pvt. James Croft, received the Medal of Honor for bravery during this battle. General Corse received a wound to his cheek in the heat of the attack.

At noon, General French received word that Yankee reinforcements were in the area and in view of the heavy casualties his forces had received, he decided to withdraw.

The cost of the day? Out of the 5,301 men engaged in the four hour battle, only 3,698 lived to talk about it–one of the bloodiest days of the entire war.

As you leave Cartersville and drive back to I-75 exit 288, note the dead end just across the interstate bridge. This is very unusual since interstate exits are only built where a substantial route crosses the freeway's path. In the 1980s however, a local judge with influence in all the right places heard that Cartersville was not going to have an exit, so a word in the right quarters...

Incidentally, this dead end is a favorite place for police cars to park.

Exit 285-Etowah Bridge and Cooper Iron Works (N): (map on page 58). Follow the map and visit remains of the Etowah Bridge where the locomotive, *Yonah* was commandeered during the Great Locomotive Chase.

Exit 285-Red Top Mountain-Eastern Bluebirds and Deer: A quarter of a mile to the east across the Bethany Bridge, you enter the Red Top Mountain State Park. Here wild deer abound. You are almost guaranteed to see them as they graze in the woodlands alongside the road. In more open stretches, the colorful Eastern Bluebirds flit across the meadows to their special "Ranger installed" nesting boxes on old farm fence posts.

At dusk, the deer often come out of the woods and graze on the grass alongside the park's roads and trails. In my mind, there is nothing better than siting on a bench watching the deer in the silvery light of the stars overhead, while listening to the night sounds coming

Baby deer are often seen in the roadside woods as you drive the roads of Red Top Mountain State Park

from the nearby woods.

Mile 283-The Georgia Gold Belt: Yep, you heard properly–gold! And there is still lode buried in this area–for it's all part of a band of rock which stretches across North Georgia, called the *Dahlonega Rift*.

Now, perhaps you didn't know the nation's first gold rush did not occur in California, but in Dahlonega, Georgia, 93 miles east along Route 52 from I-75 exit 333. In 1828, the area boomed and more than $6 million in gold coin was minted at the Dahlonega Mint before the Civil War closed it down.

Exit 283-Battle of Allatoona Pass: *(see Special Report, map is on page 60).*

Mile 281: Just a reminder, you are twenty two miles north of the point where the Atlanta bypass (I-285W) leaves I-75 to circle around the city to the west. Now is the time to start thinking about whether you are going to bypass Atlanta or stay on I-75 and go right through. Why not tune in Captain Herb on 750 AM and get a traffic report? See page 193 for Atlanta rush hour times and page 195 for the bypass map.

Mile 274-Larry McDonald Memorial Highway: You have probably just seen the roadside *"Larry McDonald Highway"* sign and may have wondered who he was. Lawrence Patton McDonald was a high profile, highly controversial Georgian Congressman, who was born and lived near Atlanta. He died in the tragic Korean Airline Flight 007, shot down by Soviet fighters in September, 1983. In 1998, the Georgia House of Representatives passed a resolution naming I-75 from the Tennessee border to the Chattahoochee River, in his honor.

Exit 273-Southern Museum of Civil War & Locomotive History: *(see* **Insider Tip***).*

Exit 267B (S/Bound), 263 (N/Bound)-Marietta: *(bold letters in this text are referenced on the map on page 61)*. Many of us zip by Marietta in our haste to get on to the "business" of Atlanta, and yet it has a charming "small town" ambiance–a pleasant grass

Insider Tip
Southern Museum of Civil War & Locomotive History

Recently re-opened after a $5.6 million expansion, this museum is now a world class facility, partnered with the Smithsonian in Washington. It houses one of the finest collections of Civil War exhibits outside the Museum of the Confederacy in Richmond, Virginia. For instance, don't miss the extremely rare 1843 Whitworth sniper's rifle, still in its original carrying case.

As you leave the Museum section, you walk through an 19th century engineer's shop and past old railroad wheel patterns, to enter a steam locomotive factory from the 1800s, where you can see an early "iron horse" being assembled.

Finally, you round a corner and pass through a tunnel ... and there she is,the famous locomotive, *General*, which was the subject of the Great Locomotive Chase *(see page 117)*. The locomotive which gave chase, the *Texas* is on display at the Cyclorama in Atlanta (phone 404-658-7625 for directions)..

The primary focus of this museum is to collect, preserve & interpret artifacts relating to the history of Southern steam locomotives, both ante and post bellum.

For details and directions, see the map on page 59.

Insider Tip–the Marietta Diner never closes

Want fried eggs and chips with a glass of wine at 3 o'clock in the morning? Then the Marietta Diner is the place for you. This authentic stainless steel and neon-lit 1950s Diner is a fun place to eat with great food presented on a thirteen page, plastic laminated menu. Breakfast, lunch, dinner, there are meals and prices to satisfy all tastes.

Owner Gus or his mother, Maria, will make you welcome regardless of when you arrive-because they never close. Share a joke with Gus, say *"hi"* to him from me and enjoy yourself...for the Marietta Diner is a unique experience not to be missed.

To find the Diner, take exit 263 (S Marietta Pkwy) west; move to the right turn lane as you approach the lights at US41 (Cobb Pkwy). Immediately after your turn, move to the left lane and look for the Diner on your left side at 306 Cobb Pkwy. ☎ 770-423-9390

square, art & craft shops, antiques, small restaurants, bed & breakfast establishments, a fine museum and of course, an excellent Welcome Center. So let's go & take a quick look.

Marietta Square-with angle parking around the perimeter and a round fountain in a parkland setting in the center, it's a great place to just sit and relax under the shady trees, or perhaps go and browse the shops and enjoy the **restaurants *(E)*** surrounding it.

One block along Church Street is an antique browser's idea of heaven for here, and also mingled in with the stores facing the Square, you'll find **antique shops *(D)*** with nooks and crannies to explore for, that special treasure.

Just one block to the west is the old railroad track and an excellent **Visitors' Center *(A)*** inside the c1898 Western & Atlantic Passenger Depot. Say *"hi"* to Mary and the other volunteers–they do a grand job. [Hrs, M-F: 9a-5p, Sa: 11-4, Su: 1-4; ☎ 770-429-1115].

Next to the Center is an historical hotel – called the **Fletcher House *(B)*** during the *"War Between the States,"* and later changed to the *Kennesaw House*. It was here that James Andrews' Raiders (Great Locomotive Chase–see page 117, item 1) stayed–in some cases, four to a bed–before boarding the train next morning, which they would steal during the breakfast stop at Big Shanty (now known as, Kennesaw).

An excellent museum upstairs, the **Marietta Museum of History *(B)*** includes the room used by James Andrews. Curator Dan Cox loves to chat with visitors and tell stories of the past. [Hrs, M-Sat, 10a-4p; Su, 1-4p; Adult/Snr/Child-$3/$2/$2; ☎ 770-528-0431].

Next door in the historic Thomas Warehouse building ***(B)***, you will find the Shaw-Tumblin **Gone With The Wind** Movie museum. Here you'll see Vivian Leigh's "Oscar," Clark Gable's contract and many other pieces of memorabilia from the famous movie. [Hrs, M-Sa,10-5; Adult/Snrs/Student/Child-$7/$6/$6/free. ☎ 770-494-5576].

If you have time, drive over to the **Confederate Cemetery *(C)*** which is about half-a-mile south from the Square *(see map)*. When you arrive, drive within the cemetery to the northern end.

More than three thousand Confederate soldiers are buried here on the tran-

Insider Tip–Drury Inn

If looking for reasonably priced lodgings in this area, try the excellent Drury Inn just east of exit 261. The rooms are large, quiet, and well equipped...and a free hot breakfast is served each morning.

Check the coupon books for special rates ☎ 770-612-0900

MARIETTA - *for Marietta Cobb, believed to have been the wife of Thomas Cobb, after whom Cobb County is named.*

Dixie Highway Motorcade

Special Report

Oct. 15, 1915–"At 4:30 o'clock this afternoon every auto owner in Atlanta is requested to meet at the Majestic Hotel for the purpose of motoring to Bolton to give the tourists the greatest road reception they have received anywhere along their route." read the Atlanta Constitution's lead. What was it all about?

DH In Georgia, the Dixie Highway project was not moving forward as quickly as some thought it should so in 1915, a group of northern tourists formed a motorcade to drive south and promote the highway's completion. A sign on the baggage truck accompanying the procession said it all, *"600,000 Automobile Owners Are Awaiting the Completion of the Dixie Highway to See the South."*

Can you imagine the sight. I'm sure you sometimes feel as I do that *"every automobile owner in Atlanta"* is on I-75 to greet us when we drive through!

quil slopes of the hill, some from a train crash, others from nearby hospitals but many from the Chickamauga and Atlanta Campaign battlefields. At least 1,000 of these soldiers were never identified; their stones are simply marked, *"Unknown."*

Exit 261-F22 Raptor: Just west of here at Dobbins AFB is Lockheed, the contractor for one of the Nation's most controversial aircraft, the F22 Raptor.

At $83.6 million each the F22 is designed to continue the USA's combat dominance in the air for the first quarter of the 21st Century, the Raptor combines stealth, extreme maneuverability, supersonic cruise speed without an afterburner and very advanced integrated avionics (aviation electronics).

The latter is very impressive. Each Raptor has the computing power of two Cray Supercomputers which provides the ability to automatically link up with other aircraft in its flight and exchange data without pilot intervention. For instance, each fighter can quickly determine on its display unit, all characteristics of the other F22's in its flight–fuel loads, weapons available, target locks, etc.–all without voice communication. The first F22 Raptor took off from Dobbins AFB on September 7, 1997, and climbed to 15,000 feet in the skies over Marietta in just a few seconds.

Mile 260-Atlanta's Advanced Traffic Management System: You have just passed under one of the electronic gantry signs of Atlanta's Advanced Traffic Management System, or ATMS, billed as the most sophisticated traffic management system in the World.

Many technologies such as video cameras and road sensors feed information into a control center where the information is analyzed. Up-to-date traffic information messages are relayed back to travelers via the overhead signs (there are five over I-75 in the Atlanta area)–and to in-car navigational displays, hand-held "Palm" personal communication devices (for people walking), on-line computer services and cable TV. The overhead signs should be a great help in driving through or around Atlanta. They will also give you a final check on whether to take the bypass (coming up in another mile) or not.

Mile 258-Atlanta Express Lanes: To help traffic move on the crowded expressway through Atlanta, the city has designated the left lane from mile marker 258 to 237 as a restricted High Occupancy Vehicle (HOV) express lane.

The HOV lane is dedicated to public and emergency vehicles, and cars with two or more people on board. Unlike many other cities though, the Atlanta Express Lanes are ***restricted to this traffic <u>24 hours a day, 7 days a week</u>.*** Watch

CHATTAHOOCHEE RIVER - *Cherokee name probably, "marked rocks," for painted stones found in the river.*

ATLANTA - *formerly named "Terminus" (in 1837 for the southern end of the Western & Atlantic Railroad), and changed to "Marthasville" in 1843 to honor Gov.. Wilson Lumpkin's daughter. Finally to "Atlanta" in 1845, suggested by the word "Atlantic" in the name of its most important industry, the W&A Railroad.*

for the black diamond sign and double dashed lines marked on the road, which identifies the restricted traffic lanes. Cross into the lane (if you are eligible) only at dashed line sections; crossing into the HOV on a solid line could earn you a traffic citation

Incidentally, the signage reads "two person car pools" but we have checked with the Atlanta authorities and any private car (even with out-of-state license plates) with two or more people in it may use the express lanes. Some readers thought a special "car pooling" permit was necessary–that's not so. Also, "AFV" (which you see on some of the signs) refers to "Alternate Fuel Vehicles" such as those powered by compressed natural gas. However, gas/electric hybrid vehicles such as the *Honda Insight* or *Toyota Prius* may not use the HOV lanes.

A small word of caution. Since the express lanes occupy the freeway's left hand lane and the I-75 running through Atlanta has some exits which also exit to the left, be very careful that you don't accidentally leave I-75 at those exits.

There are however, several points where due to the "basket weave" of other interstates joining and leaving I-75, the express lanes appear to leave the normal flow of I-75 traffic. In particular, northbound drivers should watch for this just past exits 247 and 250–the express lanes are clearly marked "I-75" with an arrow. Follow these with confidence since they rejoin I-75 a little further on. Just feel good about the fact that you are in the express lane and moving–whereas the rest of I-75 traffic is probably standing still!

I have provided separate Atlanta driving instructions–instructions (in red boxes) for those using the regular lanes and "black diamond" instructions for those in the HOV lanes.

The Varsity: at exit 249D lies one of Atlanta's famous landmarks–the Varsity drive-in restaurant.

Now there are several things you need to know about the Varsity before you decide to eat there. It can be crowded, noisy–in fact, sometimes raucous–but it's an Atlanta institution. Anybody who is anybody in Atlanta has eaten there. Presidents Carter, Bush, and most recently, Clinton have graced the Varsity dining rooms where you can choose the room according to the TV channel you would like to watch.

No matter how crowded it is–they serve over 10,000 customers and 17,000 hotdogs each day; they sell more Coke than any other single location in the World–the orders move quickly over the many sales positions along the 150' stainless steel counter.

"Whad'll ya have?? whad'll ya have??" is the constant cry. As founder/owner Frank Gordy says, *"Have your money in your hand and your order in your mind and we will get you to the game on time."*

Alternatively, you can sit in your car and one of the car-hops will come and take your order. Parking isn't always easy to find in the service area, but with a little patience you'll soon see a happy customer backing out.

You will either love or hate the Varsity, but it will be an unforgettable experience. Frank's daughter, Nancy Sims runs the Varsity along with her staff of very interesting characters–try and get Irvy Walker on the Express Counter to chant the menu for you.

If driving south on I-75, take exit 249D, turn left and the Varsity is immediately on your left just across the bridge. Pull into the first driveway (before the building) for car-hop service or regular parking.

When you leave, drive around the back out onto Spring St, cross the traffic lights at Ponce De Leon and across North Ave., stay left past the I-75 North ramp until you see the I-75 South sign–follow the I-75S ramp back down onto the freeway (also known as the Atlanta Downtown Connector).

If driving north, take exit 249D, cross Spring St and turn left when you reach West Peachtree, turn left again at North Avenue and you will see the Varsity across the road from you.

When you leave, follow the directions above for southbound travelers but take the I-75 North ramp instead.

Turner Field (Olympic Stadium): At mile 246, on your left is Turner Field (named after Atlanta's Ted Turner), site of the 1996 Summer Olympic Opening and Closing ceremonies. The stadium is home for the Atlanta Braves baseball team.

Just to the north of the Stadium is the distinctive open girder statue of the Olympic Torch, honoring the Games.

Mile 239-World's Busiest Airport: At mile 239, you might notice lights on top of stalks in I-75's median. These are the final approach lights of runway 27R, of the world's busiest airport, William B.Hartsfield International.

Built on land originally owned by Asa Chandler, the founder of The Coca-Cola Company, as the site of his auto race track, Hartsfield is the world's busiest airport, servicing more than 73.5 million passengers a year, compared to Chicago O'Hare's 72.4 million.

Plans are underway to build a fifth runway and since 1997, more than 130 businesses have been relocated to make way for this new facility. Construction is well underway but another 124 must be moved soon. Total relocation costs? Over $400 million. The 9,000ft runway is expected to be ready by 2005.

Exit 237-Georgia Farmers Market: Just to the east of I-75 lies the huge *Georgia Farmers' Market*. To reach it, take exit 237 and go east to the second traffic light. Turn left into the double gates & follow the left hand lanes marked *"Shed Area–"Georgia Farmers."*

No need to stop at the booths ahead-they are unmanned. The whole area is open to the public even though it looks commercial–follow the lanes around the building and there you will find sheds with stands selling–pecans, onions, tomatoes, peanuts... every type of fruit and vegetable you ever wanted.

Don't miss the locals very popular *Thomas Marketplace Restaurant* while there. [Hrs: 7a-8p, daily ☎ 404-361-1367]

The menu is "Southern" and as you would expect from a farmer's market restaurant, the food is always fresh and very reasonably priced. No canned produce here, everything is smoked or prepared on site.

It's a large barn of a place with friendly staff who call people they know by their first name; the rest of us are *"Honey."*

Exit 233-The "Road to Tara" Museum: We are in the Deep South and local names like *"Jonesboro"* and *"Clayton County"* strike a chord–for we are in *"Gone With The Wind"* country.

Yes, I know that Margaret Mitchell's great book was a work of fiction ... but don't bother trying to convince anybody in this neighborhood. Wasn't Jonesboro where Scarlett O'Hara used to drive her buggy five miles to catch the train to Atlanta?

While in the mood, let's go and visit the ***Road To Tara Museum*** housed in the historic Jonesboro Railroad Depot (incidentally, this same building houses the excellent ***Clayton County Information Center)***.

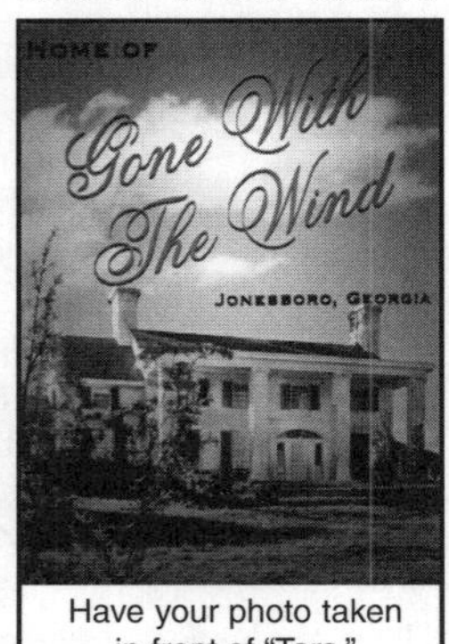

Have your photo taken in front of "Tara."

Here you will find a feast of GWTW photos, artifacts, letters and other memorabilia to satisfy the most ardent "Windie." They even run the movie continuously so you can sit and watch your favorite scene. [Hrs: M-F, 8:30am-5:30pm; Sat, 10am-4pm; Adult/Snrs/Student/Child-$5/$4/$4/free; a "package" ticket is also available covering this and 4 other Atlanta area GWTW attractions; ☎ 770-478-4800; 1-800-662-7829].

Exit 233-Morrow Welcome Center: Just east and on the north side, you'll see the *Morrow Welcome Center* building. The Center has close ties to the Jonesboro Center so you can stop and get your Jonesboro information here as well. For those who need it, there is also free internet access [Hrs, Tu-Sa, 8:30a-5p; ☎ 770-968-1623].

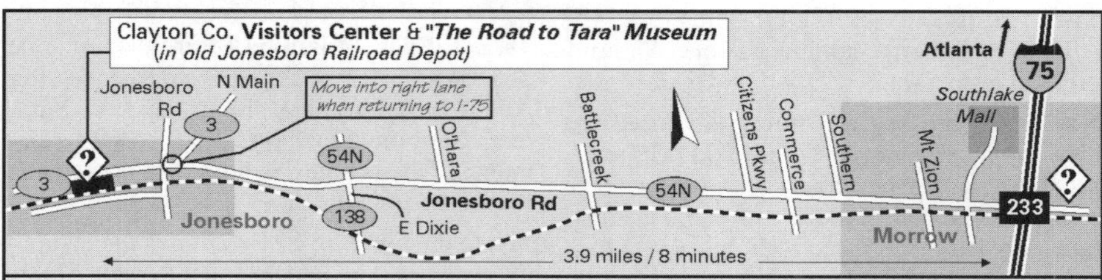

JONESBORO - *originally called "Leakesville," it was renamed after Samuel Jones, an engineer who revived the Macon & Western, a bankrupt railroad.*

FORSYTH - *for John Forsyth (1780-1841) who was Governor of Georgia in 1827 and Secretary of State between 1834-41, under Presidents Jackson and Van Buren.*

Insider Tip–Grits Cafe

I've eaten here a number of times and just love it, for here you can dine in an early 1900s setting, under real gas lights (Fall & Winter only).

Regardless of its name, most of the items on the menu–crab, lamb, steak, etc.–are not based on grits. Terri and gourmet Chef Wayne Wetendorf will ensure you have a fine meal & enjoyable experience.

Take exit 186 and drive straight ahead for 1 mile. The Grits Cafe will be on your right on the "Square" at 17 W. Johnson St, across from the Forsyth Courthouse. Hrs- ☎ 478-994-8325 Lunch: Tu-Sa, 11a-2p; Dinner: Tu-Th: 5:30-9p; F-Sa: 5:30-10p: Closed Sun/Mon.

Exit 212 - Noah's Ark: If you love children and animals then a visit to this very unusual and special place is for you. Noah's Ark is not an "attraction" but a haven which lovingly brings neglected children and injured or orphaned animals together, providing a place where through animal care therapy, they can help and heal each other.

Set in 40 acres of nature trails and natural habitat, the property includes a center where injured birds and animals are treated and if possible, rehabilitated back to health. More than 1,000 animals–some coming from Georgia's Department of Natural Resources–pass through the hands of the center's professional staff every year. You may visit many of them–domestic, farm, wildlife and exotics of all types–in the fields and pens at Noah's Ark.

At present, a group residence provides a loving foster parent home for about 24 youngsters.

The public is invited to visit the facilities and enjoy the nature trails free of charge (donation appreciated), from Tuesday to Saturday. Phone 770-957-0888 first to make sure the animal habitats are open.

Whistle Stop Cafe, Juliette

It's 4.3 miles (6.9km) from I-75. Take exit 212 and drive east via Bill Gardner Pkwy towards Locust Grove. Turn right on to US23 /SR42 (south). After .9 mile (1.4km), turn right at the Post Office onto LG Griffin Road. Noah's Ark is 2.8 miles (4.5km) west on the left side of the road.

Exit 198-High Falls State Park: Less than two miles (3.2km) east of I-75 is a pretty place to pause–perhaps for a picnic *(see* **Insider Tip** *on page 89)* beside the 100 foot waterfall–the High Falls State Park. Incidentally, an excellent overnight stop for RVers.

Exit 186-Tarleton Oaks-Gone With The Wind: I know from the letters I receive that many "Along I-75" readers have enjoyed staying at one of my past recommendations, *Tarleton Oaks*, the bed and breakfast home of Terry and Fred Crane.

Fred played "Brent Tarleton," and had the first speaking lines in the movie, *"Gone With The Wind."* He loved to regale his B&B guests with "inside" stories and his personal collection of photos from the GWTW movie set. Terry's passion was their home, Tarleton Oaks, which she had turned into arguably, the finest GWTW museum in Georgia.

But times move on. Terry and Fred have decide to take a well deserved rest and sell their B&B business. We will miss them.

Exit 186-Juliette & the Whistle Stop Cafe: *(See details on page 61)*. Do you remember the wonderful movie, *"Fried Green Tomatoes?"* If you did, then you might like to visit the tiny village and the actual cafe used as a backdrop for the film.

Whistle Stop Cafe manager Susan, Betty Clements and her son, Dean, of *The Gift shop of Southern Grace* and the *Habersham Wine Tasting Room*, Donna & Larry Pierce of *McCrackin St. Sweets*–and the many other fine people of Juliette are just as friendly and heart-warming as the folk in the movie.

The center of activity is the *Whistle Stop Cafe* (yes–they do serve fried green tomatoes as well as other Southern delicacies).

Across the street is one of my favorite places–the rocking chair in front of Betty Clement's *Southern Grace* antiques and *Habersham* wine tasting room. It's wonderful to sit here and chat with Betty and Dean, and watch the world go by. Notice the clock behind the counter. Betty keeps *"River Time"* because she doesn't like to change it in the spring or fall... *"and the nearby Ocmulgee River keeps the same time year round."*

Macon–the Song & Soul of the South

Special Report

Without a doubt, Macon is the *"Song & Soul of the South"* and yet so many travelers intent on getting to Florida, pass it by on I-475. Why not arrange to spend a night there. Located on the banks of the Ocmulgee River, it is full of history and things to do. Use the map on page 196 to orientate yourself. You'll find reasonably priced motels and inns at exits 171 & 169; many have discount coupons in the free motel books *(see saving tips on pages 68 & 134)*.

The easiest way to travel downtown is to take I-75, exit 165. At this exit, you join interstate-16 traveling east towards Savannah. Leave I-16 in 2 miles at exit 2 (MLK Blvd). This will take you across the river and into the quiet and spacious downtown area of Macon.

Drive straight across Walnut St–the **Tubman African-American Museum** is on your right–and as you round the curve, my favorite of all the museums–the **Georgia Music Hall of Fame**–is on your left. Take care here because MLK Blvd goes off to the right at the intersection of Mulberry St. Stay in the left lane and bear left onto Cherry St Plaza, which becomes 5th Street in a few blocks.

At the intersection of Cherry St and Cherry St plaza, the **Sports Hall of Fame** is on your right and immediately on your left is the imposing **Terminal Station Visitor's Center.** I suggest you park here (free parking to east of building) and pick up Macon brochures and maps, including a downtown restaurant map. The Center is open M-Sa, 9a-5p; closed Sunday. ☎ 478-743-3401.

For a short visit, I recommend you take the *"Around Town"* or *"Downtown Museum"* self-guided trolley tours. You may enter or leave the trolley as you wish throughout the day. Guides at each attraction will help and answer your questions. This is a great way to see Macon's historic sites such as the **Sidney Lanier Cottage** (Georgia's foremost poet), **Hay House** or **Cannonball House**–or the Macon museums. Tours, M-Sa. ☎ 478-743-3401 or 800-768-3401 for times.

If you enjoy ancient history, don't miss the Ocmulgee (pronounced: oak-mul-gee, like the "g" in "geese") **National Monument Indian Village** park (dated back to 9,000BC), visited by Hernando de Soto in 1540. ☎ 478-752-8257

Thirsty? Try Grandma Huber's wonderfully sweet and thirst quenching–*"lemonade made right!"* at *McCrackin Street Sweets*, just beside the Fire Hall. A photograph of Grandma (just inside the door as you enter) ensures that *"all the makins' are right."* Also try the cream fudge.

In today's hectic pace, a sidetrip to Juliette is a much needed break to recharge the soul–it's a short trip to another time and age and I heartily recommend it. Jessica Tandy's parting line in the movie mentions the Whistle Stop Cafe...*"It was never more than a little knockabout place but when I look back on it...it's funny how a tiny place like this brought so many people together."* Thanks to all the wonderful folk of Juliette, it still does.

Mile 180-Macon Welcome Center, "BJ": *(see Macon map on page 196)* The Macon Welcome Center is on the interstate just before the road splits between I-75 and the I-475 Bypass. I cannot go by here without stopping to say *"hello"* to that wonderful Southern lady, BJ–and her associate Bernice, and other staff members of the Macon Welcome Center.

BJ and I go back a few years (well...I do; she doesn't!). She has tried to teach me to pronounce *"kudzu"* in the Southern manner–but with my English accent getting in the way, I think she has given up!

Do try and visit Macon. It's an unusual and

Money Saving Tip

If planning to spend the night in Macon, tell the staff at the Macon Welcome Center). Let them make arrangements for you. Tell them what your budget is, they can often arrange much better rates (assuming availability) than you can by yourself.

MACON- *after Nai Macon (1757-1837), an American Revolutionary patriot and politician.*
ECHECONNEE CREEK - *from Creek Indian, "place where deer are trapped."*

interesting place; see my *Special Report*, on page 134 [Welcome Center Hrs, M-F, 9a-5:30p daily; Restrooms 24hrs. ☎ 478-743-3401].

I-475, Exit 3-Big Box Shopping: In the north east quadrant of exit 3, you'll find the 80 acre Eisenhower Crossing Shopping Center Stores already opened are Marshalls, Krogers, Best Buy, Target, Staples, Michaels Crafts, Old Navy and Radio Shack ... with more to come.

Exit 149-Big Peach Antiques: The antiques dealers who used to be at the antique car emporium, the *Generation Gap* have now gone and I suspect many of them moved into the huge building next door–*Big Peach Antiques*. Here you will find hundreds of booths. To reach the building, turn left on to the small road between Pizza Hut and Burger King. [Hrs. M-Sat, 10a-7p; Sun, noon-6p ☎ 912-956-6256]

Exit 146-Martin Mace Missile: A CGM-13 Martin Mace guided missile on the south eastern corner of this exit reminds us that we are close to Warner Robins, a USAF town. This used to be the exit for the Museum of Aviation, but a new exit south of here-exit 145-has been opened providing a more direct route.

New Exit 145-Warner Robins Museum of Aviation: Eight miles to the east along Russell Parkway is the Museum of Aviation. With over 93 aircraft on display, it is the second largest Air Force museum in the USA.

The best part is that you can get close. In fact a number of the larger aircraft are outside and you can walk right up and around them. The collection covers all the years from the 40's, but is not dated. For instance, you can get within touching distance of an SR-71 Lockheed *"Blackbird"* and F-15A McDonnell-Douglas *"Eagle."* Although 34 years old, the SR-71 remains one of the fastest and highest flying aircraft (that we are told about!). It can fly 15 miles above the earth's surface at 2200mph, enough speed to cross the USA from coast to coast in one hour – awesome!

Drive east on Russell Parkway until it ends at the junction ramps for US129 and SR247. Stay in the right lane and follow the ramp sign for *Macon*. At the foot of the ramp, turn left. The museum is just north of here on your right. [Hrs, 9-5, daily; Admission-free; theater-$2; ☎ 478-926-6870].

Mile 140-Forever Georgia: Once we cross *Mossy Creek*, we are in the area I call *"Forever Georgia."* Why? Well, we are now beyond the "hubbub" of the cities and into a much more relaxing part of the South. It's also an area which, apart from conscription, was not touched too badly by *The War.* Of course, you know by now that this refers to the *War Between the States*, or the *Civil War*.

Exit 136-New Perry Hotel: Readers who have traveled with me over the years will remember I used to recommend the New Perry Hotel, but sadly in the mid-1990s it started to suffer from neglect and I could no longer recommend it.

Slowly but surely this veritable "old lady" of bygone Southern hospitality is being brought back to its original splendor under the ownership of its Perry investors.

Tin Can Tourists

Special Report

Among the early users of the *Dixie Highway* were the *"Tin Can Tourists,"* the forerunners of today's RVers.

Formed at Tampa, Florida's Desoto Park in 1919, the organization got its name from the popularity of the members canned "on-the-go" meals and that many members converted the Ford Model T (the *Tin Lizzy),* into their mobile home–this was long before the availability of manufactured RVs.

TCT

TCTs had an official black & tan diamond shaped badge on their license plate, but were much easier to recognize from the tin can each soldered onto their car's radiator cap. They also had a secret handshake (sawing motion) and had an unfairly earned reputation of being vagabonds. As one member wrote, *"most people would have nothing to do with us ... many sheriffs met us at the county line."*

DH

Since the *Dixie Highway* ran through many towns between Michigan and Florida, the annual procession of TCTs was seen by some as a nuisance. Just like today, others capitalized on this mobile market.

PERRY - *"We have met the enemy and they are ours" was the naval signal sent by Oliver Hazard Perry (1785-1819) after he beat the British fleet on Lake Erie during the War of 1812. Perry is named in honor of the war hero.*

Insider Tip–Priester's

Founded by two men in 1935 with $200 and a handshake, an Alabama tradition has come to Georgia–Priester's Pecans.

Priester's at Perry is large, bright and well laid out. Here you'll find preserves, candies (made before you on a large marble table), ice cream, gifts ... and of course, pecans in just about every way imaginable. There is even a sampling table where you can "try before you buy." The store also includes an excellent cafe with very clean restrooms.

Outside the beige building, a huge lot provides parking for cars, RVs and buses; there is even a dog run.

You will see Priester's on the west side of I-75 between exits 135 & 134. Take either exit and drive down (or up) Route 41. Hrs: Su-Th, 8a-6p; F-Sa, 8a-9p

Last summer, the *New Perry Restaurant* and *Tavery Bar* operations were contracted out to an experienced Macon restaurateur, and under his on-site Food and Beverage Manager, Cass, the dining experience has improved substantially. Kathy and I had a very enjoyable evening meal while visiting a few months ago and would certainly consider eating there again on our next trip.

The New Perry Hotel itself has been listed on the *National Register of Historic Places*. This recognition will ensure that funds are shortly available to continue bringing the property back to its former glory. Much needed is an elevator and plans are underway to have this installed within the next year.

As always, the grounds are magnificent with Southern foliage and brightly colored flowers; a meal in the Restaurant or Tavery followed by a stroll around the grounds is still an excellent way to enjoy the continuing renaissance of the New Perry.

To reach the hotel, go east at exit 136; bear right onto Ball Street where the road divides and follow the route into the downtown area. You can't miss the New Perry on the corner of Ball and Main. ☎ 478-987-1000

Exit 135-Visitor Center: To the east of I-75 at this exit is an excellent Visitor Center. It is well stocked with maps and brochures, and friendly advice. [Hrs, M-F, 8:30am-5pm; Sat, 10am-4pm; in summer also open Sun, 1am-5pm; ☎ 478-988-8000]. You will also find the Georgia National Fairgrounds at this exit.

Mile 130-Hernando de Soto: At Tennessee mile 42, I explained how in 1539, Don Hernando de Soto, the Spanish explorer led his army of 600 men on a journey of exploration of the North American continent. As he moved northward through Georgia, his journal for March, 1540, records how he marched from Montezuma (about 15 miles west of I-75 mile marker 125), crossed Beaver Creek and arrived at an Indian village at Perry where he observed the women spinning silk from the fibers of mulberry trees. His army would have crossed the terrain of the modern I-75 around mile marker 130. Several days later, the army moved on towards modern Macon and crossed the "Great River"–the Ocmulgee.

Mile 133-an Epiphyte: As we travel further south the stands of conifers in the sawmill pinelands and trees draped with Hanging Moss give a much more relaxed, laid back appearance to the roadside. To me, Hanging (or Spanish) Moss (Tillandsia Usneoides) is always the guarantee that you are beyond the most southern snowline. It's a peculiar plant, not a moss and not a parasite as many people believe. It's an Epiphyte–a plant that does not grow in soil but clings to another plant or tree for support and lives on the air surrounding it.

Exit 127-Henderson Village: Barely one mile west of this exit is a fascinating 18 acre village of deluxe overnight lodging and fine dining, surrounded by formal gardens and a 3,500 acre hunting preserve (game shooting and wild boar hunting). Definitely not for the budget minded traveler, but perhaps the ultimate stopover for that special occasion-a fine way to celebrate a birthday or anniversary while on the road.

Within the village is the Langston House Restaurant–a beautifully renovated 1838 home, decorated throughout with original antiques and divided into small intimate dining rooms. The menu items change seasonally with prices within budget; a two course lunch for under $15 or three course dinner for under $35.

And now to the grounds. Henderson Village is an assembly of old historical buildings from the area–local homes and tenant farmer cottages, all completely renovated and decorated in the finest fashion for a deluxe stay. Winding brick paths meander through the

Insider Tip
A Visit to Ellis Bros.–a family Pecan Farm

"We're Nuts..." is the slogan of Ellis Bros. Pecans, and if there's anything you want to know about pecans, Elliott Ellis is your man. Just east of I-75 the Ellis family has been farming the nuts for three generations. In fact, the pecan trees in the grove just to the north of their retail store were planted in 1918, just after the end of WWI. Pecans are harvested by air blasting them onto strips of ground kept clear of cover between the trees. Elliott took me for a tour of his shelling plant behind the store and I was surprised at the control he must maintain over the humidity.

Pecan Leaf

In the store, you will find just about every type of coated pecan–coffee, honey, ginger and chocolate, to name a few. Irene Ellis has an in-house candy kitchen with four marble topped tables to supply this need. The Ellis' also grow and make the wonderful Mayhaw Jelly as well as sell almonds, cashews, peanuts–and five varieties of pecan incl. Stuart, Desirables, Papershells (Schley/Sumner). Holly at the counter will be happy to help you.

To reach Ellis Brothers, take exit 109 east (route 215) and take first left (Tippetville Rd) at the Ellis Bros. sign. Ellis Bros. is well marked, about ¾ mile on left.
The store is open 7 days a week, 8am-7pm; ☎ 1-800-635-0616 or 229-268-9041.

property, moon lights in the trees and old fashioned gaslamps light the way during the evening.

I was really taken by the "court" of six inward facing cottages. All the old architectural features that make these buildings so endearing, have been kept. Some have wooden shingle roofs while others are of tin, but all are completely modernized and weather-tight. Modern heating and air-conditioning is hidden away where you cannot see or hear it.

As you enter each, notice the wonderful aromas of cedar and bayberry. Beautiful old brick hearths (retrofitted with safe but very authentic, glowing ember gas fireplaces) along with functional antique furnishing ensure warm and comfortable interiors.

All buildings have a porch; some with double porch swings, others with rocking chairs or wicker furniture. There is something special about sitting out and quietly rocking the time away while listening to the crickets, on a warm southern night.

Our favorite tenant farmer's cottage at Henderson Village

In Henderson Village, no expense has been spared to evoke the atmosphere of a peaceful but bygone era.

General Manager Heather Bradham invites *"Along I-75"* readers to take a break from the highway, to come and enjoy the grounds, relax and wander around this unusual community and perhaps, sample some of the delicacies at the Langston House. She has special lower rates for my readers.

[Restaurant open daily for Breakfast, 7a-10a and Lunch, 11:30a-2:30p; Dinner, Su-Th, 6-9p; F-Sa, 6-10p; Information/reservations, ☎ toll free 888-615-9722, or 478-988-8696].

Mile 115-Peanuts and Irrigation: The fields just to the west (right) of you here are peanuts. The large wheeled girder units are used for irrigation.

Exit 109-Georgia Cotton Museum: The history of Georgia cotton have long been closely associated, and now a new museum ½ mile west of I-75 tells all with some very attractive exhibits. Did you know for instance, that the first Georgia cotton was brought from England in 1733 and planted in the Trustees Garden in Savannah; or that Georgia was the first state to produce cotton commercially?

Cotton Leaf

For more than 250 years, *"King Cotton"* as it was known played a major role in building the economy of Georgia–until it was almost

Insider Tip Sleep in an Antique Shop

If you love antiques, you must spend a night at this Ramada Inn (exit 101). Not only are the rates reasonable (they accept coupons) but the lobby is an antique shop which never closes!

So, if you can't sleep at 3 am, just get up and go browsing. If you see something you like, pay for it at the front desk–and then–back to bed. ☎ 229-273-5000.

wiped out by the Boll Weevil. But it has come back & today is a major Southern crop again.

The museum is more than just a collection of artifacts. Here, you'll learn about the tools used, including Eli Whitney's Cotton Gin (for removing seeds from the white cotton lint) and a weighing beam used to weigh cotton bales. Samples of cotton in various stages of growth are available so you can actually touch & feel Georgia's number one cash crop.

If you've ever wondered about cotton then you're in the right place. Museum custodian Margaret Hegidio knows cotton and loves to chat with her visitors.
[Hrs, M-F, 9am-5pm; ☎ 229-268-2045]

Insider Tip-the French Market

We visited this interesting shop in Ashburn, and found 50-60 well organized booths and sections of collectibles,small antique jewelry, interesting & unusual decorator pieces. So interesting in fact, that I purchased all the gifts for our "house & pet sitter" here.

Better still, The French Market includes a nice cafe where you can get an excellent sandwich lunch.

Owner Barbara Coley opened this market of eclectic collectibles in April, 2003, and welcomes your visit.

Drive west from exit 82 on Route 112 (Washington St) for .8 mile (1.3km). The shop is on the right side of the road just past traffic lights at Johnson St and between Ace Hardware and Movie Gallery (look for "Freds" on left)

Hrs: M-F, 10-6; Sa, 10-5; ☎ 229-567-0131

Mile 103-Pecan Orchard: If you didn't have time to stop and visit the Ellis Bros. at exit 109, here's your chance to see a grove of pecan trees beside the interstate. Look for an orchard of trees on the right (west) side as you travel south, between exits 104 and 102.

Exit 101-Cordele, Watermelon Capital of the World: Worthy of note–we are just passing our first palm tree. It's to the right (west) of the freeway, halfway between I-75 and the Holiday Inn property.

If you take this exit to buy gas, you might be surprised to see a Titan Rocket. The Titan was an early space vehicle contained many exotic but corrosive materials–sadly, the rocket is beginning to really show its age.

Exit 101-Vidalia Onions: Vidalia onions are well known the world over for their unusual sweetness and flavor. In fact they are so sweet they have a higher sugar (fructose) content than Coca-Cola. They are also tearless!

Why do they taste so different? It's due to the local sandy, low-sulphur soil in the Vidalia area (85 miles (137km) to the east along Rt280 of this exit). This was discovered by accident in 1931 when local resident Mose Coleman planted some onion seeds from Texas, and could not believe the sweet, juicy results. They're so good that they could be eaten raw.

Today, Vidalia Onions has grown into a multi-million dollar business. Just like fine wines, only onions from a certain areas are allowed to bear the Vidalia logo. The best time to buy is in the spring. Genuine Vidalia onions may be found at many outlets along I-75 in Georgia; we like to buy ours at the Georgia State Farmers Market (exit 237) if driving north.

Mile 100: Just south of this exit on the right is a cotton field which might be of interest if you don't live in the South. If you missed the Cotton Museum at exit 109, here's your chance to see a cotton field from your car.

Keep an eye on this field–green for most of the summer, it bursts into a field of thigh high cotton balls–*Southern Snow*–in mid-August.

Mile 82-The Peanut Monument: How many of you have zipped by the tall peanut just south of this exit and wondered what it is. We did a little "off-roading" and found out that it's a memorial; here's the plaque:

CORDELE - *(pronounce, "Cor-deal") after Cordelia Hawkins, daughter of Colonel Samuel Hawkins, president of the Savannah, Americus and Montgomery railroad.*

"This monument to the Peanut, Turner County's most important agricultural product is dedicated to the memory of Nora Lawrence Smith, December 25, 1886–July 17, 1971, member, Georgia Journalism Hall of Fame, Editor and Co-Publisher of the Wiregrass Farmer, Turner County's award winning newspaper, & an untiring supporter of Turner Co. and its agricultural economy."

Exit 78-Jefferson Davis Capture Site: If you were in this area in May, 1865, you were probably hunting (or helping) Jefferson Davis, ex-President of the Southern Confederacy. He had been on the run from his capital, Richmond in Virginia, since early April and had a $100,000 reward of gold on his head. With his wife, an escort of 20 men and $300,000 in gold and silver from the Confederate Treasury, the party decided to camp in a pine grove beside a stream.

Peanut leaflets

Imagine their feelings when they were woken up in the early morning by two Federal cavalries shooting at each other and everything else in sight. A soldier aimed at Jefferson but his wife offered herself as a target instead; Jefferson surrendered quickly to save her life.

Mile 63-Tifton: *(see map on page 53)*.

The Birthplace of Interstate-75: see the *Special Report* below.

Tifton–the Birthplace of Interstate-75

Have you ever wondered exactly when and where the construction of I-75 started? Well, it was here at milepost 63 in Tifton, Georgia. This is the birthplace of not only Interstate-75, but also the entire Interstate system since it was the first interstate construction project to receive Federal approval and funding! And it all came about because Tifton wanted to get rid of the heavy "snowbird" traffic flowing through town.

Like many other communities located between the northern states and Florida, the *Dixie Highway* (in this area, old US 41) went right through the center of town causing heavy congestion, especially in winter months. Cadillacs, Packards and Roadmasters from Illinois, Ohio and Michigan gave rush hour a new meaning. So Tifton decided to build a US41 bypass around town. Years of study and careful planning went into this project and in May, 1956, bids were requested & contracts awarded.

DH

Ironically a month later in Washington, President Eisenhower signed a Bill which officially launched the Interstate system *(see page 69)*. Federal transportation officials needed to get the process "off the ground" quickly and the Tifton Bypass project was a perfect place to start since legal "rights-of-way" on all the necessary land had been acquired and all the planning completed.

So, the 4 mile *Tifton US41 Bypass* became the first 4 miles of *I-75*–the first stretch of interstate constructed and completed anywhere in the USA; it ran from a point near Tifton Junior HS (north of exit 63) in the north, to Southwell Blvd (exit 59) in the south and was completed in 1960.

The Eisenhower Interstate Monument, Tifton, Georgia

Interestingly, when enacted the federal interstate planning regulations allowed only one exit every eight miles. But Tifton had designed eight for the bypass–and construction had already begun. That's why Tifton has more exits than most I-75 communities.

Some Interesting Facts about the first four miles:

- four lanes of concrete roadway
- eight planned exits
- 4.953 miles of grading and paving
- 2,138,500 cubic yds of excavation
- 129 property owners affected
- 286 acres of land cleared
- construction started in 1957
- construction completed in 1960

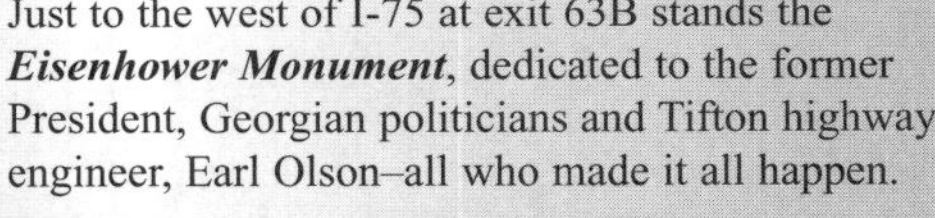

Just to the west of I-75 at exit 63B stands the ***Eisenhower Monument***, dedicated to the former President, Georgian politicians and Tifton highway engineer, Earl Olson–all who made it all happen.

TIFTON *-founded in 1841 by Capt. Henry Tift, a Yankee from Mystic, Connecticut, who sought wood for shipbuilding and built a sawmill in the area.*

Insider Tip–Charles Seafood

I love seafood. I could happily exist on a diet of shrimp, clams & mussels so when I hear about a seafood restaurant beside I-75, I've got to go and check it out.

Charles Seafood Restaurant, several blocks east of exit 62 is everything I expected...fresh seafood at reasonable prices. The menu ranges from the usual range of seafood such as grouper...to the unusual such as 'gator tail. If you're not sure about the latter, try it as an appetizer. Incidentally, there is plenty of non-seafood choice for the landlubber. All fried foods are prepared with cholesterol-free oil.

The restaurant is closed Sunday and Monday, but open the rest of the week. Lunch hours are 11-2pm; diner is served from 5-10pm. ☎ 229-382-9696.

Georgia Agrirama: Two minutes west at exit 63 (Eighth St.), country life in the late 19th century is the focus of this living outdoor museum. The town's guides wear costumes from the period and practice the trades and skills which would have been required to live in this rural community.

As you wander around the town, visit the steam-powered sawmill, water wheel grist mill, smokehouse, sugar cane mill and turpentine still, among other rural industries. All in all, a pleasant way to spend an hour or so, off the road. [Open year round: Tu-Sa, 9a-5p; Adult/Senior/Child-$10/$8/$6 ☎ 229-386-3344 or 800-767-1875].

Exit 62-Adcock Pecans: Just to the east of this exit is Adcock Pecans, the huge retail outlet of the Sunbelt Plantation company. I'm always impressed with the huge array of jellies, jams, relish, salsa, sauces and spreads on display. At the last count, there were 88 different varieties in stock, from pumpkin butter to guava jelly to chow chow-you never know what you'll find. [Hrs: 7:30a-9p, daily. ☎ 229-382-5566 or 800-348-5566].

Agrirama Steam Train

Insider Tip Pit Stop Bar-B-Que

You probably know by now that my two loves when I travel are history & eating. Some people have even subtitled this book, "Dave eats his way to Florida!" But I don't want you to miss this excellent BBQ restaurant just west of I-75 at exit 63B. After your meal, go and visit the smoke house at the back, say "hi" to owner Don Davis for me.

Hrs: Su-Th, 11a-9p; F-Sa, 11a-10p
☎ 229-387-0888

Exit 55-Magnolia Plantation: I can never seem to get my car (or my wife, Kathy) past the Magnolia Plantation without a mandatory stop to check out their large stock of local relishes, honey, jellies, jams or marmalades. We always come away with at least a few jars of Vidalia Onion relish.

Mile 32-Spanish Moss: Another stand of Hanging (Spanish) Moss to the right reminds me of the *"Legend of the Spanish Moss"*

Mile 31-Lowdnes County: For a number of years, this stretch of I-75 from here to the Florida border has been very rigidly patrolled by the Valdosta police with radar. In fact, several years ago, the AAA were very close to adding it to the infamous Waldo and Lawtey radar traps in Florida.

Due to the newly constructed concrete median wall though, times have changed. Police can no longer sit in the median monitoring oncoming traffic and quickly give chase. Now they must drive to a sliding barrier gate (notice the gates at mile 25.2 & 21), get out of their car & unlock it, drive through and re-lock it, and then chase the offender.

There will of course still be radar on this stretch but it is much more likely to follow the more normal pattern of using two vehi-

Money Saving Tip

Before you leave Georgia, fill up with gas–even if you only need a 1/4 of a tank. Georgia still has the cheapest gasoline in the USA.

There's an ancient legend
told by Southern folk
About the lacy moss
that garlands the great Live Oak;
A lovely princess and her love
upon their wedding day
Were struck-down by a savage foe
amidst a bitter fray;
Together in death they're buried
so the legends go
'Neath an oak's strong, friendly arms
protected from their foe;
There ... as was the custom
the bride's hair was cut with love
And hung in shining blackness
on the spreading boughs above;
Undisturbed it hung there
for all the world to see
And with the years
the locks turned gray,
and spread from tree to tree.

cles-one parked and the other downstream to pull offenders over.

Exit 22-Charlie Tripper's Fine Dining: A reader wrote, *"a great place - excellent food, reasonably priced - upscale dining,"* so we decided to check it out. Unfortunately, it was closed when we drove by but from a menu posted outside, noted that it's in the $15-25 dinner price range. Open Tu-Sa, 6p-10p, Lounge opens at 5p. ☎ 229-247-0366

Georgia Mile 2-Northbound Welcome Center: If you are traveling north from Florida don't forget to stop and say *"hello"* for me to my friends at the Georgia Welcome Center. Hilda, Cathy, Carol, Leigh and Patty will help make your journey northward through Georgia, as interesting as possible. If you plan any stops, they can often make reservations for you at very favorable rates.

FLORIDA Mile 472-the Florida Border: I'm sure you know by now, Florida's Department of Transport has changed the exit numbers of all its freeways, to the "milepost" system so they are consistent with other states. If you need an "old number-new number" chart, or vice versa, go to my website: **www.i75online.com** and click on *"Florida Information."*

FL Mile 471-Florida Welcome Center: *(see also the Special Report about the new Welcome Center opening in 2005)* Since Florida's major industry is tourism, the State

Insider Tip- The Hamptons

Well not quite the Hamptons of Long Island but if you are planning a stay in the Valdosta (exit 16) or Lake Park (exit 5), I know you will enjoy either of these Hampton Inns. Operated by the same owner, these properties are well furnished, clean and reasonably prices.

The Lake Park Hampton (☎ 229-559-5565) has an interesting atrium lobby with many of the rooms opening onto it. The Valdosta Hampton (☎ 229-241-1234) is larger and has more amenities. We have enjoyed both of these properties and recommend them.

Insider Tip–LuLu's

Several miles to the east of exit 16 is an excellent restaurant which received rave reviews in *"Southern Living"* magazine. With its linen table service, long narrow room & French posters, LuLu's has a definite European ambience. A large collection of wines are available by the glass and chefs work "in front" in full display of the patrons. At the door, you'll meet owner Mary Anna, who loves greeting her guests and making them feel welcome.

For dinner, Kathy and I enjoyed a very tasty Wild Mushroom soup, followed by Grilled Tuna. I selected a caramelized Creme Brule for dessert. The meal was so memorable we will definitely be back.

Lunches are $6-9; Dinner entrees range from $14-$23. Hrs: Lunch, Tu-Sa, 11-2p; Dinner, Th-Sa, 6-10p; Su Brunch, 11-2p

To find LuLu's, from exit 16 drive east on Rt84 (Hill Ave) for 2.4 miles (3.9km) to Ashley St & turn left. Drive 1 block & turn left (Central Ave), drive 1 block & turn left (N.Patterson). LuLu's is on your right at 123 N. Patterson ☎ 912-242-4000

Florida's New Welcome Center

Special Report

When you pull into the Florida Welcome Center at mile marker 471 this year, you will notice a lot of yellow construction tape, orange barrels and some sealed off parking areas. It will all be short lived and is in preparation for the new $13 million Center, scheduled for completion in the late-summer of 2005.

The new Center which is under construction south of the existing 1980-vintage building, will be three times larger to accommodate the more than 850,000 travelers who make this popular stop each year. The inside plan provides improved areas for sampling free juices and planning your Florida stops with the counter staff. Attractive alcoves have been designed to help you gather maps and brochures on a regional basis and of course, visitors will find clean and brightly lit restrooms and vending facilities. Welcome Center security is also being enhanced with the establishment of a permanent Florida Highway Patrol workstation.

Artist's rendering of the new Florida Welcome Center

has a wonderful counter staff to greet and help you. Say *"hi"* from me to manager Patrick and Barbara, the two Glendas, Helen, Rosetta, Dot and Patricia...Oh, and don't forget to pick up your free orange or grapefruit juice.

Incidentally, congratulations to Helen, Dot, Rosetta, Pat and Glenda (Bennett) who recently received letters from Governor Bush, honoring their long time service with the Center. Combined, they represent 145 years of experience, helping travelers on their way to sunny Florida destinations. Pat and Glenda, I'm sure I used to see you behind the counter while I-75 was still being built.

The Center's information section is very well stocked, and open daily from 8a-5p, daily [☎ 386-938-2981]. Restrooms are open 24 hours; the area is patrolled at night.

Incidentally, if you arrive here after hours, go over to the newspaper boxes outside the vending machine area-you will find a good supply of the free Florida motel and restaurant guides, and coupon books here.

Well–we are now in Florida. This is where I must leave you and head back north. Good news though...I'm currently writing a new book called, *"Along Florida's Freeways"* with planned publication for November, 2005.

But for now, I've enjoyed riding along with you to the Georgia border, sharing adventures and stories along the way.

Drive safely and enjoy your time in the sun.

Dave

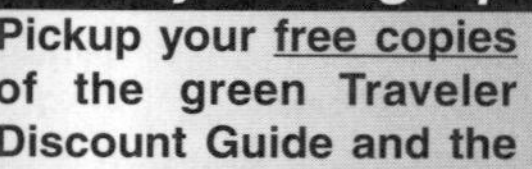

Money Saving Tip

Pickup your free copies of the green Traveler Discount Guide and the red Market America motel coupon books at the Florida Welcome Center (mile 471). Coupons in these books can save you as much as 45% off of regular motel rates.

Don't forget the special free Florida restaurant coupon books, either.

If the Welcome Center is closed, you'll find copies of all these books in the newspaper boxes, outside the vending machine area.

FLORIDA - *named by explorer Ponce de Leon, who discovered the land on Easter Sunday (Pascua Florida), in 1512. Florida means "flowering" in Spanish. Ponce de Leon's original Florida claim encompassed all the land up to and including Newfoundland in Canada.*

I-75 LODGING ALTERNATIVES

Do you sometimes get tired of the nightly motel routine? If so, you might consider several lodging alternatives: bed & breakfast (b&b), state park lodges and especially for the children, log cabins.

BED & BREAKFAST (b&b)

Bed & breakfasting is a great adult lodging alternative. For many years, Kathy and I have enjoyed staying at B&Bs; each stay has been a valuable and unforgettably pleasant experience.

B&B may not be for everybody though. The homes may be a few extra miles off the freeway; you usually have to reserve ahead and provide a deposit, and most important, you must enjoy people-spending time with your host and other guests, chatting about common interests, learning about the local countryside is one of the most enjoyable things about B&B.

Hidden in the countryside bordering Interstate-75, are some unique B&B opportunities. Here are some to try:

- ★ *Georgetown, KY:* **Bryan House B&B**, exit 125/126, 3 miles west. Hosts - Stan & Jan; ☎ 502-863-6289
- ★ *Knoxville, TN:* **Maplehurst Inn**, phone for directions. Hosts - Sonny & Becky ☎ 865-523-7773
- ★ *Tifton, GA:* **Hummingbird's Perch**, Exit 64. 2.6 miles east Host - Frances ☎ 229-382-5431

STATE PARK LODGING

Many state parks have lodging facilities and best of all, they are often subsidized by the state. Here are two to try close by I-75:

Norris State Park, TN (see page 55): this lovely Tennessee park nestled in the woods above Norris Lake has deluxe and "rustic" cabins. The units normally rent by the week, but call the Park, there may be one available for the night (range $45-$90 night). ☎ 865-426-7461

Red Top State Park Lodge, GA: just two miles east of I-75 lies a favorite Lodge of mine (we do <u>not</u> recommend the restaurant). Surrounded by hiking trails winding through the woods near Lake Allatoona, it's a wonderful place to refresh the spirit.

Please drive slowly in the park - it's full of wild deer. Kathy and I often stay here in June. At twilight, we spend an enjoyable hour just sitting quietly near the Lodge's front entrance watching families of deer grazing just south of the parking lot.

The lodge's 33 rooms cost $59-79 (Double) depending upon day-of-the-week and season. Often booked on Fri and Sat but other nights you could enjoy a peaceful night in the woods on the way to Florida (Tip: ask for a field view room). ☎ 770-975-0055.

LOG CABIN LODGINGS

Want to try something different while traveling Interstate-75? Then consider renting a log cabin or cottage in the woods. These can be found at some state parks, or at campgrounds such as Kampgrounds of America (KOA). Many in South Kentucky and Tennessee are rented privately.

Most KOA's along I-75 have log cabins or cottages for rent by the night. Some are available year round, others are closed in the winter. Most have heating and air conditioning; all have window screens, lockable doors, running cold water, electricity ... available in one room or two room layouts, they can "sleep" four-six people.

The cabins are quite basic. You cannot cook inside, but just by your private patio there is usually a BBQ unit and fire pit.

They also lack toilet facilities; instead, you use the washrooms and private showers in the campground's community building, but I've always found these to be quite clean.

The cottages are a bit more elaborate and include a well stocked kitchenette with refrigerator, dishes and silverware. They also include a bathroom with shower unit, and central heating/air conditioning.

In each case, KOA supplies the beds and mattresses; you supply bed linen (or sleeping bags) and towels.

To learn more about these lodging alternatives, pickup a free directory at any KOA campground. Rates vary according to location; I-75 cabins run from $28 (Georgia) to $50/night (Lookout Mountain, Tennessee).

Last year, Kathy and I stayed in one at the KOA in Ringgold, Georgia and had a memorable evening sitting by a campfire, just chatting while enjoying the night sounds and pine needle fragrance coming from the dark woods around us.

TRAVELING WITH PETS

During our recent I-75 travels, we've noticed that many more motels are allowing pets to stay. In fact, I would estimate that there has been a 15-20% increase in the number of "pet friendly" motels along the interstate, since last year's edition.

Many though still require a pet deposit/surcharge (usually $2-$5) basis, or allocate certain rooms as "pet" rooms.

When questioned, I have found most motel operators are not biased against pets. Damage in not an issue-after all, they do not surcharge for children! They do have concerns though with the possibility of a guest having an allergic reaction caused from staying in a room previously occupied by a pet. Proteins in pet saliva can create allergy problems for humans, and the property staff must perform special room cleaning to minimize this - so a small extra fee would seem reasonable.

As a pet owner, I understand that pets are very much part of the family. To help pet owners identify those "pet friendly" motels, I have highlighted their **names in blue** on my 25-mile colored maps.

Exits with veterinarians & animal clinics are identified with a green and blue "V" symbol.

MOTEL 1-800 NUMBERS

The chart below lists the toll free reservation phone numbers for most of the popular motel chains along the freeway. The advantage of a toll free reservation system is its convenience, but the service is often run by an independent "call-center" contractor, so be aware of two drawbacks.

First, you cannot always use a discount coupon from a free coupon books when making an 800 number reservation - some will accept them but many don't. Most reservation services will honor a senior (AARP) or AAA discount but you must mention it to them while on the phone. Make sure you mention it again when you check in, to ensure you get the lower rate.

Secondly, you may be told that the motel of your choice is full. If so, get the motel's phone number from the reservation operator, and call it. The motel can often find you a room since most *do not allocate all their rooms* to the reservation service. They usually keep back some rooms so they are available for last minute local needs. Very rarely is a motel 100% full.

Motel/Inn	Symbol	Toll Free No.
Baymont Inns	Baymnt	877-229-6668
Best Value	BestValue	888-315-2378
Best Western	BestW	800-937-8376
Comfort Inns	Comfrt	800-424-6423
Country Inns/Suites	CtyInnSte	800-456-4000
Courtyard-Marriot	CrtYrd	800-321-2211
Days Inns	Days	800-329-7466
Drury Hotels	Drury	800-378-7946
Econo Lodge	Econo	800-424-6423
Fairfield Inns	Fairfld	800-228-2800
Holiday Inns	H/Inn	800-465-4329
Hampton Inns	Hmptn	800-426-7866
Howard Johnson	HoJo	800-446-4656
Jameson Inns	Jamsn	800-526-3766
Knights Inns	Knght	800-843-5644
Microtel	MicroT	888-771-7171
Motel6	Motel6	800-466-8356
Quality Inns	QltyInn	800-424-6423
Ramada Inns	Ramda	800-272-6232
Red Roof Inns	RedRf	800-733-7663
Rodeway Inns	Rodwy	800-221-2222
Scottish Inns	Scot	800-251-1962
Signature Inns	Signtr	800-822-5252
Sleep Inns	Sleep	800-424-6423
Super 8 Motels	Supr8	800-800-8000
TravelLodge	TravL	800-578-7878

Things You Need to Know

Local Knowledge ... think about it, it's the one quality which helps you feel comfortable and in control when you travel far away from home. This book is based on local knowledge acquired over more than 38 years of I-75 travel, and from the many friends we've made along the way. In this section, I've gathered information for you which is better presented in table form, rather than on the maps or in the text sections of the book.

For instance, if you are traveling with children in the car you need to know that there have been a number of changes to seat belt law in the past year. Both Tennessee and Georgia now require ***Booster Seats for older children***; Tennessee's law which came into effect on July 1, 2004, is arguably one of the most complex child restraint safety laws in the Nation, and is being vigorously enforced. But we have all the answers for you on page 146.

If you can think of other questions which need answers, let me know (see page 203), and I will try and oblige in a future edition:

All information updated as of September, 2004

Radio on the Road

AM radio signals travel much farther in the dark. To avoid interference, the FCC requires that many stations reduce their night "distance" coverage by performing an antenna "pattern" change at dusk. By agreement, some powerful (50,000 watt) AM stations provide nighttime extended coverage and their signals can cover as much as 750 miles after dark. This is useful to know if you are on a night drive since you can stay with the same station for many miles. Here are the powerful AM stations covering your I-75 drive:

MI: Detroit, WJR-760; OH: Cincinnati, WLW-700; KY: Louisville, WHAS-840;

TN: Nashville, WLAC-1510; GA: Atlanta, WSB-750; FL: non assigned

In Ontario, Canada, I recommend the 50,000 watt station, CHWO-740

If you enjoy radio, consider one of the two satellite radio services XM or Sirius. These provide hundreds of channels of music, sports, talk, all distortion free & superb sound... and you can stay tuned to the same program for the entire trip. Receivers are available at most electronic stores (monthly service fee required) Not available in Canada

STATE	State Gas Tax (¢)	Sales Tax	Typical Lodging Taxes (accommodation & sales tax surcharges)
Michigan	.24	6%	Detroit area (Wayne Co.), 10.5%; Monroe, 8%
Ohio	.27	6%	Toledo, 14.25%; Findlay, 13.0%; Dayton, 14.0%; Cincinnati, 10.0%
Kentucky	.172	6%	Florence, 10.3%; Lexington, 12.36%; Richmond, 9.2%; London, 9.18%
Tennessee	.20	7%	Caryville, 14.25%; Knoxville, 17.25%; Chattanooga, 13.25%
Georgia	.125	4%	Dalton, 13%; Atlanta, 13.0%; Macon, 12%; Valdosta, 12%
Florida	.194S	6%	Lake City, 9.0%; Gainesville, 10.0%; Ocala, 6.0%

Notes:

State Gas Tax - this is presented to give an approximation of which states will have the lower gas prices
Sales Tax - these percentages do not include local taxes which can add another .5 - 2%
Lodging Tax Surcharges - when you pay the following morning, you just know that the cost is going to be higher than the room rate you agreed to upon arrival. The amounts in this table includes local accommodation & local/state sales taxes for sample I-75 cities. It's provided as a guide only. The figures do not include other surcharges which individual motel properties might levy, such as a charge for an in-room safe, power surcharge, etc. Always ask about miscellaneous surcharges at check-in time.

NEW SEAT BELT and CHILD RESTRAINT SEAT LAWS (see seat position & seat type codes, below)		
MI:	3yrs & under - *Any, R*	all others - *Any, Seat belt*
OH:	3yrs & under or <40lbs - *Any, R*	all others - *Any, Seat belt*
KY:	<41" tall - *Bk, R*	all others - *Any, Seat belt*
TN:	<1yr, <20lbs - *Bk, RR* 1-3yrs & >20lbs - *Bk, FR* *4-8yrs & <5ft - Bk, Bstr*	all others - *Any, Seat belt*
GA:	<5yrs & <58" - *Bk, R* 4 to 5yrs - *Any, Bstr*	all others - *Any, Seat belt*
FL:	3yrs & under - *Any, R*	all others - *Any, Seat belt*

Codes: < Less than, > Greater than. **Seat Positions:** ***Any***=any car seat, ***Ft***=Front seat, ***Bk***=Rear seat.
Seat Types (Note - all seats must meet the Federal Motor Vehicle Safety Standards): ***R***=Child restraint seat, ***RR***=Rear facing restraint seat, ***FR***=Forward facing restraint seat, ***Bstr***=Child Booster Seat.

OTHER TRAFFIC LAW NOTES:

- Radar detectors permitted in all I-75 states (except in commercial vehicles).
- Right turn on red light (after stop) permitted in all I-75 states, unless otherwise sign posted.

The Triple "A" for Help

One of the best investments you can make for a long distance drive is to join the AAA (or CAA in Canada). It doesn't cost a lot of money–annual membership fees vary by location but are usually in the $50-70 range–and yet the peace of mind provided when traveling long distances is well worth the money. Should you experience a breakdown or other car emergency, help is only a national toll free 1-800 phone call away:

USA - **1-800-AAA-HELP** (1-800-222-4357)   Canada - **1-800-CAA-HELP** (1-800-222-4357)

TORNADO WATCH

Special note: this section is not intended to alarm you - but to make sure that you are well informed and prepared should a Tornado emergency occur in your area, while traveling the I-75.

It was six o'clock in the evening. Kathy and I had checked into a motel in Miamisburg, Ohio, and were beginning to relax after a long day on the interstate . . . when we were interrupted by a loud banging on the door -

"Everybody to the basement - three tornados have been spotted in Preble County!"

Where was Preble County? We had no idea.

What should we do to minimize our risk? We didn't know.

After the emergency was over, I decided to find the answers to these very important questions & share them with you.

Over the last few years we have certainly gained a heightened awareness of tornados

Tornado Safety Tips

If in a sturdy building:

- go to the lowest level, interior room in the building.
- take a flashlight and battery radio.
- stay away from large rooms, such as auditoriums, ballrooms,etc.
- avoid rooms with windows & outside walls.
- hide under something that is sturdy.
- cover yourself with blankets, pillows, coats (to protect from flying debris).
- protect your neck and head areas. Put on a crash or safety helmet, if you have one.

If in a weak structure or RV home:

- get out and seek a sturdy shelter.

If caught in the open:

- if in a car, get right away from it.
- lay flat in a ditch face down (1st choice) or behind a sturdy hedge. Cover head with arms.

SPECIAL NOTE: recent studies indicate that it is unsafe to take shelter in the "V" created by the concrete banks of an overpass. Tornado winds can create killer suctions in this area.

Insider Tip
Your Personal Alert System

After this summer's experience, we do not travel the interstate without a Weather Radio with a weather alert feature - in the car or in our motel room. The best type to buy is a unit which receives all 7 of the National Weather Service (NWS) frequencies. It must be capable of receiving the NWS "Alert" signal - this will ensure that your unit will sound an alarm when a NWS alert signal is received. It should also have a built-in backup battery, for emergency use.

Your home unit should be capable of receiving the special Specific Area Message Encoding (SAME) signal - this signal (also known as the FIPS code) enables your unit to give you alerts for your specific area, rather than on a broad county basis. The six digit FIPS code for your area is obtained by phoning the toll-free NWS number 1-888-697-7263, and following the automated instructions. The resulting code is punched into your radio unit.

I've tested two Radio Shack units with SAME technology while on I-75, and they meet all the requirements and work very well. During our test run, we actually experienced several flood warnings and three severe thunderstorm alerts. The portable mini-unit we use in our car as we travel is Radio Shack model 12-259 (cost $49.99); it runs on 3 AAA batteries. The second unit (Radio Shack 12-261, $49.99) serves as our "plug in" unit in our motel at night since it also serves as an alarm clock. If staying for any time in one location, I obtain the FIPS code for the area. The unit has a 9v backup battery and displays alert messages on a screen as well as indicating the alert severity. *(Canadians, please note: the codes used by the SAME unit are for land areas in the U.S. only; the unit cannot be purchased from Radio Shack stores outside the U.S.A.)*.

(or twisters, as they are often known), as we travel. In April, 1996, a section of the small town of Berea was devastated by a tornado which swept across the I-75 and slammed into the "old town" area. And of course, we are all aware of the terrible damage done by a tornado which touched down just east of Kissimmee, Florida during the 1997/8 winter. Here are some tornado facts:

Tornados tend to travel from the south-west quadrant of a storm system to the north east. Never try to outrun a tornado in your

County Maps

Tornado warnings are issued by county name. I have shown all the **I-75 counties** (in yellow) through which you may travel, together with at least one other county either side (in green).

The **southwest-northeast axis** is also shown in each case, since this tends to be the general path of tornado spawning storms.

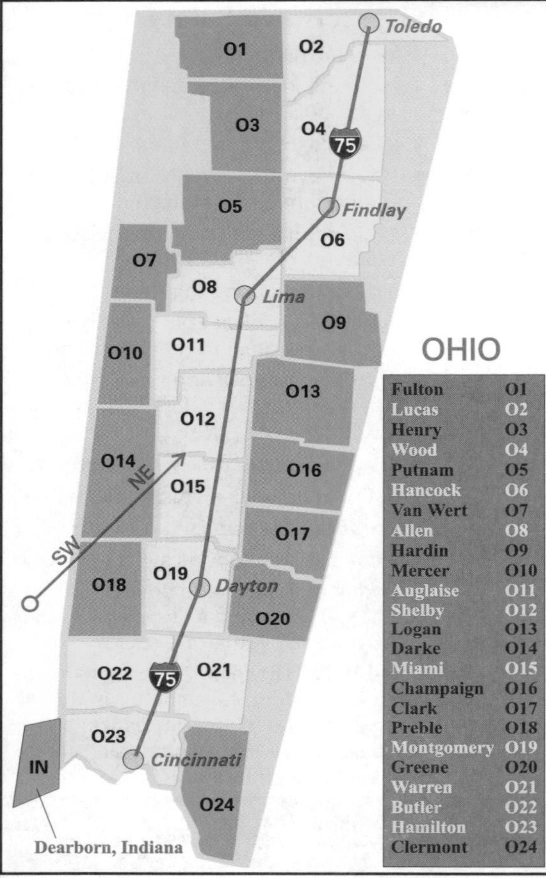

County	Code
Fulton	O1
Lucas	O2
Henry	O3
Wood	O4
Putnam	O5
Hancock	O6
Van Wert	O7
Allen	O8
Hardin	O9
Mercer	O10
Auglaise	O11
Shelby	O12
Logan	O13
Darke	O14
Miami	O15
Champaign	O16
Clark	O17
Preble	O18
Montgomery	O19
Greene	O20
Warren	O21
Butler	O22
Hamilton	O23
Clermont	O24

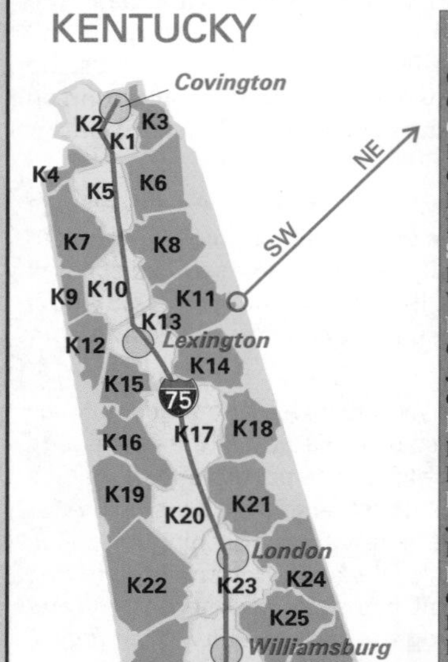

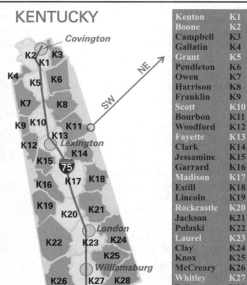

County	Code
Kenton	K1
Boone	K2
Campbell	K3
Gallatin	K4
Grant	K5
Pendleton	K6
Owen	K7
Harrison	K8
Franklin	K9
Scott	K10
Bourbon	K11
Woodford	K12
Fayette	K13
Clark	K14
Jessamine	K15
Garrard	K16
Madison	K17
Estill	K18
Lincoln	K19
Rockcastle	K20
Jackson	K21
Pulaski	K22
Laurel	K23
Clay	K24
Knox	K25
McCreary	K26
Whitley	K27
Bell	K28

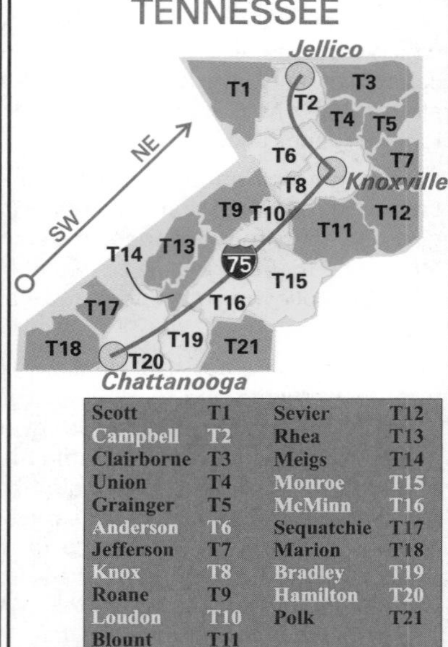

County	Code	County	Code
Scott	T1	Sevier	T12
Campbell	T2	Rhea	T13
Clairborne	T3	Meigs	T14
Union	T4	Monroe	T15
Grainger	T5	McMinn	T16
Anderson	T6	Sequatchie	T17
Jefferson	T7	Marion	T18
Knox	T8	Bradley	T19
Roane	T9	Hamilton	T20
Loudon	T10	Polk	T21
Blount	T11		

car, but if there is clear sky to your south-east, that is the direction to go.

A storm that can spawn tornados is often preceded with lightning, hail and heavy rain. They tend to happen in late afternoon, early evenings during the late-spring/early summer.

Most injuries are caused by flying debris. A tornado can come in many strengths, from one which damages light trees, branches or billboards (known as an F0) to a very rare F5 which can hurtle a wooden plank projectile at speeds up to 200 mph.

MICHIGAN
M1
M2
M3
M4
M5
M6
M7
NE
SW
Detroit
Monroe
75
Livingston M1
Oakland M2
Macomb M3
Washtenaw M4
Wayne M5
Lenawee M6
Monroe M7

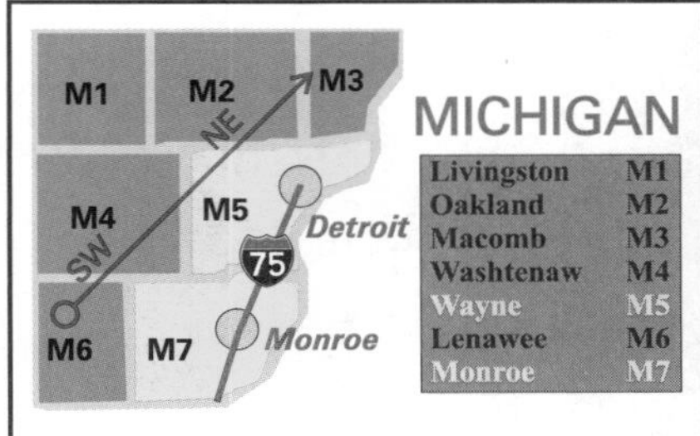

Pressure differential in tornados does not play a big role in terms of damage. Forget the dated advice about opening a window on the opposite side to the storm; experts say it makes no difference.

In terms of risk, here are annual average tornado frequencies by state, compiled by the *National Severe Storm Center* in Kansas City: Texas-189, Kansas-92, Oklahoma-64, Michigan-21, Ohio-61, Kentucky-11, Tennessee-8 and Georgia-19.

<u>Interstate-75 is no more vulnerable to tornados than any of the other major corridor routes between the mid-west and Florida.</u>

In fact, the tips in this story can be equally as well applied to your home area. I consider my home weather alert system as important as my smoke detectors or security system, and keep it running at all times.

I hope you never encounter a tornado, but if you do–you are well prepared.

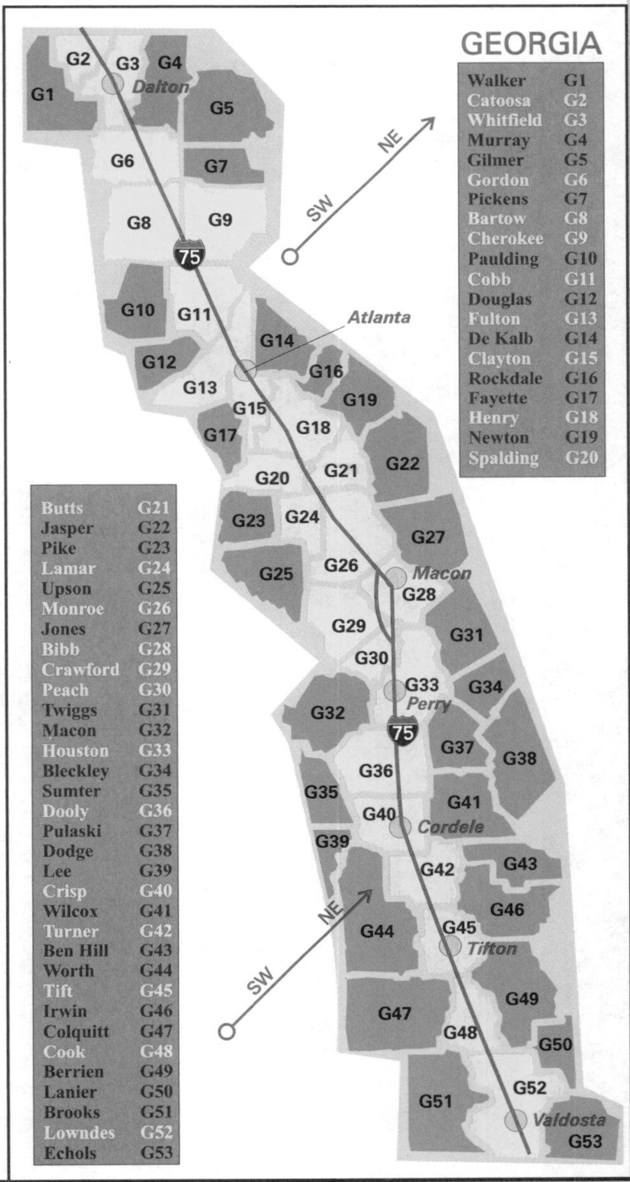

GEORGIA
Dalton
Atlanta
Macon
Perry
Cordele
Tifton
Valdosta
75
NE
SW
Walker G1
Catoosa G2
Whitfield G3
Murray G4
Gilmer G5
Gordon G6
Pickens G7
Bartow G8
Cherokee G9
Paulding G10
Cobb G11
Douglas G12
Fulton G13
De Kalb G14
Clayton G15
Rockdale G16
Fayette G17
Henry G18
Newton G19
Spalding G20
Butts G21
Jasper G22
Pike G23
Lamar G24
Upson G25
Monroe G26
Jones G27
Bibb G28
Crawford G29
Peach G30
Twiggs G31
Macon G32
Houston G33
Bleckley G34
Sumter G35
Dooly G36
Pulaski G37
Dodge G38
Lee G39
Crisp G40
Wilcox G41
Turner G42
Ben Hill G43
Worth G44
Tift G45
Irwin G46
Colquitt G47
Cook G48
Berrien G49
Lanier G50
Brooks G51
Lowndes G52
Echols G53

INTERSTATE-75 RV PARK & CAMPGROUND SITES

State	I-75 Exit	Direction	Campground	Phone	# of Sites	Open	Rates	Distance in Miles	Driving Directions
MI	11	W	Harbortown RV Resort	734-384-4700	250	all year	$28-35/family	1/2	½ mile West on Laplaisance Rd; Entrance on left
OH	179	W	Fire Lake	888-879-2267	100	4/15-10/15	$23-26/2people	2½	1½ miles W on 6; ½ m S on 25; ½ m W on Kramer Rd; on right
OH	164	E	Pleasant View	419-299-3897	300	all year	$19-23/fam.	1	¾ m E on 613; ¼ m SE on 218; Entrance on right
OH	161	E	Shady Lake	419-423-3490	139	all year	$22/fam.	2½	½ m E on 99; 1½ m N on CR 220; ½ m W on 101; Ent on right
OH	145	E	Twin Lake Park	888-436-3610	85	4/1-11/1	$26-40/fam.	.6	.1 m S on 235; ½ m E on 34; Entrance on left
OH	110	E	KOA Wapakonata	419-738-6016	73	2/4-12/4	$27-35/2p	1½	.2 m E to first intersection; ¾ m N on Cemetery Rd; Ent on left
OH	82	E	Poor Farmer's	937-368-2449	540	4/15-11/30	$17/fam.	6¾	6 m E on US36; ¾ m S on Lost Creek-Shelby Rd; Ent on left
OH	14	W	Quality Inn RV Park	513-771-5252	11	all year	$25/RV	1/4	¼ mile west on Glendale-Milford Rd; Entrance on left
OH	10	W	Woodland Trailer	513-931-8845	20	all year	$25/2p	4¼	4 m W on Galbraith; ¼ m S on Daly; Entrance on right
KY	171	W	Oak Creek Campground	859-485-9131	105	all year	$18.50-24/2p	1	1m SW on Hwy 16; Entrance on right.
KY	166	E	KOA Cincinnati - South	859-428-2000	101	all year	$22-32/2p	2¼	¼ m E on 491; 2.6 m S on US25; Entrance on right
KY	159	W	Dry Ridge Camper's Village	859-824-5836	70	all year	$20/RV	1.2	50 yds W on 22; 1 m N on Service Rd; Entrance at end of road
KY	120	E	Kentucky Horse Park SP	800-370-6416	260	all year	phone for rates	1/2	½ m E on 1973; Entrance on left
KY	95	E	Fort Boonesborough SP	606-527-3131	167	all year	phone for rates	5.9	4.9 m E on 627; ½m S on 338
KY	76	W	Oh Kentucky Campground	859-986-1150	152	all year	$10-14/RV	1/4	¼ m W on Hwy 21; Entrance on right
KY	76	W	Walnut Meadow Campground	859-986-6180	123	all year	$10-20/2p	1/2	½m W on Hwy 21; Entrance on left
KY	62	E	KOA Renfro Valley	606-256-2474	133	all year	$19-31/2p	1½	1½ m E on Hwy 25; Entrance on right
KY	62	E	Renfro Valley RV Park	800-765-7464	199	3/1-12/31	$21.20-25.44/RV	1/4	¼ mile east on Highway 25; Entrance on right
KY	38	E	Levi Jackson Wilderness Rd S/P	606-878-8000	146	all year	phone for rates	4.3	2 m E on 192; 2 3/10 m S on 25; Entrance on left
KY	29	W	KOA Corbin	606-528-1534	90	all year	$17-27/2p	1/2	¼ m W on 770; ¼ m S (follow signs); Entrance on right
KY	11	W	Williamsburg Travel Trailer Park	800-426-3267	56	all year	$12/RV	---	50 yds W on Hwy 92; Entrance on right
TN	134	W	Cove Lake SP	423-566-9701	100	all year	phone for rates	1/2	½ m NE on Hwy 25; park entrance on left
TN	141	E	Royal Blue RV Park	423-566-4847	45	all year	$19.75/RV	1/2	½ m S on Luther Seibers Rd (at the giant cross)
TN	128	E	Norris Dam State Park	865-426-7461	85	all year	phone for rates	7	see map on page 55; 7 miles east on US441; Entrance on left
TN	122	E	Big Ridge SP	865-992-5523	52	all year	phone for rates	12	12 E on Hwy 61; Entrance on left
TN	122	E	Fox Inn Campground	865-494-9386	93	all year	$16-26/2p	1/5	1/5 m E on Hwy 61; Entrance on left
TN	62	W	KOA Sweetwater Valley	865-213-3900	53	all year	$24-29/fam.	1	¾ m W on Oakland; follow signs S ¼ m; Entrance on left
TN	1	W	Holiday Trav-L-Park	800-693-2877	178	all year	$23/2p	3/4	¼ m W on Hwy 41; ½ m S on Mack Smith Rd; Ent on right

INTERSTATE-75 RV PARK & CAMPGROUND SITES

State	I-75 Exit	Direction	Campground	Phone	# of Sites	Open	Rates	Distance in Miles	Driving Directions
TN	49	E	Athens I-75 Campground	423-745-9199	60	5/15 - 9/15	$19-20/2p	1/5	1/5 m E on Hwy 30; Entrance on right
TN	20	W	KOA Cleveland	423-472-8928	92	all year	$22-28/2p	1	½ m W on county Rd; follow signs ½ m; Entrance on right
GA	350	W	KOA Chattanooga S KOA	706-937-4166	145	all year	$23-29/2p	1/4	¼m W on Hwy 2, Entrance on right (New Owner)
GA	315	E	KOA Calhoun	706-629-7511	89	all year	$21-27/2people	1½	1½ m E on Hwy 156; Entrance on right
GA	296	W	KOA Cartersville	770-382-7330	117	all year	$21-23/2p	1/4	¼ m W on Cassville Rd; Entrance on left
GA	285	E	Red Top Mountain SP	770-975-0055	92	all year	phone for rates	1¼	1 ¼ m E on Red Top Mountain Rd; follow signs in park
GA	283	E	Allatoona Landing	800-346-7305	140	all year	$19.75-28.35/4p	2	2 miles E on Allatoona Rd; Entrance on left
GA	269	W	KOA Atlanta N (Kennesaw)	770-427-2406	230	all year	$28-30/2people	2 1/10	1½ m W on Barrett; ½ m N on Hwy 41; 1/10 m Battlefield Pkwy
GA	198	W	High Falls Campground	800-428-0132	124	all year	$18/family	1/10	1/10 m W on High Falls Rd; Entrance on right
GA	186	E	KOA Forsyth	478-994-2019	141	all year	$22-24/2people	3/5	100 ft E on Juliette Rd; ½ m N on Frontage Rd; Ent on right
GA	5	W	Lake Tobesofkee Park	478-474-8770	110	all year	phone for rates	5.9	3.5 m W on Rt 74; turn left on Lower Thomaston; 2.4 m on left
GA	136	E	Boland's RV Park	478-987-3371	65	all year	$18-20/2people	1/3	¼ m E on Hwy 341; 1/10 m N on Perimeter Rd; Ent on left
GA	136	W	Crossroads Travel Park	478-987-3141	64	all year	$21/2people	1/10	1/10 m W on Hwy 341; Entrance on left
GA	135	W	Fair Harbor RV Park	877-988-8844	153	all year	$22/RV	1/4	¼ m W of exit 42; Entrance on right
GA	97	W	KOA Cordele	229-273-5454	73	all year	$24-26/2p	1/4	¼ m W on Rockhouse Rd; Entrance on right
GA	92	W	Southern Gates RV	229-273-6464	46	all year	$18/family	1/4	¼m W on Deep Creek Rd; Entrance on right
GA	84	W	Ashburn RV Park	229-567-3334	77	all year	$8.95/2people	1/10	1/10m W on Amboy Rd; Entrance on right
GA	60	W	Amy's South GA RV Park	229-386-8441	86	all year	$18/2people	1	1m W on South Central Ave; Entrance on right.
GA	39	W	Reed Bingham SP	229-896-3551	44	all year	phone for rates	6	6m W on Hwy 37; watch for sign
GA	18	W	River Park	229-244-8397	62	all year	$18-19/2people	1/10	1/10 m W on Hwy 133; Entrance on right
GA	5	E	Eagles Roost Campground	229-559-5192	140	all year	$22/2people	3/5	100 ft E; ½ m S on Frontage Rd; Entrance on left

We recommend that you purchase a current copy of ***Woodall's Campground Directory*** (available from most bookstores, or phone 1-800-323-9076). This comprehensive directory covers all the key parks and campgrounds state by state, across North America.

In addition, if you are not already a member, consider joining the ***Good Sam Club.*** The benefits are numerous, and include discounts at various campgrounds and on propane purchases, special RV insurance, etc. Good Sam publishes the ***Trailer Life Campground and RV Park & Services Directory,*** another excellent source of parks and campgrounds. Phone 1-800-234-3450 for membership information and services.

Both of these directories include information about RV services and suppliers (parts) -- and tourist attractions along the way.

INTERSTATE-75 PUBLIC GOLF COURSES

State Exit	Location	Golfcourse	Address	Phone #	Semi Prvt/ Public	Total Yds/ # Tees	Par	Fees $ Week/ Wkend	Directions	Notes (see below)
OH187	Perrysburg	Tanglewood GC	9802 Dowling Road	419-833-1725	S	5822/3	72	13/15	.6m E on 582; 1.4m N on Dunbridge; .9m on 17 to Dowling	1
OH161	Findlay	Hillcrest GC	800 West Bigelow	419-423-7211	S	6981/3	72	19/22	.5m E on Twp99; 1m S on N Main; .6 W on W Bigelow	2
OH130	Lima	Springbrook	4200 Ottawa Rd	419-225-8037	P	6045/3	71	17/19	3.5m W on Bluelick; .6 N on 65; bear right @ fork for .1m	2
OH 63	Vandalia	Castle Hills	125 Clubhouse Rd	937-890-1300	P	6617/4	71	22/26	.5m E to Brownschool; .2m N to GC	3
OH 44	Miamisburg	Mound GC	757 Mound Rd	937-866-2211	P	5605/2	72	13/14	2.7m W on 725; .4m S on S 6th to Mound Road	2
OH 29	Middletown	Pleasant Hill	6487 Hankins Rd	513-539-7221	P	6586/2	71	21/21	3.5m W on 63; 1m S on Salzman; .3m E on Hankins	2
KY 181	Florence	World of Sport	7400 Woodspoint Dr	859-371-8255	P	2997/2	58	18/18	.1m NW on Burlington Pk; .3m NE on Woodspoint	2
KY 104	Lexington	Lakeside Munic.	3725 Richmond Rd	859-263-5315	P	6844/3	72	18/18	2.5m NW on SR418; join Richmond Rd (US25) NW for .6m	2
KY 77	Berea	Berea CC	128 Lorriane Ct	859-986-7141	S	6134/3	72	14/18	2.1m E of exit - see Berea map on page 52	2
KY 38	London	Crooked Creek	781 Crooked Creek Dr	606-877-1993	S	7007/5	72	35/35	.2m E on 192; 1.7m S on 229; turn L onto Conley; .3m to GC	2
KY ---	Williamsburg	The Golf Course	690 Airport Rd	606-549-4215	S	3300/3	36	12/12	S/Bnd-exit 25 W 6.6m; N/Bnd-exit 15 W 6.8m	2
TN 76	Loudon	Riverview GC	101 Club Dr	865-986-6972	S	6072/3	72	11/16	E of exit; turn right on Hotchkiss Valley Rd 1.7m	2
TN 2	Chattanoga	Brainerd GC	5203 Old Mission Rd	423-855-2692	P	6468/4	72	13/17	1.2m on I-24W to exit 184; .3m S Moore; .9m N to GC	2
GA317	Calhoun	Calhoun Elks	143 Craigtown Rd NE	706-629-4091	S	5985/3	71	9/14	.1m E on SR225	2
GA306	Adairsville	Indian Ridge GC	4333 Adairsville Rd NE	706-291-9049	P	5720/2	72	12/22	8.6m west on Adairsville Rd (SR140)	2
GA277	Acworth	Centennial	5225 Woodstock Rd	770-975-1000	P	6849/4	72	42/52	.1m S to Baker (SR92); 1.1m E to Woodstock; .8m NW to GC	2
GA ---	Marietta	City Club	510 Powder Springs	770-528-4653	P	5738/3	71	39/49	see map on page 61 for I-75 exits and golf course location	2
GA187	Forsyth	Forsyth GC	400 Country Club Dr	478-994-5328	P	6053/3	72	10/12	.6 S on SR83; .8m W on Johnson; .7m on CountryClub to GC	2
GA ---	Macon	Barrington Hall	7100 Zebulon Rd	478-757-8358	S	7062/5	72	29/39	I-475 exit 9 - 1.9m W on Zebulon (do not turn at Lamar)	2
GA101	Cordele	Georgia Vets	2315 Hwy 280 W	229-276-2377	P	6869/4	72	17-21	6.8m W on SR280	4
GA 66	Tifton	Forest Lakes	260 Sutton Rd	229-382-7626	P	6806/4	72	22-22	3.5m E on Brighton Rd; .4m NE on Clements Simmons to GC	2
GA 22	Valdosta	Northlake G&CC	4025 Northlake Dr	229-247-8613	P	5193/2	68	9/12	E on Valdosta Rd (US41N), first turn on your left	2
GA 22	Valdosta	Stone Creek	4300 N Coleman Rd	229-247-2527	S	6705/4	72	35-45	.3 E on N Valdosta; .4 S on Coleman to GC	2
GA 5	Lake Park	Francis Lake	5366 Golf Dr	229-559-7961	S	6458/4	72	26-35	.3m E on SR376 to GC	2

I hope you enjoy this selection of Public (P) and Semi-Private (S) golf courses on your Interstate-75 drive. The fees quoted are peak season fees, so may be lower when you pass by. There are many more - the best place to find them is on the internet at www.golfcourse.com. Please refer to the codes in the last column (key below) to determine the course's season.

NOTES: **1** = Open Apr 1-Oct 31, **2** = Open all year, **3** = Open Feb 1-Dec 15, **4** =Open all year, except Mondays.

Northbound Route

First time readers: please read the *"Quick Start Hints"* on the inside of the front cover - this will quickly explain how the book is laid out in sections to help you on your journey. The Key to the road speed colors and map symbols is located on the front cover flap.

When I designed the first edition of this book in 1992, I had to make a difficult decision. Should the book be laid out so it presents information in a logical sequence for southbound travelers, or for those driving north?

Since our primary market is the *"snowbird couple"* driving to Florida for the winter, setting the book out in southbound sequence was the natural choice.

If you are **Northbound** and joining the book for the first time, I don't want you to miss important tips or helpful information, so here's a table of useful page references you should check before setting off.

Insider Tip for Northbound Travelers
Northbound Photographs

Driving north with the sun over your shoulder makes the roadside scenery much more interesting and acceptable for in-car photography. In particular, look closely at the rock cuts in north Tennessee and south Kentucky. Early morning sun angled across cuts on the west side of the interstate and late afternoon sun lighting rock cuts on the east will reveal all sorts of interesting things such as the vertical drill holes used for the dynamite charges when the road was being built.

If using an automatic camera from inside the car, don't forget to turn off the auto focusing feature (otherwise it will tend to focus on your car window glass) and set for as high a shutter speed as possible. If you don't have a high shutter speed, then try and "lock" your camera on the subject by panning as the car moves forward.

Something I sometimes forget is to make sure my windshield is clean, both inside and out...it's amazing the improvement in your photos if shooting through clean glass.

Never pull on to the soft shoulder for your photograph - an interstate shoulder is a very dangerous place to be and should only be used for emergency stops.

All information updated as of September, 2004

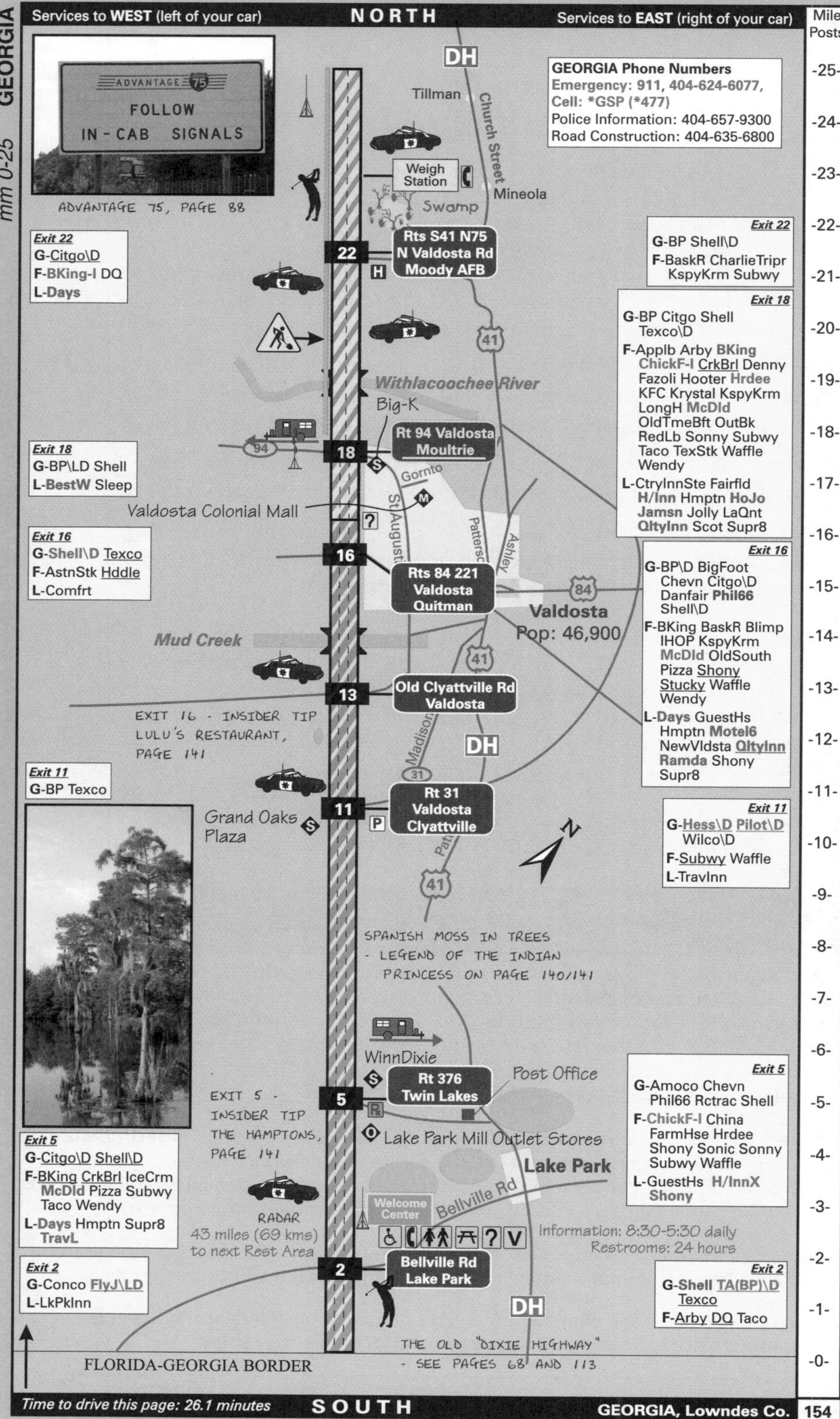
Services to WEST (left of your car)
NORTH
Services to EAST (right of your car)
Mile Posts
ADVANTAGE 75
FOLLOW
IN-CAB SIGNALS
ADVANTAGE 75, PAGE 88
GEORGIA Phone Numbers
Emergency: 911, 404-624-6077,
Cell: *GSP (*477)
Police Information: 404-657-9300
Road Construction: 404-635-6800
DH
Tillman
Church Street
Mineola
Weigh Station
Swamp
Exit 22
G-Citgo\D
F-BKing-I DQ
L-Days
22
Rts S41 N75
N Valdosta Rd
Moody AFB
H
Exit 22
G-BP Shell\D
F-BaskR CharlieTripr
KspyKrm Subwy
Exit 18
G-BP Citgo Shell
Texco\D
F-Applb Arby BKing
ChickF-I CrkBrl Denny
Fazoli Hooter Hrdee
KFC Krystal KspyKrm
LongH McDld
OldTmeBft OutBk
RedLb Sonny Subwy
Taco TexStk Waffle
Wendy
L-CtryInnSte Fairfld
H/Inn Hmptn HoJo
Jamsn Jolly LaQnt
QltyInn Scot Supr8
41
Withlacoochee River
Big-K
94
18
Rt 94 Valdosta
Moultrie
Exit 18
G-BP\LD Shell
L-BestW Sleep
Gornto
St Augustine
Valdosta Colonial Mall
Patterson
Ashley
Exit 16
G-Shell\D Texco
F-AstnStk Hddle
L-Comfrt
16
Rts 84 221
Valdosta
Quitman
84
Exit 16
G-BP\D BigFoot
Chevn Citgo\D
Danfair Phil66
Shell\D
F-BKing BaskR Blimp
IHOP KspyKrm
McDld OldSouth
Pizza Shony
Stucky Waffle
Wendy
L-Days GuestHs
Hmptn Motel6
NewVldsta QltyInn
Ramda Shony
Supr8
Valdosta
Pop: 46,900
Mud Creek
41
13
Old Clyattville Rd
Valdosta
EXIT 16 - INSIDER TIP
LULU'S RESTAURANT,
PAGE 141
Madison
DH
31
Exit 11
G-BP Texco
11
Grand Oaks
Plaza
Rt 31
Valdosta
Clyattville
P
Exit 11
G-Hess\D Pilot\D
Wilco\D
F-Subwy Waffle
L-TravInn
N
41
SPANISH MOSS IN TREES
- LEGEND OF THE INDIAN
PRINCESS ON PAGE 140/141
WinnDixie
5
Rt 376
Twin Lakes
Post Office
EXIT 5 -
INSIDER TIP
THE HAMPTONS,
PAGE 141
Lake Park Mill Outlet Stores
Lake Park
Exit 5
G-Amoco Chevn
Phil66 Rctrac Shell
F-ChickF-I China
FarmHse Hrdee
Shony Sonic Sonny
Subwy Waffle
L-GuestHs H/InnX
Shony
Exit 5
G-Citgo\D Shell\D
F-BKing CrkBrl IceCrm
McDld Pizza Subwy
Taco Wendy
L-Days Hmptn Supr8
TravL
Welcome Center
Bellville Rd
RADAR
43 miles (69 kms)
to next Rest Area
Information: 8:30-5:30 daily
Restrooms: 24 hours
Exit 2
G-Conco FlyJ\LD
L-LkPkInn
2
Bellville Rd
Lake Park
DH
Exit 2
G-Shell TA(BP)\D
Texco
F-Arby DQ Taco
FLORIDA-GEORGIA BORDER
THE OLD "DIXIE HIGHWAY"
- SEE PAGES 68 AND 113
-25-
-24-
-23-
-22-
-21-
-20-
-19-
-18-
-17-
-16-
-15-
-14-
-13-
-12-
-11-
-10-
-9-
-8-
-7-
-6-
-5-
-4-
-3-
-2-
-1-
-0-
Time to drive this page: 26.1 minutes
SOUTH

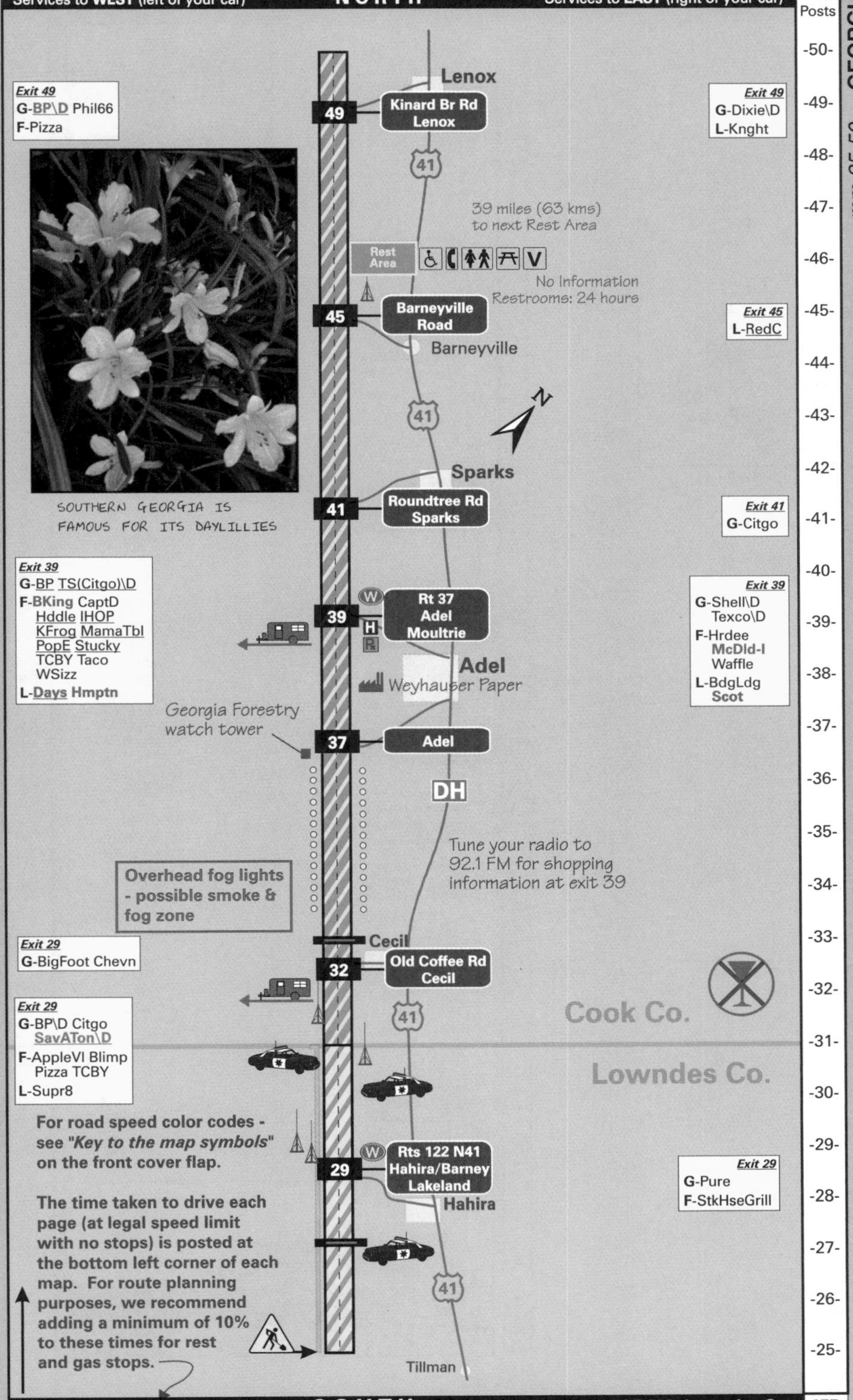

Lenox

Exit 49
G-BP\D Phil66
F-Pizza

49 Kinard Br Rd Lenox

Exit 49
G-Dixie\D
L-Knght

41

39 miles (63 kms) to next Rest Area

Rest Area

No Information
Restrooms: 24 hours

45 Barneyville Road

Barneyville

Exit 45
L-RedC

41

N

SOUTHERN GEORGIA IS FAMOUS FOR ITS DAYLILLIES

Sparks

41 Roundtree Rd Sparks

Exit 41
G-Citgo

Exit 39
G-BP TS(Citgo)\D
F-BKing CaptD Hddle IHOP KFrog MamaTbl PopE Stucky TCBY Taco WSizz
L-Days Hmptn

39 Rt 37 Adel Moultrie

Exit 39
G-Shell\D Texco\D
F-Hrdee McDld-I Waffle
L-BdgLdg Scot

Adel

Weyhauser Paper

Georgia Forestry watch tower

37 Adel

DH

Tune your radio to 92.1 FM for shopping information at exit 39

Overhead fog lights - possible smoke & fog zone

Exit 29
G-BigFoot Chevn

Cecil

32 Old Coffee Rd Cecil

Exit 29
G-BP\D Citgo SavATon\D
F-AppleVl Blimp Pizza TCBY
L-Supr8

41

Cook Co.

Lowndes Co.

For road speed color codes - see *"Key to the map symbols"* on the front cover flap.

29 Rts 122 N41 Hahira/Barney Lakeland

Hahira

Exit 29
G-Pure
F-StkHseGrill

The time taken to drive each page (at legal speed limit with no stops) is posted at the bottom left corner of each map. For route planning purposes, we recommend adding a minimum of 10% to these times for rest and gas stops.

41

Tillman

-50- -49- -48- -47- -46- -45- -44- -43- -42- -41- -40- -39- -38- -37- -36- -35- -34- -33- -32- -31- -30- -29- -28- -27- -26- -25-

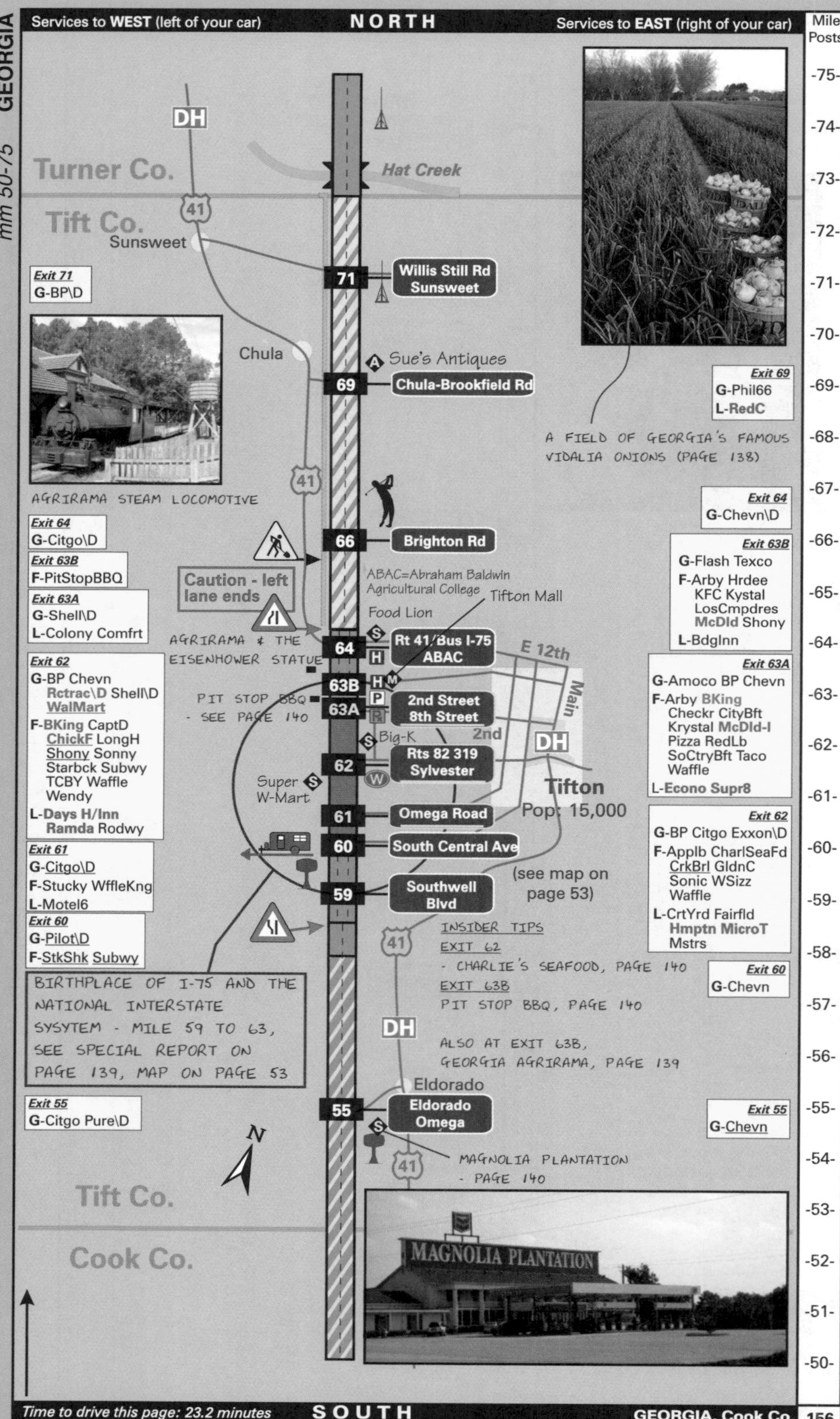
Services to WEST (left of your car)
NORTH
Services to EAST (right of your car)
Mile Posts
-75- -74- -73- -72- -71- -70- -69- -68- -67- -66- -65- -64- -63- -62- -61- -60- -59- -58- -57- -56- -55- -54- -53- -52- -51- -50-
DH
Turner Co.
Hat Creek
Tift Co.
41
Sunsweet
Exit 71
G-BP\D
71
Willis Still Rd Sunsweet
Chula
Sue's Antiques
69
Chula-Brookfield Rd
Exit 69
G-Phil66
L-RedC
A FIELD OF GEORGIA'S FAMOUS VIDALIA ONIONS (PAGE 138)
AGRIRAMA STEAM LOCOMOTIVE
Exit 64
G-Chevn\D
Exit 64
G-Citgo\D
66
Brighton Rd
Exit 63B
F-PitStopBBQ
Exit 63B
G-Flash Texco
F-Arby Hrdee
KFC Kystal
LosCmpdres
McDld Shony
L-BdgInn
Caution - left lane ends
ABAC=Abraham Baldwin Agricultural College
Tifton Mall
Exit 63A
G-Shell\D
L-Colony Comfrt
Food Lion
AGRIRAMA & THE EISENHOWER STATUE
64
Rt 41/Bus I-75 ABAC
E 12th
Main
Exit 63A
G-Amoco BP Chevn
F-Arby BKing
Checkr CityBft
Krystal McDld-I
Pizza RedLb
SoCtryBft Taco
Waffle
L-Econo Supr8
Exit 62
G-BP Chevn
Rctrac\D Shell\D
WalMart
F-BKing CaptD
ChickF LongH
Shony Sonny
Starbck Subwy
TCBY Waffle
Wendy
L-Days H/Inn
Ramda Rodwy
63B
63A
PIT STOP BBQ - SEE PAGE 140
2nd Street 8th Street
2nd
Big-K
DH
62
Rts 82 319 Sylvester
Tifton Pop: 15,000
Super W-Mart
61
Omega Road
Exit 62
G-BP Citgo Exxon\D
F-Applb CharlSeaFd
CrkBrl GldnC
Sonic WSizz
Waffle
L-CrtYrd Fairfld
Hmptn MicroT
Mstrs
Exit 61
G-Citgo\D
F-Stucky WffleKng
L-Motel6
60
South Central Ave
59
Southwell Blvd
(see map on page 53)
Exit 60
G-Pilot\D
F-StkShk Subwy
41
INSIDER TIPS
EXIT 62
- CHARLIE'S SEAFOOD, PAGE 140
EXIT 63B
PIT STOP BBQ, PAGE 140
ALSO AT EXIT 63B, GEORGIA AGRIRAMA, PAGE 139
Exit 60
G-Chevn
BIRTHPLACE OF I-75 AND THE NATIONAL INTERSTATE SYSYTEM - MILE 59 TO 63, SEE SPECIAL REPORT ON PAGE 139, MAP ON PAGE 53
DH
Eldorado
Exit 55
G-Citgo Pure\D
55
Eldorado Omega
Exit 55
G-Chevn
N
41
MAGNOLIA PLANTATION - PAGE 140
Tift Co.
Cook Co.
MAGNOLIA PLANTATION

EXIT 101 - CORDELE'S CONFEDERATE AIRFORCE TITAN MISSILE - SEE PAGE 138

Crisp Co.

41 DH

99 Rt 300 GA-FLA Pkwy

Wenona

Antiques

97 Rt 33 Wenona

Exit 97
G-TA(BP)\D
F-CPride
GtAmBft
Pizza PopE

RV Park Service

EXIT 99 - VIDALIA ONIONS - SEE PAGE 138

Plantation House

Arabi

92 Arabi

Exit 92
G-BP\D

Exit 92
G-Chevn Phil66
F-IceCrm
L-BdgInn

AN ABANDONED BRIDGE COVERED WITH VINES EVOKES THE MYSTERY AND ROMANCE OF "FOREVER GEORGIA," THIS TIMELESS SECTION OF THE "OLD SOUTH"

Crisp Co.

Turner Co.

41

W Fork Deep Creek

23 miles (37 kms) to next Rest Area

Rest Area

No Information
Restrooms: 24 hours

84 Rt 159 Ashburn Amboy

Exit 84
G-BP\D
F-Subwy

Exit 84
G-Shell\D

PEANUT? PAGE 138

Ashburn

82 Rt 112 Ashburn Fitzgerald

Exit 82
G-BP Chevn
F-Hddle Hrdee
Krystal McDld
Pizza Shony
L-BestW Days
Ramda Supr8

Levelour

EXIT 82 - INSIDER TIP ASHBURN'S FRENCH MARKET, SEE PAGE 138

80 Bussey Rd

Exit 80
G-Chevn\D

Agratech

Sycamore

78 Rt 32 Sycamore Ocilla

DH 41 N

Swamp

EXIT 78 - JEFFERSON DAVIS HISTORICAL CAPTURE SITE AND MUSEUM - 14.4 MILES EAST (19 MINS DRIVE TIME) - PAGE 139

Exit 80
G-Exxon\D Shell
F-Subwy
L-BdgInn

Inaha

75 Inaha Rd

Exit 75
G-BP
F-DQ

Exit 75
G-Chevn

Turner Co.

-100- -99- -98- -97- -96- -95- -94- -93- -92- -91- -90- -89- -88- -87- -86- -85- -84- -83- -82- -81- -80- -79- -78- -77- -76- -75-

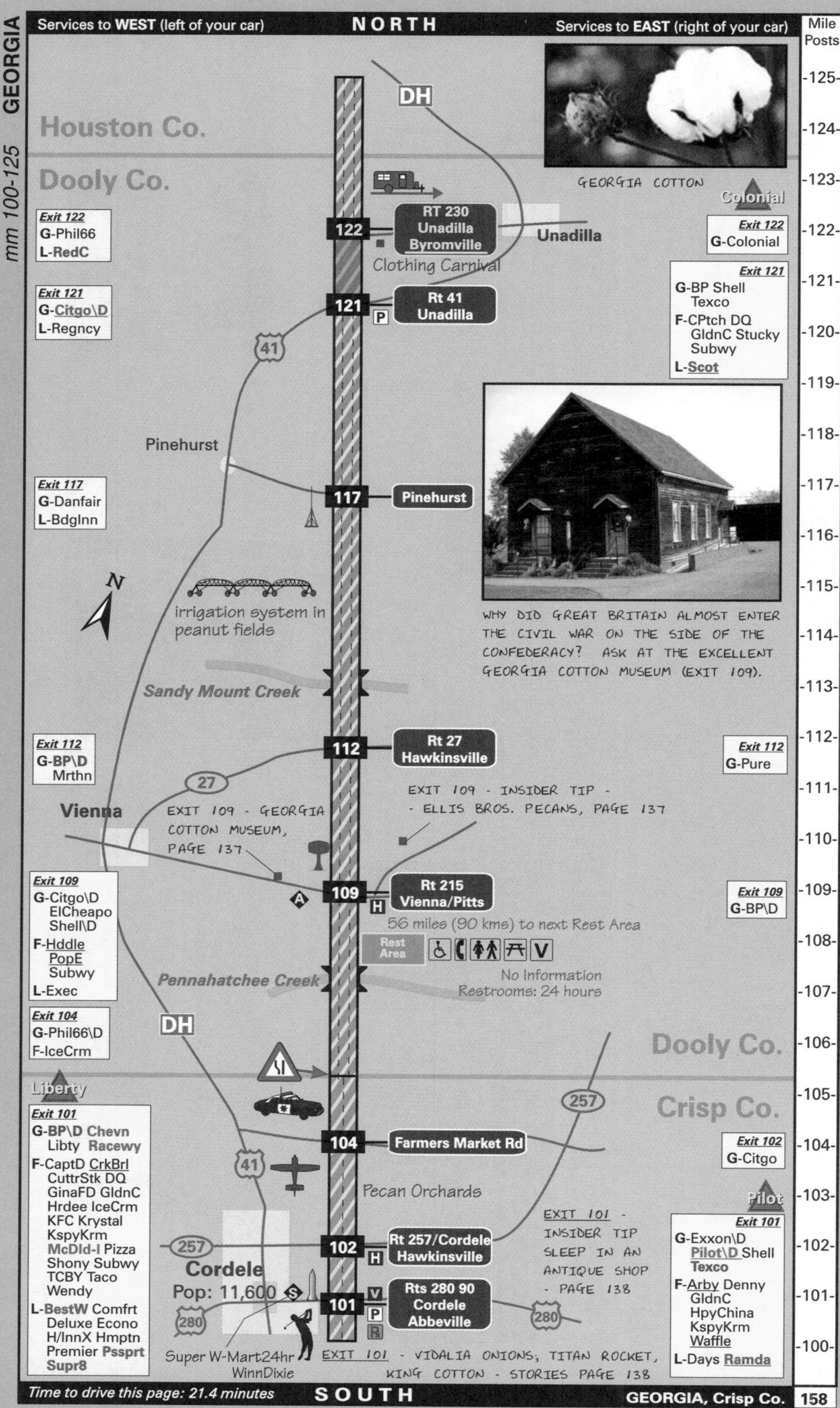
GEORGIA
mm 100-125
Services to WEST (left of your car)
NORTH
Services to EAST (right of your car)
Mile Posts
-125-
-124-
-123-
-122-
-121-
-120-
-119-
-118-
-117-
-116-
-115-
-114-
-113-
-112-
-111-
-110-
-109-
-108-
-107-
-106-
-105-
-104-
-103-
-102-
-101-
-100-
Houston Co.
Dooly Co.
DH
GEORGIA COTTON
Colonial
Exit 122
G-Phil66
L-RedC
122
RT 230 Unadilla Byromville
Unadilla
Clothing Carnival
Exit 122
G-Colonial
Exit 121
G-Citgo\D
L-Regncy
121
Rt 41 Unadilla
Exit 121
G-BP Shell Texco
F-CPtch DQ GldnC Stucky Subwy
L-Scot
41
Pinehurst
Exit 117
G-Danfair
L-BdgInn
117
Pinehurst
N
irrigation system in peanut fields
WHY DID GREAT BRITAIN ALMOST ENTER THE CIVIL WAR ON THE SIDE OF THE CONFEDERACY? ASK AT THE EXCELLENT GEORGIA COTTON MUSEUM (EXIT 109).
Sandy Mount Creek
Exit 112
G-BP\D Mrthn
112
Rt 27 Hawkinsville
Exit 112
G-Pure
27
EXIT 109 - INSIDER TIP - ELLIS BROS. PECANS, PAGE 137
Vienna
EXIT 109 - GEORGIA COTTON MUSEUM, PAGE 137
Exit 109
G-Citgo\D ElCheapo Shell\D
F-Hddle PopE Subwy
L-Exec
109
Rt 215 Vienna/Pitts
Exit 109
G-BP\D
56 miles (90 kms) to next Rest Area
Rest Area
No Information
Restrooms: 24 hours
Pennahatchee Creek
Exit 104
G-Phil66\D
F-IceCrm
DH
Dooly Co.
Crisp Co.
Liberty
Exit 101
G-BP\D Chevn Libty Racewy
F-CaptD CrkBrl CuttrStk DQ GinaFD GldnC Hrdee IceCrm KFC Krystal KspyKrm McDld-I Pizza Shony Subwy TCBY Taco Wendy
L-BestW Comfrt Deluxe Econo H/InnX Hmptn Premier Pssprt Supr8
257
104
Farmers Market Rd
Exit 102
G-Citgo
41
Pecan Orchards
Pilot
EXIT 101 - INSIDER TIP SLEEP IN AN ANTIQUE SHOP - PAGE 138
257
102
Rt 257/Cordele Hawkinsville
Cordele
Pop: 11,600
280
101
Rts 280 90 Cordele Abbeville
280
Exit 101
G-Exxon\D Pilot\D Shell Texco
F-Arby Denny GldnC HpyChina KspyKrm Waffle
L-Days Ramda
Super W-Mart24hr
WinnDixie
EXIT 101 - VIDALIA ONIONS; TITAN ROCKET, KING COTTON - STORIES PAGE 138
Time to drive this page: 21.4 minutes
SOUTH
GEORGIA, Crisp Co.
158

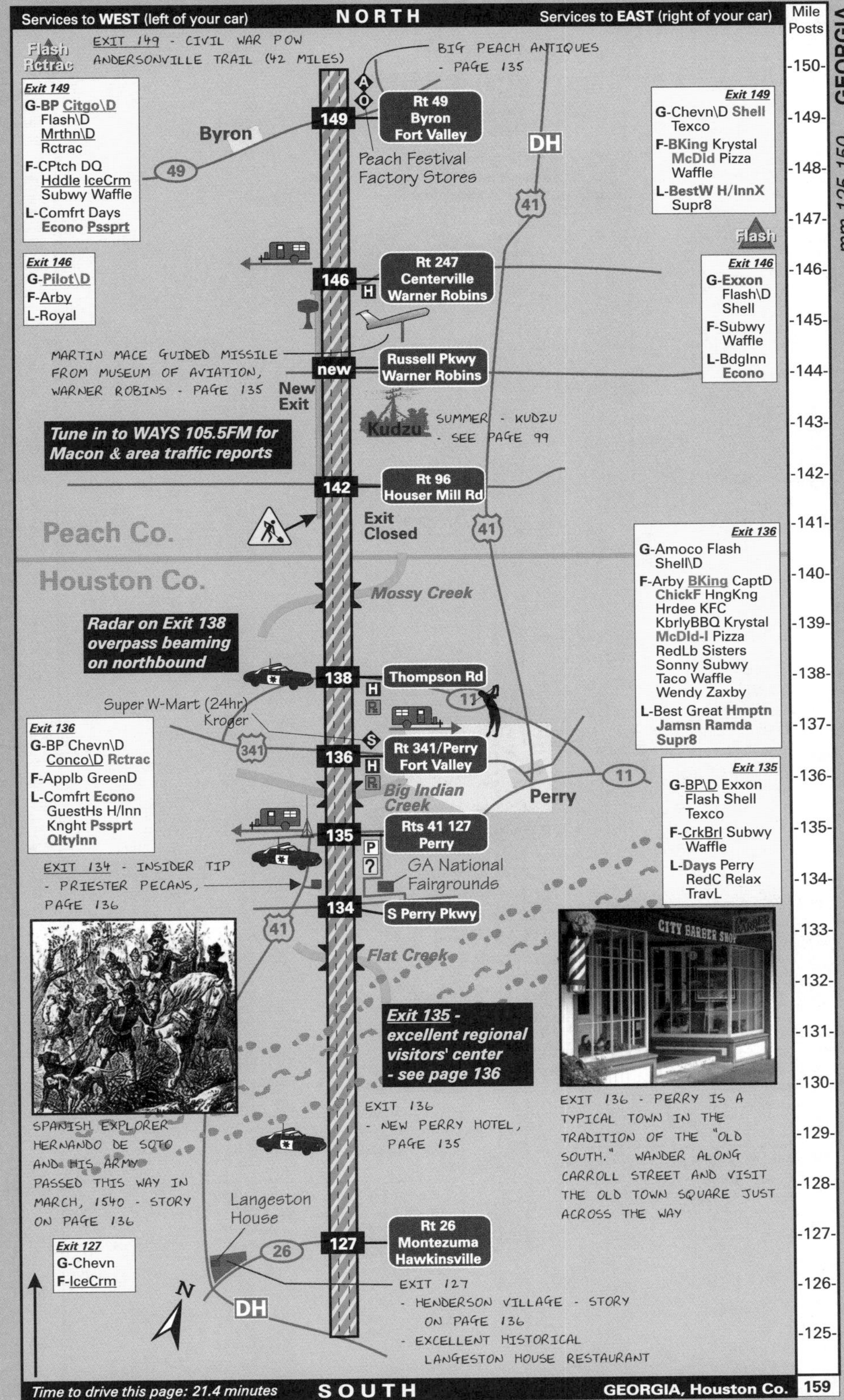

Services to WEST (left of your car)
NORTH
Services to EAST (right of your car)
Mile Posts
GEORGIA
mm 125-150
Flash Rctrac
EXIT 149 - CIVIL WAR POW
ANDERSONVILLE TRAIL (42 MILES)
BIG PEACH ANTIQUES
- PAGE 135
Exit 149
G-BP Citgo\D
Flash\D
Mrthn\D
Rctrac
F-CPtch DQ
Hddle IceCrm
Subwy Waffle
L-Comfrt Days
Econo Pssprt
Byron
49
149
Rt 49
Byron
Fort Valley
Peach Festival
Factory Stores
DH
41
Exit 149
G-Chevn\D Shell
Texco
F-BKing Krystal
McDld Pizza
Waffle
L-BestW H/InnX
Supr8
Flash
Exit 146
G-Pilot\D
F-Arby
L-Royal
146
H
Rt 247
Centerville
Warner Robins
Exit 146
G-Exxon
Flash\D
Shell
F-Subwy
Waffle
L-BdgInn
Econo
MARTIN MACE GUIDED MISSILE
FROM MUSEUM OF AVIATION,
WARNER ROBINS - PAGE 135
new
Russell Pkwy
Warner Robins
New Exit
Kudzu
SUMMER - KUDZU
- SEE PAGE 99
Tune in to WAYS 105.5FM for
Macon & area traffic reports
142
Rt 96
Houser Mill Rd
Peach Co.
Exit Closed
41
Houston Co.
Mossy Creek
Exit 136
G-Amoco Flash
Shell\D
F-Arby BKing CaptD
ChickF HngKng
Hrdee KFC
KbrlyBBQ Krystal
McDld-I Pizza
RedLb Sisters
Sonny Subwy
Taco Waffle
Wendy Zaxby
L-Best Great Hmptn
Jamsn Ramda
Supr8
Radar on Exit 138
overpass beaming
on northbound
138
H
R
Thompson Rd
11
Super W-Mart (24hr)
Kroger
Exit 136
G-BP Chevn\D
Conco\D Rctrac
F-Applb GreenD
L-Comfrt Econo
GuestHs H/Inn
Knght Pssprt
QltyInn
341
S
136
H
R
Rt 341/Perry
Fort Valley
Big Indian Creek
Perry
11
Exit 135
G-BP\D Exxon
Flash Shell
Texco
F-CrkBrl Subwy
Waffle
L-Days Perry
RedC Relax
TravL
135
P
?
Rts 41 127
Perry
GA National
Fairgrounds
EXIT 134 - INSIDER TIP
- PRIESTER PECANS,
PAGE 136
134
S Perry Pkwy
41
Flat Creek
CITY BARBER SHOP
Exit 135 -
excellent regional
visitors' center
- see page 136
SPANISH EXPLORER
HERNANDO DE SOTO
AND HIS ARMY
PASSED THIS WAY IN
MARCH, 1540 - STORY
ON PAGE 136
EXIT 136
- NEW PERRY HOTEL,
PAGE 135
EXIT 136 - PERRY IS A
TYPICAL TOWN IN THE
TRADITION OF THE "OLD
SOUTH." WANDER ALONG
CARROLL STREET AND VISIT
THE OLD TOWN SQUARE JUST
ACROSS THE WAY
Langeston
House
Exit 127
G-Chevn
F-IceCrm
26
127
Rt 26
Montezuma
Hawkinsville
N
DH
EXIT 127
- HENDERSON VILLAGE - STORY
ON PAGE 136
- EXCELLENT HISTORICAL
LANGESTON HOUSE RESTAURANT
-150- -149- -148- -147- -146- -145- -144- -143- -142- -141- -140- -139- -138- -137- -136- -135- -134- -133- -132- -131- -130- -129- -128- -127- -126- -125-
Time to drive this page: 21.4 minutes
SOUTH
GEORGIA, Houston Co.
159

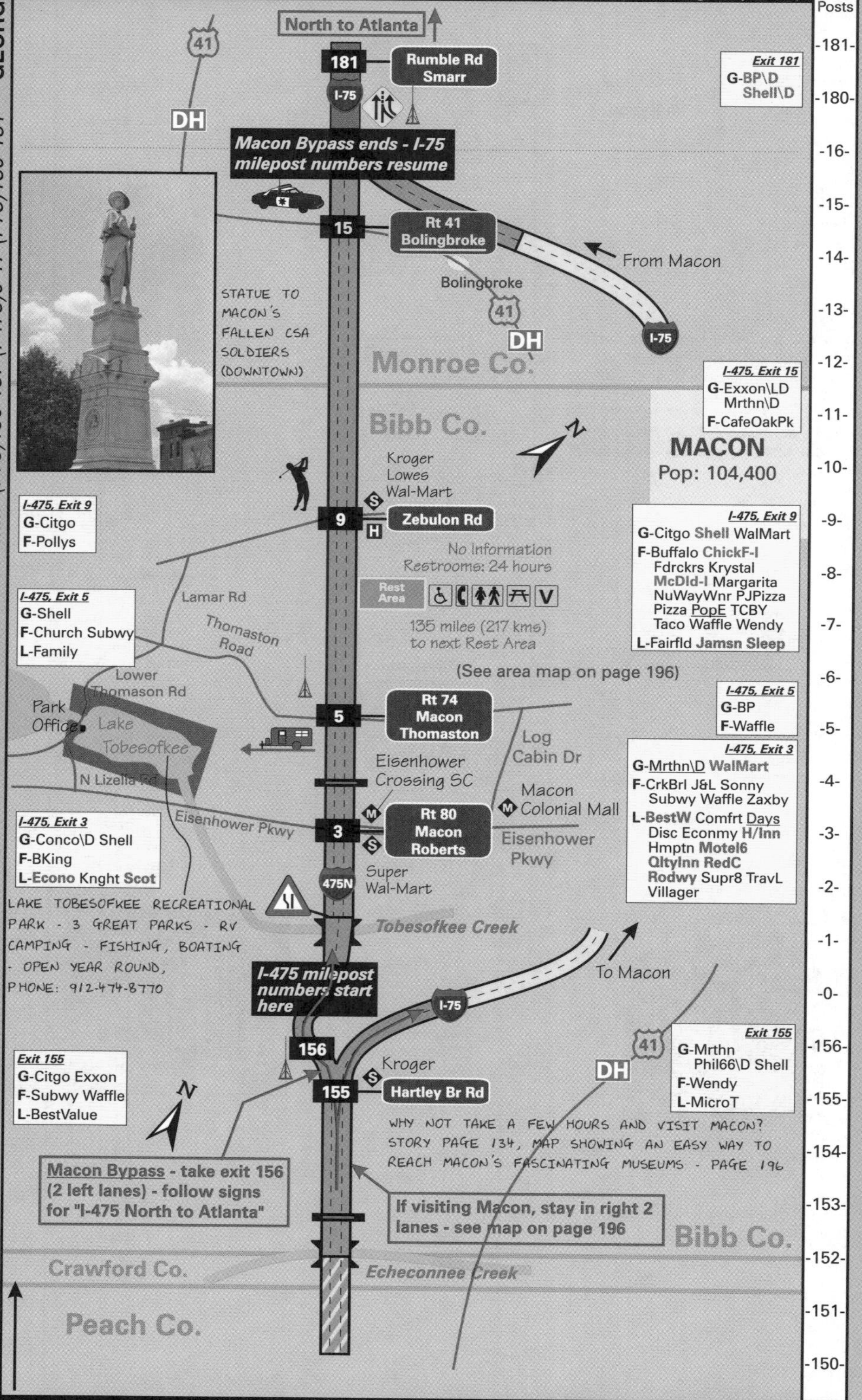

Services to **WEST** (left of your car) **NORTH** Services to **EAST** (right of your car)

Mile Posts

North to Atlanta

181 Rumble Rd Smarr

I-75

Exit 181
G-BP\D Shell\D

41

DH

Macon Bypass ends - I-75 milepost numbers resume

STATUE TO MACON'S FALLEN CSA SOLDIERS (DOWNTOWN)

15 Rt 41 Bolingbroke

From Macon

Bolingbroke

41

DH

I-75

Monroe Co.

I-475, Exit 15
G-Exxon\LD Mrthn\D
F-CafeOakPk

Bibb Co.

MACON
Pop: 104,400

Kroger Lowes Wal-Mart

I-475, Exit 9
G-Citgo
F-Pollys

9 Zebulon Rd

I-475, Exit 9
G-Citgo Shell WalMart
F-Buffalo ChickF-I Fdrckrs Krystal McDld-I Margarita NuWayWnr PJPizza Pizza PopE TCBY Taco Waffle Wendy
L-Fairfld Jamsn Sleep

No Information
Restrooms: 24 hours

Rest Area

135 miles (217 kms) to next Rest Area

I-475, Exit 5
G-Shell
F-Church Subwy
L-Family

Lamar Rd

Thomaston Road

Lower Thomason Rd

(See area map on page 196)

Park Office

Lake Tobesofkee

5 Rt 74 Macon Thomaston

I-475, Exit 5
G-BP
F-Waffle

Log Cabin Dr

N Lizella Rd

Eisenhower Crossing SC

Macon Colonial Mall

I-475, Exit 3
G-Mrthn\D WalMart
F-CrkBrl J&L Sonny Subwy Waffle Zaxby
L-BestW Comfrt Days Disc Econmy H/Inn Hmptn Motel6 QltyInn RedC Rodwy Supr8 TravL Villager

I-475, Exit 3
G-Conco\D Shell
F-BKing
L-Econo Knght Scot

Eisenhower Pkwy

3 Rt 80 Macon Roberts

Eisenhower Pkwy

475N

Super Wal-Mart

LAKE TOBESOFKEE RECREATIONAL PARK - 3 GREAT PARKS - RV CAMPING - FISHING, BOATING - OPEN YEAR ROUND, PHONE: 912-474-8770

Tobesofkee Creek

To Macon

I-475 milepost numbers start here

I-75

156

41

Exit 155
G-Mrthn Phil66\D Shell
F-Wendy
L-MicroT

DH

Kroger

155 Hartley Br Rd

Exit 155
G-Citgo Exxon
F-Subwy Waffle
L-BestValue

WHY NOT TAKE A FEW HOURS AND VISIT MACON? STORY PAGE 134, MAP SHOWING AN EASY WAY TO REACH MACON'S FASCINATING MUSEUMS - PAGE 196

Macon Bypass - take exit 156 (2 left lanes) - follow signs for "I-475 North to Atlanta"

If visiting Macon, stay in right 2 lanes - see map on page 196

Bibb Co.

Crawford Co.

Echeconnee Creek

Peach Co.

-181- -180- -16- -15- -14- -13- -12- -11- -10- -9- -8- -7- -6- -5- -4- -3- -2- -1- -0- -156- -155- -154- -153- -152- -151- -150-

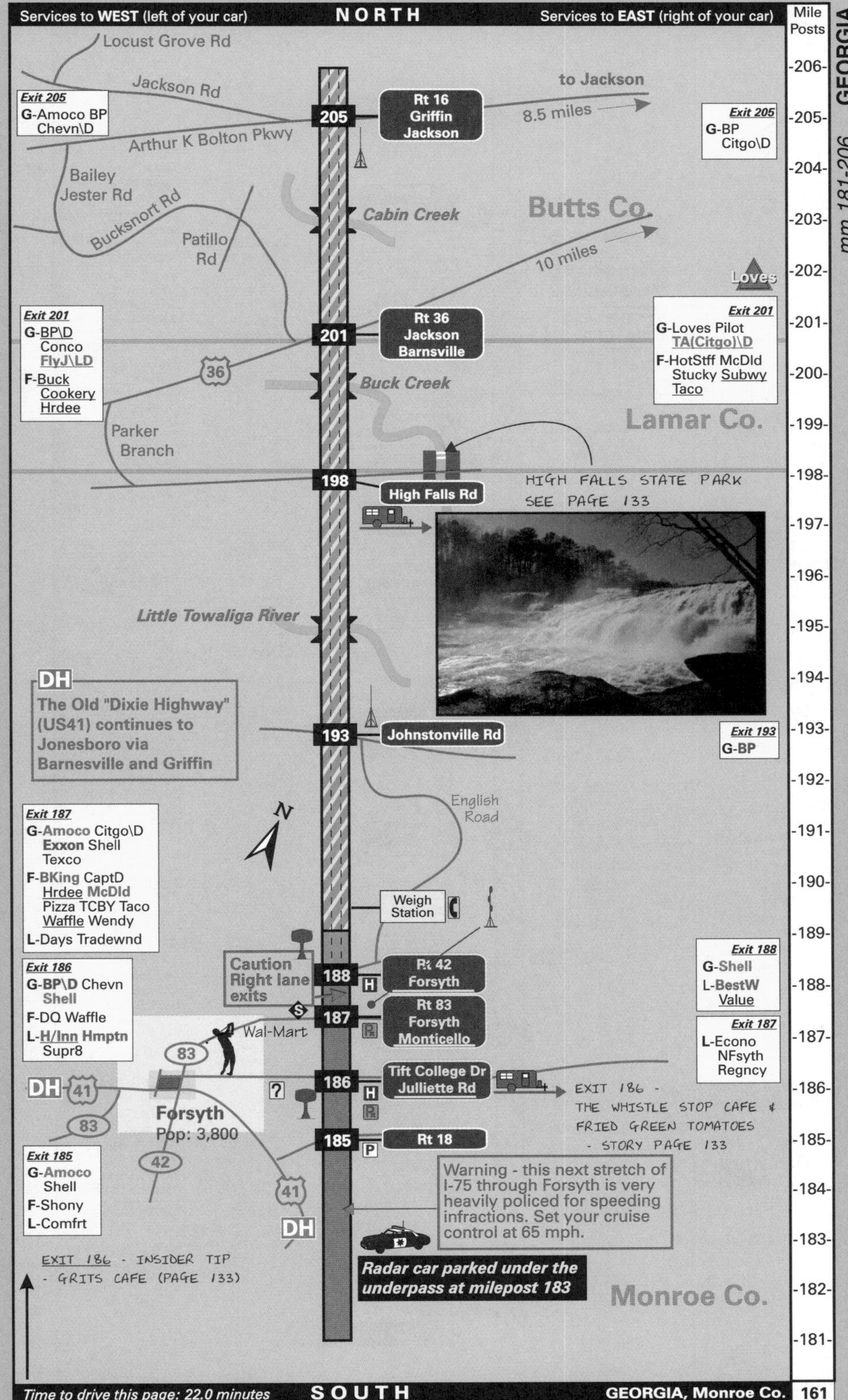
Mile Posts
Locust Grove Rd
Jackson Rd
Exit 205
G-Amoco BP
Chevn\D
205
Rt 16
Griffin
Jackson
to Jackson
8.5 miles
Exit 205
G-BP
Citgo\D
Arthur K Bolton Pkwy
Bailey
Jester Rd
Bucksnort Rd
Patillo
Rd
Cabin Creek
Butts Co.
10 miles
Loves
Exit 201
G-BP\D
Conco
FlyJ\LD
F-Buck
Cookery
Hrdee
201
Rt 36
Jackson
Barnsville
Exit 201
G-Loves Pilot
TA(Citgo)\D
F-HotStff McDld
Stucky Subwy
Taco
36
Buck Creek
Lamar Co.
Parker
Branch
198
High Falls Rd
HIGH FALLS STATE PARK
SEE PAGE 133
Little Towaliga River
DH
The Old "Dixie Highway" (US41) continues to Jonesboro via Barnesville and Griffin
193
Johnstonville Rd
Exit 193
G-BP
English
Road
N
Exit 187
G-Amoco Citgo\D
Exxon Shell
Texco
F-BKing CaptD
Hrdee McDld
Pizza TCBY Taco
Waffle Wendy
L-Days Tradewnd
Weigh
Station
Caution
Right lane
exits
188
Rt 42
Forsyth
Exit 188
G-Shell
L-BestW
Value
Exit 186
G-BP\D Chevn
Shell
F-DQ Waffle
L-H/Inn Hmptn
Supr8
187
Rt 83
Forsyth
Monticello
Exit 187
L-Econo
NFsyth
Regncy
Wal-Mart
83
DH 41
186
Tift College Dr
Julliette Rd
EXIT 186 - THE WHISTLE STOP CAFE & FRIED GREEN TOMATOES - STORY PAGE 133
83
Forsyth
Pop: 3,800
185
Rt 18
42
Exit 185
G-Amoco
Shell
F-Shony
L-Comfrt
41
DH
Warning - this next stretch of I-75 through Forsyth is very heavily policed for speeding infractions. Set your cruise control at 65 mph.
EXIT 186 - INSIDER TIP - GRITS CAFE (PAGE 133)
Radar car parked under the underpass at milepost 183
Monroe Co.
-206- -205- -204- -203- -202- -201- -200- -199- -198- -197- -196- -195- -194- -193- -192- -191- -190- -189- -188- -187- -186- -185- -184- -183- -182- -181-

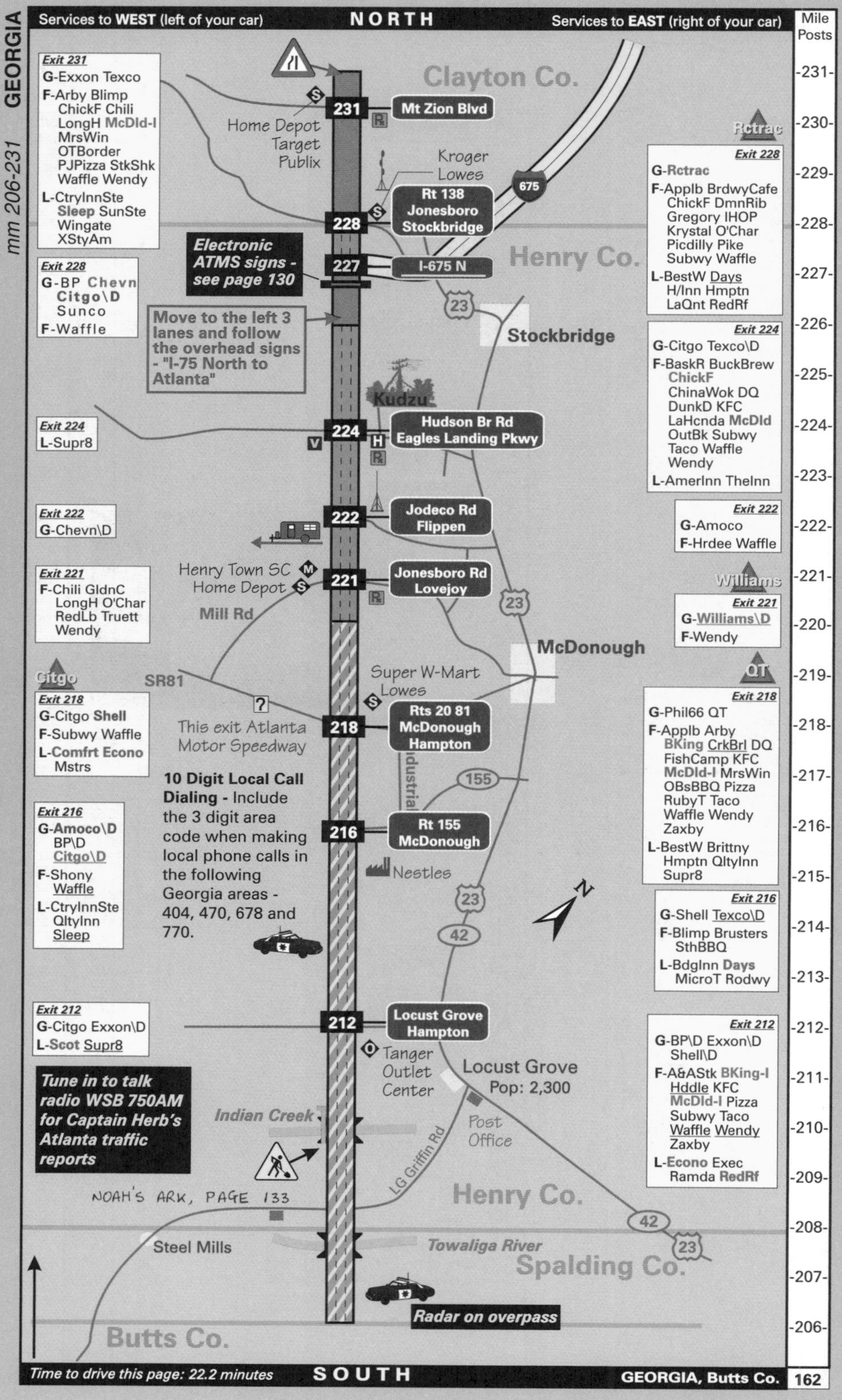

Services to WEST (left of your car)
NORTH
Services to EAST (right of your car)
Mile Posts
Clayton Co.
Exit 231
G-Exxon Texco
F-Arby Blimp ChickF Chili LongH McDld-I MrsWin OTBorder PJPizza StkShk Waffle Wendy
L-CtrylnnSte Sleep SunSte Wingate XStyAm
231
Mt Zion Blvd
Home Depot Target Publix
Kroger Lowes
675
Rctrac
Exit 228
G-Rctrac
F-Applb BrdwyCafe ChickF DmnRib Gregory IHOP Krystal O'Char Picdilly Pike Subwy Waffle
L-BestW Days H/Inn Hmptn LaQnt RedRf
Exit 228
G-BP Chevn Citgo\D Sunco
F-Waffle
228
Rt 138 Jonesboro Stockbridge
Electronic ATMS signs - see page 130
227
I-675 N
Henry Co.
23
Move to the left 3 lanes and follow the overhead signs - "I-75 North to Atlanta"
Stockbridge
Exit 224
G-Citgo Texco\D
F-BaskR BuckBrew ChickF ChinaWok DQ DunkD KFC LaHcnda McDld OutBk Subwy Taco Waffle Wendy
L-AmerInn TheInn
Kudzu
Exit 224
L-Supr8
224
Hudson Br Rd Eagles Landing Pkwy
Exit 222
G-Chevn\D
222
Jodeco Rd Flippen
Exit 222
G-Amoco
F-Hrdee Waffle
Exit 221
F-Chili GldnC LongH O'Char RedLb Truett Wendy
Henry Town SC
Home Depot
221
Jonesboro Rd Lovejoy
Williams
Exit 221
G-Williams\D
F-Wendy
Mill Rd
23
McDonough
Citgo
SR81
QT
Exit 218
G-Citgo Shell
F-Subwy Waffle
L-Comfrt Econo Mstrs
Super W-Mart Lowes
This exit Atlanta Motor Speedway
218
Rts 20 81 McDonough Hampton
Exit 218
G-Phil66 QT
F-Applb Arby BKing CrkBrl DQ FishCamp KFC McDld-I MrsWin OBsBBQ Pizza RubyT Taco Waffle Wendy Zaxby
L-BestW Brittny Hmptn QltyInn Supr8
Industrial
155
10 Digit Local Call Dialing - Include the 3 digit area code when making local phone calls in the following Georgia areas - 404, 470, 678 and 770.
Exit 216
G-Amoco\D BP\D Citgo\D
F-Shony Waffle
L-CtrylnnSte QltyInn Sleep
216
Rt 155 McDonough
Nestles
23
N
42
Exit 216
G-Shell Texco\D
F-Blimp Brusters SthBBQ
L-BdgInn Days MicroT Rodwy
Exit 212
G-Citgo Exxon\D
L-Scot Supr8
212
Locust Grove Hampton
Exit 212
G-BP\D Exxon\D Shell\D
F-A&AStk BKing-I Hddle KFC McDld-I Pizza Subwy Taco Waffle Wendy Zaxby
L-Econo Exec Ramda RedRf
Tanger Outlet Center
Locust Grove Pop: 2,300
Tune in to talk radio WSB 750AM for Captain Herb's Atlanta traffic reports
Indian Creek
LG Griffin Rd
Post Office
NOAH'S ARK, PAGE 133
Henry Co.
42
Steel Mills
Towaliga River
23
Spalding Co.
Radar on overpass
Butts Co.
-231- -230- -229- -228- -227- -226- -225- -224- -223- -222- -221- -220- -219- -218- -217- -216- -215- -214- -213- -212- -211- -210- -209- -208- -207- -206-

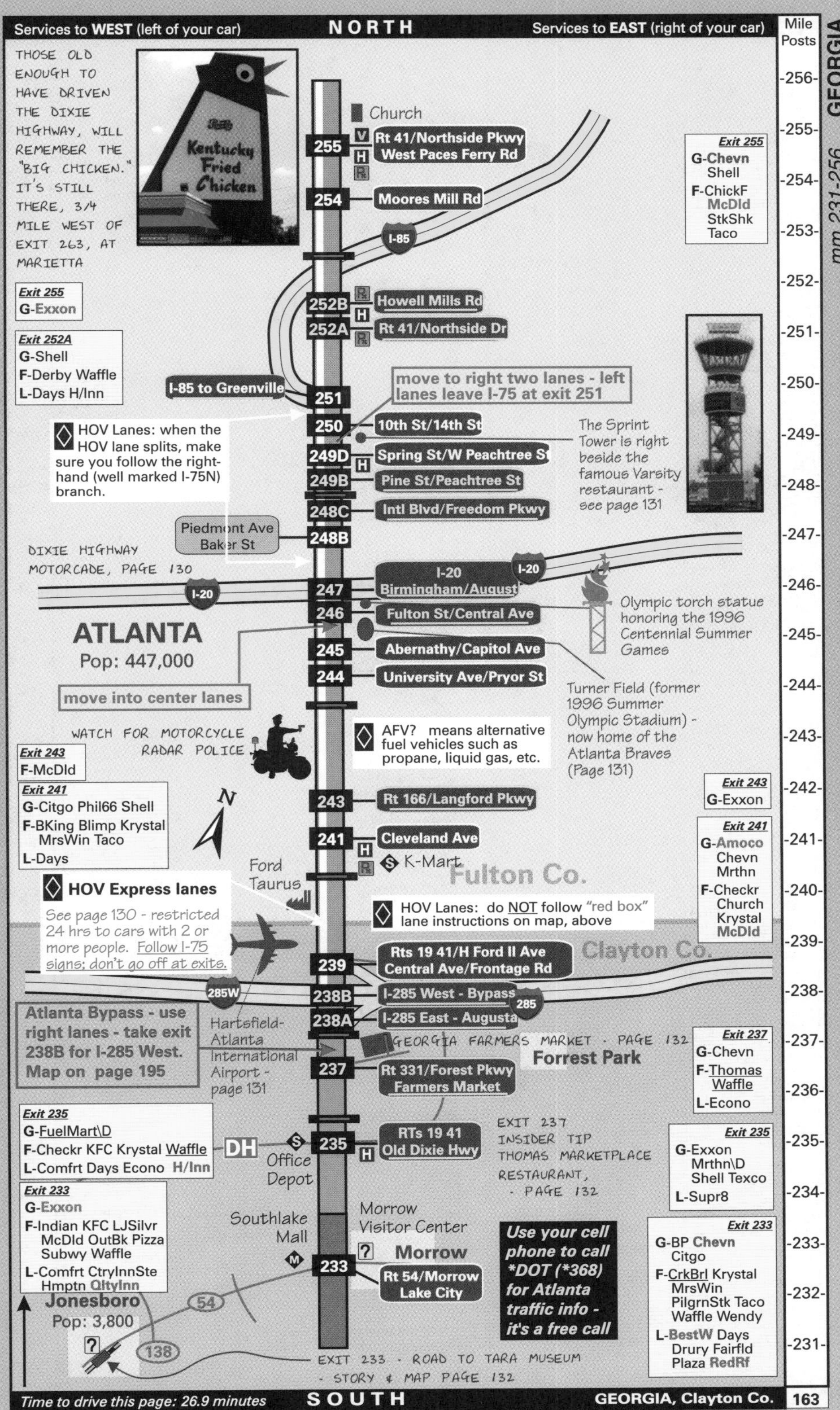

Services to WEST (left of your car)
NORTH
Services to EAST (right of your car)
Mile Posts
GEORGIA
mm 231-256
THOSE OLD ENOUGH TO HAVE DRIVEN THE DIXIE HIGHWAY, WILL REMEMBER THE "BIG CHICKEN." IT'S STILL THERE, 3/4 MILE WEST OF EXIT 263, AT MARIETTA
Kentucky Fried Chicken
Church
255
Rt 41/Northside Pkwy
West Paces Ferry Rd
254
Moores Mill Rd
I-85
Exit 255
G-Chevn Shell
F-ChickF McDld StkShk Taco
Exit 255
G-Exxon
252B
Howell Mills Rd
252A
Rt 41/Northside Dr
Exit 252A
G-Shell
F-Derby Waffle
L-Days H/Inn
I-85 to Greenville
251
move to right two lanes - left lanes leave I-75 at exit 251
250
10th St/14th St
HOV Lanes: when the HOV lane splits, make sure you follow the right-hand (well marked I-75N) branch.
249D
Spring St/W Peachtree St
249B
Pine St/Peachtree St
248C
Intl Blvd/Freedom Pkwy
The Sprint Tower is right beside the famous Varsity restaurant - see page 131
Piedmont Ave
Baker St
248B
DIXIE HIGHWAY MOTORCADE, PAGE 130
247
I-20
Birmingham/August
I-20
246
Fulton St/Central Ave
Olympic torch statue honoring the 1996 Centennial Summer Games
ATLANTA
Pop: 447,000
245
Abernathy/Capitol Ave
244
University Ave/Pryor St
move into center lanes
Turner Field (former 1996 Summer Olympic Stadium) - now home of the Atlanta Braves (Page 131)
WATCH FOR MOTORCYCLE RADAR POLICE
AFV? means alternative fuel vehicles such as propane, liquid gas, etc.
Exit 243
F-McDld
Exit 241
G-Citgo Phil66 Shell
F-BKing Blimp Krystal MrsWin Taco
L-Days
N
243
Rt 166/Langford Pkwy
Exit 243
G-Exxon
241
Cleveland Ave
K-Mart
Fulton Co.
Exit 241
G-Amoco Chevn Mrthn
F-Checkr Church Krystal McDld
Ford Taurus
HOV Express lanes
See page 130 - restricted 24 hrs to cars with 2 or more people. Follow I-75 signs: don't go off at exits.
HOV Lanes: do NOT follow "red box" lane instructions on map, above
239
Rts 19 41/H Ford II Ave
Central Ave/Frontage Rd
Clayton Co.
285W
238B
I-285 West - Bypass
285
238A
I-285 East - Augusta
Atlanta Bypass - use right lanes - take exit 238B for I-285 West. Map on page 195
Hartsfield-Atlanta International Airport - page 131
GEORGIA FARMERS MARKET - PAGE 132
Forrest Park
237
Rt 331/Forest Pkwy
Farmers Market
Exit 237
G-Chevn
F-Thomas Waffle
L-Econo
Exit 235
G-FuelMart\D
F-Checkr KFC Krystal Waffle
L-Comfrt Days Econo H/Inn
DH
Office Depot
235
RTs 19 41
Old Dixie Hwy
EXIT 237 INSIDER TIP THOMAS MARKETPLACE RESTAURANT, - PAGE 132
Exit 235
G-Exxon Mrthn\D Shell Texco
L-Supr8
Exit 233
G-Exxon
F-Indian KFC LJSilvr McDld OutBk Pizza Subwy Waffle
L-Comfrt CtryInnSte Hmptn QltyInn
Southlake Mall
Morrow Visitor Center
Morrow
233
Rt 54/Morrow Lake City
Use your cell phone to call *DOT (*368) for Atlanta traffic info - it's a free call
Exit 233
G-BP Chevn Citgo
F-CrkBrl Krystal MrsWin PilgrnStk Taco Waffle Wendy
L-BestW Days Drury Fairfld Plaza RedRf
Jonesboro
Pop: 3,800
54
138
EXIT 233 - ROAD TO TARA MUSEUM - STORY & MAP PAGE 132
-256- -255- -254- -253- -252- -251- -250- -249- -248- -247- -246- -245- -244- -243- -242- -241- -240- -239- -238- -237- -236- -235- -234- -233- -232- -231-
Time to drive this page: 26.9 minutes
SOUTH
GEORGIA, Clayton Co.
163

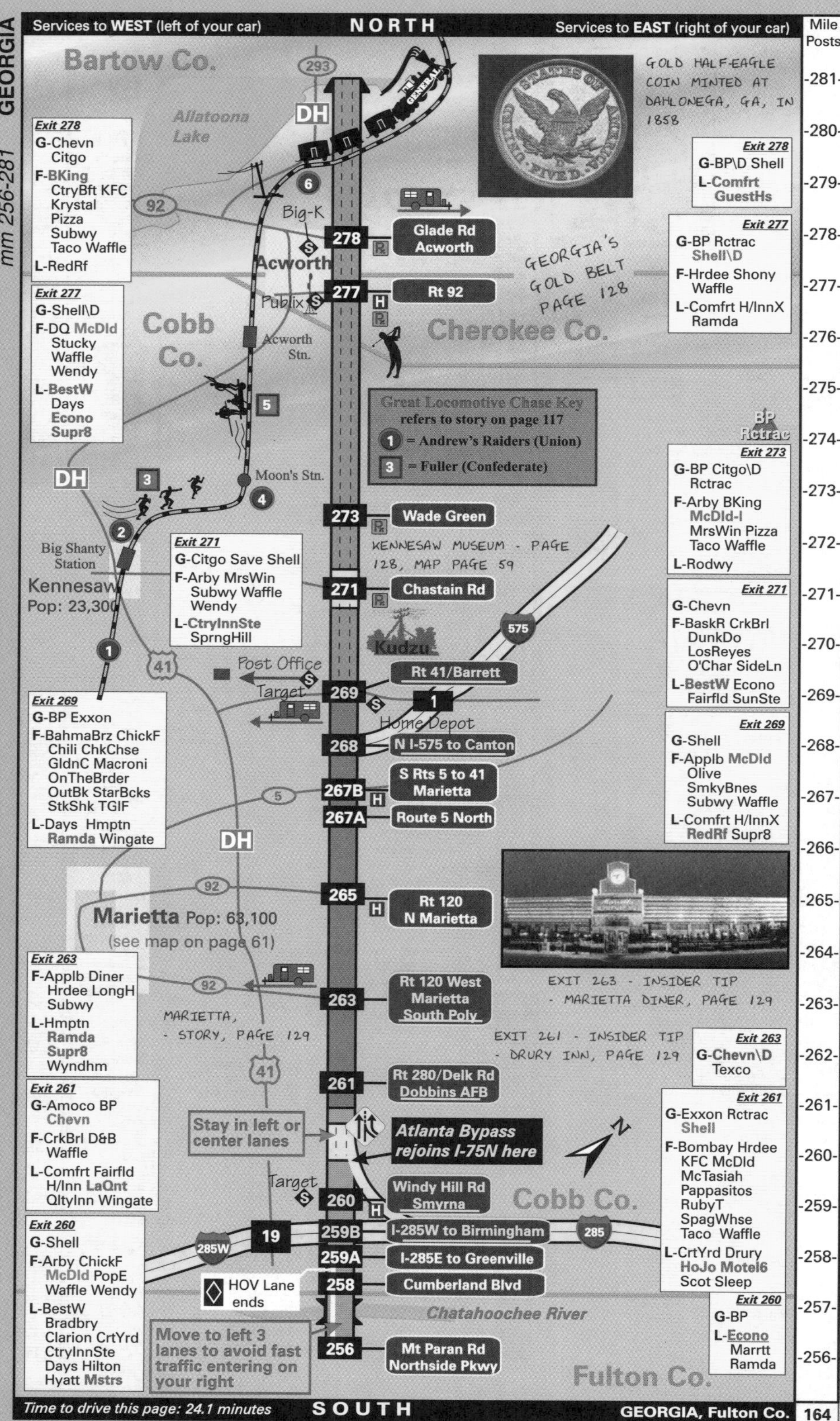
Services to WEST (left of your car)
NORTH
Services to EAST (right of your car)
Mile Posts
Bartow Co.
Allatoona Lake
GOLD HALF-EAGLE COIN MINTED AT DAHLONEGA, GA, IN 1858
Exit 278
G-Chevn Citgo
F-BKing CtryBft KFC Krystal Pizza Subwy Taco Waffle
L-RedRf
Exit 278
G-BP\D Shell
L-Comfrt GuestHs
Big-K
278
Glade Rd Acworth
Acworth
Exit 277
G-BP Rctrac Shell\D
F-Hrdee Shony Waffle
L-Comfrt H/InnX Ramda
GEORGIA'S GOLD BELT PAGE 128
Exit 277
G-Shell\D
F-DQ McDld Stucky Waffle Wendy
L-BestW Days Econo Supr8
Publix
277
Rt 92
Cobb Co.
Cherokee Co.
Acworth Stn.
Great Locomotive Chase Key refers to story on page 117
1 = Andrew's Raiders (Union)
3 = Fuller (Confederate)
BP Rctrac
Moon's Stn.
Exit 273
G-BP Citgo\D Rctrac
F-Arby BKing McDld-I MrsWin Pizza Taco Waffle
L-Rodwy
273
Wade Green
KENNESAW MUSEUM - PAGE 128, MAP PAGE 59
Big Shanty Station
Exit 271
G-Citgo Save Shell
F-Arby MrsWin Subwy Waffle Wendy
L-CtryInnSte SprngHill
271
Chastain Rd
Kennesaw Pop: 23,300
Exit 271
G-Chevn
F-BaskR CrkBrl DunkDo LosReyes O'Char SideLn
L-BestW Econo Fairfld SunSte
Kudzu
575
Post Office
Rt 41/Barrett
Target
269
Home Depot
Exit 269
G-BP Exxon
F-BahmaBrz ChickF Chili ChkChse GldnC Macroni OnTheBrder OutBk StarBcks StkShk TGIF
L-Days Hmptn Ramda Wingate
Exit 269
G-Shell
F-Applb McDld Olive SmkyBnes Subwy Waffle
L-Comfrt H/InnX RedRf Supr8
268
N I-575 to Canton
267B
S Rts 5 to 41 Marietta
267A
Route 5 North
265
Rt 120 N Marietta
Marietta Pop: 63,100 (see map on page 61)
Exit 263
F-Applb Diner Hrdee LongH Subwy
L-Hmptn Ramda Supr8 Wyndhm
MARIETTA, - STORY, PAGE 129
263
Rt 120 West Marietta South Poly
EXIT 263 - INSIDER TIP - MARIETTA DINER, PAGE 129
EXIT 261 - INSIDER TIP - DRURY INN, PAGE 129
Exit 263
G-Chevn\D Texco
Exit 261
G-Amoco BP Chevn
F-CrkBrl D&B Waffle
L-Comfrt Fairfld H/Inn LaQnt QltyInn Wingate
261
Rt 280/Delk Rd Dobbins AFB
Stay in left or center lanes
Atlanta Bypass rejoins I-75N here
Exit 261
G-Exxon Rctrac Shell
F-Bombay Hrdee KFC McDld McTasiah Pappasitos RubyT SpagWhse Taco Waffle
L-CrtYrd Drury HoJo Motel6 Scot Sleep
Target
260
Windy Hill Rd Smyrna
Cobb Co.
Exit 260
G-Shell
F-Arby ChickF McDld PopE Waffle Wendy
L-BestW Bradbry Clarion CrtYrd CtryInnSte Days Hilton Hyatt Mstrs
285W
19
259B
I-285W to Birmingham
285
259A
I-285E to Greenville
HOV Lane ends
258
Cumberland Blvd
Chatahoochee River
Exit 260
G-BP
L-Econo Marrtt Ramda
Move to left 3 lanes to avoid fast traffic entering on your right
256
Mt Paran Rd Northside Pkwy
Fulton Co.
Time to drive this page: 24.1 minutes
SOUTH

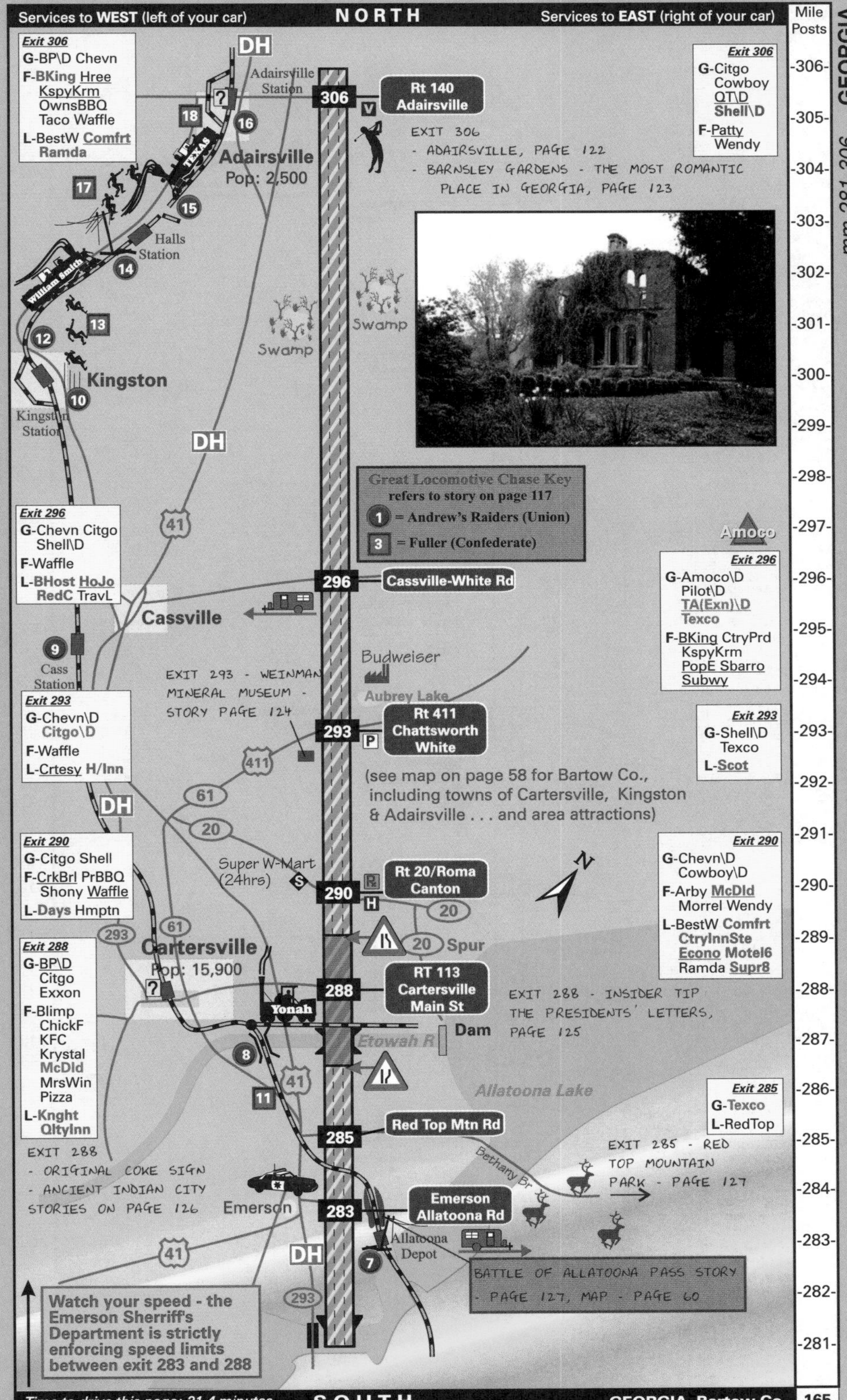
Services to WEST (left of your car)
NORTH
Services to EAST (right of your car)
Mile Posts
GEORGIA
mm 281-306
Exit 306
G-BP\D Chevn
F-BKing Hree
KspyKrm
OwnsBBQ
Taco Waffle
L-BestW Comfrt
Ramda
DH
Adairsville Station
306
Rt 140 Adairsville
V
18
16
17
15
14
13
12
10
TEXAS
William Smith
Adairsville
Pop: 2,500
Halls Station
Kingston
Kingston Station
Exit 306
G-Citgo
Cowboy
QT\D
Shell\D
F-Patty
Wendy
EXIT 306
- ADAIRSVILLE, PAGE 122
- BARNSLEY GARDENS - THE MOST ROMANTIC PLACE IN GEORGIA, PAGE 123
Swamp
Swamp
DH
41
Great Locomotive Chase Key
refers to story on page 117
1 = Andrew's Raiders (Union)
3 = Fuller (Confederate)
Amoco
Exit 296
G-Chevn Citgo
Shell\D
F-Waffle
L-BHost HoJo
RedC TravL
296
Cassville-White Rd
Cassville
Exit 296
G-Amoco\D
Pilot\D
TA(Exn)\D
Texco
F-BKing CtryPrd
KspyKrm
PopE Sbarro
Subwy
9
Cass Station
Budweiser
Aubrey Lake
EXIT 293 - WEINMAN MINERAL MUSEUM - STORY PAGE 124
Exit 293
G-Chevn\D
Citgo\D
F-Waffle
L-Crtesy H/Inn
293
P
Rt 411 Chattsworth White
Exit 293
G-Shell\D
Texco
L-Scot
411
61
20
DH
(see map on page 58 for Bartow Co., including towns of Cartersville, Kingston & Adairsville . . . and area attractions)
Exit 290
G-Citgo Shell
F-CrkBrl PrBBQ
Shony Waffle
L-Days Hmptn
Super W-Mart (24hrs)
S
290
R
H
Rt 20/Roma Canton
20
20 Spur
N
Exit 290
G-Chevn\D
Cowboy\D
F-Arby McDld
Morrel Wendy
L-BestW Comfrt
CtryInnSte
Econo Motel6
Ramda Supr8
293
61
Cartersville
Pop: 15,900
Exit 288
G-BP\D
Citgo
Exxon
F-Blimp
ChickF
KFC
Krystal
McDld
MrsWin
Pizza
L-Knght
QltyInn
Yonah
288
RT 113 Cartersville Main St
Dam
Etowah R
EXIT 288 - INSIDER TIP THE PRESIDENTS' LETTERS, PAGE 125
8
41
11
Allatoona Lake
Exit 285
G-Texco
L-RedTop
285
Red Top Mtn Rd
Bethany Br
EXIT 285 - RED TOP MOUNTAIN PARK - PAGE 127
EXIT 288
- ORIGINAL COKE SIGN
- ANCIENT INDIAN CITY
STORIES ON PAGE 126
Emerson
283
Emerson Allatoona Rd
Allatoona Depot
7
41
DH
293
BATTLE OF ALLATOONA PASS STORY - PAGE 127, MAP - PAGE 60
Watch your speed - the Emerson Sherriff's Department is strictly enforcing speed limits between exit 283 and 288
-306-
-305-
-304-
-303-
-302-
-301-
-300-
-299-
-298-
-297-
-296-
-295-
-294-
-293-
-292-
-291-
-290-
-289-
-288-
-287-
-286-
-285-
-284-
-283-
-282-
-281-
Time to drive this page: 21.4 minutes
SOUTH
GEORGIA, Bartow Co.
165

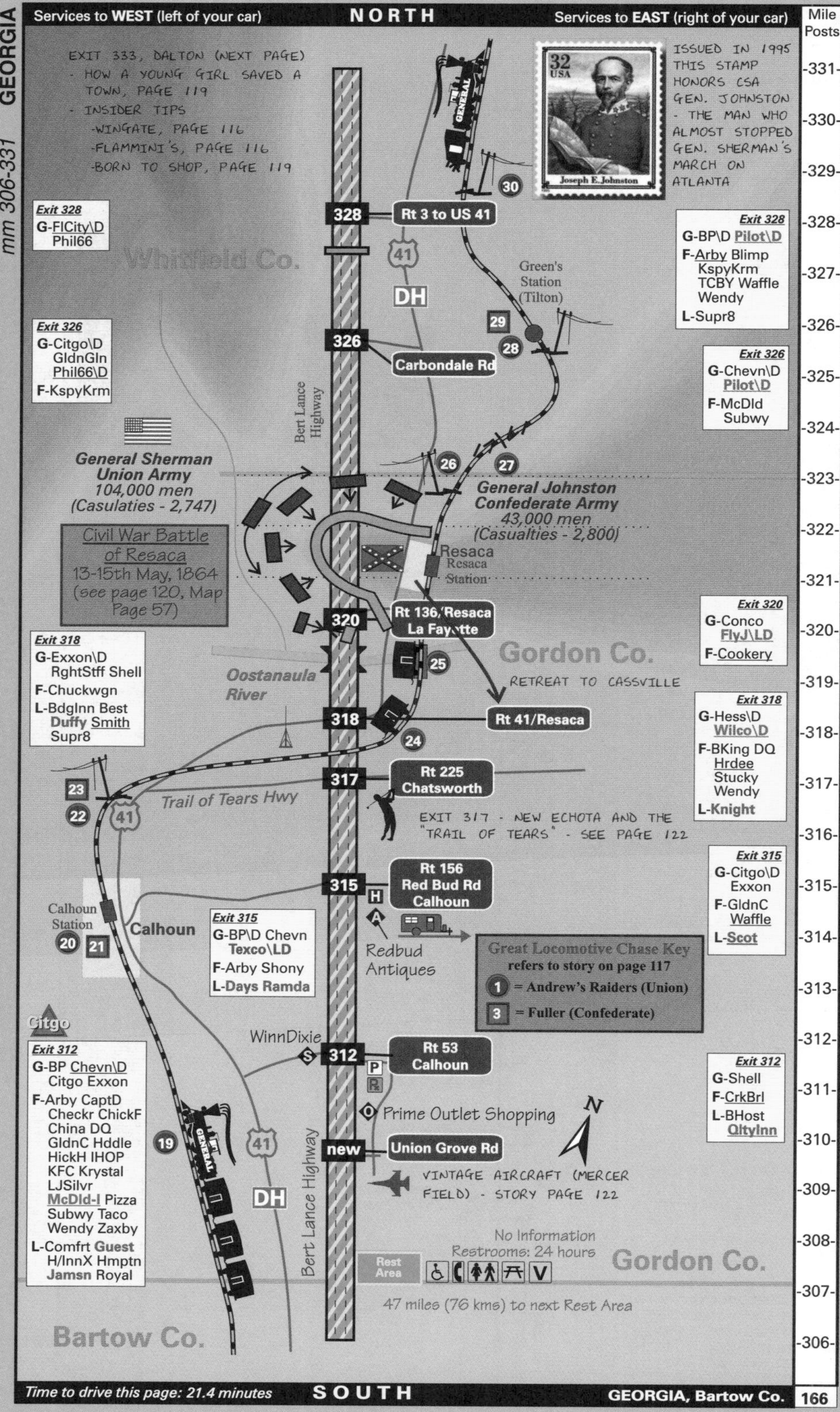
Services to WEST (left of your car)
NORTH
Services to EAST (right of your car)
Mile Posts
EXIT 333, DALTON (NEXT PAGE)
- HOW A YOUNG GIRL SAVED A TOWN, PAGE 119
- INSIDER TIPS
-WINGATE, PAGE 116
-FLAMMINI'S, PAGE 116
-BORN TO SHOP, PAGE 119
32 USA
Joseph E. Johnston
ISSUED IN 1995 THIS STAMP HONORS CSA GEN. JOHNSTON - THE MAN WHO ALMOST STOPPED GEN. SHERMAN'S MARCH ON ATLANTA
GENERAL
Exit 328
G-FlCity\D Phil66
328
Rt 3 to US 41
Exit 328
G-BP\D Pilot\D
F-Arby Blimp KspyKrm TCBY Waffle Wendy
L-Supr8
Whitfield Co.
41
DH
Green's Station (Tilton)
Exit 326
G-Citgo\D GldnGln Phil66\D
F-KspyKrm
326
Carbondale Rd
Exit 326
G-Chevn\D Pilot\D
F-McDld Subwy
Bert Lance Highway
General Sherman Union Army
104,000 men
(Casulaties - 2,747)
General Johnston Confederate Army
43,000 men
(Casualties - 2,800)
Civil War Battle of Resaca
13-15th May, 1864
(see page 120, Map Page 57)
Resaca
Resaca Station
Exit 320
G-Conco FlyJ\LD
F-Cookery
320
Rt 136/Resaca La Fayette
Exit 318
G-Exxon\D RghtStff Shell
F-Chuckwgn
L-BdgInn Best Duffy Smith Supr8
Gordon Co.
Oostanaula River
RETREAT TO CASSVILLE
318
Rt 41/Resaca
Exit 318
G-Hess\D Wilco\D
F-BKing DQ Hrdee Stucky Wendy
L-Knight
317
Rt 225 Chatsworth
Trail of Tears Hwy
41
EXIT 317 - NEW ECHOTA AND THE "TRAIL OF TEARS" - SEE PAGE 122
315
Rt 156 Red Bud Rd Calhoun
Exit 315
G-Citgo\D Exxon
F-GldnC Waffle
L-Scot
Calhoun Station
Calhoun
Exit 315
G-BP\D Chevn Texco\LD
F-Arby Shony
L-Days Ramda
Redbud Antiques
Great Locomotive Chase Key
refers to story on page 117
1 = Andrew's Raiders (Union)
3 = Fuller (Confederate)
Citgo
WinnDixie
312
Rt 53 Calhoun
Exit 312
G-BP Chevn\D Citgo Exxon
F-Arby CaptD Checkr ChickF China DQ GldnC Hddle HickH IHOP KFC Krystal LJSilvr McDld-I Pizza Subwy Taco Wendy Zaxby
L-Comfrt Guest H/InnX Hmptn Jamsn Royal
Exit 312
G-Shell
F-CrkBrl
L-BHost QltyInn
Prime Outlet Shopping
N
new
Union Grove Rd
VINTAGE AIRCRAFT (MERCER FIELD) - STORY PAGE 122
41
DH
Bert Lance Highway
No Information
Restrooms: 24 hours
Rest Area
Gordon Co.
47 miles (76 kms) to next Rest Area
Bartow Co.
-331- -330- -329- -328- -327- -326- -325- -324- -323- -322- -321- -320- -319- -318- -317- -316- -315- -314- -313- -312- -311- -310- -309- -308- -307- -306-
Time to drive this page: 21.4 minutes
SOUTH
GEORGIA, Bartow Co.

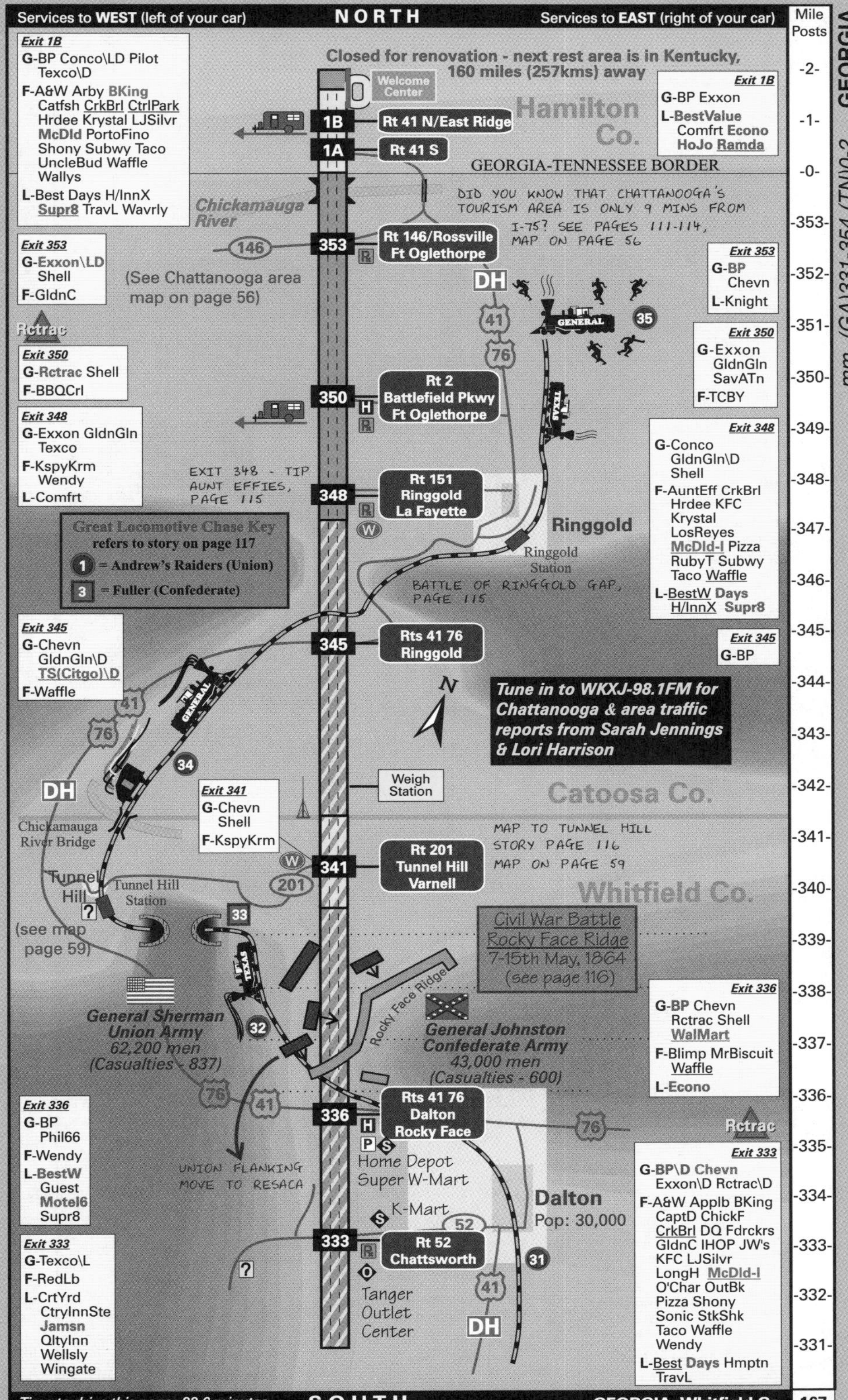

Services to WEST (left of your car)
NORTH
Services to EAST (right of your car)
Mile Posts
GEORGIA
mm (GA)331-354 (TN)0-2
Exit 1B
G-BP Conco\LD Pilot Texco\D
F-A&W Arby BKing Catfsh CrkBrl CtrlPark Hrdee Krystal LJSilvr McDld PortoFino Shony Subwy Taco UncleBud Waffle Wallys
L-Best Days H/InnX Supr8 TravL Wavrly
Closed for renovation - next rest area is in Kentucky, 160 miles (257kms) away
Welcome Center
Hamilton Co.
Exit 1B
G-BP Exxon
L-BestValue Comfrt Econo HoJo Ramda
1B
Rt 41 N/East Ridge
1A
Rt 41 S
GEORGIA-TENNESSEE BORDER
Chickamauga River
DID YOU KNOW THAT CHATTANOOGA'S TOURISM AREA IS ONLY 9 MINS FROM I-75? SEE PAGES 111-114, MAP ON PAGE 56
Exit 353
G-Exxon\LD Shell
F-GldnC
146
353
Rt 146/Rossville Ft Oglethorpe
(See Chattanooga area map on page 56)
DH
GENERAL
35
Exit 353
G-BP Chevn
L-Knight
Rctrac
41
76
Exit 350
G-Exxon GldnGln SavATn
F-TCBY
Exit 350
G-Rctrac Shell
F-BBQCrl
350
Rt 2 Battlefield Pkwy Ft Oglethorpe
TEXAS
Exit 348
G-Exxon GldnGln Texco
F-KspyKrm Wendy
L-Comfrt
EXIT 348 - TIP AUNT EFFIES, PAGE 115
348
Rt 151 Ringgold La Fayette
Exit 348
G-Conco GldnGln\D Shell
F-AuntEff CrkBrl Hrdee KFC Krystal LosReyes McDld-I Pizza RubyT Subwy Taco Waffle
L-BestW Days H/InnX Supr8
Ringgold
Great Locomotive Chase Key
refers to story on page 117
1 = Andrew's Raiders (Union)
3 = Fuller (Confederate)
Ringgold Station
BATTLE OF RINGGOLD GAP, PAGE 115
Exit 345
G-Chevn GldnGln\D TS(Citgo)\D
F-Waffle
345
Rts 41 76 Ringgold
Exit 345
G-BP
N
Tune in to WKXJ-98.1FM for Chattanooga & area traffic reports from Sarah Jennings & Lori Harrison
GENERAL
41
76
34
DH
Weigh Station
Catoosa Co.
Exit 341
G-Chevn Shell
F-KspyKrm
Chickamauga River Bridge
MAP TO TUNNEL HILL STORY PAGE 116 MAP ON PAGE 59
341
Rt 201 Tunnel Hill Varnell
201
Tunnel Hill
Tunnel Hill Station
Whitfield Co.
33
(see map page 59)
Civil War Battle Rocky Face Ridge 7-15th May, 1864 (see page 116)
TEXAS
Rocky Face Ridge
Exit 336
G-BP Chevn Rctrac Shell WalMart
F-Blimp MrBiscuit Waffle
L-Econo
General Sherman Union Army 62,200 men (Casualties - 837)
32
General Johnston Confederate Army 43,000 men (Casualties - 600)
Exit 336
G-BP Phil66
F-Wendy
L-BestW Guest Motel6 Supr8
76
41
336
Rts 41 76 Dalton Rocky Face
76
Rctrac
Home Depot Super W-Mart
UNION FLANKING MOVE TO RESACA
K-Mart
Dalton Pop: 30,000
52
Exit 333
G-BP\D Chevn Exxon\D Rctrac\D
F-A&W Applb BKing CaptD ChickF CrkBrl DQ Fdrckrs GldnC IHOP JW's KFC LJSilvr LongH McDld-I O'Char OutBk Pizza Shony Sonic StkShk Taco Waffle Wendy
L-Best Days Hmptn TravL
Exit 333
G-Texco\L
F-RedLb
L-CrtYrd CtryInnSte Jamsn QltyInn Wellsly Wingate
333
Rt 52 Chattsworth
31
Tanger Outlet Center
41
DH
-2-
-1-
-0-
-353-
-352-
-351-
-350-
-349-
-348-
-347-
-346-
-345-
-344-
-343-
-342-
-341-
-340-
-339-
-338-
-337-
-336-
-335-
-334-
-333-
-332-
-331-
Time to drive this page: 22.6 minutes
SOUTH
GEORGIA, Whitfield Co.
167

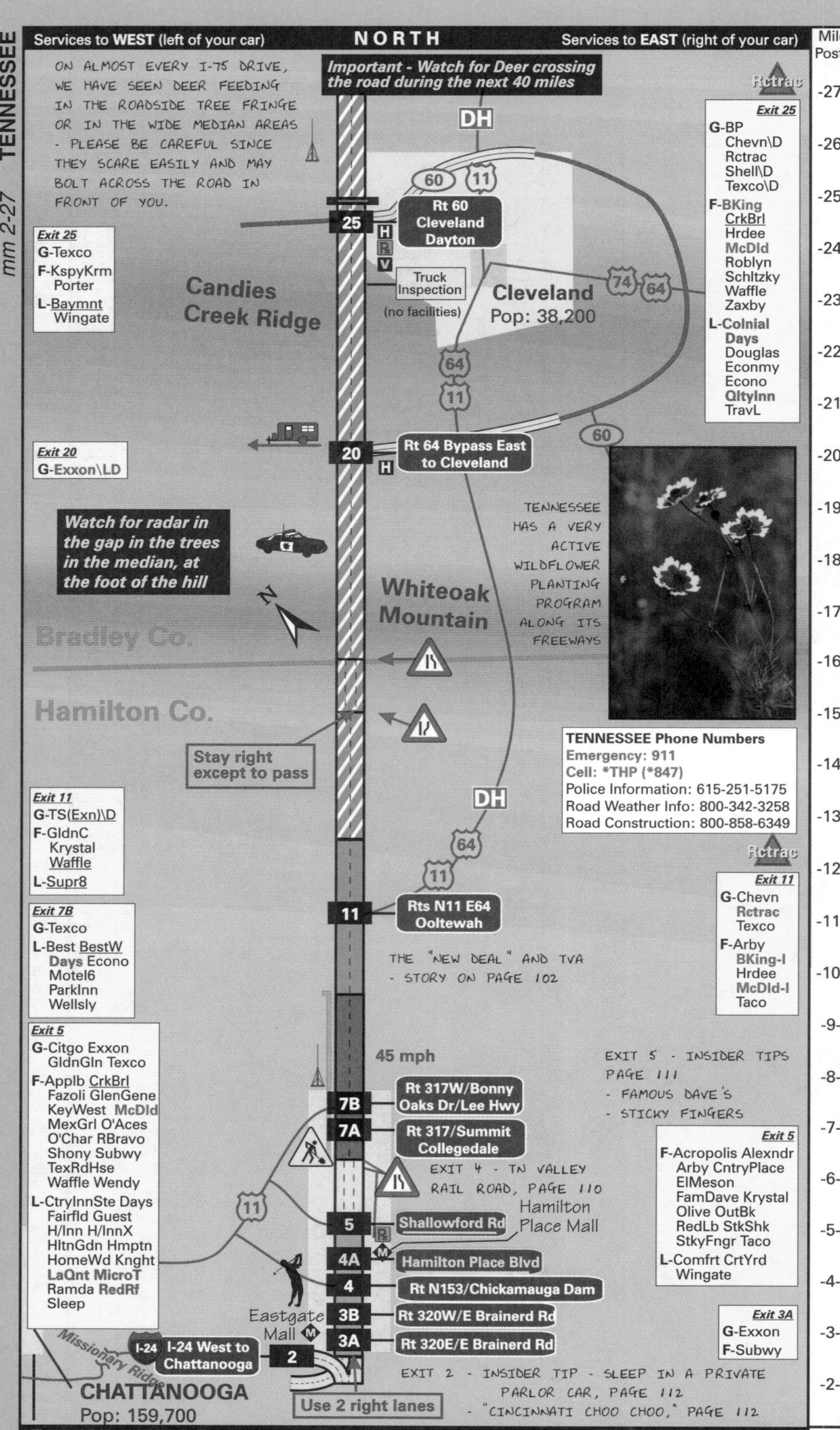
Services to WEST (left of your car)
NORTH
Services to EAST (right of your car)
Mile Posts
ON ALMOST EVERY I-75 DRIVE, WE HAVE SEEN DEER FEEDING IN THE ROADSIDE TREE FRINGE OR IN THE WIDE MEDIAN AREAS - PLEASE BE CAREFUL SINCE THEY SCARE EASILY AND MAY BOLT ACROSS THE ROAD IN FRONT OF YOU.
Important - Watch for Deer crossing the road during the next 40 miles
Rctrac
-27-
DH
Exit 25
G-BP Chevn\D Rctrac Shell\D Texco\D
F-BKing CrkBrl Hrdee McDld Roblyn Schltzky Waffle Zaxby
L-Colnial Days Douglas Econmy Econo QltyInn TravL
-26-
60
11
-25-
25
Rt 60 Cleveland Dayton
Exit 25
G-Texco
F-KspyKrm Porter
L-Baymnt Wingate
-24-
Truck Inspection
(no facilities)
74
64
Candies Creek Ridge
Cleveland
Pop: 38,200
-23-
-22-
64
11
-21-
60
Exit 20
G-Exxon\LD
20
Rt 64 Bypass East to Cleveland
-20-
TENNESSEE HAS A VERY ACTIVE WILDFLOWER PLANTING PROGRAM ALONG ITS FREEWAYS
-19-
Watch for radar in the gap in the trees in the median, at the foot of the hill
-18-
Whiteoak Mountain
-17-
Bradley Co.
-16-
Hamilton Co.
-15-
Stay right except to pass
TENNESSEE Phone Numbers
Emergency: 911
Cell: *THP (*847)
Police Information: 615-251-5175
Road Weather Info: 800-342-3258
Road Construction: 800-858-6349
-14-
Exit 11
G-TS(Exn)\D
F-GldnC Krystal Waffle
L-Supr8
DH
-13-
64
Rctrac
11
-12-
Exit 11
G-Chevn Rctrac Texco
F-Arby BKing-I Hrdee McDld-I Taco
Exit 7B
G-Texco
L-Best BestW Days Econo Motel6 ParkInn Wellsly
11
Rts N11 E64 Ooltewah
-11-
THE "NEW DEAL" AND TVA - STORY ON PAGE 102
-10-
-9-
Exit 5
G-Citgo Exxon GldnGln Texco
F-Applb CrkBrl Fazoli GlenGene KeyWest McDld MexGrl O'Aces O'Char RBravo Shony Subwy TexRdHse Waffle Wendy
L-CtryInnSte Days Fairfld Guest H/Inn H/InnX HltnGdn Hmptn HomeWd Knght LaQnt MicroT Ramda RedRf Sleep
45 mph
EXIT 5 - INSIDER TIPS PAGE 111 - FAMOUS DAVE'S - STICKY FINGERS
-8-
7B
Rt 317W/Bonny Oaks Dr/Lee Hwy
-7-
7A
Rt 317/Summit Collegedale
Exit 5
F-Acropolis Alexndr Arby CntryPlace ElMeson FamDave Krystal Olive OutBk RedLb StkShk StkyFngr Taco
L-Comfrt CrtYrd Wingate
EXIT 4 - TN VALLEY RAIL ROAD, PAGE 110
-6-
11
5
Shallowford Rd
Hamilton Place Mall
-5-
4A
Hamilton Place Blvd
-4-
4
Rt N153/Chickamauga Dam
Eastgate Mall
3B
Rt 320W/E Brainerd Rd
Exit 3A
G-Exxon
F-Subwy
-3-
I-24
I-24 West to Chattanooga
2
3A
Rt 320E/E Brainerd Rd
Missionary Ridge
EXIT 2 - INSIDER TIP - SLEEP IN A PRIVATE PARLOR CAR, PAGE 112 - "CINCINNATI CHOO CHOO," PAGE 112
-2-
CHATTANOOGA
Pop: 159,700
Use 2 right lanes

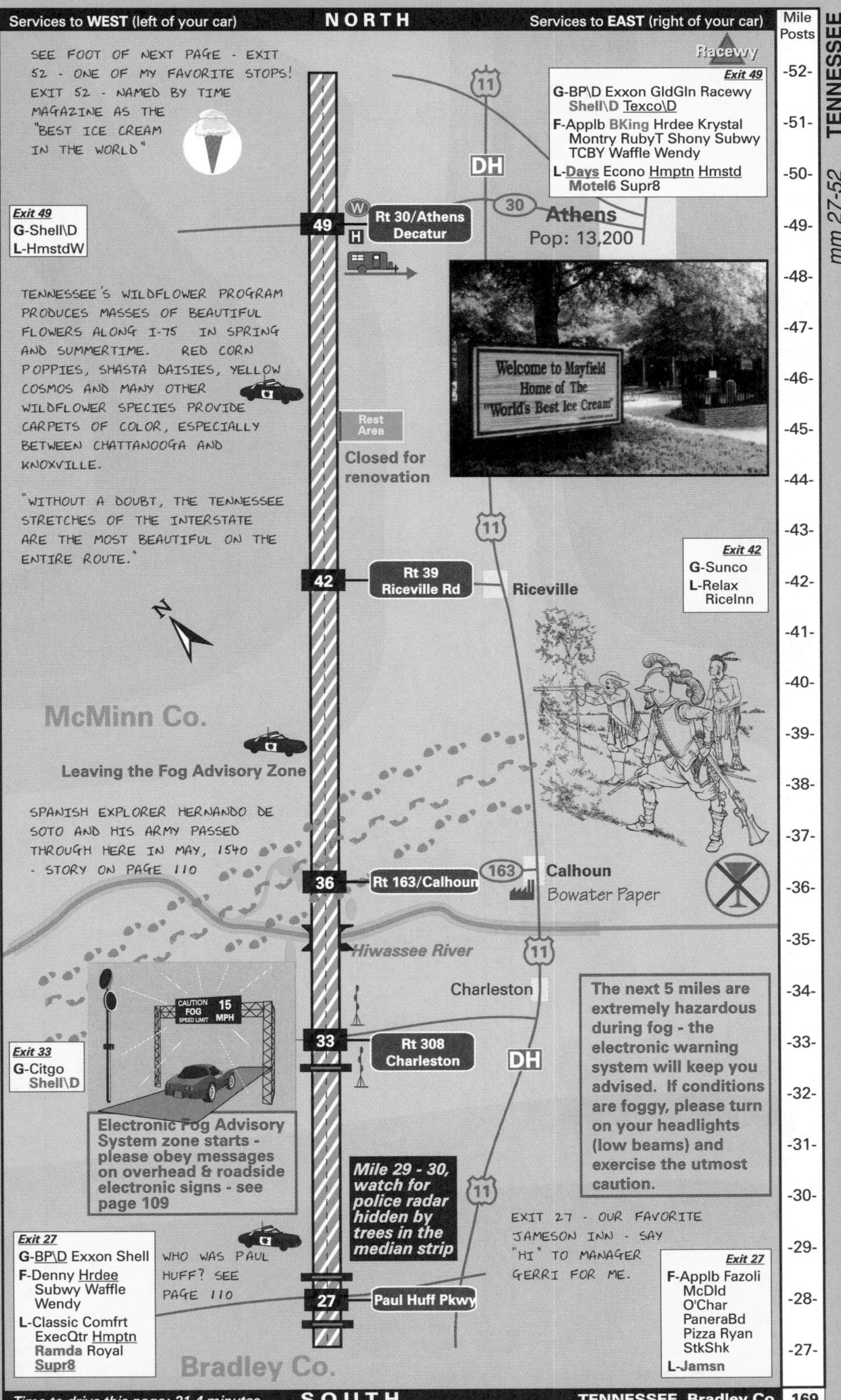
SEE FOOT OF NEXT PAGE - EXIT 52 - ONE OF MY FAVORITE STOPS! EXIT 52 - NAMED BY TIME MAGAZINE AS THE "BEST ICE CREAM IN THE WORLD"
Racewy
Exit 49
G-BP\D Exxon GldGln Racewy Shell\D Texco\D
F-Applb BKing Hrdee Krystal Montry RubyT Shony Subwy TCBY Waffle Wendy
L-Days Econo Hmptn Hmstd Motel6 Supr8
11
DH
30
Athens
Pop: 13,200
Exit 49
G-Shell\D
L-HmstdW
49
Rt 30/Athens Decatur
W
H
Welcome to Mayfield
Home of The
"World's Best Ice Cream"
TENNESSEE'S WILDFLOWER PROGRAM PRODUCES MASSES OF BEAUTIFUL FLOWERS ALONG I-75 IN SPRING AND SUMMERTIME. RED CORN POPPIES, SHASTA DAISIES, YELLOW COSMOS AND MANY OTHER WILDFLOWER SPECIES PROVIDE CARPETS OF COLOR, ESPECIALLY BETWEEN CHATTANOOGA AND KNOXVILLE.
"WITHOUT A DOUBT, THE TENNESSEE STRETCHES OF THE INTERSTATE ARE THE MOST BEAUTIFUL ON THE ENTIRE ROUTE."
Rest Area
Closed for renovation
11
Exit 42
G-Sunco
L-Relax RiceInn
42
Rt 39 Riceville Rd
Riceville
N
McMinn Co.
Leaving the Fog Advisory Zone
SPANISH EXPLORER HERNANDO DE SOTO AND HIS ARMY PASSED THROUGH HERE IN MAY, 1540 - STORY ON PAGE 110
36
Rt 163/Calhoun
163
Calhoun
Bowater Paper
Hiwassee River
11
Charleston
CAUTION FOG SPEED LIMIT 15 MPH
Exit 33
G-Citgo Shell\D
33
Rt 308 Charleston
DH
The next 5 miles are extremely hazardous during fog - the electronic warning system will keep you advised. If conditions are foggy, please turn on your headlights (low beams) and exercise the utmost caution.
Electronic Fog Advisory System zone starts - please obey messages on overhead & roadside electronic signs - see page 109
Mile 29 - 30, watch for police radar hidden by trees in the median strip
11
EXIT 27 - OUR FAVORITE JAMESON INN - SAY "HI" TO MANAGER GERRI FOR ME.
Exit 27
G-BP\D Exxon Shell
F-Denny Hrdee Subway Waffle Wendy
L-Classic Comfrt ExecQtr Hmptn Ramda Royal Supr8
WHO WAS PAUL HUFF? SEE PAGE 110
27
Paul Huff Pkwy
Exit 27
F-Applb Fazoli McDld O'Char PaneraBd Pizza Ryan StkShk
L-Jamsn
Bradley Co.
-52- -51- -50- -49- -48- -47- -46- -45- -44- -43- -42- -41- -40- -39- -38- -37- -36- -35- -34- -33- -32- -31- -30- -29- -28- -27-

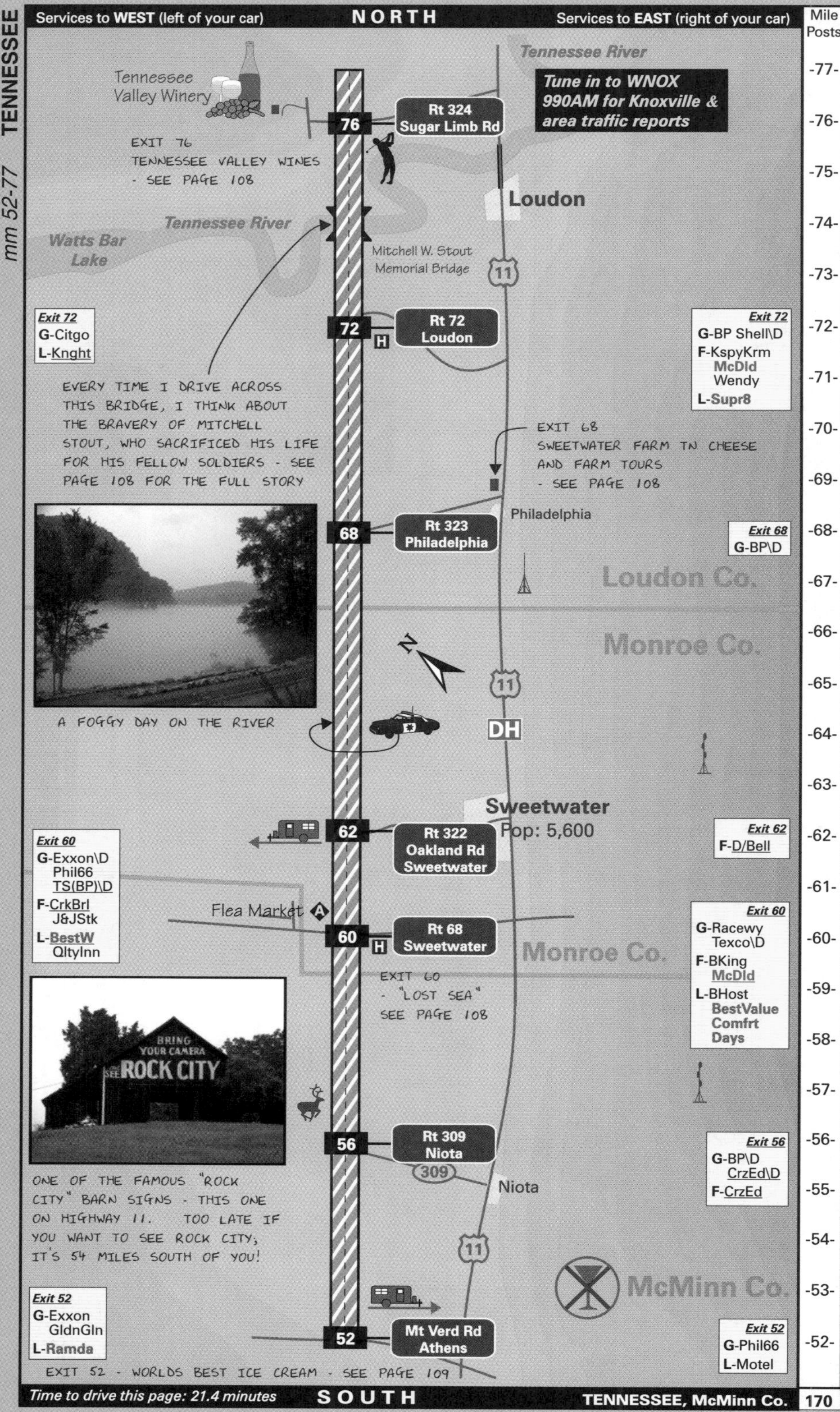
Services to WEST (left of your car)
NORTH
Services to EAST (right of your car)
Mile Posts
Tennessee River
Tune in to WNOX 990AM for Knoxville & area traffic reports
Tennessee Valley Winery
76
Rt 324 Sugar Limb Rd
EXIT 76
TENNESSEE VALLEY WINES
- SEE PAGE 108
Loudon
Tennessee River
Watts Bar Lake
Mitchell W. Stout Memorial Bridge
11
Exit 72
G-Citgo
L-Knght
72
H
Rt 72 Loudon
Exit 72
G-BP Shell\D
F-KspyKrm
McDld
Wendy
L-Supr8
EVERY TIME I DRIVE ACROSS THIS BRIDGE, I THINK ABOUT THE BRAVERY OF MITCHELL STOUT, WHO SACRIFICED HIS LIFE FOR HIS FELLOW SOLDIERS - SEE PAGE 108 FOR THE FULL STORY
EXIT 68
SWEETWATER FARM TN CHEESE AND FARM TOURS
- SEE PAGE 108
Philadelphia
68
Rt 323 Philadelphia
Exit 68
G-BP\D
Loudon Co.
Monroe Co.
N
A FOGGY DAY ON THE RIVER
11
DH
Sweetwater
Pop: 5,600
Exit 60
G-Exxon\D
Phil66
TS(BP)\D
F-CrkBrl
J&JStk
L-BestW
QltyInn
62
Rt 322 Oakland Rd Sweetwater
Exit 62
F-D/Bell
Flea Market
A
60
H
Rt 68 Sweetwater
Monroe Co.
Exit 60
G-Racewy
Texco\D
F-BKing
McDld
L-BHost
BestValue
Comfrt
Days
EXIT 60
- "LOST SEA"
SEE PAGE 108
BRING YOUR CAMERA
SEE ROCK CITY
56
Rt 309 Niota
309
Niota
Exit 56
G-BP\D
CrzEd\D
F-CrzEd
ONE OF THE FAMOUS "ROCK CITY" BARN SIGNS - THIS ONE ON HIGHWAY 11. TOO LATE IF YOU WANT TO SEE ROCK CITY; IT'S 54 MILES SOUTH OF YOU!
11
McMinn Co.
Exit 52
G-Exxon
GldnGln
L-Ramda
52
Mt Verd Rd Athens
Exit 52
G-Phil66
L-Motel
EXIT 52 - WORLDS BEST ICE CREAM - SEE PAGE 109
-77-
-76-
-75-
-74-
-73-
-72-
-71-
-70-
-69-
-68-
-67-
-66-
-65-
-64-
-63-
-62-
-61-
-60-
-59-
-58-
-57-
-56-
-55-
-54-
-53-
-52-
Time to drive this page: 21.4 minutes
SOUTH

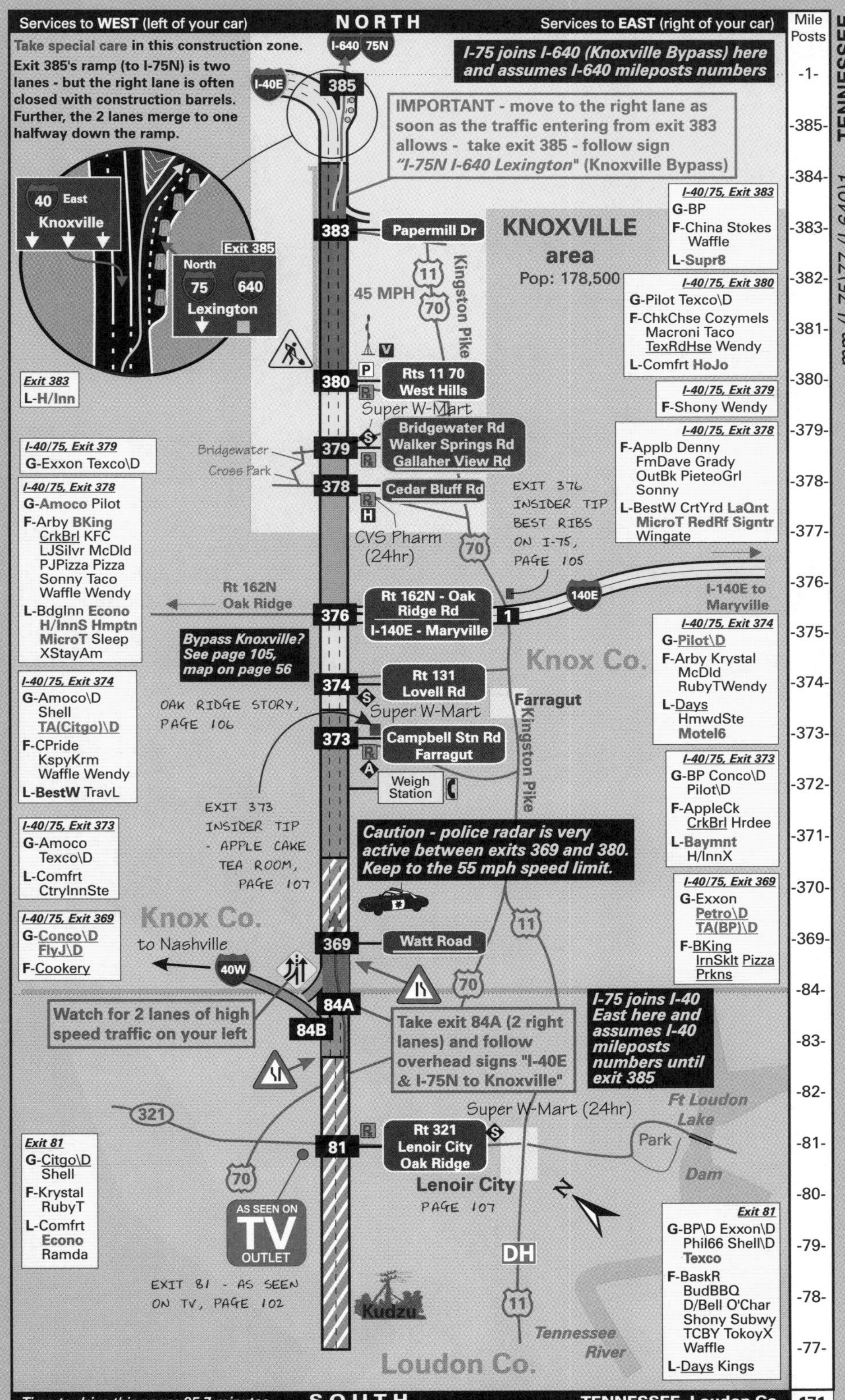

Services to WEST (left of your car)
NORTH
Services to EAST (right of your car)
Mile Posts
TENNESSEE
mm (I-75)77-(I-640)1
Take special care in this construction zone.
Exit 385's ramp (to I-75N) is two lanes - but the right lane is often closed with construction barrels. Further, the 2 lanes merge to one halfway down the ramp.
I-640 75N
I-40E
385
I-75 joins I-640 (Knoxville Bypass) here and assumes I-640 mileposts numbers
IMPORTANT - move to the right lane as soon as the traffic entering from exit 383 allows - take exit 385 - follow sign "I-75N I-640 Lexington" (Knoxville Bypass)
40 East Knoxville
Exit 385
North 75 640 Lexington
-1-
-385-
-384-
-383-
-382-
-381-
-380-
-379-
-378-
-377-
-376-
-375-
-374-
-373-
-372-
-371-
-370-
-369-
-84-
-83-
-82-
-81-
-80-
-79-
-78-
-77-
I-40/75, Exit 383
G-BP
F-China Stokes Waffle
L-Supr8
383
Papermill Dr
KNOXVILLE area
Pop: 178,500
11
70
Kingston Pike
45 MPH
I-40/75, Exit 380
G-Pilot Texco\D
F-ChkChse Cozymels Macroni Taco TexRdHse Wendy
L-Comfrt HoJo
Exit 383
L-H/Inn
380
Rts 11 70 West Hills
Super W-Mart
I-40/75, Exit 379
F-Shony Wendy
I-40/75, Exit 379
G-Exxon Texco\D
Bridgewater
Cross Park
379
Bridgewater Rd Walker Springs Rd Gallaher View Rd
I-40/75, Exit 378
F-Applb Denny FmDave Grady OutBk PieteoGrl Sonny
L-BestW CrtYrd LaQnt MicroT RedRf Signtr Wingate
I-40/75, Exit 378
G-Amoco Pilot
F-Arby BKing CrkBrl KFC LJSilvr McDld PJPizza Pizza Sonny Taco Waffle Wendy
L-BdgInn Econo H/InnS Hmptn MicroT Sleep XStayAm
378
Cedar Bluff Rd
CVS Pharm (24hr)
EXIT 376 INSIDER TIP BEST RIBS ON I-75, PAGE 105
70
Rt 162N Oak Ridge
376
Rt 162N - Oak Ridge Rd
I-140E - Maryville
1
140E
I-140E to Maryville
Bypass Knoxville? See page 105, map on page 56
I-40/75, Exit 374
G-Pilot\D
F-Arby Krystal McDld RubyTWendy
L-Days HmwdSte Motel6
Knox Co.
I-40/75, Exit 374
G-Amoco\D Shell TA(Citgo)\D
F-CPride KspyKrm Waffle Wendy
L-BestW TravL
374
Rt 131 Lovell Rd
OAK RIDGE STORY, PAGE 106
Super W-Mart
Farragut
Kingston Pike
373
Campbell Stn Rd Farragut
I-40/75, Exit 373
G-BP Conco\D Pilot\D
F-AppleCk CrkBrl Hrdee
L-Baymnt H/InnX
Weigh Station
EXIT 373 INSIDER TIP - APPLE CAKE TEA ROOM, PAGE 107
I-40/75, Exit 373
G-Amoco Texco\D
L-Comfrt CtryInnSte
Caution - police radar is very active between exits 369 and 380. Keep to the 55 mph speed limit.
I-40/75, Exit 369
G-Exxon Petro\D TA(BP)\D
F-BKing IrnSklt Pizza Prkns
I-40/75, Exit 369
G-Conco\D FlyJ\D
F-Cookery
Knox Co.
to Nashville
40W
369
Watt Road
11
70
84A
84B
Watch for 2 lanes of high speed traffic on your left
Take exit 84A (2 right lanes) and follow overhead signs "I-40E & I-75N to Knoxville"
I-75 joins I-40 East here and assumes I-40 mileposts numbers until exit 385
321
Super W-Mart (24hr)
Ft Loudon Lake
Park
Dam
Exit 81
G-Citgo\D Shell
F-Krystal RubyT
L-Comfrt Econo Ramda
81
Rt 321 Lenoir City Oak Ridge
Lenoir City
PAGE 107
70
AS SEEN ON TV OUTLET
Exit 81
G-BP\D Exxon\D Phil66 Shell\D Texco
F-BaskR BudBBQ D/Bell O'Char Shony Subwy TCBY TokoyX Waffle
L-Days Kings
DH
11
EXIT 81 - AS SEEN ON TV, PAGE 102
Kudzu
Tennessee River
Loudon Co.
Time to drive this page: 25.7 minutes
SOUTH
TENNESSEE, Loudon Co.
171

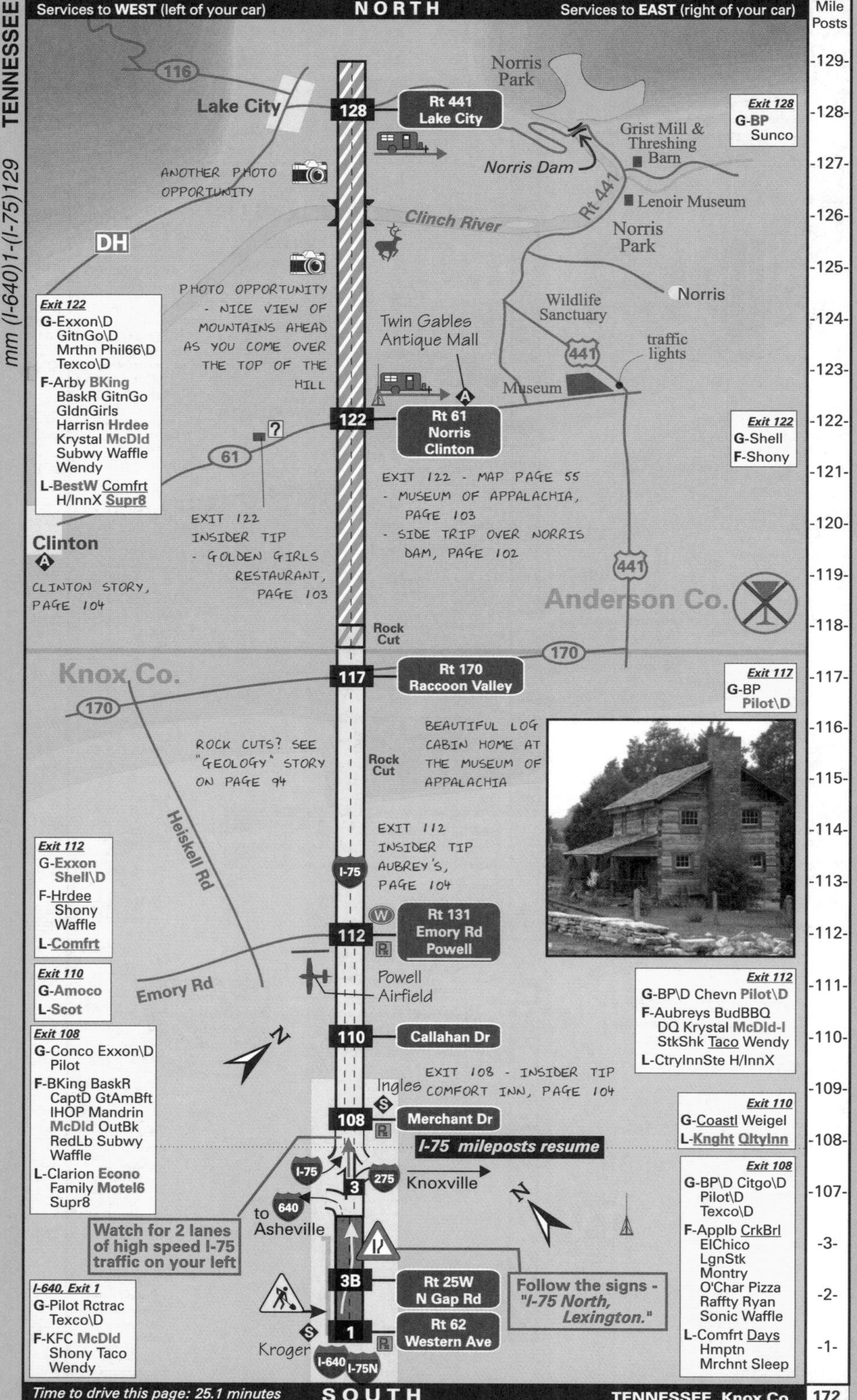

TENNESSEE
mm (I-640)1-(I-75)129
Services to WEST (left of your car)
NORTH
Services to EAST (right of your car)
Mile Posts
116
Lake City
128
Rt 441 Lake City
Norris Park
Grist Mill & Threshing Barn
Norris Dam
Exit 128
G-BP Sunco
ANOTHER PHOTO OPPORTUNITY
Clinch River
Rt 441
Lenoir Museum
Norris Park
DH
PHOTO OPPORTUNITY - NICE VIEW OF MOUNTAINS AHEAD AS YOU COME OVER THE TOP OF THE HILL
Norris
Wildlife Sanctuary
Twin Gables Antique Mall
traffic lights
441
Museum
Exit 122
G-Exxon\D GitnGo\D Mrthn Phil66\D Texco\D
F-Arby BKing BaskR GitnGo GldnGirls Harrisn Hrdee Krystal McDld Subwy Waffle Wendy
L-BestW Comfrt H/InnX Supr8
122
Rt 61 Norris Clinton
Exit 122
G-Shell
F-Shony
61
EXIT 122 - MAP PAGE 55
- MUSEUM OF APPALACHIA, PAGE 103
- SIDE TRIP OVER NORRIS DAM, PAGE 102
EXIT 122 INSIDER TIP - GOLDEN GIRLS RESTAURANT, PAGE 103
Clinton
CLINTON STORY, PAGE 104
441
Anderson Co.
Rock Cut
170
Knox Co.
117
Rt 170 Raccoon Valley
Exit 117
G-BP Pilot\D
170
BEAUTIFUL LOG CABIN HOME AT THE MUSEUM OF APPALACHIA
ROCK CUTS? SEE "GEOLOGY" STORY ON PAGE 94
Rock Cut
Heiskell Rd
EXIT 112 INSIDER TIP AUBREY'S, PAGE 104
I-75
Exit 112
G-Exxon Shell\D
F-Hrdee Shony Waffle
L-Comfrt
W
112
Rt 131 Emory Rd Powell
Exit 110
G-Amoco
L-Scot
Emory Rd
Powell Airfield
Exit 112
G-BP\D Chevn Pilot\D
F-Aubreys BudBBQ DQ Krystal McDld-I StkShk Taco Wendy
L-CtryInnSte H/InnX
Exit 108
G-Conco Exxon\D Pilot
F-BKing BaskR CaptD GtAmBft IHOP Mandrin McDld OutBk RedLb Subwy Waffle
L-Clarion Econo Family Motel6 Supr8
110
Callahan Dr
N
EXIT 108 - INSIDER TIP COMFORT INN, PAGE 104
Ingles
Exit 110
G-Coastl Weigel
L-Knght QltyInn
108
Merchant Dr
I-75 mileposts resume
I-75
3
275
Knoxville
Exit 108
G-BP\D Citgo\D Pilot\D Texco\D
F-Applb CrkBrl ElChico LgnStk Montry O'Char Pizza Raffty Ryan Sonic Waffle
L-Comfrt Days Hmptn Mrchnt Sleep
640
to Asheville
Watch for 2 lanes of high speed I-75 traffic on your left
N
I-640, Exit 1
G-Pilot Rctrac Texco\D
F-KFC McDld Shony Taco Wendy
3B
Rt 25W N Gap Rd
Follow the signs - "I-75 North, Lexington."
1
Rt 62 Western Ave
Kroger
I-640
I-75N
-129- -128- -127- -126- -125- -124- -123- -122- -121- -120- -119- -118- -117- -116- -115- -114- -113- -112- -111- -110- -109- -108- -107- -3- -2- -1-
Time to drive this page: 25.1 minutes
SOUTH
TENNESSEE, Knox Co.
172

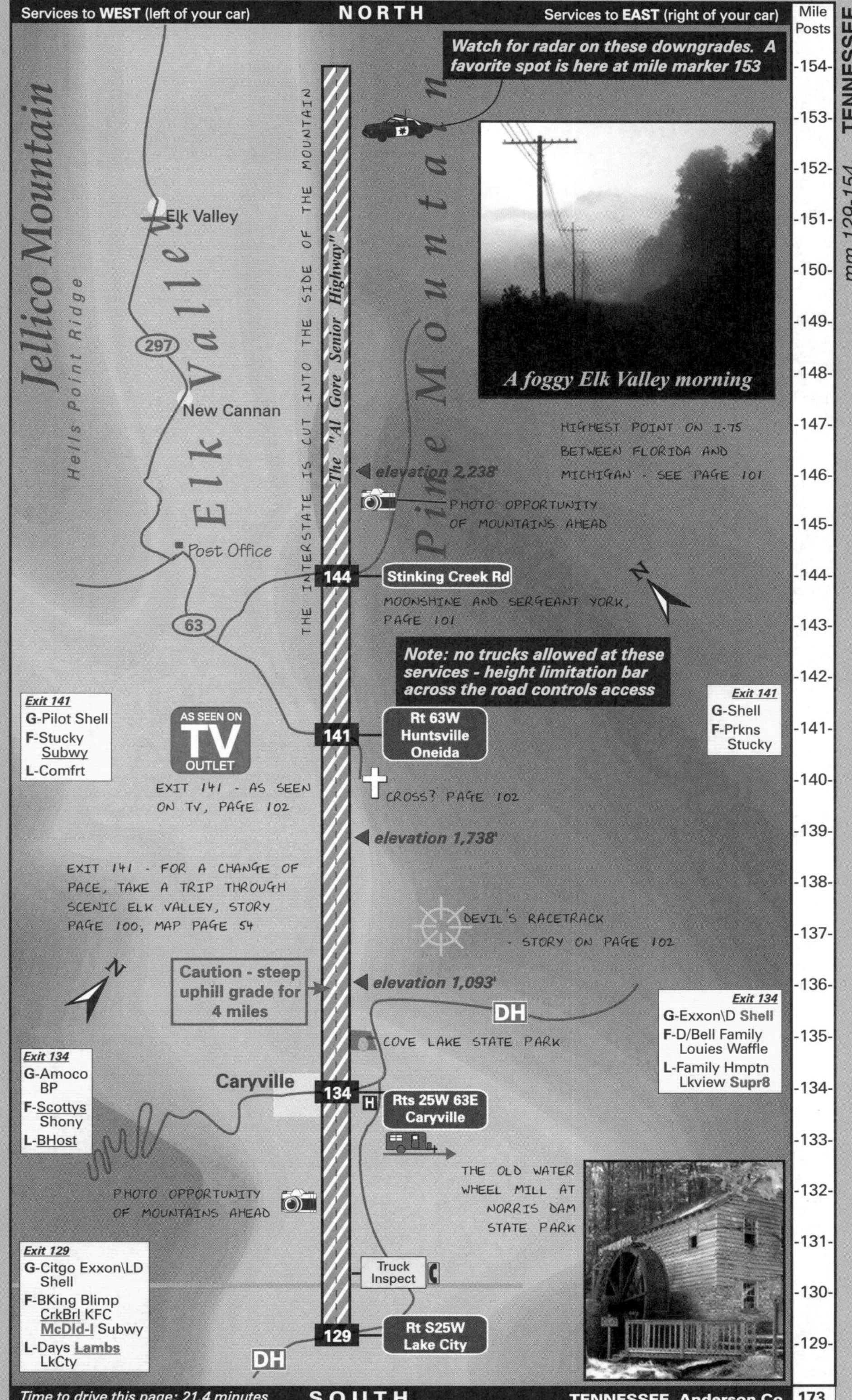

Services to WEST (left of your car)
NORTH
Services to EAST (right of your car)
Mile Posts
TENNESSEE
mm 129-154
Watch for radar on these downgrades. A favorite spot is here at mile marker 153
-154-
-153-
-152-
-151-
-150-
-149-
-148-
-147-
-146-
-145-
-144-
-143-
-142-
-141-
-140-
-139-
-138-
-137-
-136-
-135-
-134-
-133-
-132-
-131-
-130-
-129-
Jellico Mountain
Hells Point Ridge
Elk Valley
Elk Valley
297
New Cannan
Post Office
63
THE INTERSTATE IS CUT INTO THE SIDE OF THE MOUNTAIN
The "Al Gore Senior Highway"
Pine Mountain
A foggy Elk Valley morning
HIGHEST POINT ON I-75 BETWEEN FLORIDA AND MICHIGAN - SEE PAGE 101
elevation 2,238'
PHOTO OPPORTUNITY OF MOUNTAINS AHEAD
144
Stinking Creek Rd
MOONSHINE AND SERGEANT YORK, PAGE 101
Note: no trucks allowed at these services - height limitation bar across the road controls access
Exit 141
G-Pilot Shell
F-Stucky Subwy
L-Comfrt
AS SEEN ON TV OUTLET
141
Rt 63W Huntsville Oneida
Exit 141
G-Shell
F-Prkns Stucky
EXIT 141 - AS SEEN ON TV, PAGE 102
CROSS? PAGE 102
elevation 1,738'
EXIT 141 - FOR A CHANGE OF PACE, TAKE A TRIP THROUGH SCENIC ELK VALLEY, STORY PAGE 100; MAP PAGE 54
DEVIL'S RACETRACK - STORY ON PAGE 102
Caution - steep uphill grade for 4 miles
elevation 1,093'
DH
COVE LAKE STATE PARK
Exit 134
G-Exxon\D Shell
F-D/Bell Family Louies Waffle
L-Family Hmptn Lkview Supr8
Exit 134
G-Amoco BP
F-Scottys Shony
L-BHost
Caryville
134
H
Rts 25W 63E Caryville
PHOTO OPPORTUNITY OF MOUNTAINS AHEAD
THE OLD WATER WHEEL MILL AT NORRIS DAM STATE PARK
Exit 129
G-Citgo Exxon\LD Shell
F-BKing Blimp CrkBrl KFC McDld-I Subwy
L-Days Lambs LkCty
Truck Inspect
129
Rt S25W Lake City
DH

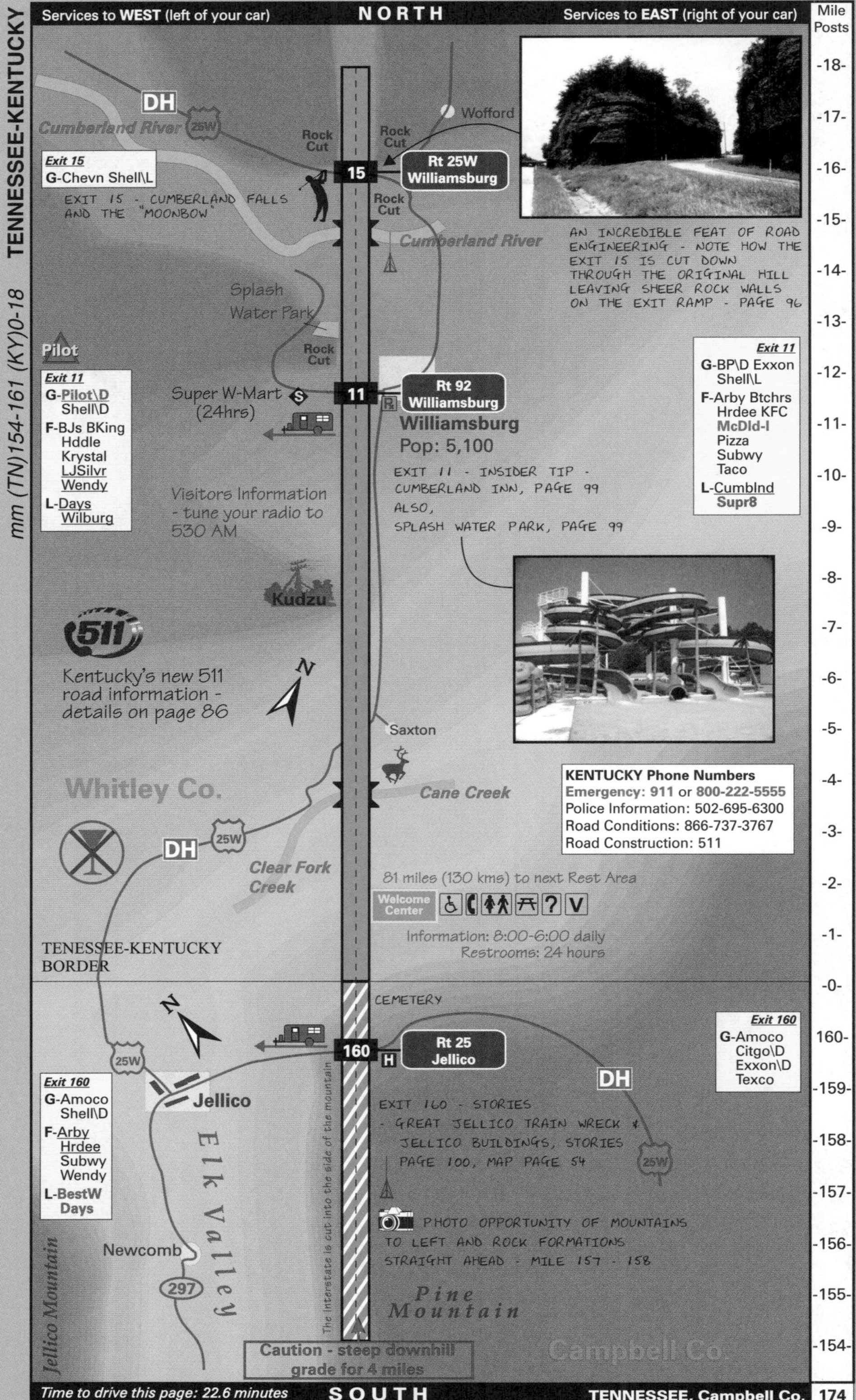
Services to WEST (left of your car)
NORTH
Services to EAST (right of your car)
Mile Posts
-18-
-17-
-16-
-15-
-14-
-13-
-12-
-11-
-10-
-9-
-8-
-7-
-6-
-5-
-4-
-3-
-2-
-1-
-0-
160-
-159-
-158-
-157-
-156-
-155-
-154-
DH
25W
Cumberland River
Wofford
Rock Cut
Rock Cut
Rock Cut
Rock Cut
Exit 15
G-Chevn Shell\L
15
Rt 25W Williamsburg
EXIT 15 - CUMBERLAND FALLS AND THE "MOONBOW"
Cumberland River
AN INCREDIBLE FEAT OF ROAD ENGINEERING - NOTE HOW THE EXIT 15 IS CUT DOWN THROUGH THE ORIGINAL HILL LEAVING SHEER ROCK WALLS ON THE EXIT RAMP - PAGE 96
Splash Water Park
Pilot
Exit 11
G-Pilot\D Shell\D
F-BJs BKing Hddle Krystal LJSilvr Wendy
L-Days Wilburg
Super W-Mart (24hrs)
S
11
Rt 92 Williamsburg
Williamsburg
Pop: 5,100
Exit 11
G-BP\D Exxon Shell\L
F-Arby Btchrs Hrdee KFC McDld-I Pizza Subwy Taco
L-Cumblnd Supr8
EXIT 11 - INSIDER TIP - CUMBERLAND INN, PAGE 99
ALSO,
SPLASH WATER PARK, PAGE 99
Visitors Information - tune your radio to 530 AM
Kudzu
511
Kentucky's new 511 road information - details on page 86
N
Saxton
Whitley Co.
Cane Creek
KENTUCKY Phone Numbers
Emergency: 911 or 800-222-5555
Police Information: 502-695-6300
Road Conditions: 866-737-3767
Road Construction: 511
DH
25W
Clear Fork Creek
81 miles (130 kms) to next Rest Area
Welcome Center
Information: 8:00-6:00 daily
Restrooms: 24 hours
TENESSEE-KENTUCKY BORDER
CEMETERY
N
160
H
Rt 25 Jellico
Exit 160
G-Amoco Citgo\D Exxon\D Texco
25W
DH
Exit 160
G-Amoco Shell\D
F-Arby Hrdee Subwy Wendy
L-BestW Days
Jellico
Elk Valley
EXIT 160 - STORIES
- GREAT JELLICO TRAIN WRECK & JELLICO BUILDINGS, STORIES PAGE 100, MAP PAGE 54
25W
The interstate is cut into the side of the mountain
PHOTO OPPORTUNITY OF MOUNTAINS TO LEFT AND ROCK FORMATIONS STRAIGHT AHEAD - MILE 157 - 158
Newcomb
297
Pine Mountain
Jellico Mountain
Caution - steep downhill grade for 4 miles
Campbell Co.
Time to drive this page: 22.6 minutes
SOUTH

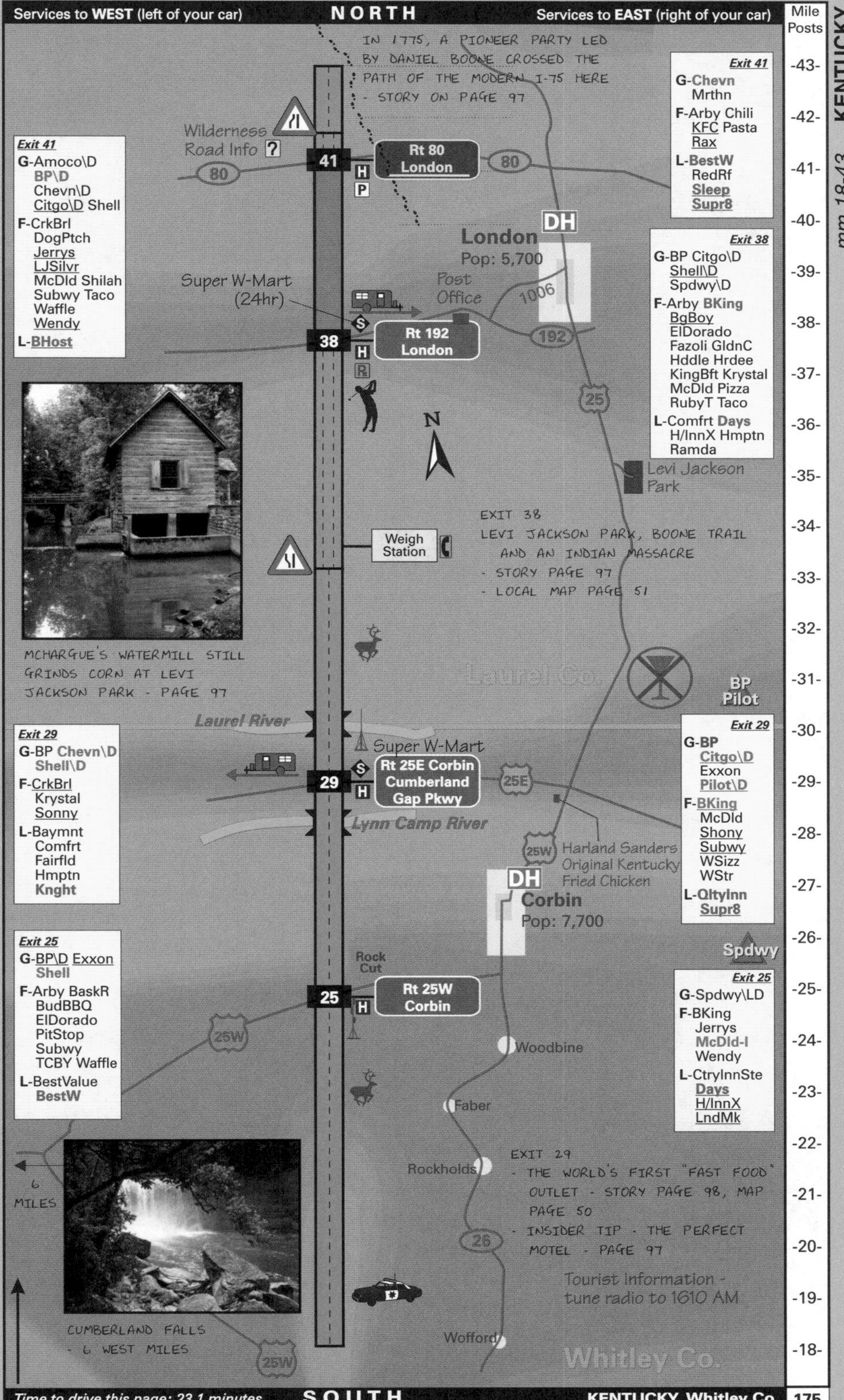

Services to WEST (left of your car)
NORTH
Services to EAST (right of your car)
Mile Posts
KENTUCKY
mm 18-43
IN 1775, A PIONEER PARTY LED BY DANIEL BOONE CROSSED THE PATH OF THE MODERN I-75 HERE - STORY ON PAGE 97
Exit 41
G-Chevn Mrthn
F-Arby Chili KFC Pasta Rax
L-BestW RedRf Sleep Supr8
Wilderness Road Info ?
Exit 41
G-Amoco\D BP\D Chevn\D Citgo\D Shell
F-CrkBrl DogPtch Jerrys LJSilvr McDld Shilah Subwy Taco Waffle Wendy
L-BHost
41
Rt 80 London
80
DH
London
Pop: 5,700
Exit 38
G-BP Citgo\D Shell\D Spdwy\D
F-Arby BKing BgBoy ElDorado Fazoli GldnC Hddle Hrdee KingBft Krystal McDld Pizza RubyT Taco
L-Comfrt Days H/InnX Hmptn Ramda
Super W-Mart (24hr)
Post Office
1006
38
Rt 192 London
192
25
N
Levi Jackson Park
Weigh Station
EXIT 38
LEVI JACKSON PARK, BOONE TRAIL AND AN INDIAN MASSACRE
- STORY PAGE 97
- LOCAL MAP PAGE 51
MCHARGUE'S WATERMILL STILL GRINDS CORN AT LEVI JACKSON PARK - PAGE 97
Laurel Co.
BP Pilot
Laurel River
Super W-Mart
Exit 29
G-BP Chevn\D Shell\D
F-CrkBrl Krystal Sonny
L-Baymnt Comfrt Fairfld Hmptn Knght
29
Rt 25E Corbin Cumberland Gap Pkwy
25E
Exit 29
G-BP Citgo\D Exxon Pilot\D
F-BKing McDld Shony Subwy WSizz WStr
L-QltyInn Supr8
Lynn Camp River
25W
Harland Sanders Original Kentucky Fried Chicken
DH
Corbin
Pop: 7,700
Spdwy
Exit 25
G-BP\D Exxon Shell
F-Arby BaskR BudBBQ ElDorado PitStop Subwy TCBY Waffle
L-BestValue BestW
Rock Cut
25
Rt 25W Corbin
Exit 25
G-Spdwy\LD
F-BKing Jerrys McDld-I Wendy
L-CtryInnSte Days H/InnX LndMk
25W
Woodbine
Faber
6 MILES
Rockholds
EXIT 29
- THE WORLD'S FIRST "FAST FOOD" OUTLET - STORY PAGE 98, MAP PAGE 50
- INSIDER TIP - THE PERFECT MOTEL - PAGE 97
26
Tourist Information - tune radio to 1610 AM
CUMBERLAND FALLS - 6 WEST MILES
Wofford
25W
Whitley Co.
-43- -42- -41- -40- -39- -38- -37- -36- -35- -34- -33- -32- -31- -30- -29- -28- -27- -26- -25- -24- -23- -22- -21- -20- -19- -18-

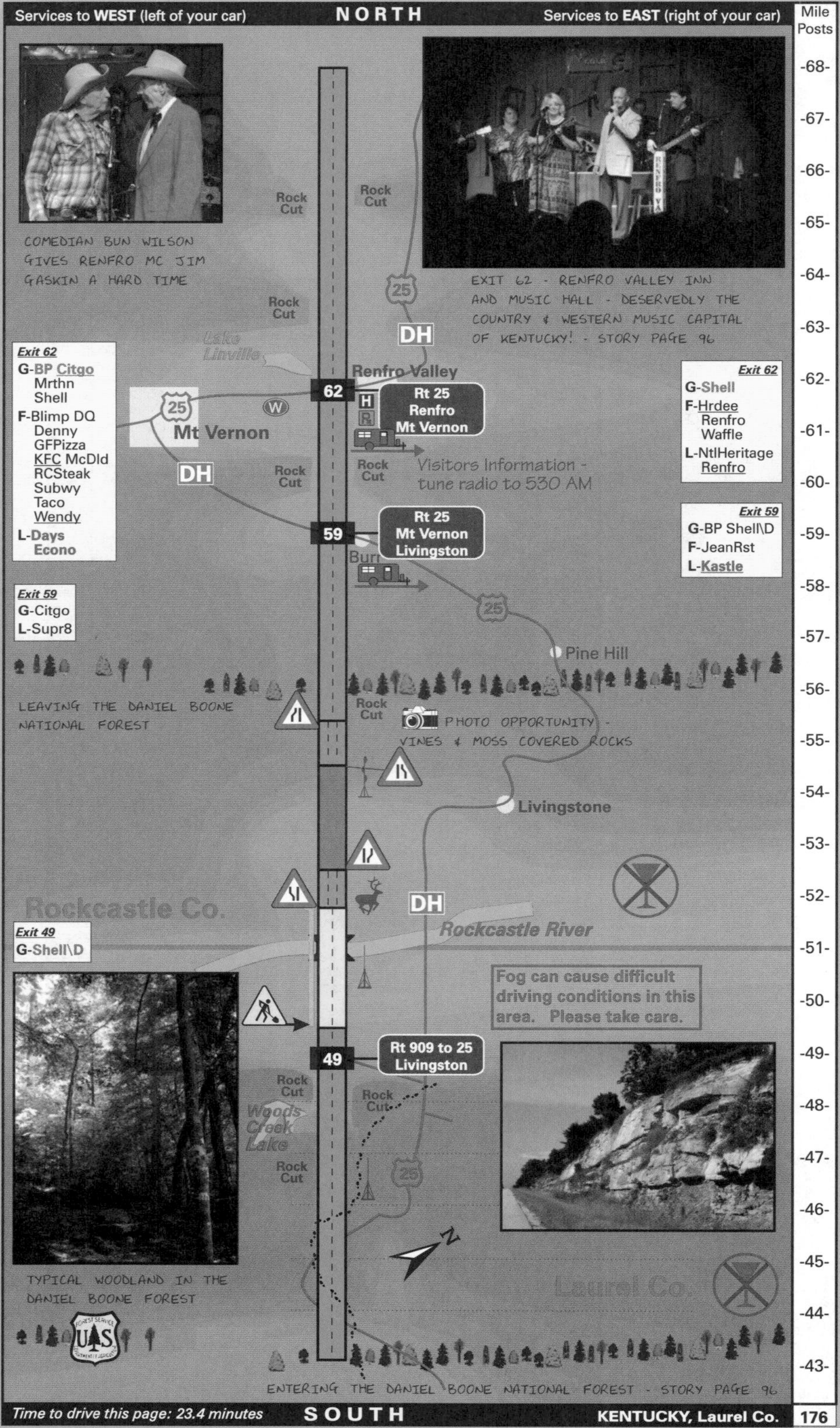
Services to WEST (left of your car)
NORTH
Services to EAST (right of your car)
Mile Posts
-68- -67- -66- -65- -64- -63- -62- -61- -60- -59- -58- -57- -56- -55- -54- -53- -52- -51- -50- -49- -48- -47- -46- -45- -44- -43-
COMEDIAN BUN WILSON GIVES RENFRO MC JIM GASKIN A HARD TIME
EXIT 62 - RENFRO VALLEY INN AND MUSIC HALL - DESERVEDLY THE COUNTRY & WESTERN MUSIC CAPITAL OF KENTUCKY! - STORY PAGE 96
Rock Cut
Lake Linville
25
DH
Renfro Valley
62
Rt 25 Renfro Mt Vernon
H
Mt Vernon
W
Visitors Information - tune radio to 530 AM
59
Rt 25 Mt Vernon Livingston
Burr
Exit 62
G-BP Citgo Mrthn Shell
F-Blimp DQ Denny GFPizza KFC McDld RCSteak Subwy Taco Wendy
L-Days Econo
Exit 62
G-Shell
F-Hrdee Renfro Waffle
L-NtlHeritage Renfro
Exit 59
G-BP Shell\D
F-JeanRst
L-Kastle
Exit 59
G-Citgo
L-Supr8
Pine Hill
LEAVING THE DANIEL BOONE NATIONAL FOREST
PHOTO OPPORTUNITY - VINES & MOSS COVERED ROCKS
Livingstone
Rockcastle Co.
Rockcastle River
Exit 49
G-Shell\D
Fog can cause difficult driving conditions in this area. Please take care.
49
Rt 909 to 25 Livingston
Woods Creek Lake
N
Laurel Co.
TYPICAL WOODLAND IN THE DANIEL BOONE FOREST
FOREST SERVICE U.S. DEPARTMENT OF AGRICULTURE
ENTERING THE DANIEL BOONE NATIONAL FOREST - STORY PAGE 96
Time to drive this page: 23.4 minutes
SOUTH

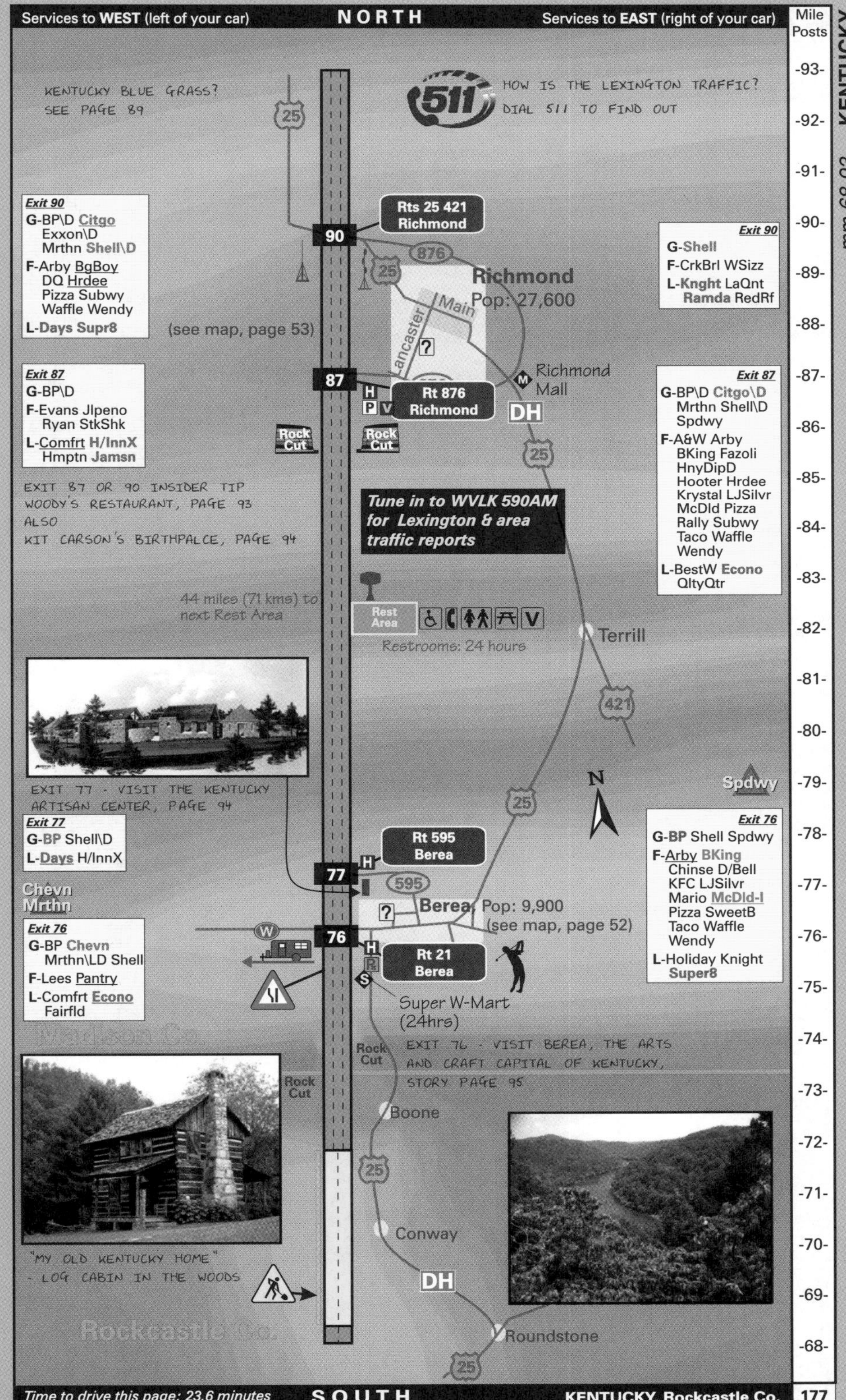
KENTUCKY BLUE GRASS?
SEE PAGE 89
HOW IS THE LEXINGTON TRAFFIC?
DIAL 511 TO FIND OUT
511
25
Exit 90
G-BP\D Citgo
Exxon\D
Mrthn Shell\D
F-Arby BgBoy
DQ Hrdee
Pizza Subwy
Waffle Wendy
L-Days Supr8
Rts 25 421
Richmond
90
876
25
Richmond
Pop: 27,600
Main
Lancaster
(see map, page 53)
Exit 90
G-Shell
F-CrkBrl WSizz
L-Knght LaQnt
Ramda RedRf
Exit 87
G-BP\D
F-Evans Jlpeno
Ryan StkShk
L-Comfrt H/InnX
Hmptn Jamsn
87
Rt 876
Richmond
Richmond
Mall
DH
Rock Cut
Rock Cut
25
Exit 87
G-BP\D Citgo\D
Mrthn Shell\D
Spdwy
F-A&W Arby
BKing Fazoli
HnyDipD
Hooter Hrdee
Krystal LJSilvr
McDld Pizza
Rally Subwy
Taco Waffle
Wendy
L-BestW Econo
QltyQtr
EXIT 87 OR 90 INSIDER TIP
WOODY'S RESTAURANT, PAGE 93
ALSO
KIT CARSON'S BIRTHPALCE, PAGE 94
Tune in to WVLK 590AM
for Lexington & area
traffic reports
44 miles (71 kms) to
next Rest Area
Rest Area
Restrooms: 24 hours
Terrill
421
EXIT 77 - VISIT THE KENTUCKY
ARTISAN CENTER, PAGE 94
25
N
Spdwy
Exit 77
G-BP Shell\D
L-Days H/InnX
Rt 595
Berea
77
595
Chevn
Mrthn
Berea, Pop: 9,900
(see map, page 52)
Exit 76
G-BP Shell Spdwy
F-Arby BKing
Chinse D/Bell
KFC LJSilvr
Mario McDld-I
Pizza SweetB
Taco Waffle
Wendy
L-Holiday Knight
Super8
Exit 76
G-BP Chevn
Mrthn\LD Shell
F-Lees Pantry
L-Comfrt Econo
Fairfld
W
76
Rt 21
Berea
Super W-Mart
(24hrs)
Madison Co.
Rock Cut
EXIT 76 - VISIT BEREA, THE ARTS
AND CRAFT CAPITAL OF KENTUCKY,
STORY PAGE 95
Rock Cut
Boone
25
Conway
DH
"MY OLD KENTUCKY HOME"
- LOG CABIN IN THE WOODS
Roundstone
Rockcastle Co.
25
-93- -92- -91- -90- -89- -88- -87- -86- -85- -84- -83- -82- -81- -80- -79- -78- -77- -76- -75- -74- -73- -72- -71- -70- -69- -68-

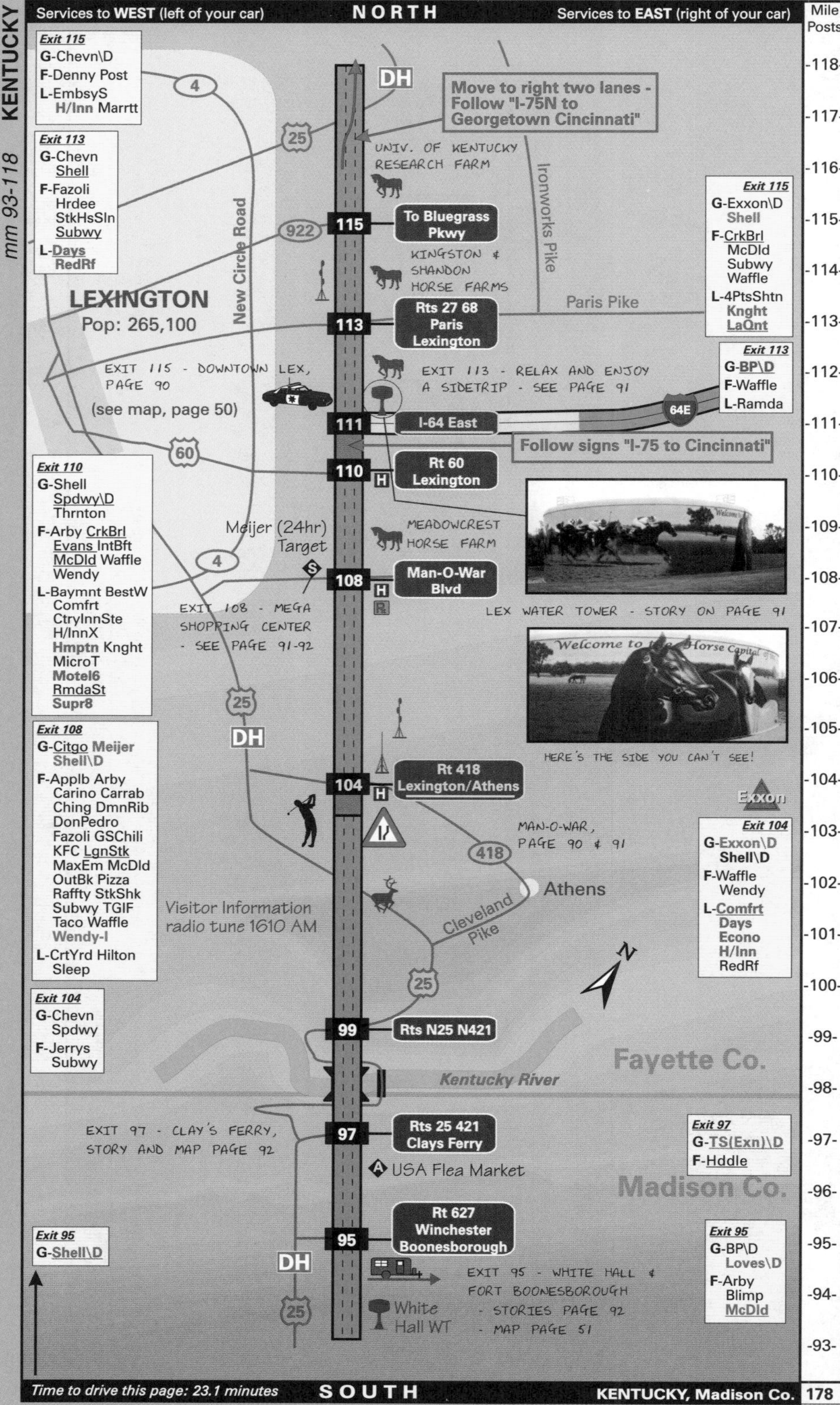
Services to WEST (left of your car)
NORTH
Services to EAST (right of your car)
Mile Posts
Exit 115
G-Chevn\D
F-Denny Post
L-EmbsyS H/Inn Marrtt
Exit 113
G-Chevn Shell
F-Fazoli Hrdee StkHsSln Subwy
L-Days RedRf
LEXINGTON
Pop: 265,100
New Circle Road
DH
Move to right two lanes - Follow "I-75N to Georgetown Cincinnati"
UNIV. OF KENTUCKY RESEARCH FARM
Ironworks Pike
115
To Bluegrass Pkwy
KINGSTON & SHANDON HORSE FARMS
Exit 115
G-Exxon\D Shell
F-CrkBrl McDld Subwy Waffle
L-4PtsShtn Knght LaQnt
Paris Pike
113
Rts 27 68 Paris Lexington
EXIT 115 - DOWNTOWN LEX, PAGE 90
EXIT 113 - RELAX AND ENJOY A SIDETRIP - SEE PAGE 91
(see map, page 50)
Exit 113
G-BP\D
F-Waffle
L-Ramda
64E
111
I-64 East
Follow signs "I-75 to Cincinnati"
Exit 110
G-Shell Spdwy\D Thrnton
F-Arby CrkBrl Evans IntBft McDld Waffle Wendy
L-Baymnt BestW Comfrt CtryInnSte H/InnX Hmptn Knght MicroT Motel6 RmdaSt Supr8
110
Rt 60 Lexington
Meijer (24hr) Target
MEADOWCREST HORSE FARM
108
Man-O-War Blvd
EXIT 108 - MEGA SHOPPING CENTER - SEE PAGE 91-92
LEX WATER TOWER - STORY ON PAGE 91
Welcome to the Horse Capital of the World
HERE'S THE SIDE YOU CAN'T SEE!
Exit 108
G-Citgo Meijer Shell\D
F-Applb Arby Carino Carrab Ching DmnRib DonPedro Fazoli GSChili KFC LgnStk MaxEm McDld OutBk Pizza Raffty StkShk Subwy TGIF Taco Waffle Wendy-I
L-CrtYrd Hilton Sleep
104
Rt 418 Lexington/Athens
Exxon
MAN-O-WAR, PAGE 90 & 91
418
Athens
Exit 104
G-Exxon\D Shell\D
F-Waffle Wendy
L-Comfrt Days Econo H/Inn RedRf
Visitor Information radio tune 1610 AM
Cleveland Pike
Exit 104
G-Chevn Spdwy
F-Jerrys Subwy
99
Rts N25 N421
Fayette Co.
Kentucky River
EXIT 97 - CLAY'S FERRY, STORY AND MAP PAGE 92
97
Rts 25 421 Clays Ferry
USA Flea Market
Exit 97
G-TS(Exn)\D
F-Hddle
Madison Co.
Exit 95
G-Shell\D
95
Rt 627 Winchester Boonesborough
Exit 95
G-BP\D Loves\D
F-Arby Blimp McDld
EXIT 95 - WHITE HALL & FORT BOONESBOROUGH - STORIES PAGE 92 - MAP PAGE 51
White Hall WT
Time to drive this page: 23.1 minutes
SOUTH

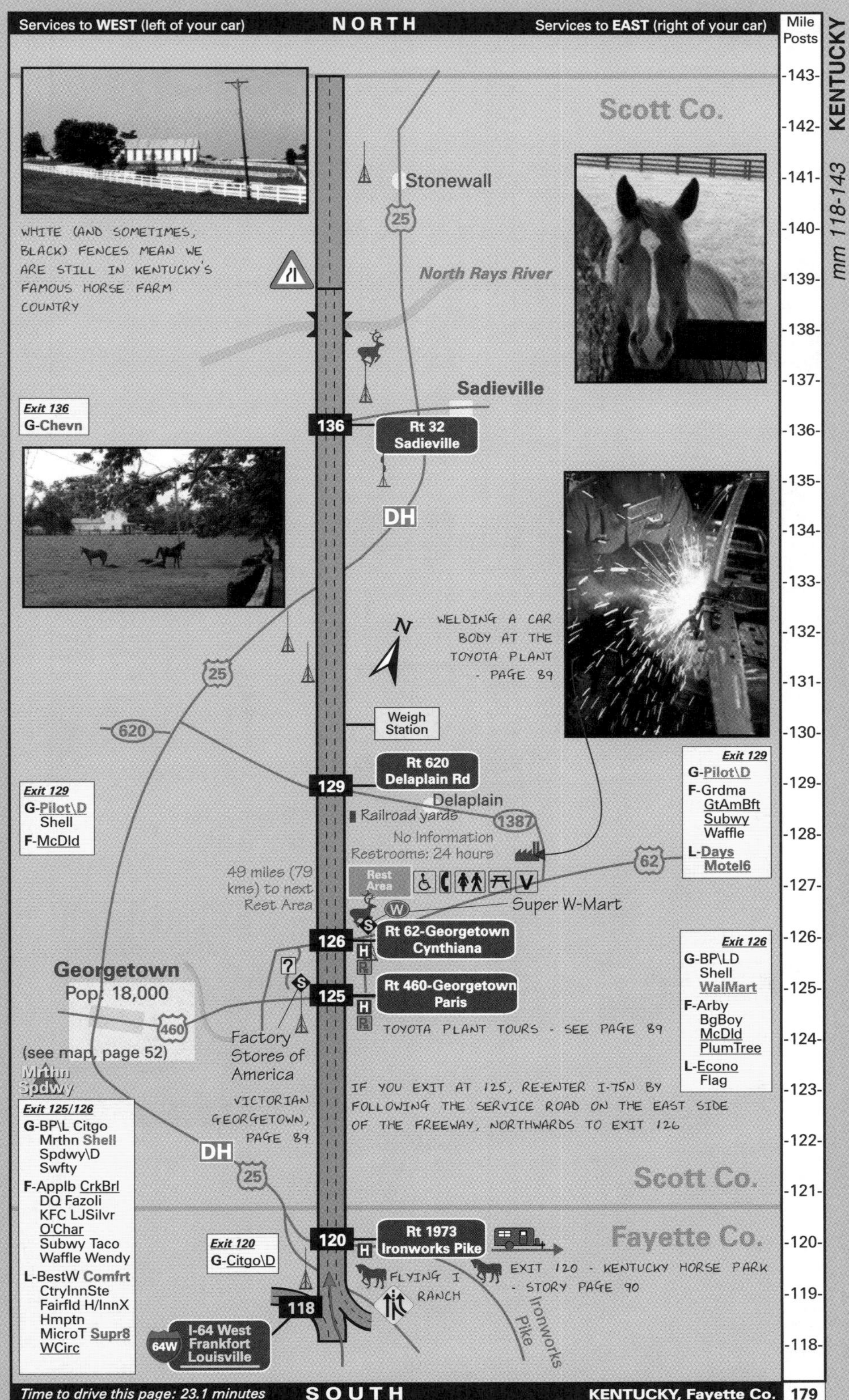
Mile Posts
-143- -142- -141- -140- -139- -138- -137- -136- -135- -134- -133- -132- -131- -130- -129- -128- -127- -126- -125- -124- -123- -122- -121- -120- -119- -118-
Scott Co.
Stonewall
25
WHITE (AND SOMETIMES, BLACK) FENCES MEAN WE ARE STILL IN KENTUCKY'S FAMOUS HORSE FARM COUNTRY
North Rays River
Sadieville
Exit 136
G-Chevn
136
Rt 32 Sadieville
DH
N
WELDING A CAR BODY AT THE TOYOTA PLANT - PAGE 89
25
620
Weigh Station
Exit 129
G-Pilot\D
F-Grdma
GtAmBft
Subwy
Waffle
L-Days
Motel6
Rt 620 Delaplain Rd
129
Exit 129
G-Pilot\D
Shell
F-McDld
Delaplain
Railroad yards
1387
No Information
Restrooms: 24 hours
62
49 miles (79 kms) to next Rest Area
Rest Area
V
W
Super W-Mart
126
Rt 62-Georgetown Cynthiana
Exit 126
G-BP\LD
Shell
WalMart
F-Arby
BgBoy
McDld
PlumTree
L-Econo
Flag
Georgetown
Pop: 18,000
?
S
125
Rt 460-Georgetown Paris
460
TOYOTA PLANT TOURS - SEE PAGE 89
(see map, page 52)
Factory Stores of America
Mrthn Spdwy
Exit 125/126
G-BP\L Citgo
Mrthn Shell
Spdwy\D
Swfty
F-Applb CrkBrl
DQ Fazoli
KFC LJSilvr
O'Char
Subwy Taco
Waffle Wendy
L-BestW Comfrt
CtryInnSte
Fairfld H/InnX
Hmptn
MicroT Supr8
WCirc
VICTORIAN GEORGETOWN, PAGE 89
IF YOU EXIT AT 125, RE-ENTER I-75N BY FOLLOWING THE SERVICE ROAD ON THE EAST SIDE OF THE FREEWAY, NORTHWARDS TO EXIT 126
DH
25
Scott Co.
Fayette Co.
Exit 120
G-Citgo\D
120
H
Rt 1973 Ironworks Pike
FLYING I RANCH
EXIT 120 - KENTUCKY HORSE PARK - STORY PAGE 90
118
64W
I-64 West Frankfort Louisville
Ironworks Pike

Kenton Co.

DH

Exit 166
G-Chevn
Shell\D
F-BKing
CntryPumkin
Subwy

166 Rt 491 Crittenden

Crittenden

Exit 166
G-BP
Citgo\D
EZyStop
Mrthn\D
F-A&W
McDld
Taco

Grant Co.

Tune in to talk radio WLW 700AM for Cincinnati traffic reports

25

Sherman

Arnolds River

Dry Ridge Outlet Mall

Exit 159
G-Spdwy\D
Sunco\D
F-CrkBrl
CtryGrll
Shony
L-H/InnX
Hmptn

159 Rt 22 Dry Ridge Owentwon

Dry Ridge WT

Super W-Mart (24 hr)

Dry Ridge

Exit 159
G-BP Mrthn
Shell\D
F-Arby BKing-I
DQ
HpyDragn
KFC LJSilvr
McDld Pizza
Subwy Taco
Waffle
Wendy
L-MicroT
Supr8

EXIT 159 - INSIDER TIP - THE COUNTRY GRILL IS AN EXCELLENT RESTAURANT - SEE PAGE 88

156 Barnes Road

New Exit

N

Exit 154
G-BP\D
Mrthn\D
F-ClassicK
L-BestValue Days

154 Rt 36 Owentown Willamstown

Exit 154
G-Citgo\LD
Shell\D
F-EZStop

36

Williamstown

22

EXIT 154 - A CIVIL WAR EXECUTION TOOK PLACE HERE - SEE PAGE 88

City of Williamsburg WT

A CIVIL WAR REPRISAL

Three Confederates were brought here from prison at Lexington and executed Aug. 15, 1864; reprisal for the guerrilla murder of Union sympathizers. Joel Skirvin and Anderson Simpson. Those executed: Wm. P. and John L. Lingenfelter, brothers of Mrs. Simpson, and George Wainscott, 1st Batt. Ky. Inf. CSA. Lingenfelter graves N.E. of Lusby's Mill, Owen County.

Mile 150: take care - radar is often hiding in the median

25

Mason

511

PHONE 511 TO FIND OUT ABOUT FLORENCE AND COVINGTON TRAFFIC CONDITIONS

DH

Corinth Lake

Mrthn

Exit 144
G-BP

144 Rt 330 Owentown Corinth

330

Corinth

Grant Co.

Exit 144
G-Mrthn\D

-168- -167- -166- -165- -164- -163- -162- -161- -160- -159- -158- -157- -156- -155- -154- -153- -152- -151- -150- -149- -148- -147- -146- -145- -144- -143-

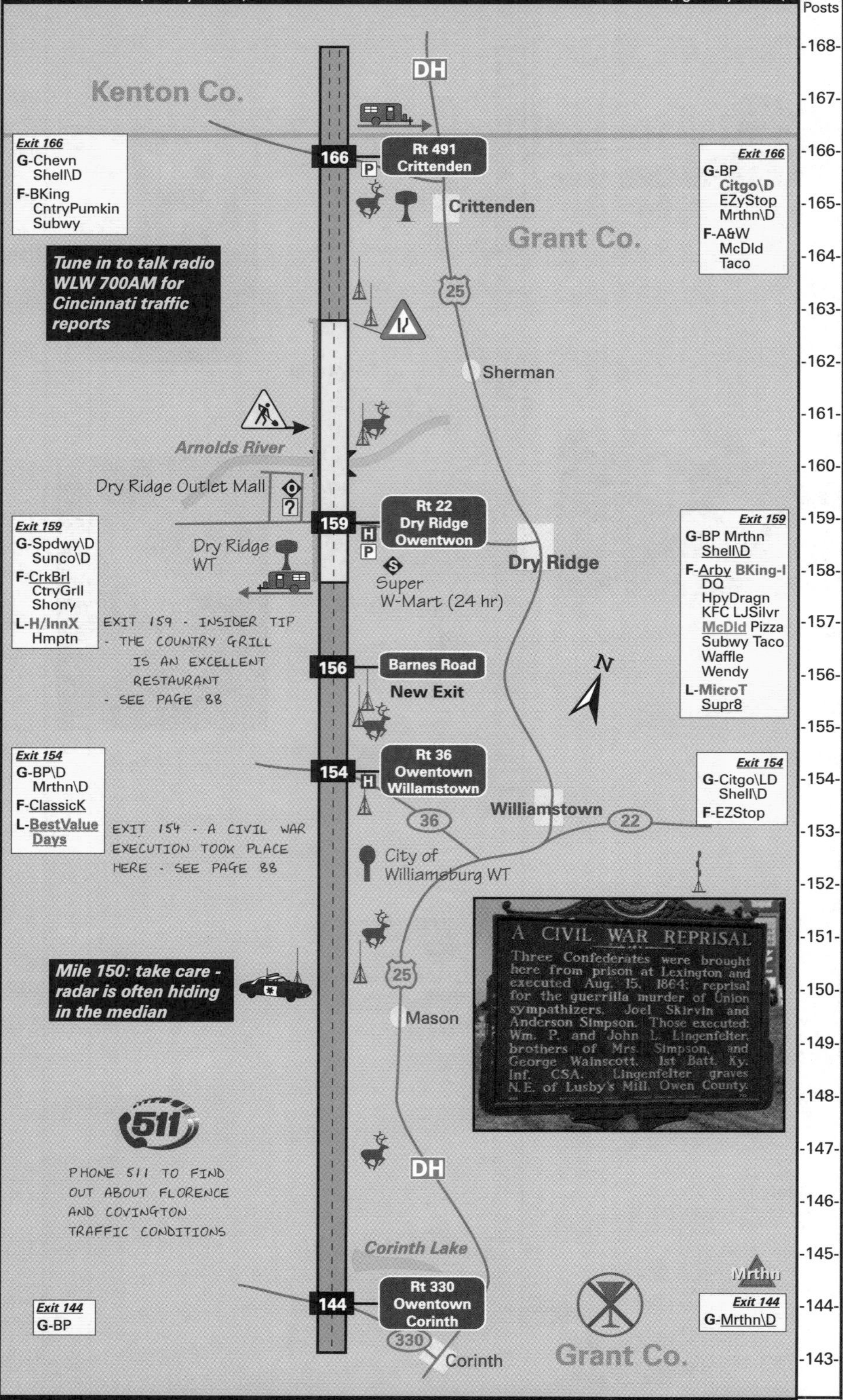

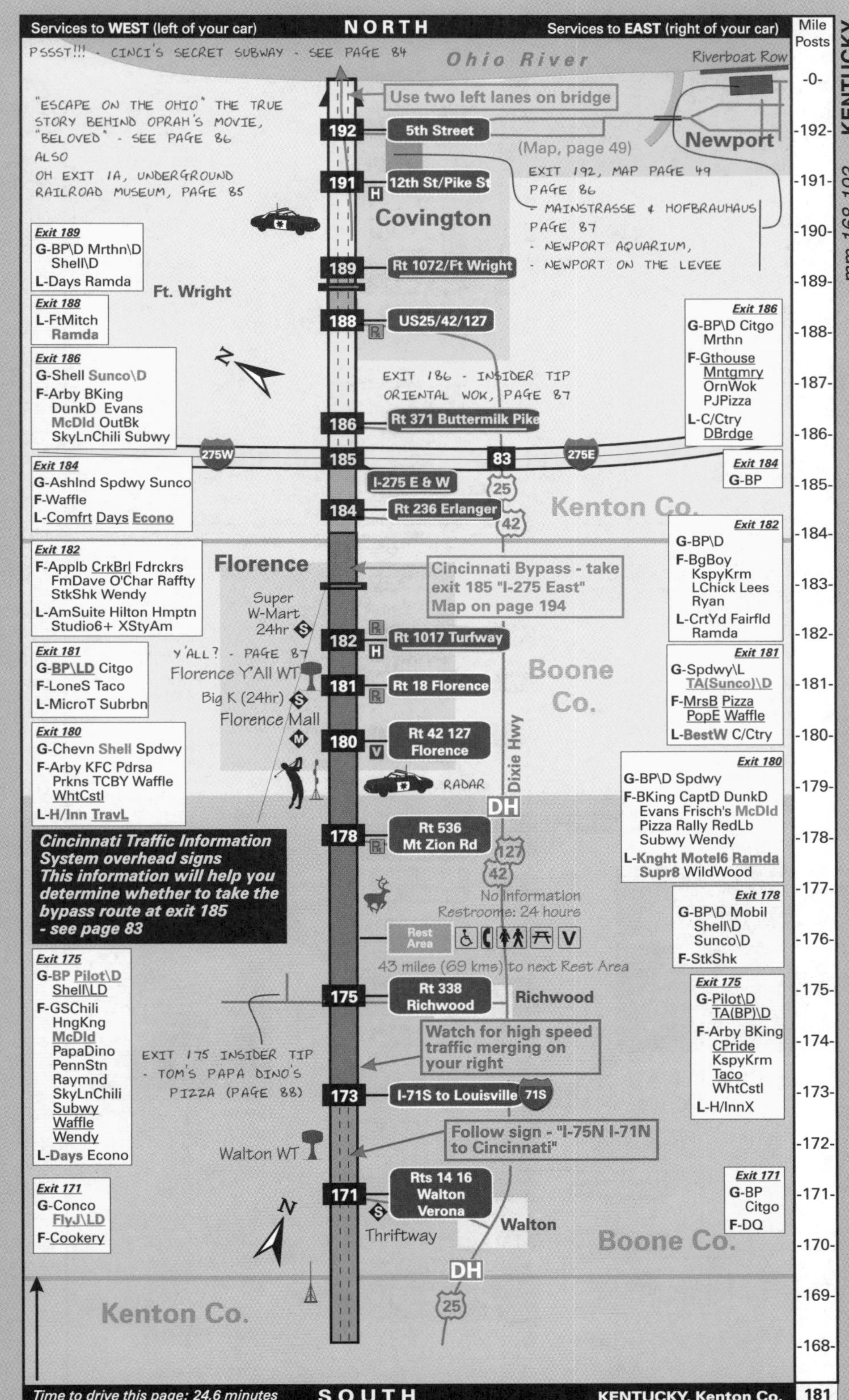

Services to WEST (left of your car)
NORTH
Services to EAST (right of your car)
Mile Posts
KENTUCKY
mm 168-193
PSSST!!! - CINCI'S SECRET SUBWAY - SEE PAGE 84
Ohio River
Riverboat Row
Use two left lanes on bridge
"ESCAPE ON THE OHIO" THE TRUE STORY BEHIND OPRAH'S MOVIE, "BELOVED" - SEE PAGE 86
ALSO
OH EXIT 1A, UNDERGROUND RAILROAD MUSEUM, PAGE 85
192
5th Street
Newport
(Map, page 49)
EXIT 192, MAP PAGE 49
PAGE 86
- MAINSTRASSE & HOFBRAUHAUS
PAGE 87
- NEWPORT AQUARIUM,
- NEWPORT ON THE LEVEE
191
12th St/Pike St
H
Covington
Exit 189
G-BP\D Mrthn\D Shell\D
L-Days Ramda
189
Rt 1072/Ft Wright
Ft. Wright
Exit 188
L-FtMitch Ramda
188
US25/42/127
Exit 186
G-BP\D Citgo Mrthn
F-Gthouse Mntgmry OrnWok PJPizza
L-C/Ctry DBrdge
Exit 186
G-Shell Sunco\D
F-Arby BKing DunkD Evans McDld OutBk SkyLnChili Subwy
N
EXIT 186 - INSIDER TIP
ORIENTAL WOK, PAGE 87
186
Rt 371 Buttermilk Pike
275W
185
83
275E
Exit 184
G-BP
Exit 184
G-Ashlnd Spdwy Sunco
F-Waffle
L-Comfrt Days Econo
I-275 E & W
25
184
Rt 236 Erlanger
42
Kenton Co.
Exit 182
G-BP\D
F-BgBoy KspyKrm LChick Lees Ryan
L-CrtYd Fairfld Ramda
Exit 182
F-Applb CrkBrl Fdrckrs FmDave O'Char Raffty StkShk Wendy
L-AmSuite Hilton Hmptn Studio6+ XStyAm
Florence
Cincinnati Bypass - take exit 185 "I-275 East"
Map on page 194
Super W-Mart 24hr
182
Rt 1017 Turfway
H
Exit 181
G-BP\LD Citgo
F-LoneS Taco
L-MicroT Subrbn
Y'ALL? - PAGE 87
Florence Y'All WT
181
Rt 18 Florence
Boone Co.
Exit 181
G-Spdwy\L TA(Sunco)\D
F-MrsB Pizza PopE Waffle
L-BestW C/Ctry
Big K (24hr)
Florence Mall
Exit 180
G-Chevn Shell Spdwy
F-Arby KFC Pdrsa Prkns TCBY Waffle WhtCstl
L-H/Inn TravL
180
Rt 42 127 Florence
V
Dixie Hwy
Exit 180
G-BP\D Spdwy
F-BKing CaptD DunkD Evans Frisch's McDld Pizza Rally RedLb Subwy Wendy
L-Knght Motel6 Ramda Supr8 WildWood
RADAR
DH
Cincinnati Traffic Information System overhead signs
This information will help you determine whether to take the bypass route at exit 185
- see page 83
178
Rt 536 Mt Zion Rd
127
42
Exit 178
G-BP\D Mobil Shell\D Sunco\D
F-StkShk
No Information
Restrooms: 24 hours
Rest Area
V
43 miles (69 kms) to next Rest Area
Exit 175
G-BP Pilot\D Shell\LD
F-GSChili HngKng McDld PapaDino PennStn Raymnd SkyLnChili Subwy Waffle Wendy
L-Days Econo
175
Rt 338 Richwood
Richwood
Exit 175
G-Pilot\D TA(BP)\D
F-Arby BKing CPride KspyKrm Taco WhtCstl
L-H/InnX
Watch for high speed traffic merging on your right
EXIT 175 INSIDER TIP
- TOM'S PAPA DINO'S PIZZA (PAGE 88)
173
I-71S to Louisville
71S
Follow sign - "I-75N I-71N to Cincinnati"
Walton WT
171
Rts 14 16 Walton Verona
Exit 171
G-BP Citgo
F-DQ
Exit 171
G-Conco FlyJ\LD
F-Cookery
N
Thriftway
Walton
Boone Co.
DH
25
Kenton Co.
-0-
-192-
-191-
-190-
-189-
-188-
-187-
-186-
-185-
-184-
-183-
-182-
-181-
-180-
-179-
-178-
-177-
-176-
-175-
-174-
-173-
-172-
-171-
-170-
-169-
-168-
Time to drive this page: 24.6 minutes
SOUTH
KENTUCKY, Kenton Co.

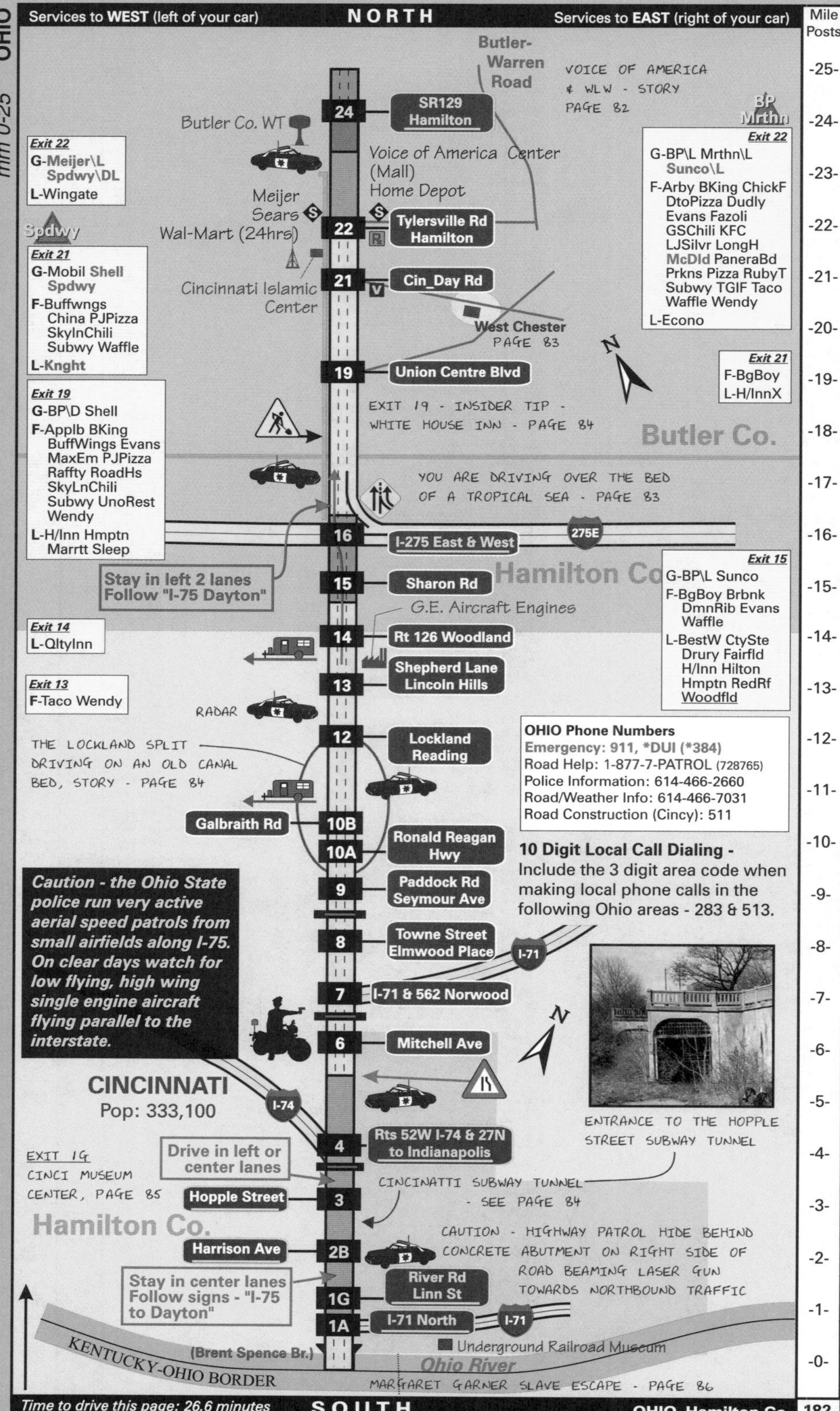
Services to WEST (left of your car)
NORTH
Services to EAST (right of your car)
Mile Posts
Butler-Warren Road
VOICE OF AMERICA & WLW - STORY PAGE 82
BP Mrthn
SR129 Hamilton
Butler Co. WT
Exit 22
G-Meijer\L Spdwy\DL
L-Wingate
Voice of America Center (Mall)
Home Depot
Exit 22
G-BP\L Mrthn\L Sunco\L
F-Arby BKing ChickF DtoPizza Dudly Evans Fazoli GSChili KFC LJSilvr LongH McDld PaneraBd Prkns Pizza RubyT Subwy TGIF Taco Waffle Wendy
L-Econo
Meijer
Sears
Wal-Mart (24hrs)
Spdwy
Tylersville Rd Hamilton
Exit 21
G-Mobil Shell Spdwy
F-Buffwngs China PJPizza SkyInChili Subway Waffle
L-Knght
Cincinnati Islamic Center
Cin_Day Rd
West Chester PAGE 83
N
Exit 21
F-BgBoy
L-H/InnX
Union Centre Blvd
Exit 19
G-BP\D Shell
F-Applb BKing BuffWings Evans MaxEm PJPizza Raffty RoadHs SkyLnChili Subway UnoRest Wendy
L-H/Inn Hmptn Marrtt Sleep
EXIT 19 - INSIDER TIP - WHITE HOUSE INN - PAGE 84
Butler Co.
YOU ARE DRIVING OVER THE BED OF A TROPICAL SEA - PAGE 83
I-275 East & West
275E
Stay in left 2 lanes Follow "I-75 Dayton"
Hamilton Co.
Sharon Rd
Exit 15
G-BP\L Sunco
F-BgBoy Brbnk DmnRib Evans Waffle
L-BestW CtySte Drury Fairfld H/Inn Hilton Hmptn RedRf Woodfld
G.E. Aircraft Engines
Exit 14
L-QltyInn
Rt 126 Woodland
Shepherd Lane Lincoln Hills
Exit 13
F-Taco Wendy
RADAR
Lockland Reading
THE LOCKLAND SPLIT DRIVING ON AN OLD CANAL BED, STORY - PAGE 84
OHIO Phone Numbers
Emergency: 911, *DUI (*384)
Road Help: 1-877-7-PATROL (728765)
Police Information: 614-466-2660
Road/Weather Info: 614-466-7031
Road Construction (Cincy): 511
Galbraith Rd
Ronald Reagan Hwy
10 Digit Local Call Dialing - Include the 3 digit area code when making local phone calls in the following Ohio areas - 283 & 513.
Caution - the Ohio State police run very active aerial speed patrols from small airfields along I-75. On clear days watch for low flying, high wing single engine aircraft flying parallel to the interstate.
Paddock Rd Seymour Ave
Towne Street Elmwood Place
I-71
I-71 & 562 Norwood
N
Mitchell Ave
CINCINNATI
Pop: 333,100
I-74
Rts 52W I-74 & 27N to Indianapolis
ENTRANCE TO THE HOPPLE STREET SUBWAY TUNNEL
EXIT 1G CINCI MUSEUM CENTER, PAGE 85
Drive in left or center lanes
Hopple Street
CINCINATTI SUBWAY TUNNEL - SEE PAGE 84
Hamilton Co.
CAUTION - HIGHWAY PATROL HIDE BEHIND CONCRETE ABUTMENT ON RIGHT SIDE OF ROAD BEAMING LASER GUN TOWARDS NORTHBOUND TRAFFIC
Harrison Ave
Stay in center lanes Follow signs - "I-75 to Dayton"
River Rd Linn St
I-71 North
I-71
Underground Railroad Museum
(Brent Spence Br.)
Ohio River
KENTUCKY-OHIO BORDER
MARGARET GARNER SLAVE ESCAPE - PAGE 86
Time to drive this page: 26.6 minutes
SOUTH
OHIO, Hamilton Co.

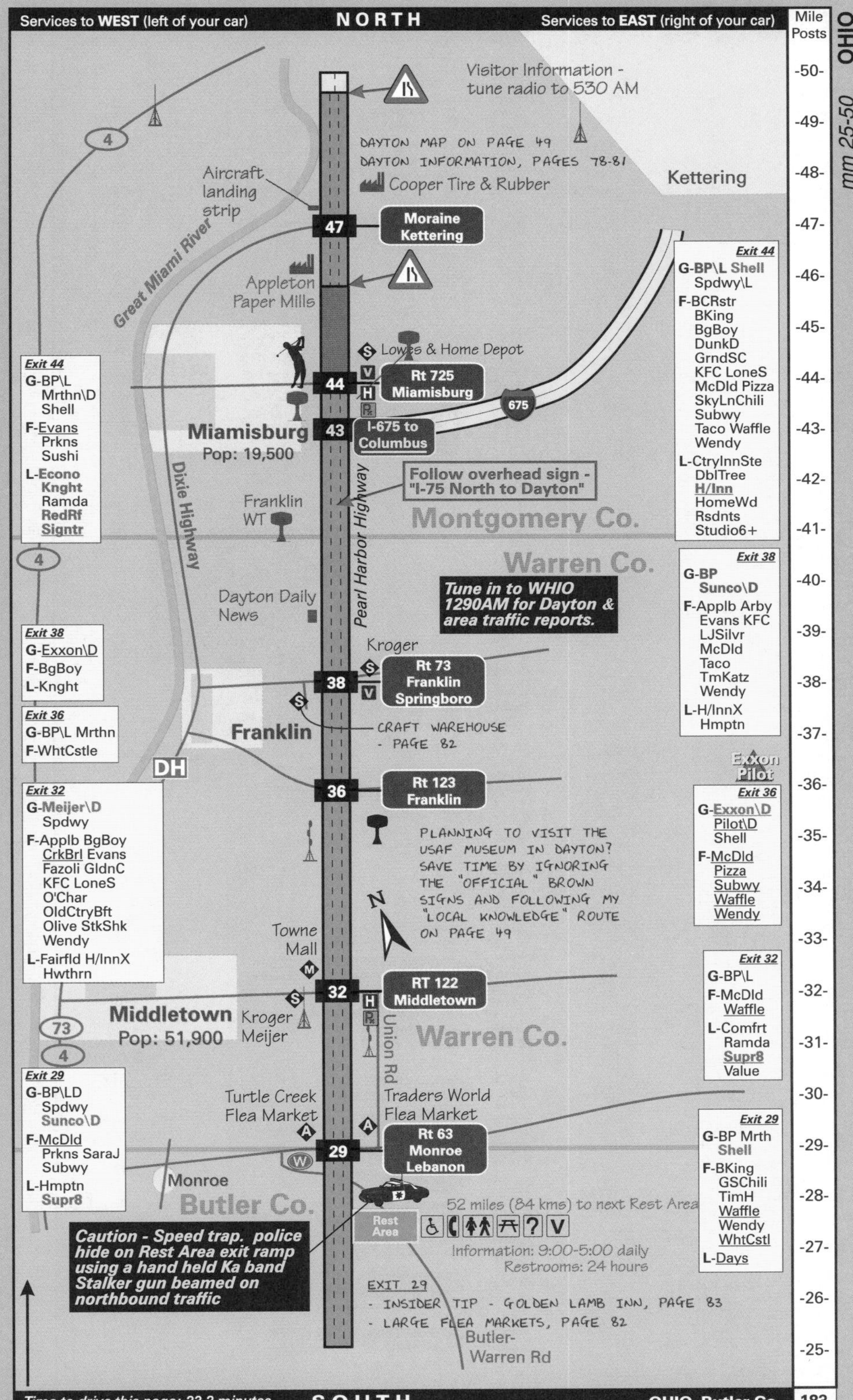

Services to WEST (left of your car)
NORTH
Services to EAST (right of your car)
Mile Posts
OHIO
mm 25-50
Visitor Information - tune radio to 530 AM
DAYTON MAP ON PAGE 49
DAYTON INFORMATION, PAGES 78-81
Cooper Tire & Rubber
Kettering
Aircraft landing strip
47
Moraine Kettering
Great Miami River
Appleton Paper Mills
4
Lowes & Home Depot
44
Rt 725 Miamisburg
675
43
I-675 to Columbus
Miamisburg
Pop: 19,500
Dixie Highway
Pearl Harbor Highway
Follow overhead sign - "I-75 North to Dayton"
Franklin WT
Montgomery Co.
Warren Co.
Dayton Daily News
Tune in to WHIO 1290AM for Dayton & area traffic reports.
Exit 44
G-BP\L
Mrthn\D
Shell
F-Evans
Prkns
Sushi
L-Econo
Knght
Ramda
RedRf
Signtr
Exit 44
G-BP\L Shell
Spdwy\L
F-BCRstr
BKing
BgBoy
DunkD
GrndSC
KFC LoneS
McDld Pizza
SkyLnChili
Subwy
Taco Waffle
Wendy
L-CtryInnSte
DblTree
H/Inn
HomeWd
Rsdnts
Studio6+
Exit 38
G-BP
Sunco\D
F-Applb Arby
Evans KFC
LJSilvr
McDld
Taco
TmKatz
Wendy
L-H/InnX
Hmptn
Kroger
38
Rt 73 Franklin Springboro
Exit 38
G-Exxon\D
F-BgBoy
L-Knght
Exit 36
G-BP\L Mrthn
F-WhtCstle
Franklin
CRAFT WAREHOUSE - PAGE 82
DH
36
Rt 123 Franklin
Exxon Pilot
Exit 36
G-Exxon\D
Pilot\D
Shell
F-McDld
Pizza
Subwy
Waffle
Wendy
Exit 32
G-Meijer\D
Spdwy
F-Applb BgBoy
CrkBrl Evans
Fazoli GldnC
KFC LoneS
O'Char
OldCtryBft
Olive StkShk
Wendy
L-Fairfld H/InnX
Hwthrn
PLANNING TO VISIT THE USAF MUSEUM IN DAYTON? SAVE TIME BY IGNORING THE "OFFICIAL" BROWN SIGNS AND FOLLOWING MY "LOCAL KNOWLEDGE" ROUTE ON PAGE 49
N
Towne Mall
32
RT 122 Middletown
Exit 32
G-BP\L
F-McDld
Waffle
L-Comfrt
Ramda
Supr8
Value
Middletown
Pop: 51,900
Kroger
Meijer
73
4
Union Rd
Warren Co.
Exit 29
G-BP\LD
Spdwy
Sunco\D
F-McDld
Prkns SaraJ
Subwy
L-Hmptn
Supr8
Turtle Creek Flea Market
Traders World Flea Market
29
Rt 63 Monroe Lebanon
W
Exit 29
G-BP Mrth
Shell
F-BKing
GSChili
TimH
Waffle
Wendy
WhtCstl
L-Days
Monroe
Butler Co.
52 miles (84 kms) to next Rest Area
Rest Area
Information: 9:00-5:00 daily
Restrooms: 24 hours
Caution - Speed trap. police hide on Rest Area exit ramp using a hand held Ka band Stalker gun beamed on northbound traffic
EXIT 29
- INSIDER TIP - GOLDEN LAMB INN, PAGE 83
- LARGE FLEA MARKETS, PAGE 82
Butler-Warren Rd
-50-
-49-
-48-
-47-
-46-
-45-
-44-
-43-
-42-
-41-
-40-
-39-
-38-
-37-
-36-
-35-
-34-
-33-
-32-
-31-
-30-
-29-
-28-
-27-
-26-
-25-
Time to drive this page: 23.2 minutes
SOUTH
OHIO, Butler Co.
183

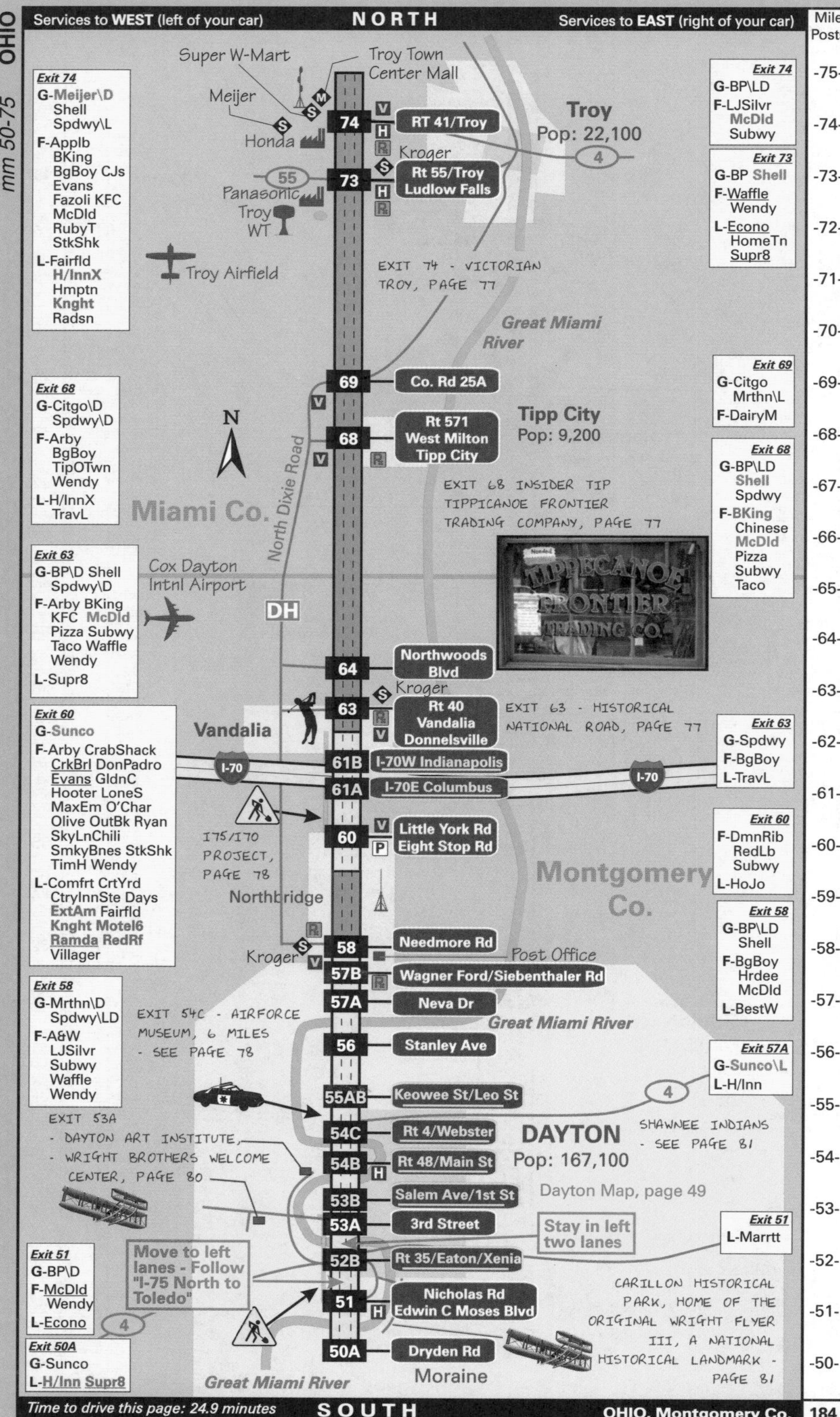
Services to WEST (left of your car)
NORTH
Services to EAST (right of your car)
Mile Posts
Exit 74
G-Meijer\D
Shell
Spdwy\L
F-Applb
BKing
BgBoy CJs
Evans
Fazoli KFC
McDld
RubyT
StkShk
L-Fairfld
H/InnX
Hmptn
Knght
Radsn
Super W-Mart
Troy Town Center Mall
Meijer
Honda
74
RT 41/Troy
Troy
Pop: 22,100
Exit 74
G-BP\LD
F-LJSilvr
McDld
Subwy
Kroger
55
73
Rt 55/Troy
Ludlow Falls
Panasonic
Troy WT
Exit 73
G-BP Shell
F-Waffle
Wendy
L-Econo
HomeTn
Supr8
Troy Airfield
EXIT 74 - VICTORIAN TROY, PAGE 77
Great Miami River
69
Co. Rd 25A
Exit 69
G-Citgo
Mrthn\L
F-DairyM
Exit 68
G-Citgo\D
Spdwy\D
F-Arby
BgBoy
TipOTwn
Wendy
L-H/InnX
TravL
N
68
Rt 571
West Milton
Tipp City
Tipp City
Pop: 9,200
Exit 68
G-BP\LD
Shell
Spdwy
F-BKing
Chinese
McDld
Pizza
Subwy
Taco
North Dixie Road
EXIT 68 INSIDER TIP
TIPPICANOE FRONTIER
TRADING COMPANY, PAGE 77
Miami Co.
TIPPECANOE FRONTIER TRADING CO.
Exit 63
G-BP\D Shell
Spdwy\D
F-Arby BKing
KFC McDld
Pizza Subwy
Taco Waffle
Wendy
L-Supr8
Cox Dayton Intnl Airport
DH
64
Northwoods Blvd
Kroger
63
Rt 40
Vandalia
Donnelsville
EXIT 63 - HISTORICAL NATIONAL ROAD, PAGE 77
Exit 60
G-Sunco
F-Arby CrabShack
CrkBrl DonPadro
Evans GldnC
Hooter LoneS
MaxEm O'Char
Olive OutBk Ryan
SkyLnChili
SmkyBnes StkShk
TimH Wendy
L-Comfrt CrtYrd
CtryInnSte Days
ExtAm Fairfld
Knght Motel6
Ramda RedRf
Villager
Vandalia
Exit 63
G-Spdwy
F-BgBoy
L-TravL
I-70
61B
I-70W Indianapolis
I-70
61A
I-70E Columbus
60
Little York Rd
Eight Stop Rd
I75/I70 PROJECT, PAGE 78
Exit 60
F-DmnRib
RedLb
Subwy
L-HoJo
Montgomery Co.
Northbridge
Exit 58
G-BP\LD
Shell
F-BgBoy
Hrdee
McDld
L-BestW
58
Needmore Rd
Kroger
Post Office
57B
Wagner Ford/Siebenthaler Rd
Exit 58
G-Mrthn\D
Spdwy\LD
F-A&W
LJSilvr
Subwy
Waffle
Wendy
57A
Neva Dr
EXIT 54C - AIRFORCE MUSEUM, 6 MILES - SEE PAGE 78
Great Miami River
56
Stanley Ave
Exit 57A
G-Sunco\L
L-H/Inn
55AB
Keowee St/Leo St
4
EXIT 53A
- DAYTON ART INSTITUTE,
- WRIGHT BROTHERS WELCOME CENTER, PAGE 80
54C
Rt 4/Webster
DAYTON
Pop: 167,100
SHAWNEE INDIANS - SEE PAGE 81
54B
Rt 48/Main St
53B
Salem Ave/1st St
Dayton Map, page 49
53A
3rd Street
Stay in left two lanes
Exit 51
L-Marrtt
Exit 51
G-BP\D
F-McDld
Wendy
L-Econo
Move to left lanes - Follow "I-75 North to Toledo"
52B
Rt 35/Eaton/Xenia
51
Nicholas Rd
Edwin C Moses Blvd
CARILLON HISTORICAL PARK, HOME OF THE ORIGINAL WRIGHT FLYER III, A NATIONAL HISTORICAL LANDMARK - PAGE 81
4
Exit 50A
G-Sunco
L-H/Inn Supr8
50A
Dryden Rd
Great Miami River
Moraine
-75-
-74-
-73-
-72-
-71-
-70-
-69-
-68-
-67-
-66-
-65-
-64-
-63-
-62-
-61-
-60-
-59-
-58-
-57-
-56-
-55-
-54-
-53-
-52-
-51-
-50-
Time to drive this page: 24.9 minutes
SOUTH
OHIO, Montgomery Co.

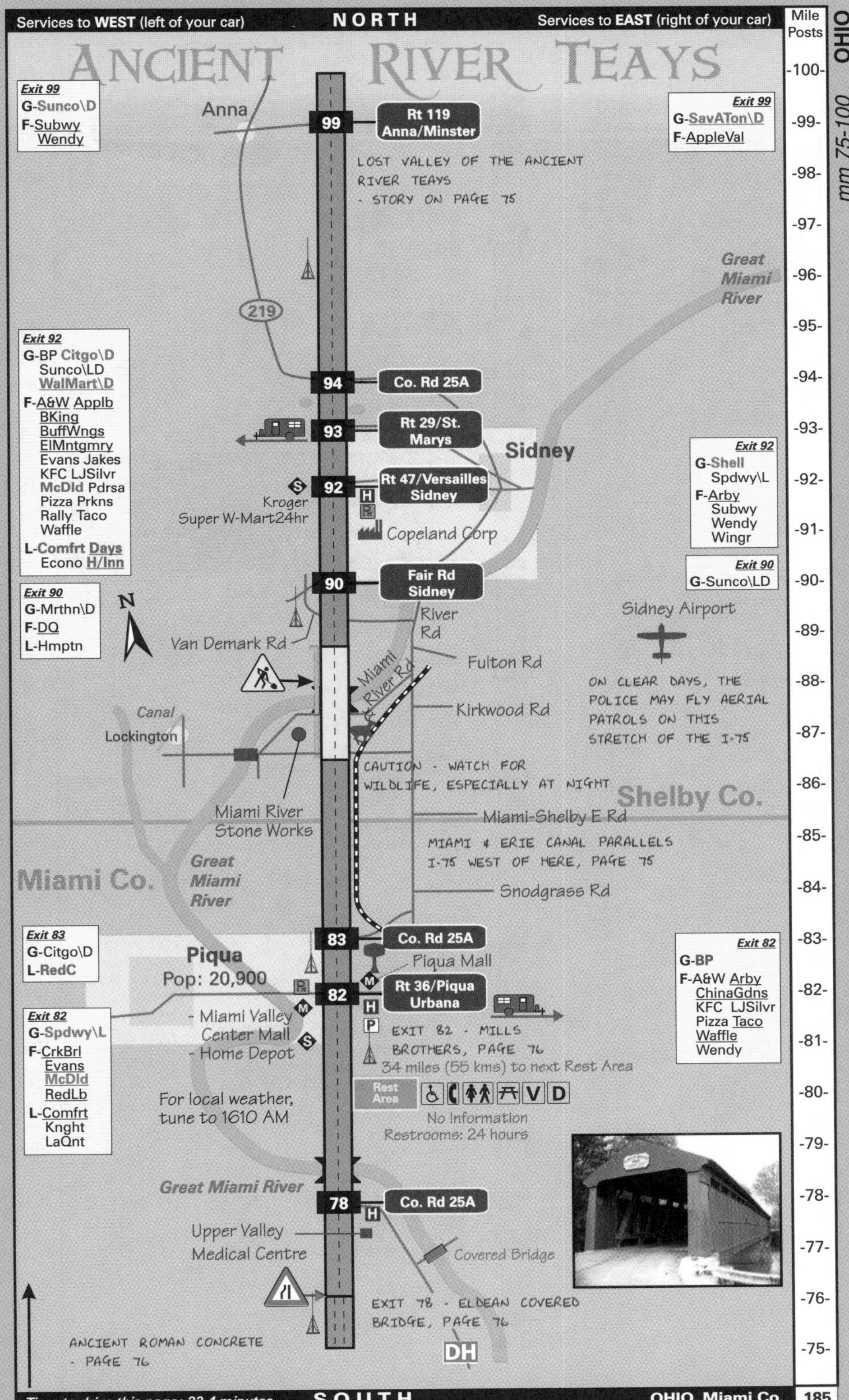
Services to WEST (left of your car)
NORTH
Services to EAST (right of your car)
Mile Posts
OHIO
mm 75-100
ANCIENT RIVER TEAYS
Exit 99
G-Sunco\D
F-Subwy
Wendy
Anna
99
Rt 119
Anna/Minster
Exit 99
G-SavATon\D
F-AppleVal
LOST VALLEY OF THE ANCIENT
RIVER TEAYS
- STORY ON PAGE 75
Great
Miami
River
219
Exit 92
G-BP Citgo\D
Sunco\LD
WalMart\D
F-A&W Applb
BKing
BuffWngs
ElMntgmry
Evans Jakes
KFC LJSilvr
McDld Pdrsa
Pizza Prkns
Rally Taco
Waffle
L-Comfrt Days
Econo H/Inn
94
Co. Rd 25A
93
Rt 29/St. Marys
Sidney
92
Rt 47/Versailles
Sidney
Kroger
Super W-Mart24hr
Copeland Corp
Exit 92
G-Shell
Spdwy\L
F-Arby
Subwy
Wendy
Wingr
Exit 90
G-Sunco\LD
Exit 90
G-Mrthn\D
F-DQ
L-Hmptn
90
Fair Rd
Sidney
N
River
Rd
Sidney Airport
Van Demark Rd
Fulton Rd
Miami
River Rd
ON CLEAR DAYS, THE
POLICE MAY FLY AERIAL
PATROLS ON THIS
STRETCH OF THE I-75
Canal
Lockington
Kirkwood Rd
CAUTION - WATCH FOR
WILDLIFE, ESPECIALLY AT NIGHT
Shelby Co.
Miami River
Stone Works
Miami-Shelby E Rd
MIAMI & ERIE CANAL PARALLELS
I-75 WEST OF HERE, PAGE 75
Great
Miami
River
Miami Co.
Snodgrass Rd
Exit 83
G-Citgo\D
L-RedC
83
Co. Rd 25A
Piqua Mall
Piqua
Pop: 20,900
82
Rt 36/Piqua
Urbana
Exit 82
G-BP
F-A&W Arby
ChinaGdns
KFC LJSilvr
Pizza Taco
Waffle
Wendy
Exit 82
G-Spdwy\L
F-CrkBrl
Evans
McDld
RedLb
L-Comfrt
Knght
LaQnt
- Miami Valley
Center Mall
- Home Depot
EXIT 82 - MILLS
BROTHERS, PAGE 76
34 miles (55 kms) to next Rest Area
Rest
Area
V D
No Information
Restrooms: 24 hours
For local weather,
tune to 1610 AM
Great Miami River
78
Co. Rd 25A
Upper Valley
Medical Centre
Covered Bridge
EXIT 78 - ELDEAN COVERED
BRIDGE, PAGE 76
ANCIENT ROMAN CONCRETE
- PAGE 76
DH
-100-
-99-
-98-
-97-
-96-
-95-
-94-
-93-
-92-
-91-
-90-
-89-
-88-
-87-
-86-
-85-
-84-
-83-
-82-
-81-
-80-
-79-
-78-
-77-
-76-
-75-
Time to drive this page: 23.4 minutes
SOUTH
OHIO, Miami Co.

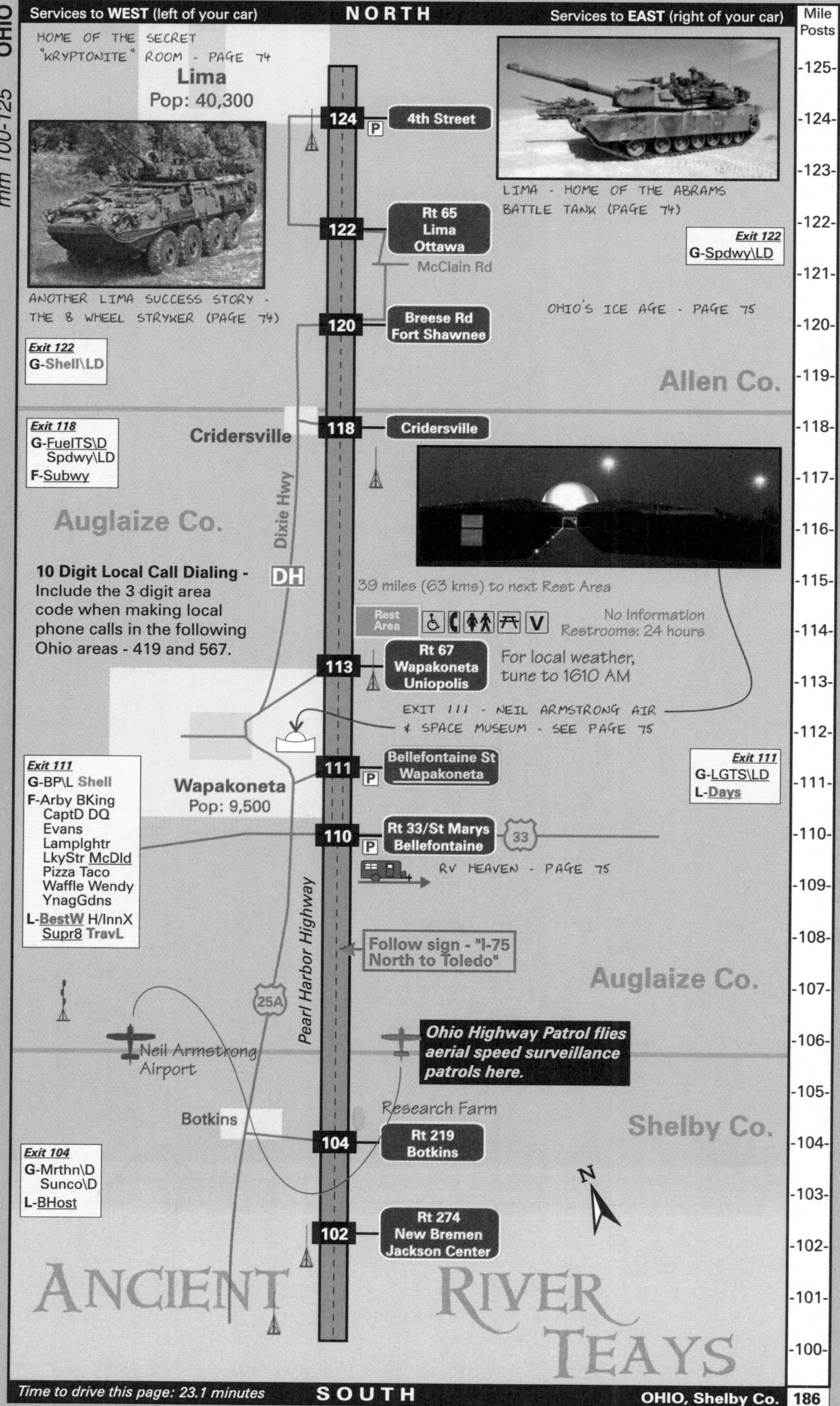
Services to WEST (left of your car)
NORTH
Services to EAST (right of your car)
Mile Posts
HOME OF THE SECRET "KRYPTONITE" ROOM - PAGE 74
Lima
Pop: 40,300
124
4th Street
LIMA - HOME OF THE ABRAMS BATTLE TANK (PAGE 74)
122
Rt 65 Lima Ottawa
McClain Rd
Exit 122
G-Spdwy\LD
ANOTHER LIMA SUCCESS STORY - THE 8 WHEEL STRYKER (PAGE 74)
120
Breese Rd Fort Shawnee
OHIO'S ICE AGE - PAGE 75
Exit 122
G-Shell\LD
Allen Co.
Exit 118
G-FuelTS\D Spdwy\LD
F-Subwy
Cridersville
118
Cridersville
Auglaize Co.
Dixie Hwy
10 Digit Local Call Dialing - Include the 3 digit area code when making local phone calls in the following Ohio areas - 419 and 567.
DH
39 miles (63 kms) to next Rest Area
Rest Area
V
No Information
Restrooms: 24 hours
113
Rt 67 Wapakoneta Uniopolis
For local weather, tune to 1610 AM
EXIT 111 - NEIL ARMSTRONG AIR & SPACE MUSEUM - SEE PAGE 75
Exit 111
G-BP\L Shell
F-Arby BKing CaptD DQ Evans Lamplghtr LkyStr McDld Pizza Taco Waffle Wendy YnagGdns
L-BestW H/InnX Supr8 TravL
Wapakoneta
Pop: 9,500
111
Bellefontaine St Wapakoneta
Exit 111
G-LGTS\LD
L-Days
110
Rt 33/St Marys Bellefontaine
33
RV HEAVEN - PAGE 75
Follow sign - "I-75 North to Toledo"
Auglaize Co.
25A
Pearl Harbor Highway
Neil Armstrong Airport
Ohio Highway Patrol flies aerial speed surveillance patrols here.
Research Farm
Botkins
104
Rt 219 Botkins
Shelby Co.
Exit 104
G-Mrthn\D Sunco\D
L-BHost
N
102
Rt 274 New Bremen Jackson Center
ANCIENT RIVER TEAYS
-125- -124- -123- -122- -121- -120- -119- -118- -117- -116- -115- -114- -113- -112- -111- -110- -109- -108- -107- -106- -105- -104- -103- -102- -101- -100-
Time to drive this page: 23.1 minutes
SOUTH
OHIO, Shelby Co.

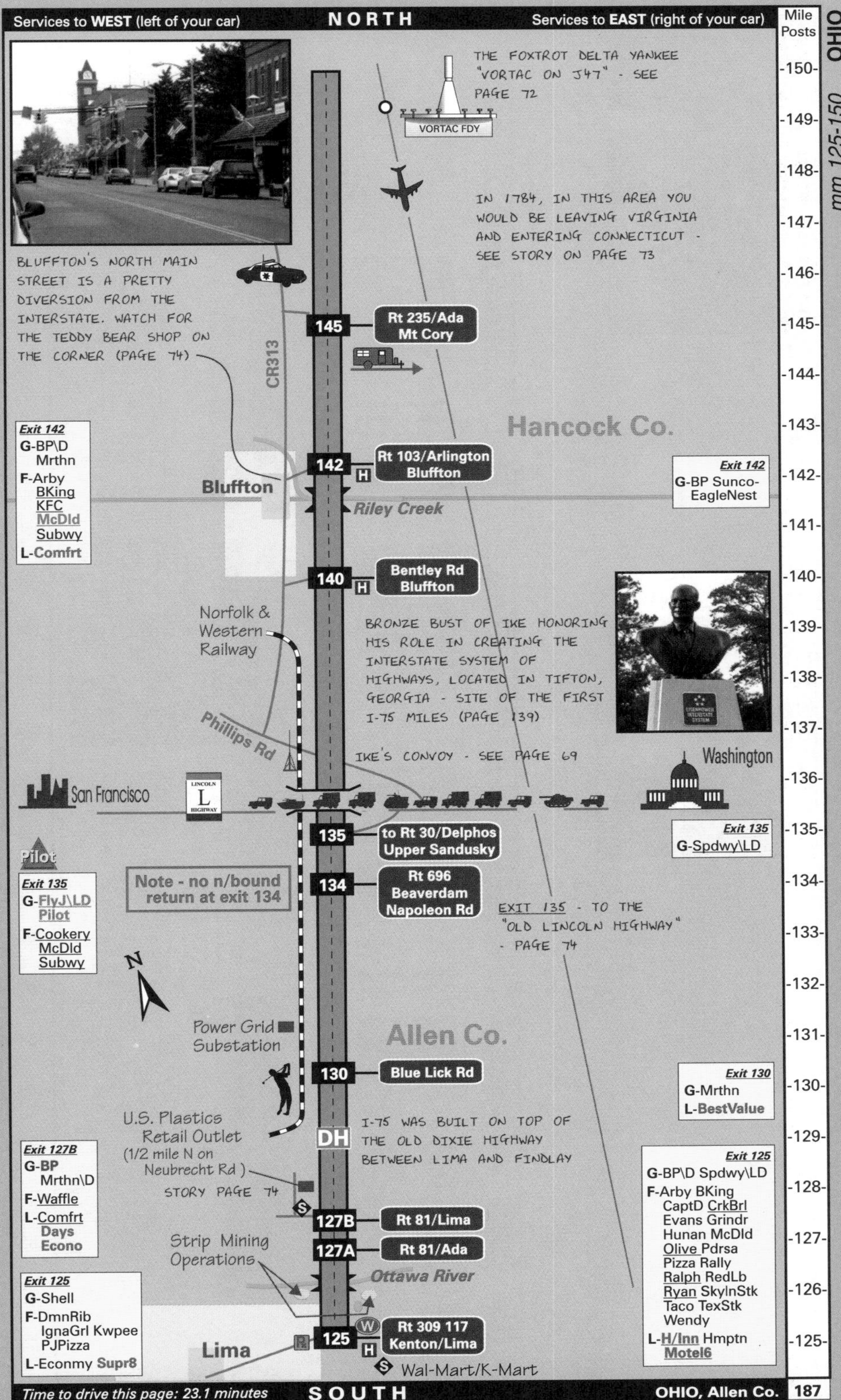
Services to WEST (left of your car)
NORTH
Services to EAST (right of your car)
Mile Posts
OHIO
mm 125-150
THE FOXTROT DELTA YANKEE "VORTAC ON J47" - SEE PAGE 72
VORTAC FDY
IN 1784, IN THIS AREA YOU WOULD BE LEAVING VIRGINIA AND ENTERING CONNECTICUT - SEE STORY ON PAGE 73
BLUFFTON'S NORTH MAIN STREET IS A PRETTY DIVERSION FROM THE INTERSTATE. WATCH FOR THE TEDDY BEAR SHOP ON THE CORNER (PAGE 74)
145
Rt 235/Ada
Mt Cory
CR313
Hancock Co.
Exit 142
G-BP\D Mrthn
F-Arby BKing KFC McDld Subwy
L-Comfrt
142
Rt 103/Arlington
Bluffton
Bluffton
Riley Creek
Exit 142
G-BP Sunco-EagleNest
140
Bentley Rd
Bluffton
Norfolk & Western Railway
BRONZE BUST OF IKE HONORING HIS ROLE IN CREATING THE INTERSTATE SYSTEM OF HIGHWAYS, LOCATED IN TIFTON, GEORGIA - SITE OF THE FIRST I-75 MILES (PAGE 139)
Phillips Rd
IKE'S CONVOY - SEE PAGE 69
Washington
San Francisco
LINCOLN L HIGHWAY
135
to Rt 30/Delphos
Upper Sandusky
Exit 135
G-Spdwy\LD
Pilot
Exit 135
G-FlyJ\LD Pilot
F-Cookery McDld Subwy
Note - no n/bound return at exit 134
134
Rt 696
Beaverdam
Napoleon Rd
EXIT 135 - TO THE "OLD LINCOLN HIGHWAY" - PAGE 74
N
Power Grid Substation
Allen Co.
130
Blue Lick Rd
Exit 130
G-Mrthn
L-BestValue
U.S. Plastics Retail Outlet (1/2 mile N on Neubrecht Rd) STORY PAGE 74
DH
I-75 WAS BUILT ON TOP OF THE OLD DIXIE HIGHWAY BETWEEN LIMA AND FINDLAY
Exit 127B
G-BP Mrthn\D
F-Waffle
L-Comfrt Days Econo
127B
Rt 81/Lima
127A
Rt 81/Ada
Strip Mining Operations
Ottawa River
Exit 125
G-BP\D Spdwy\LD
F-Arby BKing CaptD CrkBrl Evans Grindr Hunan McDld Olive Pdrsa Pizza Rally Ralph RedLb Ryan SkylnStk Taco TexStk Wendy
L-H/Inn Hmptn Motel6
Exit 125
G-Shell
F-DmnRib IgnaGrl Kwpee PJPizza
L-Econmy Supr8
125
Rt 309 117
Kenton/Lima
Lima
Wal-Mart/K-Mart
-150-
-149-
-148-
-147-
-146-
-145-
-144-
-143-
-142-
-141-
-140-
-139-
-138-
-137-
-136-
-135-
-134-
-133-
-132-
-131-
-130-
-129-
-128-
-127-
-126-
-125-
Time to drive this page: 23.1 minutes
SOUTH

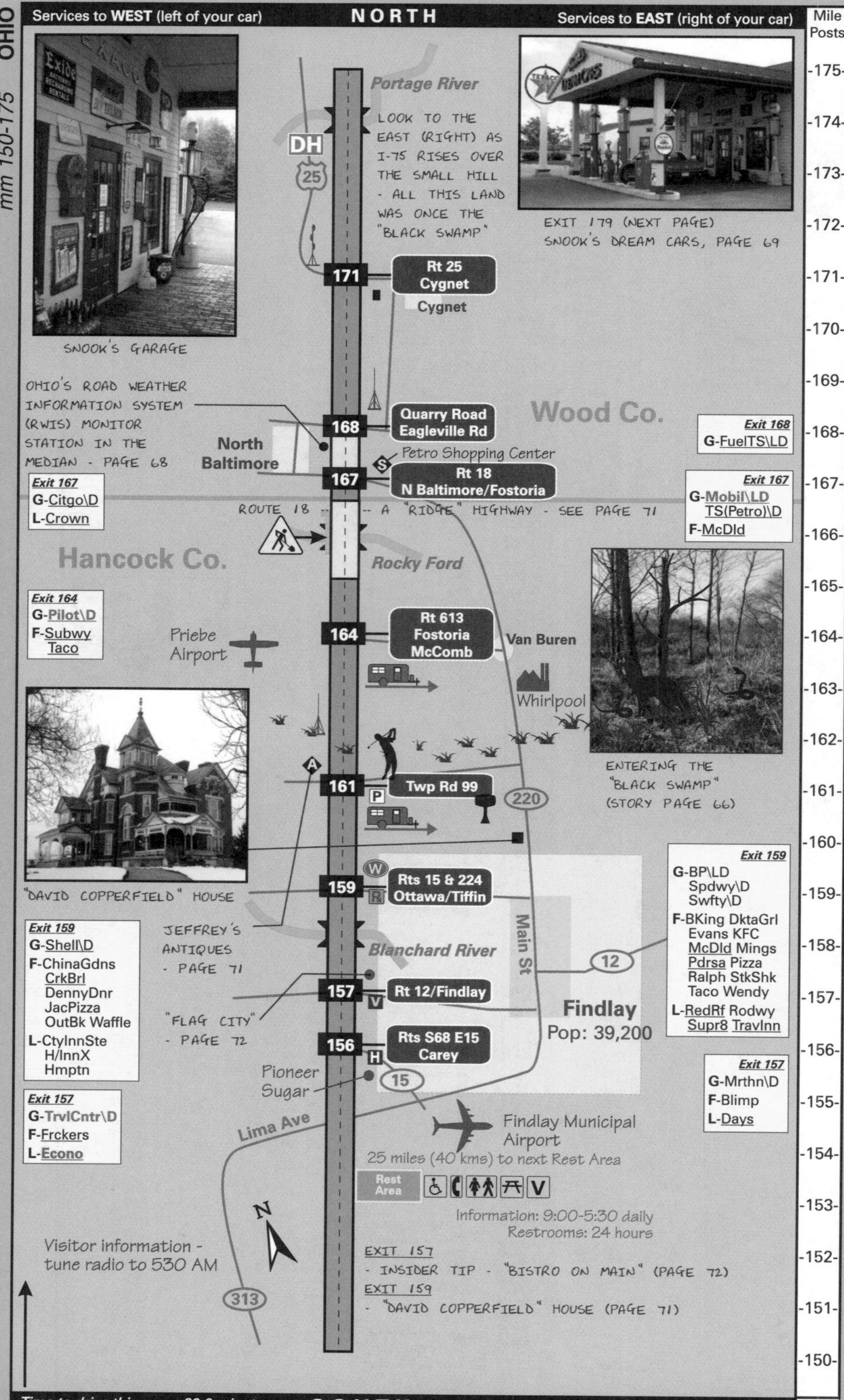

OHIO
mm 150-175
Services to WEST (left of your car)
NORTH
Services to EAST (right of your car)
Mile Posts
-175-
-174-
-173-
-172-
-171-
-170-
-169-
-168-
-167-
-166-
-165-
-164-
-163-
-162-
-161-
-160-
-159-
-158-
-157-
-156-
-155-
-154-
-153-
-152-
-151-
-150-
Portage River
DH
25
LOOK TO THE EAST (RIGHT) AS I-75 RISES OVER THE SMALL HILL - ALL THIS LAND WAS ONCE THE "BLACK SWAMP"
EXIT 179 (NEXT PAGE) SNOOK'S DREAM CARS, PAGE 69
SNOOK'S GARAGE
171
Rt 25 Cygnet
Cygnet
OHIO'S ROAD WEATHER INFORMATION SYSTEM (RWIS) MONITOR STATION IN THE MEDIAN - PAGE 68
168
Quarry Road Eagleville Rd
Wood Co.
Exit 168
G-FuelTS\LD
North Baltimore
Petro Shopping Center
167
Rt 18 N Baltimore/Fostoria
Exit 167
G-Citgo\D
L-Crown
Exit 167
G-Mobil\LD
TS(Petro)\D
F-McDld
ROUTE 18 -- A "RIDGE" HIGHWAY - SEE PAGE 71
Hancock Co.
Rocky Ford
Exit 164
G-Pilot\D
F-Subwy
Taco
Priebe Airport
164
Rt 613 Fostoria McComb
Van Buren
Whirlpool
ENTERING THE "BLACK SWAMP" (STORY PAGE 66)
A
161
Twp Rd 99
P
220
"DAVID COPPERFIELD" HOUSE
W
159
Rts 15 & 224 Ottawa/Tiffin
R
Exit 159
G-BP\LD
Spdwy\D
Swfty\D
F-BKing DktaGrl
Evans KFC
McDld Mings
Pdrsa Pizza
Ralph StkShk
Taco Wendy
L-RedRf Rodwy
Supr8 TravInn
Exit 159
G-Shell\D
F-ChinaGdns
CrkBrl
DennyDnr
JacPizza
OutBk Waffle
L-CtyInnSte
H/InnX
Hmptn
JEFFREY'S ANTIQUES - PAGE 71
Blanchard River
Main St
12
157
Rt 12/Findlay
V
Findlay
Pop: 39,200
"FLAG CITY" - PAGE 72
156
Rts S68 E15 Carey
H
Exit 157
G-Mrthn\D
F-Blimp
L-Days
Pioneer Sugar
15
Exit 157
G-TrvlCntr\D
F-Frckers
L-Econo
Lima Ave
Findlay Municipal Airport
25 miles (40 kms) to next Rest Area
Rest Area
V
Information: 9:00-5:30 daily
Restrooms: 24 hours
N
Visitor information - tune radio to 530 AM
EXIT 157
- INSIDER TIP - "BISTRO ON MAIN" (PAGE 72)
EXIT 159
- "DAVID COPPERFIELD" HOUSE (PAGE 71)
313
Time to drive this page: 23.6 minutes
SOUTH
OHIO, Hancock Co.
188

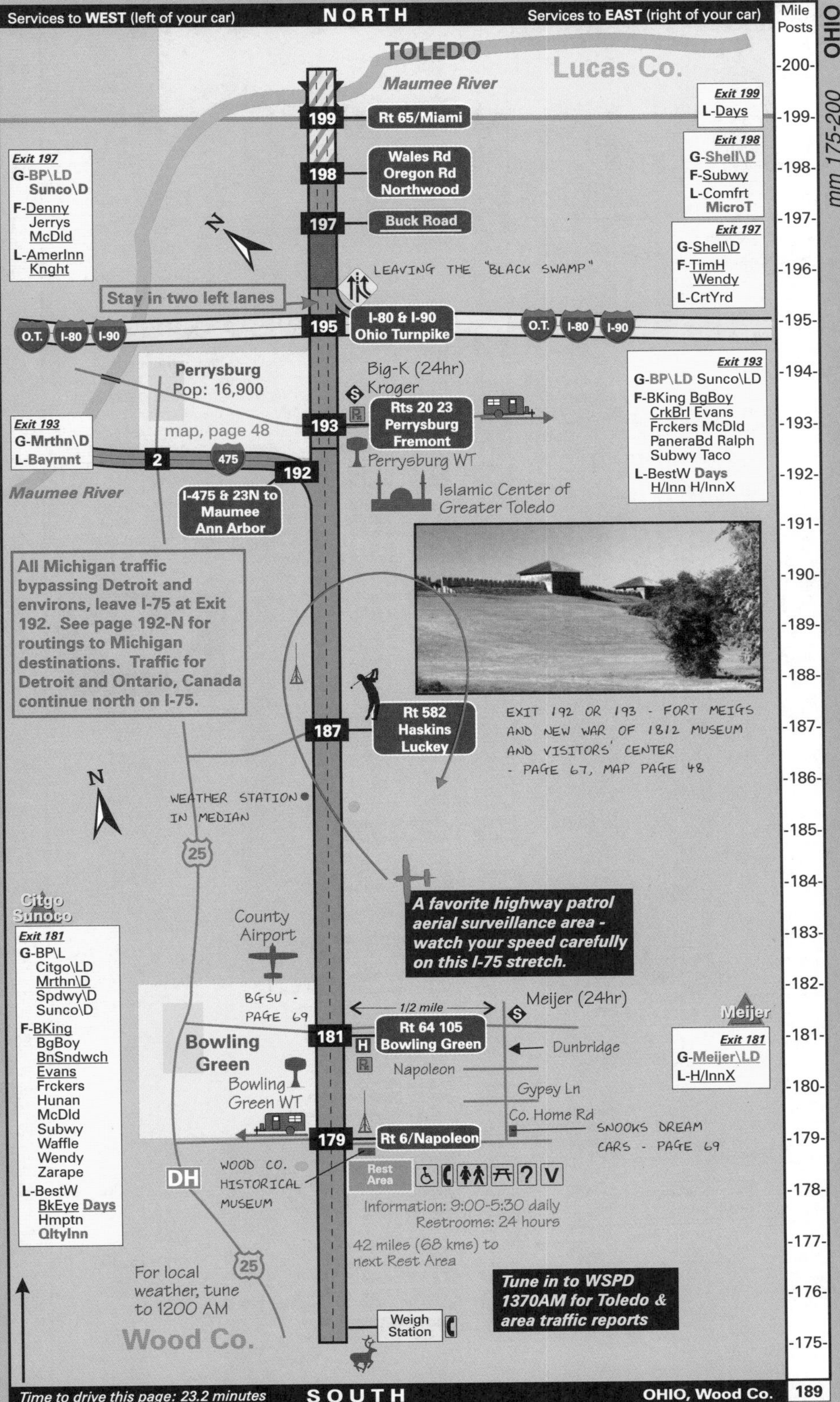

Services to WEST (left of your car)
NORTH
Services to EAST (right of your car)
Mile Posts
OHIO
mm 175-200
TOLEDO
Lucas Co.
Maumee River
199
Rt 65/Miami
Exit 199
L-Days
198
Wales Rd
Oregon Rd
Northwood
Exit 198
G-Shell\D
F-Subwy
L-Comfrt
MicroT
Exit 197
G-BP\LD
Sunco\D
F-Denny
Jerrys
McDld
L-AmerInn
Knght
197
Buck Road
Exit 197
G-Shell\D
F-TimH
Wendy
L-CrtYrd
LEAVING THE "BLACK SWAMP"
Stay in two left lanes
195
I-80 & I-90
Ohio Turnpike
O.T.
I-80
I-90
Perrysburg
Pop: 16,900
map, page 48
Big-K (24hr)
Kroger
193
Rts 20 23
Perrysburg
Fremont
Exit 193
G-BP\LD Sunco\LD
F-BKing BgBoy
CrkBrl Evans
Frckers McDld
PaneraBd Ralph
Subwy Taco
L-BestW Days
H/Inn H/InnX
Exit 193
G-Mrthn\D
L-Baymnt
2
475
192
Perrysburg WT
Maumee River
I-475 & 23N to
Maumee
Ann Arbor
Islamic Center of
Greater Toledo
All Michigan traffic bypassing Detroit and environs, leave I-75 at Exit 192. See page 192-N for routings to Michigan destinations. Traffic for Detroit and Ontario, Canada continue north on I-75.
187
Rt 582
Haskins
Luckey
EXIT 192 OR 193 - FORT MEIGS AND NEW WAR OF 1812 MUSEUM AND VISITORS' CENTER - PAGE 67, MAP PAGE 48
N
WEATHER STATION IN MEDIAN
25
A favorite highway patrol aerial surveillance area - watch your speed carefully on this I-75 stretch.
Citgo
Sunoco
Exit 181
G-BP\L
Citgo\LD
Mrthn\D
Spdwy\D
Sunco\D
F-BKing
BgBoy
BnSndwch
Evans
Frckers
Hunan
McDld
Subwy
Waffle
Wendy
Zarape
L-BestW
BkEye Days
Hmptn
QltyInn
County
Airport
BGSU - PAGE 69
1/2 mile
Meijer (24hr)
181
Rt 64 105
Bowling Green
Meijer
Exit 181
G-Meijer\LD
L-H/InnX
Bowling
Green
Bowling
Green WT
Napoleon
Dunbridge
Gypsy Ln
Co. Home Rd
179
Rt 6/Napoleon
SNOOKS DREAM CARS - PAGE 69
WOOD CO. HISTORICAL MUSEUM
DH
Rest Area
Information: 9:00-5:30 daily
Restrooms: 24 hours
42 miles (68 kms) to next Rest Area
25
For local weather, tune to 1200 AM
Tune in to WSPD 1370AM for Toledo & area traffic reports
Weigh Station
Wood Co.
-200- -199- -198- -197- -196- -195- -194- -193- -192- -191- -190- -189- -188- -187- -186- -185- -184- -183- -182- -181- -180- -179- -178- -177- -176- -175-
Time to drive this page: 23.2 minutes
SOUTH
OHIO, Wood Co.
189

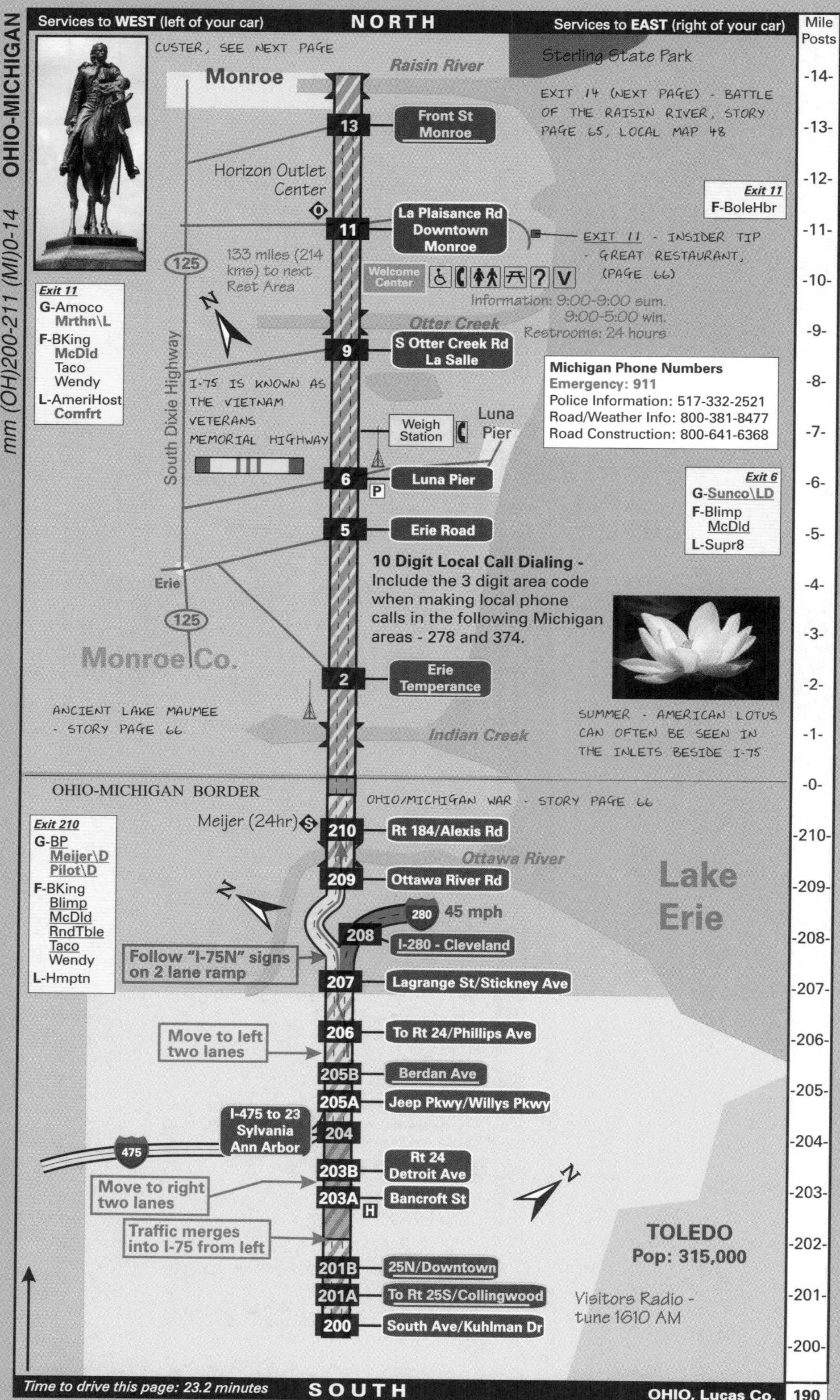
Services to WEST (left of your car)
NORTH
Services to EAST (right of your car)
Mile Posts
CUSTER, SEE NEXT PAGE
Monroe
Raisin River
Sterling State Park
EXIT 14 (NEXT PAGE) - BATTLE OF THE RAISIN RIVER, STORY PAGE 65, LOCAL MAP 48
13 Front St Monroe
Horizon Outlet Center
Exit 11 F-BoleHbr
11 La Plaisance Rd Downtown Monroe
EXIT 11 - INSIDER TIP - GREAT RESTAURANT, (PAGE 66)
125
133 miles (214 kms) to next Rest Area
Welcome Center
Information: 9:00-9:00 sum. 9:00-5:00 win.
Restrooms: 24 hours
Exit 11
G-Amoco Mrthn\L
F-BKing McDld Taco Wendy
L-AmeriHost Comfrt
Otter Creek
9 S Otter Creek Rd La Salle
South Dixie Highway
I-75 IS KNOWN AS THE VIETNAM VETERANS MEMORIAL HIGHWAY
Michigan Phone Numbers
Emergency: 911
Police Information: 517-332-2521
Road/Weather Info: 800-381-8477
Road Construction: 800-641-6368
Weigh Station
Luna Pier
6 Luna Pier
Exit 6
G-Sunco\LD
F-Blimp McDld
L-Supr8
5 Erie Road
10 Digit Local Call Dialing - Include the 3 digit area code when making local phone calls in the following Michigan areas - 278 and 374.
Erie
125
Monroe Co.
2 Erie Temperance
ANCIENT LAKE MAUMEE - STORY PAGE 66
Indian Creek
SUMMER - AMERICAN LOTUS CAN OFTEN BE SEEN IN THE INLETS BESIDE I-75
OHIO-MICHIGAN BORDER
OHIO/MICHIGAN WAR - STORY PAGE 66
Exit 210
G-BP Meijer\D Pilot\D
F-BKing Blimp McDld RndTble Taco Wendy
L-Hmptn
Meijer (24hr)
210 Rt 184/Alexis Rd
Ottawa River
209 Ottawa River Rd
Lake Erie
280 45 mph
208 I-280 - Cleveland
Follow "I-75N" signs on 2 lane ramp
207 Lagrange St/Stickney Ave
206 To Rt 24/Phillips Ave
Move to left two lanes
205B Berdan Ave
205A Jeep Pkwy/Willys Pkwy
I-475 to 23 Sylvania Ann Arbor
204
475
203B Rt 24 Detroit Ave
Move to right two lanes
203A Bancroft St
Traffic merges into I-75 from left
TOLEDO
Pop: 315,000
201B 25N/Downtown
201A To Rt 25S/Collingwood
Visitors Radio - tune 1610 AM
200 South Ave/Kuhlman Dr
-14- -13- -12- -11- -10- -9- -8- -7- -6- -5- -4- -3- -2- -1- -0- -210- -209- -208- -207- -206- -205- -204- -203- -202- -201- -200-
Time to drive this page: 23.2 minutes
SOUTH

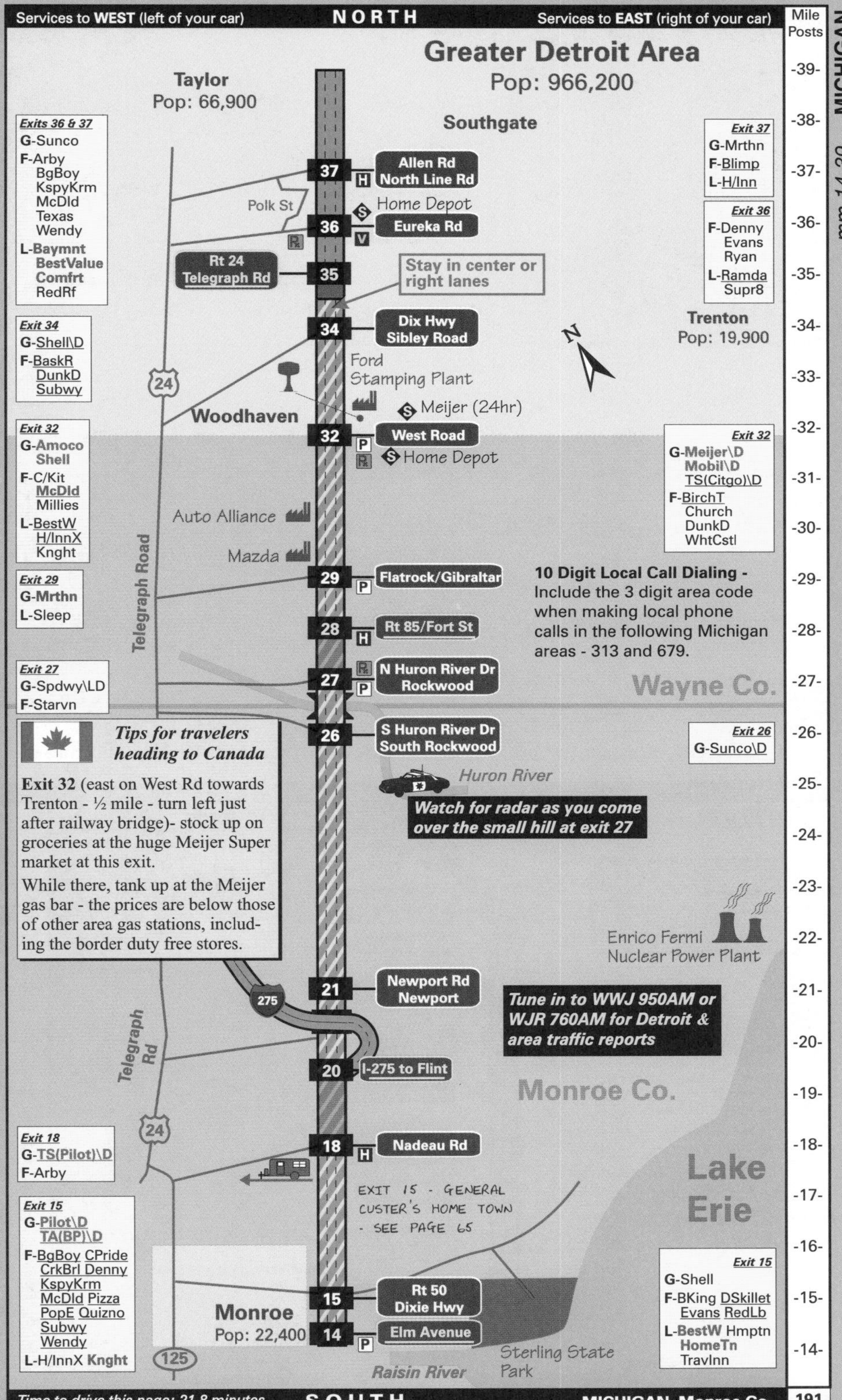
Services to WEST (left of your car)
NORTH
Services to EAST (right of your car)
Mile Posts
MICHIGAN
mm 14-39
Greater Detroit Area
Pop: 966,200
Taylor
Pop: 66,900
Southgate
Exits 36 & 37
G-Sunco
F-Arby
BgBoy
KspyKrm
McDld
Texas
Wendy
L-Baymnt
BestValue
Comfrt
RedRf
Exit 37
G-Mrthn
F-Blimp
L-H/Inn
Exit 36
F-Denny
Evans
Ryan
L-Ramda
Supr8
37
Allen Rd
North Line Rd
Polk St
Home Depot
36
Eureka Rd
Rt 24
Telegraph Rd
35
Stay in center or right lanes
Exit 34
G-Shell\D
F-BaskR
DunkD
Subwy
34
Dix Hwy
Sibley Road
Trenton
Pop: 19,900
N
24
Ford
Stamping Plant
Meijer (24hr)
Woodhaven
Exit 32
G-Amoco
Shell
F-C/Kit
McDld
Millies
L-BestW
H/InnX
Knght
32
West Road
Home Depot
Exit 32
G-Meijer\D
Mobil\D
TS(Citgo)\D
F-BirchT
Church
DunkD
WhtCstl
Auto Alliance
Mazda
Telegraph Road
Exit 29
G-Mrthn
L-Sleep
29
Flatrock/Gibraltar
10 Digit Local Call Dialing - Include the 3 digit area code when making local phone calls in the following Michigan areas - 313 and 679.
28
Rt 85/Fort St
Exit 27
G-Spdwy\LD
F-Starvn
27
N Huron River Dr
Rockwood
Wayne Co.
26
S Huron River Dr
South Rockwood
Exit 26
G-Sunco\D
Tips for travelers heading to Canada
Exit 32 (east on West Rd towards Trenton - ½ mile - turn left just after railway bridge)- stock up on groceries at the huge Meijer Super market at this exit.
While there, tank up at the Meijer gas bar - the prices are below those of other area gas stations, including the border duty free stores.
Huron River
Watch for radar as you come over the small hill at exit 27
Enrico Fermi
Nuclear Power Plant
275
21
Newport Rd
Newport
Tune in to WWJ 950AM or WJR 760AM for Detroit & area traffic reports
Telegraph Rd
20
I-275 to Flint
Monroe Co.
24
Exit 18
G-TS(Pilot)\D
F-Arby
18
Nadeau Rd
Lake Erie
EXIT 15 - GENERAL CUSTER'S HOME TOWN - SEE PAGE 65
Exit 15
G-Pilot\D
TA(BP)\D
F-BgBoy CPride
CrkBrl Denny
KspyKrm
McDld Pizza
PopE Quizno
Subwy
Wendy
L-H/InnX Knght
15
Rt 50
Dixie Hwy
Exit 15
G-Shell
F-BKing DSkillet
Evans RedLb
L-BestW Hmptn
HomeTn
TravInn
Monroe
Pop: 22,400
14
Elm Avenue
125
Sterling State Park
Raisin River
-39- -38- -37- -36- -35- -34- -33- -32- -31- -30- -29- -28- -27- -26- -25- -24- -23- -22- -21- -20- -19- -18- -17- -16- -15- -14-
Time to drive this page: 21.8 minutes
SOUTH
MICHIGAN, Monroe Co.

THANKS FOR LETTING ME RIDE WITH YOU ON YOUR JOURNEY NORTH. HAVE A SAFE TRIP, NO MATTER WHERE YOUR FINAL DESTINATION LIES.

Dave

Here is a handy guide to some *Michigan* and *Ontario* (Canada) Destinations . . .

Ann Arbor - Toledo(I-475) > MI Border(US23) > Ann Arbor = 52 miles

Lansing - Toledo(I-475) > MI Border(US23) > Brighton(I-96) > Lansing = 115 miles

Flint - Toledo(I-475) > MI Border(US 23) > Ann Arbor(US23) > Flint = 106 miles

Grand Rapids - Toledo(I-475) > MI Border(US23) > Brighton(I-96) > Grand Rapids = 179 miles

Saginaw - Toledo(I-475) > MI Border(US 23) > Ann Arbor(US23) > Flint(I-75) = 138 miles

London, ON - Windsor(Hwy401) > London = 190 Kms (118 miles)

Hamilton, ON - Windsor(Hwy401) > Exit235(Hwy403) > Brantford(Hwy2) > Jnctn(Hwy403) > Hamilton = 309 Kms (192 miles)

Kitchener, ON - Windsor(Hwy401) > = 286 Kms (178 miles)

Toronto, ON - Windsor(Hwy401) > Toronto = 350 Kms (217 miles)

Ottawa, ON - Windsor(Hwy401) > Prescott(Hwy16) > Ottawa = 800 Kms (497 miles)

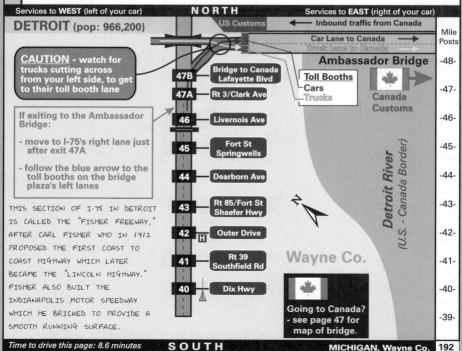

Services to **WEST** (left of your car) — **NORTH** — Services to **EAST** (right of your car)

DETROIT (pop: 966,200)

US Customs

Inbound traffic from Canada

Car Lane to Canada

Truck Lane to Canada

Mile Posts

Ambassador Bridge

CAUTION - watch for trucks cutting across from your left side, to get to their toll booth lane

Toll Booths
Cars
Trucks

Canada Customs

If exiting to the Ambassador Bridge:

- move to I-75's right lane just after exit 47A
- follow the blue arrow to the toll booths on the bridge plaza's left lanes

Exit	Services	Mile Post
		-48-
47B	Bridge to Canada Lafayette Blvd	
47A	Rt 3/Clark Ave	-47-
46	Livernois Ave	-46-
45	Fort St Springwells	-45-
44	Dearborn Ave	-44-
43	Rt 85/Fort St Shaefer Hwy	-43-
42	H Outer Drive	-42-
41	Rt 39 Southfield Rd	-41-
40	Dix Hwy	-40-
		-39-

THIS SECTION OF I-75 IN DETROIT IS CALLED THE "FISHER FREEWAY," AFTER CARL FISHER WHO IN 1912 PROPOSED THE FIRST COAST TO COAST HIGHWAY WHICH LATER BECAME THE "LINCOLN HIGHWAY." FISHER ALSO BUILT THE INDIANAPOLIS MOTOR SPEEDWAY WHICH HE BRICKED TO PROVIDE A SMOOTH RUNNING SURFACE.

N

Detroit River (U.S. - Canada Border)

Wayne Co.

Going to Canada? - see page 47 for map of bridge.

Time to drive this page: 8.6 minutes — **SOUTH**

Beating the Rush Hour Blues

Nobody likes rush hour traffic and each year it seems to get worse no matter where you are. Fortunately, I-75 cities have some of the best traffic reporters in the Nation–on the ground and in the air–to speed you through the interstate cities. I've assembled the *best-of-the-best*, as my ***I-75 Traffic Reporter Team*** to help you on your drive through their areas. You'll also find bypass maps for Cincinnati and Atlanta on the following pages, as well as a special map of the Macon area.

Detroit - morning rush hours are 7:00-9:00; afternoon, 4:00-6:30. *"On the 8's"* (every 8 minutes), tune in the team of ***John Bailey*** (on the ground) and ***Tracy Gary*** (in the air), supported by ***Jim Banner*** and ***Mike Howard***, on **WWJ-950AM.** Road construction reports at 18 and 48 minutes past each hour.

Toledo - morning rush hours are 6-9; afternoons, 3-6. **WSPD-1370AM's** ***Lynn Cassidy*** will keep you moving with her reports *"on the 10's"* (every 10 mins).

Dayton - morning rush hours are 7-9; afternoons, 4-6. Who knows traffic better than the police? Join ***Sgt. Mark Bowron,*** supported by ***Bill Kirby*** (afternoons), and ***Mike Phillips*** & **Sari Hardyal** on **WHIO-1290AM.**

Cincinnati - morning rush hours are 5:30-9:00; afternoon, 3:30-6:30. Helicopter traffic reports from **WLW 700AM**'s ***John Phillips*** every 10 minutes in rush time & *"top-of-the-hour"* at other times.

Lexington - morning rush hours are 6:30-8:30; afternoons, 4:30-6:00. **WVLK-590AM's** traffic guy in the sky is ***Scott Wilson*** who reports on the bluegrass rush traffic *"on the 6's."* Scott certainly doesn't horse around!

Knoxville - morning rush hours are 7:00-9:00; afternoon, 4:30-6:00. Listen to ***Dave Foulk*** on **WNOX-990AM's** - he'll keep you moving.

Chattanooga - morning rush hours are 6:00-9:00; afternoon, 3:30-6:30 . . . but they shouldn't bother you too much unless morning I-24 traffic backs up onto I-75. Stay tuned to **WKXJ-98.1FM's** ***Sarah Jennings*** and ***Lori Harrison,*** to check this out during rush hours *"on the 10's."*

Atlanta - morning rush hours are 6:30-9:30; afternoon, 4:00 (2:00 on Fri.)-6:30. My friend who taught me that the *"Brookwood Split"* isn't a soda fountain dessert, **WSB-750AM's** ***Captain Herb Emory*** is in the air in the WSB chopper –on the job *every 6 minutes*–all over the city and bypass routes, supported by his team of ***Mark Arum*** and ***Calandra Corder***.

Macon - You're on the I-475 Macon Bypass so you should be OK ... **WAYS-105.5FM's** ***Mike Wade*** at the Traffic Center will keep an eye on thing for you, though.

After that, it's all "downhill" to Florida, folks!

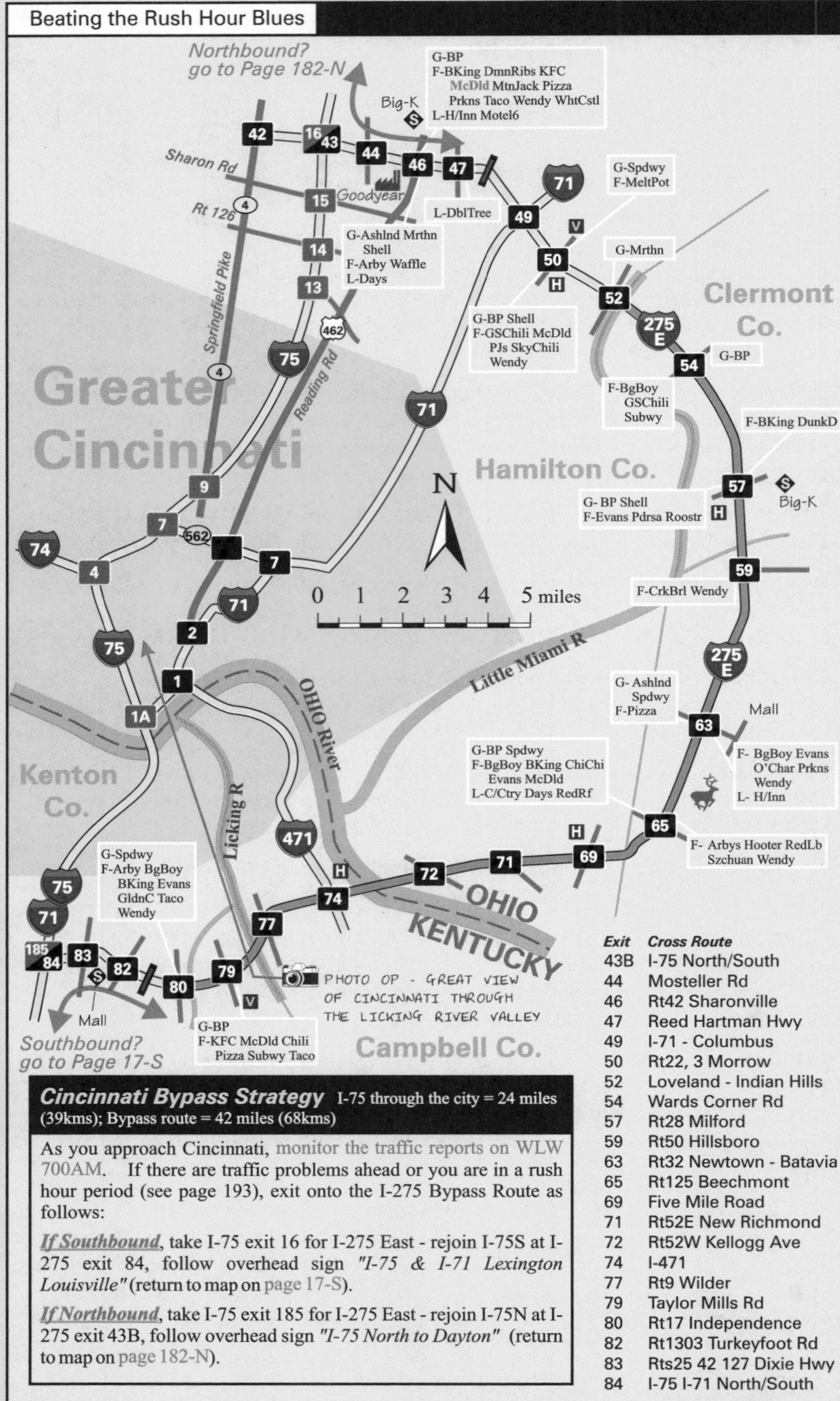

Cincinnati Bypass Strategy I-75 through the city = 24 miles (39kms); Bypass route = 42 miles (68kms)

As you approach Cincinnati, monitor the traffic reports on WLW 700AM. If there are traffic problems ahead or you are in a rush hour period (see page 193), exit onto the I-275 Bypass Route as follows:

If Southbound, take I-75 exit 16 for I-275 East - rejoin I-75S at I-275 exit 84, follow overhead sign *"I-75 & I-71 Lexington Louisville"* (return to map on page 17-S).

If Northbound, take I-75 exit 185 for I-275 East - rejoin I-75N at I-275 exit 43B, follow overhead sign *"I-75 North to Dayton"* (return to map on page 182-N).

Exit	*Cross Route*
43B	I-75 North/South
44	Mosteller Rd
46	Rt42 Sharonville
47	Reed Hartman Hwy
49	I-71 - Columbus
50	Rt22, 3 Morrow
52	Loveland - Indian Hills
54	Wards Corner Rd
57	Rt28 Milford
59	Rt50 Hillsboro
63	Rt32 Newtown - Batavia
65	Rt125 Beechmont
69	Five Mile Road
71	Rt52E New Richmond
72	Rt52W Kellogg Ave
74	I-471
77	Rt9 Wilder
79	Taylor Mills Rd
80	Rt17 Independence
82	Rt1303 Turkeyfoot Rd
83	Rts25 42 127 Dixie Hwy
84	I-75 I-71 North/South

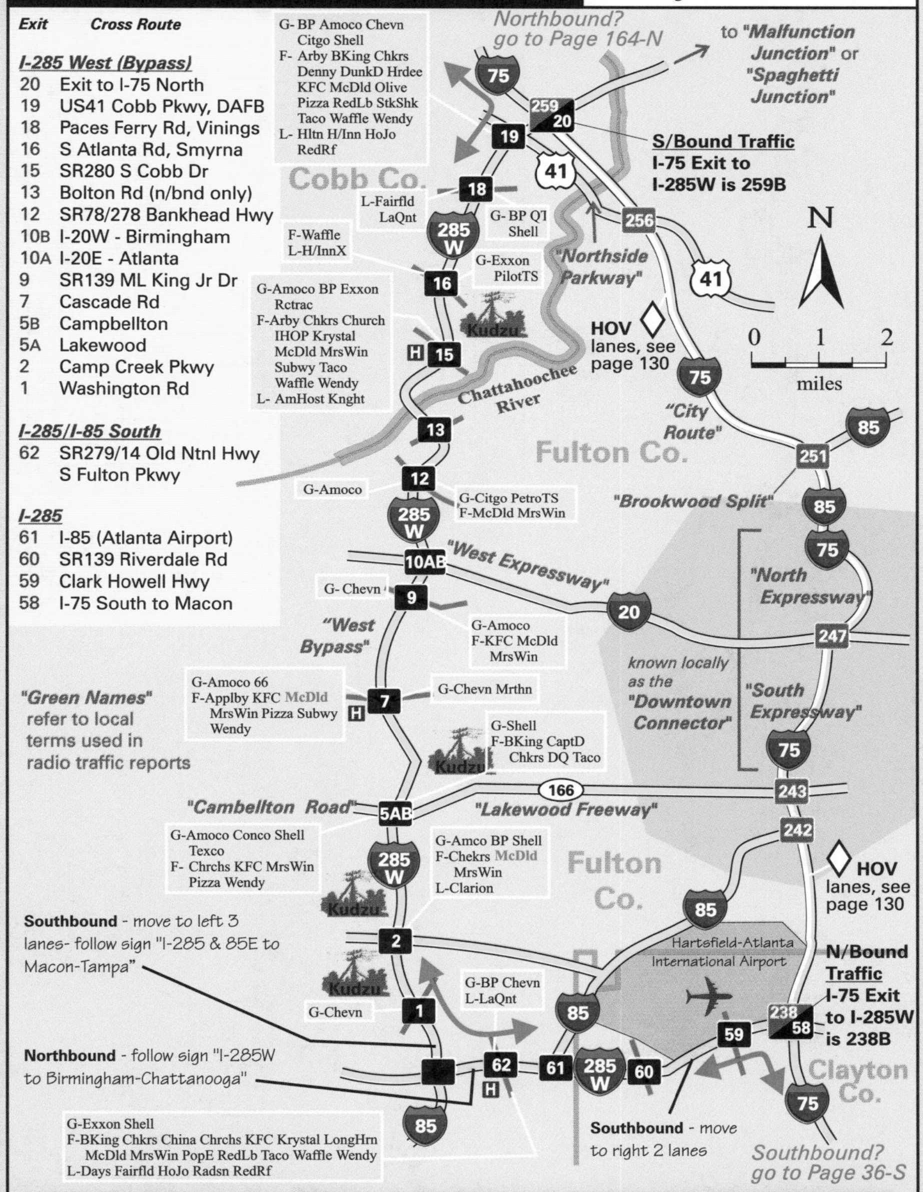

Exit	Cross Route
I-285 West (Bypass)	
20	Exit to I-75 North
19	US41 Cobb Pkwy, DAFB
18	Paces Ferry Rd, Vinings
16	S Atlanta Rd, Smyrna
15	SR280 S Cobb Dr
13	Bolton Rd (n/bnd only)
12	SR78/278 Bankhead Hwy
10B	I-20W - Birmingham
10A	I-20E - Atlanta
9	SR139 ML King Jr Dr
7	Cascade Rd
5B	Campbellton
5A	Lakewood
2	Camp Creek Pkwy
1	Washington Rd
I-285/I-85 South	
62	SR279/14 Old Ntnl Hwy S Fulton Pkwy
I-285	
61	I-85 (Atlanta Airport)
60	SR139 Riverdale Rd
59	Clark Howell Hwy
58	I-75 South to Macon

Northbound? go to Page 164-N

to "Malfunction Junction" or "Spaghetti Junction"

G- BP Amoco Chevn Citgo Shell
F- Arby BKing Chkrs Denny DunkD Hrdee KFC McDld Olive Pizza RedLb StkShk Taco Waffle Wendy
L- Hltn H/Inn HoJo RedRf

S/Bound Traffic
I-75 Exit to I-285W is 259B

Cobb Co.

L-Fairfld LaQnt

G- BP QT Shell

F-Waffle L-H/InnX

G-Exxon PilotTS

"Northside Parkway"

G-Amoco BP Exxon Rctrac
F-Arby Chkrs Church IHOP Krystal McDld MrsWin Subwy Taco Waffle Wendy
L- AmHost Knght

Kudzu

HOV lanes, see page 130

Chattahoochee River

0 1 2 miles

"City Route"

Fulton Co.

"Brookwood Split"

G-Amoco

G-Citgo PetroTS
F-McDld MrsWin

"West Expressway"

"North Expressway"

G- Chevn

"West Bypass"

G-Amoco
F-KFC McDld MrsWin

known locally as the "Downtown Connector"

"South Expressway"

G-Amoco 66
F-Applby KFC McDld MrsWin Pizza Subwy Wendy

G-Chevn Mrthn

"Green Names" refer to local terms used in radio traffic reports

G-Shell
F-BKing CaptD Chkrs DQ Taco

"Cambellton Road"

"Lakewood Freeway"

G-Amoco Conco Shell Texco
F- Chrchs KFC MrsWin Pizza Wendy

G-Amco BP Shell
F-Chekrs McDld MrsWin
L-Clarion

Fulton Co.

HOV lanes, see page 130

Southbound - move to left 3 lanes- follow sign "I-285 & 85E to Macon-Tampa"

Hartsfield-Atlanta International Airport

N/Bound Traffic
I-75 Exit to I-285W is 238B

G-BP Chevn
L-LaQnt

G-Chevn

Northbound - follow sign "I-285W to Birmingham-Chattanooga"

Clayton Co.

G-Exxon Shell
F-BKing Chkrs China Chrchs KFC Krystal LongHrn McDld MrsWin PopE RedLb Taco Waffle Wendy
L-Days Fairfld HoJo Radsn RedRf

Southbound - move to right 2 lanes

Southbound? go to Page 36-S

Atlanta Bypass Strategy I-75 through the city = 20 miles (32kms); Bypass route = 25 miles (40kms)

As you approach Atlanta, **monitor the traffic reports on WSB 750AM**. If there are traffic problems ahead or you are in a rush hour period (see page 193), exit onto the I-285 Bypass Route as follows:

Southbound - leave I-75 at exit 259, stay in ***two left lanes*** on ramp and follow *"I-285W."* On I-285W, just after exit 60, move to ***two right lanes*** - leave I-285W at exit 58 & follow overhead sign *"I-75 Macon Tampa"* - on ramp, stay right & follow *"I-75 South"* - after ramp splits, move to ***left quickly*** because ramp becomes single lane. Rejoin I-75 South at mile 238 (return to map on page 36).

Northbound - leave I-75N at exit 238B, for I-285W. At I-285W, exit 19, move to ***two right lanes*** - take exit 20 and follow overhead sign *"I-75 to Marietta/Chattanooga"* - on ramp, move to the ***two left lanes*** and - ***slow down***, very tight left corner coming up. Rejoin I-75N (return to map on page 164).

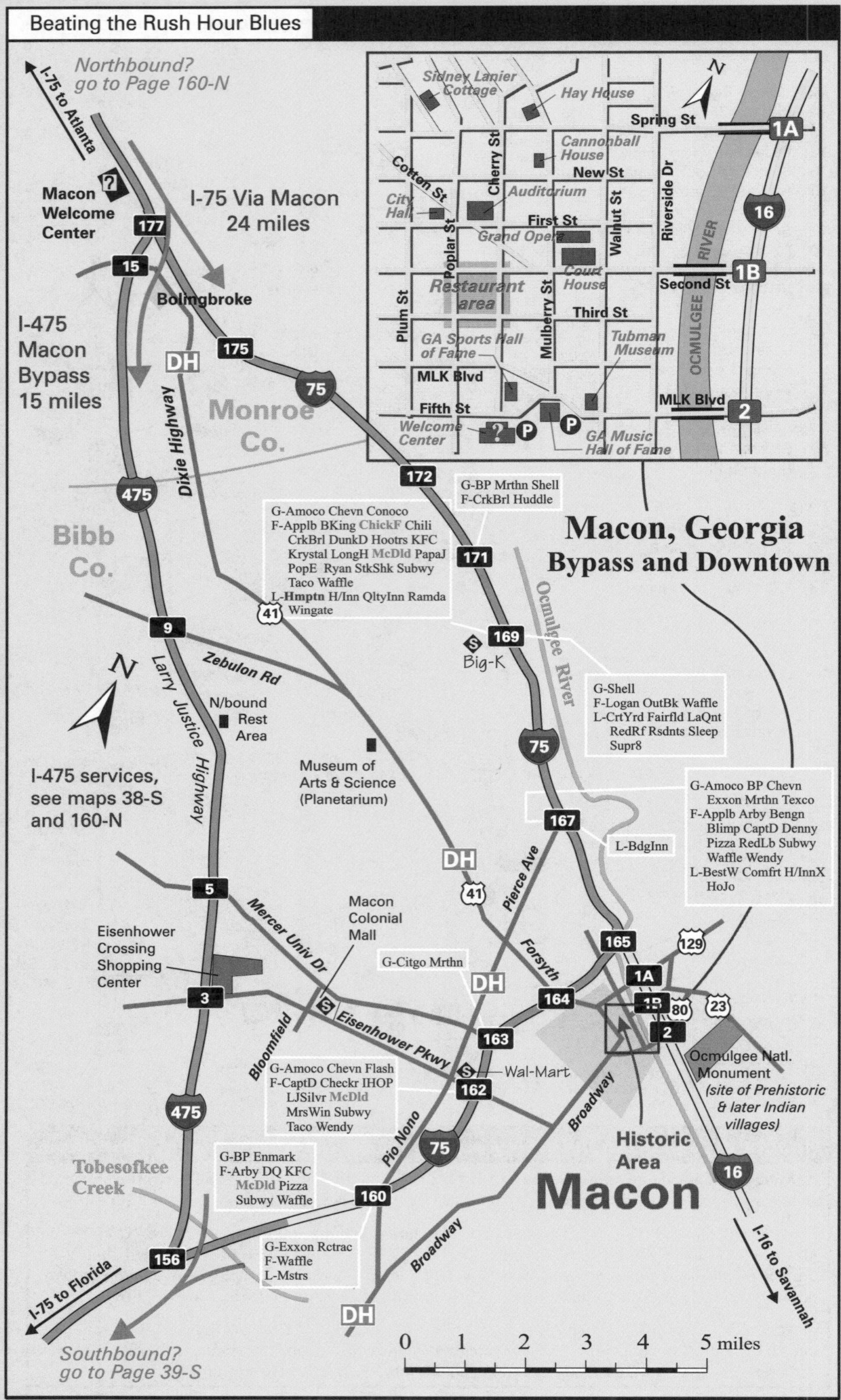
Northbound? go to Page 160-N
I-75 to Atlanta
Macon Welcome Center
I-75 Via Macon 24 miles
Bolingbroke
I-475 Macon Bypass 15 miles
Dixie Highway
Monroe Co.
Bibb Co.
Zebulon Rd
Larry Justice Highway
N/bound Rest Area
Museum of Arts & Science (Planetarium)
I-475 services, see maps 38-S and 160-N
Mercer Univ Dr
Macon Colonial Mall
Eisenhower Crossing Shopping Center
Eisenhower Pkwy
Bloomfield
Wal-Mart
Big-K
Pierce Ave
Forsyth
Pio Nono
Broadway
Tobesofkee Creek
I-75 to Florida
Southbound? go to Page 39-S
Ocmulgee River
Historic Area
Macon
Ocmulgee Natl. Monument (site of Prehistoric & later Indian villages)
I-16 to Savannah
Macon, Georgia
Bypass and Downtown
G-BP Mrthn Shell
F-CrkBrl Huddle
G-Amoco Chevn Conoco
F-Applb BKing ChickF Chili CrkBrl DunkD Hootrs KFC Krystal LongH McDld PapaJ PopE Ryan StkShk Subwy Taco Waffle
L-Hmptn H/Inn QltyInn Ramda Wingate
G-Shell
F-Logan OutBk Waffle
L-CrtYrd Fairfld LaQnt RedRf Rsdnts Sleep Supr8
G-Amoco BP Chevn Exxon Mrthn Texco
F-Applb Arby Bengn Blimp CaptD Denny Pizza RedLb Subwy Waffle Wendy
L-BestW Comfrt H/InnX HoJo
L-BdgInn
G-Citgo Mrthn
G-Amoco Chevn Flash
F-CaptD Checkr IHOP LJSilvr McDld MrsWin Subwy Taco Wendy
G-BP Enmark
F-Arby DQ KFC McDld Pizza Subwy Waffle
G-Exxon Rctrac
F-Waffle
L-Mstrs
Sidney Lanier Cottage
Hay House
Spring St
Cannonball House
New St
Cotton St
Cherry St
Auditorium
City Hall
First St
Poplar St
Grand Opera
Walnut St
Riverside Dr
Ocmulgee River
Court House
Second St
Restaurant area
Plum St
Mulberry St
Third St
GA Sports Hall of Fame
Tubman Museum
MLK Blvd
Fifth St
Welcome Center
GA Music Hall of Fame
0 1 2 3 4 5 miles

A word about these listings

The Internet's World Wide Web has become such an information resource that wherever possible, I've included the appropriate website address. Book titles followed by *"Amzn"* indicate that the book is available through **www.amazon.com**. Don't forget that during the winter months, you can obtain the most recent Interstate-75 information - gas prices, construction updates, tips, etc., by visiting our website at - www.i75online.com.

"Allatoona Pass" by William Scaife - pub: Etowah Valley Historical Society. A very well researched book detailing the horrendous Civil War battle at Allatoona Pass in Georgia [excellent website at **www.evhsonline.org** where you may also purchase the book].

American Association of Retired Persons (AARP) - [**www.aarp.org**] - 601 E Street NW, Washington DC 20049.. Everybody 50 or older should join this organization; the annual membership is so low and the benefits broad. Phone: 1-800-687-2277.

American Automobile Association (AAA) - [**www.aaa.com**] - Check your phone book for number of your local club. Emergency road number: **1-800-AAA-HELP** I wouldn't consider traveling by car without my membership. I have had to use AAA emergency services on several occasion and always found them to be responsive and my problems solved easily. Great peace of mind!

"Battlefield Atlas of the Civil War" by Craig Symonds (*Amzn*) - pub: NAPCA, 8 W Madison St, Baltimore MD 21201 (phone: 301-659-0220) - ISBN: 0-933852-40-1.

"Battle of Resaca, The" by Philip Secrist (*Amzn*) - pub: Mercer Univ. Press, Macon, GA. ISBN" 0-86554-601-0. An excellent book which not only explains the entire battle in great detail, but also deals with the archaeological situation (and subsequent reports) resulting from the I-75 construction in the battlefield area. [**www.ResacaBattlefield.org**].

Canadian Association of Retired Persons (CARP) - [**www.fifty-plus.net**] - 27 Queen Street East, Suite 1304, Toronto ON M5C 2M6. Phone: 416-363-8748.

Canadian Automobile Association (CAA) - [**www.caa.ca**] - See my comments under "AAA." Emergency road number: **1-800-CAA-HELP.** Check your phone book for your local club.

Canadian Snowbird Association - [**www.snowbirds.org**] - 180 Lesmill Road, Toronto ON M3B 2T5 (phone: 1-800-265-3200). If you are Canadian, and spend your winters in the South, you should consider becoming a member of this organization. Low annual membership fees, many discounts and benefits, this 100,000+ members organization is the "voice" of the Canadian "snowbird."

"City Behind A Fence, Oak Ridge TN 1942-1946" (*Amzn*) - Indispensable source for anybody interested in the development of the atomic bomb, and the role played by Oak Ridge during the war years. Available through the Univ. of TN Press - ISBN: 0-87049-309-4

"Civil War Battlefield Guide" (*Amzn*) - pub: by Mariner Books - ISBN: 0-395-740-12-6

DeLorme Mapping Company - [**www.delorme.com**] - Box 298, Freeport, MN 04032; phone: 1-800-227-1656. Available at many truck stops and bookstores. DeLorme issues a superb set of large scale map guides, state by state. All states area available; we wouldn't travel to Florida without our DeLorme large scale guide (Atlas and Gazetteer) in our car. See also my Insider Tip about the DeLorme Street Atlas USA GPS system - page 73.

Florida's New Exit Numbers - visit my site, **www.i75online.com** for information about the new exit numbers on ALL Florida interstates.

Georgia, North - Planning to spend any time in Georgia north of Atlanta? If so, you must visit this exceptional website - **www.ngeorgia.com**. It's one of the best source of information for the area. Webmaster Randy Golden provides interesting side trips & much information about the history, flora and fauna of this fascinating part of the Peach State.

Interstate-95 - Yes, I-95! Many people who drive the "eastern" route to Florida have written to me wishing there was a similar book for "their" route. Now there is. Several years ago, I mentored Sandra Phillips and Stan Posner, two journalist friends of mine, and the result is an excellent and similar driving guide, *"Drive I-95."* It has already won several awards and I heartily recommend it. See for yourself at **www.driveI95.com**. It may also be purchased through bookstores, or ordered by phoning toll-free, **888-484-3395**.

MA - Market America Motel Discount Coupon Books - Box 7069, Gadsden AL 35906 (phone: 256-547-4321). The familiar red covered motel discount coupon books available at I-75 welcome centers. MA also has a website where you can print and clip your discount coupons before you travel. Visit **www.travelcoupons.com**.

"PassPorter Walt Disney World 2004" by Jennifer Watson & Dave Marx (*Amzn*) - pub: PassPorter Travel Press (ISBN: 0-58771-004-8). This superb book is highly recommend to those planning a visit to WDW. Winner of four major awards, it's a WDW travel guide, planner, organizer . . . and unusual journal and keepsake, providing a wonderful memento of your visit. Supported by an excellent website - **www.PassPorter.com**.

State Travel Information - how to get official travel information for each I-75 state.

Michigan:	1-888-78-GREAT (784-7328);	**www.Michigan.org**
Ohio:	1-800-BUCKEYE (282-5393);	**www.OhioTourism.com**
Kentucky:	1-800-225-TRIP (225-8747);	**www.tourKY.com**
Tennessee:	1-800-GO2-TENN (462-8366);	**www.TNvacation.com**
Georgia:	1-800-VISIT-GA (847-4842);	**www.Georgia.org/tourism**
Florida:	1-888-7FLA USA (735-2872);	**www.FlaUSA.com**

Traveler Discount Guide Hotel Coupons - - [**www.roomsaver.com**]. 4205 NW 6th Street, Gainesville FL 32609; phone: 1-800-332-3948. The familiar green covered motel discount coupon books available at I-75 welcome centers and rest areas. The company also has an excellent website where you can print your discount coupons before you travel.

"Traveling With Your Pet" (The AAA PetBook) (*Amzn*) - Contains many pet travel tips and 466 pages listing "pet friendly" motels. An excellent resource book for people traveling with pets - available from any AAA (or CAA) office. ISBN: 1-5625-1406-7.

"Trailer Life RV Park & Services Directory" (*Amzn*) - Box 11097, Des Moines IA 50336 phone: 1-800-234-3450. One of the two essential campground and RV services guides to have aboard your RV [**www.goodsamclub.com**]. (see also, *"Woodall's"*).

"Unofficial Guide to Walt Disney World" by Bob Sehlinger (*Amzn*) - pub: John Wiley. Order through most bookstores. Don't consider a visit to WDW without this book. Far superior to any of the other guides ("official" and "unofficial") because of its objective point of view. Many money and time saving tips. ISBN: 0-764-52631-6.

Valentine Research - [**www.valentine1.com**]. - 10280 Alliance Road, Cincinnati OH 45242 (order: 1-800-331-3030). Annual tests conducted by major car magazines, consistently rate the Valentine One radar detector with laser warning as the best detection equipment available, by far. This is the *"Rolls Royce"* of detectors.

"War of 1812 - "The Invasion of Canada" (ISBN: 0-385-65839-7) and ***"Flames Across the Border"*** (*Amzn*) - (ISBN: 0-385-65838-9) by Pierre Berton (Doubleday) are excellent, very readable books about the War of 1812. Well researched; great detail.

"Wilderness Road, The" by Robert Kincaid (available through **www.abebooks.com**). The definitive book about the Wilderness Road which was used by many pioneers in the 1700s for their journeys across the mountains and into Kentucky and Tennessee.

"Woodall's Campground Directory" (*Amzn*) - [**www.woodalls.com**] - 2575 Vista Del Mar Drive, Ventura CA 93001 (order: 1-877-680-6155). Available at RV dealers, most large bookstores or at Woodall's website, this is one of the two essential campground and RV services guides to have aboard your RV (the other is *"Trailer Life"* - see above).

"Wheelchairs on the Go - Accessible fun in Florida" (ISBN:0-9664356-5-6, published by Access Travel Guide, FL) (*Amzn*) - the definitive book for anybody with a disability visiting Florida. This well researched book stems from experience since one of the author's husband is a quadriplegic; they both travel extensively throughout the Sunshine State. To order, visit **www.wheelchairsonthego.com**, or phone 888-245-7300 (727-573-0434).

Abbreviations used in our maps

Space limitations on the maps necessitate the use of abbreviations for many of the fuel stations, restaurants and motels listed. For your convenience, the abbreviations used are listed on the next two pages.

GAS, DIESEL & LPG

Ashlnd. . . . . Ashland Oil
BP. . . . . BP Oil
Chevn . . . Chevron USA
Coastl . . . . Coastal
Conco . . . . Conoco
Fina. . . . . Fina Oil
FlyJ . . . . FlyingJ
FlCty . . . . Fuel City
FuelMrt . . . . . . FuelMart
GldnGln . Golden Gallon
Hess . . . . Hess Oil
Libty . . . . Liberty
Mrthn . . . . Marathon Oil
Phil66 . . . . Philips66
Pilot . . . . Pilot Gas
QT . . . . Quick Time Gas
Racewy. . . . . . Raceway
Rctrac . . . . Racetrac
RghtStff . . . . . RightStuff
SavATn . . . . Save A Ton
Shell. . . . . Shell Oil
Spdwy. . . . . . Speedway
Sunco . . . . Sunoco
Swfty . . . . Swifty
TA(brand) . . . . . . Travel-
. . . . Centers of America
Texco . . . . Texaco
Thrntn . . . . . . Thorntons

This symbol on the colored maps indicates those filling station where we have observed lower priced gas during our many I-75 trips.

Citgo

NOTE:

1. Gas Stations offering Diesel or LPG (propane) are listed on the maps with a "\D" or "\L" after their name. For example, "BP\DL" indicates a BP station with diesel pump(s), and stocking propane.
2. Unless otherwise designated, Truck Stops are listed as "TS" followed by the gas brand . . . e.g., TS(BP).

FOOD

A&AStk . . . . A&A Steak
A&W. . . A&W Fast Food
Alexndr . . . . . Alexander
Applb . . . . . . Applebee's
Arby . . . . Arbys
AuntEff . . . . Aunt Effie's
BKing . . . . . Burger King
BaskR . Baskin-Robbins Ice Cream
BelairGrl . . . . Belair Grill
BgBoy . . . . Big Boy Family Restaurant
Blimp . . . . Blimpies
Brbnk. . . Burbanks BBQ
BudBBQ. . . . Bud's BBQ
BuffWngs Buffalo Wings
C/Kit. . . Country Kitchen
CPride. . . Country Pride
CPtch . . . . Cotton Patch Restaurant
CaptD . . . . . Captain D's
CharlSeaFd . . . Charles Sea Food
Checkr . . . . . . Checkers
ChickF . . . . . Chick-Fil-A
Chili. . . . . GoldStar Chili
China. . . . . China Buffet
ChinaGdns. . . . . . China Gardens
ChkChse . . . . . Chuck E Cheese's
Church . . . . Chicken Cookery
CityBft. . . . . . City Buffet
CrkBrl. . . Cracker Barrel
CrzEd. . Crazy Eds Rest
CtrlPark . . . Central Park
CtryBft . . Country Buffet
CtryGrill. . . Country Grill
CuttrsStk . . . . . . Cutters Steakhouse
D/Bell. . . . . . Dinner Bell
DQ . . . . . . Dairy Queen
Denny. . . . . Denny's
DennyDnr . . . . . Denny's Diner
DktaGrl. . . . Dakota Grill
DmnRib . . . . . . Damons
Dudly . . . . Dudley's
DunkD . . . . Dunkin Doughnut
Evans. . . . . . Bob Evans
FamDave . . . . . Famous Dave's
Family. . . . . Family Rest
Fazoli . . . . Fazzoli's
Fdrckrs . . . Fuddruckers
Frckers. . . Fricker's Rest
GFPizza . . . . Godfather Pizza
GSChili. . Gold Star Chili
GinaFD . . . . Gina's Fine Dining
GitnGo . . . . . . Git 'n Go
GldnC . . . Golden Corral
GldnGrls . . Golden Girls
Grdma . . . . . Grandma's Kitchen
Grindr . . . . WJ Grinders
GrndSC . . . Grindestone Charlies
GtAmBft . . . . Great American Buffet
Gthouse. . . . Gatehouse
Hddle . . . Huddle House
HickH . . . Hickory House
HngKng . . . . Hong Kong
HnyDipD. . . . Honey Dip Donuts
Hooter. . . . . Hooters
Hrdee . . . Hardee's Rest
Hunan. . Hunan Chinese
IHOP . . . . . International House of Pancakes
IceCrm . . . . . Ice Cream Churn
IntBft . . . . . International Buffet
IrnSklt. . . . . . Iron Skillet
J&L . . . . . . J&L Famous Pit BBQ
Jerry's . . . . Jerry's Rest
Jlpeno . . . . . . Jalepenos
KFC . . . . Kentucky Fried Chicken
Knapp . . . . Bob Knapp's
Krystal . . . . Krystal Rest
KspyKrm . . KrispyKreme Doughnuts
LChick. . . Lee's Country Chicken
LJSilvr . . . . . Long John Silver
Lees . . Lees Restaurant
LgnStk. . . . Logan Steak
LkyStr. . . . . Lucky Steer Restaurant
LoneS . . . . . . Lone Star Steaks
LongH . . . . . . Longhorn Steaks
LosR. . . . . . . Los Reyes
Louie's . . . . Louie's on the Lake
Macroni. . . . . Macaronis
MamaTbl . Mama's Table
MaxEma . Max&Emma's
McDld . . . . . McDonalds
MexGrl . . . Mexican Grill
Montry. . . . . . Monterrey
Morrel . . . . Morrel's Restaurant
Mntgmry . . Montgomery
MrsWin . . . Mrs Winners Chicken
NuWyWnr . . . . NewWay Weiner
O'Char . . . . . O'Charlies
OldCtryBft . Old Country Buffet
Olive. . . . . Olive Garden
OTBorder OnThe Border
OrnWok . . Oriental Wok
OutBk. . . . . Outback Steakhouse
PJPizza . . . Papa Jones Pizza
PaneraBd. . . . . . Panera Bread
Pantry. . . . . Pantry Rest
PapaDino . . PaPaDino's Pizza
Patty . . . . . Patty's Buffet
Pdrsa . . . . . . Ponderosa Steaks
Picdilly . . . . Picadilly
PitStop . . . PitStop BBQ
Pizza . . . . Pizza Hut
PopE . . . . Popeye's
Prkns. . . Perkin's Family Restaurant
RCSteak . . . Rockcastle Steak
Raffty . . . . Rafferty's
Rally . . . . Rally Drive-In
Ralph. . . . . Ralphies
Rax. . . Rax Restaurants
RedLb . . . . Red Lobster
RoadHs . . . Road House
RubyT . . . Ruby Tuesday
Ryan . . . . Ryan's Family Steakhouse
SaraJ . . . . . . Sara Jane
Sbarro . . . . Sbarro's
Schltzky. . . . Schlotzky's Deli
Shony . . . . Shoney's
SkyLnChili . . . . . Skyline Chili
SmkyBnes . . . . . Smoky Bones BBQ
Sonic . . . . . 50's Drive In
Sonny. . . . Sonny's BBQ
SpagWhse . . . Spaghetti Warehouse

Continued on next page

FOOD, continued

Starbcks . . . . Starbuck's
Starvn . . Starvin' Marvin
StkHsSln. . Steak House Saloon
StkShk. . Steak & Shake Burgers
StkyFngr. Sticky Fingers
Stucky . . . . . . Stuckey's
Subwy. . . . . Subway
TCBY . . . The Country's Best Yogurt
TGIF. . . . . . . TGI Friday
Taco . . . . Taco Bell
TexRdHse . . . . . . Texas Roadhouse
TexStk. . . . . West Texas Steakhouse
ThomasMkt . . . Thomas Fresh Market Rest
TimH . . . . . . Tim Horton
TipOTwn . . . Tip O' Town
WSizz . Western Sizzlin'
WStr. . . . Western Steer Steakhouse
Waffle. . . . Waffle House
Wendy . . . . Wendy's
WfflKing . . . Waffle King
WhtCstl. . . White Castle Hamburgers
Wingr . . . . Wingers
Zaxby . Zaxby's Chicken

LODGING

4PtsShtn . . . Four Points Sheraton
Ambssdr . . Ambassador Motel
AmerInn. . American Inn
BHost . . . . Budget Host
Baymnt . . . . . . Baymont Inns & Suites
BdgInn . . . Budget Inn of America
Best . . . . Best Inns
BestValue . . . BestValue Motel
BestW . . . Best Western
BkEye . . . . Buckeye
Bradbry. . . . . . Bradbury
Brittny . . . Brittany Motor Inn
C/Ctry. . . Cross Country
Clarion . . . . Clarion
Colnial . . . . Colonial Inn
Comfrt . . . . Comfort Inn
Crown . . . . . . Crown Inn
CrtYrd . . . . . . Courtyard by Marriot
Crtesy. . . . . . . Courtesy
CtryInnSte . . . . Country Inns & Suites
Cumberlnd . . . . Cumberland Inn
DBrdge . . . . Drawbridge
Days . . . . Days Inn
DblTree . . . . DoubleTree
Drury . . . . . Drury Motel
Duffy. . . . . Duffy's Motel
Econmy . . . . . Economy Motel
Econo. . . . Econo Lodge
EmbsyS . . . . . Embassy Suites
Exec. . . . . Executive Inn
Fairfld . . . . . Fairfield Inn
Family . . . . . Family Inns of America
Flag . . . . Flag Inn
Guest. . . . . . . Guest Inn
GuestHs . . Guest House Inn
H/Inn . . . . . . Holiday Inn
H/InnS . . . . . Holiday Inn Select
H/InnX . . . . . Holiday Inn Express
Hilton . . . . Hilton Hotels
HltnGdn . . . . Hilton Garden
Hmptn. . . . Hampton Inn
Hmstd . . . . . Homestead
HoJo. . Howard Johnson
Hol/M. . . . Holiday Motel
HomeTn . . . . Hometown Motel
HomeWd . . . Homewood Motel
Hrtge . . . Heritage Motel
Hwthrn . . . . . Hawthorne Suites
Hyatt . . . . . Hyatt Hotels
Jamsn. . . . Jameson Inn
Jolly . . . . Jolly Inn
Kings . . . . Kings Inn
Knght. . . . . . Knights Inn
LaQnt. . . . La Quinta Inn
LkCty . . . . Lake City
Lkview . . . Lakeview Inn
LndMk . . . . . . Landmark
Marrtt . . . Marriot Hotels
MicroT. . . . Microtel Inns
Motel. . any independent unknown motel
Motel6. . . . . Motel6
Mstrs . . . . . Masters Inn
NFsyth. . . . New Forsyth Inn
Pssprt . . . . Passport Inn
QltyInn . . . . . Quality Inn
QltyQtr . . . . Quality Quarter Inn
Radsn. . . . Radisson Inn
Ramda. . . . Ramada Inn
RedC . . . . . Red Carpet Inns
RedRf. . . . Red Roof Inn
Regncy . . . Regency Inn
Relax . . . . Relax Inn
Renfro . . . Renfro Valley Motel
RmdaSt . . . . . . Ramada Suites
Rodwy . . . Rodeway Inn
Rsdnts. . . Residents Inn
Scot . . . . . . Scottish Inn
Shony . . . . Shoney's Inn
Signtr . . . . Signature Inn
Sleep . . . . Sleep Inn
Studio6+ . . Studio6 Plus
Supr8 . . Super 8 Motels
TradeWd . . Trade Winds Motel
TravInn. . . . . . Travel Inn
TravL . . . . . . Travelodge
Value . . . . . . Value Inns
Villager . . . . Villager Inn
Wavrly. . . . . Waverly
Wellsly . . . . . . Wellesley
Wilburg . . . Williamsburg Motel
Wingate . . . Wingate Inn
WldWd. . . Wildwood Inn
Woodfld . . . . . Woodfield
Wyndm . . . . . Wyndham
XstayAm. . . . . Extended Stay America

A Word to our Readers . . .

Please note: we have not listed gas, food or lodgings in the downtown areas of Detroit, Toledo, Dayton, Cincinnati and Atlanta. We feel that access to such facilities (and easy return to the Interstate) is often difficult for those not familiar with streets in the area.

Also, downtown facilities tend to be higher priced, catering more to the business traveler than vacationer - travel bargains will generally be found elsewhere. This Guide has been written with the long distance interstate traveler in mind, and accordingly we recommend staying or eating at facilities outside these areas.

Nobody has paid to be listed or recommended in this guide; furthermore, we do NOT accept advertising. *"Along I-75"* contains no commercial content.

Unless a facility or service is specifically mentioned in an **Insider Tip**, inclusion in this book does not constitute a recommendation on the part of the publisher or author. We are however, interested in receiving your comments about facilities

Finally - every effort has been made to ensure the accuracy of the Guide's listings. Prior to printing this edition, three personal trips have been made along I-75, cross-checking information and ensuring that services were where they were supposed to be. The most recent survey was completed just a month prior to publication. We have included all major road construction projects encountered on this trip, although many may be completed before you head south.

DATE		MILEAGE			FUEL	DAILY EXPENSE RECORD						OVERNIGHT STOP			
(M/D)	DAY	START	STOP	DIFF	(Gals)	B/FAST	LUNCH	DINNER	GAS	MISC	TOTAL	STATE	EXIT#	LOCATION	MOTEL
A	B	C	D	E	F	G	H	I	J	K	L	M	N	O	P

- Enter the **Date** (month/day), and the **Day** of the week (e.g.. Mon, Tues, etc.) in columns A & B.
- At the beginning of the first day, record your car's odometer reading in **Mileage Start** (column C). After finishing with the car each evening, record the odometer reading in **Mileage Stop** (column D). Post the same number in column C for the next day.

  To calculate the number of miles driven during the day, deduct column C from column D, and enter the result in **Difference** (column E).
- To calculate your daily **Miles per Gallon**, make sure you fill up your tank before you start your journey (do not enter these gallons on the chart).

  Keep a note of the number of fuel gallons purchased during each day.

  Each morning before you start, fill up your car and add these gallons to the fuel purchased during the previous day's run. Record this total for the previous day in column F.

  Divide the total number of miles driven during the previous day (column E) by the total number of gallons used (column F). The result will be your Miles per Gallon for the previous day.
- **Daily expenses** can be recorded in columns G to K, and totaled for the day in column L. Post your motel costs and sundry expenses in column L.
- Record details of your **Overnight Stops** in columns M to P.

Personal Log - Northbound

DATE		MILEAGE			FUEL	DAILY EXPENSE RECORD						OVERNIGHT STOP			
(M/D)	DAY	START	STOP	DIFF	(Gals)	B/FAST	LUNCH	DINNER	GAS	MISC	TOTAL	STATE	EXIT#	LOCATION	MOTEL
A	B	C	D	E	F	G	H	I	J	K	L	M	N	O	P

- Enter the **Date** (month/day), and the **Day** of the week (e.g.. Mon, Tues, etc.) in columns A & B.
- At the beginning of the first day, record your car's odometer reading in **Mileage Start** (column C). After finishing with the car each evening, record the odometer reading in **Mileage Stop** (column D). Post the same number in column C for the next day.

  To calculate the number of miles driven during the day, deduct column C from column D, and enter the result in **Difference** (column E).
- To calculate your daily **Miles per Gallon**, make sure you fill up your tank before you start your journey (do not enter these gallons on the chart).

  Keep a note of the number of fuel gallons purchased during each day.

  Each morning before you start, fill up your car and add these gallons to the fuel purchased during the previous day's run. Record this total for the previous day in column F.

  Divide the total number of miles driven during the previous day (column E) by the total number of gallons used (column F). The result will be your Miles per Gallon for the previous day.
- **Daily expenses** can be recorded in columns G to K, and totaled for the day in column L. Post your motel costs and sundry expenses in column L.
- Record details of your **Overnight Stops** in columns M to P.

Help me write our 14th - 2006 - edition of . . .

. . . "Along Interstate-75"

Please help me continue to make this your book. Each year, I receive many interesting letters from our readers. Before going to press, Kathy and I review every suggestion and try and incorporate as many of them as possible into the next edition. We can then make sure that the guide continues to meet your needs.

Please use the space below to record your recommendations or changes to the book's information. Use the other side for your comments and other suggestions. Tell me what you like about the guide, or what you don't like — we are constantly trying to improve it for you. To be considered for the 2006 guide though, we must have your submission by April 30, 2005.

Dave

To: *Dave Hunter, c/o Mile Oak Publishing Inc.,*
Suite 81, 20 Mineola Road East,
Mississauga ON Canada L5G 4N9

From: ☐ ✔ Please add my name to your mailing list.
Please note, we do **not** give your mailing information to others; we only send one mailing per year . . . which includes a **discount coupon** for your next book.

Name: Phone:

Address:

City: State/Prov: Zip/PC:

e.mail address:

My recommendation or change in information:

(if recommending a facility, please include as much information as possible - thanks).

Facility Name:

Owner or Manager's Name: Phone:

Where is it? - State: Exit#: East/West?:

Recommendation or Information to be changed:

Please use the other side for your comments or suggestions

My comments and suggestions for the 2006 edition:

Free Offer

Offer expires July 31, 2005

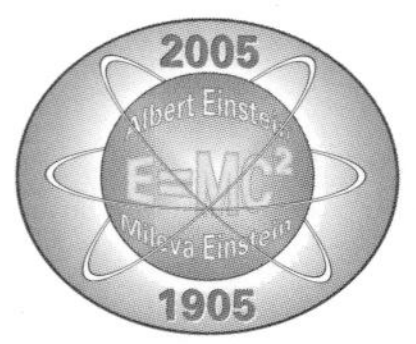

2005 is the centenary of Einstein's Special Theory of Relativity, which presented the famous equation E=MC to the World

FLORIDA 75 Florida's I-75 Map

and our Annual Newsletter

with news for Florida's winter visitors

☐ Check (✔) box to left; fill in your name & address in the space below, and mail or fax this form to Mile Oak Publishing (see address and fax number below) - we will send you a free copy of Dave Hunter's black & white panel strip-map of the *I-75 to Tampa, Florida*, *his new Gas Buying Tips to Save Money and his Winter 2004/2005 Florida Newsletter* . . . all mailed within 48 hours of receipt of this form.

Name: ....

Address: ....

....

City: .... State/Prov.: ....

ZIP/Postal Code: .... Phone: ....

E.Mail Address: ....

BOOK ORDER FORM

Need another copy of *Along Interstate-75*?

. . . either, **phone 1-800-431-1579** (fast service; book mailed within 24hrs),
or, use this handy **Mail Order Form**

Please send me ☐ copies of *Along Interstate-75, 13th edition* to my address shown above. I enclose my check for $ ☐ (see below for prices).

Please make your check payable to *Mile Oak Publishing Inc.* We mail within 24 hrs of receiving your order.

Orders shipped to US addresses: # of books x $23.95 + s&h ($4.50 first book/$1.25 each addnl). Amount payable in US funds.

Orders shipped to Canadian Addresses: # of books x $29.95 + s&h ($4.00 first book/$1.00 each additional) - add 7% GST to cost of total order. Amount payable in Canadian funds.

Buying a gift copy for a friend? Visit our website at **www.i75online.com** *to learn how to order an autographed gift copy personalized with your friend's name.*

How to contact us:

By mail: **Mile Oak Publishing Inc.,**
Suite 81, 20 Mineola Road East,
Mississauga, ON Canada L5G 4N9

Phone: **905-274-4356**; Fax: **905-274-8656**; Email: **mile_oak@compuserve.com**

NOTES